D1637249

THE PAPERS OF ALEXANDER HAMILTON

THE WORKS OF ALEXANDER HAMILTON.

Alexander Hamilton, *circa* 1786. Oil portrait by Robert Edge Pine.
Courtesy E. J. Rousuck

THE PAPERS OF

Alexander Hamilton

VOLUME VIII

FEBRUARY 1791–JULY 1791

HAROLD C. SYRETT, EDITOR

JACOB E. COOKE, ASSOCIATE EDITOR

Assistant Editors

JEAN G. COOKE   CARA-LOUISE MILLER

DOROTHY TWOHIG   PATRICIA SYRETT

 COLUMBIA UNIVERSITY PRESS

NEW YORK AND LONDON, 1965

FROM THE PUBLISHER

The preparation of this edition of the papers of Alexander Hamilton has been made possible by the support received for the work of the editorial and research staff from the generous grants of the Rockefeller Foundation, Time Inc., and the Ford Foundation, and by the far-sighted cooperation of the National Historical Publications Commission. To these organizations, the publisher expresses gratitude on behalf of all who are concerned about making available the record of the founding of the United States.

ACKNOWLEDGMENTS

SINCE the publication in 1963 of Volume VII of *The Papers of Alexander Hamilton,* the editors have incurred several obligations which they wish to take this opportunity to acknowledge. Mr. John Knowlton of Washington, D.C., has answered our countless questions and performed a great variety of other tasks with remarkable alacrity and unfailing good humor. The editors also wish to express their indebtedness to Mr. Michael Becksha, chief of the Federal Records Center, Boston; Mr. Clifford P. Monahon and Mr. Clarkson A. Collins III, who serve respectively as director and librarian of The Rhode Island Historical Society; Mr. H. G. Jones, State Archivist, North Carolina Department of Archives and History; and Miss Helen Gittleman, who until recently was a member of the staff of Butler Library, Columbia University. The editors are especially grateful to Dr. Oliver W. Holmes, Executive Director, National Historical Publications Commission, for his continued support, understanding, and encouragement.

PREFACE

THIS EDITION of Alexander Hamilton's papers contains letters and other documents written by Hamilton, letters to Hamilton, and some documents (commissions, certificates, etc.) that directly concern Hamilton but were written neither by him nor to him. All letters and other documents have been printed in chronological order. Hamilton's legal papers are being published under the editorial direction of Julius Goebel, Jr., George Welwood Murray Professor Emeritus of Legal History of the School of Law, Columbia University. The first volume of this distinguished work, which is entitled *The Law Practice of Alexander Hamilton,* was published by the Columbia University Press in 1964.

Many letters and documents have been calendared. Such calendared items include routine letters and documents by Hamilton, routine letters to Hamilton, some of the letters or documents written by Hamilton for someone else, letters or documents which have not been found but which are known to have existed, letters or documents which have been erroneously attributed to Hamilton, and letters to or by Hamilton that deal exclusively with his legal practice.

Certain routine documents which Hamilton wrote and received as Secretary of the Treasury have not been printed. The documents that fall within this category are warrants or interest certificates; letters written by Hamilton acknowledging receipts from banks, endorsing margins of certificate of registry, and enclosing sea letters; letters to Hamilton transmitting weekly, monthly, and quarterly accounts, or enclosing certificates of registry and other routine Treasury forms; and drafts by Hamilton on the treasurer. Statements of facts from the judges of the District Courts on cases concerning violations of the customs laws and warrants of remission of forfeiture issued by Hamilton have generally been omitted unless they pertain to cases discussed in Hamilton's correspondence.

The notes in these volumes are designed to provide information concerning the nature and location of each document, to identify Hamilton's correspondents and the individuals mentioned in the text, to explain events or ideas referred to in the text, and to point out textual variations or mistakes. Occasional departures from these standards can be attributed to a variety of reasons. In many cases the desired information has been supplied in an earlier note and can be found through the use of the index. Notes were not added when in the opinion of the editors the material in the text was either self-explanatory or common knowledge. The editors, moreover, did not think it desirable or necessary to provide full annotation for Hamilton's legal correspondence. Finally, the editors on some occasions were unable to find the desired information, and on other occasions the editors were remiss.

GUIDE TO EDITORIAL APPARATUS

I. SYMBOLS USED TO DESCRIBE MANUSCRIPTS

AD	Autograph Document
ADS	Autograph Document Signed
ADf	Autograph Draft
ADfS	Autograph Draft Signed
AL	Autograph Letter
ALS	Autograph Letter Signed
D	Document
DS	Document Signed
Df	Draft
DfS	Draft Signed
LS	**Letter Signed**
LC	Letter Book Copy
[S]	[S] is used with other symbols (AD[S], ADf[S], AL[S], D[S], Df[S], L[S]) to indicate that the signature on the document has been cropped or clipped.

II. MONETARY SYMBOLS AND ABBREVIATIONS

bf	Banco florin
V	Ecu
f	Florin
₶	**Livre Tournois**
medes	Maravedis (also md and mde)
d.	Penny or denier
ps	Piece of eight

£	Pound sterling or livre
Ry	Real
rs vn	Reals de vellon
rdr	Rix daller
s	Shilling, sou or sol (also expressed as /)
sti	Stiver

III. SHORT TITLES AND ABBREVIATIONS

Annals of Congress, I, II, III	*The Debates and Proceedings in the Congress of the United States; with an Appendix, Containing Important State Papers and Public Documents, and All the Laws of a Public Nature* (Washington, 1834–1849).
Arch. des Aff. Etr., Corr. Pol., Etats-Unis	Transcripts or photostats from the French Foreign Office deposited in the Library of Congress.
Archives Parlementaires	*Archives Parlementaires de 1787 à 1860* (Paris, 1868–).
ASP	*American State Papers, Documents, Legislative and Executive, of the Congress of the United States* (Washington, 1832–1861).
Bayley, *National Loans*	Rafael A. Bayley, *The National Loans of the United States from July 4, 1776, to June 30, 1880* (Washington, 1882).
Bemis, *Jay's Treaty*	Samuel Flagg Bemis, *Jay's Treaty, a Study in Commerce and Diplomacy* (New York, 1923).
Brymner, *Canadian Archives,* 1890	Douglas Brymner, ed., *Report on Canadian Archives,* 1890 (Ottawa, 1891).
Carter, *Territorial Papers*	Clarence E. Carter, ed., *The Territorial Papers of the United States* (Washington, 1934–).
Clark, *State Records of North Carolina*	Walter Clark, ed., *The State Records of North Carolina* (Goldsboro, North Carolina, 1886–1907).

Davis, *Essays*	Joseph Stancliffe Davis, *Essays in the Earlier History of American Corporations* ("Harvard Economic Studies," XVI [Cambridge, 1917]).
Executive Journal, I	*Journal of the Executive Proceedings of the Senate* (Washington, 1828).
Ferguson, *Power of the Purse*	E. James Ferguson, *The Power of the Purse* (Chapel Hill, 1961).
Freeman, *Washington*	Douglas Southall Freeman, *George Washington* (New York, 1948–1957). Volume VII of this series was written by John Alexander Carroll and Mary Wells Ashworth.
GW	John C. Fitzpatrick, ed., *The Writings of George Washington* (Washington, 1931–1944).
Hamilton, *History*	John C. Hamilton, *Life of Alexander Hamilton, a History of the Republic of the United States of America* (Boston, 1879).
Hamilton, *Intimate Life*	Allan McLane Hamilton, *The Intimate Life of Alexander Hamilton* (New York, 1910).
Hamilton, *Life*	John C. Hamilton, *The Life of Alexander Hamilton* (New York, 1840).
Hazard, *Pennsylvania Archives*	Samuel Hazard, ed., *Pennsylvania Archives* (Philadelphia, 1852–1856).
HCLW	Henry Cabot Lodge, ed., *The Works of Alexander Hamilton* (New York, 1904).
Hunt, *Calendar of Applications*	Gaillard Hunt, *Calendar of Applications and Recommendations for Office During the Presidency of George Washington* (Washington, 1901).
Hunt and Scott, *Debates*	Gaillard Hunt and James Brown Scott, eds., *The Debates in the Federal Convention of 1787 Which Framed the Constitution*

	of the United States of America. Reported by James Madison (New York, 1920).
JCC	*Journals of the Continental Congress, 1774–1789* (Washington, 1904–1937).
JCH Transcripts	John C. Hamilton Transcripts. These transcripts are owned by Mr. William H. Swan, Hampton Bays, New York, and have been placed on loan in the Columbia University Libraries.
JCHW	John C. Hamilton, ed., *The Works of Alexander Hamilton* (New York, 1851–1856).
Journal of the House, I	*Journal of the House of Representatives of the United States* (Washington, 1826).
Laws of the State of New York, III	*Laws of the State of New York Passed at the sessions of the Legislature Held in the Years 1789, 1790, 1791, 1792, 1793, 1794, 1795, and 1796, Inclusive, Being the Twelfth, Thirteenth, Fourteenth, Fifteenth, Sixteenth, Seventeenth, Eighteenth and Nineteenth Sessions* (Albany, 1887).
Mitchell, *Hamilton*	Broadus Mitchell, *Alexander Hamilton* (1957–1962).
Pennsylvania Archives, 9th ser.	*Pennsylvania Archives,* 9th ser. (n. p., 1931–1935).
Pennsylvania Statutes	James T. Mitchell and Henry Flanders, eds., *The Statutes at Large of Pennsylvania from 1682 to 1801* (Harrisburg, 1896–1908).
PRO: F.O., or PRO: C.O.	Transcripts or photostats from the Public Records Office of Great Britain deposited in the Library of Congress.
Records of Rhode Island	John Russell Bartlett, ed., *Records of the State of Rhode Island and Providence Plantations in New England* (Providence, 1856–1865).

Smith, *St. Clair Papers*   William Henry Smith, ed., *The St. Clair Papers: The Life and Public Services of Arthur St. Clair* (Cincinnati, 1882).

1 *Stat.*   *The Public Statutes at Large of the United States of America* (Boston, 1845).

IV. INDECIPHERABLE WORDS

Words or parts of words which could not be deciphered because of the illegibility of the writing or the mutilation of the manuscript have been indicated as follows:

1. ⟨– – – – –⟩ indicates illegible words with the number of dashes indicating the estimated number of illegible words.
2. Words or letters in broken brackets indicate a guess as to what the words or letters in question may be. If the source of the words or letters within the broken brackets is known, it has been given in a note.

V. CROSSED-OUT MATERIAL IN MANUSCRIPTS

Words or sentences crossed out by a writer in a manuscript have been handled in one of the three following ways:

1. They have been ignored, and the document or letter has been printed in its final version.
2. Crossed-out words and insertions for the crossed-out words have been described in the notes.
3. When the significance of a manuscript seems to warrant it, the crossed-out words have been retained, and the document has been printed as it was written.

VI. TEXTUAL CHANGES AND INSERTIONS

The following changes or insertions have been made in the letters and documents printed in these volumes:

1. Words or letters written above the line of print (for example, 9th) have been made even with the line of print (9th).

2. Punctuation and capitalization have been changed in those instances where it seemed necessary to make clear the sense of the writer. A special effort has been made to eliminate the dash, which was such a popular eighteenth-century device.

3. When the place or date, or both, of a letter or document does not appear at the head of that letter or document, it has been inserted in the text in brackets. If either the place or date at the head of a letter or document is incomplete, the necessary additional material has been added in the text in brackets. For all but the best known localities or places, the name of the colony, state, or territory has been added in brackets at the head of a document or letter.

4. In calendared documents, place and date have been uniformly written out in full without the use of brackets. Thus "N. York, Octr. 8, '99" becomes "New York, October 8, 1799." If, however, substantive material is added to the place or date in a calendared document, such material is placed in brackets. Thus "Oxford, Jan. 6" becomes "Oxford [Massachusetts] January 6 [1788]."

5. When a writer made an unintentional slip comparable to a typographical error, one of the four following devices has been used:

   a. It has been allowed to stand as written.

   b. It has been corrected by inserting either one or more letters in brackets.

   c. It has been corrected without indicating the change.

   d. It has been explained in a note.

6. Because the symbol for the thorn was archaic even in Hamilton's day, the editors have used the letter "y" to represent it. In doing this they are conforming to eighteenth-century manuscript usage.

1791

To Benjamin Lincoln [1]

Treasury Department
February 1st. 1791.

Sir

The Trustees of the sinking fund have thought fit to commit to you the making of purchases of the public debt to the amount of fifty thousand Dollars pursuant to the Act making provision for the reduction of the public debt.[2]

To enable you to execute this trust (which I doubt not you will chearfully undertake) I have directed the Treasurer [3] to forward to you fifty thousand dollars in Notes of the bank of North America, payable to yourself on order. You will not only receive *these* particular notes on the terms heretofore prescribed, but you will exchange them for any specie which may at any time be in your hands, though a return may have been made of it to this office.

You will observe by the Act a copy of which accompanies this that the purchases are to be made *openly* and at the *market price*.

The first has been construed to mean that they are to be made by a *known agent* acting avowedly on behalf of the public. Other Circumstances have been considered as matters of discretion and accordingly have been varied. Sometimes the Treasurer (who has been charged with the business at the seat of Government) has gone to the Coffee house and purchased such as offered at the price of the day; at other times he has advertised for proposals and taken the lowest except where special reasons have recommended a small variation from that rule &ca. With these intimations the mode is left to your judgment.

By the market price has been understood the most common rate at which securities are sold at the time and place when and where the purchases are made. On this point it has been deemed most consistent with the general view of the act to be liberal, rather than to manifest a disposition unfavourable to the Creditor.

One of the objects of the Act is to raise the funds. And when it is considered, that every penny at which foreigners purchase our debt below its value is absolute loss to the Community, and that what is gained by the Government in its purchases is lost to the Citizens of whom they are made, it must appear, that there is a greater national Interest in the rise of the funds, than in the saving to the Government. Hence it has been deemed not expedient to act in a manner which should evince that the Government was not disposed *to press* the object of profit at the expence of the Creditor.

These hints can only serve to indicate to you the spirit with which the purchases heretofore made have been conducted. Their Application must be left to your discretion.

You will observe that the purchases are to be confined to the debt of the United States which cannot comprehend the State debt 'till it has been subscribed and new certificates given for it.

You are also to keep an exact account of the disbursements and purchases made by you specifying the *place* where, the times when, the prices at which, and the parties of whom they are made.

The manner in which you shall dispose of the securities which you shall purchase shall be the subject of a future instruction.

I am sir   your obedient servant   Alexander Hamilton
                                                Secy of the Treasy

P.S. It has been suggested to me that Persons desirous of making Remittances to Philadelphia will be disposed to furnish specie for these Notes [4] to facilitate their Remittance hither. You will be pleased to accommodate them with such exchanges when applied for.

Benjamin Lincoln Esq.

LS, RG 36, Collector of Customs at Boston, Letters from the Treasury, 1789–1808, National Archives; copy, RG 56, Letters to Collectors at Small Ports, "Set G," National Archives; copy, RG 56, Letters to the Collector at Boston, National Archives.

1. For background to this letter, see "Meeting of the Commissioners of the Sinking Fund," January 18, 1791.

Lincoln was collector of customs at Boston.

2. 1 *Stat.* 186–87 (August 12, 1790).

3. Samuel Meredith served as the first United States treasurer from September, 1789, to December, 1801.

4. The Bank of North America notes.

To Charles Lee [1]

Treasury Department
February 2d. 1791

Sir

I have made a remittance to William Heth Esq. Collector of Bermuda Hundred in Notes of the Bank of North America, made payable to him, which I request you to exchange for specie should any of them be offered by the holders. The Cash *included in your returns* as well as that received in the current week may be used for that purpose, if requisite.

I am Sir,   your obedient servant.   A Hamilton

LS, Charles Lee Papers, Library of Congress.
1. Lee was collector of customs at Alexandria, Virginia.

From Arthur Fenner [1]

Providence Feby. 3 1791

Sir

Your letter of the 14th Jany.[2] I recd. In February 1786 a Committee appointed by the Legislature of the State of Rhode Island settled the Accounts with the Agent for the Rhode Island line of the late Army.[3] There appeared in his hands certificates to the amount of three thousand seven Dollars and seventy three Ninetieths which were delivered over and lodgd in the Treasury of this State to be deliverd to the absentees or their representatives when called for. Since their being lodged in the Treasury the greatest part I am informed have been deliverd either to the original Proprietors or their representatives. The exact amount (if any) remaining in the Treasury I cannot at present ascertain the Treasurer living at Newport. I have wrote him on the subject, and as soon as I receive his Answer shall forward to you the amount.

With sentiments of esteem your Obedient Friend   A Fenner Govr
                                                          S R

A Hamilton Secry
Treasury U States

Copy, The John Carter Brown Library, Providence, Rhode Island.

1. Fenner was governor of Rhode Island.

2. "Treasury Department Circular to the Governors of the States," January 14, 1791.

3. See the "Report of the Committee appointed by the General Assembly relative to the services of Major John S. Dexter, as agent of the Rhode Island regiment" (*Records of Rhode Island,* X, 156–57).

From William Seton [1]

New York 3d February 1791

Dear sir

The note you inclosed to Mr Troup [2] for discount was immediately done & passd to your Credit. The dft to Mr. Francis [3] has not yet appeared, but should have been punctually attended to & honored at all Events. Your present ballance in Bank including the discount is 2907 Dolls. & $^{44}/_{100}$. Therefore the 3000 Dolls. dft will overrun 92. Do: $^{56}/_{100}$ which I mention for your Government. The letters you entrusted to my Care relating to our *Senator* [4] were duly delivered as you would find by the answer our friend D——— [5] wrote you, but the point had been absolutely decided long before as the other party had been undermining for Months & the Coalition between the G——— [6] & C——— [7] secured the Election. All your friends here lamented it, foreseeing the impediments it would throw in your way. Some say he [8] will act otherwise, but what is bad in the bone will appear in the flesh. I anticipate (tho' no politician) great opposition to every salutary system.

The Goldsmiths inform me (contrary to your expectation & contrary to what would seem reasonable) that the Standard they mean in their Assays is British Standard, which is 11 parts fine Gold & 1 part alloy.

I am induced from motives of friendship to a very valuable Character, to take a liberty with you that I can scarcely justify to my own feelings considering our two situations, but friendship will sometimes lead a man beyond the bounds of discretion.

There is a Gentleman in business residing at Leghorn of the Name of Philip Feliechj who married in this City a Miss Cowper. A worthier or more respectable Character in the mercantile Line does not exist. (I have some faint idea that he is personally known to you). He has done a great deal of business with this Country & still continues to do it, is every way attached to it, & few men his Superiors in abilities. I conceive it would be of great advantage to my friend if he could get the appointment of Consul for The United States of America to Leghorn,[9] or say the Duke of Tuscanys Dominions. I am convinced no man would do more honor to the appointment; perhaps it may be in your power to procure me this favour or to point out to me what path to pursue to obtain it. I hope you will pardon this liberty & believe me ever

   Your devoted Hule Svt   Wm Seton

P.S. Of the last Bills on Amsterdam we have sold 81,000 Guilders, hope to run off the remainder of the 200,000 in a few days.

Alexr. Hamilton Esqr.

ALS, Hamilton Papers, Library of Congress.
1. Seton was cashier of the Bank of New York.
2. Robert Troup at this time was practicing law in Albany.
3. Tench Francis was cashier of the Bank of North America.
4. Aaron Burr, who had just been elected United States Senator. For background to this election, see William Duer to H, January 19, 1791.
5. William Duer.
6. Governor George Clinton.
7. Chancellor Robert R. Livingston.
8. Aaron Burr.
9. Feliechj (or Feliechy) received this appointment in 1794.

From Richard Harison [1]

New York 4 Febry 1791

Sir,

It is a Misfortune in our Legislation that particular Regulations of other Countries have been adopted without considering their Dependence upon the System to which they belong. Hence our Laws in many instances become unprovisional & Questions important in their Consequences & difficult to be resolved must necessarily arise. The fifth Section of the Registring Act [2] is nearly copied from the eighth Section of an Act passed in Great Britain since the late War,[3] the Operation of which I conclude is directed by a Clause of the Navigation Act, subjecting foreign Ships to Seizure in certain Cases.[4] I take it too that in Great Britain the Certificate of Registry is only prima Facie Evidence of Conformity to the Laws of Trade, but may be contradicted by Proof that it is applied to improper Purposes.

I should think that a similar Principle must be implied in our present System with Respect to registring Vessels, and granting Certificates. Supposing a Certificate to have been obtained by Perjury, and the Person to abscond upon whose Oath it was granted, surely it could not avail to exempt the Vessel from Payment of the foreign Duty.

By applying this Principle to the fifth Section of the Act, I think that the Question contained in your Letter of the 29th. Ultimo may be resolved. It is clearly the Intention of the Legislature that Citizens residing in foreign Countries should be upon the Footing of Foreigners in Respect to the Ships which they possess. If the Register obtained before their Removal is to be considered as conclusive, the Intention of the Legislature must be defeated; & the same Inconvenience would arise in Case of Transfers to Foreigners, the Remedy upon the Bond being inadequate in many supposeable Instances.

I think that the Register must be considered as a Caution against Frauds, but cannot with Propriety serve as a Cover to any; and the Acts of Trade must be explained liberally so as to render them most effectual.

Upon the whole, therefore, I am of Opinion that in the Case expressed in your Letter, the Vessel would lose the Benefit of her Register during the Residence of the Owner in a foreign Country. But it would be adviseable to procure an explicit Act of the Legislature to prevent any Question upon this & similar Subjects.

I am with the utmost Respect   Sir   Your most obedt. humb Servt.

Hon. Alexr. Hamilton Esqr.

ADf, New-York Historical Society, New York City; LC, New-York Historical Society.

1. This letter was written in reply to H to Harison, January 29, 1791. Harison, a prominent New York lawyer, had served as a delegate to the New York Ratifying Convention. In 1789 he was appointed United States attorney for the District of New York.

2. "An Act for Registering and Clearing Vessels, Regulating the Coasting Trade, and for other purposes" (1 Stat. 55–65 [September 1, 1789]). Section 5 of this act reads as follows: "And be it further enacted, That no ship or vessel owned in whole or in part by any citizen of the United States, usually residing in any foreign country, shall, during the time he shall continue so to reside, be deemed a vessel of the United States, entitled to be registered by virtue of this act, unless he be an agent for, and partner in, some house or co-partnership,

consisting of citizens of the United States, actually carrying on trade in the said States."

3. 26 Geo. III, C. 60 (1786). Section 8 of this act reads as follows: "And be it enacted by the authority aforesaid, That no subject of his Majesty, his heirs and successors, whose usual residence is in any country not under the dominion of his Majesty, his heirs and successors, shall be deemed or intitled, during the time he shall continue so to reside, to be the owner in whole or in part of any *British* ship, or vessel, required and authorised to be registered by virtue of this act, unless he be a member of some *British* factory, or agent for, or partner in, any house or copartnership, actually carrying on trade in *Great Britain* or *Ireland*."

4. Section 6 of the Navigation Act of 1660 reads as follows: "And be it further enacted by the Authority aforesaid, That from henceforth it shall not be lawful to any Person or Persons whatsoever, to load or cause to be loaden and carried in any Bottom or Bottoms, Ship or Ships, Vessel or Vessels whatsoever, whereof any Stranger or Strangers-born (unless such as shall be Denizens or Naturalized) be Owners, Part-Owners or Master, and whereof three forths of the Mariners at least shall not be *English,* any Fish, Victual, Wares, Goods, Commodities or Things, of what Kind or Nature soever the same shall be, from one Port or Creek of *England, Ireland, Wales,* Islands of *Guernsey* or *Jersey,* or Town of *Berwick* upon *Tweed,* to another Port or Creek of the same, or of any of them; under Penalty for every one that shall offend contrary to the true Meaning of this Branch of this present Act, to forfeit all such Goods as shall be loaden and carried in any such Ship or Vessel, together with the Ship or Vessel, and all her Guns, Ammunition, Tackle, Furniture and Apparel; one Moiety to his Majesty, his Heirs and Successors, and the other Moiety to him or them that shall inform, seize or sue for the same in any Court of Record, to be recovered in Manner aforesaid" (12 Car. II, C. 18 [1660]).

From Nathaniel Appleton [1]

[*Boston*] *February 5, 1791.* "I wrote you 26 Ulto. This serves to inclose Duplicate Receipt for Certificates received from the Register dated 22d Jany 1791—also first receipt for Certificates dated 29th. Jany 1791. By this Post I transmitt to the Auditor an Abstract of Certificates Indents & Bills of Old Emission, recd into the Office in the Month of November last for which Certificates of the Funded Debt have been issued agreeably to the Act of Congress 4 August 1790. . . . The Loaning is so fast & the Transfers so many that I find myself unavoidable much behind hand in my returns & am very apprecencive that the month of April, when there is a universal expectation of Interest, will be upon me before it will be possible to get all the abstracts registered & the Book posted up, unless I have a sessation of business from abroad, longer then the fourteen days mentioned in your instructions. I think the whole month of March will be little enough to get the Books into a readiness to discharge the Interest by the first of April when I am sure of having a croud of applicants. Therefore unless I shall receive your orders to the contrary, I propose to inform all applicants to Loan or to Transfer That no Certificates can be Loaned or Transfers made in the Month of March. . . . I have seen the Secrety of War's advertisement that Pentions are to be paid at this Office in the month of March. If that should be the case it is an additional reason why Loaning & transfers should be suspended during that month. All which is humbly submitted to your opinion. Permitt me to express my earnest hopes That Congress will speedily make some provision for Clerks otherwise I cannot see how the public buisness can be carried on. . . ."

LC, RG 53, Massachusetts State Loan Office, Letter Book, 1785–1791, Vol. "259–M," National Archives.

1. In the course of this letter, Appleton, who was commissioner of loans for Massachusetts, discusses some of the routine problems that he and the commissioners of loans in other states encountered. Although most of the matters in this letter are self-explanatory, some mention should be made of the "Certificates Indents & Bills of Old Emission," which were the three distinct forms in which the old Continental debt was subscribed to the new Federal loan in each state.

The variety of paper included under the heading "Certificates" is described in Section 3 of "An Act making provision for the (payment of the) Debt of the United States." Sums subscribed to the new Federal loan were payable in the following types of certificates:

"Those issued by the register of the treasury.

"Those issued by the commissioners of loans in the several states, including certificates given pursuant to the act of Congress of the second of January, one thousand seven hundred and seventy-nine, for bills of credit of the several emissions of the twentieth of May, one thousand seven hundred and seventy-seven, and the eleventh of April, one thousand seven hundred and seventy-eight.

"Those issued by the commissioners for the adjustment of the accounts of the quartermaster, commissary, hospital, clothing, and marine departments.

"Those issued by the commissioners for the adjustment of accounts in the respective states.

"Those issued by the late and present paymaster-general, or commissioner of army accounts." (1 Stat. 139–40 [August 4, 1790].)

"Indents" were another form of paper issued in the persistent, but futile, effort to solve the financial problems of the Confederation government. Unlike either the certificates or the bills of old emissions, the indents were issued for interest rather than principal on the loan office debt. In addition, although indents were authorized by the Continental Congress and were printed by the Treasury, they were issued under local authority in each state. At the outset Congress stipulated that indents would be accepted in payment of the requisitions of the Continental Congress on the states only if a specified proportion of specie accompanied the indents when they were sent to the Treasury. Eventually even this requirement was removed, and indents were received without qualification. Certificates "issued for the payment of interest, commonly called indents of interest" were included among the certificates described in Section 3 of the act of August 4, 1790, as receivable in subscriptions to the new Federal loan. Section 5 of the act provided for the establishment of an issue of three percent stock exchangeable for the indents and accrued interest (1 Stat. 140). Under Section 4 of the act two thirds of the value of certificates which were accepted as principal of the old Continental debt were exchanged for the new six percent Federal stock, and the remaining one third of the certificates was exchanged for the new six percent deferred stock (1 *Stat.* 140).

"Bills of Old Emission" are described in Section 3 of the act of August 4, 1790, as "bills of credit issued by the authority of the United States in Congress assembled, at the rate of one hundred dollars in the said bills, for one dollar in specie" (1 *Stat.* 140). The term "old emission" served to distinguish bills of credit issued before 1780 from those issued subsequently. In the spring of 1780 a new system of issuing bills of credit was proposed and passed by Congress on March 18, 1780 (*JCC*, XVI, 263–67). This measure provided for "new emission" bills to be issued at the rate of two dollars for each forty dollars of the "old emissions" returned by the states to Congress to be destroyed. Because of the financial problems of the Continental Congress other types of certificates were issued in excessive quantities, and bills of the "old emission" failed to come back to the Continental Treasury in quantities sufficient either to reduce the number of "old emissions" in circulation or to issue the new bills in aid of Continental finances.

The number of certificates on the books of the commissioners of loans varied from one loan office to another. Speculation, fluctuations in the securities markets, and the routine purchase and sale of the Federal debt were some of the reasons for these transfers. The provision which a particular state had made for its citizens who were Continental creditors during the Confederation was a major source of variation in the number of transfers among the various loan officers during the subscriptions to the new Federal loan. Many of the states had made some kind of provision for the Continental debts during the Confederation. Where the state had confined these benefits to its own citizens, as was usually the case, there was a tendency for public creditors to hold their certificates in the name of a citizen of the state or to have them recorded with the register of the Treasury in order to receive "certificates in lieu of indents" which were issued by that officer for citizens of all the states. Under the new funding system state citizenship ceased to be important to Federal creditors, and some transfers to the loan offices most convenient to the creditor occurred. In addition, in some states during the Confederation, state certificates had been issued in lieu of Continental certificates. Under the new funding system certificates which appeared in the loan office books to the credit of a state officer were transferred back to the creditor who held the state certificate issued in lieu of the Continental one. Other special conditions in some states placed an additional burden on the work of the commissioners in charge of the loan offices in those states.

For a discussion of the problems of government finance during the Confederation period and the financial difficulties in 1790 which arose from the Revolutionary War debt, see Ferguson, *Power of the Purse*. For H's proposals for funding the public debts, see "Report Relative to a Provision for the Support of Public Credit," January 9, 1790. For the establishment of the loan offices as well as the funding program adopted by Congress, see "An Act making provision for the (payment of the) Debt of the United States" (1 *Stat.* 138–44).

From Isaac Sherman [1]

[*February 5, 1791.* On January 23, 1792, Sherman wrote to Hamilton: ". . . subsequent to my letter of 5th of February last. . . ." *Letter not found.*]

1. Sherman was the son of Roger Sherman of Connecticut. In 1787 and 1788 he was employed as one of the surveyors of the Northwest Territory, and he subsequently held a minor position in the Treasury.

From Joseph Whipple [1]

Portsmouth, New Hampshire, February 5, 1791. "In compliance with the directions given in your Circular letter of the 20th. January 1790 I enclosed you the 18th. of February following a Statement of the emoluments of the officers of the Customs in this district for one year; but as that Statement was founded partly on Calculation it could not be accurate. I flattered myself however that such dependence could be had upon it, as would make Some impression on Such Committees of the Legislature as might have matters of that kind before them. I have now enclosed a precise accot. of those emoluments accruing in the Year 1790, which I beg you will please to make such use of as you conceive proper & which I hope will be productive of the end proposed in troubling you with it. In the early times of the Revolution it was not an uncommon thing to see Services performed without reward & fortunes Sacrificed to the great objects then in Contemplation. But at this period when necessity does not call for such Sacrifices, when a peaceful & happy establishment of government is effected & a fortunate System of Revenue established and improving, it will not be expected that those employed in the execution of the Laws will be left without an adequate support. The office to which I am attached requires constant and diligent attention. It has my exertions that it shall be executed according to Law. It will be needless for me to Say after refering you to the Statement enclosed that I am oblig'd to draw from other resources the greater part of my Support. . . ."

LC, RG 36, Collector of Customs at Portsmouth, Letters Sent, 1790–1791, Vol. 2, National Archives; copy, RG 56, Letters from the Collector at Portsmouth, National Archives.

    1. Whipple was collector of customs at Portsmouth, New Hampshire.

From William Short [1]

Amsterdam. Feb. 7. 1791.

Sir

    I had the honor of writing to you on the 25th. of last month by the English packet. This, inclosed to the Secretary of State, will be sent also by the way of England. I mentioned in my last what I repeat here for greater certainty. "1093.   450.   264.   1405.   224.   264. 1405.   319.   1065.   224.   239.   1210.   1340.   426.   1336. 839.   1590.   224.   531.   1388.   224.   708.   227.   527.   224. 564.   566.   1340.   426.   1336.   1568.   948.   540.   422. 1648.   1416.   1233.   1336.   1236.   607.   224.   64.   1683. 508.   1330.   1208.   1460.   137."   —1413.   365.   294.   1000. 527.   1416.   1340.   176.   426.   1681.   1416.   1215.   763. 783.   224.   508.   1330.   1208.   1460.   224.   1357.   224. 1195.   1638.   1233.   115   1093.   168.   977.   1208.   105. 947.   1286.[2]

I have lately recieved a letter from M. de Montmorin [3] in which he informs me that at the request of Messrs. Schweizer &c.[4] he had given instructions to M. Otto [5] respecting that business, with which I have already made you acquainted.[6] He sends me a copy of these instructions which I don't doubt M. Otto will have already communicated. You will see by them the dispositions of the French ministry on this subject with which you will be perfectly satisfied, as every thing is rendered entirely subservient to the views of the President. I suppose it certain that the minister has no idea the plan proposed by Messrs. Schweizer &c. will be entered into.

I beg leave to refer you to my letter of this day to the Secretary of State [7] for information respecting the change of duties on American oils imported into France. Opinions were much divided but a majority were for increasing to an excessive degree these duties, so far as related to American oils, & prohibiting entirely those of other countries. The Nantucket fishermen settled in France may be considered as the principal cause of this measure—others conspired also to effect it. I have no doubt however that as soon as the French shall have organised their government they will correct many errors into which the parties that now rage in the assembly, force them. Each decree may be considered as a resolution carried by storm in which of course there is much chance work. Until they change this manner of proceeding no regulations that they adopt with respect to themselves or others can be considered as permanent. The article of tobacco is now under their discussion. The opinions are divided between admitting it to be cultivated freely in France & imported subject to a duty & prohibiting the culture & confining its importation to a monopoly. It is impossible to conjecture which will predominate. Appearances vary daily with respect to it.

I have &ca

The Honble Alexander Hamilton, Secretary of the Treasury.

[E N C L O S U R E]

Comte de Montmorin to Louis G. Otto [8]

Paris le   [9] Janvier 1791

Je vous adresse, M, plusiéres piéces qui m'ont été envoyées par les Srs. Jeanneret et Schweizer, Banquiers à Paris; vous y verrez l'offre que ces particuliers ont faite de Se charger de l'emprunt que le Congrès a ouvert en hollande, principalement pour acquiter notre créance; vous verrez également la correspondance qu'ils ont suivie sur cet objet avec M. Short; les motifs qui ont déterminé ce dernier à ne pas accepter leur Soumission, et le parti qu'il doit avoir pris de demander les ordres du Président des Etat-unis.

Vous voudrez bien, M, entretenir M. Jefferson sur la proposition des Ms. Jeanneret et Schweitzer. Nous devons désirer naturellement, vû la position gênée de nos finances, qu'elle puisse entrer dans les vues de M. le Gnal Washington et qu'il se détermine à l'agréer: mais vous observerez que nous Subordonnons notre convenance à celle des Etats Unis, et que, si, ceque je ne saurois juger d'avance, l'opération proposée y est contraire, notre intention n'est point d'y insister. Lorsque l'on a voulu nous engager à transmettre notre créance à des étrangers, nous nous y sommes refusés de crainte de faire chose désagréable au congrès: le cas présent n'est pas le même, puisqu'il s'agit simplement de remplir un emprunt que cette assemblée à elle même décreté. Je recommande, M, cette affaire à votre Zèle et à votre prudence.

Je suis &a.

ALS, letterpress copy, William Short Papers, Library of Congress; ALS, letterpress copy, William Short Papers, Library of Congress.

1. Short had accompanied Thomas Jefferson to Paris in 1784 as his secretary and later served as secretary of legation. In 1789 he was appointed chargé d'affaires at Paris.

2. In the second letterpress copy, William Short Papers, Library of Congress, this section is decoded as follows:

"In general terms the terms on which the loan is to be made are the same with the last except that the commission is to be ½ p. cent lower. It will be opened the middle or latter part of Febry. At present I may add that it is agreed to bring it into public the latter part of the month—the interest will begin for no part before March. 1."

3. Armand Marc, Comte de Montmorin Saint-Herem, to Short, January 24, 1791. This letter is printed as an enclosure to Short to H, March 11, 1791.

4. The Paris banking firm of Jean Gaspar Schweizer and François Jeanneret. See Short to H, December 18, 30, 1790, and January 15, 1791.

5. Louis G. Otto, French chargé d'affaires at Philadelphia. See enclosure.

6. See Short to H, January 15, 1791.

7. On February 7, 1791, Short wrote to Thomas Jefferson:
"They have at length fixed the duties on the importation of several foreign articles—instead of adopting the report of the committee in the mass as there was reason to expect, they discussed the articles separately. The committees of commerce & imposition adhered to their idea of subjecting the American oils to a moderate duty, in consequence of their second opinion, of which I have formerly given you an account—finding that it would be opposed in the assembly they agreed to augment it in hopes of succeeding by that means—the opposition however still continued. It was finally decided to exclude all foreign oils except the American & to subject them to a duty of twelve livres the quintal. This may be considered as a prohibitive duty, but the partisans of the plan knowing that a majority of the assembly would be against the exclusion of the American oils made use of this strategem. There are many who wish to make an experiment to see whether the national fishery can be made adequate to the national consumption & others who wish to make us purchase by a general commercial treaty a market for this particular article." (ALS, William Short Papers, Library of Congress.)

The following decree concerning oil was adopted on January 24, 1791:
"Les huiles de poissons étrangères, venant de tout autre pays que des Etats-Unis d'Amérique continueront d'être prohibées.

"A l'exception de celles qui entreront par les bureaux établis sur la Meuse, et de là jusqu'au Rhin, qui y seront admises en payant un droit de 12 livres du quintal.

"Les huiles venant des Etats-Unis d'Amérique, et importées par bâtiments français ou américains, payeront le même droit de 12 livres par quintal." (*Archives Parlementaires*, XXII, 475.)

8. Copy, William Short Papers, Library of Congress.

9. Space left blank in MS.

To Nathaniel Appleton

Treasury Department, February 8, 1791. Announces that Appleton has been selected by the President to pay "Pensions to Invalids for the space of one year." [1]

LS, with an insertion in H's handwriting, MS Division, New York Public Library.

1. The United States had assumed the payment of military pensions to invalids "who were wounded and disabled during the late war" by "An Act providing for the payments of the Invalid Pensioners of the United States" (1 *Stat.* 95 [September 29, 1789]) which provided payment of invalids until March 4, 1790. The payment of invalids for the years 1790 and 1791 was continued in "An Act further to provide for the Payment of the Invalid Pensioners of the United

States" (1 *Stat.* 129–30 [July 16, 1790]) and "An Act to continue in force the act therein mentioned, and to make further provision for the payment of Pensions to Invalids, and for the support of lighthouses, beacons, buoys, and public piers" (1 *Stat.* 218 [March 3, 1791]).

This letter, except for the sums specified as due to invalids, is the same as H to Jedediah Huntington, January 30, 1790.

To Sharp Delany [1]

Treasury Department,
February 8. 1791

Sir,

I received yesterday an application from Messrs. R & J Potter, Knox, Henderson & others,[2] relative to the claim of additional duties on Goods ℔ the ship Kitty from London. Having no statement of facts from your office, I am uncertain how far all those things, that may concern the rights of the United States, have occurred to the Applicants, & can, therefore, only give a conditional instruction to you.

It is proper in this & similar cases, that the concerned be requested to adduce all such testimony as you or they conceive to affect the question. If, on a *careful* examination into the facts, it shall *appear* that the vessel was within the United States (& if in this case the Ship Kitty shall be proved to have been within the Capes of Delaware bay) on the thirty first of Decemr last, I do not conceive that the additional duties can be lawfully demanded. The Goods, tho' not entered will be to be considered as those brought into the United States, which is the language of the Act of Congress.[3]

I must repeat to you, on this occasion, my wish that no application, in any case arising within your district, be made to the Treasury, with your knowledge, without a statement of facts from your office. Matters very interesting to the United States, & decisive upon questions, may often be overlooked, misconceived or omitted by the parties.

I am, sir,   Your Obedient Servant.   Alexander Hamilton

Sharp Delany esqr.

LS, Bureau of Customs, Philadelphia; copy, RG 56, Letters to the Collector at Philadelphia, National Archives; copy, RG 56, Letters to Collectors at Small Ports, "Set G," National Archives.
   1. Delany was collector of customs at Philadelphia.

2. This application has not been found. These were the Philadelphia mercantile houses of David Knox and James Henderson, and Richard and James Potter.

3. "An Act making further provision for the payment of the debts of the United States" (1 *Stat.* 180–82 [August 10, 1790]), which increased the duties on specific goods, went into effect on January 1, 1791.

To Thomas Smith [1]

[*Philadelphia, February 8, 1791.* On February 14, 1791, Smith wrote to Hamilton: "I am honored with your favor of 8th Inst." [2] *Letter not found.*]

1. Smith was commissioner of loans for Pennsylvania.
2. This was probably the same as the letter which H sent to Nathaniel Appleton on this date and to Jedediah Huntington on January 30, 1790.

From Otho H. Williams [1]

Baltimore, February 8, 1791. Explains apparent discrepancy in "last Weekly return of monies received and paid . . . from the 29th January to the 4. February 1791." States that the "credit for Forfeitures" in "the preceeding return, to wit from the 22nd. to the 28 January . . . arises upon the Sales of two parcels of condemned Merchandize which ought to have been credited last year."

ADfS, RG 53, "Old Correspondence," Baltimore Collector, National Archives.
1. Williams was collector of customs at Baltimore.

From Nathaniel Appleton

Boston, February 9, 1791. "As I understand all public papers must pass under cover to you, this incloses a duplicate receipt for Certificates received from the Registers and letter to the Auditor respecting cancelled Certifts & Indents forwarded to him by this Post. . . ."

LC, RG 53, Massachusetts State Loan Office, Letter Book, 1785–1791, Vol. "259–M," National Archives.

From Joseph Whipple

Portsmouth, New Hampshire, February 9, 1791. "In Conformity
with the directions given in your Circular letter of the 17th. May last
respecting Seizures, I have to inform you that a Small Seizure has been
made in this district, consisting of one Barrel, one half Barrel & three
Small Bags Coffee. . . ."

LC, RG 36, Collector of Customs at Portsmouth, Letters Sent, 1790–1791, Vol. 2,
National Archives; copy, RG 56, Letters from the Collector at Portsmouth,
National Archives.

To Henry Marchant [1]

Treasury Department
February 10. 1791.

Sir

You will find under this cover an act [2] remitting the forfeiture in
the case of the Schooner Fly, on the petition prefered to your court
by Wm. Brightman.

This vessel being under thirty tons cannot be employed in the
importation of goods from foreign ports. Nor can she pursue the
coasting trade without the burden of the foreign tonnage duty. She
may, however, with any papers that she may have brought in, export
a cargo to some foreign place in which vessels of her size are enter-
able and may there be sold. It is not probable that the legislature will
at any time put vessels, that shall be granted to their former owners,
on a footing better than that on which they were before.

I am, Sir, very respectfully   Your obedt. servant   Alex Hamilton

The Honorable Henry Marchant Esq.
District Judge of Rhode Island Newport.

LS, Hamilton Papers, Library of Congress.
   1. This letter is in reply to Marchant to H, December 20, 1790.
   2. H does not mean a legislative statute. "An Act to provide for mitigating or
remitting the forfeitures and penalties accruing under the revenue laws, in certain cases therein mentioned" (1 *Stat.* 122–23 [May 26, 1790]) permitted the
Secretary of the Treasury to decide such cases.

From Samuel Paterson [1]

Edinr. 10 Feby. 1791

Respectd. Sir

When I wrote you formerly,[2] It was Just when a Trunk was packing up for my freind Robt. Campbell [3] Bookseller. My hasty Scrawll & Dr. Prices [4] Pamphlet, in the way it was Sent, I hope youll Excuse. Their is No clean Copy of it to be got. At that Period I did not know that the inclosed State of the British Custom house Dutys &c. was published. Youll Notice this now Sent is by Authority of the British Government. Their is no other List of the Inland Taxes but that by *Kearsly* [5] which is Said to be very exact. Youll receive along with these Two Vollumes of Sir John Sinclair upon the Revenue of Great Britain.[6] He is a Member of the British House of Commons or Parliment.

I by no Means wish to engage your Most valuable time, by answering me, but I have to Sollicitt you upon an affair, that if it is not hurtfull, Very hurtfull to the Intrests of the United States, I know your own humanity will be a powerful Agent in My behalf. This will I find Make My letter longer then I intended, But it is Respected Sir On the footing that a Bystander will often Notice what reall Actors doe not discern. Nay Solomon, that Wise King, Says "that a fooll May teach a Wise man wisdom at a time". I theirfore doe it with that deference, that becomes me when writing you on any affair belonging to the United States, and with a Sense of that Ignorance I must have at this distance of the true Intrests of America.

ALS, Hamilton Papers, Library of Congress.
  1. Although Paterson was identified in an earlier volume of *The Papers of Alexander Hamilton* as an Edinburgh merchant (see Paterson to H, September 30, 1790), it is more likely he was the prominent British bookseller, cataloguer, and auctioneer of that name. Until he sold off his stock in 1769, Paterson was one of London's leading bookdealers. After 1769 he prepared bibliographies of a number of England's most extensive private libraries and for some years acted as librarian at the Bowood estate of Lord Shelburne.
  2. Paterson to H, September 30, 1790.
  3. Campbell was a Philadelphia bookseller.
  4. Richard Price, an English divine and polemicist. For Price's pamphlet, see Paterson to H, September 30, 1790.
  5. G. Kearsley, *Kearsley's Tax Tables & Stamp Duties* (London, 1789).
  6. Sir John Sinclair, *History of the Public Revenue of the British Empire*, 2 Vols. (London, 1784).

I beg to Sollicit you, in behalf of the Poor, hard wrought, half fed Inhabitants of Europe And would humbly propose, as they are Utterly unable to pay for a Passage to America, the only thing that Stopts thousands of them from Emigrating. I beg theirfore, that you would Imploy & use you Intrest to procure a Grant of Some Bounty or Relaxation of the Duties, to European Shipping bringing over Poor Industrious workmen to America.

Suppose the Tonnage Duty, upon Foreign Vessells Should be re-laxed, to answer as a Bounty. Suppose for every 15 or 20 Passengers Brought from Europe the Vessell was to have an Exemption of the Tonnage Duty upon 100 or 130 Tons & So on. Nay not only that But as Passengers often want to goe to a Certain Port, Say Philadelphia for Instance, & the Owners of the Vessell want to bring a Cargo of Tob-bacco from Virginia, The foreign Vessell or the Extent of Tonnage in proportion to the passengers she brought, Might be allowed without any duty to take in goods for the Port she designed to Load at. This or some other Plan is Neccessary to assist Emigrants from Europe to America, Journeymen of all Professions (a few of the fine arts ex-ceptd) are unable ever to Collect or save out of their Wages, a Sum equall to paying their whole freight to America, From Greenock or Glasgow to America. It is Six Guineas for a Steerage Passenger.

It may be answered Why not grant, priviledges or Bounties to the American Bottoms, *only* for bringing over tradesmen? In answer I say its impossible for the American Ships, to Carry over emigrants from Europe So well as Foreign Ships. The Penalties & Forfeitures, are so very heavy & so easily incurred, that No person Unacquaint with the Laws durst Venture upon Such a Measure. But the European Captain & owners know how to agree with Passengers so as to Escape the Penalties. In Britain the Penalties are £ 500 Str. & 6 mo. imprison-ment for every person Indented to goe out of the Kings Dominions, & I know not the Laws of Ireland, far less of any other Part of Europe, with regard to this.

I have hitherto only Mentioned the Poor of Britain but in other parts of Europe I am informed, their working people are in a Worse State, & less able to pay for their Passage to America. The Germans are a most Industrious people, the United States, would I hope be greatly benefeted by a Number of Germans imported every Year. I think the draining one part of Europe of these Industrious poor, that may be said to be able with every exertion they Can make only to be able to Keep Soull & Body together would have a Beneficiall effect upon the Treatment the poor would have in other Parts. No Doubt a few would goe also from Britain if encouragement was given, & I hope they would be found also Very industrious Subjects for here we are overstocked with people.

O Let the Name of the United States Rise high in the Annalls of Fame, by Extending her Bounties to enable the Industrious Poor of Europe to Sitt down on her fruitfull Soill, & be feed liberally by produce of her Lands. But as the Proverb says a Word to the wise is Enough.

I hope Respected Sir that filled with admiration of your Conduct, as Exhibited in Congressionall Register &c. youll pardon this freedom. My Zeall for the good of Mankind, & my Esteem for one who endeavours to Remove a Load of Debt from a Rising Nation of Free Men, have emboldened me to write this. Again I will Not trouble you Nor engross your Valuable time. If you knew the State of the Laborious Poor in Europe, as well as I, your own Compassion & humanity would not need to be desired to Remember them. by Respected Sir, Yr. Most hle Sert   Saml. Paterson

PS. A half penny or even a farthing, upon every pound of Tobbacco Exported from the United States, would not affect the Consumpt. & would be a good Fund for Bounties to Emigrants. If the United States Cannot impose it, the States that export Tobbacco Might by such a Tax, provide an Excellent fund for Publick Roads, Canalls &c. & the Sale would never be a Singlue pound less in Europe.

Many people here are of opinion, That the Prosperity & flourishing State of Britain, Is owing far more to the Establishment of *Bank's* then to the Nationall Debt. Certain it is that Scotland alone owes allmost all its Improvement in Agriculture, Commerce & Manufactures to the Institution of Banks. Their Are about Fifty Banks in England and about Thirty Banks in Scotland, that Issue out Notes.

S. Paterson

Report on the Petition of the
Merchants of Philadelphia
Trading to India and China

[Philadelphia, February 10, 1791
Communicated on February 10, 1791] [1]

[To the Speaker of the House of Representatives]

The Secretary of the Treasury in obedience to the order of the House of representatives of the twentieth day of January last referring to him the petition of the Merchants of Philadelphia trading to India and China; [2]

Respectfully reports:

That the subject of the said petition involves the consideration of the general policy, which ought to be pursued by the United States, in relation to the trade with India and China; concerning which, questions of equal delicacy and importance arise, requiring a more careful and deliberate investigation, than can be performed consistently with the view of the House of Representatives, respecting the termination of their present Session.

That, under this impression, the Secretary, if permitted by the House, will defer a report on the said subject, generally, till the next Session of Congress, and will confine himself, for the present, to a particular article of the said trade, namely, Teas.

That it appears, upon enquiry, that considerable quantities of Bohea tea have been brought into the United States, from Europe, notwithstanding the additional duties laid upon that article, when so imported, by the laws heretofore passed: [3] which have contributed both to overstock the market, and to reduce the price below the standard, at which it can be afforded, by the merchants trading to China; producing, consequently, a material discouragement to the trade with that country: in which the article of Bohea-tea is one of principal importance. As an additional and extensive field for the enterprize of our merchants and mariners, and as an additional outlet for the commodities of the country, the trade to India and China appears to lay claim to the patronage of the Government. And it's proceedings hitherto have countenanced the expediency of granting that patronage; in pursuance of which principle, the fact, which has been stated, would seem to render it advisable for the present, that a farther duty should be laid on Bohea-tea, brought from Europe: Three Cents per pound, it is conceived, would be an adequate increase.

But to form a satisfactory judgment of the propriety, either of pursuing or extending the system of granting particular favors to the trade in question, it is necessary that a full and accurate examination should be had into the nature and tendency of that trade, in order to ascertain the extent, to which it may require, or be entitled to encouragement.

All which is humbly submitted.   Alexander Hamilton,
                                       Secretary of the Treasury

Treasury-Office,
February, 10th. 1791.

Copy, RG 233, Reports of the Treasury Department, 1791–1792, Vol. II, National Archives.
    1. *Journal of the House*, I, 375.
    2. On January 20, 1791, "A memorial of the merchants of Philadelphia, trading to India and China, was presented to the House and read, praying that an additional duty may be laid upon goods imported from thence in foreign bottoms; and also on articles the growth and produce of India or China, which are imported from Europe either in American or foreign bottoms. . . .
    "*Ordered*, That the said memorial . . . be referred to the Secretary of the Treasury, with instruction to examine the same, and report his opinion thereupon to the House." (*Journal of the House*, I, 358.)
    3. Section 1 of "An Act making further provision for the payment of the debts of the United States" provided that, when merchants imported bohea tea from China and India in ships of the United States, they paid a duty of ten cents a pound. When they imported it from Europe in vessels of the United States, they paid twelve cents a pound. When they imported it from any other place or in ships of another country, they paid fifteen cents a pound (1 *Stat.* 180 [August 10, 1790]).

From Thomas Rodney [1]

Poplar Grove [Delaware] Feby. 10th 1791.

Dr. Sir

It is very True that I was not an advocate for the Fedœral Government being adopted so soon altho I was very sensible of great defects

ALS, Delaware Historical Society, Wilmington.
    1. Rodney had served as a colonel in the Delaware militia during the Revolution and had represented Delaware in the Continental Congress from 1781 to 1783 and from 1785 to 1787.

in the Old confederation, Yet I was apprehensive it would be dangerous to Our Independence to attempt Changing that principle of Government which had conducted us Safe through the Revolution,
because I was persuaded that the local attachment of The people to
their State governments would prevent their consenting to a Regular
& Uniform General government and that if a partial form was Established the peoples local attachment to their State government would
operate Strongly against it so as to render its Operations weak & in
Effectual. I find in both Instances my apprehensions well founded.
The States have deligated great powers to Congress but have reserved
Enough to them selves to keep up their Old local attachments and
indeed to increase them. And we already see that the State legislatures
of Virginia and Pensylvania are attempting to controle Congress in
the Exercise of their Constitutional powers, and as the locale Attachments of the people will natural⟨ly⟩ incline them to Side with their
State governments, ⟨such⟩ conduct however unconstitutional will have
a Tendency to weaken the general Government; for no resolut⟨ion⟩ of
the States unless agreed to by all the States ought to have any Controle
on the General Government. The Fedœral powers being Established
by all the States, cannot be constitutionally controled by any number
of them less than all. Therefore Such conduct in the Seperate States
Should have no Other weight with the general Legislature than as
Counsels Advising them to Consider the Subject, they Object to, with
the greatest wisdom and impartiallity always giving, in their results,
the general welfare of all the States the preference.

Since all the States have adopted the Fedœral Constitution and
it is now the Only existing principle of Union, The same reasons that
induced me to be against it now induces me as Strongly to support
and maintain it. Being a firm Unalterable friend to the Revolution;
and believing that the Union of the States is the Only thing that can
secure their Independance for a long time; I consider every measure
that Indangers this Union as Adverse to the Welfare of America.
Therefore I was against the Fedœral Constitution on Account of the
danger of its having this Effect, but Since it has become the only
principle of Union it is plain that the same reason induces me to be a
firm friend to it. And Certainly every friend to the Liberty and Independance of America ought to consider the Subject in this point
of view. The Opinion and information of the Several States would

Certainty be of great use to the general government if Communicated in a proper manner as advisce or Counsel but may have a very different Effect if Couched in Terms of Censure. The legislature of Pensylvania for Instance Might have advised Congress in the most friendly manner that they considered the Excise Law [2] as prejudicial to the Liberties of the peoples & desiring them if posible to prefer Some other Subject of revenue that would answer their purpose less adverse to the private liberty and rights of Individuals and without pointing out what other Subject the legislature of the State prefered to the Excise.[3] Such Counsel as this would Not be adverse to, but useful to the general government. There is no Law more adverse to the rights & liberty of a free people than excise Laws for however gentle they be in their Commencement it will be found that they Cannot be Executed without a great number of petty officers, and those Officers vested with powers greatly adverse to the Liberty and private rights of Individuals. I therefore as an Individual would prefer a Land Tax or poll Tax far before an Excise. Yet perhaps the great Councils of the nation may be induced by Sufficient considerations to think other wise. In England where the rights of Individuals are more respected and better secured by the Laws then ever they were in any other nation, they have long had excise Laws and altho the petty officers of excise are vested with frightful powers yet if we may Judge by the quiet Acquiessence of the people the Exercise of them are not So adverse to the people as the appearance of them Seem to indicate. Atho there is greater Objections to excise Laws than to Imports & duties on commerce yet there is the same reason in Support of them.

2. "An Act repealing, after the last day of June next, the duties heretofore laid upon Distilled Spirits imported from abroad, and laying others in their stead; and also upon Spirits distilled within the United States, and for appropriating the same" (1 *Stat.* 199–214 [March 3, 1791]). The bill had been presented in the House on December 30, 1790.

3. On January 14, 1791, a motion remonstrating against the excise bill was presented to the Pennsylvania House of Representatives. On January 22 the Pennsylvania House of Representatives agreed to a modified version of this motion which reads in part: "That these sentiments be communicated to the Senators representing the state of *Pennsylvania* in the Senate of the United States, with a hope that they will oppose every part of the excise bill now before Congress, which shall militate against the just rights and liberties of the people." The state senate did not concur (*Journal of the First Session of the House of Representatives of the Commonwealth of Pennsylvania, Which Commenced at Philadelphia, on Tuesday, the Seventh Day of December, in the Year of our Lord One Thousand Seven Hundred and Ninety* [Philadelphia: Printed by Hall and Sellers, No. 51 Market-Street—1790], 94–95, 108, 138).

It is difficult to draw Sufficient revenues from the pepole for the support of the government of a great nation by direct Taxation therefore it is found necessary to apply to Subjects that afford it by indirect Taxation, and upon this principle perhaps the Excise may be as necessary as the Impost. Yet in my Own Opinion direct Taxation is absolutely necessary in every government for this calls forth that information from Society which is necessary to direct the Government; And I am fully convinced that the annual Support of the Civil Government of every free State ought to be by direct Taxation; I mean the Annual support of all the Civil Officers of Government. This is without doubt an Essential principle in a free Government; How much further it might be prudent to pursue direct Taxation must always depend on the wisdom of the Legislature, and the information and Sentiments of the Community Which would naturally flow on that Subject; beside if direct Taxation was felt and carried as far as the people would Chuse to bare it according to the Exigences of the Nation; they would the more willingly submit afterwards to indirect Taxation, where more revenue was Necessary, and this in all probability is the True reason that indirect Taxation is so quietly Acquiessed to in England. It therefore appears advisable to Charge the Whole Support of Civil government on direct Taxation and if the people did not Chuse to bare more in this way, then they would naturally become Advocates for Indirect Taxation. I am therefore pursuaded that to propose a Direct Land Tax and Poll Tax for the Support of Civil government would Set the People right with respect to Taxation, for this would draw forth the True Sentiments of the people towards what kind of Taxation they would prefer, and for this reason every kind of Taxation ought to be pursued at the same Time because the Sentiments of the people would then plainly direct the Minister to those kinds where they would Chuse he should Seek the most revenue. A free people will always grumble at every Species of Taxation but nevertheless will always bare What appears Necessary to answer the purposes of government if wisely conducted.

I am Sir with great respect   your most Obedient   Thomas Rodney

Honble Alexandr. Hamilton Esqr.
Secretary of the Treasury.

To Otho H. Williams

Treasury Department
February 10th 1791.

Sir,

A petition from Mr John Hollins,[1] of Baltimore, to the House of representatives has been refered to me on which I shall report [2] that in my opinion the existing law admits of the relief desired by the petitioner. Annexed to the petition are legal Testimonies that the Schooner John was before the first of January 1791. within the Capes of Chessapeak bay, whence it follows that the Cargo on board her was "brought into the United States" before the expiration of the 31st December 1790.[3] You will therefore only [4] claim from Mr. Hollins the duties imposed by the impost Act of the first of June 1789.[5]

I am sir   Your Obedient Servant   Alexander Hamilton

Otho. H. Williams Esquire

LS, Columbia University Libraries.
 1. On February 4, 1791, the House of Representatives received "A petition of John Hollins, praying an abatement of the additional duties, which took place the first of January last, arising on a cargo imported in a vessel, which, although she arrived before that period, was prevented by the ice from getting to her port of entry till some time after.
 "*Ordered*, That the said [petition] be referred to the Secretary of the Treasury, with instruction to examine the same, and report his opinion thereupon to the House." (*Journal of the House*, I, 370.)
 2. See "Report on the Petition of John Hollins," February 12, 1791.
 3. January 1, 1791, was specified as the effective date for "An Act making further provision for the payment of the debts of the United States" (1 *Stat.* 180 [August 10, 1790]).
 4. This word is in H's handwriting.
 5. The act H is referring to is "An Act for laying a Duty on Goods, Wares, and Merchandises imported into the United States" (1 *Stat.* 24–27 [July 4, 1789]).

To ————

Treasury Department
February 11. 1791

Sir

The Treasurer has been directed to draw *in favour* of the Commissioner of Loans for your State in order to the payment of the

Pensions to Invalids which will become payable the fifth of March next.[1] His drafts however will not in the first instance be directed to any particular Collector; but will be transmitted with blanks to be filled up by the Commissioner. This is mentioned lest the manner of the Direction should occasion suspicion of Counterfeit. Such as may be presented to you you will of course pay with whatever money may be in your hands.

In order that the Commissioner may know how to address the bills it is requisite that you should inform him *immediately* on the receipt of this of the Specie in your hands and of the sums which you may receive from time to time 'till the end is answered. This being a matter in which humanity is concerned I shall be glad that there may be as little delay as possible.

I am, Sir,   Your Obedt. servant   Alexander Hamilton

LS, The Huntington Library, San Marino, California.
   1. See H to Appleton, February 8, 1791.

From John Habersham [1]

[*February 11, 1791*. In a letter to Hamilton, dated May 20, 1791, Habersham referred to "my letter of the 11th. of February last." *Letter not found.*]

   1. Habersham was collector of customs at Savannah.

From Thomas Jefferson

[*Philadelphia, February 11, 1791. Letter not found.*]

Letter listed in Jefferson's record of letters written and received, Thomas Jefferson Papers, Library of Congress.

To William Seton

[*Philadelphia, February 11, 1791.* On February 16, 1791, Seton wrote to Hamilton: "I am honored with your letter of the 11th." *Letter not found.*]

To William Lewis

Treasury Department February 12th 1791

Sir

The following case [1] occours in the transactions of the Treasury.

The husband of a deceased Administratrix *after her death* applies at the Treasury for the settlement of an account which was relative to the *administration* of the wife. The Officers of the Treasury, without notice of her decease, make settlement and grant a Certificate for a balance due, in the name of the husband.

Other parties have since taken out administration *de bonis non*, upon the estate to which the balance was due, and now apply for a settlement, and a certificate.

Are they entitled to it? or can it with propriety be refused?

The parties all belonged to the state of massachusetts. It is agreed that by the laws of that state, if the wife had been living at the time of the settlement it would have been well made with the husband without her cooperation. The Question therefore turns on her death and the want of notice.

I have the honor to be   with great consideration   sir   Your obedt servt   Alexander Hamilton

William Lewis Esqr
Attorney for the district
of Pennsylvania

LS, RG 217, Miscellaneous Treasury Accounts, 1790–1894, Account No. 1268, National Archives.

1. This case concerned a claim against the estate of Dr. Daniel Scott of Boston by "Samuel Cobb, Mercht. & Abijah Cheever, Physician both of the Town of Boston, . . . as administrators to the Estate . . . For . . . the balance which appeared due to the said Estate, for sundry Medicines & Chirugical Instruments, furnished for the use of the Department of the late General Hospital. . . ." Margaret Scott Page, Scott's widow, had acted as administratrix, and after her death the amount due the estate was paid by the Treasury Department to "the Credit of John Page, as Administrator on the Estate of the said Daniel Scott." The documents pertaining to this case may be found in RG 217, Miscellaneous Treasury Accounts, 1790–1894, Account No. 1268, National Archives.

To Edmund Randolph

[Philadelphia, February 12, 1791. In a letter dated February, 1791, Randolph referred to Hamilton's "letter of February, 12th: 1791." Letter not found.]

Report on the Petition of John Hollins

Treasury Department; February 12th: 1791.
[Communicated on February 12, 1791] [1]

[To the Speaker of the House of Representatives]
The Secretary of the Treasury, in obedience to the Order of the House of Representatives of the 4th Instant, relative to the petition of John Hollins,[2] of the Town of Baltimore, Merchant,
Respectfully reports;

That after duly examining the late and existing laws imposing duties on goods imported into the United States, with a view to their application in the case, wherein the said John Hollins has sought relief, he is of opinion, that the additional duties, from which the petitioner prays to be exonerated, are not legally demandable from him, and that he has transmitted an explanatory instruction to the Collector of Baltimore.[3] He, therefore, humbly submits to the House, the propriety of giving leave that the said petition be withdrawn.[4]

All which is humbly submitted,   Alexander Hamilton
                                         Secretary of the Treasury

Copy, RG 233, Reports of the Treasury Department, 1791–1792, Vol. II, National Archives.

1. *Journal of the House*, I, 377.
2. See H to Otho H. Williams, February 10, 1791, note 1.
3. H to Williams, February 10, 1791.
4. An entry in the *Journal of the House* for February 12, 1791, reads as follows: "The Speaker laid before the House a letter from the Secretary of the Treasury, covering his report on the petition of John Hollins, . . . Whereupon, *Ordered*, That the petitioner have leave to withdraw his said petition" (*Journal of the House*, I, 377).

From Nathaniel Appleton

Boston, February 13, 1791. ". . . I hope by next Post to be able to transmitt you the amount of the Certift of Funded Debt issued in the month of December & Jany last for your information tho' I shall not be able to send a regular Abstract of the Same."

LC, RG 53, Massachusetts State Loan Office, Letter Book, 1785–1791, Vol. "259–M," National Archives.

Election to American Philosophical Society

[Philadelphia, February 14, 1791]

To all Persons to whom These Presents shall come,
Greeting.

The American Philosophical Society held at Philadelphia for promoting useful Knowledge, desirous of advancing the Interest of the Society by associating to themselves Men of distinguished Eminence, and of conferring Marks of their Esteem upon Persons of literary Merit, have Elected The Honourable Alexander Hamilton Secretary of the United States for the Department of the Treasury. a Member of the said Philosophical Society, hereby granting unto him all the Rights of Fellowship, with all the Liberties and Privileges thereunto belonging.

In Testimony whereof the said Society have caused the Seal of their Corporation to be annexed to this Certificate, and the same to be attested by the Names of the proper Officers this fourteenth Day of February in the Year of our Lord One Thousand Seven Hundred and Ninety One.

Attested James Hutchinson ⎞ Secretaries   Davd. Rittenhouse President
          R. Patterson | John Ewing ⎞
          Sam. Magaw | William Smith ⎬ Vice Presidents
          Jono Williams ⎠   Th: Jefferson ⎠

Elected 21 January 1791.

DS, Hamilton Papers, Library of Congress.

From Henry Marchant

Newport, Rhode Island, February 14, 1791. Encloses the petition of Hezekiah Usher and George Usher, captain and mate of the brigantine *Ruth,* who had been prosecuted for landing goods which they did not declare. States that the "said Hezh. Usher, Master of sd. Brige. is a young Man, twenty six years old, and, that this was first Voyage he was ever Captain, that the Mate, is but twenty three years old, and this was but the second Voyage he was ever Mate."

ADfS, Rhode Island Historical Society, Providence.

From Jeremiah Olney [1]

Providence, February 14, 1791. "The enclosed Letter to the Treasurer, covers the second Moieties (the first being transmitted the 10th. instant) of Two Bank Notes, amounting, ℔ triplicate List herewith, to 127 Dollars. . . . I have . . . received your Letter of the 31st. Ulto., relative to the appointment of Mates to the Revenue Cutters. I have in view Two or Three Persons whom I could recommend as suitable for those births; and if, on conversing with them, I find they will accept thereof, you shall be made acquainted with their Names by the next Post."

ADfS, Rhode Island Historical Society, Providence; copy, RG 56, Letters from the Collector at Providence, National Archives.
  1. Olney was collector of customs at Providence.

To Edmund Randolph

[*Philadelphia, February 14 1791.* In a letter dated February, 1791, Randolph referred to Hamilton's "letter of the 14th: February." *Letter not found.*]

Report on Compensation to the Commissioners of Loans

Treasury Department,
February, 14. 1791.
[Communicated on February 15, 1791] [1]

[To the Speaker of the House of Representatives]

The Secretary of the Treasury, in obedience to the Order of the House of Representatives, of the 13th. Ultimo, relative to compensation to the Commissioners of Loans [2] for the extraordinary expenses, that may, in the first instance, be incurred by them in the execution of the Act making provision for the public debt; [3]

Respectfully reports,

That as the allowances to the several Commissioners of loans must be considered, as intended to compensate them for their services, and for those expenditures only, which are ordinarily incident to the execution of their respective offices, it may be deemed reasonable and just, that they should be indemnified for all such extraordinary expenditures, as shall appear to have been necessarily incurred, in the first stages of the business.

That these extraordinary expenditures will consist of additional Stationary, and additional Clerk-hire.

That with regard to the first, as the quantity of Stationary, which will be consumed in a common year, after the first will bear a very inconsiderable proportion, to that which will be necessarily provided and consumed during the first year, and as much additional labor and exertion, on the part of the Commissioners themselves, will be required, during the same period, it is humbly conceived, that it will be proper to reimburse those officers, for whatever expense they shall necessarily have incurred, in procuring Stationary for the use of the first year of their service.

That with regard to the second part, namely, additional Clerk-hire, it is presumable, from the rates of the compensations, that it was in contemplation of the Legislature, that some of the Commissioners would stand in need of Clerks, and that others of them would be able to perform the requisite services, themselves. The first Class may be supposed to include only the Commissioners of Massachusetts, New York, Pennsylvania, and Virginia; a Clerk to each of whom will, probably, be indispensable, at all times; perhaps, to some of them, more than one may be found so. If this supposition be well-founded, the rule for determining the extra-Clerk-hire may be, to consider, in this light, all that may have been necessarily paid by the several Commissioners, except the wages of one Clerk, by each of the Commissioners of Massachusetts, New York, Pennsylvania and Virginia.

If these suggestions shall be appproved by the House, it will be proper, that provision should be made by law, for admitting to the credit of the several Commissioners of Loans, in the settlement of their respective accounts, all such sums as shall appear to have been necessarily expended by them in the purchase of stationary, and for the hire of Clerks, in relation to the execution of their offices, from the commencement of the same to the first day of October next, deducting the salary of one Clerk, in respect to each of the Commissioners of Massachusetts, New York, Pennsylvania and Virginia.

All which is humbly submitted.   Alexander Hamilton
                                     Secretary of the Treasury

Copy, RG 233, Reports of the Treasury Department, 1791–1792, Vol. II, National Archives.

1. *Journal of the House*, I, 379.

2. The House ordered: "On a motion made and seconded, 'That a committee be appointed to consider and report whether any, and what, further compensation is necessary to be made to the Commissioners of Loans, to defray the extraordinary expense occasioned to them, in the first instance, in the execution of the act making farther provision for the debt of the United States.'

"*Ordered*, That the said motion be referred to the Secretary of the Treasury, with instruction to examine the same, and report his opinion thereupon to the House." (*Journal of the House*, I, 354.)

3. 1 *Stat.* 138–44 (August 4, 1790).

From Thomas Smith

Loan Office [Philadelphia] Feby. 14th 1791

Sir,

This accompanys Abstract of Certificates Old Emissions & Indents [1] received on subscriptions to the Loan proposed by act of Congress 4 Augt 1790 [2] from the 1st to the 31st January inclusive.

The subscriptions are encreasing very fast, which with the payment of Indents to the Citizens of this State to enable them to possess themselves of their original Certificates in order to fund them; together with the great number of Transfers that are daily making encreases the business of this office to so great a degree that without great assistance whilst the pressure of business continues it must be much retarded if not greatly embarrassed. I am honored with your favor of 8th Inst.[3] also with Genl. Knox's [4] of 9th with his Instructions & Warrant for the payment of the Invalids. I shall most chearfully execute that & every other duty in the power of

Sir your &c.

Honble Alex. Hamilton Secy. Treasy. U.S.

LC, RG 53, Pennsylvania State Loan Office, Letter Book, 1790–1794, Vol. "615–P," National Archives.

1. The monthly abstract which Smith enclosed with this letter provided a summary of the routine work of the Pennsylvania loan office. For a discussion of "Certificates Old Emissions & Indents," see Nathaniel Appleton to H, February 5, 1791, note 1.

In the second paragraph of this letter Smith is referring to conditions in the Pennsylvania loan office which differed somewhat from those in the loan offices of other states. In several offices the indents of interest, which had become due before January 1, 1788, continued to be issued after the institution of the new Federal Government. In Pennsylvania a more complete issue of indents was made because of Section 2 of the Pennsylvania law of March 27, 1789, entitled "An Act to Repeal So Much of Any Act or Acts of Assembly of This Commonwealth as Directs the Payment of the New Loan Debt or the Interest Thereof Beyond the First Day of April Next, and for Other Purposes Therein Mentioned," which provided that "new loan" certificates issued by Pennsylvania during that state's assumption of the Continental debt might be returned to the office of the comptroller general and exchanged for the Continental certificates originally loaned to Pennsylvania or "other certificates to the like amount." Section 2 concluded with the proviso that "no certificates shall be so returned or delivered until the interest paid by this state on the certificate or certificates issued by this commonwealth as aforesaid shall be equalized and the overplus or balance beyond what has been in every such case received by this state from the United States shall be repaid in indents of the United States to the comptroller-general for the use of this state, and in every case where this state shall have received more interest from the United States than shall have been paid on the certificates so as aforsaid issued by this state the comptroller-general shall and he is hereby required to pay such overplus in indents of the United States to the holder or holders of such certificates" (*Pennsylvania Statutes,* XIII, 266).

2. "An Act making provision for the (payment of the) Debt of the United States" (1 *Stat.* 138–44).

3. Letter not found.

4. Henry Knox, Secretary of War.

Treasury Department Circular
to the Commissioners of Loans

Treasury Department,
February 14. 1791

Sir,

I have directed the Treasurer of the United States to forward to you drafts payable to you or your order for the Sum of fifty thousand Dollars.

These Drafts will be transmitted to you with blanks for the Direction of each as the case may require, and may be filled up either with the name of Tench Francis Esquire, Cashier of the Bank of North America, or with that of William Seton Esquire, Cashier of the Bank of New York, or with that of the Collector of [Boston, being first informed in respect to the latter that he is in Cash to pay them.] [1]

They are intended as one mean of putting you in Cash for paying the first Quarters interest on the public debt, which will become payable on the first day of April next to the Creditors in your State.

There are ample funds deposited in the Banks of North America & New York, for answering the bills on demand. So that you may direct the whole or any part of them to the Cashier of either of those banks.

It is conceived that you will be able to Sell these bills, or a proportion of them to persons who may have occasion to remit money to New York or to Pennsylvania. You will of course understand that they are to be sold at par only.

Immediately on receipt of the bills, you will do well to give public notice that you have bills drawn by the Treasurer of the United States to dispose of for Cash, on either of the Banks of New York or North America, at the option of the purchaser.

It appears to me that it will be advisable for you to deposit the bills in the Bank of Massachusetts, if the Directors of it shall be willing to receive & sell them on the public Account, passing the proceeds to your credit. This method is constantly pursued with the banks of N America & New York in similar matters. In this case the notice you give ought to specify that the bills are lodged in the Bank.

It need not be observed that the drafts being payable to you or order they are to be indorsed by you previous to the *Sale; of which* you will *not fail* to make me a return by every post.

If there are any circumstances which lead to a judgment of the amount of the debt on which interest will be to be paid in your State, I shall be glad of immediate information, & shall thank you for your opinion by the first post after this reaches you how far the timely Sale of the bills can be relied on. In order to this you will do well to converse with some of your best informed Merchants.

I am, Sir,   Your Obt Hbe Servt.   Alexander Hamilton

LS, to Nathaniel Appleton, The Bostonian Society, Boston; LS, to Jabez Bowen, from the original in the New York State Library, Albany.
   1. Bracketed material is in H's handwriting. In the letter to Bowen H inserted the words "Providence or New Port being first informed that such Collector is in Cash to answer them."

From Otho H. Williams

Baltimore 14th February 1791

Sir

In answer to remarks of the Comptroller,[1] on my account Current, ending the 30th September last, I have had occasion to reply at some length. There will not probably be any essential difference between the final Opinion of the Comptroller and my own, on the subjects of his remarks, unless it may be on a charge for the rent of a publick warehouse. On that subject I had the honour to address you in October last.[2] In addition to what I have written to you, Sir, and to the Comptroller, permit me to remark that the want of a publick *wharf, and Warehouse* in this place, subjects the Officers of the Customs to very great inconvenience, and sometimes, even distress, in the execution of their duty.

For want of a publick landing place, particular places must be mentiond in the permits for landing, or Owners are exonerated, in some respect, from the penalty for removing goods without permission; and the weigher is occasionally to remove his scales from Wharf to Wharf, make use of others, or to subject importers to an extraordinary expence for retransportation of their Merchandise; and the Gauger is, in like manner, to go from place to place, to perform his duty. The Surveyor ⟨is⟩ necessarily much on board Vessels; the Connection however between that Officer and the Collector, and the reciprocal duties of the latter, and the Naval Officer, make it requisite that they should be often together. It is to be regretted that their several duties and Compensations are not more distinct. But in any case the having all their Offices in the same house, would be a very Considerable Convenience, as their *Official documents ought* reciprocally to check each other.

Inspectors are, in certain cases, Comptrollers of the Customs; they are together with the Collector, and Naval Officer, to examine and sign all manifests after delivery of the Cargos. And their duty on Other Occasions requires their attendance at the Custom House; which is a consideration in favour of a place both commodious and Convenient to the Harbour. The Measurer is, at this Port, an unnecessary Officer. There is no regular tide to bring into Port the inward bound Vessels, and they are often detained by contrary Winds, until multiplied to a fleet of a dozen, or more. If three, or four happen to have salt, and Coal, which is not uncommon, it becomes necessary to prevent delays, and expence to Importers, that more than One or two Measurers be apointed and more than one Cannot be reasonably rewarded for the service by *all* that is allowed by law for the measuring all the salt and Coal imported to this place.[3]

Every vessel must be in charge of an *Inspector*, and a vessel having salt, or coal, only, must have a *measurer* also on board. Two Officers are therefore, in such Case, on board the same Vessel, and for the same purpose.

Inspectors are, in every respect, as well qualified for the service as the nature of it requires, and the quantity of Coal or Salt, or other thing, could certainly be as truely ascertained by an Inspector constantly employed, as by a Man occasionally appointed. The terms of the allowance to an Inspector, which is not to exceed One Dollar and One fourth ℔ day for "every day he shall be employed in aid of the Customs." [4] implies that he may on some days be *not* employed. The nature of the service, in this District, where there are many ports, and landing places, requires that Inspectors should be constantly employed, and considering the manner of their creation, and conditions upon which they hold their appointments, I believe that to allow them fixed Sallaries, payable monthly, would be no less eligible on account of their industry, and integrity than the present plan: and might all things considered, be more to the advantage of the revenue.

Those considerations are not all perhaps strictly pertinent to the Subject upon which this letter was particularly intended, but if any of them afford you information you will excuse the trouble of them. My wish to see the department of the Customs upon an eligible and respectable establishment must be my apology.

I am Sir   Your most Obedient   Humble Servant

Alexr. Hamilton Esqr.
Secretary of the Treasury

ADf, RG 53, "Old Correspondence," Baltimore Collector, National Archives.
     1. Nicholas Eveleigh.
     2. Letter not found.
     3. Section 53 of "An Act to provide more effectually for the collection of the duties imposed by law on goods, wares and merchandise imported into the United States, and on the tonnage of ships or vessels" provided that measurers would be paid forty cents for the measurement of each hundred bushels of salt and fifty cents for the measurement of each hundred bushels of coal (1 *Stat.* 172 [August 4, 1790]).
     4. 1 *Stat.* 172.

From William Ellery [1]

Custom House [Newport, Rhode Island]
Feby. 15th 1791

Sir,

I received your letter of the 31st. of last month [2] on the 12th of this. It will be impossible for me to give the names of persons of this State suitable for 1st. 2nd. & 3d. mates of the Cutter now building in Connecticut by this Post. I will do it the next.

When I sent forward a statement of the Cases of Hezekiah Usher & George Usher [3] I was unacquainted with some circumstances which appeared on the examination of the Inspector of Bristol [4] before the District Judge. I mean that upon his discovering the Hhd of Rum not mentioned in the Permit, and mentioning it to the Capt., the Capt. said it might be water, and that the said Rum, and the three bags of Coffee were unladed in the absence of the Inspector, that he had locked up the hatchways, and taken the key with him, and that when he returned he found the Hatchways had been open'd, and the Rum and Coffee stored. If these circumstances had been known to me at the time I wrote I should most certainly have mentioned them in the Statement.

Inclosed is a weekly return of Cash on hand; and also a List of one Bank note and of two Post notes of the bank of North America amounting to eighty dollars, Moieties of which are now transmitted to the Treasr. The other moieties of them were transmitted by the last Post.

I have the honour to be   Sir   Yr. most obedt. servt.

W Ellery Collr

Secry of the Treasy.
of the U. States

LC, Newport Historical Society, Newport, Rhode Island.
   1. Ellery, who had served as Continental loan officer for Rhode Island during the Confederation, was collector of customs at Newport.
   2. Letter not found, but see H to Jeremiah Olney, January 31, 1791.
   3. Ellery had forwarded this statement to H on January 17, 1791. Ellery's letter of January 17 had not been found when Volume VII of *The Papers of Alexander Hamilton* was published. It has since been located in the Newport Historical Society and will be printed in a supplementary volume. See also Henry Marchant to H, February 14, 1791.
   4. William Munro.

To Cyrus Griffin [1]

[*Philadelphia, February 15, 1791.* "I am under the necessity of returning you the papers in the cases of Messrs. McRae and Morrison,[2] which you will find enclosed. There is no legal proof that the goods have ever paid duty. The Collectors & Deputy Collectors of the customs are not vested with the *general* power of administring oaths. The Deposition of Mr. Fraser [3] before the Deputy Collector of Baltimore [4] however true it may be is not therefore legal testimony. The Deposition moreover should have been that the goods were the contents or part of the contents of certain *specified packages* under *specified marks* and *Numbers* imported in *specified vessels* the same on which the official documents shews the duties had been paid or secured, and should have been taken before a Magistrate or Judge authorized to administer Oaths. It is observable that the deposition and manifest given as it is presumed after the seizure do not say when the goods were shipt, and that there is no proof or statement of the time of said seizure." *Letter not found.*]

Extract, Columbia University Libraries.
  1. Griffin was judge of the Federal District Court of Virginia.
  2. John McRae and John Morrison had applied to Griffin under the provisions of "An Act to provide for mitigating or remitting the forfeitures and penalties accruing under the revenue laws, in certain cases therein mentioned" (1 *Stat.* 122 [May 26, 1790]) for a remission of penalties on imported goods seized in Baltimore.
  3. Thomas Fraser, a Baltimore importer. See H to Otho H. Williams, June 4, 1791; Williams to H, June 10, 1791.
  4. Daniel Delozier.

Reports on Exports for the Year Ending September 30, 1790

Treasury Department, Feb. 15, 1791.
[Communicated on February 15, 1791] [1]

[To the Speaker of the House of Representatives]
Sir,

  I do myself the honour to transmit thro' you to the House of Representatives, a General Return of the Exports of the United States,[2] abstracted from Custom-House Returns, commencing on the various days in August, 1789, whereon they were respectively opened, and ending on the 30th of September last. From inadvertence in some of those offices, the space of time prior to the 1st of October 1789, was blended with the quarter following, which prevented an uniform commencement of this abstract on that day; and there is yet a deficiency of many of the returns for the last quarter of the year 1790, which confines the abstract to the 30th of September last. The progress which was made in this form of statement of the exports, prior to the order of the house, and the impossibility of having it completed in the form directed by them before the fourth of March next, have occasioned me to offer it in its present shape.

  I have the honour to be, With the greatest respect, Sir, your most obedient and   Most humble servant. Alexander Hamilton
                                              Secretary of the Treasury.

The Hon. the Speaker of the House of Representatives of the United States.

The New-York Daily Gazette, March 7, 1791. A somewhat briefer version of this letter is printed in *ASP, Commerce and Navigation*, I, 23.
  1. *Journal of the House*, I, 379.
  2. Copy, RG 233, Reports of the Secretary, First Congress, National Archives. This document, which was drawn up and signed by Tench Coxe, is printed in full in *ASP, Commerce and Navigation*, I, 24–34. There is an abbreviated version in *The New-York Daily Gazette*, March 7, 1791.

From Joseph Whipple

Portsmouth New Hamp. Feb. 15th 1791

Sir

Your letter of the 23rd Ulto.[1] I have received and in pursuance of your directions have agreed for the Hull of a Vessel for a Cutter for this Station of 44 feet Keel payable (say 46 Straight rabbet) 15 Beam & 6½ hold at 9 Dollars pr. Ton.

I could find no person on whom I could depend for a *good* Vessel that would undertake the whole equipments fit for Sea at 22½ Dollrs. per Ton, or indeed at any rate, it not being customary in this port ever to connect the Carpenters with all, or any other bills. I hope I shall be able to finish the Vessel at your limits but this must depend on the prices of Materials in the purchase of which no pains shall be spared in the exercise of the aconomy which you recommend. I found it of advantage in my agreement with the Carpenter to make him a payment of 100 Dollars.

It is the opinion of some sea men that a Sloop rigged Vessel would answer better the purpose than a Schr. If any directions on this point should be thought proper or if it may be left to the officer who is to command her, be pleased to direct me. The Vessel is to be delivered the 10th of May next.

I am Sir, very respectfully   your Most Obedt. servt.

Honble. Alex Hamilton Esqr.

LC, RG 36, Collector of Customs at Portsmouth, Letters Sent, 1790–1791, Vol. 2, National Archives; copy, RG 56, Letters from the Collector at Portsmouth, National Archives.
  1. Letter not found, but see H to Jedediah Huntington, January 23, 1791.

From Nathaniel Appleton [1]

United States Loan Office
Boston 16th Feby 1791

Sr.

I wrote you 13th instant—this serves to enclose first Rect. 12th. Feby for Certifts. received from the Register—agreable to my engagement by last Post I have added up the Receipts for Certificates of Funded Dept issued in the Months of December and January for your information, tho' it is impossible for me yet to transmitt regular Abstracts of the same. Amount is as follows

	six ℔ C Stock	Defered	3 ℔ Sent Stock
December	314,916.85	157 458.74	267,715.48
January	278,524.60	139 262.62	224 090.86
	593,441.45	296,721.36	491,806.34

with great respect I have the honor to be   Sr. your most hum Servt
N A

LC, RG 53, Massachusetts State Loan Office, Letter Book, 1785–1791, Vol. "259–M," National Archives.
  1. For background to the loan office business to which Appleton is referring, see Appleton to H, February 5, 1791, note 1.

Conversation with George Beckwith [1]

[Philadelphia, February 16, 1791]

The Secretary of the Treasury
February 16th.

Lt. Colonel Beckwith. The newspapers of yesterday and of this day mention communications to the two Houses, from The President, on the subject of a commercial treaty with us, and although no particulars are stated, yet enough is expressed to convey an impression to

D, PRO: F.O., Series 4, Vol. 12, Part I.
  1. This document was enclosed in the letter Beckwith wrote to Lord Grenville, March 3, 1791.
  Beckwith was the informal representative of the British government in the United States.

the public mind, that we are not disposed to form any such treaty.[2]

I have in former conversations had the honor of declaring my sentiments with respect to Mr. Morris,[3] I continue in the same way of thinking concerning this gentleman, I believe him to be a man of genius, of knowledge and of discernment, but like other men of strong faculties, I suspect him liable to be led away by his vivacity, to form tenacious opinions and to act upon them; I assume it as a fact, that the information laid before your Legislature, is founded on Mr. Morris's communications, and as there have been no late arrivals from England, I am further led to conceive, that this information is not recent, and that it refers to accounts from thence, pending our negotiations with Spain; without pretending to more than an ordinary share of discernment, I am induced to consider the motives, which have led to such communications by your Executive at this period, in preference to a more early one, and to reflect on the public questions now before Congress, particularly the House of Representatives; I am carried to the following conclusions.

The measure either stands alone, or it is connected with others; if the latter, I find two which attract my observation; the Indian War— and an application from another Foreign Power; it is my duty and my wish to speak in terms of the highest respect of the Chief Magistrate of this country, as well as of the government itself, but I should be guilty of insincerity, if I did not declare, I cannot avoid suspecting, that this communication (tending as it does to convey an impression of there being a coldness in our Administration towards The States) has been made in order to influence gentlemen in a popular Assembly

2. On February 14, 1791, George Washington addressed the House of Representatives and the Senate on the subject of a commercial treaty with England. The President stated: "Soon after I was called to the administration of the Government, I found it important to come to an understanding with the court of London, on several points interesting to the United States; and particularly to know whether they were disposed to enter into arrangements, by mutual consent, which might fix the commerce between the two nations on principles of reciprocal advantage. For this purpose, I authorized informal conferences with their ministers; and from these, I do not infer any disposition, on their part, to enter into any arrangements merely commercial. I have thought it proper to give you this information, as it might, at some time, have influence on matters under your consideration" (*Journal of the House*, I, 377–78).

On the same day, the President sent a separate message to the Senate in which he discussed the failure of Gouverneur Morris's mission to England (*Executive Journal*, I, 73). This message is printed in *GW*, XXXI, 214–15.

3. See, for example, Beckwith's conversation with H, September 25–30, 1790.

with ideas which may operate on other questions; whether this may have been the effect of accident or of design, I do not presume to determine.

Mr. _____. I have frequently mentioned to you that there was a difference of sentiment with us, respecting our having a strict national or commercial friendship with Great Britain, my opinions as I have told you, are directly in favor of it, because I think it for the best interests of this Country; your ideas of the communications from The President to the two Houses, being founded on Mr. Morris's letters are natural and just, undoubtedly the information comes from this gentleman; he tells us, that there is a great diversity of opinion in your Cabinet on the subject of American commerce,   [4] that he does not think a commercial treaty attainable unless it shall be formed or bottomed upon a treaty of Alliance offensive and defensive, and that on the most extended scale; but from his letters although the thing will not succeed without it, yet we have no assurances that it will be secured by it.

I told you on a former occasion, that we have no treaty whatever with France, but the printed one universally known, and whatever construction may be put on that treaty; we do not view it here, as binding us down to grant any peculiar advantages to that Power, to the exclusion of other Nations: there are indeed certain stipulations in favor of prizes in time of war, which are particularly expressed, but nothing on the former subject.

I cannot bring myself to believe that The President's mind is the least influenced by any set of prejudices whatever; he indeed is of opinion from Mr. Morris's letters, *that no commercial treaty is attainable with England*, but I am sure he is not led to make these communications to the Legislature at this time, from any idea of assimilating this with other questions, yet I do not pretend to say that such views may not have struck the minds of certain persons, who have recom-

---

4. Space left blank in MS. A letter to Lord Grenville, dated March 3, 1791, states: "The blank in the ninth page of the Appendix, after the words American Commerce, may be filled up as follows:—'As well as in a higher quarter, that, in short, the K[ing] is much opposed to it, but that the Q[ueen] is more favourably inclined to the measure, as well as Mr. Pitt himself' *Nota Bene.* Such are Mr. Morris' opinions and communications; and they have weight in this country" (Historical Manuscripts Commission, *The Manuscripts of J. B. Fortescue, Esq., Preserved at Dropmore*, Fourteenth Report, Appendix, Part V [London, 1894], II, 37).

mended this measure; whether I personally approved of this business or not it is neither necessary, nor would it be proper in me to express.

It is difficult to speak with precision of what may be the determinations of a popular Assembly, but I am strongly inclined to think, no immediate warmth will arise from it, on the contrary; and in the Senate, I am sure, none will be effected.

In the present state of things, nothing has happened between us and France, to give a tolerable pretence, for breaking off our treaty of Alliance with that Power and immediately forming one with you. A regard for National decorum, puts such a decisive step as this, out of our reach, but I tell you candidly as an individual, that I think the formation of a treaty of commerce, would by degrees have led to this measure, which undoubtedly that Party with us, whose remaining animosities and French partialities influence their whole political conduct, regard with dissatisfaction.

Lt. Colonel Beckwith. It is essential to remark, that these communications are the opinions of Mr. Morris, formed whilst we were on the eve of a war; is it quite clear that this gentleman is really thoroughly acquainted with the intentions of our government? For my own part my instructions from Lord Dorchester [5] authorise me to think and to say, that we have the most friendly dispositions towards the States, of which our liberality in Commercial matters is a decisive proof, notwithstanding the existing difficulties, relative to the treaty of peace; I know that gentlemen in a French interest, are not disposed to admit the force of this, as they do not view our commercial conduct in this light, but I am instructed to hold a different language on this subject.

I cannot help viewing the present communication as an attempt to check the growing friendship, evidently likely to take place between us, to prevent possibly a mutual ministerial appointment, and to give a bias to a French interest. Hitherto, I have thought it my duty to be silent on all political matters, and have shunned explanations even to gentlemen in your Legislature, but in the present moment, I should think it wrong to adhere to this, I feel myself compelled to speak out, and I wish to have my sentiments on this subject known, where they ought to be, for this reason I shall write you a letter on this important question, of which you may make what use you please, I

5. Lord Dorchester was Governor General of Canada.

shall state my sentiments candidly and I trust in a way not to give any offense to your government.[6]

6. The letter which Beckwith wrote to H on the following day, February 17, is almost a verbatim report of the conversation printed above. Beckwith enclosed a copy of the letter to H in his letter to Grenville of March 3, 1791, in which he also recorded the conversation on the same subject.

From Benjamin Hawkins [1]

Senate Chamber 16 Feby. 1791.

Dear Sir

I have just received an authentic copy of the Resolutions of the general assembly of North Carolina which I shewed to you in a news-paper some time past, containing among other Items the following instructions to the Senators from that State.

"Resolved that they strenuosly oppose every excise and direct taxation law should any be attempted in Congress." [2]

Being of Opinion that the Constitution marks the line of my duty, and that is obligatory on my honor to make my own Judgment the ultimate standard after paying suitable respect to the Opinions and observations of others, I have acted in conformity on a recent occasion. Altho' it is much to be wished that a discussion of this sort should never have happened, yet in the present case being inevitable, a right decision is of the utmost consequence to the Union. If the States have a right to instruct, why are we bound by oath support to the Constitution?

As no one has contributed more than yourself to the elucidation of the principles of the government I take the liberty to request the service of you, if you should have leisure from the important functions of your office to give me your opinion on this Subject.

I have the honor to be   with the highest respect   Dear Sir   Yr. most obedient   Humble servant   Benjamin Hawkins

The Honble. Alexander Hamilton

ALS, Hamilton Papers, Library of Congress.
    1. Hawkins was a Federalist Senator from North Carolina.
    2. On November 24, 1790, the North Carolina legislature passed several resolutions and requested the governor to send copies to the North Carolina Senators and to the legislatures of each state. In addition to the resolution quoted by

Hawkins, the Senators were instructed to use their influence to improve mail service in North Carolina, to increase the number of district and state courts, and to correspond regularly with the legislature. They were also instructed to ". . . use their utmost endeavours to effect economy in the expenditure of the public monies, and to decrease the monstrous salaries given to the public officers and others; who, however much they may be deserving of the public gratitude or liberality for the eminence of past or present services, ought only to be compensated agreeable to republican economy, not enriched with the bounty of regal spendour" (Clark, *State Records of North Carolina*, XXI, 962).

From Thomas Newton, Junior [1]

Norfolk [Virginia] February 16, 1791. Proposes that a "comfortable house" be built for the keeper of the Cape Henry lighthouse.

ALS, RG 26, Lighthouse Letters Received, Vol. "A," Pennsylvania and Southern States, National Archives.

1. This letter was enclosed in Josiah Parker to H, March 5, 1791. Newton, a Norfolk lawyer, was nominated inspector of Survey No. 4 in Virginia on October 31, 1791.

Notes on Edmund Randolph's Opinion on the Constitutionality of an Act to Establish a Bank [1]

[Philadelphia, February 16–21, 1791]

Power to lay & Collect taxes
ascertain subject of taxation
   declare Quantum
   prescribe mode of Collection
   ordain the manner of accounting

This an infinite chapter
   creation of districts & ports
      of officers
         duties powers & capacities
         compensation
         penalties
         exemption
         what places to be paid at
         oaths
☞   in what to be paid
         Drawback
         Cutters
         Mode of recovery
☞   Farming Revenue

Power to borrow Money
1 Stipulate a sum to be lent
2 An interest or no interest to be paid
3 The time & manner of repayt.
   unless irredeemable

consideration to be paid or performed including collaterateral conditions & inducement. Lottery Tickets

No   Dutch loans
1   exemption from taxes

Regulation of Trade
with foreign Country
1 To prohibit foreigners or their
commodity
2 to impose duties [3]
3 to subject them to Custom house
Regulations or
4 To grant them any exemp ~ or
privileges which policy may suggest

Between the States
1 to establish the *forms* of Com ~ Intercourse
2 to preserve the prohibitions in the
constitution

With the Indians

1 To prohibit the Indians from coming into or trading with the U
States
2 To admit them with or without restrictions
3 To prohibit *Citizens* from Trading
with them or
4 To permit it with or without restrictions

Rules & Regulations concerning property
1 To exert an Owner over Territory
& *institute a Government* therein
2 To exert ownership Over other
property which may signify
3   1 personal property *however* acquired or
2 real property *aptly* denominated
territory
But it cannot signify
1 Debts due from the U States
2 Nor money arising from the sources
of Revenue. The disposal and regulation of money is the final cause
for raising it.

2   from sequestration in time of
war
3   mortgage of all lands [2]
Fund by way of security
this Fund may be vested in
lenders & they may be made
a Corporation
Institute a lottery

omissions
prohibition of exports

regulate the characteristics & privileges
of American Vessels

The manner in which they shall be
navigated
The inspection of our Com ~ with a
view to exportation

Bounties upon ships or goods
Internal trans of foreign goods
                    policies of Insurance
                    bills of exchange from
f Coun &   between states
                    Salvage
                    light house pilots
                    ransom Contracts
     medium of exchange
                    To erect trading Com-
                    panies

ADf, Hamilton Papers, Library of Congress.

1. These notes were apparently part of a larger body of comments by H on the Attorney General's opinion on the constitutionality of the act establishing the Bank of the United States. Randolph's opinion had been enclosed in George Washington to H, February 16, 1791.

H placed Randolph's points in the left-hand column and his own answers to them in the column on the right. The part or section of Randolph's opinion with which H is dealing in this document reads as follows:

"We ask then, in the second place, whether upon any principle of fair construction, the specified powers of legislation involve the power of granting charters of incorporation? We say charters of incorporation, without confining the question to the Bank; because the admission of it in that instance, is an admission of it in every other, in which Congress may think the use of it equally expedient.

"There is a real difference between the rule of interpretation, applied to a law & a constitution. The one comprises a summary of matter, for the detail of which numberless Laws will be necessary; the other is the very detail. The one is therefore to be construed with a discreet liberality; the other with a closer adherence to the literal meaning.

"But when we compare the modes of construing a state, and the federal, constitution, we are admonished to be stricter with regard to the latter, because there is a greater danger of Error in defining partial than general powers.

"The rule therefore for interpreting the specified powers seems to be, that, as each of them includes those details which properly constitute the whole of the subject, to which the power relates, the details themselves must be fixed by reasoning. And the appeal may on this occasion be made to common sense & common language.

"Those powers, then, which bear any analogy to that of incorporation, shall be examined separately in their constituent parts; and afterwards in those traits, which are urged to have the strongest resemblance to the favorite power.

"1. Congress have power to lay & collect taxes &ca.—the heads of this power are,

1. to ascertain the subject of taxation &c.
2. to declare the quantum of taxation &c.
3. to prescribe the mode of collection; &
4. to ordain the manner of accounting for the Taxes &c:

"2dly. Congress have also power to borrow money on the credit of the United States—the heads of this power are,

1. to stipulate a sum to be lent
2. —   "   an interest, or no interest to be paid, &
3. —   "   the time & manner of repayment, unless the Loan be placed on an irredeemable fund.

"3. Congress have also power to regulate commerce with foreign Nations, among the several states, and with the Indian tribes.

"The heads of this power with respect to foreign nations, are;

1. to prohibit them or their commodities from our ports.
2. to impose duties on them, where none existed before, or to increase existing Duties on them.
3. to subject them to any species of Custom house regulations: or
4. to grant them any exemptions or privileges which policy may suggest.

"The heads of this power with respect to the several States, are little more, than to establish the *forms* of commercial intercourse between them, & to keep the prohibitions, which the Constitution imposes on that intercourse, undiminished in their operation: that is, to prevent taxes on imports or Exports; preferences to one port over another by any regulation of commerce or revenue; and duties upon the entering or clearing of the vessels of one State in the ports of another.

"The heads of this power with respect to the Indian Tribes are

1. to prohibit the Indians from coming into, or trading within, the United States.
2. to admit them with or without restrictions.
3. to prohibit citizens of the United States from trading with them; or
4. to permit [the trade] with or without restrictions.

"4. Congress have also power to dispose of, & make all needful rules and regulations, respecting the territory or other property belonging to the United States: the heads of this power are,

1. to exert an ownership over the territory of the United States, which may be properly called the property of the united States, as is the western Territory; and to institute a government therein; or
2. to exert an ownership over the other property of the United States.

"This property may signify,

1. Personal property of the United States howsoever acquired; or
2. real property, not aptly denominated territory, acquired by cession or otherwise.

"It cannot signify.

1. *Debts* due from the United States.
2. Nor money, arising from the sources of revenue, pointed out in the Constitution. The disposal and regulation of money is the final cause for raising it by taxes &c."

(LC, George Washington Papers, Library of Congress.)

H's arguments in the right-hand column should be compared with both the draft and the final version of his "Opinion on the Constitutionality of an Act to Establish a Bank," February 23, 1791.

2. At this point H wrote and crossed out the word "security."
3. At this point H wrote and crossed out the words "or increase."

From William Seton

Bank of New York 16th. Feby 91

Sir

I am honored with your letter of the 11th.[1] and agreable to your desire enclose a return of the Treasurers Bills on the Collectors now in Bank undispos'd of. You will please to observe that there are of these Bills

No 882 on Newbern for   900 dollars ⎤
   883 on Edenton   200   ⎬ dated 7 Jany 1791
   884 on Savanah   400   ⎦

have been already credited to the Treasurers Account in Bank being part of Bills for 5300 Dollars which The Treasurer sent here on the 11th. January, desiring they might be instantly passed to his Credit or returned to him. Of course if the negotiation of these Bills is stopt, the Treasurers Account must be debited with the amount, or any arrangement shall be made that you may please to point out.

I have the honor to be

LC, Bank of New York, New York City.
1. Letter not found.

From George Washington

Philadelphia Feby. 16th: 1791

Sir,

"An Act to incorporate the Subscribers to the Bank of the United States" [1] is now before me for consideration.

The constitutionality of it is objected to. It therefore becomes more particularly my duty to examine the ground on wch. the objection is built. As a mean of investigation I have called upon the Attorney General of the United States in whose line it seemed more particularly to be for his official examination and opinion.[2] His report [3] is, that the Constitution does not warrant the Act. I then applied to the Secretary of State for his sentiments on this subject.[4] These coincide with the Attorney General's; and the reasons for their opinions having been submitted in writing, I now require, in like manner, yours on the validity & propriety of the above recited Act: and that you may know the points on which the Secretary of State and the Attorney-General dispute the constitutionality of the Act; and that I may be fully possessed of the Arguments *for* and *against* the measure before I express any opinion of my own, I give you an opportunity of examining & answering the objections contained in the enclosed papers. I require the return of them when your own sentiments are handed to me (which I wish may be as soon as is convenient); and further, that no copies of them be taken, as it is for my own satisfaction they have been called for.

Go: Washington

The Secretary of the Treasury.

ALS, Connecticut Historical Society, Hartford; LC, George Washington Papers, Library of Congress.
1. 1 *Stat.* 191–96 (February 25, 1791).
2. Although Congress sent the bill to Washington on February 14, the President had acted beforehand on the question of the statute's constitutionality.

Edmund Randolph replied to Washington's request on February 12. Washington, therefore, had received his first legal advice on the bill two days before Congress had sent it to him.

3. Randolph to Washington, February 12, 1791 (LC, George Washington Papers, Library of Congress). In this letter, Randolph enclosed two documents, neither of which has a title. The first was Randolph's opinion on the constitutionality of the bank. The second consists of additional considerations which Randolph in an introductory paragraph describes as "several topics, which have more or less influenced the friends & enemies of the bank-bill." These two documents can be found in Washington's letter book, George Washington Papers, Library of Congress. See also "Notes on Edmund Randolph's Opinion on the Constitutionality of an Act to Establish a Bank," February 16–21, 1791.

4. ADS, letterpress copy, Thomas Jefferson Papers, Library of Congress; LC, George Washington Papers, Library of Congress.

Jefferson's opinion on the constitutionality of the bank is available in any of the multivolumed editions of his works.

From George Beckwith [1]

Philadelphia, February 17, 1791. Repeats statements made to Hamilton in conversation on preceding day.[2]

D, PRO: F.O., Series 4, Vol. 12, Part I.
1. This document was enclosed in the letter Beckwith wrote to Lord Grenville, March 3, 1791.
2. See "Conversation with George Beckwith," February 16, 1791, note 6.

From Jeremiah Olney

Providence, February 17, 1791. "In conformity to your Letter of the 31st. of January I now beg leave to make Jeremiah Greenman and Daniel Bucklin Junr., both of this Town, as Persons well qualified to fill the stations of First and Second Mates onboard the Revenue Cutter building in Connecticut. . . ."

ADfS, Rhode Island Historical Society, Providence; copy, RG 56, Letters from the Collector at Providence, National Archives.

From William Short

Amsterdam Feb. 17. 1791.

Sir

My two last letters were of Jan. 25. & Feb. 7. They were sent by the way of England. Since then I learn that a momentary change of the wind has permitted two of the American vessels which had my letters for you, to leave the Texel. There were other letters on board of another vessel which I am told still remains there, the wind having again become contrary. I have been much mortified by the unexampled delay of these letters, but I should have been still more so if those which I sent by the way of England had not informed you of the cause of it.

I have the honor to inform you at present that a loan for the U.S. for two millions & an half of guilders was brought on the market the day before yesterday morning.[1] The terms are the same with the last [2] except that the commission is reduced one half p. cent. The form of the bond is now making out & as soon as completed I will send you a copy of it. I think you will learn with pleasure Sir that this loan (of which the rate of interest is the same with that paid by the most accredited powers here, & of which the commission is one half of that paid by some & lower than that paid by any except the Emperor, who has no further occasion for money, & who paid the same) was all taken up & contracted for in less than two hours after being published on the exchange; a celerity of which I am told there has been no instance here before in loans for any country. This circumstance cannot fail to give a very favorable impulsion to the credit to which the U.S. are so justly entitled & facilitate the views they may have here in future. I must add also that the accounts which are recieved here of the happy effects of

ALS, letterpress copy, William Short Papers, Library of Congress.

1. Rafael Bayley describes this loan as follows: "This loan . . . was contracted under the authority given by the acts of August 4 and 12, 1790. . . . After some negotiation . . . the commission and brokerage were reduced to 4 per cent. It was determined to open a loan for two and a half million of guilders ($1,000,000), at 5 per cent. interest, the reimbursement to begin in ten years and to be completed in five, the United States to have the right to reimburse the whole at an earlier period if deemed proper. . . . The original contract, as confirmed by the President . . . provided that the loan should run for eleven years, at 5 per cent. interest, then to be redeemable in the city of Amsterdam, on the 1st day of March in each year until paid, at the rate of 500,000 guilders per annum, the United States to have the privilege of reimbursing the whole sum or any part thereof at any earlier date if they should wish so to do. Two thousand five hundred bonds of the United States, for 1,000 guilders each, were to be issued to the subscribers to the loan, and it was to be determined by lot which of these should be redeemed in any one year" (Bayley, National Loans, 23).

2. The terms for the first loan, which was authorized in August, 1790, were five percent interest and four and one-half percent commission charges. For a description of this loan, see H to Willink, Van Staphorst, and Hubbard, November 29, 1790, note 1.

our new constitution & the confidence which its present administration has inspired at this place are the real & efficient causes of the prosperous situation of the credit of the U.S. This consideration is the more agreeable as it shews that it is dependent on themselves & not merely on the management or credit of Agents or other temporary & uncertain means which other powers are sometimes obliged to employ. It cannot be denied however that the times & manner of bringing a loan on the market has much influence on the facility with which it is carried through & that the present is a favorable moment for loans in general & for those of the U.S. in particular.

I mentioned to you in my letter of Dec. 2. that the commissioners of the U.S.[3] wished much to fix the loans at three instead of two and an half millions of guilders. I was sensible of the propriety of their observations which I have already communicated to you, but I declined acceding without mentioning to them the only true reason, which was your instruction on that head.[4] On the loan being carried off with so much rapidity they have renewed their observations & joined to them other reasons for extending it to three millions which they have pressed on me repeatedly since with a warmth which I did not expect. The principal reason & that on which they seemed to dwell with most earnestness, is the necessity of keeping the undertakers well disposed —that in order to do this it is found necessary to give them all a part in loans which are recieved favorably that they may be disposed to take a part also if at any time the moment should be less favorable— that not foreseeing the very great demand there would be for this loan they had allowed the undertakers as they presented themselves to subscribe for as much as they chose, by which means there was no part left for those who came last. They add that by extending it to three millions they could satisfy them & that otherwise these people at a future time should the U.S. wish to make a loan might from ill humor or resentment decline their aid. Whether this be the true cause or not of the tenacity with which the commissioners adhere to this desire I cannot say. I am sensible however of the weight of the undertakers in loans & of the propriety of not disobliging them. Still I cannot apprehend much from their resentment in a case like this. It

3. The Amsterdam banking firms of Wilhem and Jan Willink, Nicholaas and Jacob Van Staphorst, and Nicholas Hubbard.
4. See H to Short, September 1, 1790.

seems to me on the contrary that the loan being not pushed now as far as it might be, would rather render them more forward in the case of another being brought on the market. The commissioners however seem to be fully of a different opinion & as it is an affair of meer locality they must necessarily be better acquainted with it than I am. They seem somewhat mortified that I should not therefore follow their advice respecting it. They gave me to understand that I might extend the loan if I judged proper to make use of this favorable moment to four millions, which is beyond the ordinary size of loans & are much astonished at my not doing it. I have not informed them of the true cause of it for a reason which seems to me sufficient, that it is not necessary.

It has seemed to me proper to make you acquainted with this circumstance because I wish you to be completely possessed of all the facts which arise relative to the business on which I came here. Although I have not the same apprehensions of the inconveniences which may accrue from my not complying with the request of the commissioners which they seem to entertain, yet I am free to confess that I think it would have hastened the completion of the wishes of the U.S. if I had done it; & that if I had had the honor of having been longer in relation with you & better acquainted with your views I should have been probably induced to have taken on myself this additional degree of responsability. But my desire in general to follow rigorously the instructions I recieve & the circumstances of this case in particular have made me make this sacrifice of what appeared to me the public interest to my personal tranquillity. In this I hope Sir you will think me justifiable even if the fears of the commissioners should be realized.

I mentioned in my last that the loan would be opened in such a manner that interest would begin for no part before the 1st of March; & this had been agreed on between the commissioners & myself, but at their meeting with the brokers the evening before it was brought on the market they insisted on the propriety of conforming to constant usage in such cases—viz of recieving immediately such sums as should be offered & of allowing the interest to date from the first day of such month in which any part is recieved. The term which they have allowed the undertakers is five months. They have no doubt however that the money will be all recieved long before the expiration of the

term; & will accept any bills you may draw for its amount after recieving this letter from thirty to sixty days sight. Having not had the
honor of hearing from you relative to the appropriation since your
Letter of Sep. 1, I, did not think it necessary to press this matter, & the
less so as it is always thought best to give the undertakers the time
they ask. 1. because it is their interest to deliver the money as soon as
possible & 2. because if they are forced in this delivery & obliged thereby to hasten, in placing the obligations they would injure the market-
price.

I suppose it useless to mention to you the advantage that would result from knowing as soon as possible your intentions as to the particular destination of the monies which are from time to time in the hands
of the commissioners here, in order to avoid paying uselessly a double
interest on such parts as are to follow those appropriated in your letter of Aug. 29. You will readily concieve also that the loans of Congress here being well known to those interested in that appropriation,
their expectations will be graduated by these loans; & that it is essential to have some general idea of your intentions in order to know how
to meet questions that may be asked & which certainly will be asked.

I have lately recieved a letter from Mr. Gov. Morris [5] at Paris in
wch. he informs me that he is well persuaded a loan for about a million
of dollars could have been made for the U.S. some months ago in a
place not in Holland (he does not say what place) on the following
terms "The sum to have been at the order of the Secretary of the
Treasury at fixed terms & the interest to commence from those terms
at 5 p. cent. For commissions, charges & bonus with the express undertaking, for the money about four p. cent." He adds that having understood from me that my powers were confined to Holland he gave
those who had applied to him information that nothing could be done
for the present—viz at the time of his speaking to me, which was a day
or two before I left Paris. I did not suppose from what he then said
that any proposals had been made to him & I should not have thought
it prudent to have risked an experiment any where without an absolute certainty of success; for a variety of reasons which will naturally
present themselves to you. Under those circumstances I did not per-

5. Gouverneur Morris to Short, February 6, 1791 (ALS, William Short Papers,
Library of Congress).

haps go into any explanations which could give Mr. Morris a true idea of the nature of my powers. This appeared to me the less necessary also because having no intention of making more than one loan before I again heard from you & not being able to entertain a doubt that that could be done more advantageously here than elsewhere, I did not see any means at that time of making an experiment elsewhere. Mr. Morris adds also in his letter that he "will not pretend to say whether such a loan could be made at present because a great part of the disposable cash is probably applied but that if I wish to know he will make enquiry, but would not wish to meddle in it unless I think it could be brought to something." I am so fully sensible of the advantages which would result from the U.S. being able to make loans, if they should chuse it, in more than one place that I have thought Mr. Morris's idea not to be neglected & yet I see no means of making use of it at present. I have therefore answered him [6] that my wishes were that he would make such enquiries as would reduce that matter to as much certainty as possible, as nothing could justify an experiment without the success being previously ascertained—that I had no reason to believe at present that I should wish to undertake such a loan before April or May—but that there was so great a presumption that a loan out of Holland would then or sooner be agreeable that I thought myself authorized in asking him to make the enquiry—that as to the terms I would say nothing at present as they would of course be to be settled at the time of making the loan. I hope that letters from you in consequence of such as I have formerly written, mentioning the terms on which the loan would be opened here, or of this, stating the terms on which it is opened, will arrive in May or sooner so as to enable me to make use of Mr. Morris's proposition if it should be found practicable & proper. I must add here also that Mr. Morris mentions in his letter that he is unwilling it should be known here that he has mentioned this circumstance, lest it should expose him uselessly to the resentment of those whose interests it opposes. Although I consider myself authorized to mention his name to you & suppose it proper at the same time as your acquaintance will enable you to form a more perfect judgment of the value of the proposition, yet I think it my duty to do it with the caution he desires. As soon as I know any thing

6. Short to Morris, February 13, 1791 (ALS, Columbia University Libraries).

further in this business I will inform you of it. In the mean time I have the honor to be with the most perfect respect & attachment Sir, your most obedient & most humble servant

W: Short

The Honble. Alexander Hamilton Secretary of the Treasury.

From William Ellery

[*Newport, Rhode Island*] *February 21, 1791.* "Agreeably to your request [1] I now give the names of such persons as have offered, and I think are suitable to hold offices on board the Cutters. . . ."

LC, Newport Historical Society, Newport, Rhode Island.
   1. Letter not found. H had requested this information on January 31. See Ellery to H, February 15, 1791.

From William Seton

Bank of New York
21st. Feby. 1791

Sir.
   The Goldsmiths who made the Assays [1] have furnished the enclosed Account, which they submit to be paid upon the same footing as the others you may have had done at Philadelphia.
   I have the honor to be.

LC, Bank of New York, New York City.
   1. Assays of coins for H's "Report on the Establishment of a Mint," January 28, 1791.

To George Washington

[Philadelphia, February 21, 1791]

The Secretary of the Treasury presents his respects to the President of the United States to request his indulgence for not having yet furnished his reasons on a certain point.[1] He has been ever since sedulously engaged in it, but finds it will be impossible to complete before Tuesday or Wednesday *morning* early. He is anxious to give the point a *thorough examination*.

Monday.

LC, George Washington Papers, Library of Congress.
 1. H's opinion on the constitutionality of the act establishing the Bank of the United States. See Washington to H, February 16, 1791.

From William Short

Amsterdam Feb. 22. 1791.

Sir

When I had the honor of writing to you on the 17th. I expected that I should have been able to have sent you by this post a copy of the obligation which will be given on the part of the U.S. in consequence of the loan which I then announced to you. The form of the obligation having been delayed, I inclose you at present the prospectus of the loan, original & translation, as it is the basis of the obligation, which I hope still to be able to send you by the next post, so that it may go by the English March Packet.

I am happy to learn that all the letters which I wrote you by the American vessels have at length left the Texel. You will find them prolix but I wished to be as particular as possible as to the objects I presented to you that you might have all the data I could collect in order to form your own judgment on them. My stay here has only served to confirm me in the several communications I then made to you.

The present price of the five p.cent stock of the principal borrowing powers is Emperor 102½. for an 100. U.S. & Poland 99½ to 100. Russia 99 to 99½. Sweden 96 to 97. The 4.p.cent loan of the U.S. with the lottery [1] is 108. In the loan at present contracted for [2] the undertakers are bound not to sell any of the bonds under par viz. 100. with a deduction of ½. p.cent brokerage. This is a prudent regulation to prevent their injuring the market price by selling them at a loss, or

ALS, letterpress copy, William Short Papers, Library of Congress.
 1. This is a reference to the Holland loan of 1784. For a description of this loan, see H to Short, September 1, 1790, note 22.
 2. See Short to H, February 17, 1791.

which is the same thing by sacrificing a part of their profits on the American bonds in order to raise money on any emergency for other speculations. This they could have been the more enabled to do as they are allowed half a per cent more on this loan than the last, This added to the ½.p.cent less which the bankers recieve on the whole shews that they (the bankers) have 1.p.cent less on this loan than the last. The brokerage is always ½.p.cent.

Many people here have made purchases of the American domestic debt in America & intend recieving their interest there. I should think it probable that most of them would change this stock of 6.p.cent payable in America for the obligations of the U.S. at five p.cent payable here. If you think it adviseable to make such an exchange it would be worth while perhaps to have the offer made. I must observe however that the houses employed here by the U.S.[3] think the holders of these funds would not do it—that is to say in answer to me on that question one of them doubted & the other asserted they would not— still I cannot help inferring from what the same house has told me on other occasions that it is probable many would be glad to make such an exchange. It is true this could have the effect of tending to depreciate the obligations of the U.S. by increasing their number but I should suppose that their increasing resources becoming every day more & more developed here would be sufficient to counteract this tendency. This however is simply an idea that I submit to your consideration.

One of the houses employed here (Messrs. Willink) thinks that some of the States of America might make loans here advantageously. Those which he mentions as being most likely to do it are N. York— Pennsylvania—Maryland—Virginia. The reasons on which his opinion is founded arise from the comparison always made in the minds of the people here between the government of these provinces & of the U.S. As they see that the credit of the province of Holland is better than that of the provinces united, many of them conclude by a false analogy that it should be the same in America. This house thinks that loans proposed here for the States individually could not injure those proposed by the U.S. because they would embrace a different class of money holders. He intends submitting this to some of the states mentioned above & has asked me to certify to the Governor of the

3. Willink, Van Staphorst, and Hubbard.

State of Virginia [4] that the house may be relied on as to its capital & credit. This is sufficiently demonstrated by its being employed by the U.S. & therefore I see no impropriety in giving them such a certificate. As far as I can judge from former circumstances relative to that state they will not be disposed to make loans abroad; yet I have thought it proper to give you this information as you may possibly combine it with your general system of assuming the State debts so as to make it useful.

Your report for the establishing a national bank [5] has been recieved here by one house & is much approved of by those to whom they have thought proper to communicate it. It is a great misfortune that such papers are not more generally circulated here. There seems to be a strong disposition to take shares in the bank if established by Congress on the basis you propose.

I beg leave to refer you to my letter of to day to the Secretary of State for information of what the national assembly have decided relative to tobacco as an article of Commerce.[6]

I have the honor to be with the most perfect respect & attachment Sir, your most obedient & most humble servant   W: Short

The Honble Alexander Hamilton Secretary of the Treasury.

4. Beverley Randolph.

5. "Second Report on the Further Provision Necessary for Establishing Public Credit (Report on a National Bank)," December 13, 1790.

6. On February 22, 1791, Short sent Jefferson the following information concerning the tobacco decrees: "It was accordingly brought on & decided that the cultivation [of tobacco] should be free for every person in France—the manufacture and sale of it to be subject to such modifications as the assembly shall fix. By which is meant licenses that are to be granted for that purpose & from which the committee count on a revenue of two millions only. These modifications however, have not yet been discussed in the Assembly: but the foreign & homemade Tobacco will probably be put on the same footing as to these modifications. The second article decreed without a division was that the importation of foreign manufactured tobacco should continue to be prohibited. The third which passed after much debate as to the rate of duty is in these terms. 'Il sera libre d'importer par les ports qui seront designés du tabac en feuille, moyennant une taxe de 25 ₶ par quintal. Les navires françois qui importeront directement du tabac d'Amerique, ne seront soumis qu'aux trois quarts du droit.' Nothing further was then decided, & the Assembly according to its desultory mode of proceeding took up other business. It is in the sequel of the plan of the committee, which I should suppose the Assembly would again soon resume, to form a national regie to purchase, manufacture & sell this article for public profit. Such tobacco as the regie shall import from abroad to be subject to no duty. They are to have no monopoly except such as they may acquire by this exemption from foreign duty, their superior capital & greater skill in the manufacture of this

article. It remains still for the Assembly to decide with respect to this regie"
(LC, RG 59, Despatches from United States Ministers to France, 1789–1869,
January 16, 1791–August 6, 1792, National Archives).

From Nathaniel Appleton

Boston, February 23, 1791. Acknowledges receipt of Hamilton's
letters of February 8 and 14, 1791. Will carry out instructions in those
letters. Encloses "Duplicate rec't for Certifts received from the Registers 12 instant & first receipt of Ditto rec'd 23 instant." Will "inquire
respecting the Sale of Bills on New York or Philadelphia."

LC, RG 53, Massachusetts State Loan Office, Letter Book, 1785–1791, Vol.
"259–M," National Archives.

From Stephen Higginson [1]

Boston, February 23, 1791. Wishes to obtain a position in the executive branch of the government, but will not accept a post that pays
less than two thousand dollars. Congratulates Hamilton on the success
of Hamilton's "measures & projections." Has heard that Hamilton
plans "to establish deposits of Cash here & in york, at least, to exchange
the Notes of the Proposed Bank." Approves of this plan, for without
it "the notes will never answer all the purposes of money, or be equal
to those of our own Bank." [2]

ALS, Hamilton Papers, Library of Congress.
   1. Higginson was a Boston merchant and a Federalist.
   2. The Bank of Massachusetts.

From Benjamin Lincoln

Boston, February 23, 1791. "Since my return I have attended to the
subject matter of your letter of the 22nd ultimo.[1] The Gentleman
with whom I contracted for the Cutter being in this Town, he lives at
Newbury-port. I have had a good opportunity thus early to review
the whole proceeding and to know from him that he could not now
alter his plan, that he would take her to himself, though he thought the
loss to him would be three hundred dollars at the least. . . . On the
whole he has concluded to finish the vessel, hopeing she will be re-

ceived. If I was now to contract for a Vessel of fifty tons to be built in this Town, she would cost I am very confidant as much as this will finally cost us. . . ."

Copy, RG 56, Letters from the Collector at Boston, National Archives; LC, RG 36, Collector of Customs at Boston, Letter Book, 1790–1797, National Archives; copy, RG 56, Letters from the Collector at Boston, National Archives.
    1. Letter not found.

From William Lewis [1]

[Philadelphia, February 23, 1791]

I am of opinion, that by the death of the Administratrix, the power which the husband had by his intermarriage acquired in her right, to intermeddle with the effects of the Intestate, immediately and without notice ceased; and that as the power was only in consequence of the marriage, and of but equal duration in point of time with it, it was incumbent on all Persons indebted to the Intestate to inform themselves whether she was alive or not before making payments to the Husband. I therefore think that in the case stated the Administrator de bonis non &c. is clearly entitled to a Settlement and Certificate.

Wm Lewis

Feb: 23rd. 1791

ALS, RG 217, Miscellaneous Treasury Accounts, 1790–1894, Account No. 1268, National Archives.
    1. For the background to this document, see H to Lewis, February 12, 1791.

To George Washington [1]

[Philadelphia, February 23, 1791]

The Secretary of the Treasury presents his respects to the President and sends him the opinion required [2] which occupied him the greatest part of last night.

The Bill for extending the time of opening subscriptions passed yesterday unanimously to an order for engrossing.[3]

LC, George Washington Papers, Library of Congress.
    1. In the George Washington letter book this letter follows H's signature on the "Opinion of the Constitutionality of an Act to Establish a Bank," February 23, 1791.

2. See Washington to H, February 16, 1791, and "Opinion of the Constitutionality of an Act to Establish a Bank," February 23, 1791.
3. See *Journal of the House*, I, 386.

Opinion on the Constitutionality of an Act to Establish a Bank

[Philadelphia, February 23, 1791]

Introductory Note

There are at least eight manuscript versions of this famous document. One of these is an incomplete draft in Hamilton's handwriting. The other seven are copies. The two versions that are printed below are the draft and that copy which it is assumed is the final version that was sent to George Washington.

The seven copies of this document are located as follows:

1. Copy, Mr. John R. Dillard, Philadelphia.
2. Copy, Historical Society of Pennsylvania, Philadelphia.
3. LC, George Washington Papers, Library of Congress.
4. Copy, Hamilton Papers, Library of Congress (subsequently referred to as the first copy in the Hamilton Papers).
5. Copy, Hamilton Papers, Library of Congress (subsequently referred to as the second copy in the Hamilton Papers).
6. Copy, Massachusetts Historical Society, Boston.
7. Copy, Columbia University Libraries.

It is impossible to determine with certainty which of the seven copies is closest to Hamilton's original document or which of these copies—if, indeed, any of them—was sent to Washington. Nevertheless, most evidence points to the copy owned by Mr. Dillard. It is in Henry Kuhl's handwriting (John C. Fitzpatrick in a note attached to this document mistakenly states that it is in Hamilton's handwriting), and Kuhl was a clerk in the Treasury Department. In addition, aside from insignificant differences in punctuation, capitalization, and paragraphing, it is practically identical with Washington's letter book copy, which, in turn, was undoubtedly copied from the version sent to the President.

Because of errors by the copyists these documents contain variations, and they can, therefore, be divided into three groups. The Dillard copy, the copy in the Historical Society of Pennsylvania, and the Washington letter book copy are essentially the same; the first copy in the Hamilton Papers, Library of Congress, and the copy in the Massachusetts Historical Society are essentially the same; and the second copy in the Hamilton Papers and the copy in the Columbia University Libraries are essentially the same. The version used by J. C. Hamilton (*JCHW*, IV, 104–38) and Lodge (*HCLW*, III, 445–93) is the second copy in the Hamilton Papers, Library of Congress.

Substantive notes have been made for the Dillard copy but not for the draft. For background to Hamilton's "Opinion on the Constitutionality of an Act to Establish a Bank," see Washington to H, February 16, 1791.

DRAFT OF AN OPINION ON THE CONSTITUTIONALITY
OF AN ACT
TO ESTABLISH A BANK

The Secretary of the Treasury has perused with great attention the opinions of the Secretary of State and of the Attorney General concerning the constitutionality of the bill for establishing a National Bank and proceeds to execute the order of the President for submitting the reasons which have induced him to view the subject in a different light.

It will naturally have been ~~expected~~ anticipated that in performing this task he must feel uncommon solicitude. Personal considerations alone, arising from ~~were~~ ~~suggested~~ by ~~from~~ the reflection that the measure originated with him would be sufficient to produce it. The sense which he has manifested of the great importance of the institution to the successful administration of the ~~Finances, under more particularly under his~~ department committed to his care ~~charge the conviction,~~ ~~care~~ the serious and extensive consequences which he believes would attend the failure ~~which he entertains that its failure will materially retard the apprecia-~~ of the ~~plan~~ measure ~~tion of the public debt and the rise of public debt credit and will be~~ ~~an occasion would~~ do not permit him to be without anxiety on ~~a~~ public accounts. ~~ground~~ ~~account.~~ But his chief solicitude arises from a persuasion that if the principles of ~~constitut~~ construction which ~~are~~ ~~insisted~~ ~~upon~~ ~~the~~

ADf, Hamilton Papers, Library of Congress.

regulate
~~foundations of~~ ^the opinions of the Secretary of State and the Attorney

and indispensable
just^authority of the
General should prevail, the^~~government of~~ the United States must re-

deep and dangerous The
ceive a^~~serious~~ wound. ~~Its~~ future operations ~~must be fatally clogged.~~
~~And~~ of the government must be fatally clogged. And it must in the

end   purposes   been
^find itself incapable of answering the ~~ends~~ for which it has^instituted.

~~It was frequently under the confeder~~

It has often been regretted by the decided friends of an efficient na-

American late
tional government that Congress in the early stages of the^revolution
exercised the powers entrusted to them with too sparing and ~~a~~ feeble
a hand. It is earnestly to be hoped, after so much has been done for
retrieving the prostrate affairs of the Union, that no similar cause of

again
regret may be^furnished.

incontrovertible position
It may be laid down as an^~~indisputable truth~~, that all the powers
contained in a constitution of Government, which concern the general
administration of the affairs of a country its finances its trade its de-

in
fence &c ought to be construed liberally, ~~for the~~^advancement of the
general good. This maxim does not depend on the particular form of

or   particular
the government ~~or on~~ on the ~~definition~~ particular delineation or
demarkation of the boundaries   condition of
~~definition or boundaries~~ of its powers but on the ~~state~~^~~of human~~

itself
society, on the *nature* and *objects* of ~~all~~ government^. The means by
which national exigencies are to be satisfied, national inconveniences

extent
obviated, national prosperity promoted are of such infinite variety^
and complexity, that there must of necessity be great latitude of dis-

the selection and application of   essential
cretion in ~~those selecting and applying~~ those means. It is ~~necessary~~
to the public good that the power of providing for it should be
commensurate
^~~in these respects as little fettered as possible~~ ~~coextensive~~ with the
diversity
~~variety~~ of circumstances by which it may be affected—and conse-

quently that the authorities confided to the government should be

exercised ~~according to the rules of~~ ^a^ ~~liberal construction.~~ on principles
of liberal ~~considera~~ construction. ~~The only exception to this rule is of
cases in which priva the security of private property and personal
liberty is concerned.~~

The Attorney General admitting the rule here laid down takes a
distinction between a state and the Fœderal constitution and thinks
the latter ought to be construed with greater strictness because there
is more danger of error in defining *partial* than *general* powers.

But if the *reason* of the rule is ~~resorted~~ ^adverted^ to it must be concluded that
this distinction cannot be admitted. That reason is founded on the
variety ^and extent^ of ~~national exigencies and~~ ^public~~ public concerns, and public exigencies; ~~comparing the objects of the Fœderal with those of a state gov-
ernment~~ a ~~much~~ ^far^ greater proportion of which and of a ~~much more~~
far more critical and important ~~nature~~ ^kind^ ~~than~~
~~interesting kind~~ are objects of National ~~and~~ of State administration.
If therefore the supposition of greater danger of error be acceded to
it could only operate as a ^prudential^ *motive* to ~~greater~~ caution in administering
the powers of the National government not as a principle of *restrictive* interpretation.

It will be shewn hereafter that the rule abovementioned has ~~pre-
vailed in go~~verned ~~in a variety of~~ ~~cases the~~ various acts of Congress
which have received the Sanction of ~~Congress~~ the Chief Magistrate;
and it is not to be doubted that every days experience will evince it
to be indispensable to the ~~con~~ prosperous conduct of the affairs of the
Union.

Another position equally incontrovertible is this—That though
the Government of the ~~United States~~ Union does not possess complete
and intire sovereignty ^in every respect^ it nevertheless possesses ~~a variety of~~ sovereign
powers in a variety of respects; and these of a high and transcendent
nature. ~~Such~~ ^as^ ~~are~~ ^are true^ ~~the indefinite power of taxation~~ Of these the most
important are the powers of taxation, of regulating commerce with ^that^
foreign nations, between the several states and with the indian tribes,

that   it
of making war and as ~~a~~ incidents to ~~this~~ of raising supporting and governing armies and fleets, ~~of making trea~~ and that of making treaties. If
  it were not evident that   as applied to ~~a~~ nations are
government and *sovereignty* ~~were not~~ *convertible* terms; if the idea
of sovereignty were not necessarily included in the powers which have
        mentioned
been ~~stated~~—if it were ~~necess~~ requisite to confirm the position which
has been advanced by proof, there is a clause in the constitution ~~w~~
                                                    is
which would put the matter out of all doubt. It that which declares
that the Constitution, and the laws of the United States made in pursuance of it and all treaties made or which shall be made under their
authority shall be the *Supreme Law of the Land*. The power which
can create the Supreme law of the land, in any case, is doubtless
sovereign ~~as far as it goes~~ in relation to such case.
        plain
The inference to be drawn from this position is this, that in carrying into execution the powers vested in the national Government, it
has a right to employ all the *means* which are ~~calcu~~ fairly and truly
calculated to effect the objects of those powers, in as full and ample
a manner as can be done by any Government whatever; or in other
                                                        which
words it can do, in *relation to those objects* every thing ~~that~~ is
~~implied in the idea of Sovereign~~ power ~~authority; subject only to~~
not contrary to
the *limitations* and *exceptions* ~~which are~~ specified in the constitution—or which is not in itself immoral ~~or subversive of the personal~~
                                            political
~~rights~~ or inconsistent with the ends of society.

This idea enters into the very definition of sovereignty or government; and though that ~~Government~~ of the United States cannot do
all that some other governments can do it can do all that any other
government can do *in relation to the objects* entrusted to its management; except so far as these may be ~~express~~ specified restrictions.

If this be not the true rule there is then no rule at all. It must become
impossible to determine what can or cannot be constitutionally done.
The legality of the means to be made use of in each case must be a
subject of vague and endless controversy; ~~and~~ in which caprice and
                                    influence
prejudice must have much greater ~~sway~~ than ~~than~~ reason or principle.

to this,

To urge as an objection˄that "all powers not delegated to the US by the constitution, nor prohibitted by it to the states are reserved to the States or to the People" ~~is to do nothi~~ is to do nothing. This is only saying in another form that ~~Congress possess no~~ the United States *possess no powers* not *delegated* to them; a position ~~equally~~ alike applicable to all popular constitutions of Government and to that of each state equally with that of the ~~United~~ Union. It resolves itself

general

into this ~~fundamental~~˄maxim, ~~of republican Gov liberty~~ that all government is a *delegation* of power. How much is delegated in any case

determined ~~resolved~~ by

is always a question of fact to be ~~made out from~~ the particular ~~tener~~ provisi⟨ons⟩ of a constitution and by fair construction up⟨on⟩ those provisions.

It certainly will not be pretended that the proposition which has been quoted was designed to exclude the ~~use of~~ doctrine of implied powers. There is nothing in the manner of expression which indicates

it

such a meaning and it is known that it was not the intention of ~~these the proposed~~ amendment.

from

Hence no inference can be drawn˄it against the position which has been deduced from the nature of sovereign power.

may lawfully

To say that such things only ~~are to~~ be done as are "necessary and proper" ~~would~~ amounts to nothing. This is in truth only to say that all *requisite* and *fit* means may be employed; which brings the matter precisely to the ~~point~~ issue of a right to do whatever is fairly and truly calculated to effect the objects of the powers vested in the government.

The Secretary of State has annexed a more strict sense to the word necessary which he considers as restricting the government to the

grant of the

employment of those means without which "the˄power would be nugatory." In this however he is neither warranted by the grammati-

meaning

cal nor popular˄~~sense~~ of the word, nor by considerations of political

most   ~~aspect~~ import

expediency nor by the˄obvious aspect˄of the clause which contains

expression

~~by~~ the ~~word~~ nor by the practice of the Government upon it.

Not by the grammatical sense because this, in many, and in relation to political subjects in most cases ~~makes~~ establishes the word *neces-*
sary as equivalent only to *requisite* or *needful* or *conducive to* ~~a particular~~
be said   be
~~end.~~ Thus if it should ~~that it is necessary to France~~ observed "that it is necessary to ~~France to maintain her connection with Spain~~" this
that
~~would only imply that~~ connection ~~is in a conseq~~ to Great Britain to maintain a good understanding with Holland" this would only mean
a thing
that the maintenance of that good understanding is useful to her or conducive to her interests. It would not signify ~~it~~ that it it is *essentially* or *indispensable* or *absolutely* requisite; or a thing without which she could not exist or prosper as a nation.

Neither does ~~the popular~~ such a signification accord with the popular use of the term. ~~It is often said for instance~~ A man will ~~often~~ say
that
for instance "It is necessary I should breakfast before I go to business." This would not mean that he *could not do* business without having first breakfasted; but merely that his habits are such as to render it *inconvenient* to him to enter upon the business of the day before he has made that meal.

Considerations of political expediency do not favour such a construction; because it tends to create a disability in the government to pursue measures which though highly useful may not be ~~absolutely~~ absolutely essential; and of course abriges its power of doing good
reference
even in ~~respect~~ to the objects which are particularly confided to it.

It must ever be a matter of infinite uncertainty when a measure is necessary in the sense in which the word is understood by the secretary of state. Many very intelligent men have contended that all regulations of trade are ~~pericious.~~ pernicious. There are many in this country who now maintain that all ~~burthens~~ extra burthens
That   most
~~That~~ construction does not consist with the obvious import of the clause ~~in question~~ containing the expression. ~~Placed at the end~~ No person who should read it without an eye to any particular question
to his judgment   be inclined to
that might give a bypass but would infer that it was intended to give
rather
latitude to the enumerated powers than to confine their operation.

Placed at the end of them it is couched in these comprehensive terms "To make *all* laws which shall be necessary and proper for *carrying into execution* the foregoing powers, and *all other* powers vested by the constitution in the government of the United States or *in any department* or *officer* thereof." The turn of the expressions as well as the familiar and popular sense of the ˄words forbids a restrictive interpretation.

If it were proper to go out of the instrument into what passed in the course of the debates in the Convention or even to resort to the minutes of that body ample confirmation would be found of the ~~reasonings~~ sense here contended for. But a recourse of that kind is not admissible. Nor ~~is~~ it be ~~at~~ ˄can requisite. The clause itself speaks a language not easily to be mistaken. It is evidently ~~inten~~ designed ~~to ena~~ to place on an unequivocal footing the power of the government to employ all the means ~~appertaining to the~~ *fairly* ~~relav~~ *relative* to the execution of its specified powers and to the ~~fulfilm most prosperous conduct of the affairs entrusted~~ fulfilment of the objects entrusted to its direction.

The Attorney General indeed ~~appears to~~ concedes that no such restrictive effect ought to be ascribed to the clause; and defines the word necessary thus—"To be necessary is to be *incidental* or in other words may be denominated the natural means of executing a power."

As on the one hand the sense put upon the clause by the Secretary of State cannot be admitted to be just [1]

The practice of the government has contradicted such an interpretation. The act for the establishment and support of light houses beacons buoys and public piers may be cited as an example. This doubtless must be ~~reported~~ referred to the power which ˄respects the regulation ˄of trade and it is certainly fairly relative to it. But it cannot be affirmed that it was *absolutely* necessary that provision should be made for this object by the National Government or that the interests of Trade would have essentially suffered if it had been left upon its ~~foot~~ former footing or that the power of regulating trade would be *nugatory* without that of regulating establishments of this nature. ~~The states continue~~

1. In the margin opposite this paragraph H wrote "Inspection laws."

~~competent~~ All that can be said is that as ~~establis~~ such establishments
relate to & ~~relative and~~
‸are‸useful to trade, ~~were~~ they were a proper object of the care of that
authority which is charged with the trust of promoting its interests.

To affix the sense advocated by the Secretary of State to the word
necessary would lead to infinite uncertainty. There are persons who
maintain for instance that all regulations of Trade are pernicious. ~~It
is notorious that~~ There are others who are of opinion that ~~measures
the favours~~ immunities
~~privileges~~ which have been granted to certain branches of trade and
restraints
the ~~restrictions~~ which have been laid upon others are hurtful to the
general interests of ~~trade~~ commerce. There ~~exist~~ are wide differences
and proper
of opinion about the measures which are or are not necessary‸to ~~the~~
the
promote ~~of our~~ navigation of this country—How shall it be determined what is *strictly* necessary? because it seems nothing else is
supposed
to be ~~deemed~~ to be included in the power to regulate trade.

Nothing can better shew the fallacy of the doctrine espoused by
the Secretary of State than some of the arguments which he makes use
of to enforce it. One of these is that there are existing banks in some
of the states which may serve the purposes of a National Bank, and
therefore render the establishment of one unnecessary. Here the constitutional right of exercising a power is made to depend on certain
arrangements which *happen* to have been made by particular States
may disappear.   rights &
and which ~~may~~ ere long ~~totally disappear cease~~. Surely the‸powers of
fortuitous   and foreign
a government cannot depend upon such ~~adventitious‸and~~ casual‸cir-
cumstances. Surely a right to establish a Bank ~~cannot be less inherent
in a Government~~ which does not exist to day ~~can~~ because institutions
of that kind in which the Government has had no agency happen to
exist, ~~will~~ cannot be created to morrow by their disappearance.
Surely therefore a principle which turns on such an argument cannot
just
be‸~~well founded~~.[2]

2. In the margin opposite this paragraph H wrote "Take in here what relates
to manner of construing Constitution."

The Attorney General indeed concedes that no restrictive operation is to be ascribed to the word necessary. He defines it thus "To be
necessary is to be *incidental* and may be denominated the natural
means of executing a power."

But while on the one hand the construction of the Secretary of
State cannot be allowed, it will not be contended on the other that
the clause in question confers any *new* or *substantive* power. It is

                been
conceived to have ^only intended to obviate the embarrassments
which had been experienced under the confederation from the clause
declaring   ³

and to give an express ~~recognition that~~ sanction to the exercise of *implied* powers fairly ~~incli~~ *incidental* or *relative* to the declared ones.

      however
~~And~~ This ^it is conceived, is equivalent to an admission ~~that~~ of the
proposition that the Government *as to its specified objects* ~~has sovereign and plenary authority, except so far as restrictions appear~~
where no restrictions are annexed to them has sovereign and plenary
authority; in some cases paramount to that of the states in others
coordinate with it. Indeed as has been remarked this principle
seems inseparable from the idea of a legislative or sovereign
power.

~~If this principle be a just one~~

It is no valid objection to this principle to say that it ~~would lead to~~
might ~~be extended~~ lead to an extension of the powers of the general
government throughout the intire sp[h]ere of state legislation. The
same thing has been said and may as justly be said with regard to ~~the
exe~~ every exercise of power by *implication* or *construction.* Wherever
the literal meaning is departed from there is a chance of error and
abuse. And yet an adhererence to the letter of its powers would

      arrest the motion of the
speedily ~~bring the~~ government ~~to a full stop.~~ and destroy its utility. It
is agreed on all hands that the exercise of implied or constructive
powers is indispensable. Every act that has been past is more or less

  exemplification
an ^~~example~~ of it. That which declares the Power of the President to
remove ~~the~~ officers at pleasure is a signal one.

The truth ~~that~~ is that difficulties on this point are inherent in the

3. Space in MS left blank by H.

nature of the National Constitution ~~which~~ which is founded on a division of the legislative power assigning certain ~~powers~~ portions of sovereignty to the Union and leaving the rest with the particular members. The consequence of this will be that there will be some cases clearly within the power of the National government such as the right to lay duties on imported articles; some clearly not within its power such as a provision to convey water by pipes through the city of Philadelphia for the accommodation of its ~~parti~~ inhabitants, which
which
is a matter purely local; and there are others will admit of room for
reasonable
dispute and difference of sentiment and in regard to which a ~~sound~~ discretion must be exercised.

The position which has been stated does not assert that the National Goverment is sove[re]ign in all respects, but that it has sovereign
extent
powe[r] to a certain ; that is as far as its specified objects extend.

There is therefore always a criterion of what is constitutional and
end
what is not constitutional. This criterion is the ~~object~~ to which the
as a mean.   end   clearly
measure relates ^. If the ~~object~~ ^ is one ^ entrusted to the National Gov-
reference
ernment and if the measure has any obvious ^ ~~relation~~ to that ~~object~~ end and is not forbidden by any particular provision of the constitution—
it may be deemed to be within the compass of the National authority.
also these
These are ~~these other erit~~ criteria which ought to have ~~great~~ weight in the decision. Does the proposed measure abrige a preexisting *right* of any state or of any individual?—if this question can be answered in
will always
the negative it ^ affords a strong presumption in favour of the con-
thing
stitutionality of the ^ ~~measure~~ and slighter relations to any declared object of the constitution may be permitted to turn the scale.[4]

The objectors to the rule which has been stated may be confidently asked what other can be adopted? What is there in the nature of things to render the declared powers in the national constitution less sovereign than the powers in the state constitutions? What are the

4. In the margin opposite this paragraph H wrote "Is any state competent to doing what is proposed to be done?"

distinguish
characteristics which ~~define~~ the means that sovereign or legislative

attain an　　　　　　　　attain
power may employ to ~~end~~ ~~committed~~ ~~attend~~ ‸and end within its
acknowleged ~~allowed~~
province from those which it may not employ?

It is observable that both the Secretary of State and the Attorney General build their objections wholly upon a supposed inability in the National government to erect a Corporation; ~~The Attorney General acknowleges~~
~~indeed allows that if there be any~~ and this not in the particular case

whatever
only but in every case. Indeed the Attorney General acknowleges "that if any part of the bill does either encounter the constitution or is not warranted by it, the clause of the Corporation is the only one."

How it has come to pass that the power of erecting corporations has been conceived to be of so *peculiar* or *transcendent* a nature, as to form an *implied* exception to *every* power granted to the United States and in *every case* is not easy to be conjectured and remains un-

much an
explained. Why it should not be as ‸incident to legislative authority to erect a corporation, if a *necessary* and *proper*, or a *requisite* and *fit*

a given
mean to ~~an~~ end, as to do any other thing, is, to say the best of it, not obvious.

Congress for example have power to *regulate Trade* with foreign nations. This power is not supposed to be confined merely to the

of
prescribing ‸rules for the ~~ordering~~ *orderly conducting* of Commerce between the United States and other Countries; but it is agreed ~~agreed~~ on all hands to ~~mean~~ extend to the adoption of proper measures for the advancement of Navigation & foreign commerce. To this end are various regulations in the revenue laws that have been passed.

be
Let it ‸supposed that it were demonstrable that there was ~~a particular~~

of Trade
an opportunity for opening a particular branch ‸with some foreign

highly
country, which would be ~~particularly~~ beneficial to the United States; but that in order to entering upon it, it was absolutely necessary there

and
should be an union of the capitals of a number of Individuals; ~~let it be~~

added ~~to this that~~ that in order to engage ~~those individuals~~ proper persons to embark on it it was ~~indispensable~~ equally necessary that they should be incorporated & should for a ~~certain~~ time be permitted to enjoy certain peculiar privileges and exemptions—in such a state of things as this, can there be any reasonable ground of doubt that it would be within the *compass* of the general *power* of regulating ~~an~~ commerce with foreign nations to erect such a corporation and to grant to it the requisite privileges and immunities? It is apprehended that there cannot be any such ground of doubt.

~~The~~ It would not be a good answer to say that such a case cannot be supposed. It is certainly a possible one. It has been believed to exist in other countries, and has produced ~~such~~ institutions of the kind contemplated which remain to this day. The possibility of it is enough for the argument. It would doubtless be expedient to be well assured that the circumstances were such as to require and justify it; but this would be a mere question of expediency not of right or power.

~~If the sense of a number of the state conventions acts of the different state Conventions which who be consulted it will be pere~~

As far as the sense of the different state Conventions can be supposed to have weight ~~on this point~~ in the question, it will appear that there was a ~~prevail~~ prevalent idea that Congress had power to erect trading companies or corporations. Hence is found among the amendments proposed by them, generally, a clause to this effect "That Congress shall not grant monopolies nor *erect* any *company with exclusive* advantages of commerce." thus tacitly admitting the power of Congress to erect such Corporations or companies, and objecting no further than to the grant of *exclusive* privileges. The existence of such a power is indeed a natural and obvious inference from that of regulating Trade.

Neither the Origin of the power of erecting corporations nor the practice respecting ~~in~~ it in the couuntry from which we have borrowed our ~~ideas~~ notions of it are of a nature to warrant the conclusion that it is of so preeminent a nature as to ~~be~~ lie beyond the reach of the ~~ext portions of sov~~ powers of the United States.

Its *origin* is traced to the Roman empire where a *voluntary associa-tion* of individuals was alone sufficient to produce a Corporation. In England the power of erecting corporations forms a part of the ex-ecutive authority and the exercise of it may even be delegated to that Authority to other persons. Certainly then ~~it may be fairly presumed~~ there is something not a little forced in the supposition ~~there is no colour to suppose~~ that the whole Legislative power ~~authority~~ of the ~~Unit~~ Union is *unequal* to it. *[incapable of]*

The Secretary of State ~~affirms~~ asserts indefinitely that the power of erect-ing corporations ~~is ex~~ remains exclusively with the states; but he certainly has not provdd. *[it]* The arguments already ~~produce~~ adduced are sufficient it is presumed to shew that this is at least a very questionable position. But ~~there are~~ that it is not true in the extent in which ~~he advances~~ is advanced may be reduced to ~~absolute~~ precise demonstration. And it is not doubted ~~in~~ that in the progress of the investigation the ~~progress of~~ contrary of it will appear more and more clearly.

Congress are empowered "to exercise *exclusive* legislation *in all cases whatso-ever* over ~~such~~ the district which shall become the seat of of the Govern-ment of the United States and over all places purchased for the erection of forts magazines arsenals dockyards and other needful buildings" By what process of reasoning can it be made a doubt that a power of exercising *exclusive legislation in all cases whatsoever* must include that of erecting a corporation within the limits which ~~is~~ are embraced by it? There can be none.

Here then are cases in which it is certain that Congress may erect corporations. And if ~~they~~ a direct power of ~~erecting~~ instituting a Bank in other places is denied to the government it has only to establish one at ~~one~~ some place which it may have acquired exclusive ~~legislation~~ jurisdiction and the matter may be so managed as to have the administration of it where it ~~may~~ shall be found be most convenient. Doctrines which lead to ~~such~~ like consequences like these are at least to be ~~embraced with caution~~ suspected of error.

There is indeed a case in which Congress have exercised the power of erecting a Corporation and that, one of the most important kind; ~~and~~ one not less important than the establishment of a Government. The "Act for the Government of the Territory of the United States South of the River Ohio" is here alluded to. A constitution of Government is a Corporation of the highest nature—and that act establishes one; proceeding as is presumed upon

Gov of the | has

If then it| ~~can it~~ ought to be admitted that the U States ~~have~~ the power of erecting Corporations in cases relative to the objects entrusted to it, it remains to see

the 2d. Clause of the 3d. Section of the Constitution which declares that Congress shall have power to dispose of and make *all needful rules and regulations* respecting the territory or other property belonging to the United States.

Let it now be seen what are the objections to the power of erecting corporations *generally*.

The sum of them as respects the Secretary of State seems to be that they contain certain capacities properties or attributes; which are against the laws of *mortmain* against the laws of *Alienage* ~~which~~

against the law
~~change the course~~ of *descents*, ~~which are~~ against the laws of *forfieture* and *escheat* against the law of distribution, and as respects the particular institution contemplated against the laws of *Monopoly:* And it is added to the rest that a power is given ~~conferred~~ to make laws *paramount* ~~of~~ to the *laws of the States.* Nothing but a *necessity invincible*

means,
*by others*ₐcan justify it is said such a *prostration of laws* which constitute the pillars of our whole system of jurisprudence and are the foundation laws of the State governments.

Let it ~~first~~ be seen, how far these observations are correct, and ~~then~~ what force they have.

~~The law & bill is said to be again~~

The power of erecting Corporations is nothing more than that of giving *individuality* to a number of persons. ~~The common~~ When once this *individuality* is created the *Common law* of *every state* annexes to it those *incidents* which produce the effects above-mentioned ~~as~~

~~they~~ as far as they ~~reality~~ really exist. It establishes that ~~foreigners may~~

Aliens

notwithstanding the laws of Alienage

~~hold laws~~ in the artificial capacity thereby created may hold lands ˰ —
that the lands shall be ~~transacte~~ transmitted to the successors of the

corporators

first ~~holders in their~~ in the same *capacity* not to the heirs of the individuals—notwithstanding the ~~laws~~ of descents—that the corporate
property in case of the dissolution of the corporation shall revert to
the donors, not to the sovereign, ~~notw~~ as in the case of a failure of heirs
of private persons—notwithstanding the law of escheat & that it shall
not be forfieted for the crimes of the individual members; notwith-

forfietures.

standing the laws of ~~foreigners~~. All these circumstances too are mere
consequences of the creation of an *artificial* person. The distinction

real

between *citizen* and *alien* can only apply between ~~natural~~ persons.
Such an artificial person may have successors but can have no *heirs*—
therefore the laws of descent cannot reach it, and, for the same reason,
it is equally out of the reach of the law of escheat which relates wholly

person

to a *failure* of *heirs*. An artificial ~~person~~ cannot commit a crime—
therefore its property cannot be liable to forfieture.

inaccurate

This shews that it is ˰~~incorrect~~ to say, that ~~a~~ the erection of a corporation is *against* those *different heads* of the state laws. It is in fact only
to create a certain *Artificial* or *legal entity*, to which ~~the fundamental~~
~~law maxims of~~ the law of every state itself, annexes an ~~emptio~~
exemption from the operation of the rules that fall under those heads,
as being *inapplicable to* it. It is only to put a certain number of individuals with their own consent in a situation ~~with~~ which subjects

to

their property ˰a different regulation from that which would attend
it if they had not consented to enter into this State.

But if the thing were not truly to be viewed in this right—if the

a   heads

creation of corporation were really against those different ˰of the

really

state laws, if it ~~really~~ made an alteration in them ~~laws~~ in ~~those respects~~
the particulars which have been ~~mad~~ mentioned—what would be the
consequence of all this? Is it meant to be maintained that Congress

cannot make alterations _{in no case} in the state laws. If this is intended all the powers of the national government become nugatory. For almost every new law must ~~is~~ be an alteration in some way or other ~~other~~ of ~~one su one or more old laws~~ some other law either common or statute.

There are laws concerning bankruptcy in several states—several states have laws concerning the values of foreign Coins—Congress are empowered to _{establish} uniform laws concerning bankruptcy throughout the United States and to regulate the value of foreign coin. The exercise of either of these powers, by Congress, necessarily involves an alteration of the laws of those states; and in respect to bankruptcies in cases that affect real property and _{involve} penalties of the highest nature.

Again ~~Congress under~~ every person by the *common-law* of each state may now export his ~~property commodities~~ property to foreign countries at pleasure. But Congress may without doubt in pursuance of the power of regulating Trade prohibit the exportation of commodities; in ~~doing~~ which they would certainly alter the common law of each state in abrigement of individual rights.

This being the case it can never be good reasoning to say—the doing of *this* or *that act* is unconstitutional because it alters *this* or *that* law of the states. It must always be shewn that the thing which makes the alteration is unconstitutional in its own nature not *because* it makes the alteration. Hence an argument which ~~objects the~~ makes that _{circumstance} such ~~an effect~~ an objection to the ~~ex~~ constitutional right of exercising any power must be rejected.

Two things are advanced by the Secretary of State which are peculiarly incorrect. These are that the proposed incorporation is against the laws of monopoly and that power is given by it to *make laws paramount* to the laws of the states. As to the first the only part of the bill which can give colour to the suggestion is that which ~~stipulating~~ stipulates that the U States will not ~~not~~ erect any similar institution or grant similar privileges to any other. But does this prohibit any state from erecting itself a bank. Does it even prohibit any number of individuals from associating themselves to carry~~ing~~ on ~~other~~ the banking

free
business? It does neither and consequently is altogether⌃from the

The supposition of a
charge of establishing a monopoly. ~~A~~ consequential interference with
the Banks of other states if founded would not make good a charge—
For Monopoly implies a *legal impediment* to the carrying on of the
Trade by others than those to whom it is granted. ~~That supposition
however would be a forced one.~~ Such an interference indeed might
tend to prevent rather than to create monopoly by dividing the business—~~But it is not probable that the~~ but whether any ~~species of~~ com-
in this way
petition⌃will exist is altogether problematical.

The idea of the Corporation having power to make laws *paramount*

Its
to those of the states is still less colourable. ~~Their~~ bye laws of regulations from the nature of the institution can operate only upon ~~the
members themselves~~ its own members can relate only the disposition
of its own property & ~~can be little more than the private~~ will essentially resemble the private rules of a mercantile partnership. They are
expressly not to be contrary to *law*—and ~~this~~ law here must necessarily mean the law of each state ~~so far as it dos not contravene that of
the U States~~ as well as of the U States so far as the formerly does not
improperly contravene the latter. If there should be a repugnancy between any state law and that of the U States the Courts as in every
similar case must decide ~~between them~~ on the their respective validity.
There may be questions between an interfering law of a state & that
of the U States but there can be none between ~~a state and~~ a law of a
state and a law of the Corporation.

a
The ~~sum of the~~ Arguments of the Attorney General against ~~the~~
power of incorporation in the National Government generally are to
this effect.

First that it is not *expressly* given to Congress.

This is admitted. There ~~are no war~~ is no clause of the constitution
declaring in *~~direct terms~~* express terms that Congress may make corporations.

point
It was said upon this⌃in argument in the House of Representatives—
that if a power of so transcendent a nature was meant to be conferred
upon Congress it would have been expressly mentioned.

But this idea of the transcendant nature of the power is all exageration. It has been seen that it is only to give *individuality* to a number of persons *voluntarily* associated for a particular purpose or to substitute an artificial to a natural ^capacity *person*. It has been seen that in its origin a voluntary association of Individuals was capable of producing ~~it~~ ^the effect without the help of ^a particular act of ~~positive~~ law—And that in England it is a part of the Executive authority.

Perhaps the best definition that can be given of a Corporation is this. It is a *legal* person or a person created by ^act of law, ~~to hold property or a franchise in succession~~ consisting of one or more ~~individuals~~ natural persons ~~capable of~~ ^empowered to ~~holding~~ property or a franchise in *succession* in a legal ^as contradistinguished ~~as distinct~~ from ~~their~~ ^a natural, capacity. According to this ^definition ~~idea of it~~, of legislation if the United States should declare that all bonds for duties should be given to the Collector of each district by the name of the Collector of the District of A or B and that ^every such bond ~~the sai~~ should enure to such *Collector* and his *successors in office,* in trust for the U States, this would be to constitute a Corporation in each district; and it is presumed, that if it had been ~~thought~~ ^proposed ~~expedient~~ to put the Collection of the duties in this train, however the expediency of it might be called in Question, the constitutional right of doing it would never have been disputed.

A still plainer case is this—Congress are empowered to establish post roads. Let it be supposed that it were to be resolved to establish a turn pike road throughout the united ^States under the direction of certain Commissioners by a Certain denomination to be appointed as other officers are; and that certain funds including a portion of *Western* lands should be vested in them and their *successors in office* to be disposed of for the purpose of defraying the expences of making the road—this certainly would be a corporation; and can it be doubted that it is within the constitutional power of Congress to make such an arrangement. It is repeated that the expediency of doing it or not doing it is never a test of constitutional right; for the consequence of such a principle would be that every inexpedient or injudicious measure which a government may adopt is unconstitution[ally] an absurdity of the first magnitude.

Again: ~~There are certain~~ The Western lands are pledged ~~for~~ as a
                                                    in order
fund to sink the public debt. Suppose to render the application of the
                              repeatedly
fund still more inviolable, ~~as has been~~ proposed ~~by able men~~ by giving it the *character* and *sanction* of *private property*, as has been repeatedly proposed by able men in Great Britain & if rightly recollected
                                           a
practiced upon in ~~the~~ the late instance, it had been judged expedient ~~expedient~~ by Congress to vest those lands in certain Commissioners to be appointed as ~~off~~ other officers and in their *successors in office* to be disposed of & the proceeds applied to the redemption of the public debt, ~~could have an~~ could any objection have been made to the constitutionality of the measure? Certainly none—probably none would have even been thought of from the obvious futility of it. And yet here would have been most manifestly a corporation.

Instances of a similar kind may be multiplied without number in which a natural construction of the powers of Congress would author-ise the erection of Corporations as very simple *means* to ~~declared ends~~ the specified ends of the governt.

The erection of a Corporation is plainly then
~~It is therefore plainly~~ one of those *incidental* things, one of those
          operations
ordinary ~~objects~~ one of those *mere means* to an *end,* which was best left to be implied as an *ingredient* in a general power. Particularly as there might exist prejudices on the point. And it was not prudent to encounter any by unnecessary specifications.

This is not an improper place to take notice of an observation made by the Secretary of State concerning ~~a~~ the proposition in the Convention to insert specifically a power to make Corporations which he uses as an argument against the power.

                                        or what the reasons for refusing it
What the precise nature, or extent of the proposition, was is not ascertained by any authentic document. As far as any such document exists it only specifies *canals.* The ~~memories~~ recollections of individuals do not correspond either as to the *import* of the proposition or the reasons for not adopting it. Some affirm that ~~it~~ there was an ob-

jection to granting power to erect corporations others that it was thought unnecessary as being incidental to the powers granted and ~~migh~~ inexpedient to be specified as involving a new topic of objection; others that the purposes of it, being canals and obstructions in rivers were thought irrelative to fœderal ~~objects~~ regulation. Thus stands the manner, and certainly in this situation there is no inference to be drawn from the fact.

The Secretary of State also knows, that whatever may have been the true state of that fact it is of no weight in the question, that whatever may have been the intention of the framers of a Constitution, or of a law, that intention must be sought for in the instrument _{itself} and must be ~~gene~~ deter~~dimined~~_{mined} by general principles of construction ~~& the~~ applied to the tenor & objects of ~~the~~ _{such} instrument. _{Nothing is more com⌐} If then a power to
_{than for laws to express & effect more or less than was intended.}
erect corporations is deducible by fair inference from the whole or any part of the constitution of the United States ~~the intention of the Conven~~ arguments drawn from extrinsic circumstances regarding the intention of the Convention must be rejected.

~~The Attorny Gener~~

The power of making corporations not being expressly granted The Attorney General proceeds to infer that it can only exist from one of three causes

1   Because the *nature* of the *Fœderal Government* implies it or
2   Because it is involved in some of the specified powers of legislation or
3dly.   Because it is necessary and proper to carry into execution some of the specified powers.

With regard to the first he argues that to be implied in the *nature* of the Fœderal Government would beget a doctrine so indefinite as to grasp every power.

Let it be remarked in the first place that neither of these ~~provisions~~ propositions is ~~essentially~~ precisely or substantially *that* which ~~has been relied upon~~ is relied upon here—*This* is that the right of erecting corporations is incidental to *sovereign power*, not to the particular *nature* of the *fœderal Government*. None of the reasonings of the Attorney General do therefore reach this proposition.

But let it be supposed that he would consider the two propositions
in the same light and that the answer which has been stated _{as given} to the
one is to be applied to the other.

Then the answer _{to that} is, that it is not true that the Doctrine would be
so indefinite as to grasp every power—Because the ~~quality~~ qualification which has stated to the Doctrine is that it must be *in relation to
the objects confided to the government.* A *general legislative power*
_{includes a}
~~is a~~ *power* to erect corporations *in all cases* where they shall appear
necessary or expedient to the legislature. A legislative power as to
certain objects includes a power only to erect corporations in relation
to *those* objects—not in relation to *other* objects. Hence therefore to
contend that the legislative power of the U States extends to the erection of Corporations in relation to the objects of the Fœderal Government does not imply a claim that it shall extend to things not
relative to the objects of that Government. Thus a power to erect a
corporation relatively to *Trade* is not a power to erect one relatively
to *Religion.* The first is a declared and leading object of the Regulation of the Fœderal Government. The last it has no power concerning.

The object therefore is in every case as already remarked to test and
characterise the proper exercise of the power. As reasonably might
be argued that a right to prescribe penalties for a breach of the laws of
Trade is a right to prescribe penalties for violations of the laws of
~~Chasting~~ Chastity.

The Attorney General after combating the first proposition relatively to the nature of the Fœderal Government which has been just
examined in its *true sense* proceeds _{next} to shew that ~~it is not within~~ the
power of erecting corporations is not involved in any of the specified
powers of legislation.

In order to accomplish this, he makes an *enumeration ~~according to
his own ideas~~* of the *particulars* which ~~are included~~ *in his opinion,* ~~are~~
for *so only* it must be considered are comprehended in several of the
principal general powers; and ~~including in~~ _{excluding from} this enumeration ~~only such~~
~~particulars only as appeared to him~~ _{very} *the particular in controversy* as

well as many others that may be imagined and many more that no

imagination can ~~reach in perspective~~ _{anticipate} and that occasions only can suggest he fairly *begs the question.*

It is not meant to represent this as intentional. It is a natural consequence of attempting to try ~~a power by a fallacious test~~ a general
power ~~by an enum~~ which always includes an *infinite number of*
particulars by ~~an~~ _{precise} enumeration. Every such enumeration must be more
or less ~~important~~ imperfect; because the human imagination is inadequate to the detail. Even every particular that may be specified must
be in itself a general that must include a vast variety of other particulars. The intent of this enumeration is *doubtless* to shew what is contained in each power & then to infer that the power of incorporation
not corresponding with either of the _{specified} particulars does not exist. The
force of this conclusion must depend on the accuracy of the enumer-
ation—the pointing out of inaccuracy and defects must therefore destroy it. It was from a Conviction of this very difficulty that the Convention forebore to attempt such a specification.

A ~~critial~~ critical ~~examssion~~ examination of the detail into which he
enters would involve too voluminous a discussion. It will ~~be sufficient~~
~~to destroy all possibl~~ the ~~effect intended to be produced by this enu-~~
~~meration~~ _{suffice} to state certain palpable *defects* and *omissions*—some ~~less~~ _{not equally} *pal-*
pable or *certain* but ~~still~~ probable ones. ~~and~~ In the couse of this to cor-
robarate but some new & particular view, the _{more} general doctrines which
have been advanced.

The first power descanted upon is that of laying and collecting
Taxes which indeed is the most accurately subdivided.

One subdivision of it is "to prescribe the mode of Collection"—an
immense *chapter* which involves a variety of details and among others
the very ~~power~~ _{thing} in question. It includes—the establishment of districts
and ports—the creation of officers and the appointment of their duties
powers and *legal capacities,* modes of proceeding, exemptions penalties modes of prosecution & recovery—*species of money ~~or other~~*

~~thing~~ in which the taxes are to be paid—And it may *legally* include

the erection of_∧corporations charged with the Collection, upon certain conditions stipulated between the Government and them.

~~This last point shal~~

        noted
It has been already ~~stated~~ in what manner the Officers of the customs might be made a Corporation for the purposes of taking bonds & receiving the monies payable upon them. It shall be explained in another place how far the power of establishing *the species of money* in which the taxes shall be paid is connected with the institution of a Bank. It shall now be shewn that by a fair construction of the power of *laying* & *collecting taxes* a corporation may be instituted charged with the collection upon certain conditions stipulated with the Government.

It is a common practice in some countries and has been practiced in this—to farm particular taxes. This is to sell or mortgage the product of them to an individual or company for a certain ~~spef~~ specified
                    of it
sum, leaving ~~it~~ the collection_∧to that individual or company. Let it be
                                          in any case
supposed that it ~~was~~ was *manifest* that this mode of proceeding was_∧
                    in the view of revenue
the most eligible to the government_∧and equally convenient & safe for the citizens—let it also be supposed that a number of individuals were disposed to undertake the matter upon condition of being incor-
                                persons
porated. An incorporation, if a number of ~~individuals~~ were concerned would be a natural and a necessary ingredient in the arrangement—
        for
~~but~~ it would be essential to the security of the undertakers that the property in the fund should be definitively vested in them and that
                                          and managing
they should have an easy method of recovering_∧the taxes—to which a corporate capacity would be indispensable. It must be extremely difficult to assign a reasy why ~~the Legislature~~ Congress might not adopt this mode of Collection as well as any other, and might not as a necessary ingredient in it incorporate the undertakers. It would not
                    might be constity. ~~be~~ *done*
be doubted that this ~~could~~_∧by ~~any~~ an other government and why not

by that of the United States which has as plenary a power of taxation
as any in the world ^except with respect to duties on exports & with these~~ with only~~ two qualifications shall all duties that
direct shall be apportioned according to ~~a fixed rule & that no dut~~ taxes ^determinate~~
a certain ratio of population.

The specification of particulars ~~incident~~ next relates to the power of borrowing money, and is materially defective. It confines that power to
three points—the *stipulation of a sum to be lent,* of an *interest* or no
interest to be paid and of the *time* and *manner* of repayment.

A palpable omission strikes the eye at once the *pledging* or *mortgaging* of a *fund* for the security of the money lent. Here is a common
& in most cases an essential requisite which is overlooked.

The idea of ~~a~~ the stipulation of *an interest* or *no interest* is too confined. The *phrase* should have been to stipulate the *consideration* of
the loan. Individuals often borrow upon considerations different from
the payment of interest sometimes in addition to it sometimes independent of it—So may governments, and so they often find it necessary to do. Every one recollects the lottery tickets and other douceurs
often given in Great Britain as collateral inducements to the lending
of money to the government.

There are also frequently collateral conditions not falling within
any of the enumerated particulars. Every Contract for monies borrowed in Holland, stipulates that the sum due shall be free from all
taxes and from sequestration in time of war and mortgages all the
lands & property of the United States for the reimbursement.

It is also known that a lottery is a very common expedient for borrowing money, which is certainly not included under either of the
specified heads.

These things are mentioned to shew the defectiveness of the specifi-
cation & that any ~~inference drawn from them not comprehending~~ argument built upon them against
the power of erecting a corporation must be ~~unfun~~ unfounded. It is
reserved in the sequel to shew the relation between this power and the
institution of a bank.

The enumeration respecting the power of regulating trade is still
more defective and inconclusive.

~~First as it relates to the Trade with foreign Countrys~~ Here is a total *omission* of every thing that regards the Citizens of the United States —their vessels and Merchandize.

1   The power of *prohibitting* the *exportation* of domestic commodities of which there cannot be a shadow of doubt and which in time of war it would be necessary to exercise, sometimes temporarily in ~~a~~ the shape of an embargo sometimes altogether—as with reference to Naval and other warlike stores which might be wanted at home

2   The prescribing rules concerning the characteristics and privileges of an American *bottom* and the manner in which she shall be navigated as to the composition of her Commander and Crew what proportion of Citizens to foreigners.

3   The prescribing of regulations concerning the ∧ police of Ships terms on which persons shall be engaged & the on their Voyages &c as by the "Act for the Government & regulation of Seamen in the Merchants service."

4   The granting of bounties to certain species of vessels and certain kinds of Merchandize. This has been actually done in respect to dried & pickled fish & salted provision.

There are other things which occur that appear to be within the power of regulating trade though not as certainly as those which have been mentioned.

These are ~~the regulation of policies of insurance~~

1   The prescribing rules for the *Inspection* of Commodities to be exported. Though the states individually are competent to this there appears no reason in *point of authority* why a general System might not be adopted for the purpose by the United States.

2   The regulation of policies of Insurance

3   The prohibition of *wearing* as well as importing foreign Commodities

4   The Regulation of salvage upon goods found at Sea

5   The Regulation of pilots

6   The Regulation of bills of Exchange drawn by a Merchant in one State upon a Merchant in another.

~~And as it respects the Trade between the Fe states y The power of~~

Hence is seen the imperfection of the enumeration under the second head and the impossibility of deducing from it any argument against

leaves in full force the arguments that
the power of incorporation contended for ~~and~~ which ~~it is presumed~~
have been offered to shew that it exists & particularly
~~has been shewn to exist~~ in relation to Trading Companies—which
therefore ought to be classed ~~under~~ as one of the particulars comprehended in the power of regulating Trade. The relation which it has
to a Bank in particular is reserved to ~~be shewn~~ future discussion.

The last specification relates to that clause which empowers Con-
dispose of &
gress to ^make all needful rules and regulations respecting the territory
or other property belonging to the U States.

The remaks here will relate less to the defectiveness in the enumeration of particulars than to some errors of reasoning.

~~It is admitted as one of the Items of this head of powers~~

The *institution* of a *Government* in the western Territory is admitted to belong to this head of the powers of the Fœderal Government. Now to admit the right of *instituting* a *Government* and to deny
that of erecting a corporation appears to be a contradiction in terms.
For a Government as already remarked is a Corporation of the highest
nature. It is a Corporation which can itself create other corporations.

How it could be imagined that the National Legislature could in-
could not   a
stitute a government in the Western Territory and ~~cannot~~ erect ~~an~~
~~in~~corporation for clearing obstructions ~~in its Ri~~ in the Rivers which
run through it, or for any other purpose there confounds all conjecture. ~~It directly overturns~~ Or how it can be admitted that there is a
power to *institute* a *goverment* and denied that there is a power to
erect a Corporation requires to be reconciled.

Here then by an ~~express~~ express concession of the Atty General is
a power to erect a Corporation in one case at least; a power too which
has in fact been carried into operation.

It is said that the property contemplated in the clause *may signify
personal property* of the United States *however acquired;* and yet it
is affirmed that it *cannot signify money* arising from the sources of
revenue pointed out in the Constitution.

This opposition in terms is not remarked for the sake of any verbal
~~critical~~ criticism. It is only meant to make use of *what is conceded*
to oppose it to *what is denied.*

The concession is that *property* in the ~~general~~ sense of the clause
extends generally to *personal* as well as _{to} real property.

The denial is that it extends to *money* raised by taxes ~~me~~ which
therefore is to be considered as excepted out of the general term property though comprehending personal property.

For this exception the reason given is——. "That the disposal and
regulation of money is the *final cause* ~~of~~ for raising it by taxes" ~~But
this reason is not satisfactory~~. This reason which is rather subtile, and
against the *letter* of the clause, must be combatted by reasoning that
may perhaps itself seem to savour of subtilty and refinement.

It would certainly be a more accurate and more just mode of ex-
pression to say "that the *object* to which money is _{intended} to be applied is the
final cause for raising it" than that the *disposal* and *regulation* of it is
such. Now the *objects* for which the Constitution authorises the raising of money are *common defence* and *general welfare*. The _{actual} disposi-
tion and *regulation* of it when raised are therefore the *steps* by which
it is ~~app~~ *in fact* applied to the objects for which it was raised. Hence
therefore the money to be raised by taxes as well as any other personal
property may be supposed to be comprehended within the meaning
as they certainly are within the letter of the ~~provisio~~ authority to dispose of and make all needful rules and regulations concerning the
property of the U States—for _{that is to say,} the purposes of the common defence
and general welfare.

The terms *general welfare* are of very comprehensive import. They
must ~~necessary~~ necessarily embrace every object of general concern-
ment —whatever has a *general* operation, relating either to the _{general} order
of the national finances or to the general interests of Trade Agriculture or manufactures.

A case will make this plainer. Certain revenues are now established,
in relation to the public debt. Suppose the whole or a considerable
part of this debt discharged & the funds now pledged for it or a considerable part of them liberated. ~~Here then would be monies in the
public Treasury to be *disposed of* and *regulated*.~~ _{In such a case} ~~It is true~~ the taxes
might be repealed; ~~but in some~~ and in certain _{instances} ~~cases~~ it might be wise to

do so but in others it ~~will~~ might be more wise to retain them, as the repeal might injure our own manufactures and industry. ~~It would~~

would

~~then remain to cause such a disposition as might consist with general utility or *general welfare*.~~ Here then would be monies to be *disposed of* & *regulated* in the strictest sense of the clause.

under this clause,

What then would there be in such case to prevent, the investiture of those monies in a Bank, if such an institution should appear ~~calcuted~~ calculated to promote the general ~~good?~~ welfare? Evidently the want

what

of a power to ~~erected~~ a *corporation* would not be an obstacle. For‸

is equivalent or more,

the power to erect a *government* is admitted to exist and has been exercised under it.

~~Here then is plainly a case~~

Hence it is evident, that under this clause alone a Bank may be erected. For as has been before remarked the existence of a constitu-

unless

tional power cannot depend on times & circumstances; ~~only~~ the Constitution ~~explicitly~~ marks out the conditions on which it is to begin to exist.

Hitherto except in this *last instance* the arguments which have used

~~designed~~   designed to

have been ~~intended to prove that~~‸establish the general proposition that the Government of the U States has power to erect Corporations in certain cases. This it is confided has been satisfactorily done and all the objections to it satisfactorily removed. And as all the Arguments of the Secretary of State & Attorney General are built on a denial of that proposition, as far as their objections are concerned there might be no necessity to proceed further.

But something more is proper to be done to satisfy the judgment of

of the   is desireable to illustrate still further

the President United States. It ~~remains to shew~~ that there is a power to erect such a *species* of Corporation as a *Bank* by shewing that it has a fair relation to some one or more of the specified powers. ~~This indeed has been in part done~~

~~Previous to this it will be useful briefly to analise~~ A few preliminary observations may be proper.

is to   for the purpose of creating

The proposed bank ~~will~~ consist of an association of persons ~~to certain~~ a joint capital to be employed chiefly and essentially in loans.

There is no doubt that it is lawful for any number ~~so to associate~~ of individuals so to associate and dispose of their money or property. The Bank of New York is an example of this. That Bank is not incorporated. The Bill proposes in respect to the government that it shall become a joint proprietor in this undertaking; that it shall permit the bills of the Bank payable on demand ~~& that~~ to be received in payment of its Revenues, and that it will not grant a similar privilege to any other Bank.

All this is indubitably within the ~~wise~~ compass of the discretion of the Governt. The only Question is has it a right to incorporate this company the more effectually to enable it to accomplish ends which are in themselves lawful.

Its power of making Corporations in all the cases relative to its proper objects has been proved. Let it now be examined to which of those objects the proposed institution relates.

No person who reads with an impartial eye the powers vested in the National Government but must be satisfied that it is intended by its constitution to vest it with all the powers ~~that are~~ which necessary for ~~the~~ what may be called the *Administration* of its Finances.

It is authorised to raise *money* by taxes to an indefinite extent to borrow money to an indefinite extent, to coin money, regulate the value thereof and of foreign coin, to dispose of and make all needful rules and regulations concerning the property of the United States and to pass all laws necessary and proper for carrying into execution those powers.

It has a direct relation to the power of *collecting* taxes; to that of *borrowing* money, to that of regulating Trade between the States and ~~to that~~ and as a consequence of the two first to that of raising supporting and maintaining fleets and armies for the common defence. And it is ~~within the letter of the~~ clearly within the provision which respects the disposal and regulation of the *property* of the U States as the same has been practiced upon by the Government.

It relates to the collection of taxes in two ways, indirectly by ~~the facility which rep~~ increasing the quantity of circulating medium— ~~in~~directly by creating a *convenient species of medium* in which they are to be *received*.

It is undeniably within the power of providing for the *collection of the taxes* to appoint the *money* or *thing* in which they are to be paid. Accordingly Congress have declared ~~that~~ in the Collection law that ~~they shall~~ the duties on imports and tonnage shall be payable in gold and silver at certain rates. But while it was a necessary part of the work to declare in what they should be payable, ~~there was cert~~ it was mere matter of discretion what that medium of payment should be. It might have been, though inconvenient, in the commodities themselves. Taxes in kind are not without precedents even in the United States. It might have been in the paper emissions of the several States; ~~and it or it might have been in the bills of the Ban It might have been~~

or

~~in notes issued under bills~~ it might have been in the bills of the Banks of North America New York Massachusettes all or any of them or it

issued

might have been in bills ~~emitted~~ under the ~~immediate~~ *Authority* of the United States.

It is presumed there is not a tittle of this which can be controverted. The appointment then of the *money* or *thing* in which the taxes are

discretion

to be paid is an object within the ~~power~~ of the Government as incident to the power of Collection. And among the expedients which occur is that *of bills issued under the authority of the United States.*

Now the manner of issuing these bills must be again matter of discretion. There must be agents employed for the purpose. These Agents may be ~~stand~~ officers of the Government or they may be *Directors of a Bank*. If the notes of the ~~Bank~~ Bank of North America were made receiveable in the taxes, the Directors of that Bank would thereby become ipso facto Agents of the Government for this purpose.

deemed a   mean of preserving

Suppose it were ~~judged~~ necessary ~~to preserve~~ the Credit of the bills that they should be made payable in gold and silver *on demand* and

~~in order to this~~ a sum of money should be

that it ~~were thought expedient to~~ *appropriated* and set *apart* ~~a sum of money~~ as a fund for answering them; ~~Certainly all this would be clearly within the power of~~ designating certain officers of the Government who were to issue the bills and administer the fund. The constitutionality of all this could certainly not be called in question. And yet it would amount to the institution of a Bank, with a view to the more convenient collection of taxes. For a Bank in the simplest idea of it is a *deposit* of money or other property as a fund for ~~circum~~ circulating a credit upon it ~~as~~ equivalent to money. The reality of this character would become the more obvious if the ~~officers~~ place in which the fund was kept should be made the receptable of the monies of all other persons who should incline to deposit them there for safe keeping; and if in addition to the rest the officers of this fund were authorised to make discounts at the usual rate of interest upon good security. The first would be an operation within the discretion of the officers themselves and to deny the power of the Government to authorise the last would be to refine away all government.

This process serves to establish the natural and direct relation between the Institution of a *Bank* and the Collection of taxes and to shew that it is a mean which may with constitutional propriety be employed in reference to that end.

~~in reference to it~~. It is true that the species of Bank which has been just designated does not involve the idea of incorporation. But the argument intended to be founded upon it is this, that the *institution* or *thing* comprehended in the definition of a *Bank* being one ^immediately^ relative to the collection of taxes, as it *regards the appointment of the money* or ~~thing~~ in which they are to be ^medium^ ^paid^, the sovereign power of passing all laws necessary and proper ^for the collection of taxes^ includes that ~~incorporation of a Bank~~ *incorporating* ^of^ such an institution as ~~it~~ a *requisite* to its greater security utility and more convenient management.

^A^ ~~Some~~ further process will still more clearly illustrate this point. Suppose when the species of Bank ^which has been described^ was about to be instituted it were to be ~~remarked~~ urged that in order to securing to it a proper degree of confidence, the fund ought not ~~no~~ only to ^be^ set apart and appropriated generally, but ought to be specifically vested in those who were to have the Direction ^of it^ and ^in^ their successors in office, to the end that it might become of the nature of private property incapable of being touched without invading the sanctions by which the rights of property are protected and occasioning more serious and general

the apprehension of
alarm˄which might operate as a check upon the Government. Such a
proposition might be opposed by arguments against the expediency of
it or the solidity of the reason assigned for it; but it is not easy to conceive what could be said against the constitutionality of it, unless it
should be ~~by~~˄a general denial of the power of incorporating in any case.
But this it is presumed has been satisfactorily refuted. Here then by a
very simple and natural step the quality of a corporation would be
given to the institution.

Let the argument proceed a step farther. Suppose a Bank of the
foregoing nature with or without ~~an~~ incorporation had been insti-
that
tuted; and˄experience had demonstrated as it is very probable it
op
would˄that it wanted the confidence requisite to the Credit of its bills
~~Suppose~~ ~~at this conjuncture~~ ~~also~~ being wholly on a public foundation.
Suppose in this state of things that by some of those adverse conjunc-
nations
tures which occasionally attend˄there had been a very great drain of
the specie of the Country so as to cause general distress for want of
an adequate medium of circulation & defalcation in the product of the
revenue as a consequence of it. Suppose also that there was no Bank
position
instituted in any state—in such a ~~state~~ of things would it not be ~~mani-~~
Bank
~~fest~~ most ~~manifest~~ evident that the Incorporation of a ~~such~~ on the
general principle of that proposed by the Bill namely the Union of

the Capitals of a number of individuals under a private manage˄would
be a measure immediately relative to the *effectual Collection* of the
taxes?
would render
If it be said that such a state of thing˄that *necessary* and therefore
constitutional which is not now *so* now. The solid answer to this is
that *circumstances* may affect the *expediency* of ~~the~~ a measure but
not the constitutionality of it.

It has been shewn that the word *necessary* is not to be taken in so
strict a sense. ~~An addition~~ ~~Though~~ ~~the~~ ~~Attorny~~ ~~General~~ *~~in~~* *~~fact~~* ~~con-~~
he
~~cedes this,~~ ~~yet~~ ~~it falls into~~ ~~a use of the word in the sense~~ he ~~regrets in~~
~~relation to this particular point.~~ Of this a further illustration may be

the *thing*
given here. Congress are to appoint the ~~medium~~ medium in which the
taxes are to be paid. This as has been remarked may be commodities
                                                    authorised
or gold & silver or ~~various kinds of~~ paper. If Congress are ˄to do nothing but what is strictly necessary they cannot require the payment of
taxes in gold or silver only because ~~som~~ other commodities may answer—nor can they allow them to be ~~necessary~~ received in paper, un-
            be   or
less there ~~was~~ no gold ~~and~~ silver.

                        such as that proposed
    The institution of a Bank ˄is directly relative to the borrowing of
                        business
money. ~~It~~ Its main ~~design~~ is to lend money. It is *essential*, especially in
a Country like this, to the ~~obta~~ procuring of loans in sudden imer-
gencies. It is the usual instrument relied upon for this purpose in different nations.

    A nation is threatened with a war. Considerable sums are wanted
on a sudden to make the requisite preparations. Taxes are laid for the
purpose; but it requires time to obtain the benefit of them. ~~A loan is~~
                                            be
Anticipation is indispensable. If there ~~is~~ a Bank the supply can at once
            be
can be had. If there ~~is~~ none ~~individ~~ loans of individuals must be re-
sorted to. The progress of these is often too slow for the exigency. In
some situations indeed they are not practicable. Often when they are
it is of great importance to be able to anticipate the product of them
by advances from a Bank.

    The essentiality of this institution as an instrument of loans is exem-
plified at this very moment. An Indian expedition is to be prosecuted.
~~all the~~ The only fund out of which the money can arise consistently
with the public engagements is a tax which will only begin to be collected in July next. The preparations ~~were~~ are instantly to be made.
The ~~tax mu~~ money must therefore be borrowed. And of whom could
it borrowed if there were no public banks?

    It happens that there are institutions of this kind but if there were
none it would be indispensable to create one. ~~And can it be believed~~
~~that the Government would be destitute of the power of doing it?~~
            then
    Let it ˄be supposed that the necessity existed (as but for a casualty

it would) that proposals were made for a loan that a number of individuals came forward and said—We are willing to accommodate the Government with this money—with what we have in hand and

                                                              can
the Credit we ~~should be~~ ~~might~~ raise upon it, we ~~sho~~ doubt not of being able to furnish the sum required but in order to this it is absolutely

                                                with the capacity
        that   & be
necessary we should be incorporated ~~in order to the established~~ of a bank. This will not only be a *consideration* with us for the loan but it is

FINAL VERSION OF AN OPINION ON THE CONSTITUTIONALITY OF AN ACT TO ESTABLISH A BANK [5]

The Secretary of the Treasury having perused with attention the papers containing the opinions of the Secretary of State and Attorney General concerning the constitutionality of the bill for establishing a National Bank [6] proceeds according to the order of the President to submit the reasons which have induced him to entertain a different opinion.

It will naturally have been anticipated that, in performing this task he would feel uncommon solicitude. Personal considerations alone arising from the reflection that the measure originated with him would be sufficient to produce it: The sense which he has manifested of the great importance of such an institution to the successful administration of the department under his particular care; and an expectation of serious ill consequences to result from a failure of the measure, do not permit him to be without anxiety on public accounts. But the chief solicitude arises from a firm persuasion, that principles of construction like those espoused by the Secretary of State and the Attorney General would be fatal to the just & indispensible authority of the United States.

In entering upon the argument it ought to be premised, that the objections of the Secretary of State and Attorney General are founded

5. Copy, Mr. John R. Dillard, Philadelphia.
6. Both Edmund Randolph's and Thomas Jefferson's opinions were enclosed in a letter from George Washington to H, February 16, 1791, which is found in the George Washington letter book, Library of Congress.

on a general denial of the authority of the United States to erect corporations. The latter indeed expressly admits, that if there be any
thing in the bill which is not warranted by the constitution, it is the
clause of incorporation.[7]

Now it appears to the Secretary of the Treasury, that this *general
principle* is *inherent* in the very *definition* of *Government* and *essential* to every step of the progress to be made by that of the United
States; namely—that every power vested in a Government is in its nature *sovereign*, and includes by *force* of the *term*, a right to employ
all the *means* requisite, and fairly *applicable* to the attainment of the
ends of such power; and which are not precluded by restrictions &
exceptions specified in the constitution; or not immoral, or not contrary to the essential ends of political society.

This principle in its application to Government in general would
be admitted as an axiom. And it will be incumbent upon those, who
may incline to deny it, to *prove* a distinction; and to shew that a rule
which in the general system of things is essential to the preservation
of the social order is inapplicable to the United States.

The circumstances that the powers of sovereignty are in this country divided between the National and State Governments, does not
afford the distinction required. It does not follow from this, that each
of the *portions* of powers delegated to the one or to the other is not
sovereign *with regard to its proper objects*. It will only *follow* from
it, that each has sovereign power as to *certain things*, and not as to
other things. To deny that the Government of the United States has
sovereign power as to its declared purposes & trusts, because its power
does not extend to all cases, would be equally to deny, that the State
Governments have sovereign power in any case; because their power
does not extend to every case. The tenth section of the first article of
the constitution exhibits a long list of very important things which
they may not do. And thus the United States would furnish the singular spectacle of a *political society* without *sovereignty*, or of a people
governed without *government*.

If it would be necessary to bring proof to a proposition so clear as
that which affirms that the powers of the fœderal government, *as to*

7. Randolph stated: "It must be acknowledged, that, if any part of the bill
does either encounter the Constitution, or is not warranted by it, the clause of
incorporation is the only one."

its objects, are sovereign, there is a clause of its constitution which would be decisive. It is that which declares, that the constitution and the laws of the United States made in pursuance of it, and all treaties made or which shall be made under their authority shall be the supreme law of the land. The power which can create the *Supreme law* of the land, in any case, is doubtless sovereign *as to such case.*

This general & indisputable principle puts at once an end to the *abstract* question—Whether the United States have power to *erect a corporation?* that is to say, to give a *legal* or *artificial capacity* to one or more persons, distinct from the natural. For it is unquestionably incident to *sovereign power* to erect corporations, and consequently to *that* of the United States, in *relation to the objects* intrusted to the management of the government. The difference is this—where the authority of the government is general, it can create corporations in *all cases;* where it is confined to certain branches of legislation, it can create corporations only in those cases.

Here then as far as concerns the reasonings of the Secretary of State & the Attorney General, the affirmative of the constitutionality of the bill might be permitted to rest. It will occur to the President that the principle here advanced has been untouched by either of them.

For a more complete elucidation of the point nevertheless, the arguments which they have used against the power of the government to erect corporations, however foreign they are to the great & fundamental rule which has been stated, shall be particularly examined. And after shewing that they do not tend to impair its force, it shall also be shewn, that the power of incorporation incident to the government in certain cases, does fairly extend to the particular case which is the object of the bill.

The first of these arguments is, that the foundation of the constitution is laid on this ground "that all powers not delegated to the United States by the Constitution nor prohibited to it by the States are reserved to the States or to the people", whence it is meant to be inferred, that congress can in no case exercise any power not included in those enumerated in the constitution. And it is affirmed that the power of erecting a corporation is not included in any of the enumerated powers.

The main proposition here laid down, in its true signification is not to be questioned. It is nothing more than a consequence of this republican maxim, that all government is a delegation of power. But how much is delegated in each case, is a question of fact to be made out by fair reasoning & construction upon the particular provisions of the constitution—taking as guides the general principles & general ends of government.

It is not denied, that there are *implied*, as well as *express* powers, and that the former are as effectually delegated as the latter. And for the sake of accuracy it shall be mentioned, that there is another class of powers, which may be properly denominated *resulting* powers. It will not be doubted that if the United States should make a conquest of any of the territories of its neighbours, they would possess sovereign jurisdiction over the conquered territory. This would rather be a result from the whole mass of the powers of the government & from the nature of political society, than a consequence of either of the powers specially enumerated.

But be this as it may, it furnishes a striking illustration of the general doctrine contended for. It shews an extensive case, in which a power of erecting corporations is either implied in, or would result from some or all of the powers, vested in the National Government. The jurisdiction acquired over such conquered territory would certainly be competent to every species of legislation.

To return—It is conceded, that implied powers are to be considered as delegated equally with express ones.

Then it follows, that as a power of erecting a corporation may as well be *implied* as any other thing; it may as well be employed as an *instrument* or *mean* of carrying into execution any of the specified powers, as any other instrument or mean whatever. The only question must be, in this as in every other case, whether the mean to be employed, or in this instance the corporation to be erected, has a natural relation to any of the acknowledged objects or lawful ends of the government. Thus a corporation may not be erected by congress, for superintending the police of the city of Philadelphia because they are not authorised to *regulate* the *police* of that city; but one may be erected in relation to the collection of the taxes, or to the trade with foreign countries, or to the trade between the States, or with the Indian Tribes, because it is the province of the fœderal government to regulate those objects & because it is incident to a general *sov-*

ereign or *legislative power* to *regulate* a thing, to employ all the means which relate to its regulation to the *best & greatest advantage.*

A strange fallacy seems to have crept into the manner of thinking & reasoning upon the subject. Imagination appears to have been unusually busy concerning it. An incorporation seems to have been regarded as some great, independent, substantive thing—as a political end of peculiar magnitude & moment; whereas it is truly to be considered as a *quality, capacity,* or *mean* to an end. Thus a mercantile company is formed with a certain capital for the purpose of carrying on a particular branch of business. Here the business to be prosecuted is the *end;* the association in order to form the requisite capital is the primary mean. Suppose that an incorporation were added to this; it would only be to add a new *quality* to that association; to give it an artificial capacity by which it would be enabled to prosecute the business with more safety & convenience.

That the importance of the power of incorporation has been exaggerated, leading to erroneous conclusions, will further appear from tracing it to its origin. The roman law is the source of it, according to which a *voluntary* association of individuals at *any time* or *for any purpose* was capable of producing it. In England, whence our notions of it are immediately borrowed, it forms a part of the executive authority, & the exercise of it has been often *delegated* by that authority. Whence therefore the ground of the supposition, that it lies beyond the reach of all those very important portions of sovereign power, legislative as well as executive, which belong to the government of the United States?

To this mode of reasoning respecting the right of employing all the means requisite to the execution of the specified powers of the Government, it is objected that none but *necessary* & proper means are to be employed, & the Secretary of State maintains, that no means are to be considered as *necessary,* but those without which the grant of the power would be *nugatory.*[8] Nay so far does he go in his restrictive

8. Jefferson stated: "It has been much urged that a bank will give great facility, or convenience in the collection of taxes: Suppose this were true; yet the Constitution allows only the means which are 'necessary' not those which are merely 'convenient' for effecting the enumerated powers. If such a latitude of construction be allowed to this phrase, as to give any non-enumerated power, it will go to every one, for there is no one which ingenuity may not torture into a *convenience, in some way or other to some one* of so long a list of enumerated powers; it would swallow up all the delegated powers, and reduce the whole to

interpretation of the word, as even to make the case of *necessity* which shall warrant the constitutional exercise of the power to depend on *casual* & *temporary* circumstances, an idea which alone refutes the construction. The *expediency* of exercising a particular power, at a particular time, must indeed depend on *circumstances;* but the constitutional right of exercising it must be uniform & invariable—the same to day, as to morrow.

All the arguments therefore against the constitutionality of the bill derived from the accidental existence of certain State-banks: [9] institutions which *happen* to exist to day, & for ought that concerns the government of the United States, may disappear to morrow, must not only be rejected as fallacious, but must be viewed as demonstrative, that there is a *radical* source of error in the reasoning.

It is essential to the being of the National government, that so erroneous a conception of the meaning of the word *necessary*, should be exploded.

It is certain, that neither the grammatical, nor popular sense of the term requires that construction. According to both, *necessary* often means no more than *needful, requisite, incidental, useful,* or *conducive to.* It is a common mode of expression to say, that it is *necessary* for a government or a person to do this or that thing, when nothing more is intended or understood, than that the interests of the government or person require, or will be promoted, by the doing of this or that thing. The imagination can be at no loss for exemplifications of the use of the word in this sense.

And it is the true one in which it is to be understood as used in the constitution. The whole turn of the clause containing it, indicates,

---

one phrase as before observed. Therefore it was that the Constitution restrained them to the *necessary* means; that is to say, to those means, without which the grant of the power would be nugatory."

9. Jefferson stated: "Besides, the existing banks will without a doubt, enter into arrangements for lending their agency: & the more favorable, as there will be a competition among them for it; whereas the bill delivers us up bound to the National bank, who are free to refuse all arrangement, but on their own terms, & the public not free, on such refusal, to employ any other bank. That of Philada., I believe, now does this business, by their post notes, which by an arrangement with the Treasury are paid by any State collector to whom they are presented: this expedient alone suffices to prevent the existence of that *necessity*, which may justify the assumption of a non-enumerated power as a means for carrying into effect an enumerated one. The thing may be done, and has been done, and well done, without this assumption: therefore it does not stand on that degree of *necessity* which can honestly justify it."

that it was the intent of the convention, by that clause to give a liberal latitude to the exercise of the specified powers. The expressions have peculiar comprehensiveness. They are—"to make *all laws,* necessary & proper for *carrying into execution* the foregoing powers & all *other powers* vested by the constitution in the *government* of the United States, or in any *department* or *officer* thereof." To understand the word as the Secretary of State does, would be to depart from its obvious & popular sense, and to give it a *restrictive* operation; an idea never before entertained. It would be to give it the same force as if the word *absolutely* or *indispensibly* had been prefixed to it.

Such a construction would beget endless uncertainty & embarassment. The cases must be palpable & extreme in which it could be pronounced with certainty, that a measure was absolutely necessary, or one without which the exercise of a given power would be nugatory. There are few measures of any government, which would stand so severe a test. To insist upon it, would be to make the criterion of the exercise of any implied power a *case of extreme necessity;* which is rather a rule to justify the overleaping of the bounds of constitutional authority, than to govern the ordinary exercise of it.

It may be truly said of every government, as well as of that of the United States, that it has only a right, to pass such laws as are necessary & proper to accomplish the objects intrusted to it. For no government has a right to do *merely what it pleases.* Hence by a process of reasoning similar to that of the Secretary of State, it might be proved, that neither of the State governments has a right to incorporate a bank. It might be shewn, that all the public business of the State, could be performed without a bank, and inferring thence that it was unnecessary it might be argued that it could not be done, because it is against the rule which has been just mentioned. A like mode of reasoning would prove, that there was no power to incorporate the Inhabitants of a town, with a view to a more perfect police: For it is certain, that an incorporation may be dispensed with, though it is better to have one. It is to be remembered, that there is no *express* power in any State constitution to erect corporations.[10]

10. Jefferson stated:
"But let us examine this *convenience,* & see what it is, the report on subject (page 3) states the only *general* convenience to be the preventing the transportation & re-transportation of money between the States and the Treasury, (for I pass over the increase of circulating medium, ascribed to it as a merit, and which,

The *degree* in which a measure is necessary, can never be a test of the *legal* right to adopt it. That must ever be a matter of opinion; and can only be a test of expediency. The *relation* between the *measure* and the *end*, between the *nature* of *the mean* employed towards the execution of a power and the object of that power, must be the criterion of constitutionality not the more or less of *necessity* or *utility*.

The practice of the government is against the rule of construction advocated by the Secretary of State. Of this the act concerning light houses, beacons, buoys & public piers, is a decisive example.[11] This doubtless must be referred to the power of regulating trade, and is fairly relative to it. But it cannot be affirmed, that the exercise of that power, in this instance, was strictly necessary; or that the power itself would be *nugatory* without that of regulating establishments of this nature.

This restrictive interpretation of the word *necessary* is also con-

---

according to my ideas of paper money, is clearly a demerit.) Every State will have to pay a sum of tax-money into the Treasury; and the Treasury will have to pay, in every State, a part of the interest on the public Debt, & Salaries to the officers of government resident in that state. In most of the States there will still be a surplus of tax-money to come up to the seat of government for the officers residing there: the payments of interest & Salary in each State may be made by Treasury-orders on the State-collector; this will take up the greater part of the money he has collected for his State, & consequently prevent the great mass of it from being drawn out of the State. If there be a balance of commerce in favor of that State against the one in which the government resides, the surplus of taxes will be remitted by the bills of exchange drawn for that commercial balance: and so it must be if there was a bank: but if there be no balance of commerce, either direct or circuitous, all the banks in the world, could not bring up the surplus of taxes but in the form of money. Treasury orders then, and Bills of exchange may prevent the displacement of the main mass of the money collected, without the aid of any Bank: and where these fail, it cannot be prevented even with that aid.

"Perhaps indeed bank bills may be a more *convenient* vehicle than treasury-orders, but a little *difference* in the degree of *convenience,* cannot constitute the *necessity* which the constitution makes the ground for assuming any non-enumerated power. . . .

"It may be said that a bank, whose bills would have a currency all over the states, would be more convenient than one whose currency is limitted to a single State: so it would be still more convenient that there should be a Bank whose bills should have a currency all over the world: but it does not follow from this superior conveniency that there exists any where a power to establish such a bank; or that the world may not go on very well without it."

11. "An Act for the establishment and support of Lighthouses, Beacons, Buoys, and Public Piers" (1 *Stat.* 53–54 [August 7, 1789]).

trary to this sound maxim of construction namely, that the powers contained in a constitution of government, especially those which concern the general administration of the affairs of a country, its finances, trade, defence &c ought to be construed liberally, in advancement of the public good. This rule does not depend on the particular form of a government or on the particular demarkation of the boundaries of its powers, but on the nature and objects of government itself. The means by which national exigencies are to be provided for, national inconveniencies obviated, national prosperity promoted, are of such infinite variety, extent and complexity, that there must, of necessity, be great latitude of discretion in the selection & application of those means. Hence consequently, the necessity & propriety of exercising the authorities intrusted to a government on principles of liberal construction.

The Attorney General admits the *rule*, but takes a distinction between a State, and the fœderal constitution. The latter, he thinks, ought to be construed with greater strictness, because there is more danger of error in defining partial than general powers.[12]

But the reason of the *rule* forbids such a distinction. This reason is—the variety & extent of public exigencies, a far greater proportion of which and of a far more critical kind, are objects of National than of State administration. The greater danger of error, as far as it is supposeable, may be a prudential reason for caution in practice, but it cannot be a rule of restrictive interpretation.

In regard to the clause of the constitution immediately under consideration, it is admitted by the Attorney General, that no *restrictive* effect can be ascribed to it. He defines the word necessary thus. "To

---

12. Randolph stated:

"There is a real difference between the rule of interpretation, applied to a law & a Constitution. The one comprises a summary of matter, for the detail of which numberless Laws will be necessary; the other is the very detail. The one is therefore to be construed with a discreet liberality; the other with a closer adherence to the literal meaning.

"But when we compare the modes of construing a state, and the federal, constitution, we are admonished to be stricter with regard to the latter, because there is a greater danger of Error in defining partial than general powers.

"The rule therefore for interpreting the specified powers seems to be, that, as each of them includes those details which properly constitute the whole of the subject, to which the power relates, the details themselves must be fixed by reasoning. And the appeal may on this occasion be made to common sense & common language."

be necessary is to be *incidental,* and may be denominated the natural means of executing a power." [13]

But while, on the one hand, the construction of the Secretary of State is deemed inadmissible, it will not be contended on the other, that the clause in question gives any *new* or *independent* power. But it gives an explicit sanction to the doctrine of *implied* powers, and is equivalent to an admission of the proposition, that the government, *as to its specified powers* and *objects,* has plenary & sovereign authority, in some cases paramount to that of the States, in others coordinate with it. For such is the plain import of the declaration, that it may pass *all laws* necessary & proper to carry into execution those powers.

It is no valid objection to the doctrine to say, that it is calculated to extend the powers of the general government throughout the entire sphere of State legislation. The same thing has been said, and may be said with regard to every exercise of power by *implication* or *construction.* The moment the literal meaning is departed from, there is a chance of error and abuse. And yet an adherence to the letter of its powers would at once arrest the motions of the government. It is not only agreed, on all hands, that the exercise of constructive powers is indispensible, but every act which has been passed is more or less an exemplification of it. One has been already mentioned, that relating to light houses &c.[14] That which declares the power of the President to remove officers at pleasure,[15] acknowlidges the same truth in another, and a signal instance.

13. Randolph stated:
"The general qualities of the fœderal government, independent of the Constitution, and the specified powers, being thus insufficient to uphold the incorporation of a bank; we come to the last enquiry, which has been already anticipated, whether it be sanctified by the power to make all Laws which shall be necessary and proper for carrying into execution the powers, vested by the Constitution. To be necessary is to be incidental, or in other words may be denominated the natural means of executing a power.

"The phrase, 'and proper', if it has any meaning, does not enlarge the powers of Congress, but rather restricts them. For no power is to be assumed under the general clause, but such as is not only necessary but proper, or perhaps expedient also, but, as the friends to the bill ought not to claim any advantage from this clause, so ought not the enemies to it, to quote the clause as having a restrictive effect: both ought to consider it, as among the surplusage, which as often proceeds from inattention, as caution."

14. See note 11.

15. The President was given the power "to remove officers at pleasure" in the following acts establishing the departments of the Federal Government: Section

The truth is that difficulties on this point are inherent in the nature of the fœderal constitution. They result inevitably from a division of the legislative power. The consequence of this division is, that there will be cases clearly within the power of the National Government; others clearly without its power; and a third class, which will leave room for controversy & difference of opinion, & concerning which a reasonable latitude of judgment must be allowed.

But the doctrine which is contended for is not chargeable with the consequence imputed to it. It does not affirm that the National government is sovereign in all respects, but that it is sovereign to a certain extent: that is, to the extent of the objects of its specified powers.

It leaves therefore a criterion of what is constitutional, and of what is not so. This criterion is the *end* to which the measure relates as a *mean*. If the end be clearly comprehended within any of the specified powers, & if the measure have an obvious relation to that end, and is not forbidden by any particular provision of the constitution—it may safely be deemed to come within the compass of the national authority. There is also this further criterion which may materially assist the decision. Does the proposed measure abridge a preexisting right of any State, or of any individual? If it does not, there is a strong presumption in favour of its constitutionality; & slighter relations to any declared object of the constitution may be permitted to turn the scale.

The general objections which are to be inferred from the reasonings of the Secretary of State and of the Attorney General to the doctrine which has been advanced, have been stated and it is hoped satisfactorily answered. Those of a more particular nature shall now be examined.

The Secretary of State introduces his opinion with an observation, that the proposed incorporation undertakes to create certain capacities properties or attributes which are *against* the laws of *alienage, descents, escheat* and *forfeiture, distribution* and *monopoly,* and to confer a

---

2 of "An Act for establishing an Executive Department, to be denominated the Department of Foreign Affairs" (1 *Stat.* 29 [July 27, 1789]); Section 2 of "An Act to establish an Executive Department, to be denominated the Department of War" (1 *Stat.* 50 [August 7, 1789]); Section 7 of "An Act to establish the Treasury Department" (1 *Stat.* 65–66 [September 2, 1789]); Section 1 of "An Act to provide for the Government of the Territory Northwest of the river Ohio" (1 *Stat.* 52–53 [August 7, 1789]).

power to make laws paramount to those of the States.[16] And nothing says he, in another place, but a *necessity invincible by other means* can justify such a *prostration* of *laws* which constitute the pillars of our whole system of jurisprudence, and are the foundation laws of the State Governments.[17]

If these are truly the foundation laws of the several states, then have most of them subverted their own foundations. For there is scarcely one of them which has not, since the establishment of its particular constitution, made material alterations in some of those branches of its jurisprudence especially the law of descents. But it is not conceived how any thing can be called the fundamental law of a State Government which is not established in its constitution unalterable by the ordinary legislature. And with regard to the question of necessity it has been shewn, that this can only constitute a question of expediency, not of right.

To erect a corporation is to substitute a *legal* or *artificial* to a *natural* person, and where a number are concerned to give them *in-*

16. Jefferson stated:

"The Bill for establishing a national bank undertakes among other things,

"1. To form the subscribers into a Corporation.

"2. to enable them, in their corporate capacities to receive grants of Land; and so far is against the laws of *Mortmain*. . . .

"3. to make *alien* subscribers capable of holding lands, & so far is against the laws of *Alienage*.

"4. to transmit these lands, on the death of a proprietor, to a certain line of sucessors: & so far changes the course of *Descents*.

"5. to put the lands out of the reach of forfeiture or escheat: & so far is against the laws of *Forfeiture & Escheat*.

"6. to transmit personal chattels to successors, in a certain line; and so far is against the laws of *Distribution*.

"7. to give them the sole & exclusive right of banking under the National authority: and so far is against the Laws of *monopoly*.

"8. to communicate to them a power to make laws paramount to the laws of the States: for so they must be construed, to protect the institution from the controul of the state Legislatures: & so probably they will be construed.

"I consider the foundation of the Constitution as laid on this ground, that, 'all powers not delegated to the U.S. by the constitution, nor prohibited by it to the States, are reserved to the states or to the people,' (XIIth. Amendmt.) to take a single step beyond the boundaries thus specially drawn around the powers of Congress, is to take possession of a boundless field of power, no longer susceptible of any definition."

17. Jefferson stated: "Nothing but a necessity invincible by any other means, can justify such a prostration of Laws, which constitute the pillars of our whole System of jurisprudence. Will Congress be too strait-laced to carry the Constitution into honest effect, unless they may pass over the foundation-laws of the state-governments for the slightest convenience to theirs?"

dividuality. To that legal or artificial person once created, the common law of every state of itself *annexes* all those incidents and attributes, which are represented as a prostration of the main pillars of their jurisprudence. It is certainly not accurate to say, that the erection of a corporation is *against* those different *heads* of the State laws; because it is rather to create a kind of person or entity, to which *they* are inapplicable, and to which the general rule of those laws assign a different regimen. The laws of alienage cannot apply to an artificial person, because it can have no country. Those of descent cannot apply to it, because it can have no heirs. Those of escheat are foreign from it for the same reason. Those of forfeiture, because it cannot commit a crime. Those of distribution, because, though it may be dissolved, it cannot die. As truly might it be said, that the exercise of the power of prescribing the rule by which foreigners shall be naturalised, is *against* the law of alienage; while it is in fact only to put them in a situation to cease to be the subject of that law. To do a thing which is *against* a law, is to do something which it forbids or which is a violation of it.

But if it were even to be admitted that the erection of a corporation is a direct alteration of the State laws in the enumerated particulars; it would do nothing towards proving, that the measure was unconstitutional. If the government of the United States can do no act, which amounts to an alteration of a State law, all its powers are nugatory. For almost every new law is an alteration, in some way or other of an old *law*, either *common*, or *statute*.

There are laws concerning bankruptcy in some states—some states have laws regulating the values of foreign coins. Congress are empowered to establish uniform laws concerning bankruptcy throughout the United States, and to regulate the values of foreign coins. The exercise of either of these powers by Congress necessarily involves an alteration of the laws of those states.

Again: Every person by the common law of each state may export his property to foreign countries, at pleasure. But Congress, in pursuance of the power of regulating trade, may prohibit the exportation of commodities: in doing which, they would alter the common law of each state in abridgement of individual rights.

It can therefore never be good reasoning to say—this or that act is unconstitutional, because it alters this or that law of a State. It must be shewn, that the act which makes the alteration is unconstitutional on other accounts, not *because* it makes the alteration.

There are two points in the suggestions of the Secretary of State which have been noted that are peculiarly incorrect. One is, that the proposed incorporation is against the laws of monopoly, because it stipulates an exclusive right of banking under the national authority. The other that it gives power to the institution to make laws paramount to those of the states.[18]

But with regard to the first point, the bill neither prohibits any State from erecting as many banks as they please, nor any number of Individuals from associating to carry on the business: & consequently is free from the charge of establishing a monopoly: for monopoly implies a *legal impediment* to the carrying on of the trade by others than those to whom it is granted.

And with regard to the second point, there is still less foundation. The bye-laws of such an institution as a bank can operate only upon its own members; can only concern the disposition of its own property and must essentially resemble the rules of a private mercantile partnership. They are expressly not to be contrary to law; and law must here mean the law of a State as well as of the United States. There never can be a doubt, that a law of the corporation, if contrary to a law of a state, must be overruled as void; unless the law of the State is contrary to that of the United States; and then the question will not be between the law of the State and that of the corporation, but between the law of the State and that of the United States.

Another argument made use of by the Secretary of State, is, the rejection of a proposition by the convention to empower Congress to make corporations, either generally, or for some special purpose.[19]

What was the precise nature or extent of this proposition, or what the reasons for refusing it, is not ascertained by any authentic document, or even by accurate recollection. As far as any such document exists, it specifies only canals. If this was the amount of it, it would at most only prove, that it was thought inexpedient to give a power to incorporate for the purpose of opening canals, for which purpose a special power would have been necessary; except with regard to the Western Territory, there being nothing in any part of the con-

18. See note 16.
19. Jefferson stated:
"It is known that the very power now proposed as *a means,* was rejected *as an end* by the Convention which formed the Constitution: a proposition was

stitution respecting the regulation of canals. It must be confessed however, that very different accounts are given of the import of the proposition and of the motives for rejecting it. Some affirm that it was confined to the opening of canals and obstructions in rivers; others, that it embraced banks; and others, that it extended to the power of incorporating generally. Some again alledge, that it was disagreed to, because it was thought improper to vest in Congress a power of erecting corporations—others, because it was thought unnecessary to *specify* the power, and inexpedient to furnish an additional topic of objection to the constitution. In this state of the matter, no inference whatever can be drawn from it.

But whatever may have been the nature of the proposition or the reasons for rejecting it concludes nothing in respect to the real merits of the question. The Secretary of State will not deny, that whatever may have been the intention of the framers of a constitution, or of a law, that intention is to be sought for in the instrument itself, according to the usual & established rules of construction. Nothing is more common than for laws to *express* and *effect*, more or less than was intended. If then a power to erect a corporation, in any case, be deducible by fair inference from the whole or any part of the numerous provisions of the constitution of the United States, arguments drawn from extrinsic circumstances, regarding the intention of the convention, must be rejected.

Most of the arguments of the Secretary of State which have not been considered in the foregoing remarks, are of a nature rather to apply to the expediency than to the constitutionality of the bill. They will however be noticed in the discussions which will be necessary in reference to the particular heads of the powers of the government which are involved in the question.

Those of the Attorney General will now properly come under review.

---

made to them to authorise Congress to open canals: & an amendatory one to empower them to incorporate: but the whole was rejected, & one of the reasons of rejection urged in debate was that then they would have a power to erect a bank, which would render the great Cities where there were prejudices or jealousies on this subject, adverse to the reception of the Constitution."

On September 14, 1787, in the Constitutional Convention the following debate took place:

"Docr. Franklin moved to add after the words 'post roads' Art I. Sect. 8. 'a power to provide for cutting canals where deemed necessary'

"Mr. [James] Wilson 2ded. the motion

"Mr. [Roger] Sherman objected. The expence in such cases will fall on the

His first observation is, that the power of incorporation is not *expressly* given to congress.[20] This shall be conceded, but in *this sense* only, that it is not declared in *express terms* that congress may erect a *corporation*. But this cannot mean, that there are not certain *express* powers, which *necessarily* include it.

For instance, Congress have express power "to exercise exclusive legislation in all cases whatsoever, over such *district* (not exceeding ten miles square) as may by cession of particular states, & the acceptance of Congress become the seat of the government of the United states; and to exercise *like authority* over all places purchased by consent of the legislature of the State in which the same shall be for the erection of forts, arsenals, dock yards & other needful buildings."

Here then is express power to exercise *exclusive legislation in all cases whatsoever over certain places;* that is to do in respect to those places, all that any government whatever may do: For language does not afford a more complete designation of sovereign power, than in

---

U. States, and the benefit accrue to the places where the canals may be cut.

"Mr. Wilson. Instead of being an expense to the U. S. they may be made a source of revenue.

"Mr. Madison suggested an enlargement of the motion into a power 'to grant charters of incorporation where the interest of the U. S. might require & the legislative provisions of individual States may be incompetent.' His primary object was however to secure an easy communication between the States which the free intercourse now to be opened, seemed to call for. The political obstacles being removed, a removal of the natural ones as far as possible ought to follow. Mr. Randolph 2ded. the proposition

"Mr. [Rufus] King thought the power unnecessary.

"Mr. Wilson. It is necessary to prevent a State from obstructing the *general* welfare.

"Mr. King. The States will be prejudiced and divided into parties by it. In Philada. & New York, It will be referred to the establishment of a Bank, which has been a subject of contention in those Cities. In other places it will be referred to mercantile monopolies.

"Mr. Wilson mentioned the importance of facilitating by canals, the communication with the Western Settlements. As to Banks he did not think with Mr. King that the power in that point of view would excite the prejudices & parties apprehended. As to mercantile monopolies they are already included in the power to regulate trade.

"Col. [George] Mason was for limiting the power to the single case of Canals. He was afraid of monopolies of every sort, which he did not think were by any means already implied by the Constitution as supposed by Mr. Wilson.

"The motion being so modified as to admit a distinct question specifying & limited to the case of canals,

"N. H. no. Mas. no. Ct. no. N. J. no. Pa. ay. Del. no. Md. no. Va. ay. N.C. no. S. C no. Geo. ay." (Hunt and Scott, *Debates*, 563–64.)

20. Randolph stated: "That the power of creating Corporations is not *expressly* given to Congress, is obvious."

those comprehensive terms. It is in other words a power to pass all laws whatsoever, & consequently to pass laws for erecting corporations, as well as for any other purpose which is the proper object of law in a free government. Surely it can never be believed, that Congress with *exclusive power of legislation in all cases whatsoever,* cannot erect a corporation within the district which shall become the seat of government, for the better regulation of its police. And yet there is an unqualified denial of the power to erect corporations in every case on the part both of the Secretary of State and of the Attorney General. The former indeed speaks of that power in these emphatical terms, that it is *a right remaining exclusively with the states.*[21]

As far then as there is an express power to do any *particular act of legislation,* there is an express one to erect corporations in the cases above described. But accurately speaking, no *particular power* is more than *implied* in a *general one.* Thus the power to lay a duty on a *gallon of rum,* is only a particular *implied* in the general power to lay and collect taxes, duties, imposts and excises. This serves to explain in what sense it may be said, that congress have not an express power to make corporations.

This may not be an improper place to take notice of an argument which was used in debate in the House of Representatives. It was there urged, that if the constitution intended to confer so important a power as that of erecting corporations, it would have been expressly mentioned.[22] But the case which has been noticed is clearly one in

21. Jefferson stated: "The negative of the President is the shield provided by the Constitution to protect against the invasions of the legislature. 1st. the rights of the Executive 2, of the Judiciary. 3. of the States & State-Legislatures. The present is the case of a right remaining exclusively with the States, & is consequently one of those intended by the Constitution to be placed under his protection."

22. On February 2, 1791, during the debate on the Bank Bill in the House of Representatives, Madison stated: "From this view of the power of incorporation exercised in the bill, it could never be deemed an accessory or subaltern power, to be deduced by implication, as a means of executing another power; it was in its nature a distinct, an independent and substantive prerogative, which not being enumerated in the Constitution, could never have been meant to be included in it, and not being included, could never be rightfully exercised. . . . In fine, if the power were in the Constitution, the immediate exercise of it cannot be essential; if not there, the exercise of it involves the guilt of usurpation, and establishes a precedent of interpretation, levelling all the barriers which limit the powers of the General Government, and protect those of the State Governments. . . . It appeared on the whole, he concluded, that the power exercised by the bill was condemned by the silence of the Constitution . . ." (*Annals of Congress,* II, 1950–52).

which such a power exists, and yet without any specification or ex-press grant of it, further than as every *particular implied* in a general power, can be said to be so granted.

But the argument itself is founded upon an exaggerated and er-roneous conception of the nature of the power. It has been shewn, that it is not of so transcendent a kind as the reasoning supposes; and that viewed in a just light it is a mean which ought to have been left to *implication,* rather than an *end* which ought to have been *ex-pressly* granted.

Having observed, that the power of erecting corporations is not expressly granted to Congress, the Attorney General proceeds thus . . . .

"If it can be exercised by them, it must be

  1. because the nature of the fœderal government implies it.
  2. because it is involved in some of the specified powers of legis-lation or
  3. because it is necessary & proper to carry into execution some of the specified powers." [23]

To be implied in the *nature of the fœderal government,* says he, would beget a doctrine so indefinite, as to grasp every power.

This proposition it ought to be remarked is not precisely, or even substantially, that, which has been relied upon. The proposition relied upon is, that the *specified powers* of Congress are in their nature sovereign—that it is incident to sovereign power to erect corpora-tions; & that therefore Congress have a right within the *sphere* & *in relation to the objects of their power, to erect corporations.*

It shall however be supposed, that the Attorney General would consider the two propositions in the same light, & that the objection made to the one, would be made to the other.

To this objection an answer has been already given. It is this; that the doctrine is stated with this express *qualification,* that the right to erect corporations does *only* extend to *cases* & *objects* within the *sphere* of the *specified powers* of the government. A general legisla-tive authority implies a power to erect corporations *in all cases*—a particular legislative power implies authority to erect corporations, in relation to cases arising under that power only. Hence the affirming, that as an *incident* to sovereign power, congress may erect a corpora-

23. This is a direct quotation.

tion in relation to the *collection* of their taxes, is no more than to affirm that they may do whatever else they please; than the saying that they have a power to regulate trade would be to affirm that they have a power to regulate religion: or than the maintaining that they have sovereign power as to taxation, would be to maintain that they have sovereign power as to every thing else.

The Attorney General undertakes, in the next place, to shew, that the power of erecting corporations is not involved in any of the specified powers of legislation confided to the National government.[24]

24. Randolph stated:
"Those powers, then, which bear any analogy to that of incorporation, shall be examined separately in their constituent parts; and afterwards in those traits, which are urged to have the strongest resemblance to the favorite power.
"1. Congress have power to lay & collect taxes &c—the heads of this power are,
    1. to ascertain the subject of taxation &c.
    2. to declare the quantum of taxation &c.
    3. to prescribe the mode of collection, &
    4. to ordain the manner of accounting for the Taxes &c:
"2. Congress have also power to borrow money on the credit of the United States—the heads of this power are,
    1. to stipulate a sum to be lent
    2. "   "   an interest, or no interest to be paid, &
    3. "   "   the time & manner of repayment, unless the Loan be placed on an irredeemable fund.
"3. Congress have also power to regulate commerce with foreign Nations, among the several states, and with the Indian tribes.
"The heads of this power with respect to foreign nations, are,
    1. to prohibit them or their commodities from our ports.
    2. to impose duties on them, where none existed before, or to increase existing Duties on them.
    3. to subject them to any species of Custom house regulations: or
    4. to grant them any exemptions or privileges which policy may suggest.
"The heads of this power with respect to the several States, are little more, than to establish the *forms* of commercial intercourse between them, & to keep the prohibitions, which the Constitution imposes on that intercourse, undiminished in their operation: that is, to prevent taxes on imports or Exports; preferences to one port over another by any regulation of commerce or revenue; and duties upon the entering or clearing of the vessels of one State in the ports of another.
"The heads of this power with respect to the Indian tribes are
    1. to prohibit the Indians from coming into, or trading within, the United States.
    2. to admit them with or without restrictions.
    3. to prohibit citizens of the United States from trading with them; or
    4. to permit with or without restrictions.
"4. Congress have also power to dispose of & make all needful rules and regulations, respecting the territory or other property belonging to the United States: the heads of this power are:
    1. to exert an ownership over the territory of the United States, which

In order to this he has attempted an enumeration of the particulars which he supposes to be comprehended under the several heads of the *powers* to lay & collect taxes &c—to borrow money on the credit of the United States—to regulate commerce with foreign nations—between the states, and with the Indian Tribes—to dispose of and make all needful rules & regulations respecting the territory or other property belonging to the United States; the design of which enumeration is to shew *what is* included under those different heads of power, & *negatively*, that the power of erecting corporations is not included.

The truth of this inference or conclusion must depend on the accuracy of the enumeration. If it can be shewn that the enumeration is *defective*, the inference is destroyed. To do this will be attended with no difficulty.

The heads of the power to lay & collect taxes, he states to be

1. To ascertain the subject of taxation &c
2. to declare the quantum of taxation &c
3. to prescribe the *mode* of *collection*.
4. to ordain the manner of accounting for the taxes &c [25]

The defectiveness of this enumeration consists in the generality of the third division "*to prescribe the mode* of collection"; which is in itself an immense chapter. It will be shewn hereafter, that, among a vast variety of particulars, it comprises the very power in question; namely to *erect corporations*.

The heads of the power to borrow money are stated to be

1. to stipulate the sum to be lent.
2. an interest or no interest to be paid.
3. the time & manner of repaying, unless the loan be placed on an irredeemable fund.[26]

---

may be properly called the property of the United States, as is the western Territory; and to institute a government therein; or
2. to exert an ownership over the other property of the United States.
"This property may signify,
1. Personal property of the United States howsoever acquired; or
2. real property, not aptly denominated territory, acquired by cession or otherwise.
"It cannot signify,
1. *Debts* due from the United States.
2. Nor money, arising from the sources of revenue, pointed out in the Constitution. The disposal and regulation of money is the final cause for raising it by taxes &c."
25. For this list, see note 24.   26. For this list, see note 24.

This enumeration is liable to a variety of objections. It omits, in the first place, the *pledging* or *mortgaging* of a fund for the security of the money lent, an usual and in most cases an essential ingredient.

The idea of a stipulation of *an interest or no interest* is too confined. It should rather have been said, to stipulate *the consideration* of the loan. Individuals often borrow upon considerations other than the payment of interest. So may government; and so they often find it necessary to do. Every one reCollects the lottery tickets & other douceurs often given in Great Britain, as collateral inducements to the lending of money to the Government.

There are also frequently collateral conditions, which the enumeration does not contemplate. Every contract which has been made for monies borrowed in Holland includes stipulations that the sum due shall be *free from taxes*, and from sequestration in time of war, and mortgages all the land & property of the United States for the reimbursement.

It is also known, that a lottery is a common expedient for borrowing money, which certainly does not fall under either of the enumerated heads.

The heads of the power to regulate commerce with foreign nations are stated to be

1. to prohibit them or their commodities from our ports.
2. to impose duties on *them* where none existed before, or to increase existing duties on them.
3. to subject *them* to any species of custom house regulation
4. to grant *them* any exemptions or privileges which policy may suggest.[27]

This enumeration is far more exceptionable than either of the former. It omits *every thing* that relates to the *citizens vessels* or *commodities* of the United States. The following palpable omissions occur at once.

1. Of the power to prohibit the exportation of commodities which not only exists at all times, but which in time of war it would be necessary to exercise, particularly with relation to naval and warlike stores.
2. Of the power to prescribe rules concerning the *characteristics* & *priviledges* of an american bottom—how she shall be navigated,

27. For this list, see note 24.

as whether by citizens or foreigners, or by a proportion of each.

3. Of the power of regulating the manner of contracting with seamen, the police of ships on their voyages &c of which the act
for the government & regulation of seamen in the merchants
service is a specimen.[28]

That the three preceding articles are omissions, will not be doubted.
There is a long list of items in addition, which admit of little, if any
question; of which a few samples shall be given.

1. The granting of bounties to certain kinds of vessels, & certain
species of merchandise. Of this nature is the allowance on dried
& pickled fish & salted provisions.[29]

2. The prescribing of rules concerning the *inspection* of commodities to be exported. Though the states individually are competent
to this regulation, yet there is no reason, in point of authority at
least, why a general system might not be adopted by the United
States.

3. The regulation of policies of insurance; of salvage upon goods
found at sea, and the disposition of such goods.

4. The regulation of pilots.

5. The regulation of bills of exchange drawn by a merchant of *one
state* upon a merchant of *another state*. This last rather belongs
to the regulation of trade between the states, but is equally
omitted in the specification under that head.

The last enumeration relates to the power "to dispose of & make
all needful rules and regulations respecting the territory *or other property* belonging to the United States."

The heads of this power are said to be

1. to exert an ownership over the territory of the United States,
which may be properly called the property of the United States,
as in the Western Territory, and to *institute a government therein:* or

2. to exert an ownership over the other property of the United
States.[30]

28. "An Act for the government and regulation of Seamen in the merchants
service" (1 *Stat.* 131–35 [July 20, 1790]).

29. Section 4 of "An Act making further provision for the payment of the
debts of the United States" provided a bounty of ten cents per quintal on dried
fish and ten cents per barrel on pickled fish and other salted provisions (1 *Stat.*
181–82 [August 10, 1790]).

30. For this list, see note 24.

This idea of exerting an ownership over the Territory or other property of the United States, is particularly indefinite and vague. It does not at all satisfy the conception of what must have been intended by a power, to make all needful *rules* and *regulations;* nor would there have been any use for a special clause which authorised nothing more. For the right of exerting an ownership is implied in the very definition of property.

It is admitted that in regard to the western territory some thing more is intended—even the institution of a government; that is the creation of a body politic, or corporation of the highest nature; one, which in its maturity, will be able itself to create other corporations. Why then does not the same clause authorise the erection of a corporation in respect to the regulation or disposal of any other of the property of the United States? This idea will be enlarged upon in another place.

Hence it appears, that the enumerations which have been attempted by the Attorney General are so imperfect, as to authorise no conclusion whatever. They therefore have no tendency to disprove, that each and every of the powers to which they relate, includes that of erecting corporations; which they certainly do, as the subsequent illustrations will more & more evince.

It is presumed to have been satisfactorily shewn in the course of the preceding observations

1. That the power of the government, *as to* the objects intrusted to its management, is in its nature sovereign.
2. That the right of erecting corporations is one, inherent in & inseparable from the idea of sovereign power.
3. That the position, that the government of the United States can exercise no power but such as is delegated to it by its constitution, does not militate against this principle.
4. That the word *necessary* in the general clause can have no *restrictive* operation, derogating from the force of this principle, indeed, that the degree in which a measure is, or is not necessary, cannot be a *test* of *constitutional* right, but of expediency only.
5. That the power to erect corporations is not to be considered, as an *independent* & *substantive* power but as an *incidental* & *auxiliary* one; and was therefore more properly left to implication, than expressly granted.

6. that the principle in question does not extend the power of the government beyond the prescribed limits, because it only affirms a power to *incorporate* for *purposes within the sphere of the specified powers.*

And lastly that the right to exercise such a power, in certain cases, is unequivocally granted in the most *positive* & *comprehensive* terms.

To all which it only remains to be added that such a power has actually been exercised in two very eminent instances: namely in the erection of two governments, One, northwest of the river Ohio, and the other south west—*the last, independent of any antecedent compact.*[31]

And there results a full & complete demonstration, that the Secretary of State & Attorney General are mistaken, when they deny generally the power of the National government to erect corporations.

It shall now be endeavoured to be shewn that there is a power to erect one of the kind proposed by the bill. This will be done, by tracing a natural & obvious relation between the institution of a bank, and the objects of several of the enumerated powers of the government; and by shewing that, *politically* speaking, it is necessary to the effectual execution of one or more of those powers. In the course of this investigation, various instances will be stated, by way of illustration, of a right to erect corporations under those powers.

Some preliminary observations maybe proper.

The proposed bank is to consist of an association of persons for the purpose of creating a joint capital to be employed, chiefly and essentially, in loans. So far the object is not only lawful, but it is the mere exercise of a right, which the law allows to every individual. The bank of New York which is not incorporated, is an example of such an association. The bill proposes in addition, that the government shall become a joint proprietor in this undertaking, and that it shall permit the bills of the company payable on demand to be receivable in its revenues & stipulates that it shall not grant privileges similar to those which are to be allowed to this company, to any others. All this is in-

31. "An Act to provide for the Government of the Territory Northwest of the river Ohio" (1 *Stat.* 50–53 [August 7, 1789]); "An Act for the Government of the Territory of the United States, south of the river Ohio" (1 *Stat.* 123 [May 26, 1790]).

controvertibly within the compass of the discretion of the government. The only question is, whether it has a right to incorporate this company, in order to enable it the more effectually to accomplish *ends*, which are in themselves lawful.

To establish such a right, it remains to shew the relation of such an institution to one or more of the specified powers of the government.

Accordingly it is affirmed, that it has a relation more or less direct to the power of collecting taxes; to that of borrowing money; to that of regulating trade between the states; and to those of raising, supporting & maintaining fleets & armies. To the two former, the relation may be said to be *immediate*.

And, in the last place, it will be argued, that it is, *clearly*, within the provision which authorises the making of all *needful* rules & *regulations* concerning the *property* of the United States, as the same has been practiced upon by the Government.

A Bank relates to the collection of taxes in two ways; *indirectly*, by increasing the quantity of circulating medium & quickening circulation, which facilitates the means of paying—*directly*, by creating a *convenient species* of *medium* in which they are to be paid.

To designate or appoint the money or *thing* in which taxes are to be paid, is not only a proper, but a necessary *exercise* of the power of collecting them. Accordingly congress in the law concerning the collection of the duties on imports & tonnage, have provided that they shall be payable in gold & silver.[32] But while it was an indispensible part of the work to say in what they should be paid, the choice of the specific thing was mere matter of discretion. The payment might have been required in the commodities themselves. Taxes in kind, however ill judged, are not without precedents, even in the United States. Or it might have been in the paper money of the several states; or in the bills of the bank of North America, New York and Massachusetts, all or either of them: or it might have been in bills issued under the authority of the United States.

No part of this can, it is presumed, be disputed. The appointment, then, of the *money* or *thing*, in which the taxes are to be paid, is an incident to the power of collection. And among the expedients which

32. This was provided in Section 56 of "An Act to provide more effectually for the collection of the duties imposed by law on goods, wares and merchandise imported into the United States, and on the tonnage of ships or vessels" (1 *Stat.* 145–78 [August 4, 1790]).

may be adopted, is that of bills issued under the authority of the United States.

Now the manner of issuing these bills is again matter of discretion. The government might, doubtless, proceed in the following manner. It might provide, that they should be issued under the direction of certain officers, payable on demand; and in order to support their credit & give them a ready circulation, it might, besides giving them a currency in its taxes, set apart out of any monies in its Treasury, a given sum and appropriate it under the direction of those officers as a fund for answering the bills as presented for payment.

The constitutionality of all this would not admit of a question. And yet it would amount to the institution of a bank, with a view to the more convenient collection of taxes. For the simplest and most precise idea of a bank, is, a deposit of coin or other property, as a fund for *circulating* a *credit* upon it, which is to answer the purpose of money. That such an arrangement would be equivalent to the establishment of a bank would become obvious, if the place where the fund to be set apart was kept should be made a receptacle of the monies of all other persons who should incline to deposit them there for safe keeping; and would become still more so, if the Officers charged with the direction of the fund were authorised to make discounts at the usual rate of interest, upon good security. To deny the power of the government to add these ingredients to the plan, would be to refine away all government.

This process serves to exemplify the natural & direct relation which may subsist between the institution of a bank and the collection of taxes. It is true that the species of bank which has been designated, does not include the idea of incorporation. But the argument intended to be founded upon it, is this: that the institution comprehended in the idea of a bank being one immediately relative to the collection of taxes, *in regard to the appointment* of *the money or thing* in which they are to be paid; the sovereign power of providing for the collection of taxes necessarily includes the right of granting a corporate capacity to such an institution, as a requisite to its greater security, utility and more convenient management.

A further process will still more clearly illustrate the point. Suppose, when the species of bank which has been described was about to be instituted, it were to be urged, that in order to secure to it a due degree of confidence the fund ought not only to be set apart & appropriated generally, but ought to be specifically vested in the officers who were to have the direction of it, and in their *successors* in office, to the end that it might acquire the character of *private property* incapable of being resumed without a violation of the sanctions by which the rights of property are protected & occasioning more serious & general alarm, the apprehension of which might operate as a check upon the government—such a proposition might be opposed by arguments against the expediency of it or the solidity of the reason assigned for it, but it is not conceivable what could be urged against its constitutionality.

And yet such a disposition of the thing would amount to the erection of a corporation. For the true definition of a corporation seems to be this. It is a *legal* person, or a person created by act of law, consisting of one or more natural persons authorised to hold property or a franchise in succession in a legal as contradistinguished from a natural capacity.

Let the illustration proceed a step further. Suppose a bank of the nature which has been described with or without incorporation, had been instituted, & that experience had evinced as it probably would, that being wholly under public direction it possessed not the confidence requisite to the credit of its bills— Suppose also that by some of those adverse conjunctures which occasionally attend nations, there had been a very great drain of the specie of the country, so as not only to cause general distress for want of an adequate medium of circulation, but to produce, in consequence of that circumstance, considerable defalcations in the public revenues—suppose also, that there was no bank instituted in any State—in such a posture of things, would it not be most manifest that the incorporation of a bank, like that proposed by the bill, would be a measure immediately relative to the *effectual collection* of the taxes and completely within the province of the sovereign power of providing by all laws necessary & proper for that collection?

If it be said, that such a state of things would render that necessary & therefore constitutional, which is not so now—the answer to this, and a solid one it doubtless is, must still be, that which has been already stated—Circumstances may affect the expediency of the measure, but they can neither add to, nor diminish its constitutionality.

A Bank has a direct relation to the power of borrowing money, because it is an usual and in sudden emergencies an essential instrument in the obtaining of loans to Government.

A nation is threatened with a war. Large sums are wanted, on a sudden, to make the requisite preparations. Taxes are laid for the purpose, but it requires time to obtain the benefit of them. Anticipation is indispensible. If there be a bank, the supply can, at once be had; if there be none loans from Individuals must be sought. The progress of these is often too slow for the exigency: in some situations they are not practicable at all. Frequently when they are, it is of great consequence to be able to anticipate the product of them by advances from a bank.

The essentiality of such an institution as an instrument of loans is exemplified at this very moment. An Indian expedition is to be prosecuted.[33] The only fund out of which the money can arise consistently with the public engagements, is a tax which will only begin to be collected in July next.[34] The preparations, however, are instantly to be made. The money must therefore be borrowed. And of whom could it be borrowed; if there were no public banks?

It happens, that there are institutions of this kind, but if there were none, it would be indispensible to create one.

33. On January 27, 1791, Washington sent to the Senate and the House the following message:

"In order that you may be fully informed of the situation of the frontiers, and the prospect of hostility in that quarter, I lay before you the intelligence of some recent depredations, received since my message to you, upon this subject, of the twenty-fourth instant." (*Journal of the House*, I, 364.)

The papers which he enclosed described an Indian attack on Big Bottom near Fort Harmer and Marietta in the Northwest Territory (*ASP, Indian Affairs*, I, 121–22).

Congress then took steps to prepare for an expedition against the Indians, and on February 12, 1791, the Senate received the following message from the House of Representatives:

"The House of Representatives have passed a Bill, entitled, 'An Act for raising and adding another regiment to the military establishment of the United States, and for making further provision for the protection of the frontiers.'" (*Journal of the Third Session of the Senate of the United States of America* [Philadelphia, 1791], 95.)

This bill was passed on March 3, 1791 (1 *Stat.* 222-24).

34. This increase in the military establishment for the protection of the frontier was to be paid for from funds obtained under the terms of "An Act repealing, after the last day of June next, the duties heretofore laid upon Distilled Spirits imported from abroad, and laying others in their stead; and also upon Spirits distilled within the United States, and for appropriating the same" (1 *Stat.* 199–214 [March 3, 1791]).

Let it then be supposed, that the necessity existed, (as but for a casualty would be the case) that proposals were made for obtaining a loan; that a number of individuals came forward and said, we are willing to accommodate the government with this money; with what we have in hand and the credit we can raise upon it we doubt not of being able to furnish the sum required: but in order to this, it is indispensible, that we should be incorporated as a bank. This is essential towards putting it in our power to do what is desired and we are obliged on that account to make it the *consideration* or condition of the loan.

Can it be believed, that a compliance with this proposition would be unconstitutional? Does not this alone evince the contrary? It is a necessary part of a power to borrow to be able to stipulate the consideration or conditions of a loan. It is evident, as has been remarked elsewhere, that this is not confined to the mere stipulation of a sum of money by way of interest—why may it not be deemed to extend, where a government is the contracting party, to the stipulation of a *franchise?* If it may, & it is not perceived why it may not, then the grant of a corporate capacity may be stipulated as a consideration of the loan? There seems to be nothing unfit, or foreign from the nature of the thing in giving individuality or a corporate capacity to a number of persons who are willing to lend a sum of money to the government, the better to enable them to do it, and make them an ordinary instrument of loans in future emergencies of the state.

But the more general view of the subject is still more satisfactory. The legislative power of borrowing money, & of making all laws necessary & proper for carrying into execution that power, seems obviously competent to the appointment of the *organ* through which the abilities and wills of individuals may be most efficaciously exerted, for the accommodation of the government by loans.

The Attorney General opposes to this reasoning, the following observation. "To borrow money presupposes the accumulation of a fund to be lent, and is secondary to the creation of an ability to lend." [35] This is plausible in theory, but it is not true in fact. In a great number of cases, a previous accumulation of a fund equal to the whole sum required, does not exist. And nothing more can be actually presupposed, than that there exist resources, which put into

35. This is a direct quotation.

activity to the greatest advantage by the nature of the operation with the government, will be equal to the effect desired to be produced. All the provisions and operations of government must be presumed to contemplate things as they *really* are.

The institution of a bank has also a natural relation to the regulation of trade between the States: in so far as it is conducive to the creation of a convenient medium of *exchange* between them, and to the keeping up a full circulation by preventing the frequent displacement of the metals in reciprocal remittances. Money is the very hinge on which commerce turns. And this does not mean merely gold & silver, many other things have served the purpose with different degrees of utility. Paper has been extensively employed.

It cannot therefore be admitted with the Attorney General, that the regulation of trade between the States, as it concerns the medium of circulation & exchange ought to be considered as confined to coin. It is even supposeable in argument, that the whole, or the greatest part of the coin of the country, might be carried out of it.

The Secretary of State objects to the relation here insisted upon, by the following mode of reasoning—"To erect a bank, says he, & to regulate commerce, are very different acts. He who erects a bank, creates a subject of commerce,[36] so does he, who makes a bushel of wheat, or digs a dollar out of the mines. Yet neither of these persons regulates commerce thereby. To make a thing which may be bought & sold is not to *prescribe* regulations for *buying* & *selling*: thus making the regulation of commerce to consist in prescribing rules for *buying* & *selling*.

This indeed is a species of regulation of trade; but is one which falls more aptly within the province of the local jurisdictions than within that of the general government, whose care must be presumed to have been intended to be directed to those general political arrangements concerning trade on which its aggregate interests depend, rather than to the details of buying and selling.

Accordingly such only are the regulations to be found in the laws of the United States; whose objects are to give encouragement to the entreprise of our own merchants, and to advance our navigation and manufactures.

And it is in reference to these general relations of commerce, that

36. At this point Jefferson wrote "in its bills," which H omitted.

an establishment which furnishes facilities to circulation and a convenient medium of exchange & alienation, is to be regarded as a regulation of trade.

The Secretary of State further argues, that if this was a regulation of commerce, it would be void, *as extending as much to the internal commerce of every state as to its external*.[37] But what regulation of commerce does not extend to the internal commerce of every state? What are all the duties upon imported articles amounting to prohibitions, but so many bounties upon domestic manufactures affecting the interests of different classes of citizens in different ways? What are all the provisions in the coasting act,[38] which relate to the trade between district and district of the same State? In short what regulation of trade between the States, but must affect the internal trade of each State? What can operate upon the whole but must extend to every part!

The relation of a bank to the execution of the powers, that concern the common defence, has been anticipated. It has been noted, that at this very moment the aid of such an institution is essential to the measures to be pursued for the protection of our frontier.

It now remains to shew, that the incorporation of a bank is within the operation of the provision which authorises Congress to make all needful rules & regulations concerning the property of the United States. But it is previously necessary to advert to a distinction which has been taken by the Attorney General.

He admits, that the word *property* may signify personal property however acquired. And yet asserts, that it cannot signify money arising from the sources of revenue pointed out in the constitution; because, says he, "the disposal & regulation of money is the final cause for raising it by taxes." [39]

But it would be more accurate to say, that the *object* to which money is intended to be applied is the *final cause* for raising it, than that the disposal and regulation of it is *such*. The support of Government; the support of troops for the common defence; the payment of

37. This is a direct quotation.
38. "An Act for Registering and Clearing Vessels, Regulating the Coasting Trade, and for other purposes" (1 *Stat.* 55–65 [September 1, 1789]) and "An Act to explain and amend an Act, intituled 'An Act for registering and clearing Vessels, regulating the Coasting Trade, and for other purposes' " (1 *Stat.* 94–95 [September 29, 1789]).
39. See note 24.

the public debt, are the true *final causes* for raising money. The disposition & regulation of it when raised, are the steps by which it is applied to the *ends* for which it was raised, not the ends themselves. Hence therefore the money to be raised by taxes as well as any other personal property, must be supposed to come within the meaning as they certainly do within the letter of the authority, to make all needful rules & regulations concerning the property of the United States.

A case will make this plainer: suppose the public debt discharged, and the funds now pledged for it liberated. In some instances it would be found expedient to repeal the taxes, in others, the repeal might injure our own industry, our agriculture and manufactures. In these cases they would of course be retained. Here then would be monies arising from the authorised sources of revenue which would not fall within the rule by which the Attorney General endeavours to except them from other personal property, & from the operation of the clause in question.

The monies being in the coffers of the government, what is to hinder such a disposition to be made of them as is contemplated in the bill or what an incorporation of the parties concerned under the clause which has been cited.

It is admitted that with regard to the Western territory they give a power to erect a corporation—that is to institute a government. And by what rule of construction can it be maintained, that the same words in a constitution of government will not have the same effect when applied to one species of property, as to another, as far as the subject is capable of it? or that a legislative power to make all needful rules & regulations, or to pass all laws necessary & proper concerning the public property which is admitted to authorise an incorporation in one case will not authorise it in another? will justify the institution of a government over the western territory & will not justify the incorporation of a bank, for the more useful management of the money of the nation? If it will do the last, as well as the first, then under this provision alone the bill is constitutional, because it contemplates that the United States shall be joint proprietors of the stock of the bank.

There is an observation of the secretary of state to this effect, which may require notice in this place. Congress, says he, are not to lay taxes *ad libitum for any purpose they please,* but only to pay the debts, or provide for the *welfare* of the Union.[40] Certainly no inference can be drawn from this against the power of applying their money for the institution of a bank. It is true, that they cannot without breach of trust, lay taxes for any other purpose than the general welfare but so neither can any other government. The welfare of the community is the only legitimate end for which money can be raised on the community. Congress can be considered as under only one restriction, which does not apply to other governments—They cannot rightfully apply the money they raise to any purpose *merely* or purely local. But with this exception they have as large a discretion in relation to the *application* of money as any legislature whatever. The constitutional *test* of a right application must always be whether it be for a purpose of *general* or *local* nature. If the former, there can be no want of constitutional power. The quality of the object, as how far it will really promote or not the welfare of the union, must be matter of conscientious discretion. And the arguments for or against a measure in this light, must be arguments concerning expediency or inexpediency, not constitutional right. Whatever relates to the general order of the finances, to the general interests of trade &c being general objects are constitutional ones for *the application* of *money*.

A Bank then whose bills are to circulate in all the revenues of the country, is *evidently* a general object, and for that very reason a constitutional one as far as regards the appropriation of money to it. Whether it will really be a beneficial one, or not, is worthy of careful examination, but is no more a constitutional point, in the particular referred to; than the question whether the western lands shall be sold for twenty or thirty cents ℔ acre.

A hope is entertained, that it has by this time been made to appear, to the satisfaction of the President, that a bank has a natural relation to the power of collecting taxes; to that of borrowing money; to that of regulating trade; to that of providing for the common defence: and that as the bill under consideration contemplates the government in the light of a joint proprietor of the stock of the bank, it brings the case within the provision of the clause of the constitution which immediately respects the property of the United States.

Under a conviction that such a relation subsists, the Secretary of

40. This is a direct quotation.

the Treasury, with all deference conceives, that it will result as a necessary consequence from the position, that all the specified powers of the government are sovereign as to the proper objects; that the incorporation of a bank is a constitutional measure, and that the objections taken to the bill, in this respect, are ill founded.

But from an earnest desire to give the utmost possible satisfaction to the mind of the President, on so delicate and important a subject, the Secretary of the Treasury will ask his indulgence while he gives some additional illustrations of cases in which a power of erecting corporations may be exercised, under some of those heads of the specified powers of the Government, which are alledged to include the right of incorporating a bank.

1. It does not appear susceptible of a doubt, that if Congress had thought proper to provide in the collection law,[41] that the bonds to be given for the duties should be given to the collector of each district in the name of the collector of the district A. or B. as the case might require, to enure to him & his successors in office, in trust for the United States, that it would have been consistent with the constitution to make such an arrangement. And yet this it is conceived would amount to an incorporation.

2. It is not an unusual expedient of taxation to farm particular branches of revenue, that is to mortgage or sell the product of them for certain definite sums, leaving the collection to the parties to whom they are mortgaged or sold. There are even examples of this in the United States. Suppose that there was any particular branch of revenue which it was manifestly expedient to place on this footing, & there were a number of persons willing to engage with the Government, upon condition, that they should be incorporated & the funds vested in them, as well for their greater safety as for the more convenient recovery & management of the taxes. Is it supposeable, that there could be any constitutional obstacle to the measure? It is presumed that there could be none. It is certainly a mode of collection which it would be in the discretion of the Government to adopt; though the circumstances must be very extraordinary, that would induce the Secretary to think it expedient.

41. "An Act to provide more effectually for the collection of the duties imposed by law on goods, wares and merchandise imported into the United States, and on the tonnage of ships or vessels" (1 *Stat.* 145–78 [August 4, 1790]).

3. suppose a new & unexplored branch of trade should present itself with some foreign country. Suppose it was manifest, that, to undertake it with advantage, required an union of the capitals of a number of individuals; & that those individuals would not be disposed to embark without an incorporation, as well to obviate that consequence of a private partnership, which makes every individual liable in his whole estate for the debts of the company to their utmost extent, as for the more convenient management of the business—what reason can there be to doubt, that the national government would have a constitutional right to institute and incorporate such a company? None.

They possess a general authority to regulate trade with foreign countries. This is a mean which has been practiced to that end by all the principal commercial nations; who have trading companies to this day which have subsisted for centuries. Why may not the United States *constitutionally* employ the means *usual* in other countries for attaining the ends entrusted to them?

A power to make all needful rules & regulations concerning territory has been construed to mean a power to erect a government. A power to *regulate* trade is a power to make all needful rules & regulations concerning trade. Why may it not then include that of erecting a trading company as well as in the other case to erect a Government?

It is remarkable, that the State Conventions who have proposed amendments in relation to this point, have most, if not all of them, expressed themselves nearly thus—"Congress shall not grant monopolies, nor *erect any company* with exclusive advantages of commerce;" thus at the same time expressing their sense, that the power to erect trading companies or corporations, was inherent in Congress, & objecting to it no further, than as to the grant of *exclusive* priviledges.

The Secretary entertains all the doubts which prevail concerning the utility of such companies; but he cannot fashion to his own mind a reason to induce a doubt, that there is a constitutional authority in the United States to establish them. If such a reason were demanded, none could be given unless it were this—that congress cannot erect a corporation; which would be no better than to say they cannot do it, because they cannot do it: first presuming an inability, without reason, & then assigning that *inability* as the cause of itself.

Illustrations of this kind might be multiplied without end. They shall however be pursued no further.

There is a sort of evidence on this point, arising from an aggregate view of the constitution, which is of no inconsiderable weight. The very general power of laying & collecting taxes & appropriating their proceeds—that of borrowing money indefinitely—that of coining money & regulating foreign coins—that of making all needful rules and regulations respecting the property of the United States—these powers combined, as well as the reason & nature of the thing speak strongly this language: That it is the manifest design and scope of the constitution to vest in congress all the powers requisite to the effectual administration of the finances of the United States. As far as concerns this object, there appears to be no parsimony of power.

To suppose then, that the government is precluded from the employment of so usual as well as so important an instrument for the administration of its finances as that of a bank, is to suppose, what does not coincide with the general tenor & complexion of the constitution, and what is not agreeable to impressions that any mere spectator would entertain concerning it. Little less than a prohibitory clause can destroy the strong presumptions which result from the general aspect of the government. Nothing but demonstration should exclude the idea, that the power exists.

In all questions of this nature the practice of mankind ought to have great weight against the theories of Individuals.

The fact, for instance, that all the principal commercial nations have made use of trading corporations or companies for the purposes of *external commerce*, is a satisfactory proof, that the Establishment of them is an incident to the regulation of that commerce.

This other fact, that banks are an usual engine in the administration of national finances, & an ordinary & the most effectual instrument of loans & one which in this country has been found essential, pleads strongly against the supposition, that a government clothed with most of the most important prerogatives of sovereignty in relation to the revenues, its debts, its credit, its defence, its trade, its intercourse with foreign nations—is forbidden to make use of that instrument as an appendage to its own authority.

It has been stated as an auxiliary test of constitutional authority, to try, whether it abridges any preexisting right of any state, or any

Individual. The proposed incorporation will stand the most severe examination on this point. Each state may still erect as many banks as it pleases; every individual may still carry on the banking business to any extent he pleases.

Another criterion may be this, whether the institution or thing has a more direct relation as to its uses, to the objects of the reserved powers of the State Governments, than to those of the powers delegated by the United States. This rule indeed is less precise than the former, but it may still serve as some guide. Surely a bank has more reference to the objects entrusted to the national government, than to those, left to the care of the State Governments. The common defence is decisive in this comparison.

It is presumed, that nothing of consequence in the observations of the Secretary of State and Attorney General has been left unnoticed.

There are indeed a variety of observations of the Secretary of State designed to shew that the utilities ascribed to a bank in relation to the collection of taxes and to trade, could be obtained without it, to analyse which would prolong the discussion beyond all bounds.[42] It shall be forborne for two reasons—first because the report concerning the Bank [43] may speak for itself in this respect; and secondly, because all those observations are grounded on the erroneous idea, that the *quantum* of necessity or utility is the test of a constitutional exercise of power.

One or two remarks only shall be made: one is that he has taken no notice of a very essential advantage to trade in general which is mentioned in the report, as peculiar to the existence of a bank circulation equal, in the public estimation to Gold & silver. It is this, that it renders it unnecessary to *lock* up the money of the country to accumulate for months successively in order to the periodical payment of interest. The other is this; that his arguments to shew that treasury orders & bills of exchange from the course of trade will prevent any considerable displacement of the metals, are founded on a partial view of the subject. A case will prove this: The sums collected in a state may be small in comparison with the debt due to it. The balance of its trade, direct & circuitous, with the seat of government may be even or nearly so. Here then without bank bills, which in that state

42. See note 10.
43. "Second Report on the Further Provision Necessary for Establishing Public Credit (Report on a National Bank)," December 13, 1790.

answer the purpose of coin, there must be a displacement of the coin, in proportion to the difference between the sum collected in the State and that to be paid in it. With bank bills no such displacement would take place, or, as far as it did, it would be gradual & insensible. In many other ways also, would there be at least a temporary & inconvenient displacement of the coin, even where the course of trade would eventually return it to its proper channels.

The difference of the two situations in point of convenience to the Treasury can only be appreciated by one, who experiences the embarassments of making provision for the payment of the interest on a stock continually changing place in thirteen different places.

One thing which has been omitted just occurs, although it is not very material to the main argument. The Secretary of State affirms, that the bill only contemplates a re-payment, not a loan to the government.[44] But here he is, certainly mistaken. It is true, the government invests in the stock of the bank a sum equal to that which it receives on loan. But let it be remembered, that it does not, therefore, cease to be a proprietor of the stock; which would be the case, if the money received back were in the nature of a repayment. It remains a proprietor still, & will share in the profit, or loss, of the institution, according as the dividend is more or less than the interest it is to pay on the sum borrowed. Hence that sum is manifestly, and, in the strictest sense, a loan.

Philadelphia February 23d. 1791.

44. Jefferson stated: " 'To borrow money.' But this bill neither borrows money, nor ensures the borrowing it. The proprietors of the bank will be just as free as any other money holders, to lend or not to lend their money to the public; the operation proposed in the bill, first to lend them two millions, & then borrow them back again, cannot change the nature of the latter Act, which will still be a payment, and not a loan, call it by what name you please."

From George Washington

[Philadelphia] Wednesday noon 23d. Feby. 1791.

Sir

I have this moment received your sentiments with respect to the constitutionality of the Bill "to incorporate the subscribers to the Bank of the United States." [1]

This bill was presented to me by the joint Commee. of Congress at 12 o'Clock on Monday the 14th. instant. To what precise period, by legal interpretation of the constitution, can the president retain it in his possession, before it becomes a Law by the lapse of ten days?

Go: Washington

LC, George Washington Papers, Library of Congress.
1. "Opinion on the Constitutionality of an Act to Establish a Bank," February 23, 1791.

To George Washington

[Philadelphia] Feby. 23d. 1791.

Sir

In answer to your note of this morning, just deliver'd me, I give it as my opinion that you have ten days exclusive of that on which the Bill was delivered to you, and sundays. Hence in the present case if it is returned on Friday at any time while Congress are setting, it will be in time.

It might be a question, if returned after their adjournment on Friday.

I have the honor to be   with perfect respect   Sir   Yr. most Obedt. Servant   A. Hamilton

LC, George Washington Papers, Library of Congress.

From Alexander Dallas [1]

Philadelphia, February 24, 1791. Forwards "copy of a letter from the Comptroller Genl. of Penna... respecting the final Certificates... paid over to this State by the agents for settling the Accts. of the Penna. line in the late Army." [2]

ADfS, Division of Public Records, Pennsylvania Historical and Museum Commission, Harrisburg; LC, Division of Public Records, Pennsylvania Historical and Museum Commission.
1. Dallas came to the United States from the West Indies in 1783 and settled in Philadelphia, where he eventually became a lawyer. During the Pennsylvania Ratifying Convention he aroused the criticism of Federalists by publishing Antifederalist views of the convention. From the spring of 1787 to May, 1789, he was editor of the *Columbian Magazine*, and by publishing court cases, including those of the United States Supreme Court, enhanced his legal reputation. Late

in 1790 he became secretary of the Commonwealth of Pennsylvania, a position he held until 1801. During this period he became the leader of the Republicans in Pennsylvania.

2. John Nicholson, who had come to Philadelphia from Wales before the American Revolution, was appointed comptroller general of Pennsylvania in 1782. In April, 1790, members of the Pennsylvania Supreme Executive Council made an unsuccessful attempt to remove him from his position. Impeachment proceedings against him in 1794 were equally unsuccessful, but led to Nicholson's resignation as comptroller general. He then gave his full attention to the encouragement of immigration and to land speculation in partnership with Robert Morris. He died in debtors' prison in 1800.

Nicholson's letter was in answer to "Treasury Department Circular to the Governors of the States," January 14, 1791, and stated that the certificates amounted to "one hundred and fifty one thousand three hundred and fifty six Dollars and nine ninetieths of a Dollar" (*Pennsylvania Archives*, 9th ser. I, 39).

On May 4, 1784, Major Thomas B. Bowen and Ercurius Beatty had been appointed Continental agents for issuing certificates for the arrears of pay to the officers of the Pennsylvania line (*JCC*, XXVI, 341). Bowen later deposited the remaining unused certificates with Nicholson. This deposit and Nicholson's subsequent refusal to send the unused certificates to the Pennsylvania legislature until the accounts had been settled with the United States were cited among the complaints of the Pennsylvania House of Representatives during the impeachment proceedings against Nicholson in 1794.

Report on the Holland Loan of Three Million Florins

[Philadelphia, February 24, 1791 [1]
Communicated to the House on February 25, 1791 [2]
Communicated to the Senate on February 25, 1791] [3]

[To the Speaker of the House of Representatives and the President of the Senate]

The Secretary of the Treasury in obedience to the orders of the President of the United States as signified in his speech at the opening of the present session [4]

Respectfully informs the Senate and House of Representatives

That the terms of the Loan of Three Millions of florins mentioned by the President as having been negotiated in Holland [5] are as follow.

The rate of Interest is five per Cent, but the charges form a deduction from the principal sum of 4½ per Cent which will occasion the real interest to be paid on the sum actually received by the United States to be equal to five and a quarter per Cent nearly.

The reimbursement is to be made in six equal installments commencing in the Year 1800 and ending in the Year 1804. But it is in the option of the United States to reimburse the whole or any part of the sum borrowed at any time they may think proper.

That the disposition which has been made of the above mentioned sum is as follows.

One Million five hundred thousand Florins has been applied pursuant to the directions of the President of the United States as a payment to France.

A further sum of about One hundred and sixty thousand Florins will also have been appropriated towards a payment on account of the Dutch Loans, which became due on the first day of February last, including a premium of Seventy thousand Florins.

The residue is in a situation to be disposed of as may be judged expedient.

A doubt arises how far this loan may be within the meaning of the Act making provision for the reduction of the public Debt on account of the limitation of the rate of Interest,[6] which taking the charges of the loan into calculation would be somewhat exceeded; and though it is presumed that that limitation was not intended to exclude the addition of the ordinary charges, yet a point of so much delicacy appears to require Legislative explanation.

The Secretary of the Treasury begs leave to observe that it is in his judgment highly expedient and very important to the general operations of the Treasury that the abovementioned loan should be deemed to be included within the meaning of the aforesaid Act.[7] The residue may in this case be applied with material advantage to the purposes of that Act and the part which has been otherwise applied may be hereafter replaced.

All which is humbly Submitted.

Alexander Hamilton
Secy of the Treasy

Treasury Department
February 24th. 1791

DS, RG 46, Second Congress, 1791–1793, Reports of the Secretary of the Treasury, National Archives; copy, RG 233, Reports of the Treasury Department, 1791–1792, Vol. II, National Archives.

1. This date is taken from the copy in RG 233, National Archives.

2. *Journal of the House*, I, 391.

3. *Annals of Congress*, II, 1810–11.

4. In his second annual message to Congress on December 8, 1790, Washington said: "In conformity to the powers vested in me by acts of the last session, a loan of three millions of florins, towards which some provisional measures had

previously taken place, has been completed in Holland. . . . The Secretary of the Treasury has my direction to communicate such further particulars as may be requisite for more precise information" (*Journal of the House*, I, 331).

5. The Holland loan of 1790. See H to Willink, Van Staphorst, and Hubbard, November 29, 1790.

6. 1 *Stat.* 186–87 (August 12, 1790). This statute limited the interest on the loan to five percent.

7. Congress enacted the necessary legislation. See "An Act supplementary to the act making provision for the reduction of the Public Debt" (1 *Stat.* 218–19 [March 3, 1791]).

Report on the Petition of Comfort Sands and Others

Treasury-Department.
February 24th. 1791.
[Communicated on February 25, 1791] [1]

[To the Speaker of the House of Representatives]

The Secretary of the Treasury, pursuant to the order of the House of Representatives of the 20th. of January last,[2] referring to him, among other things, a petition of Comfort Sands, and others,

Respectfully reports,

That it is true, as represented by the said petitioners, that sometime in the year 1782, they contracted with the Superintendant of the Finances [3] for the supply of rations for the use of the garrison of West point, and it's dependencies, and also for the use of the main army.[4]

Copy, RG 233, Reports of the Treasury Department, 1791–1792, Vol. II, National Archives.

1. *Journal of the House*, I, 391.

2. On January 20, 1791, the House received "A petition of Comfort Sands and others, praying that the proceedings of the former Congress upon a claim of the petitioners against the United States, may now be confirmed, and payment of the said claim granted to them.

"*Ordered,* That the said memorial and petitions be referred to the Secretary of the Treasury, with instruction to examine the same, and report his opinion thereupon to the House." (*Journal of the House*, I, 358.)

3. Robert Morris.

4. These contracts are described in *ASP, Claims,* I, 272, 595–96, 669, 708–28.

A number of contractors were associated with Comfort Sands in the execution of these contracts. So far as is known, the major associates were the Sands brothers (Comfort, Joshua, and Richardson), Walter Livingston, Daniel Parker, William Duer, Thomas Lowrey, Charles Stewart, Oliver Philps, Timothy Edwards, and Tench Francis. Other merchants bought into the contracts; these included John Holker, Jonathan Lawrence, and Melancton Smith.

That it is likewise true that, before the expiration of the term of their contract, it was deemed proper or necessary by the said Superintendant, that the business of supply should be withdrawn from them, and placed in other hands.

That a claim to be indemnified for damages and losses, alledged to have been sustained, was made on the part of the said Contractors; in consequence of which the several resolutions, recited in the said petition, were passed, and nearly at the times specified therein.[5]

That it further appears, that four of the Referees, appointed by, and in pursuance of the said resolutions, namely, Isaac Rosevelt, William Malcolm, Elbridge Gerry, and Henry Remsen, did, in the year 1787, make an award or report, expressive of their decision or opinion, that the United States ought to pay to the said Contractors the sum of forty thousand two hundred and ninety seven dollars, and four ninetieth parts of a dollar.[6]

That it is also true, as stated in the said petition, that the said award or report was, by Congress, referred for examination to a Committee,[7] who reported in favour of its being confirmed; but that report was afterwards committed to another committee who never, as

5. Apparently the contractors first petitioned Congress on February 28, 1785. On May 27, 1785, Congress resolved to authorize three men to "enquire into the particulars, and to determine what damages, if any, have been sustained by Tench Francis, Comfort Sands, and others, late contractors for the moving army, from the late Superintendent of finance having failed to make good the stipulated payments, or from his withdrawing the contract; and make report to Congress." Two resolutions of June 27 gave the final authorization to the hearing and directed the comptroller of the Treasury to attend on behalf of the Government. On November 4, 1785, Congress voted to add two more referees to the group:

"*Resolved*, That the secretary of Congress be, and hereby is authorised, in conjunction with Walter Livingston and Comfort Sands, and their associates, to agree upon and appoint two disinterested referees to be added to those heretofore appointed, to decide certain controversies between the United States, and the said Walter Livingston and Comfort Sands, and their associates, who, or a majority of whom, shall be competent to report their opinion to Congress." (*JCC*, XXIX, 870.)

See *JCC*, XXVIII, 109, note 1; 233–34; 321, note 2; 360; 397; 482–83; XXIX, 630, note 1; 860.

6. The arbitrators heard the evidence in October, 1787, but the Government did not present a rebuttal. The arbitrators divided four to one over the decision, but only the majority, cited here by H, wrote an opinion at this time. John D. Mercier, the dissenter, did not write his opinion until June 10, 1788. See *ASP, Claims*, I, 725–26.

7. H was a member of the committee to which Congress referred, on February 29, 1788, the arbitrators' opinion. Although the committee submitted its report on March 25, 1788, the report was not read. On June 11, Congress recommitted the report of March 25. See *JCC*, XXXIV, 75, note 1; 113, note 1; 211, note 6.

far as can be traced, made any report. Neither has there been any decision of Congress on the subject. That the reasons, which induced the reference to a second Committee do not appear; but it is within the recollection of the Secretary, who was then a member of that body, that it was not attended with any circumstances indicating an opinion, either favorable or unfavorable to the merits of the award, but was done for the sake of farther enquiry.

That it is likewise true that application having been made to the accounting officers of the Treasury, for a determination on the said award, it has been concluded, that they were not competent to the same without the special authority of the Legislature.[8]

That in judging of the light in which this transaction ought to be viewed, the following particulars seem to claim attention.

That the course pursued was similar to that which is usual in the submission of controversies between individuals by arbitration.

That there was a mutual election and consent in the appointment of the persons who were to make the investigation.

That they are expressly denominated referees.

That they acted under oath.

That the proper officer, representing the government, was empowered to employ Council if necessary.

That the referees are authorized by the first resolution, to determine, what damages, if any, were sustained by the Contractors, and by the last Resolution, their duty or business is designated to be "to decide certain controversies" between the United States and the Contractors.

That these characteristics, and the general spirit of the transaction, appear to the Secretary, to denote that the report of the referees, in the case, ought to be considered, as equivalent to an Award between individuals, possessing the same validity and equally open to exceptions.

That, as to the provision, made by the several resolutions, that the Referees should report their opinion to Congress, this, it is conceived, could only have been intended to reserve to Congress a right of re-

8. Only one of the documents involved in this Treasury accounting has been found. It is the opinion of the auditor, Oliver Wolcott, Jr., which he gave to the comptroller, Nicholas Eveleigh, on March 15, 1790. Wolcott thought the referees' award was binding on the Government. See *ASP, Claims*, I, 595.

viewing the Award, on the same principles, bona fide, as would prevail in a Court of Justice.

That entertaining a doubt, how far Congress, under the present Constitution of the United States, may think it advisable to exercise, themselves, the power so reserved, the Secretary forbears to enter into a detail of the circumstances which attended the Award; desirous of submitting, in the first instance, to the consideration of the House, whether it will not be expedient to repose elsewhere, the exercise of that power.

Two modes of doing this have occurred, which are also respectfully submitted.

One is, to authorize the accounting officers of the Treasury, on the application of the parties, to decide upon the Award, on principles, similar to those which would prevail, in a controversy concerning it at Law.

The other is, to authorize its being made, with consent of parties, a rule of the Supreme Court of the United States, for the determination of the said Court; in which case, it will, of course, be determined according to those principles.

All which is humbly submitted. Alexander Hamilton,
Secry. of the Treasy.

Report on the Petition of William Simmons [1]

Treasury Department,
February 24th: 1791.
[Communicated on February 24, 1791] [2]

[To the Speaker of the House of Representatives]
The Secretary of the Treasury, pursuant to the Order of the House of Representatives of the seventh day of January,[3] referring to him the petition of William Simmons;
Respectfully reports:

That on comparing the services to be performed, by the chief Clerk of the Auditor, with those to be performed by the chief Clerk of the Comptroller, and the qualifications requisite in each case, he does not perceive any reason for a difference in their respective compensations: [4] And as the variety and importance of the business, committed to those Officers, require that they should have able assistance, it does not appear to the Secretary, that the allowance to the chief Clerk of the Comptroller is greater, than it ought to be: He is therefore of opinion, that it will be expedient to raise that of the chief Clerk of the Auditor, to the same standard.[5]

All which is humbly submitted

Alexander Hamilton. Secy. of the Treasy.

Copy, RG 233, Reports of the Treasury Department, 1791–1792, Vol. II, National Archives.

1. William Simmons was chief clerk to the auditor of the Treasury.

2. *Journal of the House*, I, 388.

3. On January 7, 1791, "A petition of William Simmons was presented to the House and read, praying an augmentation of his salary, as principal Clerk in the office of the Auditor of the Treasury.

"Ordered, That the said petition be referred to the Secretary of the Treasury, with instruction to examine the same, and report his opinion thereupon to the House." (*Journal of the House*, I, 350.)

4. "An Act for establishing the Salaries of the Executive Officers of Government, with their Assistants and Clerks" provided that the salary of the chief clerk of the comptroller be eight hundred dollars; that of the chief clerk of the auditor was to be six hundred dollars (1 *Stat.* 68 [September 11, 1789]).

5. Following H's report, Congress adopted "An Act supplemental to the act 'establishing the Treasury Department,' and for a farther compensation to certain officers." Section 3 of this act provided that "it shall and may be lawful for the principal in any of the offices of the United States, who is authorized by law to appoint clerks under him, to allow to each clerk such compensation for his services, as he shall, in the opinion of such officer, deserve for the same: *Provided*, That the whole sum to be expended for clerks in any such office (except the chief clerk) shall not exceed a sum equal to five hundred dollars per annum for every clerk employed therein" (1 *Stat.* 215 [March 3, 1791]).

To George Washington

[Philadelphia, February 24, 1791] [1]

Sir,

The Bill supplementary to the Bank bill[2] passed the House of representatives yesterday. General Schuyler[3] informs me that the friends of the Bank proposed that it should pass to a second reading immediately, and that *Mr. Carroll* [4] opposed it, and moved that it should be printed—that by rule of the House it was of necessity to comply with Mr. Carroll's objection, a departure requiring unanimous consent.[5] That accordingly the bill was deferred till to day, & in the mean time ordered to be printed.

It will doubtless pass, if there are not *studied* delays on the part of the *opposers of the Bank.*

I have the honor to be   With perfect respect Sir   Your Obedt. Servt.   A. Hamilton

Thursday [6]
Feby. 25th. 1791.

LC, George Washington Papers, Library of Congress.
1. The MS is incorrectly dated February 25. The bill, which H in the first sentence states passed the House "yesterday," passed the House on February 23 (*Journal of the House,* I, 387).
2. "An Act to incorporate the subscribers to the Bank of the United States" (1 *Stat.* 191 [February 25, 1791]).
3. Philip Schuyler, H's father-in-law, had been elected to the Senate from New York in 1789.
4. Charles Carroll of Carrollton, Senator from Maryland.
5. Senate Rule XIII provided that "readings [of a bill] shall be on three different days, unless the Senate unanimously direct otherwise" (*Annals of Congress,* I, 21).
6. February 25, 1791, was a Friday. See note 1.

To George Washington

Philadelphia Feby 24. [1791]

Sir

I have just heared from the Senate that the Bill supplementary to that for incorporating the Bank went through a second reading and a question was taken upon it & only three or four *dissentients:* among these, Mr. *Carrol* and Mr. *Monroe.*[1]

It would have been passed this day without doubt; but the opponents insisted on the rule of the House,[2] which made it impossible. It will be passed the first thing tomorrow.

The Yeas and Nays were taken in order to *pledge* the members.

I have the honor to be   Most respectfully & Affecty.   Sir   Your obedt. Servant   A. Hamilton

LC, George Washington Papers, Library of Congress.
1. The question was whether the bill should pass to the third reading. In addition to Charles Carroll and James Monroe, James Gunn of Georgia voted against the bill. Twenty-two Senators voted in favor of it (*Annals of Congress,* II, 1809).
2. See note 5 in the first letter which H wrote to Washington on February 24, 1791.

From Benjamin Lincoln

From the Collector of Boston
Febry 25d 1791.

Sir

I have completed the business you assigned me [1] and purchased up so much of the public debt as could be bought for the fifty thousand dollars Bank Bills which you put into my hands for that purpose. I have carefully attended to your instructions & have I presume neither lowered or raised the price. I have received a number of six per cents and other paper, all nearly on the same principles, 6 per cents @ 18s/ 9d Defered & interest @ 9/9. Some friends here wish to exchange Some loan office certificates of other States for the Six pr cents & other Stocks at the rate they were received. I cannot comply with their wishes while I attend to my instructions. I therefore wish to know, whether such may be made or not.

To Secy of the Treasury.

Copy, RG 56, Letters from the Collector at Boston, National Archives; copy, RG 56, Letters from the Collector at Boston, National Archives.
   1. See H to Lincoln, February 1, 1791.

Report on Certificates of Debt Issued After January 1, 1790

[*Philadelphia, February 25, 1791.* An entry in the *Journal of the House* for February 25, 1791, reads as follows: "The Speaker laid before the House a letter from the Secretary of the Treasury, covering his report respecting certificates or evidences of debt issued after the first of January, one thousand seven hundred and ninety; which were read, and ordered to lie on the table." [1] *Letter and Report not found.*]

Journal of the House, I, 392.
   1. The House requested this report on February 3, 1791. The entry in the *Journal of the House* reads as follows:
   "On a motion made and seconded, that the House do come to the following resolution:
   " 'Whereas certain certificates or evidences of debt, dated after the first of

January, one thousand seven hundred and ninety, have been issued by one or more of the States, which certificates purport that they were issued in lieu of certain other certificates, dated prior to the first of January, one thousand seven hundred and ninety; and the certificates of the first description are, on account of their date, not received by the Loan Officers, as subscriptions to the loan proposed by the United States, although the certificates, in lieu of which they were issued, are clearly within the description of the law, and would, if not cancelled, be recoverable at the Loan Office: Therefore,

" 'Resolved, That all certificates of the first description above, be received at the Loan Offices, as other evidences of the debt of the several States are, by law, receivable:'

"Ordered, That the said motion be referred to the Secretary of the Treasury, with instruction to examine the same, and report his opinion thereupon to the House." (Journal of the House, I, 369.)

Supplement to the Report on Exports for the Year Ending September 30, 1790 [1]

Treasury Department
February 26th. 1791.

[To the Speaker of the House of Representatives]
Sir,

In obedience to the order of the House of Representatives of the 24th. Instant,[2] I have the honor to transmit to you a supplement [3] to the return of the exports of the United States of the 15th. of the present month. This contains the substance of the several quarterly returns, which have been received at the Treasury, since the day, on which the former abstract was completed. Quarterly returns from some inconsiderable districts are yet to be transmitted by the Collectors.

I have the honor to be, with the greatest respect,   Sir,   Your most obedient and   Most Humble Servant   Alexander Hamilton.

The Honorable
The Speaker of the House of Representatives.

Copy, RG 233, Reports of the Treasury Department, 1791–1792, Vol. II, National Archives.

1. A note at the bottom of this letter states: "This Letter and the supplementary Abstract of Exports which accompanied it were not received till after the Adjournment, and of course no entry of them appears on the Journal."

2. The House "Ordered, That the Secretary of the Treasury report whether any, and what, additions are to be made to his return of the exports of the United States" (Journal of the House, I, 389).

3. This supplement was signed by Tench Coxe and may be found in RG 233, First Congress, Reports Submitted by the Secretary of the Treasury, National Archives.

To Nathaniel Appleton

Treasury Department
Philadelphia Feby 27. 1791

Sir

Mr. H LeRoy [1] informs me that he will probably have a sum of money in Boston for which he will be glad to receive an equal sum here. I have told him that if he will cause it to be placed in your hands you will receive it and give duplicate receipts upon one of which the amount received will be reimbursed here. This you will accordingly do to the extent of thirty thousand dollars.[2]

If you should have on hand bills of the Treasurer as far as they go, you will deliver them in payment directed to either Cashier of the Bank of North America or New York as may be desired of you. In this case any receipt you give will of course only be for a ballance   I am Sir   Your Obedient servt   Alexander Hamilton

N Appleton Esqr

ALS, The Bostonian Society, Boston.
   1. Herman Le Roy was a partner with William Bayard in the New York mercantile firm of Le Roy and Bayard.
   2. Le Roy and Bayard drew a bill of exchange on Stephen Higginson on February 28, 1791, for ten thousand dollars. H endorsed this bill payable to Appleton (D, The Bostonian Society).

From Tobias Lear [1]

[Philadelphia, February 28, 1791]

Sir

The President has commanded me to transmit the enclosed to you from Mr. Thatcher [2] and request that you will give it the considera-tion it may merit. The President also requests that you will take occasion to converse with some others of the gentlemen from Mas-sachusetts on this subject and to mention it likewise to some from New Hampshire.

I have the honor to be   very respectfully & sincerely   Your Most
Obedt. Servant   Tobias Lear

28th. Feby. 1791

LC, George Washington Papers, Library of Congress.
  1. Lear, a native of Portsmouth, New Hampshire, and a graduate of Harvard,
was Washington's secretary.
  2. George Thacher, member of the House of Representatives from the District
of Maine.

From Jeremiah Olney

Providence, February 28, 1791. Asks Hamilton's opinion on the
"Construction of the Law, relative to the 12 ⅌ Cent allowed for
Tare on Sugars &c." [1] Asks if the same "deduction for Tare is al-
lowed" for "Cocoa in Bags" as for coffee.

ADfS, Rhode Island Historical Society, Providence; copy, RG 56, Letters from
the Collector at Providence, National Archives.
  1. This is provided in Section 35 of "An Act to provide more effectually for
the collection of the duties imposed by law on goods, wares and merchandise
imported into the United States, and on the tonnage of ships or vessels" (1 *Stat.*
166 [August 4, 1790]).

To Sharp Delany [1]

Treasury Department [February, 1791]

Sir,
    I have considered the case of the two vessels belonging to the port
of Philadelphia which have arrived at the capes of Delaware.
    The law does not authorize the receiving in any custom house, re-
ports and entries of vessels that are not within the district to which it
appertains.[2] The Only method therefore, as it appears to me, by which
the owners can effect an entry in this or any other case is to apply to
the Custom house, within the limits of which the vessels are.
    I am, Sir,   Your Obedt Servant   Alex. Hamilton

Sharp Delany Esquire

Copy, RG 56, Letters to the Collector at Philadelphia, National Archives; copy,
RG 56, Letters to Collectors at Small Ports, "Set G," National Archives.
  1. This letter is in reply to Delany to H, December 20, 1790.

2. For the regulations governing the reports and declarations required of ship captains upon entry into a port, see Section 16 of "An Act to provide more effectually for the collection of the duties imposed by law on goods, wares and merchandise imported into the United States, and on the tonnage of ships or vessels" (1 *Stat.* 158–59 [August 4, 1790]).

From Edmund Randolph

[Philadelphia, February, 1791]

The Attorney General of the United States does himself the honor of replying to the questions propounded to him by the Secretary of the Treasury, as follows:

1st. To the statement in the letter of February, 12th: 1791.[1]

It does not appear whether the deceased Administrix be interested personally in the estate of her deceased husband. If she were so, although the whole legal right vested in her as administratrix, yet if she had an equitable right in a part, the administrator de bonis non. ought at any rate to liberate the Treasury so far as that part goes.

I mention this, however, not from a supposition, that you will have any difficulty. For as money paid through mistake, may be recovered, so may an engagement to pay money through mistake, be cancelled. Therefore the administrator de bonis non, ought to have a settlement made with him, and a certificate granted accordingly.

But I think it would be proper immediately to have a suit instituted against the husband, and publication made, to prevent sale and deception.

2d. To the statement in the letter of the 14th: February.[2]

By a general power of attorney is, I presume, meant a power to do all things in the transfer of stock, which the principal might do, were he personally present. Now the principal might transfer it, were he present, to the person who is his attorney. But can a man with his right hand perform an act to his left? When two rights concur in the same person, they are on the same footing, as if they were in different persons. The attorney subscribes the name, or affixes the seal of the principal. He accepts in his own mere character. The law then does not seem to forbid the transfer; and altho' the attorney has a great opportunity for fraud, by being permitted to sell to himself, yet the principal declares his confidence in him by the letter of substitution, and the difference between an immediate transfer to himself, and a circuitous one thro' a third person, presents little or no difference of difficulty in committing fraud. The power thus exercised, will indeed be scanned with more rigor; but it is not therefore unexerciseable.

3d: To the letter from the Comptroller, dated February 10th. 1791. inclosed in Secry's letter of 14th. February.

An Additional fact has been stated to me: that before Willing, Morris, and S.[3] accepted the original Certificates, Mr. Milligan the Comptroller under the former government of the United States [4] was consulted upon their genuineness, and that he affirmed them to be genuine. I mention this circumstance as one, which may seem to have real weight, and for a moment had some with me. But the United States not being bound by extra-official opinions, at least by opinions on points, which it was not the actual duty of their officers to answer, I discard it from my consideration.

The important ingredient, is, that registered certificates were issued upon the forged ones to W. M. & S.

But I must take the liberty of witholding my opinion, until I can receive a reply from you on the following hints.

I have been told that W. M. & S. refused to take original certificates from young, until the continental officer had transferred their amount to them; and that they were thereby prevented from pushing Young, and recovering from him a debt, which but for the transfer, they might perhaps have secured some other way.[5] Now altho' I cannot say, that in *every* case, the United States can investigate the genuineness of the original certificates, it is no less impossible for me to assert, that there is no case, in which this investigation ought to be made. I wish to try each case by itself; and I must therefore beg you to add by what means the cancelled certificates can *now* be proved to have been counterfeited?

The secretary knows that the foregoing was written some time ago; and nothing has prevented it from being sent earlier, but some public calls, which seemed more pressing, and prevented, an earlier transcription by his clerk.[6]

Edm. Randolph

LS, RG 60, Copies of Opinions, National Archives.

1. Letter not found, but see H to William Lewis, February 12, 1791, and Lewis to H, February 23, 1791.
2. Letter not found.

3. The Philadelphia mercantile firm of Thomas Willing, Robert Morris, and John Swanwick.

4. James Milligan, who served as comptroller from October, 1781, until the abolition of the office in November, 1787.

5. In a letter dated August 4, 1785, from Willing, Morris, and Swanwick to Richard Henry Lee, President of Congress, this case was described as follows:

"We beg leave through your Excellency to Communicate to the United States in Congress the following Facts.

"Sometime in November last at the Instance of a certain William Young we agreed to purchase of him sundry certificates Signed by John Pierce Esqr. Paymaster General Amounting in the whole to Twenty five thousand One hundred thirty five Dollars and fifteen Ninetieths of a Dollar provided they Should be passed on due Examination at the Treasury office of the United States—And in that case we agreed to give for the same four thousand three hundred Ninety Eight Dollars and fifty-three Ninetieths of a Dollar.

"The certificates were accordingly presented to James Milligan Esqr. the Comptroller of the Treasury for Examination, and after the due Investigation thereof We Received new certificates in Exchange signed by the Register of the Treasury (of which copies are enclosed) and thereupon paid to the said William Young the Sum Stipulated. By this Means we became Creditors of the United States on Record for the sums and on the terms in these Certificates Specified. Several Months after this Transaction we learnt that the Certificates delivered by William Young had been altered or Forged and thereupon Immediately took Measures to secure as much as possible of his Property. By our attention and care the sum of One thousand Nine hundred thirty six Dollars and fifteen Ninetieths of a Dollar in Money and a Note from a certain Samuel Lyning to him now in the Possession of Thos Russell Esqr. of Boston for One hundred thirteen and one third Dollars have been secured and are now Ready at the Order of Congress. But we must pray Your Excellancys Permission to Observe that it does not consist with our Feelings to derive Benefit from an affair of such Nature as the present and therefore altho our Right to the sums Mentioned in the said Certificates is Indisputable We will not hold them without the approbation of the United States in Congress but on the Contrary if that shall be thought most Eligible will Readily deliver them up on Receiving the Principal and Interest of the sum paid to William Young who is now Insolvent and a Prisoner for Debt in the Gaol of this City." (LS, Papers of the Continental Congress, National Archives.)

This letter was referred to the Board of Treasury on August 22, 1785 (JCC, XXIX, 650–51). On March 28, 1787, the Board reported to Congress: "It appears to the Board that the Memoralists have no Claim against the United States for the value of the Counterfeit Certificates (which they purchased through mistake) and Registered in the Books of the Treasury; since no error of a Public Officer in admitting an improper Credit, can make the United States chargeable therewith, when the same is discovered. . . . That the Application of Messrs. Willing, Morris, and Swanwick . . . cannot be complied with; the Memoralists having on that account no Claim whatsoever against the United States" (JCC, XXXII, 140–41).

6. This paragraph is in Randolph's handwriting.

To George Washington

[Philadelphia, March 1–4, 1791]

The Secretary of the Treasury presents his respects to The President of the United States. He has just ascertained that General Matthews [1] would not accept. His son is older than was believed 29 years of age & has a family. As he will have the benefit of his fathers influence which is considerable and is a young man of real merit & as the appointment of any other candidate would be subject to the uncertainty of acceptance or not, the nomination of the son is perhaps the best thing that can be done.

Major Butler [2] has just called on me to say that he has reason to believe General Huger [3] the present Martial if appointed Supervisor would accept, & he is of opinion would give popularity to the measure. Should this appear adviseable *Stevens* may be Marshall & would in all probability discharge the office well. But this communication is for the information of the President merely, not from any conviction that an alteration of the first arrangement would be an improvement. It [is] however admitted on all hands that General Huger is a worthy man & has claims on the public on the score of sacrifices.

Since writing the above the inclosed has come to hand. [4]

AL, George Washington Papers, Library of Congress.
    1. Although "General Matthews" is identified by Gaillard Hunt as Joseph Matthews (*Calendar of Applications*, 84), a letter, dated February 9, 1791, from William Matthews of Baltimore to George Washington encloses letters from William Smith, member of the House of Representatives from Maryland, and a group of Baltimore citizens recommending William Matthews for the post of inspector of the revenue (George Washington Papers, Library of Congress).
    2. Senator Pierce Butler of South Carolina.
    3. Isaac Huger was a South Carolina planter and Federal marshal for South Carolina. At this time he was being considered for the post of supervisor of the revenue in that state. On March 4, 1791, however, Daniel Stevens was appointed to the post, and Huger remained Federal marshal.
    4. See Butler to H, March 1–4, 1791.

From Pierce Butler [1]

[Philadelphia, March 1–4, 1791]

Dear sir.

However inconsistant it may appear I am under a necessity of re-calling what I wrote [2] on the subject of General Huger. Judge Burke [3] has Calld on me to Say that on reflection He is of opinion that the Sallery woud be no object to General Huger and therefore woud not wish to name Him.

I write in a Debate. You will Excuse the inaccuracy.

I am   Dear sir   sincerely Yrs.   P Butler

Mr Coxe's [4] affair is settled to our wish.

ALS, George Washington Papers, Library of Congress.
    1. This letter was enclosed in H to George Washington, March 1–4, 1791.
    2. Butler's undated recommendation of Isaac Huger may be found in the George Washington Papers, Library of Congress.
    3. Ædanus Burke of South Carolina was a judge of the state Circuit Court and a Representative in the First Congress.
    4. Presumably Tench Coxe.

From Wilhem and Jan Willink, Nicholaas and Jacob Van Staphorst, and Nicholas Hubbard [1]

[*Amsterdam, March 1, 1791.* "You'll thereby see, that after de-ducting

2 Pr. Cent Premium
½ ℔ Ct. Brokerage
½ ℔ Ct. for Seals, Notary's Signatures, Charges &c. Advertise-
        ments, Papers for the Bonds and other incidental Expences,
        there remains but
1 "   " for our Commission

———

4 Per Cent that We fixed with Mr. Short to do the Business for: We at that time calculated to give but 1½ per Cent Premium to the Under-takers, But when It was question of only a Sacrifice of our Interest, to accelerate Mr. Short's Wish to open the Loan immediately, We did

not balance a Moment to make it, by allowing Two per Cent premium, the least We could obtain the Money for." *Letter not found.*]

Extract from a letter from Willink, Van Staphorst, and Hubbard to William Short, August 25, 1791 (Short Family Papers, Library of Congress). The letter from which this extract is taken is printed as an enclosure to Short to H, August 31, 1791.

1. On November 29, 1790, H had written to Willink, Van Staphorst, and Hubbard for the information contained in this letter.

To Nathaniel Appleton [1]

Treasury Department
March 2. 1791.

Sir

You will find enclosed LeRoy and Bayard's first bill at five days sight on Stephen Higginson for ten thousand dollars dated Philadelphia the 28th. of February payable to my order as Secretary of the Treasury of the United States, with which you are charged in the Books of the Register. This sum is to be applied to the discharge of the interest on the public debt that will be payable at your office on the 1st. of April.

You will present the draught for acceptance, and if not accepted you will cause it to be duly noted and transmit me a notarial copy of the protest. Should it be accepted and not paid the same precaution must be observed as to the protest for non payment. You will acknowledge the receipt of this bill by the first post after acceptance.

I am, Sir,   Your obedt. servant   Alexander Hamilton

Nathaniel Appleton Esq.
Commissioner of Loans
Boston.

LS, Essex Institute, Salem, Massachusetts.
1. For background to this letter, see H to Appleton, February 27, 1791.

To Nathaniel Appleton

Treasury Department, March 2, 1791. "You will find enclosed Le-Roy and Bayard's second bill. . . ." [1]

LS, The Bostonian Society, Boston.
    1. The remainder of this letter is exactly the same as the other letter which H sent to Appleton on this date.

From Nathaniel Appleton

Boston, March 2, 1791. "I had the honor to write you 23d Ulto. since which I have received Drafts from the Treasury for fifty thousand Dollars. I find they will meet with a ready Sale. I have already sold & Engaged 24000 Dollr. The drafts on the Collector [1] & the Massachusetts Bank are recd. & deposited in the Bank to my credit by which I am supplied with means to pay the Pensioners which business commences the 5 instant. . . ."

LC, RG 53, Massachusetts State Loan Office, Letter Book, 1785–1791, Vol. "259–M," National Archives.
    1. Benjamin Lincoln was the collector of customs at Boston.

Report on the Petition of Conyngham, Nesbitt and Company, and James Crawford

Treasury-Department.
March 2nd. 1791.
[Communicated on March 2, 1791][1]

[To the Speaker of the House of Representatives]
The Secretary of the Treasury, in obedience to the Order of the House of Representatives of the nineteenth Ultimo,[2] relative to the petition of Conynghame, Nesbitt & Co.,[3] and James Crawford, of the City of Philadelphia, Merchants;
Respectfully reports
    That he has examined into the facts, stated in the said petition, and has had the same under consideration.
    That it is admitted by the Collector of the District of Wilmington,[4] that the Deputy-Collector had mistaken the time of enacting the Tonnage-law, of the fourth of August 1790, for the commencement of it's operation, which was the first day of October.[5] That in this interval, the several vessels, mentioned in the petition, arrived under orders to proceed to the District of Philadelphia, without stopping at New Castle, to land the passengers, with which they were prin-

cipally occupied. That these orders had been given in consequence of their having been subjected to tonnage, both in Wilmington and Philadelphia in their former voyages. That they were induced by the acknowledged misinformation of the Deputy-Collector to enter in Delaware, and proceeded afterwards, without taking in any goods, to Philadelphia, where they were again subjected to tonnage.

On due consideration of these circumstances, which shew that the lawful intentions of the petitioners were frustrated by the oversight of the officer, the Secretary humbly conceives, that it will comport with the justice of the House, to authorize a return of the duties of tonnage, on the vessels specified in the petition, which were collected in the District of Wilmington.

All which is humbly submitted   Alexander Hamilton
                                        Secretary of the Treasury.

Copy, RG 233, Reports of the Treasury Department, 1791–1792, Vol. II, National Archives.

1. *Journal of the House*, I, 400.

2. On February 19, 1791, the House received "A petition of Coningham, Nesbitt and Company, and James Crawford, of the city of Philadelphia, praying to be relieved against the payment of second tonnage on certain vessels, the double entry of which was occasioned by the mistake of the Deputy Collector at New Castle. . . .

"*Ordered*, That the said [petition] be referred to the Secretary of the Treasury, with instruction to examine the same, and report his opinion thereupon to the House." (*Journal of the House*, I, 383.)

3. The firm of David H. Conyngham and John M. Nesbitt.

4. George Bush.

5. This date was specified in Section 74 of "An Act to provide more effectually for the collection of the duties imposed by law on goods, wares and merchandise imported into the United States, and on the tonnage of ships or vessels (1 *Stat.* 178).

Report on the Petition of Elias Hasket Derby

Treasury Department
March 2nd. 1791.
[Communicated on March 2, 1791] [1]

[To the Speaker of the House of Representatives]

The Secretary of the Treasury in obedience to an order of the House of Representatives of the 26th. Ulto.[2] relative to the petition of Elias Hasket Derby, of the town of Salem Merchant;

Respectfully reports

That he has duly considered the allegations contained in the said petition, and the prayer thereof.

That he finds an insuperable difficulty in recommending to the consideration of the House, an act of particular indulgence, relative to the public dues, in favor of an individual.

That, however, it is true, that the importers of Teas, in the year 1790, have been embarrassed and injured by the difficulty of immediately obtaining prices adequate to cover the duties which have been imposed on those articles.

That an apprehension of such difficulties had induced him, to suggest to the House, in his report of the thirteenth of December last,[3] the extension of the credit for the duties thereafter to accrue upon this Article.

From a view of the cases of the petitioner and other importers of Teas, by whom representations have been made to him, the Secretary begs leave to suggest, for the consideration of the House, the propriety of giving a retrospect to that clause in the pending Bill,[4] which extends, in future, the credit allowed upon the Impost on Teas, in favor of all the Importers of that Article in the last Year.

All which is humbly submitted   Alexander Hamilton,
                                        Secretary of the Treasury

Copy, RG 233, Reports of the Treasury Department, 1791–1792, Vol. II, National Archives.

1. *Journal of the House,* I, 400.

2. On February 26, 1791, "A petition of Elias Hasket Derby was presented to the House and read, praying relief in the payment of the impost on certain cargoes of tea, imported by the petitioner.

"*Ordered,* That the said petition be referred to the Secretary of the Treasury, with instruction to examine the same, and report his opinion thereupon to the House." (*Journal of the House,* I, 393.)

3. "First Report on the Further Provision Necessary for Establishing Public Credit," December 13, 1790.

4. This bill became law. See "An Act making farther provision for the collection of duties by law imposed on Teas, and to prolong the term for the payment of the Duties on Wines" (1 *Stat.* 219–21 [March 3, 1791]). H's recommendation was not, however, adopted by Congress.

Report on the Petition of Gosuinus Erkelens

Treasury-Department,
March 2nd. 1791.
[Communicated on March 2, 1791] [1]

[To the Speaker of the House of Representatives]
The Secretary of the Treasury, to whom was referred the petition of
Gosuinus Erkelens,[2]
Respectfully reports thereupon;

That authentic documents produced by the petitioner shew, that,
at an early period of the late Revolution, he espoused with zeal the
cause of this country, and became a medium of communication between Governor Trumbull [3] and Livingston; [4] and one or more distinguished political characters in Holland, which contributed to the
events that finally connected the United Netherlands and the United
States in a common cause.[5]

That, in the course of this agency, it is presumable, expenses were
incurred; but to what extent, is not explained; neither is it easy, at
this time, to ascertain all the circumstances, which ought to decide the
propriety of indemnification.

That the petitioner concedes, that the services, which were rendered by him, were originally without a view to reward, and pleads
his distresses as the reason for his departure from that ground, and as
a motive to the United States for conferring gratuitously what is not
claimed as matter of obligation on their part.

That in this state of things, and at this late period, the Secretary
does not perceive any ground sufficiently definite or precise to justify,
on his part, a suggestion favorable to a compliance with the prayer
of the petitioner.

All which is humbly submitted,   Alexander Hamilton
                                        Secretary of the Treasury.

Copy, RG 233, Reports of the Treasury Department, 1791–1792, Vol. II, National
Archives.
  1. *Journal of the House*, I, 400.
  2. On February 2, 1791, "A petition of Gosuinus Erkelens was presented to
the House and read, praying compensation for services rendered to the United
States during the late war. . . ,

"Ordered, That the said [petition] be referred to the Secretary of the Treasury, with instruction to examine the same, and report his opinion thereupon to the House." (*Journal of the House,* I, 368.)

3. Jonathan Trumbull, Revolutionary War governor of Connecticut.

4. William Livingston, Revolutionary War governor of New Jersey.

5. In 1778, Erkelens and J. G. Dericks proposed to negotiate a loan of two million pounds from the Netherlands. Dericks went to Holland in 1778–1779, but Congress had not authorized him to negotiate a loan (see, *JCC,* XVI, 42; XXVIII, 151–52).

From Tobias Lear

[*Philadelphia*] *March 3, 1791.* Encloses a letter to the President "from the Senators . . . of Rhode Island [1] recommending Mr. Thompson [2] as a proper person for Supervisor of excise in that District."

LC, George Washington Papers, Library of Congress.

1. Joseph Stanton and Theodore Foster to George Washington, March 3, 1791 (LS, George Washington Papers, Library of Congress).

2. Ebenezer Thompson, naval officer of the port of Providence.

From Jeremiah Olney

Providence, March 3, 1791. "Enclosed are my Weekly Return of Cash No. 30, and Monthly Schedule of Bonds for Feby. . . . I have also just received your Letter of the 18th. of December last,[1] together with the Hydrometer, intended as a substitute to Dycas's, the Directions for their use. . . . Particular attention shall be paid to your Directions relative to this Instrument. . . ."

ADfS, Rhode Island Historical Society, Providence; copy, RG 56, Letters from the Collector at Providence, National Archives.

1. "Treasury Department Circular to the Collectors of the Customs," December 18, 1790.

From William Short

Amsterdam March 4th. 1791

Sir

I had the honor of informing you on the 17th. of the last month of the loan of 2½. millions of guilders being brought on the market & on the 22d. I inclosed you a prospectus of that loan. It is not till now that

I have been able to get a copy of the bonds which are to be given on the part of the U.S. & of which I forward you one at present by the way of England, for your examination, & to obtain on it the promised ratification. A duplicate & triplicate will be sent by other conveyances.

You will find the instrument verbose & of a barbarous style. This is occasioned by the profits of those employed being proportioned to its length & on its being a translation from the Dutch in which it is thought necessary to conform literally to the original. It is the form to which the money lenders here are accustomed & which it is neither necessary or proper to change. The conditions of the loan being clearly expressed in it I suppose you will consider its form & language as of little importance.

You will have seen by the letter of the two houses employed here which I inclosed you in mine of the 15th. of January, as well as by several letters I have written you since, that the commission on this loan is to be ½ p. cent lower than on that made in Jan. 90.[1]

I learn from the agents that about one fourth of the money on this loan has been already subscribed viz during the month of February & that of course agreeably to constant usage the interest on it will commence from the 1st. of that month. I can add nothing here which will not occur of itself to you on the propriety of your views being made known to me as soon as possible, with respect to this loan. One circumstance however which I cannot omit is that the committee of finance of the national assembly are informed of your late draughts & that these, probably much exagerated as to their amount & as explanatory of your future intentions, excited there disagreeable reflexions. I learn this only by a private letter, & shall say nothing unless I should be applied to officially. If you will consider that I have not had the honor of hearing from you since the 1st. of Sep. 90. & that I have no other data whatever on which to form my conjectures as to your intentions, you will readily concieve that I should wish as much as possible to avoid going into explanations on the subject: The more so as explanations, in such cases, which are not complete, produce the same effect as those which are dissatisfactory.

I am waiting now only for the printing of the bonds in order that I may sign them, & shall then return immediately to Paris. I am promised them for the day after to-morrow, so that I shall probably leave this place in five days.

You will have seen by my letters to the Secretary of State of the

22d. & 25th of february, the decision of the national assembly respecting tobacco.[2] He will have recieved also from Paris the debates of the national assembly on this question.[3] The preference given there to French vessels & which if it subsists will exclude entirely the American, was produced by a combination of hazard & design. It was proposed to the assembly during the debate & adopted without examination. It was suggested by those merchants probably who are owners of vessels. The assembly certainly were not aware that the difference in the duty was more than the full freight, & of course that as to this article, they were passing with respect to us a navigation act more severe than that of their neighbors which they consider so unjust. I have taken measures to engage them to change this decree as well as that with respect to the oils,[4] & on my return to Paris shall pursue those measures in person. I must add however what you will easily concieve that in an assembly which is composed, & which deliberates like that, it is impossible to foresee the steps into which they are often unavoidably surprized, or to conjecture whether they may be induced to return on them. You know also that they have adopted as a kind of principle that the assembly cannot change its decrees; yet they violate this, as well all the other principles they have adopted, when they find it convenient. I have no doubt that time & experience will correct the errors into which the national assembly have been drawn with respect to our commerce. If I could go into a full explanation of their causes, you would see that accident & the circumstances of the moment have contributed principally to them.

I have the honor to be with sentiments of perfect respect & attachment Sir, Your most obedient & most humble servant W: Short

The Honble Alexander Hamilton Secretary of the Treasury

ALS, letterpress copy, William Short Papers, Library of Congress.
1. See Short to H, January 15, 1791, note 1; Willink, Van Staphorst, and Hubbard to H, January 25, 1790; and H to Willink, Van Staphorst, and Hubbard, August 28, 1790. The commission on the Holland loan of 1790 was four and one-half percent.
2. For the information Short sent to Thomas Jefferson on February 22, 1791, see Short to H, February 22, 1791, note 6.
On February 25, 1791, Short sent to Jefferson the following additional decrees and information concerning tobacco:
"1. Le tabac en feuilles provenant de l'etranger pourra être mis en entrepot

pendant un an dans les magasins de la regie qui seront destinés à cet usage & re-exporté à l'etranger sans payer aucun droit.

"2. Une regie nationale fera fabriquer & vendre du tabac au profit du tresor public & *payera les mêmes droits que les particuliers.*

"The committee had proposed that the tobacco imported by the regie should be exempted from duty but the Assembly rejected it by the amendment under-lined. The article respecting licenses of manufacture & retail was not decided when my last letters left Paris. It is possible that the post which will arrive this evening after the english mail, in which this letter goes, shall have set off, may bring an account of its decision." (LC, RG 59, Despatches from United States Ministers to France, 1789–1869, January 16, 1791–August 16, 1792, National Archives.)

3. For a summary of the debate on tobacco in the French National Assembly, see Frederick L. Nussbaum, *Commercial Policy in the French Revolution* (Washington, 1923), 47–49.

4. See Short to H, February 7, 1791, note 7.

To Nathaniel Appleton [1]

Treasury Department
March 5th. 1791

Sir

You have been instructed fourteen days before interest becomes due in each quarter, to close your office and balance your books.

As the provision for the payment of interest in each state for the ensuing quarter must be regulated by the sums which shall appear on the books of each Commissioner at the period of closing them either as "funded" or "unfunded" stock or in other words as stock subscribed to the proposed loan or as stock for which certificates shall have been issued to *non-subscribers,*[2] I am to desire that you will im-mediately after your office shall be closed as abovementioned trans-mit to me the total amount of the different kinds of stock funded and unfunded which shall be borne on your books distinguishing each kind under a separate head.

As this is only for my information towards a general arrangement, the *transmission* is not to wait for the revision of your books but is to be made without delay from the first face of them.

You will at the same time inform me of the amount of the cash which you will then have in hand from whatever source; together with the amount of the Treasurer's draughts if any which then re-main undisposed of.

My wish is that as far as practicable the Bank of Massachusetts may be the place of deposit of whatever money you may have and the medium of your payments.

The day for closing your office will be the seventeenth instant. On that day the post leaves Boston and arrives here the 25th. You will forward the statement required by that post.

I am, Sir,　Your obedt. servant　　　　　Alexander Hamilton

Nathanl. Appleton Esq.
Commissioner of Loans
Boston

LS, The Bostonian Society, Boston.
　1. This letter is a reply to Appleton to H, February 5, 1791.
　2. For the provision made for "non-subscribers," see Andrew Porter to H, April 23, 1791, note 2.

From Josiah Parker [1]

March 5, 1791. Forwards a letter from Thomas Newton, Jr., to Hamilton.[2]

ALS, RG 26, Lighthouse Letters Received, Vol. "A," Pennsylvania and Southern States, National Archives.
　1. Parker was a large landholder in Virginia and an Antifederalist member of the House of Representatives.
　2. Newton to H, February 16, 1791.

Treasury Department Circular to the Collectors of the Customs

Treasury Department,
5 March 1791

Sir,

The arrangements towards the payment of the ensuing Quarters interest to the public Creditors within your state require that the Commissioner of Loans for your state should be advised by every opportunity of the monies in your hands. This you will not fail to do by every post, & even by *every private* opportunity which shall present. I shall count on your punctuality.

You will also pay to the order of the said Commissioner whatever specie may be in your hands at any time during the present month.

Your returns to the Treasury will continue with exact punctuality.

I remain with great consideration sir,   your obt servant

A Hamilton

LS, to Jeremiah Olney, Rhode Island Historical Society, Providence; copy, to John Daves, RG 56, Letters to the Collector at New Bern, National Archives; copy, to John Daves, RG 56, Letters to Collectors at Small Ports, "Set G," National Archives; copy, to Jeremiah Olney, RG 56, Letters to the Collector at Providence, National Archives; copy, to Jeremiah Olney, RG 56, Letters to Collectors at Small Ports, "Set G," National Archives.

From William Ellery

Custom House
Newport [Rhode Island] March 7th 1791

Sir,

Inclosed is a weekly return of Cash on hand, and also a Certificate of Registry No. 13 issued at the Port of Dighton by H Baylies [1] Collector Mh. 27th 1790, and delivered up on account of transfer of property.

The Genl. Assembly of this State met at East Greenwich the last week. Previous to their meeting I requested two of the Deputies of this town to move for a cession of the right of the State to the Light-House and the Dwelling House adjoining; [2] but a House was not formed until Thursday, and the Assembly rose on Saturday night, so that, it seems, there was no opportunity to bring this matter on the carpet. The Assembly will sit in course the first Wednesday in May next.

I have not as yet had an opportunity to sound Mr. Bowers [3] who claims the land on which the Light House and Dwelling House stand. When I last wrote respecting this matter the Surveyor of this Port [4] was about going to Swansey where Mr. Bowers lives, and through him I hoped to learn his sentiments; but he did not go. Since that time One of my Sons was at his House, but he was at Boston attending the General Court of which he is a member. I shall embrace the first opportunity for obtaining the information you desired.

In a Statement and remarks on my accounts I find monies I have furnished for the Light-House are carried to my account as *Super-*

intendant of Light House. I wish to know in what relation I stand to the Light-House.[5]

I am, Sir,   Yr. most obedt servant   W Ellery Collector

A Hamilton Esqr
Secry &c.

LC, Newport Historical Society, Newport, Rhode Island.
   1. Hodijah Baylis had been appointed collector of customs at Dighton, Massachusetts, in 1789.
   2. "An Act for the establishment and support of Lighthouses, Beacons, Buoys, and Public Piers" provided for the payment of the expenses of lighthouses by the Treasury Department with the provision, however, that "none of the said expenses shall continue to be so defrayed by the United States, after the expiration of one year from the day aforesaid, unless such lighthouses, beacons, buoys and public piers, shall . . . be ceded to and vested in the United States, by the state or states respectively in which the same may be, together with the lands and tenements thereunto belonging, and together with the jurisdiction of the same" (1 *Stat.* 53–54 [August 7, 1789]).
   3. Jerathmeel Bowers.
   4. Daniel Lyman.
   5. The letter book copy of this letter is endorsed by Ellery "Answered." H's reply has not been found.

From Tobias Lear

[*Philadelphia*] *March 7, 1791.* Transmits "all the letters of application which have come to the President's hands for appointments on board the cutters."

LC, George Washington Papers, Library of Congress.

To John Brown [1]

Treasury Department, March 8, 1791. "In answer to your Enquiry, I am to inform you that the Contract for the Supply of Articles in the Quarter Masters Department was made with Messrs. Elliot & Williams.[2] That they are considered as the persons to whom the Government is responsible for all purches of such Articles. . . . That accordingly *very liberal advances* of money for all those purposes have been made to them . . . no accounts having been yet rendered in relation to the Expenditures for the late Expedition.[3] I stand ready the moment any balance shall satisfactorily appear to be due, to pay it."

Copy, Maryland Historical Society, Baltimore.

1. Presumably this is the John Brown of Frankfort, Kentucky, who represented the Kentucky district of Virginia in the House of Representatives.

2. In 1789 Robert Elliot and Elie Williams had contracted to supply the western posts. See Williams to H, October 10, 1789, H to Williams, October 17, 1789.

3. This is presumably a reference to Brigadier General Josiah Harmar's unsuccessful expedition against the Indians in the Northwest Territory.

To Catherine Greene [1]

Philadelphia March 8. 1791

Your letter of the 26th of January did not reach me till the 4th instant, the day after the adjournment of Congress; of course it was impossible that I could obey your wish, by making a report on your Memorial.

But my dear friend, I love you too well not be be very candid with you. I am afraid my report will not promote your interest. I had too much reverence as well as friendship for General Greene, ever to admit any supposition injurious to his fame without a degree of proof of misconduct which I am confident will never be possible. The labouring point therefore in my judgment is this—It does not appear that General Greene gave notice *at the time* of the engagement, he had entered into, to any of the public departments. In proportion as he stepped aside from the *authorised path*, it became incumbent upon him to notify the proceeding and assign the reasons. The not having done it opposes a tremendous bar to the claim of indemnification. The precedent of granting such indemnification upon a *subsequent disclosure* of facts, when the danger of loss had *already exploded* would be of a most delicate and hazardous kind.

Colonel Wadsworth [2] is the only person beside yourself to whom I have hinted this difficulty. He promised to have a search made in the Offices and among General Greenes papers; but has not informed me of the result. I fear it will not have been successful. As far as regards the public Offices my attention shall not be wanting.

You are at liberty to communicate this letter to Mr. E. Rutlege.[3] I wish he may be able by proof or argument to obviate the objection I have stated. I should be glad to be convinced that it is not valid, that it is consistent with my duty and reputation to surmount it. It is impossible that I can have stronger motives than I have to view the matter in conformity to your Interests. At the same time I confide in Mr. Rutleges candour that if he sees the point in the same light, [as] I at present do, he will tell you so. For of all things I desire to stand justified in your judgment and feelings.

When shall we have the pleasure of seeing you this way? I need not tell you how much Interest I should take in it; as I am sure you do not doubt the attachment of

Your sincere friend

JCH Transcripts.
1. Catharine Greene was the widow of Major General Nathanael Greene. She was petitioning Congress for reimbursement of funds expended by Greene for supplies for the Army during the American Revolution.
2. Jeremiah Wadsworth, a prominent merchant of Hartford, Connecticut. During the Revolution Wadsworth had been commissary general of purchases and was associated with Greene in several speculative enterprises.
3. Edward Rutledge, brother of John Rutledge, was a lawyer, landowner, and politician of South Carolina.

From Tobias Lear

[*Philadelphia*] *March 8, 1791*. Transmits "a commission for Stephen Keyes, Collector of Allburgh [1] in Vermont."

LC, George Washington Papers, Library of Congress.
1. Vermont was admitted to the Union on March 4, 1791. On the same day Keyes, a Burlington, Vermont, merchant, was appointed collector of Alburg.

From Nathaniel Hazard [1]

[New York, March 9, 1791]

Sir

Mr. White Matlack, who is one of our first Ale Brewers in this City, goes to Philadelphia on Business, of what Nature I know not, which I understand, will lead him to wait upon you. One Part of his private Business he tells me, is to review the Operations of a Steel Furnace which he erected there, & has lain d⟨or⟩mant for some Months. This Article is of very great Consumption in America. It is made of various Kinds, as good as english, & afforded cheaper. There are some Kinds not yet introduced, particularly that of the german Mode &

Temper, which may easily be done. Mr. Matlack is not averse to a moderate Excise on american, provided, a proportionably heavy one, is laid on foreign Steels. I have been for several Years, Agent for the Sale of that made at Matlack's Furnace. I apprehend the Consumption of Steel in America is little short of 3000 Tons per Annum. The Use of american Porter & Beer is rapidly increasing, *particularly in the Southern States*. The Vend of Snuff is not inconsiderable, & confined to the Northern, principally. Of these Articles I speak professionally, or occupationally; having dealt extensively in them for several Years. Of Course, I have been led to examine the principal Markets for them, from Boston, ⟨to⟩ Savanna, with Attention. Mr. Maxwell [2] has no Objection to Ten Cents pr. Pound Weight of Snuff, which I think however too high, for a Beginning.[3] Mr. Lispenard [4] has none to a moderate Excise on Porter; nor Mr. Matlack to one on Ale & american Steel. If capital Manufacturers do not object, I conceive others cannot complain. I have Minutes on these Subjects in my Possession, that have lain by me many Months, which I wish to arrange & compress, & submit to your leisureable Inspection. In August last were published in Childs's Paper, "Hints &c on an american Excise" signed "Columbianus" [5] containing Sentiments, *exactly similar to mine on that Subject;* they were republished in Carey's Museum for September last.[6] I can furnish from my own Experience, Facts, which appear to me convincing Data, that a Revenue may be raised of above 80,000 Dollars per Annum, from the Articles I have mentioned, & they be excised agreeably to the Makers Wishes. Mr. Matlack is a Man of Candor, Enterprize & Information, & nearly related to Mr. Haines [7] a considerable Brewer in Philadelphia. Perhaps it may not be useless to converse with him *on this Subject*, as he has other Business he tells me, which will lead him to wait upon you. I am Sir with as much Truth, Esteem & Respect, as Talents, Virtue & Perseverance combined, alone ought to excite, in the Hearts of honest, unambitious, independent Men, who only can judge of, & do Honor to real Merit, your Friend & most obedient Servant   Nathl. Hazard

Newyork 9th. March 1791

ALS, Hamilton Papers, Library of Congress.
    1. Hazard was a New York City merchant and ironmonger.
    2. William Maxwell of New York City was a snuff and tobacco manufacturer.
    3. Hazard is referring to an excise of ten cents on snuff.

4. Anthony Lispenard was a prominent brewer of New York City.

5. *The* [New York] *Daily Advertiser*, August 3, 1790. Francis Childs was the publisher of this newspaper.

6. "Hints and Conjectural Observations on the Subject of an American Excise," *The American Museum*, VIII (September, 1790), 136-40. Mathew Carey was the publisher of *The American Museum*.

7. Caspar Haines.

From Robert Leslie [1]

Philadelphia, March 9, 1791. Applies for a position as a mechanic in the mint "that Congress have resolved to establish."

ALS, Hamilton Papers, Library of Congress.

1. Leslie was a Philadelphia clockmaker. See Tench Coxe to H, December 31, 1790.

From Benjamin Lincoln

From the Collector of Boston
March 9th. 1791

Sir

By the 32nd. Section of the late Collection Act,[1] no exporter of Goods, wares & merchandise imported could be allowed the Draw Back of Duties paid, unless the goods were exported in the same casks &c & from the Port or District into which they were originally imported, these restrictions very much embarrassed trade & were a source of daily complaints of the Merchants, especially that part, where the exportation must be from the Port or District into which the Goods were originally imported.

The existing law [2] is penned differently, but how far, even in this the Merchant is relieved, I cannot determine; permit me Sir, to state to you a case. Suppose a Merchant of Salem comes into Boston & here purchases twenty chests of Tea, imported originally into this District, enters it here for exportation in the Ship America of Salem for London & complies in all respects with the Law. After this the Collector causes the Goods to be inspected & finding them to correspond with the notice & proof concerning the same, can a permit be granted for lading them and an officer be appointed to see them on board the Ship in Salem? If this cannot be done, can a Captain receive part of his Cargo in Salem & come into this District & complete his load? In short, is there any method whereby a Merchant loading his Cargo in one District can secure the Draw back on Good exported in the same Vessel which were imported into a different District.

To Secy of the Treasury.

Copy, RG 56, Letters from the Collector at Boston, National Archives.
1. "An Act to regulate the Collection of the Duties imposed by law on the tonnage of ships or vessels, and on goods, wares and merchandises imported into the United States" (1 *Stat.* 45–46 [July 31, 1789]).
2. "An Act to provide more effectually for the collection of the duties imposed by law on goods, wares and merchandise imported into the United States, and on the tonnage of ships or vessels" (1 *Stat.* 145–78 [August 4, 1790]). Sections 57, 58, 59, 60, and 61 of this act describe the terms under which drawbacks may be paid.

Treasury Department Circular to the Commissioners of Loans

Treasury Department
March 9. 1791

Sir

The Comptroller of the Treasury being prevented by sickness from executing the duties of his Office I have found it necessary to instruct Mr. Joseph Hardy his first Clerk, to sign all such papers as are requisite to transfer Stock from one Loan Office to another, and to and from the Books of the Treasury. You will therefore proceed upon warrants signed by me and counter signed by him, as if they were countersigned by the Comptroller himself till further orders.
I am Sir   Your Obedient servant   Alex Hamilton

LS, Mr. Hall P. McCullough, North Bennington, Vermont.

To Meletiah Jordan [1]

[*Philadelphia, March 10, 1791.* On July 1, 1791, Jordan wrote to Hamilton and referred to "Your letter of March the 10th." *Letter not found.*]

1. Jordan was collector of customs at Frenchman's Bay, District of Maine.

From William Short

Amsterdam March 11. 1791

Sir

I have the honor of writing to you at present for the last time from this place. I am now signing the bonds [1] as fast as I recieve them from the notary. It is possible they may be finished to-morrow & in that case I shall set out the day after for Paris.

In my last of the 4th. inst. sent by the way of England was inclosed a translation of the bonds of the present loan. I now add a copy of the original in the Dutch language. Duplicates will be sent by the bankers.

In a former letter sent by the way of England I mentioned to you a letter which I had recieved from M. de Montmorin relative to the offers of Jeanneret & Co.[2] You will recieve enclosed at present a copy of the same No. 1.[3] together with the instructions therein alluded to No. 2.[4] It is probable M. Otto [5] will have previously communicated them. I have learned lately what I had before reason to suspect that Jeanneret & Co. are entirely without capital or credit & further of a character which shews it would be unsafe to treat with them their offers being supported by the minister is the only circumstance which entitles them to any kind of attention. They are besides of a nature which there is no probability of your being disposed to accept. You will observe by the instructions of M. de Montmorin that the ministry is in the disposition you would desire with respect to this affair.

I mentioned in my last that the committee of finance might be led into a different disposition by those who have an interest in the purchase of the American debt. The day after I wrote that letter I recieved from the Chargé des affaires of France at the Hague,[6] one of which I inclose you a copy No. 3.[7] & my answer No. 4.[8] I am persuaded that this letter was written at the instigation of the committee of finance.

ALS, letterpress copy, William Short Papers, Library of Congress.
1. See Short to H, March 4, 1791.
2. See Short to H, February 7, 1791.   3. See enclosure.
4. See Short to H, February 7, 1791, note 7, and enclosure.
5. Louis G. Otto, French chargé d'affaires in the United States.
6. Antoine Bernard Caillard.   7. See enclosure.   8. See enclosure.

They had been told that your draughts were for the loan now making. Those who wish to make this purchase & of whom some are probably in that committee imagined that if this could be ascertained that the assembly would perhaps force the government to treat for the sale of the debt, & that they would treat on more favorable terms on finding that the loans made here by the U.S. were destined for other purposes. My complete ignorance of your views on this subject disabled me from giving any other answer to M. Caillard. I know not as yet whether it will be thought satisfactory at Paris, where so much is done at present by intrigue & corruption, & where there are so many who are endeavouring to speculate on this debt. So far as it depends on the ministry I have no apprehension of any thing being done contrary to your wishes but the ministry have no weight against a decree of the assembly & these decrees are easily surprized by a committee, or a few members of a committee.

I have lately recieved from Mr. Grand [9] of Paris a letter of which I inclose a copy *No. 5* [10] & my answer *No. 6.*[11] These letters will suffice to explain themselves & the present situation of the subject which gave rise to them. They are submitted to you Sir that you may give such instructions relative thereto as you may think proper. Mr. Grand will probably persist in his complaint & carry it to the cognizance of the government of the United States. I have learned since I wrote my letter to him that the house here in which I supposed him interested has the name of Grand from his son's [12] being one of the partners & that he himself is not concerned in it.

The moment for making loans at present has been found so favorable that Russia has opened one for six millions of guilders instead of three as was intended; & it is already filled. The policy of Hope [13] who conducts the business of that country with much propriety has always been never to bring on a loan at an improper moment & never to let slip unemployed one that was favorable. By the date of the bonds used in the late loan it appears that it was to have been made in August

9. Ferdinand Le Grand, French banker, who through his brother was connected with Hogguer, Grand, and Company.

10. See enclosure.

11. See enclosure.

12. Apparently Short is mistaken. Ferdinand Le Grand's brother, George Le Grand, was a partner in the house of Hogguer, Grand, and Company.

13. Henry Hope, head of the House of Hope, a long-established Amsterdam banking firm.

last. He found it proper to hold them up until now notwithstanding the exigencies of the Court of Petersburg. It is by the prudent & judicious conduct of this house that the credit of Russia has been maintained here throughout the war, & in such a manner that it is much superior now to what it was when the war begun. Hence it is that the services of Hope, for which however he is most extravagantly remunerated, are considered as more essential to Russia than an alliance with any of the secondary powers of Europe.

The city of Amsterdam have lately made a loan here of six millions of guilders to restore order to the affairs of their bank which have for some time appeared in an alarming posture. The interest is only 3½. p cent. The principal merchants have taken the most of it on themselves so that it was soon filled. This produced a good effect for a few days on the paper of the bank. It is again declining, which would seem to indicate that the root of the evil is deeper than had been supposed.

The price of foreign stock on this market is as when I wrote you on the 22d. of February. That of the loans made on the liquidated debt of the U.S. varies from 1 to 40 p cent above par, according to the conditions of these loans. In them the liquidated debt is alienated at different prices according to the time at which the loan was made. The present rate of the loan is graduated accordingly & will follow the rise of the funds in America.

I have had several occasions of observing during my stay here that the distance of the United States is a considerable drawback on their credit in the minds of the people in general. The idea of this distance consisting for the most part in the communications from thence being rare. The inconvenience would be much diminished if authentic papers & information were regularly sent here & published in the gazettes in the Dutch language. This might be done by some of your clerks & an arrangement made here with a gazetteer. The people being thus accustomed to have something respecting the U. S. before their eyes regularly two or three times a week would insensibly suppose America nearer to them—they would necessarily become better acquainted with the real situation of the U.S. & of course be more disposed to judge for themselves. This would contribute more than any thing else to emancipate your foreign operations from a dependence on the agents employed here. At present it cannot be denied that a combination among a few of the more powerful & more enlightened would much embarass, perhaps totally defeat any loan the U. S. might wish to make. I have formerly explained to you [14] in what manner their influence operates on the money lenders, which will have convinced you also that the best manner of counteracting such inconveniences is to unfold the U.S. fully to the public view, & keep them constantly in their sight. You will easily believe that the houses here who recieve the most constant information from America, & who are four or five only, can have no inducement to disseminate the knowlege they thus acquire, & of which the principal value consists in the exclusion.

There has been an apprehension, here some time past that the states of Holland intended laying a tax of 2½ p. cent on foreign loans negotiated in the province. The idea is abandoned for the present year at least & it is thought it will not be again resumed. Yet if the exigencies of the country should increase, by their being drawn into a war, of which the probability has become greater within a day or two, I should not be surprized that this resource should be tried on foreign loans made in future. If adopted in Holland it wd of course be extended to the other provinces.

I beg leave to refer you to my letters to the secretary of State, (one of this date, which goes by the way of England & to one which I shall write to him to-morrow to go by the American vessel which carries this) for information relative to some decrees of the national assembly on navigation & commerce, & also relative to the present alarming situation of the affairs of that country.[15] You will easily see from thence that there is little probability of the exchange rising for some time & that the payments which you may order to be made in future will be on as advantageous terms as the last.

I have the honor to be with sentiments of the most profound respect,   Sir,   Your most obedient & most humble servant   W Short

The Honble. Alexander Hamilton Secretary of the Treasury.

14. See Short to H, December 2, 18, 1790.
15. On March 11, 1791, Short wrote to Thomas Jefferson:
"A letter which I received by the last post from my Secretary in Paris, informs me that the National Assembly have changed their decree with respect to the american oils imported into France, on the representation of the committees they have reduced the duty from 12 ₶. to 6 ₶. the quintal. I do not find this cir-

cumstance mentioned in the journals of the Assembly, but he gives it to me as having that moment recieved it from the member of the diplomatic committee who was most instrumental in obtaining this reduction & who desired him to communicate it to me. The committees were for some time determined to propose the reduction to 8 ₶ only. The Secretary whom I left at Paris urged the reduction to 6 ₶ with so much force that he at length prevailed on them to risk it. Their greatest objection was the fear of its not passing in the Assembly, & that the aversion of the members to change any of their decrees together with so considerable a reduction would defeat the plan altogether. I can have no doubt that this reduction has been decreed, from the manner in which it is communicated to me, still I should have been better satisfied, if it had not been omitted in the journal. The committees calculate that the internal duties hitherto paid on oils & to which the american were subject (independent of the duty of 11 ₶. 5s. the barrel on entering the kingdom) were upwards of 5 ₶. the quintal. By the *arret du conseil,* the duty would have been at present only 7 ₶. 10. the barrel of 500 lb. Still the 6 ₶. being in lieu of all other duties is considered as giving greater facilities to the importation of the american oils than they would have had under the former government.

"I received also by the last post an account of some alterations made by the Assembly in their decree concerning the importation of tobacco. It is confined to french vessels & those of the country where it is made, except that from the Levant which can be imported in french vessels only. With respect to that made in the United States it must be brought immediately from thence to France. The difference of duty on this article imported in french or foreign vessels remains as when I last wrote to you viz: 6 ₶ 5s. the quintal. The ports at which foreign tobacco is allowed to be entered are very numerous as well in the atlantic as the mediterranean, & indeed are all where any american vessel would wish to go.

"I am making use of the same means to get changed that part of the decree that makes so great a difference between french and american vessels which I did with respect to the oils. I have long ceased however even attempting to conjecture what the Assembly will do in any case. There are many arguments to be used for inducing them to put the vessels of the two nations on the same footing—the objection however which will be constantly made will be the foreign tonnage to which their vessels are subjected with us. They will insist probably on making a similar difference in their ports, but as I am sure that they were surprized into the fixing a difference which exceeds the value of the freight I have some hopes of inducing them to lower it.

"Scenes of disorder and riot are exhibited from time to time in Paris of the most alarming kind. The departure of the king's aunts is one of the pretexts. It is not yet known here whether they have been allowed to quit the kingdom. The repairing of the Chateau de Vincennes in order to transport there some of those confined in the different prisons of Paris gave rise lately to a mob which threatened bloodshed between the rioters and the Garde Nationale. At the same time a number of persons either totally unknown or known as enemies to the present order of things entered in crowds into the king's apartments. It being found that they had arms concealed under their clothes, they were disarmed, & some of them arrested. The reason they give for their conduct is a desire to defend the king whom they supposed in danger in that moment of disorder. It is probable that was the true cause—but many suspect an intention in them to make use of that moment for carrying off the king to some other part of the kingdom or perhaps out of it. Such scenes must be expected so long as the present anarchy continues & it is certain that the Assembly either from inability or design do nothing to prevent it.

"The Bishop of Spire, one of those foreign princes who suffer by the decrees of the National Assembly has refused absolutely to enter into negotiation for an indemnity. The manner in which he has answered the propositions of the Minister of France would induce a belief that he counts on being well supported. This however will probably depend on circumstances. The disorders of France may in time beget so much internal discontent as to invite foreign interference, but I cannot think they would have any thing of that sort to fear if their Government were properly organised & order restored. Even the greatest enemies of the revolution wish now for peace & personal security at the expence of the sacrifices they have been obliged to make." (LC, RG 59, Despatches from United States Ministers to France, 1789–1869, January 16, 1791–August 6, 1792, National Archives.)

On March 12, 1791, Short wrote to Jefferson:

"I mentioned to you in my letter of yesterday, sent by the way of England, the reduction made by the Assembly in the duty on oils. The post which arrived last night, after the departure of that letter, brought a journal which contained the decree. It is so concise as to oils that it would appear to me obscure if I did not find that the Secretary whom I left at Paris, considers it as a substitution for the duty of 12 ₶. formerly fixed by the Assembly. The decree is as follows, copied literally from the journal.

" 'Sur le rapport fait par M. Vernier le decret suivant est rendu.

" 'Les toiles de chanvre & de lin, importées de l'etranger, seront assujettiés au droit de 70 ₶. le quintal.

" 'Celles importées par terre de la Flandre Autrichienne & de l'Allemagne seront assujetties au droit de 36 ₶. le quintal et les toiles blanches à 45 ₶. *le droit sur les* huiles & savons sera de 61 ₶. . . . .'

"This letter will be sent by an american ship which is here & will contain one for the Secretary of the Treasury. The bonds are signed & I leave this place tomorrow for Paris. When there I shall be better able to judge of the real situation of the affairs of that country. At present I can not do better than to send you the following extract of a letter received from the Secretary whom I left at Paris. I have already told you that he is a man much to be relied on & enjoying fully the confidence of M. de la Fayette. I must add also that he is in general subject to be easily alarmed, & of course that some allowance must be made for that disposition in the writer. The letter is dated March 7, 1791. 'Les journées sont orageuses. Jamais les partis n'ont eu un développement si violent. Depuis leur derniere avanture (the entering armed into the king's apartments as mentioned in my last) les aristocrates sont dans une fureur qu'ils ne cherchent point á dissimuler, l'interieur des Thuilleries est en combustion. Les Jacobins & 89 (two clubs composed of the popular part of the Assembly) se livrent un combat a mort pendant ce tems lá on a de justes allarmes sur les rives du Rhin. Un courier arrivé hier m'apprend qu'il y un corps de 5000 hommes rassemblé en souable prés Basle, que l'on recrute à force chez le Margrave de Bade, qu'a Carlsruhe & Worms on ne parle que d'invasion, que Coubourg annonce ouvertement qu'il va commander une armée, que toute l'Alsace ce defie de plusieurs des commandants militaires, & que l'ennemi entretient des correspondances allarmantes & presque à decouvert avec les facteux de l'interieur. Les insurrections les plus violentes menacent ici nous ne pourrons éviter une explosion ces jours ci & elle pourra être terrible. S'il se fait une invasion, on ne peut prevoir combien de tetes tomberont. M. de La Fayette est maintenant en bonne posture, mais l'assassinat le menace de tous les côtés. Jacobins & Aristocrates dechainent contre lui tous les coupe jarrets. Dans l'affaire de Vincennes (mentioned in my last) il a pensé deux fois être tué.'

"Two persons have been arrested in Alsace recruiting troops for what they

[ENCLOSURE]

Comte de Montmorin to William Short [16]

A Paris le 24. Janvier 1791.

J'ai reçu, Monsieur, la lettre que vous m'avez fait l'honneur de m'écrire le 19. du mois.

Les Srs. Jeanneret et Schwietzer en me communiquant la réponse que vous leur avez faite,[17] m'ont prié d'appuyer auprès du Président des Etats-Unis la proposition que vous vous êtes déterminé à lui transmettre. J'ai fait d'autans moins de difficulté de me prêter à leur demande, que je l'ai entierement subordonneé aux convenances du Congrès: Vous en jugerez par la copie qui je joins ici des instructions que je viens d'addresser à Mr. Otto. C'est à vous à juger, Monsieur, si vous croyez être suffisamment autorisé pour prendre dès à présent des arrangemts conditionels avec les Srs. Jeanneret et Schweitzer.

Je suis très sincerement, Monsieur votre très humble et très affectionné serviteur.

Montmorin

Je crois devoir vous informer, Monsieur, que le Roi vient de nommer Mr. de Ternant Son Ministre plénipre auprès des Etats-unis de l'amérique.[18]

---

call *l'arme des Princes*. It becomes every day more probable that the discontented joined by whatever troops they can collect, will enter France & seize on some frontier place. The object will be probably merely to feel the pulse of the people & to retire if they find it unsafe to advance. In such a case much is to be apprehended for the Queen's life—after such a calamitous scene, should it take place, it is impossible to say what would be the denouement, but certainly terrible." (LC, RG 59, Despatches from United States Ministers to France, 1789–1869, January 16, 1791–August 6, 1792, National Archives.)

16. LS, William Short Papers, Library of Congress. Montmorin was French Minister for Foreign Affairs.

17. See Short to Schweizer, Jeanneret, and Company, December 17, 1790. This letter is printed as an enclosure to Short to H, December 18, 1790.

18. Jean Baptiste de Ternant did not arrive in the United States until August, 1791.

[ENCLOSURE]

Antoine Bernard Caillard to William Short [19]

La Haye le 4 Mars 1791.

Monsieur

Le Gouvernement de france a grand interet de Savoir Si l'emprunt que font en ce moment à Amsterdam les Etats unis de l'Amerique par votre ministere a pour objet le rebousement d'une partie des sommes qu'ils doivent à la france, et il me charge de vous demander un mot d'eclaircissement à ce Sujet. J'ose vous prier, Monsieur, le vouloir bien m'honorer d'une reponse Sur cela—et de me mettre en etat de donner au Ministere l'information qu'il desire le plus promptement qu'il sera possible. Je me felicite de cette circonstance qui me met a portée de Correspondre avec vous. J'espere que vous ne quitteres pas la Hollande sans venir Faire un tour à La Haye. Je Serai enchanté de vous y recevoir et de vous donner des preuves des Sentimens distingués et da la haute consideration avec la quelle j ai l'honneur d'etre Monsieur   Votre très humble et   très obeissant Serviteur   Caillard

M. Short

[ENCLOSURE]

William Short to Antoine Bernard Caillard [20]

Amsterdam le 6. Mars 1791.

Monsieur

En reponse à la lettre que vous m'avez fait l'honneur de m'ecrire avant hier je puis vous informer que l'emprunt dont il est question a été fait en consequence de deux votes du Congres passés le 4. & le 12. du mois d'Aoust dernier & qui autorisent des emprunts en y designant leurs objets. J'ai eu l'honneur avant mon depart de Paris de porter a la connaissance de votre ministere les intentions de notre gouvernment autant qu'elles m'etaient connues alors—à mon trés grand etonnement je n'ai pas jusqu'a present reçu des ordres ulterieurs quoique j'en attends comme j'en ai attendu journellement depuis quelque tems. Quand à mon opinion particuliere je crois que cet emprunt sera em-

19. ALS, William Short Papers, Library of Congress.
20. AL, letterpress copy, William Short Papers, Library of Congress.

ployé, ainsi que ceux qui se feront successivement, à rembourser sans delai la partie de la dette Americaine envers la France, qui est echue; & je n'ai nul doute que je recevrai des ordres à cet effect avant qu'il ne soit rempli. Je conte passer par la Haye sous peu de jours en m'en retournant à Paris. Je ne manquerai pas Monsieur de profiter de cette occasion pour vous aller faire ma cour & avoir l'honneur de vous assurer de mes voeux

M. Caillard.

[E N C L O S U R E]

Ferdinand Le Grand to William Short [21]

[Paris, February 25, 1791]

Jaime a croire Monsieur que vous ne vous etes pas rappelle les conditions du traité passé dans le temps entre le roi & Monsieur Francklin il porte que le remboursement des Sommes pretées aux etats unis Seront faites a mon domicile pour etre ensuite versées au tresor royal, j'ai appris avec peine que cette condition na pas été observée dans le payement qui S'est effectué dernierement, independament du droit que j'ai a ce quelle Soit executée, c'en est un aussi de justice puisque cest moi Seul qui ait Sollicité & obtenu tous les Secours de notre gouvernement & que depuis l'origine je nai cessé de rendre avec le Zele le plus actif & le plus Soutenu les Services les plus Importans en tous le genres. & Successivement a tous les Ministres des Etats unis jusqua ce quils aient été reçus a la Cour. Je ne puis croire dapres cela que L'intention due Congrès fut daller contre Ses engagemens vis a vis du banquier quil a adopté a paris & qui la bien merité, cependant S'il en etoit autrement je vous prie Monsieur de vouloir bien m'en Informer & de me croire plus que personne.
Votre Tres Humble &   Tres Obeissant Serviteur   Grand

Paris le 25 fevr 1791

P. S.   Je desirerois Savoir Si nous n'aurons pas bientot le plaisir de vous voir, comme aussi Si dans l'emprunt actuel on reçoit des papiers, & de quelle nature.

21. ALS, letterpress copy, William Short Papers, Library of Congress.

[ENCLOSURE]

William Short to Ferdinand Le Grand [22]

Amsterdam le 3. Mars 1791

Votre lettre du 25. du mois dernier, Monsieur, m'est parvenue hier. Les remboursements dont vous me parlez ont eté faits depuis plusieurs moi & d'apres les mesures prises de concert avec M. le Directeur du Trésor Royal [23] selon le desir du Ministre des Affaires étrangéres. Les seules parties que me paraissoient interesseés s'etant ainsi concerteés, je suis obligé de vous avouer, Monsieur, que je ne m'attendois pas aux reclamations que vous venez de faire, & cela d'autant moins qu'un tems considerable s'est passé depuis & qu'une partie de ces remboursements a eté faite par l'intermedaire même de votre maison etablie ici. Quand à l'intention du Congrés dont vous desirez être informé je ne puis en juger que par les ordres que j'ai recu & qui ont reglé ma conduite dans cette affaire. Je vous prie Monsieur de me faire la justice de croire que je suis trés sincérement votre trés humble & trés obiessant serviteur.

W. Short

P. S.   Je conte partir la semaine prochaine pour Paris & y aller en droiture. Dans l'emprunt dont vous me parlez on ne reçoit pas de papiers.

M. Grand

22. LS, William Short Papers, Library of Congress.   23. Bertrand Dufresne.

From Thomas Jefferson

Philadelphia Mar. 12. 1791.

Dear Sir

The President has thought proper to appoint Colo. David Humphreys,[1] minister Resident for the U.S. at the court of Lisbon, with a salary of 4500. dollars a year, and an outfit equal to a year's salary. Besides this, by a standing regulation, he will be allowed his disbursements for gazettes transmitted here, translating & printing papers where that shall be necessary, postage, couriers, & necessary aids to *poor* American sailors. An opportunity ocurring, by a vessel sailing for Lisbon within a few days, to send him his commission, I shall be obliged to you to enable me to convey to him at the same time the means of recieving his outfit in the first instance, and his salary & disbursements above described in quarterly paiments, afterwards.

An act of Congress [2] having authorised the President to take measures for procuring a recognition of our treaty from the new Emperor of Morocco, arrangements for that purpose have been decided. The act allows 20,000 Dollars for this object, but not more than 13,000 Dollars will be called for in the first instance, if at all, and these, or the means of drawing for them not till six weeks hence. I thought it proper however to apprise you of the call at the earliest day possible, and while the President is here, and to ask your attention to it. I have the honor to be with sentiments of the most perfect respect & esteem   Dear Sir   your most obedt. & most humble servt.   Th: Jefferson

The Secretary of the Treasury.

ALS, letterpress copy, Thomas Jefferson Papers, Library of Congress; LC, Papers of the Continental Congress, National Archives.
1. Humphreys, a resident of Connecticut, had been a lieutenant colonel and an aide-de-camp to George Washington during the American Revolution. In 1790, Washington had appointed him as a special agent in England, Spain, and Portugal.
2. "An Act making an appropriation for the purpose therein mentioned" (1 *Stat.* 214 [March 3, 1791]).

To Jeremiah Wadsworth

Philadelphia March 12. 1791

Dr Sir

Persuaded that there was nothing better to be done with Mr Chaloner, I approve the arrangement you have made as far as Mr Church's interest is concerned.[1]

Yrs with great regard   A Hamilton

Philadelphia
Jeremiah Wadsworth Esqr

ALS, Connecticut Historical Society, Hartford.

1. During the American Revolution Wadsworth and John B. Church had formed a business partnership which had been dissolved in 1785. From the time of his retirement from the Army in 1782 H managed the American business affairs of Church, who had returned to Europe at the end of the war. The property in Philadelphia owned by Church and Wadsworth was handled by John Chaloner, a Philadelphia merchant. When Church returned to the United States in 1785, he disapproved of Chaloner's management and removed his affairs from Chaloner's control. This letter refers to the liquidation of Chaloner's debts to Wadsworth and Church.

To George Washington

Treasury Department
March 12th. 1791

The Secretary of the Treasury has the honor respectfully to submit to the President of the United States a contract which has been recently transmitted from South Carolina for the Keeping of the Light house in that State. The terms are some what less than those of the Lighthouse Keeper at Cape Henlopen, and considering the expences of living in South Carolina it is humbly conceived they are not immoderate at this time. The Secretary, however, begs leave to suggest the expediency of confirming the Contract for one year only from its commencement, as there appears some reason to expect a diminution of the highest of this class of compensations.

Alex: Hamilton

LC, George Washington Papers, Library of Congress.

To George Washington

Treasury Department
March 12th. 1791

The Secretary of the Treasury has the honor respectfully to submit to the President of the United States a Contract made by the Collector of New London,[1] with Nathaniel Richards for supplying the Light house belonging to that Port.

This Contract not having been originally made in a manner sufficiently explanatory of the business, was returned for the purpose of being put into such form as should place before the President the particulars on which he is to decide. The Secretary humbly offers an opinion that the terms are not unfavorable to the United States.

Alexander Hamilton
Secy. of the Treasury

LC, George Washington Papers, Library of Congress.
  1. Jedediah Huntington.

To Wilhem and Jan Willink, Nicholaas and Jacob Van Staphorst, and Nicholas Hubbard

Treasury Department,
March 12th. 1791.

Gentlemen,

This serves to desire, that the interest, which will become payable on the Dutch loans, upon the first day of June next, may be discharged out of the funds, which will remain in your hands, of the last loan of three millions of Florins.[1]

I am &c.   Alexander Hamilton.

Messrs. Willink, Van Staphorst and Hubbard.

Copy, RG 233, Reports of the Treasury Department, 1792–1793, Vol. III, National Archives. This letter was enclosed in H's "Report on Foreign Loans," February 13, 1793.
  1. The Holland loan of 1790. For a description of this loan, see H to Willink, Van Staphorst, and Hubbard, November 29, 1790, note 1.

From Nathaniel Appleton

Boston, March 13, 1791. ". . . Mr. Higginson presented me with a letter from you of 27 Feby. Agreably thereto I shall recei⟨ve of⟩ him whatever he inclines to pay me to the extent of thirty thousand Dolls. . . . I am in hopes to be ready to pay Interest on the 1st April but it will require our utmost exertions to accomplish it, for on the last of Feby they crowded upon me very large sums to Loan & transfer, & the payment of the Pensioners immediately commenced."

LC, RG 53, Massachusetts State Loan Office, Letter Book, 1785–1791, Vol. "259–M," National Archives.

From Tobias Lear

[*Philadelphia*] *March 14, 1791.* Returns two lighthouse contracts [1] which George Washington has approved.

ALS, RG 26, Lighthouse Letters Received, "Segregated" Lighthouse Records, Lear, National Archives; copy, George Washington Papers, Library of Congress.
  1. These contracts were for supplying the lighthouses at New London, Connecticut, and Charleston, South Carolina. See H to Washington, March 12, 1791.

To George Washington

[Philadelphia, March 14, 1791]

The Secretary of the Treasury presents his respects to the President of the United States and sends him the Draft of a power concerning the intended Loans.[1] If any thing more particular should occur to the President it may be the subject of a distinct instruction.

Monday

LC, George Washington Papers, Library of Congress.
  1. For the enclosure, see Washington to H, March 15, 1791.

From William Ellery

Custom House
Newport [Rhode Island] March 15 1791

Sir,

This will be accompanied by a weekly return of Cash, and by a Certificate of Registry No. 5 dated Jany. 22. 1790, granted by the Collector of Dighton,[1] and delivered up on account of the transfer of property, and also the copy of an Endorsment of an Enrollment of the change of Master said Enrollment being No. 11 and issued from this office.

Yesterday arrived here a Schooner named the Charming Sally James Reed Master from St. John New Brunswick, and reported One hundred & twenty nine smoaked Salmon and one Box of books; and that she was destined for New York. Upon examining her Register it appeared that She was British Plantation built, her length forty three [feet] and seven Inches, her breadth Twelve feet and nine Inches, and her Height between decks & ceiling in the hold Five feet & Six Inches, and that She admeasured Thirty tons. A suspicion arising I desired the Surveyor [2] to admeasure her, and by his Certificate of her admeasurement she is Twenty six Tons and 54/95. Whereupon I seized both vessel & cargo for a breach of the 70th. Sect. p. 40 of the last Collection Law [3] and have applied to the attorney of this District [4] to libel them accordingly. The Libel will be prosecuted at the next District Court; which will sit in Providence on the first monday in May next unless you should think proper to countermand it. If a foreign built vessel should be condemned would the purchaser, being a citizen of the United States, be entitled to a register, enrollment or license of such vessel? [5]

I have the honor to be   Sir   Yr. most obedt. servt: W Ellery Collr

A Hamilton Esqre
Secry of the Treasy

LC, Newport Historical Society, Newport, Rhode Island.
   1. Hodijah Baylis.
   2. Daniel Lyman.
   3. Section 70 of "An Act to provide more effectually for the collection of the duties imposed by law on goods, wares and merchandise imported into the United States, and on the tonnage of ships or vessels" provided that "no goods, wares or merchandise of foreign growth or manufacture, subject to the payment of duties, shall be brought into the United States from any foreign port or place in any other manner than by sea, nor in any ship or vessel of less than thirty tons burthen" (1 *Stat.* 177 [August 4, 1790]).
   4. William Channing.
   5. Ellery endorsed the letter book copy of this letter "Answered." H's reply has not been found.

To Richard Harison

Treasury Department
March 15. 1791

Sir

You will find under this cover a letter of particular importance to this department,[1] the business of which will I doubt not receive your early attention.

I am, Sir,   Your Obedient servant   Alexander Hamilton

Richard Harison Esqr.
Attorney of the United States
for the district of New York

LS, New-York Historical Society, New York City.
    1. William Lewis to Harison, March 14, 1791 (ALS, New-York Historical
Society). In this letter, Lewis, United States attorney for the District of Pennsylvania, asked for Harison's assistance in apprehending a band of counterfeiters.

From Samuel Henshaw [1]

Northampton [*Massachusetts*] *March 15, 1791.* Asks to be appointed inspector of revenue in Massachusetts.

ALS, Hamilton Papers, Library of Congress.
    1. Henshaw had served as state collector of customs at Boston in the seventeen-
eighties.

From Thomas Jones, Brockholst Livingston, and John H. Livingston [1]

New York, March 15, 1791. "Mr. Philip Henry Livingston of this
City together with his Father in law Walter Livingston [2] having assumed certain debts due from us as administrators on the estate of the
late Philip Livingston deceased, we have agreed to execute to him an
assignment of his Father's bonds & mortgage to our Testator. To
perfect this Assignment we are advised that it is essential that you
should join in the execution of it. We therefore enclose one for that
purpose. . . . As we have now a prospect of settling our testators
Affairs we are afraid we shall often be under the disagreable necessity,
of troubling you upon that subject & thereby diverting your attention from the more important & useful pursuits in which you are engaged. We know not any way of preventing this interruption but by
an application to our Legislature which is now sitting: If an application of this kind be agreeable to you, & not otherwise, we will make
it. . . ." [3]

LS, Hamilton Papers, Library of Congress.
    1. Jones was a New York City physician who had married Margaret Living-
ston, the daughter of Philip Livingston. Brockholst Livingston was a well-known
New York City attorney and the son of William Livingston, former governor

of New Jersey. John H. Livingston was a New York City clergyman and the husband of Sarah Livingston, Margaret Livingston Jones's sister. H had extensive correspondence in the seventeen-eighties concerning the estate of Philip Philip Livingston, who died in 1787. See Ezekiel Forman to H, August 23, 1788, December 1, 1788; H to Richard Morris, September 8, 1788; William Livingston to H, December 22, 1788.

2. Philip Henry Livingston, son of Philip Philip Livingston, married Walter Livingston's daughter, Maria.

3. H endorsed this letter: "Answered 22d March 91." Letter not found.

From George Washington [1]

[Philadelphia, March 15, 1791]

By Virtue of the several Acts, the one entitled "An Act for raising and adding another regiment to the military establishment of the United States and for making further provision for the protection of the frontiers," [2] and the other entitled "An Act making an appropriation for the purpose therein mentioned," [3] I do hereby authorise and empower you by yourself or any other person or persons to borrow on behalf of the United States, within the said States or elsewhere a sum or sums not exceeding in the whole, three hundred and thirty two thousand six hundred & eighty six Dollars and twenty Cents,[4] and to make or cause to be made for that purpose such Contract or Contracts as shall be necessary, and for the interest of the said States in conformity to the said several acts subject to the restrictions and limitations therein respectively contained; and also to this further restriction, that the United States shall have a right to reimburse the principal & interest of the monies which shall be borrowed in pursuance hereof, at the end of the present year or as soon thereafter as they shall think fit. And for so doing this shall be your sufficient warrant.

Given under my hand at the City of Philadelphia this fifteenth day of march in the year of our Lord one thousand seven hundred and ninety one.

Go. Washington

LC, George Washington Papers, Library of Congress.

1. Either this warrant or a draft of it had been drawn up by H. See H to Washington, March 14, 1791.

2. 1 *Stat.* 222–24 (March 3, 1791).   3. 1 *Stat.* 214 (March 3, 1791).

4. Congress provided a maximum of $20,000 for the Moroccan mission and $312,686.20 for the Army.

From George Washington [1]

[Philadelphia, March 15, 1791]

Having thought fit, pursuant to the powers vested in me by the Act intitled "An Act repealing after the last day of June next the duties heretofore laid upon distilled Spirits imported from abroad and laying others in their stead, & also upon spirits distilled within the United States and for appropriating the same" [2] to divide the United States into the following fourteen districts, namely one to consist of the state of New hampshire, another to consist of the State of Massachusetts another to consist of the State of Rhode Island and Providence Plantations another to consist of the State of Connecticut another to consist of the State of Vermont another to consist of the State of New York another to consist of the State of New Jersey another to consist of the State of Pennsylvania another to consist of the State of Delaware another to consist of the State of Maryland another to consist of the State of Virginia another to consist of the State of North Carolina another to consist of the State of South Carolina and another to consist of the State of Georgia, and having by and with the advice and consent of the Senate appointed the following persons to be Supervisors of the said Districts respectively, that is to say—for the District of New hampshire Joshua Wentworth, for the District of Massachusetts Nathaniel Gorham, for the District of Rhode Island & Providence Plantations John S. Dexter, for the district of Connecticut John Chester, for the district of Vermont Noah Smith, for the district of New York William S. Smith, for the district of New Jersey Aaron Dunham, for the district of Pennsylvania George Clymer, for the district of Delaware Henry Latimer, for the district of Maryland George Gale, for the district of Virginia Edward Carrington, for the district of North Carolina William Polk, for the district

LS, RG 58, General Records, 1791–1803, National Archives; LC, George Washington Papers, Library of Congress.

1. There is a Washington memorandum, dated March 15, 1791 (LC, George Washington Papers, Library of Congress), some of the details of which differ from the contents of Washington's letter to H. For these variations, see *GW*, XXXI, 239–40, note 88.

2. 1 *Stat.* 199–214 (March 3, 1791).

of South Carolina Daniel Stevens, and for the district of Georgia John Matthews.

I do hereby in further execution of the said powers make and establish the following supplementary arrangements, viz:

First—That the Compensations to the said Supervisors respectively shall be as follows:

To the Supervisor of New hampshire a Salary of Five hundred Dollars and a Commission of one half ℔ Cent.

To the Supervisor of Massachusetts a salary of Eight hundred Dollars and a Commission of one half per Cent.

To the Supervisor of Rhode Island and Providence Plantations a Salary of Five hundred Dollars and a Commission of one half per Cent.

To the Supervisor of Connecticut a Salary of Six hundred Dollars and a Commission of one half per Cent.

To the Supervisor of Vermont a Salary of Four hundred Dollars and a Commission of one half per Cent.

To the Supervisor of New York a salary of Eight Hundred dollars and a Commission of one half per Cent.

To the Supervisor of New Jersey a salary of Four hundred Dollars and a Commission of one half per Cent.

To the Supervisor of Pennsylvania a Salary of One thousand Dollars and a Commission of one half per Cent.

To the Supervisor of Delaware a Salary of Four hundred Dollars and a Commission of one per Cent.

To the Supervisor of Maryland a Salary of Seven hundred Dollars and a Commission of one per Cent.

To the Supervisor of Virginia a Salary of One thousand Dollars and a Commission of One per Cent.

To the Supervisor of North Carolina a Salary of Seven hundred Dollars and a Commission of One per Cent.

To the Supervisor of South Carolina a salary of Seven hundred Dollars and a Commission of one per Cent.

To the Supervisor of Georgia a Salary of Five hundred dollars and a Commission of One per Cent.

Secondly—That the States hereafter-mentioned shall be distributed into the following Surveys of Inspection and under the dispositions and regulations which follow, viz:

The districts of New hampshire, Rhode Island and Providence

Plantations, of Connecticut, Vermont, New York, New Jersey, Delaware, Maryland for the present, and Georgia shall severally form each one survey and the duties of Inspector of each Survey shall be performed by the Supervisor of the district comprehending the same.

Massachusetts shall form three Surveys No. 1. 2. & 3, the first consisting of the province of Maine, the second of the counties of Essex, Middlesex, Worcester, Hampshire and Berkshire, the third, of the residue of the State.

The duties of Inspector of the Survey No. 1 shall for the present be performed by the Supervisor.

For the Survey No. 2. there shall be an Inspector, whose compensation shall be a Salary of Five hundred Dollars and a Commission of one half per Cent. To this Office I shall appoint Jonathan Jackson.

For the Survey No. 3 there shall also be an Inspector whose compensation shall be a Salary of Five hundred Dollars and a Commission of one half per Cent. To this Office I shall appoint Leonard Jarvis.

Pennsylvania shall form four surveys No. 1. 2. 3 & 4: the first consisting of the City and County of Philadelphia and the Counties of Bucks and Montgomery. The duties of Inspector of this Survey shall for the present be performed by the Supervisor. The second consisting of the Counties of Berks Northampton, Luzerne & Northumberland; the third, consisting of the Counties of Delaware, Chester, Lancaster, York, Dauphin, Cumberland, Franklin, Mifflin and Huntington; the fourth consisting of the Counties of Bedford, Westmoreland, Fayette, Washington and Alleghany. To each of the three last Surveys there shall be an Inspector whose compensation shall be a Salary of Four hundred and fifty Dollars and a Commission of one per Cent. I shall appoint for No. 2 James Collins, and for No. 4 John Neville. It is my wish to appoint for No. 3 Edward Hand. But as his acceptance of the office is doubted and some inconveniences might attend a refusal, I have concluded to leave a Commission with a blank for his name; desiring that you will take measures to ascertain the disposition of the said Edward Hand, and if this should appear to be in favour of an acceptance that the blank be filled with his name; if against it with the name of John McDowel.

With regard to the district of Virginia I shall postpone any further arrangement till my arrival within that State.

North Carolina shall form five Surveys No. 1. 2. 3. 4 & 5, the first consisting of the Counties of Wilmington, Onslow, New Hanover,

Brunswick, Bladen, Duplin, Anson, Richmond, Moore, Cumberland, Robertson and Sampson. The second of the Counties of Carteret, Hyde, Beaufort, Pitt, Craven, Jones, Dobbs, Johnson, Wayne; the third of the Counties of Kurrituck, Cambden, Pasquotank, Perquimans Chowan Gates Hartford Tyrrell; the fourth of the Counties of Northampton Martin Hallifax Nash Edgecomb Warren Franklin Caswell Orange, Randolph Grandville Wake & Chatham; the fifth of the Counties of Mecklenbergh Montgomery Roan Iredel Surrey Stokes Rockingham Gilford Lincoln Rutherford Burke Wilkes. I shall appoint for the present the Collector of Wilmington as Inspector of Survey No. 1. The Collector of Newbern as Inspector of No. 2. The Collector of Edenton as Inspector of Survey No 3. And the compensation in each case shall be a Commission of two per Cent. To each of the Surveys No. 4 and 5 there shall be an Inspector whose compensation shall be a Salary of Four hundred and fifty dollars and a Commission of One per Cent. It is my present intention to appoint for No. 4 John Whitaker and for No. 5 John McDowell.[3] But as I shall have an opportunity of further enquiry in the course of my Journey through the State I shall leave Commissions with blanks which are not to be filled up till after the tenth day of June next; but if nothing to the contrary is learned from me by that day, the blanks are severally to be filled with the names above mentioned.

The State of South Carolina shall form three Surveys No. 1. 2 and 3, the first consisting of the counties of Colleton Berkley, Washington, Marion Bartholomew Charleston, Granville Hilton Lincoln Shrewsbury, Winton Orange Lexington and Lewisburgh; the second consisting of the Counties of Winyaw, Williamsburgh Liberty Kingston, Darlington, Chesterfield, Marlborough Clarendon Clermont Lancaster Kershaw Richland Fairfield, Chester, York; the third consisting of the counties of Edgefield Abbeville Newbury Laurens Union Spartanburgh Greenville Pendleton. The duties of Inspector of Survey No. 1 to be performed by the Supervisor. The Collector of Georgetown to be Inspector of No. 2 with a salary of Three hundred dollars and a Commission of two per Cent. And for Survey No. 3 there shall be an Inspector whose compensation shall be a Salary of Five hundred and fifty dollars and a Commission of One per Cent. To this office I shall appoint Andrew Pickens.

3. Washington is referring to Joseph McDowell, Sr.

The Commission in each case shall be computed upon the Nett product of the duties, distilled within the United States and within the jurisdiction of the Officer to whom it is allowed; which nett product shall be determined by deducting at each Stage of the computation all antecedent charges.

Thirdly—That at every port where there is a Collector and Surveyor, the Surveyor shall be an Inspector, and at every port where there is a Collector only he shall be an Inspector and at every port where there is a Surveyor only he shall be an Inspector. The duties of these Inspectors except in the cases hereinbefore specified shall extend only to Spirits imported from Foreign Countries.

Fourthly—That for the sake of uniformity the Officers to be appointed by the respective Supervisors shall be denominated Collectors of the Revenue.

Fifthly—That the compensation to those Officers respectively shall be a Commission on the sums which shall from time to time be collected by each, of two per Centum on the duties arising on spirits distilled from foreign Materials and of four per Centum on the duties arising on spirits distilled from Materials of the Growth or production of the United States.

Having thus made known to you the arrangements which I have thought fit to adopt, you will proceed to notify them to whomsoever it may concern. And you will add such instructions to the respective officers in conformity to the law and to the tenor of these presents as shall appear to you necessary.

Given under my hand at the City of Philadelphia the fifteenth day of March in the year One thousand seven hundred and ninety one. Go: Washington

From Nathaniel Appleton

United States Loan Office
Boston 16th March 1791

Sr.

I had the honor to write you 13th instant since which Mr Higginson has paid LeRoy & Bayards draft for ten Thousand Dollrs. He has also purchased five thousand Dollrs of the Treasurers Drafts and proposes soon to make a further purchase. The money as fast as I recive it is deposited in the Massts Bank. I have this minute recd yours of 5th instant. I note what you say of closing the Office tomorrow. I have sat my people to form a General Abstract of the several Stocks stand-ing on my Books & which if possible shall be transmitted to you by the Post this Evening agreable to your request. The following is a general statement of Cash on hand Vizt

	Dollrs	Cents
Recd for the Treasurers draft on Benjn Lincoln Esqr collector for this Port for the purpose of paying Invalid Pensioners	8586.75	
For Treasurers draft on Massts Bank for the above purpose	4000	
	12586.75	
out of which has been paid to Invalids	5360.41	
	7226.34	
For Sale of drafts on the North American Bank and the Bank at New York	32.600	
For Messrs LeRoy & Bayards draft on Stephen Higgin-son Esqr paid	10.000	
Treasurers draft on hand	17.400	
	60 000	

I shall make the Bank a mediun of all my payments as much as is pos-sible. With great respect I have the honor to be Sr Yr Humle Sert

N A

P.S I have also reced yours 2d instant inclosing Messrs LeRoys and Bayards second Bill Exchange.

LC, RG 53, Massachusetts State Loan Office, Letter Book, 1785–1791, Vol. "259–M," National Archives.

From Nathaniel Appleton

United States Loan Office
Boston 16 March 1791

Sr.

I have already wrote you this Evening & as it is now past the close of the Mail am in hopes to convey this by the Stage Driver. Inclosed is as accurate Statement of the Stocks standing on my Books as the time would permitt the Books not being posted up. Part of the Ac-count are taken from original entries & therefore subject to error. But I believe it is not far from the truth.

Issues of Certificates [1] as follows Viz

	Six p cent	Deferred	Three p Cent
October	209 047.12.	104 524–51	270.562 21
Nov	235,171–34	117.585–81.	262.877–53
Decr.	314.916.85	157 458–74	267.715–48
Jany	278.524–60	139 262.62	224 090.86
Feby & March	367.630 89	183,816.54	425 912 20
	1,405.290.80	702 648.22	1,451.158–28
Transfers into Office	37 019.14	10.307.59	69.437–67
	1,442.309.94	712,955.81	1,520,595.95
Transfers out	12,559.46	18,308 76	3 143–13
	1,429,750.48	694,647.05	1 517,452.82

LC, RG 53, Massachusetts State Loan Office, Letter Book, 1785–1791, Vol. "259-M," National Archives.

1. For background to the issue of these certificates, see Appleton to H, February 5, 1791, note 1.

From Jedediah Huntington

[*New London, Connecticut, March 16, 1791*. On April 10, 1791, Hamilton wrote to Huntington: "I observe in your letter of the 16th. ultimo." *Letter not found.*]

From Blair McClenachan et al.

[Philadelphia, March 16, 1791] [1]

Sir

The underwritten holders of Loan office Certificates given for Money lent the United States to carry on the late War between Sepr 1st 1777 & March 1st. 1778 conceiving themselves aggrieved by the opperation of certain instructions reced from you [2] by the Commis-

Copy, Division of Public Records, Pennsylvania Historical and Museum Commission, Harrisburg; Df, in the handwriting of John Nicholson, Division of Public Records, Pennsylvania Historical and Museum Commission.

1. This letter is undated, but it has been endorsed by John Nicholson, comptroller of Pennsylvania, "Copy of A Letter to The Honble A Hamilton Esqr secy Treasy March 16th. 1791."

2. See "Treasury Department Circular to the Commissioners of Loans," November 1, 1790.

sioner of loans, beg leave to represent their Situation and at the Same time to assure you that they have not the most distant idea that what you have done proceeded either from want of attention to the Public faith to the laws of Congress or to the rights of this Class of Public Creditors.

By Sundry Acts of Congress the holders of these Certificates were promised the Interest thereof in Specie untill the principal shall be ready to be discharged,[3] we need not recite these engagements they are well known to you. All the Interest hitherto dischargd. hath been paid conformably thereto, And in observance thereof you have in the Instructions alluded to directed the Interest upon the nominal Sum to be allow'd the holders untill the first of the year 1791 but we complain that you should prevent its continuance afterwards to non-Subscribers and are well assur'd that there is no law to warrant it; indeed the Manner which the arrears of Interest 'till Jany. 1791 hath been allow'd, Strongly evinces that the principles adopted which fulfils this obvious engagement untill Jany 1791 and which would deprive the owners of the Same in future are not conformable to the law for by the instructions given a Certificate of 1000 Dollars issued on the 28th. Feby 1778 the Interest whereof hath been paid to 31st Decr. 1787 will intitle the bearer to a Certificate on Interest from the beginning of Augt. 1785 by which means the Public would be charged with the Interest twice from Augt. 1785 till Jany 1788 on the Same Debt but there is another proof that the principles adopted are not only unauthorised by the law but that they are directly repugnant to it. And that is the act itself which declares that nothing therein contained shall be *construed* in any wise to *alter abridge* or *impair* the *rights* of those Creditors of the United States who shall not Subscribe to the Said Loans or the *Contracts* upon which their respective *claims* are founded; [4] for can any thing be more evident than that the *construction* which hath been given thereof does materially *Alter Abridge* and *impair* the rights of those Creditors and therefore is contrary to the law.

The Said Act directs that a Sum equal to the Interest payble to Subscribing creditors shall also be paid to non-Subscribers in the

---

3. See, for example, *JCC*, VIII, 724–25, 730–31; XI, 513–14; XVII, 568; XXXI, 465.

4. See Section 9 of "An Act making provision for the (payment of the) Debt of the United States" (1 *Stat.* 141 [August 4, 1790]).

present year on Accot. of the Interest due them,[5] and that allowance we claim.

In order to entitle us thereto by the Said Act as non-Subscribers it is nevertheless necessary that the Certificates we possess should be exchanged for others to be issued in lieu thereof but it is by Said Law provided and Secured to the holders that in this exchange, the rights of the Creditors shall not be *altered Abridged* or *impaired* nor the *contracts* upon which their respective claims are founded but the Said Contracts and rights (which in their Nature were unalterable by the United States) are in and by the Said Act recognized and declared to remain in full force & virtue.[6]

Having thus clearly Shown that the proposed defalcation from our Interest from and After Jany 1791 is not agreeable to Law, we are fully convinced that you will revise these Instructions which were given when the Subject was yet new and untried and with all when a Multitude of presing Business must have prevented you from considering so fully the operations & effects thereof.

It is certain that according to the engagements of the United States the Scale of depreciation is not to affect Certificates for Moneys loan'd between Sepr. 1777 & March 1778 untill the United States shall be ready to Discharge the principal and untill that period they are to all intents & purposes Specie Debts therefore the Certificates to be granted in liu of them should be for the same Sums and to the Same Amot., otherwise the law will not be complied with.[7]

When by a Similar Law of the State of Penna. these Certificates were allow'd to be Exchanged for others of that State in like manner as is by this act directed, The holders recei[ve]d a New Certificate for the *Same Amot.* with those they gave up.[8] By that act a provision

5. See Section 10 of "An Act making provision for the (payment of the) Debt of the United States" (1 *Stat.* 141–42).

6. See Section 9 of "An Act making provision for the (payment of the) Debt of the United States" (1 *Stat.* 141).

7. See *JCC*, XVII, 566–69.

8. Section III of "An Act for the Further Relief of the Public Creditors Who are Citizens of This State by Receiving on Loan Certain Debts of the United States of America and for Funding the Same and for Paying the Annual Interest of Such Loans and the Interest of Certain Debts of This State Every Six Months" reads in part as follows: "And whereas certain of the loan office certificates aforesaid which bear date between the first day of September in the year of our Lord one thousand seven hundred and seventy-seven and the first day of March in the year of our Lord one thousand seven hundred and seventy-eight are subject to liquidation by the aforesaid scale of depreciation on the final re-

was made stating that whereas certain of the Loan Office Certificates aforesaid and which bear Date between the first day of Sepr. 1777 and the first Day of March, 1778 are Subject to a liquidation of the aforesaid Scale of depreciation on the final redemption and payment of the principal Sums thereof respectively altho the possessors of the Same Certificates be intitled to receve the annual Interest thereof At full Value on the nominal Sums therein expressed untill Such Redemption and payment of the principal be made and it may be necessary to distinguish and set forth this particularity on the Certificates to be given for Loans to be made as aforesaid in such Certificates in order that the paper liquidation of the principal Monies thereof may be made on the final payment & discharge "of the Same;" they then proceed to declare that an endorsment Shall be made on each Certificate so exchanged in such manner as to enable the proper liquidation to be made when the Public are authorized to make it, Altho provision is not so expressly made in the Act of the United States of the 4 Augt. 1790. Yet the principles are the Same and as you are Authorized to direct the forms of the Certificates it will be easily done by instructing the Commissioners respectively when they issue Certificates to non-Subscribers for Certificates presented of this description to note on the back of each the Sum for which the United States will be Authorized to redeem them respectively. We pray that you will take the Subject into your Consideration and are well assur'd that you will be of Opinion that we are intitled by law and by Justice to what we ask and that you will alter the Instructions given accordingly that so we may not be debar'd from recving the part Allowed us by the United States of what is due to us from them.

We have the Honor   to be Sir   With great Respect   Your mo. obt. & very Hume. Servant

Blair McClenachen
Catherine Keppele
Edwd Bartholomew

---

demption and payment of the principal sums thereof respectively althought the possessors of the same certificates be entitled to receive the annual interest thereof at full value on the nominal sums therein expressed until such redemption and payment of the principal be made; and it may be necessary to distinguish and set forth this particularity on the certificates to be given for loans to be made as aforesaid in such certificates in order that the proper liquidation of the principal moneys thereof may be made on the final payment and discharge of the same" (Pennsylvania Statutes, XII, 160–61 [March 1, 1786]).

Isaac Snowden
John Tromberger
Paul Coxe
Walter Stewart
Andw. Caldwell
Willm. Bell
John Nixon
John Nicholson [9]

To the Honble Alexr. Hamilton Esqr. secy Treas

9. The signatures on the copy are in the handwriting of John Nicholson.

From Richard Harison

New York 17 March 1791

Sir,

I have been honored by your Letter of the 15th., and beg Leave to assure you that the Business it alludes to, & every other Subject in which the Public is interested will at all Times command the Attention of

Sir   Your most obedt Servt.

Honble. A. Hamilton Esqr.
Secry Treasury &ca.

LC, New-York Historical Society, New York City.

From Jeremiah Olney

Providence, March 17, 1791. "I have received your Letter of the 5th. instant,[1] relative to the Payment of Money in my hands to the Commissioner of Loans for this State: [2] Your directions therein shall be punctually attended to. . . ."

ADfS, Rhode Island Historical Society, Providence; copy, RG 56, Letters from the Collector at Providence, National Archives.
1. "Treasury Department Circular to the Collectors of the Customs," March 5, 1791.
2. Jabez Bowen.

Treasury Department Circular
to the Commissioners of Loans

Treasury Department
March 17. 1791.

Sir

It has been represented to me by the officers of this department, that some of the Commissioners of Loans, who have received on loan certificates of *the Register* of the Treasury, have issued new loan certificates therefor, without a previous transmission of them to the Treasury for examination. You will find by a recurrence to the circular letter of the 16th September,[1] that it is therein directed *"that all certificates issued by the Register of the Treasury* and all other certificates of which you have no checks or registers, or of the authenticity of which you entertain doubts *are previously to a settlement in your office to be transmitted to the Treasury for examination,"* to accomplish which with safety and dispatch the form (I) was prepared and forwarded to all the Commissioners.

Considerations which regard the public safety, dictated this precaution. It is still deemed indispensible, and it is much feared that injury or inconvenience may arise from the deviations, which may have taken place. The danger to the loan officer is no less serious than to the public, for if a certificate, which has been received in a manner contrary to the instructions, should prove to have been counterfeited or altered, responsibility in the receiving Commissioner will necessarily take place.

The importance of the above caution has induced me to make it circular, though it is not said that you have overlooked the instructions.

I am, Sir,   your Obedt Servant.   Alex Hamilton

LS, to Nathaniel Appleton, Washington University Libraries, St. Louis, Missouri.
    1. Circular not found.

To Nathaniel Appleton

Treasury Department
March 18th. 1791.

Sir

Your Letter of the second Instant is before me. I trust mine of the 5th. will have duly reached you and I doubt not you will have paid an exact attention to its contents.

Lest other resources might fail of placing in time in your hands the requisite funds for payment of the ensuing Quarters interest I have obtained a Credit with the Bank of Massachusetts for any sum you may want not exceeding Fifty-thousand dollars.

But as it is desireable to avoid incurring a charge of Interest to the United States, unless it be indispensable to preserve *punctuality, which is a primary consideration,* you will before you make application to the Bank examine the State of your means, and if they are found sufficient you will forbear to make it, or if a deficiency appear you will confine your application within the limits of that deficiency. Towards this examination you will obtain information of the Bank of Massachusetts of the sum in their possession on account of the United States, arising from remittances from the Collectors of the Customs and you will know from the Collector of Boston,[1] (whom you will do well to consult as to the necessity of having recourse to the aid of the bank) what sums can be certainly depended upon from him to the close of this month and *early in the ensuing.* I mention early in the *ensuing;* because some *little* delay in paying the dividends will be unavoidable, and it is to be expected that a part of the Creditors may not come immediately forward to claim their Interest. So that the Custom House Receipts within the first ten or fifteen days of April may probably be reckoned upon.

But while I give this intimation I would have nothing put to the hazard, as it concerns *strict* punctuality in the payment of the Interest. To this, other considerations must yield. I am nevertheless in great expectation, that the extra aid of the bank will not be wanted.

The bank is authorized to pay to you any sum, they may have received on account of the United States, to the end of the Month and such further sum as you may require not exceeding One hundred thousand dollars. The Collector of Boston is also authorized to pay to you any Sums, which shall have been received by him up to the 15th. of April next.

But you will of course understand that you are not to draw into your hands from any of the resources put within your reach any greater sum than is necessary to satisfy the ensuing quarters interest and to enable you to comply with what is mentioned below.

You will lose no time in ascertaining and giving notice to the bank whether you will stand in need of aid from that institution and to what extent. And you will without delay advise me of all the steps you have taken including a statement of your receipts and from what sources. You are to give duplicate Receipts for whatever sums you may receive either from the bank of Massachusetts or from the Collector of Boston.

I have authorized William Gardner commissioner of Loans for New Hampshire to draw upon you for any sum he may want not exceeding ten thousand dollars; to do which he is at Liberty either to direct to you some Treasurers bills which have been remitted to him or to draw himself. These drafts whether of the one kind or of the other you will accordingly satisfy; and you will take this sum into your calculations; though I do not expect you will be called upon for any part of it.

I am sir,   your obt. servant   Alexander Hamilton

Nathl. Appleton Esqr.
commr. of Loans
Massachusetts.

LS, National Library of Scotland, Edinburgh; copy, RG 56, Letters to the Collector at Boston, National Archives; copy, RG 56, Miscellaneous Letters Sent, "Set K," National Archives.
   1. Benjamin Lincoln.

To John Daves

Treasury Department
March 18th 1791.

Sir,

The President of the United States may have occasion to direct one of the Gentlemen of his family to apply to you for Cash, in exchange for notes of the Bank of North America, in the course of a tour which he intends to make thro' the Southern States. Should any such application be made, you will immediately furnish the money for the notes, which the President may desire to have exchanged, out of the funds in your Office, whether the same shall have been included in your Weekly Return to this department or not.

I am, Sir,   Your Obt. Servant   A. Hamilton

John Daves Esqr.
Collector
New Bern N. C.

Copy, RG 56, Letters to the Collector at New Bern, National Archives; copy, RG 56, Letters to Collectors at Small Ports, "Set G," National Archives.

To William Gardner [1]

Treasury Department,
March 18, 1791

Sir,

The certificate of your having taken the Oaths to support the Constitution of the United States and faithfully to execute the duties of your Office has been received.

You will observe my instructions as to the Sufficiency of Mr. Gilman's [2] Sureties, which are extended to you also. You will therefore present the names of Messrs. Brackett & Hill [3] to the Attorney of the United States, for the District of New Hampshire,[4] & in the mean time I shall cause further enquiries to be made.

All Subscribers to the loan, & other persons who have applied as
Non Subscribers,[5] before the time of closing your Office, Antecedent
to the April Quarter day, (which was the 17 instant) will be entitled
to receive their interest, be they numerous or few; and all persons who
shall not have applied as loaners or non Subscribers, on or before that
day, will have to wait 'till the next Quarter day, the first of July.

It will be necessary to the perfect understanding of the case of the
state paper issued for interest on the New Hampshire separate debt,
that I be furnished with a small one or with a full & true copy of one,
with its endorsements, if any, which will perfectly exhibit the form
& substance of that species of paper; also with copies or sufficient
extracts from all the laws relative thereto. The same will also be
necessary in the case of "the Colony bills" or "bills of Credit." I must
however in the mean time inform you that I do not consider any state
paper, of the nature of *money*, as assumable.[6]

I am, sir,   Your obt Servant.   Alexander Hamilton

Wm. Gardner Esqr.
Commr of Loans,
New Hampshire.

LS, Massachusetts Historical Society, Boston.
    1. Gardner was appointed commissioner of loans for New Hampshire on
December 24, 1790.
    2. Presumably John T. Gilman of New Hampshire, who was one of the
three commissioners for settling the accounts between the United States and the
individual states.
    3. James Brackett and James Hill of New Hampshire.
    4. Samuel Sherburne.
    5. For the provision made by Congress for "non-subscribers," see Andrew
Porter to H, April 23, 1791, note 2.
    6. For the legislative provision concerning the assumption of state debts, see
Thomas Smith to H, June 6, 1791, note 1.

To Richard Harison

Treasury Department
March 18. 1791

Sir,

    The President of the United States having under consideration the
petition of Samuel Dodge,[1] an inspector of the Customs in the District

of New York, I have to request that you will consent, on the part of
the United States, to the suspension of the judgment in the case of the
petitioner, 'till you shall be further advised.[2]

I am, sir,   Your Obedt. Servant   A Hamilton

Richard Harrison Esqr.
Attorney of the U States,
for the District of New York,
New York

LS, New-York Historical Society, New York City.
  1. Dodge had been suspended from his post and was threatened with prosecution for recovery of a penalty incurred through his violation of the customs
laws. On November 5, 1790, he submitted a petition to the United States District
Court for the Southern District of New York claiming the violation had occurred through ignorance of the law and not with fraudulent intent, and appealing for relief under the provisions of Section 1 of "An Act to provide for
mitigating or remitting the forfeitures and penalties accruing under the revenue
laws, in certain cases therein mentioned" (1 *Stat.* 122–23 [May 26, 1790]). On
February 22, 1791, Dodge was indicted by the United States Circuit Court for
the Southern District of New York and pleaded guilty to the charge against him.
Judgment against Dodge, however, was suspended until the next session of the
court in order that he might appeal to the President for relief. Dodge's petition
to Washington, dated February 24, 1791, may be found in RG 59, Miscellaneous
Letters, 1790–1799, National Archives. On September 14, 1791, Tobias Lear informed Edmund Randolph, the Attorney General, that "the President thinks
proper to have a pardon issued to Saml. Dodge which the Atty Genl. is requested to prepare accordingly" (ALS, RG 59, Miscellaneous Letters, 1790–
1799, National Archives).
  2. This word is in H's handwriting.

To Charles Lee

Treasury Department, March 18, 1791. Directs Lee to supply funds
for any notes George Washington may desire to exchange on the
President's southern tour.[1]

LS, RG 56, Letters to and from the Collector at Alexandria, National Archives;
copy, RG 56, Letters to Collectors at Small Ports, "Set G," National Archives.
  1. This is the same letter that was sent to John Daves on this date.

To Benjamin Lincoln

Treasury Department, March 18, 1791. "Inclosed is a copy of a
Letter of the same date with this to the Commissioner of Loans [1] for

the State of Massachusetts. You will do what is therein mentioned in reference to yourself. . . ."

L[S], RG 36, Collector of Customs at Boston, Letters from the Treasury, 1789–1808, National Archives; copy, RG 56, Letters to the Collector at Boston, National Archives; copy, RG 56, Letters to Collectors at Small Ports, "Set G," National Archives.
    1. H to Nathaniel Appleton, March 18, 1791.

From Benjamin Lincoln

Boston, March 18, 1791. Describes case of a schooner from Nova Scotia, which was seized because it was under thirty tons.[1] Tells of vessel from the West Indies whose captain attempted to smuggle six barrels of sugar and one barrel of coffee. Encloses petition from Christopher Saddler which "by some accident has been delayed it should have been forwarded to you some months since."

LC, RG 36, Collector of Customs at Boston, Letter Book, 1790–1797, National Archives; two copies, RG 56, Letters from the Collector at Boston, National Archives.
    1. Section 70 of "An Act to provide more effectually for the collection of the duties imposed by law on goods, wares and merchandise imported into the United States, and on the tonnage of ships or vessels" provided that no foreign goods subject to duty could be imported from a foreign port in vessels of less than thirty tons (*1 Stat.* 177 [August 4, 1790]).

Treasury Department Circular to the Commissioners of Loans

[*Philadelphia, March 18, 1791.* On March 30, 1791, Nathaniel Appleton wrote to Hamilton: "I am this Evening favoured with your Circular Letters of 17th and 18 instant." *Circular of March 18 not found.*]

To Wilhem and Jan Willink, Nicholaas and Jacob Van Staphorst, and Nicholas Hubbard

Treasury Department,
March 18th. 1791.

Gentlemen,
    The Treasurer of the United States has been directed to draw upon

you, a Bill, at ten days sight, in favor of the Secretary of State, for ninety nine thousand Guilders, which you will dispose of, according to directions to be given you by, Mr. Jefferson.[1]

I am &c. Alexander Hamilton.

Messrs. Willink, Van Staphorst and Hubbard.
Amsterdam.

Copy, RG 233, Reports of the Treasury Department, 1792–1793, Vol. III, National Archives. This letter was enclosed in H's "Report on Foreign Loans," February 13, 1793.
1. On March 19, 1791, Jefferson wrote to Willink, Van Staphorst, and Hubbard: "Congress having appropriated the sum of 40,000 Dollars annually to the department of state in the transaction of it's foreign business, I inclose you the Treasurer's bill on you for 90,000 florins supposed equivelent to the beforementioned sum of dollars. You will be pleased to open an account therefore with the 'Secretary of State for the United States of America' wherein you will credit him this draught. This arrangement being taken only this day, & the vessel by which this goes, sailing early tommorow morning I have only time to observe to you that the allowances to mr Short, mr Carmichael, Collo. Humphreys, & mr Dumas, with some special expences from the 1st. day of July 1790. to July 1, 1791. are to be debited to this account, as I shall more particularly explain to you by the first conveyance which shall occur: and that, till I send you such explanation, you are desired to answer any draughts of theirs for the above purposes. Colo. Humphreys will have to draw on you immediately for 4500. dollars his outfit, & about a thousand dollars salary, and it is principally to advise you of his draught and to authorise you to answer it that I hasten to forward the bill on you before I have time to direct specially what demands you are to answer from it, but this shall soon follow" (ALS, Thomas Jefferson Papers, Library of Congress).

From James Jarvis [1]

Philadelphia, March 19, 1791. Applies for "the appointment . . . to go and reside within the Emperor of Morrocco's dominions."

ALS, Hamilton Papers, Library of Congress.
1. Jarvis was a New York speculator whose most notorious financial transaction was the abortive contract made with the Board of Treasury in 1787 to supply the United States with copper coin. See Samuel Broome to H, August 13, 1788.

From George Washington

United States of America [March 19, 1791]

Pay or cause to be paid to the Secretary of State Forty thousand Dollars to be applied to the purposes of the Act, intitled "An Act providing the means of Intercourse between the United States and foreign Nations," [1] for which this shall be your warrant.

Given under my hand at Philadelphia the nineteenth day of March, in the year one thousand seven hundred & ninety one.

G: Washington

To the Secretary of the Treasury.

LC, George Washington Papers, Library of Congress.
   1. Congress provided forty thousand dollars annually for the diplomatic service (1 *Stat.* 128–29 [July 1, 1790]).

To Otho H. Williams

Treasury Department
March 19th. 1791.

Dupe
Sir

I have placed in the hands of the Commissioner of Loans in the State of Maryland [1] sundry draughts the direction of which he is instructed to fill with the name of the Cashier of either of the Banks of North America or New York or with your name as he may find the demand of the purchasers to be. The bills drawn upon you which were suspended when you were last here will continue to be suspended. It is my wish that on the receipt hereof you give Mr. Harwood immediate advice of the Monies in your hands, and that you can pay any of those bills which he may fill up with your direction to such amount—also that you are instructed to pay him any sum over the draughts he may have, not exceeding Five thousand Dollars provided you have or shall have the same within the time of his making payment of the ensuing April quarters interest.

You will keep him advised by post and by good private opportunities of the State of your Cash till he informs you that he has sufficient provision for the interest which he is to pay.

I am, Sir,   Your Obedt. servant   Alexander Hamilton

Otho H. Williams Esqr.
Collector of the Customs
Baltimore.

LS, Columbia University Libraries.
　1. Thomas Harwood.

From Nathaniel Appleton

Boston, March 20, 1791. "I wrote you twice the 16 instant. . . . I now send you copy of the same lest the original should miscarry. . . . I have issued no Certificate to non-subscribers or for Deposits. . . ." [1]

LC, RG 53, Massachusetts State Loan Office, Letter Book, 1785–1791, Vol. "259–M," National Archives.
　1. See H to Appleton, March 5, 1791.

To Edward Carrington

[*Philadelphia, March 21, 1791.* "The compensation annexed to that office [1] is to consist of a Salary of One Thousand dollars per Annum and one per Cent of the product of the duties on the Spirits which shall be distilled within your district. . . . The subdivision of your district into surveys of Inspection has been deferred by the President, to be done, in the course of his journey. He will write to you from Georgetown fixing a period at which you are to meet him at Richmond. . . . The law [2] contemplates three descriptions of Officers; a Supervisor, who is to have chief direction within a district, Inspectors, who under him are to manage the business within certain Surveys." *Letter not found.*] [3]

LS, sold by the American Art Association, November 24, 1924, Lot 331.
　1. Carrington had been appointed supervisor of the District of Virginia.
　2. See Section 4 of "An Act repealing, after the last day of June next, the duties heretofore laid upon Distilled Spirits imported from abroad, and laying others in their stead; and also upon Spirits distilled within the United States, and for appropriating the same" (1 *Stat.* 199–200 [March 3, 1791]).
　3. Text taken from an extract in the dealer's catalogue.

To Edward Carrington

[*Philadelphia, March 21, 1791.* On April 4, 1791, Carrington wrote to Hamilton: "The private letter which you was so good as to accompany your Official communication [1] with. . . ." *Private letter not found.*]

　1. H to Carrington, March 21, 1791.

From William Ellery

Custom House
Newport [Rhode Island] Mh. 21 1791

Sir,

This will be accompanied by my weekly return of Cash, the copy of a memorandum of the change of master on a Certifict. of Registry No. 5 which issued from this Office, and with a draft No. 728 dated 9th Novr 1789 drawn upon me by Saml. Meredith Tr. in favour of the Cashr. of bank of New york for one hundred Dollars.

Your letter of the 5th. of this month [1] did not come to hand until the 18th. On the day I recd. it, by a private opportunity, I advised the Commr. of Loans [2] of the money in my hands, and will by every post and by every private opportunity, give him similar advice, and will pay to his order whatever specie may be in my hands at any time during the present month; and my returns I will continue with exact punctuality.

On the 17th. instant I recd. a letter from the Commr. of Loans dated the 16th. in which, agreeably to your direction, he inquired of me what monies I should probably have in my office the last day of this month, and to which I gave an immediate answer.

I have the honour to be   Sir   Yr. most obedt servt.   W Ellery Collr

A Hamilton Esqr.
Secry of Treasy

LC, Newport Historical Society, Newport, Rhode Island.
   1. See "Treasury Department Circular to the Collectors of the Customs," March 5, 1791.
   2. The commissioner of loans for Rhode Island was Jabez Bowen.

To William Seton

[*Philadelphia, March 21, 1791.* In his letter to Hamilton on March 28, 1791, Seton referred to "the Bond endorsed in your letter of the 21st." *Letter not found.*]

Treasury Department Circular
to the Collectors of the Customs

[*Philadelphia, March 21, 1791.* On July 1, 1791, Meletiah Jordan wrote to Hamilton: "Your Letter (Circular) of the 21st March, observes I should inform you what Post Office would be most convenient for me to get my Letters from." *Circular not found.*]

From Alexander Dallas

[Philadelphia, March 22, 1791]

Sir.

In compliance with the Resolution of the Senate and House of Representatives of the United States, approved the 23d of September 1789,[1] the Legislature of this Commonwealth passed a law, to provide for the custody of Prisoners, committed under the authority of the United States, in which the respective Gaolers were directed to transmit a Calender of such prisoners to the Executive, that order might be taken for the payment of the allowances and expences, on the part of the United States,[2] agreably to the assumption contained in the above mentioned resolution.

I have now the honor, in obedience to the orders of the Governor,[3] to inclose a copy of the Calender which has been transmitted to him, by the Gaoler of the Debtors apartment of the prison of the City and County of Philadelphia, and to request, that measures may be taken for discharging the sum, that appears to be due from the United States on this account.

I am, Sir   Your mo: obedt hble Servt.   A J Dallas.

Philada., March 22d., 1791.
Alexander Hamilton, Esquire,
Secretary of the Treasury, &c.

LC, Division of Public Records, Pennsylvania Historical and Museum Commission, Harrisburg.
 1. Resolution 2, 1 *Stat.* 96–97.
 2. *Pennsylvania Statutes*, XXIII, 419–20.
 3. Thomas Mifflin.

To Thomas Jones, Brockholst Livingston, and John H. Livingston

[*Philadelphia, March 22, 1791.* On the back of a letter dated March 15, 1791, from Jones and Brockholst and John H. Livingston, Hamilton wrote: "Answered 22d March 91." *Letter not found.*]

To John Beale Bordley [1]

Treasury Department, March 23, 1791. "The President having been pleased to appoint you one of the Commissioners [2] to receive subscriptions to the Bank of the United States, you will find in this inclosure his commission. . . ."

LS, Maryland Historical Society, Baltimore.
 1. Bordley, a lawyer and landholder on the Eastern Shore of Maryland, moved to Philadelphia in 1791.
 2. See H to Tobias Lear, March 23, 1791.

To Tobias Lear

Treasury Department
March 23d. 1791

Sir
   I find it necessary to request of you the Commissions of the several gentlemen, whom the President was pleased to appoint as Commissioners to receive subscriptions to the Bank of the United States. The persons appointed are

> Thomas Willing ⎫
> David Rittenhouse ⎬ of Pennsylvania
> Saml. Howell ⎭

John Beale Bordley of Maryland and
Lambert Cadwalader of New Jersey.
   You will oblige me by procuring the Seals to be affixed and the Commissions sent to this Office by two oClock this day.
   I am sir   Yr. most Obt. Servt.   Alexander Hamilton

LC, George Washington Papers, Library of Congress.

From Tobias Lear

[*Philadelphia*] *March 23, 1791.* "I have the honor to transmit you agreeably to your request [1] the five commissions for the Commissioners to receive subscriptions to the Bank of the United States. . . ."

LC, George Washington Papers, Library of Congress.
 1. H to Lear, March 23, 1791.

From John Nicholson

Comptroller General's Office [Philadelphia] March 23d. 1791

Sir

I was yesterday informed by the Auditor [1] that the quarterly payment will be made from the Treasury of the United States for the Interest of Certificates of the registered Debt as the Credits of the same appear on the Books of the Treasury as to non subscribers on the first of April next. By an Act of the Legislature of Pennsylvania passed in 1786 a Loan was opened by this State for Certificates of Debts due by the United States to Citizens of this Commonwealth: [2] And in virtue thereof a great number of Certificates of the Registered debt as aforesaid was so loaned; and in most cases they were not assigned by the party before Loaning to the Commonwealth, but a power to transfer them to the State in the usual forms in which I am named attorney was executed and filed with the Certificates: These yet appear on the Register's Books to the Credit of those persons respectively altho in fact are the Property of the Commonwealth. I did not make the transfer of them to the State because where the new loan Certificate of this State hath not been redeemed the holder on delivering up the others is intitled to those identical Certificates again from me and where the holder is not an alienee nothing more is necessary than to return him his own Certificates and renew his letter of Attorney.[3] Whereas had they been assigned to the State such person must have waited a reassignment from the State which would have required two transfers at the Office both which by this mode hath been saved; with alienees this double transfer is indispensable. I am making out a Schedule of all Certificates of the above description the

Property of the State or remaining unexchanged which will be furnished immediately, and would in behalf of the State request that you
would either suspend directing payment of the Interest on the Credits
contained in said Schedule for this quarter or that they might be
directed previously to be transferred to the Commonwealth in toto,
so as to appear to this State's Credit on the Books.

I am   Sir   Yr &c

J. N.

The Honble. Alexr. Hamilton Esqr.
Secy. Treasury United States.

LC, Division of Public Records, Pennsylvania Historical and Museum Commission, Harrisburg.
  1. Oliver Wolcott, Jr.
  2. "An Act for the Further Relief of the Public Creditors who are Citizens
of This State By Receiving on Loan Certain Debts of the United States of
America and for Funding the Same and for Paying the Annual Interest of Such
Loans and the Interest of Certain Debts of This State Every Six Months"
(*Pennsylvania Statutes*, XII, 158–64 [March 1, 1786]).
  3. See Thomas Smith to H, February 14, 1791, note 1.

To Nathaniel Appleton

[*Philadelphia, March 24, 1791*. On April 9, 1791, Appleton wrote
to Hamilton: "Your special Letter 24th March . . . and also your
Circular Letter 25th March are this minute come to hand." *Letter of
March 24 not found.*]

From John Cochran [1]

[*New York, March 24, 1791*. On March 28, 1791, Hamilton wrote
to Cochran: "Yours of the 24th is just come to hand." *Letter not
found.*]

  1. Cochran was commissioner of loans for New York.

From Rufus King [1]

[*New York, March 24, 1791*. "The Legislature of this State have
incorporated the Bank,[2] limiting its capital to a million of Dollars and
its duration to *twenty years*.[3] The Treasurer is authorised to subscribe to the Loan proposed to Congress all the Continental paper in

the Treasury [4] and by a bill that passed the Legislature this morning, he is directed to take in behalf of the State, *one hundred and ninety shares* in the *National* Bank.[5] I have seen a letter from Mr. John Taylor [6] of Albany which has created some uneasiness on account of our frontier settlements. He says 'there is great reason to apprehend danger from the Indians in this quarter;' but does not mention, nor have I been able to learn the grounds of this apprehension. You are sensible that almost every person here is interested in our Western Lands; their value depends upon the settlement of the frontiers, these settlements depend on Peace with the Indians, and indeed the bare possibility of a war with the six Nations, would break up our whole frontier. It is from this state of things that the war with the Wabash Indians is so much disrelished here. The Legislature have authorised the Governor to draw money from the Treasury and to take such measures as he may judge suitable to *preserve the good will* of the neighbouring Indians.[7] I have said, and I presume it will be the case, that all prudent steps will be pursued to keep the six Nations quiet; that we were embarked and that it had become necessary to go forward with the War, if peace could be obtained by no other means; but I am more and more convinced that it behoves the government if practicable to finish this Indian business, in the course of the summer."
Letter not found.]

Extract from H to George Washington, March 27, 1791 (LC, George Washington Papers, Library of Congress). A shorter extract, dated "about 1 Ap. 1791," may be found in the New-York Historical Society, New York City.

1. At this time King was a Federalist Senator from New York.
2. The Bank of New York.
3. See "An Act to incorporate the stockholders of the Bank of New York" (*Laws of the State of New York*, III, 237–41 [March 21, 1791]).
4. "An Act for the relief of the creditors of this State" (*Laws of the State of New York*, III, 214–16 [February 23, 1791]). Gerard Bancker was treasurer of New York State.
5. "An Act directing the treasurer of this State to subscribe to the bank of the United States" (*Laws of the State of New York*, III, 256 [March 24, 1791]).
6. Tayler was an Albany merchant and land speculator.
7. After the failure of the Harmar expedition against the western Indians in the fall of 1790, Indian attacks against the frontier settlements increased in intensity. The settlements in Ohio and Kentucky were not the only ones to suffer. In the spring of 1791 a group of white men attacked a party of Seneca at Big Beaver Creek in western Pennsylvania and killed three men and a woman (*ASP, Indian Affairs*, I, 145). Several similar instances resulted in a series of raids on Pennsylvania settlements above Pittsburgh. Officials of New York became alarmed that the fighting might spread to their state, and on March 24, 1791, the New York legislature authorized Governor George Clinton to draw up to one thousand pounds to be applied "in such manner as he shall judge most expedient, to prevent any incursion of hostile Indians into this State" (*Laws of the State of New York*, III, 252).

To John Nicholson

[*Philadelphia, March 24, 1791.* On March 25, 1791, Nicholson wrote
to Hamilton: "Your favor of the 24th with which I was honored. . . ."
Letter not found.]

To Abraham Wilkerson

[Philadelphia, March 24, 1791]

Sir

I left in the hands of Robert Troupe Esquire all the papers relative
to the business of *Mr. Charles Godwin* which he was directed to deliver to you, in conformity to Mr. Godwin's request. If you have not
yet received the papers, you may have them by applying to Mr.
Troupe. I am   Sir   Your Obed. &   hum. Servt   A. Hamilton

March 24, 1791
Mr. Abraham Wilkerson

ALS, anonymous donor.

From John Beale Bordley

Philadelphia, March 25, 1791. Acknowledges receipt of commission [1] to receive subscriptions to the stock of the Bank of the United
States.

ALS, Maryland Historical Society, Baltimore.
  1. See H to Bordley, March 23, 1791.

From John Nicholson

[Philadelphia, March 25, 1791]

Sir,

Your favor of the   [1] with which I was honored had placed
the certificates of Registered debt the property of Penna. but not yet
assigned into as good a situation I thought as we could have desired,[2]
but it hath been since suggested to me that the arrangement with

the bank [3] is to be considered as payment of one quarter Interest, whether the party apply for it or not. If this should be the case and when these Certificates come afterwards to be assigned they should be granted for one quarters Interest less. Altho the party would be debared from receivg. his interest the state would likewise be preclued therefrom. A power of attorney would be wanting from the persons who appear as the creditors on the books. Altho I flatter myself that this is the case, yet the possibility of a measure which so much concerns the interest of this state must plead my excuse for troubling you again on the subject, as it may be possible now to devise some remedy which could not be done when the business shall be farther advanced.

I have the honor to be   &ca.   J N

The Honble Alex. Hamilton Esqr.   Mar 25th. 1791
Secy. Try.

ADf, Division of Public Records, Pennsylvania Historical and Museum Commission, Harrisburg; LC, Division of Public Records, Pennsylvania Historical and Museum Commission.
    1. Space left blank in MS. In the letter book copy the date is given as "the 24th." Letter not found.
    2. See Nicholson to H, March 23, 1791.
    3. Nicholson is referring to the Bank of North America.

Treasury Department Circular to the Commissioners of Loans

[*Philadelphia, March 25, 1791.* On April 9, 1791, Nathaniel Appleton wrote to Hamilton: "Your special Letter 24th March . . . and also your Circular Letter 25th March are this minute come to hand." *Circular of March 25 not found.*]

From Jonathan Burrall [1]

General Post Office
Phila Mar. 26th 1791

Sir
    In the absence of the Postmaster General [2] I have received your letter respecting a Balance due from the Estate of Edwd Davies late Depy. Postmaster in Savannah.

The situation in which the late P. M. G.[3] left his business, makes it peculiarly necessary, in my opinion, that he should be called upon for a settlement of his Accounts.

There are balances due from his Deputies to the Amount of 15,000 Dollars, or upwards, a considerable part of which will be lost. The Ordinance of Congress of the 18th October 1782 [4] Vests the post-master General with the power of appointing his Deputies, and makes him responsible for their conduct. He has generally taken Bonds as security for their fidelity, which are made payable to him, his Heirs Executors &c. It may therefore be a question whether suits can be commenced against them on behalf of the United States, as Debts due to the public. In several instances however those Bonds are greatly short of the Sum due. One Deputy in particular owes 4000 Dollars, and the Bond given by him is for 1,000 Dollars.

Edward Davies's Account is closed in the Books. It appears that he never rendered any Accounts from the time of his appointment to the Day of his Death. That Mr. Watt [5] the present postmaster at Savannah, examined his Books and informed the Postmaster General, that there was 632 44/90 Dollars due from him—that the late Board of Treasury drew a Warrant on the late Postmaster General for this sum in favor of the Commissioner of Loans—and his order on the Representative of Mr. Davies was taken in payment. In June last this order was re-turned to the Treasury Office unpaid and the Amt carried to the Debits of Mr. Hazards Account. The Bond given by Mr. Davies is for *300 Dollars*. There are no Documents in this Office from which an Account can be formed against his Estate and it appears to me very doubtful whether any thing more than the Penalty of the Bond can be recovered.

The Postmaster Generals responsibility for the fidelity of his Depu-ties will doubtless be considered as a *qualified responsibility* and the public Interest requires that the matter should be brought to a decis-sion and effectual means be taken to secure as much of the money as possible.

I am sir &c   J B.

LC, RG 28, Letter Books, 1789–1794, National Archives.
   1. Burrall was first Assistant Postmaster General.
   2. Samuel Osgood. Letter not found.
   3. Ebenezer Hazard had been Postmaster General from 1782 to 1789.
   4. JCC, XXIII, 670–79.
   5. Alexander Watt.

To Tobias Lear

[Philadelphia, March 26, 1791]

Dr: Sir

I have just received information that General Hand [1] will serve as Inspector of the revenue, in which case it was the Presidents pleasure that his name should be inserted in the Blank commission, which was to be left for the purpose. You will please accordingly to have the name of Edward Hand inserted, & to get the commission completed. I shall be glad to receive it this forenoon.

Yrs. sincerely   A Hamilton

Philada. March 26. 1791.

LC, George Washington Papers, Library of Congress.
   1. Edward Hand. See George Washington to H, March 15, 1791.

From Tobias Lear

[*Philadelphia*] *March 27, 1791.* "About two hours ago I had the honor to receive your letter of yesterday, which the door keeper of your Office says he forgot to deliver sooner. This will account for your not receiving the commission for General Hand yesterday forenoon as you requested. I have now the honor to enclose it. . . ."

LC, George Washington Papers, Library of Congress.

To George Washington

[*Philadelphia*] *March 27, 1791.* "I have embraced the first moment of leisure to execute your wish, on the subject to which the enclosed notes are applicable. They are neither so accurate nor so full, as I should have been glad to make them; but they are all that my situation has permitted. Nothing new has occurred in my Department worth mentioning. I thought that the following extract of a letter from Mr. King might not be wholly uninteresting, and I therefore make it. . . .[1] The clue to Mr. Taylors apprehensions seems to be a late

LC, George Washington Papers, Library of Congress.
   1. For this extract, see Rufus King to H, March 24, 1791.

murder of some friendly indians within the limits of this State;[2] the
particulars of which I take it for granted will be made known to you
by the Secretary at War."

[ENCLOSURE]

Notes on the Advantages of a National Bank[3]

[Philadelphia, March 27, 1791]

The Report to the House of representatives proposing the plan of
a Bank,[4] enters fully into the advantages attending institutions of this
nature. They are summarily these.

1. They tend to increase the active or productive capital of a
country by keeping it in more constant employment and by adding
to the real, an artificial capital in the credit of the Bank which answers
equally with specie the purpose of money.

2. They increase and quicken circulation from the foregoing cause
from the introduction of Bank notes as money, from the greater
facility of remittances in notes than in money, from their obviateing
the necessity in a great number of cases of transporting specie back-
wards and forwards, from their rendering it unnecessary to lock up
specie for the periodical payments of interest &c. whence a greater
plenty of specie is left in circulation and an additional medium is
furnished. And thence

3. They assist industry and Trade. This they also do by facilitating
loans to individuals within the spheres of their immediate operation.
Accordingly whereever they have been established they have given a

2. This is a reference to the murder by white men of four friendly Indians at
Big Beaver Creek. An entry in the executive minutes of Governor Thomas Mifflin for April 23, 1791, describes this incident as follows: "The Governor having
received information upon oath that four friendly Indians were murdered on
the Ninth of March last by a body of armed men, under the Command of Samuel
Brady and Francis McGuire, who had fled from Justice into the State of Virginia
addressed His Excellency Beverly Randolph Esquire upon the subject and required that the above named two persons should be delivered up to this State
having jurisdiction of their crime according to the Provisions contained in the
second Section of the fourth Article of the Constitution of the United States"
(*Pennsylvania Archives*, 9th ser., I, 89).
3. LC, George Washington Papers, Library of Congress.
4. "Second Report on the Further Provision Necessary for Establishing Public Credit (Report on a National Bank)," December 13, 1790.

new spring to Agriculture, Manufactures & Commerce. This has been most remarkably exemplified of late years in Scotland & Ireland; and has been confirmed by the experience of the United States.

4. They facilitate the payment of taxes by keeping the circulation more full and active every where, and by direct loans to the Merchants to pay their duties.

5. They aid the Government *in ordinary*, by facilitating the Collection of taxes; by rendering remittances to and from the Treasury more easy, safe, and free from expence, and lastly, in extraordinary cases by being an instrument of loans in sudden emergencies. The drawing a large capital to a point, and the vast credit annexed to it enable Banks to come at once to the aid of the Government in a manner that no individual resources are equal to. This was felt during the latter periods of the late war in the most important operations; and even at this moment it is the only resort for whatever pecuniary aids may be found necessary for carrying into execution the measures taken for the defence of the frontier.

But it is said admitting the utility of Banks in general, why establish a new one, since there are such institutions already in being? The answers to this are,

1. That all these institutions now rest on state foundations and may cease to exist if the State Legislatures shou'd not be inclined to continue. That of Pennsylvania has virtually surrendered its old charter [5] by accepting a new one incompatible with it. It is therefore neither compatible with the dignity nor interest of the United States to suffer so important an engine of its administration to depend on so precarious a tenure & one so foreign from itself.

2. By being mere local institutions they cannot serve as engines of a general circulation. For this they have neither sufficient capital nor have they enough of the confidence of all parts of the Union. As *local* institutions they are rather objects of jealousy.

3. They would be improper foundations on which to rest the security of the Public revenue by suffering their paper to be receivable in all payments to the public.

1. Because they have not adequate capital.

2. Because their continuance or discontinuance does not depend on the will of the U. States.

5. The charter of 1787.

3. Because the Government of the Union can have no *inspection* of their proceedings, consequently no security for their prudent administration of their affairs.

4. They are too limitted in their capital to afford such extensive aid to the United States as they may require in future emergencies. They may answer well enough for an Indian War; but in a War with an European power they could do nothing adequate to the public necessities.

5. Their constitutions have not those precautions which are calculated to guard against the abuses to which such institutions are subject. They are therefore in this light also insecure reliances for national circulation.

But admitting a National Bank ought to be instituted, the Duration is said to be too long, and contrary to precedent; too long because the affairs of this country from its peculiar situation must change so rapidly as to render it questionable, whether a good thing now will continue to be a good thing for twenty Years. With regard to precedent it is presumed that the matter is mistaken. The Banks of Venice, Genoa, Hamburgh & Amsterdam are understood to be indefinite in point of duration. The Bank of England indeed has been limitted to different periods under different circumstances: the assertion that it was in its first creation limited to 11 years is not founded. It was incorporated for an indefinite period; but there was a right reserved to the Government at the end of eleven Years to *pay off* the Debt which constituted its Capital and *thereby* to dissolve the corporation. But it could not be dissolved nor was it to cease in any other way.

With regard to the argument drawn from the changing situation of the Country, the answer is, that Banks are not novel institutions. They have been long tried, and in different Countries. They had eleven [6] years experience in their favour in this Country: their *effects* therefore can *now* be perfectly judged of and pronounced upon with certainty. They are *necessary* in Countries little advanced in wealth; they have been found very *useful* in Countries greatly advanced in wealth.

In a Country like this, which having vast tracts of vacant land

6. In MS "even." Presumably this is a reference to the fact that the Bank of North America had been established in 1781.

and few manufactures, can have no great abundance of specie; the auxiliary circulation of Banks must be peculiarly useful. Though the Country may advance in manufactures & in wealth considerably in the course of twenty years, yet very obvious causes must leave it, during all that period, in a condition to stand in need of the same auxiliary. Besides as has been remarked, Banks are at this day found useful in the wealthiest Countries—Holland, England, France.

If the nature of the institution is attended to, it must be perceived that its relations to the future are as easy to be comprehended and pronounced upon, as its relations to the present. Its operation must be always of the same tendency, and there is no more difficulty in pronouncing that it will be good for twenty Years to come, as easily as that it is good at the present moment.

How far one place or another may be the proper seat of it, may be a thing variable by time: but the time which can vary this must evidently be more than twenty years. It is manifest that a *large commercial City* with a great deal of *capital* and *business* must be the fittest seat of the Bank. It is morally certain that for twenty years to come Philadelphia will continue to have as good pretensions as any of the principal trading Cities now established. And with regard to the future seat of the Government, it is morrally impossible that it can become in less than twenty years a place of sufficient trade and capital to be the principal scene of the operations of the National Bank. Governments must always act upon reasonable probabilities and in doing so, they can hardly fail to do right.

The motives to a considerable duration to the Charter of the Bank were these—to strengthen the inducement to men of property throughout the United States to embark in it, and to enhance the value of the public stock by a prospect of greater advantage.

This last idea is of great moment. All those acquainted with the operation of the thing will admit that the institution in question has been a main cause of the rise of the public Debt. It operated upon it like a charm. Now it is evident that its effect in this way must have been greater or less in proportion to the prospect of advantage which a long or short duration afforded.

The raising of the public Debt is a circumstance of immense importance in the affairs of the Country. It is tantamount to the establishment of public credit. No man can be in credit whose Bonds are selling for one third or one half their value: the same thing in respect to a Government. Besides, while the Debt is low, foreigners become possessed of the property of the Citizens of this Country greatly below its true value. And every shilling which they pay less for the Debt than its true value is so much loss to the Country. The distress to this Country would have been prodigious in time to come if it had had to pay millions to foreigners for which they had given little or no value. And the existence of a public Debt would have been truly a curse.

As far as this essential object might have been made to give way to the speculative possibility of a better arrangement of the Bank in reference to future changes in the situation of the Country, it would have been to sacrifice substance to shadow, reality to supposition.

Objection. The advantages of the Bank will not be *equal* in all the States.

This is hardly even an objection to a measure of Government, because there is scarcely one to which it may not be objected. Is there a law for the advancement of Navigation? It will benefit *most* those states which have *most* aptitudes for Navigation. Is there a Law for the encouragement of manufactures? The same thing may be observed—Is there *one* for the encouragement of particular objects of Agriculture? The same observation applies. What is the duty upon foreign Cotton? As far as its operation may correspond with its intention it will be a direct bounty upon the Industry of a few of the States. For there are only particular states adapted to the raising of Cotton.

In short such is the state of human affairs that public measures unavoidably benefit or injure some part more than others. Consequently, that must be a good public measure which *benefits* all the *parts* of a Country, though some more than others. If *all* gain, the general mass of public prosperity is promoted, though some gain more than others.

It is certain the operations of the proposed Bank will be most directly useful to the spot upon which they are carried on; but by aiding general circulation, and establishing a convenient medium of remittance & exchange between the States, all will be benefitted in different degrees.

If branches are established the immediate benefit will be diffused still more extensively.

Objection. It will interfere with the several State Banks. This cannot happen, unless branches are established in the same States. If this is done no inconvenience to the community can accrue. Either the State Bank and the branch of the National Bank can go on together, and then Trade, & Industry will be promoted by larger supplies, or the one will subvert the other. If the state Bank subverts the branch the injury is at least temporary. If the Branch subverts the State Bank, it furnishes to the commerce & industry of the place a better substitute; one which, to all the common advantages, will add this peculiar one, the affording a medium of circulation which is useful in all the States and not merely on the spot, and can of course be employed in the intercourse with other States.

But in fact all this is exaggerated supposition. It is not probable, except at the immediate seat of the Bank, where the competition will be compensated by obvious advantages, that there will be any interference. It can never be the interest of the National Bank to quarrel with the local institutions. The local Institutions will in all likelihood either be adopted by the national Bank or establishments where they exist will be foreborne.

Lastly an attentive consideration of the tendency of an institution, immediately connected with the national Government which will interweave itself into the *monied* interest of every State, which will by its notes insinuate itself into every branch of industry and will affect the interests of all classes of the community; ought to produce strong prepossessions in its favor in all who consider the firm establishment of the National Government as necessary to the safety & happiness of the Country, and who at the same time believe that it stands in need of additional props.

To John Cochran

Treasury Department
March 28th 1791

Sir

Yours of the 24th [1] is just come to hand.

I have directed the Treasurer [2] to transmit by tomorrow's post a draft in your favour on the Bank of New York for Twenty six thousand two hundred and fifty dollars; which according to your statement will enable you to pay the ensuing quarters interest.

I am content with the plan you intend to pursue with the Bank; though my idea was that the business might have been shortened and trouble saved to yourself and the Creditor, by your engaging the Bank to transact *in the first instance* with the Creditors, taking for you the receipts which are required as your vouchers with the Treasury. This is the mode pursued here.

I shall cause to be shortly transmitted to you a form for the rendering of your accounts concerning stationary and Clerk hire.

I am with great consideration   Sir   Your obedient servant

Alexander Hamilton

John Cochran Esquire
Commissioner of Loans
New York

ALS, Charles Roberts Autograph Collection of the Haverford College Library, Haverford, Pennsylvania.
1. Letter not found.
2. Samuel Meredith.

From William Ellery

Custom House
Newport [Rhode Island] Mh 28 1791

Sir,

Inclosed is my weekly return of Cash and a Certificate of Registry No. 15, dated at the Port of Dighton March 30 1790, and delivered up on account of transfer of property.

On the Twenty first day of this month I received a letter from the Commr. of loans [1] informing me that on inquiry of Col. Olney [2] he found, that he would be able to furnish as much money as would be wanted to pay the first Quarters interest, and that it would be therefore unnecessary for me to furnish him with any further account of the State of my funds.

On the 25th. of this month I recd. a letter from the Assist. Secry [3] expressing your wish that I would transmit as soon as might be convenient the most exact returns of decked vessels built in this District &c., and that I might forward from time to time as they may come into my hands any documents that have relation to the commerce navigation, fisheries, manufactures or productions of this State &c.

I have put matters in train to obtain information on the first object, and shall attend to the last. Letters &c similar to those I have heretofore inclosed to you I will in future put into the mails addressed to the Comptroller the Treasurer, and Auditor.

I am   Sir   Yr. most obedt. servant   Wm Ellery Collr

A Hamilton Esqr
Secry of Treasy.

LC, Newport Historical Society, Newport, Rhode Island.
  1. Jabez Bowen.
  2. Jeremiah Olney, collector of customs at Providence.
  3. A copy of this circular letter from Tench Coxe to the collectors of the customs, dated March 10, 1791, may be found in the Hamilton Papers, Library of Congress.

From William Ellery

Custom House
Newport [Rhode Island] Mh. 28th. 1791

Sir,

On the 26th. of this month arrived in this Port the Sloop Betsy of Providence James Munro junr. master.

He reported that he took in his Cargo consisting of Fifty four Hogsheads & ten bbls of Molasses, One hundred and thirty five barrels of sugar, part of a piece of broad Cloth, and one Umbrella at Cape Francois, proceeded therewith to Charleston So. Carolina, but not finding a suitable market, after laying there three Days, he sailed for Providence in this State where the said sloop is owned, and to which port she was destined, without landing any part of his Cargo at said Charleston. I asked him for a certified copy of the Report he made at Charlestown, he told me that he had none, that he was not called upon by the Collector of that District [1] for a report, that he did not know he was obliged by Law to produce a certified copy of a report made at the first District where he arrived to the Collector of the second, and that he received a pass for the Fort from the Collector of Charlestown.

I consider Capt. Munros not having made a report, and obtained a certified copy thereof from the Collector at Charlestown and not having produced the same to me as a breach of the 20 Sect: of the existing Collection Law; [2] but as he appeared to be honest in his declaration, and his neglect seemed to be owing to his ignorance of the Law, I think it adviseable to ask your direction, and not to institute a prosecution against him until your pleasure shall be known.

I am with great esteem   Sir   Yr. most obedt. servt.   W Ellery Collr

A Hamilton Esqr
Secry of the Treasy.

LC, Newport Historical Society, Newport, Rhode Island.
 1. George Abbot Hall.
 2. Section 20 of "An Act to provide more effectually for the collection of the duties imposed by law on goods, wares and merchandise imported into the United States, and on the tonnage of ships or vessels" provided that "before any ship or vessel shall depart from the district in which she shall first arrive, for another district, with goods, wares or merchandise brought in such ship or vessel from a foreign port or place, the duties whereof shall not have been paid or secured, the master or person having the charge or command of such ship or vessel, shall obtain from the collector of the district from which she shall be about to depart (who is hereby required to grant the same) a copy of the report made by such master or person having the charge or command of such ship or vessel, certified by the said collector, together with a certificate of the quantity and particulars of the goods which shall appear to him to have been landed within his district. And within twenty-four hours after the arrival of such ship or vessel within any other district, the said master or person having the charge or command of such ship or vessel shall make report or entry to or with the collector of such other district, producing and showing the said certified copy of his said first report, together with a certificate from each collector of any other district within which any of the goods, wares or merchandise brought in such ship or vessel shall have been before landed, of the quantity and particulars of such of the said goods, wares and merchandise as shall have been so landed in each district respectively" (1 *Stat.* 160 [August 4, 1790]).

From William Seton

Bank of New York 28 March 1791

Sir

Mr. William Hill [1] with two competant Surities have duely executed the Bond endorsed in your letter of the 21st.[2] and I have deliver'd to him the Contract. As you do not desire the Bond to be returned, I hold it for your further orders. Mr. Hill expected he was to receive immediately from this Bank a payment of Five thousand Dollars, but he was informed your orders did not extend to the payment. The letter for Amsterdam goes by the Brig Rebecca, Captn Codwise,[3] now waiting for a wind; those for London went by the Packet. I have the honor to be &c.

LC, Bank of New York, New York City.
1. Hill, a New York City merchant, had been awarded a contract to supply clothing to the Army.
2. Letter not found.
3. George Codwise, a ship captain of New York City. H had first met Codwise when H was still a boy working for Nicholas Cruger's mercantile firm in St. Croix. See H to Nicholas Cruger, October 31, 1771.

From Nathaniel Appleton

Boston, March 30, 1791. "I wrote you 20 instant when I transmitted a duplicate Statement of the Stock apparently standing on my Books. I am this Evening favour'd with your Circular Letters of 17th & 18 instant.[1] In answer to the former, I have recd Register Certificates & admitted them upon the new Loan persuming that your instructions of 19th November [2] permitted it. In evry case I have conformed to the mode therein prescribed. If I am wrong in this, I materially mistook your design. Your instructions of 18 instant respecting powers Attorney shall be duely attended to. I am also favoured with your special Letter 18th. I have disposed of all the Treasurer Drafts & I have since my last recd. of Mr. Higginson [3] on account of Mess Le Roy & Bayard 2500 Dollrs [4] all of which is deposited in the Bank...."

LC, RG 53, Massachusetts State Loan Office, Letter Book, 1785–1791, Vol. "259–M," National Archives.
1. Circular of March 18, 1791, not found.
2. "Treasury Department Circular to the Commissioners of Loans," November 19, 1790.
3. Stephen Higginson.
4. See H to Appleton, March 2, 16, 1791.

From William Playfair [1]

To the Honourable—Hamilton

Paris 30th March 1791

Sir

I take the liberty of writing to you on an affair which concerns a great number of Ividuals as well as myself which liberty I would

ALS, Hamilton Papers, Library of Congress.
1. Playfair was an English adventurer who in 1789 was associated with Joel Barlow in the formation of a French company to sell the Scioto lands. Although

not take if it were not that from the total want of letters in answer to mine to Mr Duer of Newyork I am left in the most Cruel Situation Possible as well as a great number of individuals who have their near Relations in America.

I undertook eighteen Months ago to lay the Foundation of a Colony on the Sioto Lands for the Sale of which M: M: Cutler, Sergent [2] & Duer had given a Procuration of Mr Barlow who himself was without Any of the Means necessary to put in Practice Such a Plan. The Lands were not paid to congress; Mr Barlow had never seen them & knew little about them; he had no money to Expend on the affair, no connexions and did not Speak french. He was made known to me by a third Person [3] & told me his Plan was to sell 3 millions of acres of Land. This was certainly an Idea formed without Reflection as neither an Individual nor any Company could be supposed to pay 18 millions [4] for lands uninhabited & unknown & which did not belong to the Persons who were to sell them.[5] It was three Months after I knew Mr Barlow before I conceived that their was any Means of Undertaking such a thing with any degree of success but the Revolution in France gave me the Idea that an Emigration would be possible & that Individual purchasers might be found. To abridge the History I undertook for 15 Pr cent on the Sales [6] to begin the affair at my own Expence. It was begun but it appeared necessary to give facilities to the First Purchasers who might set an Example to the others, this was done upon the Idea that the affair would go on which in the fact

---

Barlow was William Duer's agent in this business, Duer did not maintain close contact with the proceedings. The venture collapsed in 1790.

2. The Reverend Manasseh Cutler and Winthrop Sargent were both founders of the Ohio Company. Cutler had helped draw up the articles of agreement of the company and went to Ohio in July, 1788, to aid in the establishment of the early Ohio settlements. He returned to Massachusetts in 1789. Sargent, who had surveyed in the Ohio country in 1786, was elected secretary of the Ohio Company in 1787 and was active in the planting of the Ohio settlements. In 1787 Congress appointed him secretary of the Northwest Territory.

For the relationship between the Ohio and Scioto groups, see Davis, *Essays*, I, 130–43.

3. Colonel Samuel Blackden, an American who was selling Kentucky lands in Paris.

4. Eighteen million livres.

5. The Scioto Associates held an option on the land.

6. There is a difference of opinion concerning Playfair's remuneration. See Thomas T. Belote, "The Scioto Speculation and the French Settlement at Gallipolis," *University Studies Published by the University of Cincinnati*, III, No. 3 (September-October, 1907), 24; Davis, *Essays*, I, 213; Milton Cantor, "Life

it did for several months in an astonishing Manner but was stoped short by the want of preparations in America as was promised & Expected. Our Errors in the Prices of Cattle & other things have created great discontents great Expences & merited complaints. The Total want of Letters from America has suspended the affair.[7] There are several hundreds of People who have their Relations in America & who are in the most unquiet state which as I have nothing to show respecting their Relations who are gone is rather an ill looking piece of business. Add to that that Mr Barlow who was here has Run away in debt without informing me or any other Person.

I have on all sides heard the Best character of Mr Duer & I am informed that he Runs a great Risque of Being Burned by the advances he has made. It is Clear likewise that the whole Colony will suffer if the affair stops where it is but I am afraid it will do so as there has been a Mr Walker here who said he was commissioned by the Company to look into things but who *Refused to shew his power of attorney or procuration* and who Refused to Enter with any degree of frankness or Candor into the Nature of the affair but who would considder it as goods bought & sold at a fixed Price on Each side. The fact is that he was disappointed as to some personal views & that from Mr Barlows want of Informing Mr Dewer the quantity of sales Mr Dewer had immagined when Walker left new york that there were one million of acres sold when their was not one hundred & fifty thousand acres & one 4th of that not paid for in values that are yet Realized.

I know that the Engagement taken with the Treasury of the United States by the company at New-york [8] is not, nor cannot be fulfilled in the original terms therefore I am Ignorant Whether Messrs Duer & Co continue in the affair or not. I have the honour therefore Sir to adress myself to you & to send a memoir on the subject which is in

of Joel Barlow" (Unpublished Ph.D. Dissertation, Columbia University, 1954), 101.

7. Duer did not reply to Barlow's letters, but in 1790 he and his associates sent Benjamin Walker to France to straighten out the company's affairs.

8. In his study of the Scioto purchase, Theodore Belote described this transaction as follows:

"On October 27, 1789, Manasseh Cutler and Winthrop Sargent completed their negotiations with the Treasury Board for nearly six million acres of land. Two distinct contracts were drawn. One of these consisted in an absolute purchase of a million and a half acres of land lying along the Ohio River. . . . The

French & which I take to be a justification of My Intentions & of my
Conduct viewing the affair in its whole Extent which I did & I am
surprised that any Person can do otherwise as the small affairs done
were but to begin a colony and I will venture to say that if that
Colony[9] is in a thriving State & the People Contented and if at the
same time a method is taken to Sell here without any great derangement in the Present form of sales there will be more than half the
lands sold in Six months & Sold upon advantageous terms. If so then
the United states would gain a number of Inhabitants, their Treasury

---

second contract, like the first, was drawn between the Treasury Board and
Manasseh Cutler and Winthrop Sargent, the latter acting for themselves and
associates. This second contract was an option to purchase all the lands lying between the Ohio and Scioto rivers and the western boundary of the seventeenth
range of townships, extending north to the tenth township from the Ohio. This
contract included also the tract of land west of the seventeenth range of townships, south of the tenth township from the Ohio River, and north of the Ohio
Company's purchase. . . . From the river at its back, this was termed the
'Scioto Tract.' . . .

"In the eyes of Congress, officially at least, the two contracts described above
were parts of one and the same transaction, and the Ohio Company was responsible for both. The Ohio Company had bought outright the first tract which was
supposed to contain a million and a half of acres. The second or Scioto tract
was to be paid for in six equal installments. The prompt payment by the Ohio
Company for its one and a half millions of acres was the condition of the long
term of credit allowed the Scioto Company by Congress. To make sure of the
second contract, the first one had to be carried out, and William Duer advanced
one hundred and forty-three thousand dollars to assist the Ohio Company in
paying Congress, in order that his own interests in connection with the second
contract might thereby be advanced. . . .

"On October 27, 1787, Manasseh Cutler and Winthrop Sargent 'for themselves
and associates' transferred to William Duer and his associates 'one equal moiety
of the Scioto tract of land mentioned in the second contract above.' By the
terms of the transfer it was provided that the respective parties to the transaction were to be equally concerned in the disposal of the said lands either in
Europe or America, as the circumstances would best admit. They were to share
equally in any profit or loss which might arise in attempting to negotiate the
sale of the same and in paying the purchase money to the United States. The
property in question was the residue of the large tract purchased by Cutler and
Sargent, namely, that not included in the actual purchase of the Ohio Company.
It was to be divided into thirty shares, thirteen of which were to be the property of Duer. He was at liberty to admit such associates to his shares as he
might think proper. In like manner thirteen shares were to become the property of Manasseh Cutler and Winthrop Sargent. The remaining four shares
were to be disposed of in Europe. . . ." (Belote, "The Scioto Speculation,"
17–19.)

A copy of the transfer from Cutler and Sargent to Duer, dated October 29,
1787, is printed in Belote, "The Scioto Speculation," 65–67.

9. The colony was Gallipolis on the Ohio River, a few miles below the mouth
of the Kanawha.

would be paid amply for the Lands & Messrs Duer & co after being Repaid their advances would gain a large sum.

To accomplish these Points it would be well to renew the Arrangement with Messrs Duer & Co on other terms that the names may not appear to change & as it has already been Announced in a new Prospectus here which has been distributed every where that 9/10ths of the Price will be deposited untill possession is given it is not possible that any Risque can be Run of Giving Possession of Lands that will not be paid for so that the affair is Simple Plain & without any inconveniency.[10] The Fears that Walker [11] Pretends to have about not being Paid are as ill founded as they are unjust. It is impossible to touch here the 9/10ths in question & surely the 10th that remains is not more than is necessary to cover the Expences and pay whoever sells it. With Regard to the Plan that Walker has to Endeavour to Substitute Some of his Freinds in my Place, it is impracticable & in justice to all concerned as well as to My self I must say so.[12] I have done nothing that merits such treatment. I have begun the affair & suffered the disagreable part & Run all the Risques. I have a Correspondence with & know the most Part of those who would go out the First upon good news ariving and as I have Contracted debts to support the thing till the news that arives shall determin whether in itself it is good or bad, I cannot think of submitting to so great an Injustice as it would be to substitute Mr Morris or any other of those Persons who have all along been the Enemies of the affair in My Place.[13] I should therefore make my apeal to the Public & defend myself in the tribunals at the same time. The Affair would then be stopt as till the Bye past were settled nothing could go on and that it would take a prodigious time to do as none of the affairs here have been done in the Name of individuals but of a Fictitious Company which Circumstance alone would involve & render prodigiously Expensive & Tedious all the operations of a law suit. In a word this affair is only to be Carried on with Faith & Confidence. Nothing will be more agreable to me than that a Person should be sent over to verify

10. Apparently this is a reference to the proceedings of the second Scioto Company, which Barlow organized in July, 1790, to succeed the bankrupt first company.

11. Walker disapproved of the reorganization.

12. Walker sought to establish a third Scioto Company, but this came to nothing.

13. Gouverneur Morris was hostile to the company.

& sign every sale & to Receive into his own hands the Titles to the deposit of the 9/10ths. In short there is no precautions possible for the surety of the affair that I would not with the Greatest Eagerness embrace; neither do I insist upon the Portion of Profit which by my original agreement with Mr Barlow was ceded to me *for future sales.* I only demand a Confidential honourable arrangement on both sides for the Carrying on the affair.

If on the Contrary it is determined to Stop short where we are, I have titles to deliver & quittances for money paid, which, deduction being made of the Percentage that was allowed to me by the original agreement *do more than Balance the account for Lands Sold* and which account I have Ready, tho' as I told Mr Walker we could not with any degree of Propriety or common sence Balance the account untill the affair was stopt or the Plan of going on was settled. I nevertheless should have at the last agreed to settle with him if he would have shewn his Procuration & declared his intentions. I was obliged to summons him to shew them; he did not make any Answer. A Messanger waited upon him to obtain a verbal answer at least & to the messanger he only said that he had an advertisement Ready to put in the News papers against me & that his powers were deposed with a notaire whose name he gave. I went to the Notaire to see the Powers & took the Messanger with Me but Mr Walker had been there half an hour before & withdrawn the Powers which the Notaire declared he had not Read. After that I had nothing to do with Mr Walker & if he chuses to insert his advertisement he may do it but it will be answered in a Manner that will be more disagreable to him than he Expects because No Man has a Right to come and act as he has done in Paris. The circumstance of Mr Barlows evasion is sufficiently disagreable & disgracefull to his constituents without adding the Ruin of the affair by a Public Explanation of all the difficulties under which the affair lyes.[14]

I know that Mr Duer has been told lyes on My Account & as he does not know me I cannot wonder at his believing them this has been the Cause of his not writing to me [15] but he can never give a Reason for

14. Walker "became convinced that Playfair was a scoundrel and in a published advertisement denounced him and warned the public to purchase no Scioto lands from him. Playfair replied in kind the next day and attempted to assure the public that he alone had 'any authority to sell those lands or negotiate the effects,' but soon, it seems, disappeared with what funds remained unspent" (Davis, *Essays*, I, 244).

15. Playfair wrote to Duer on December 27, 1790, declaring that the company had sold only one hundred and forty-three thousand acres, but he did not ex-

not writing *to some one Else* to prevent those Ruinous mistakes that have been made and of which he himself will probably be the first victim.

I have taken the liberty to trouble you with this long letter. I send inclosed the account up to the time that the sales stopt and I have done the same to Mr Jefferson [16] to whom I had the honour of being known when he was in France and I request your Interference in the affair in order to Enable some arrangement to take Place that will not Prevent the affair from terminating in the Ruin & disgrace of those who have begun it.

I am Sir with Respect your most obedient & most humble servant   William Playfair

Paris 30th March 1791

---

plain what happened to the money he had received in payment for the land. See Belote, "The Scioto Speculation," 42–43; Davis, *Essays*, I, 244, note 4.

16. See Playfair to Thomas Jefferson, March 20, 1791 (ALS, Thomas Jefferson Papers, Library of Congress).

From Thomas Smith [1]

Loan Office [Philadelphia] Pennsa March 30th 1791

Sir,

The amount of the several kinds of Stock on the books of this office on which Interest is payable is as follows with Interest Calculated to 1st April 1791 Viz.

	Principle		Interest
Funded 6 ⅌ Cent	864 203.54	——	12961.97
Funded 3 ⅌ Cent	364 890.61	——	2735.40
Deferred 6 ⅌ Cent	410.369.31		. . . .
Non subscription Stock	29 573.77 ⎫		
Interest	5 323.25 ⎭		335.66
			16033. 3

The abstract at large &c. will be compleated this Night & delivered in to-morrow morning.

I have the honor &c.

Honble. Alex. Hamilton Esqr. secy of the Treasury.

LC, RG 53, Pennsylvania State Loan Office, Letter Book, 1790–1794, Vol. "615–P," National Archives.

1. For background to the loan office business to which Smith is referring, see Nathaniel Appleton to H, February 5, 1791, note 1.

From George Thacher

Biddeford [District of Maine] March 30, 1791. ". . . The Bonds which Mr. Cutts [1] gave the Collector for the port of Biddeford & Pepperellborough [2] will become payable about the 10th of May, & he is anxious to have your opinion on the justice of paying them as early as possible."

ALS, Maine Historical Society, Portland.
   1. Thomas Cutts.
   2. Jeremiah Hill.

Agreement with John McComb, Junior

Philadelphia, March 31, 1791. A contract for the construction of the Cape Henry lighthouse by McComb.

Copy, RG 26, Lighthouse Letters Received, Lighthouse Deeds and Contracts, National Archives.

To John Habersham

[*Philadelphia, March 31, 1791.* On May 20, 1791, Habersham wrote to Hamilton: "I have to acknowledge the receipt of your letter of the 31st of March last." *Letter not found.*]

From Thomas Jefferson

Department of state Mar. 31. 1791.

Sir

The publication of the laws of the U.S. and the purchase of those of the several states call on us immediately for about five hundred dollars, for which sum I must ask a warrant from you to be accounted for. The contingent expenses of my department to the 1st. inst. are

now stated and will be settled with the Auditor tomorrow. I have the
honor to be with great esteem & respect   Sir
   Your most obedt   & most humble servt   Th: Jefferson

The Secretary of the Treasury

ALS, letterpress copy, Thomas Jefferson Papers, Library of Congress; LC, Papers
of the Continental Congress, National Archives.

From Jeremiah Olney

Providence, March 31, 1791. "I have received Mr. Coxe's circular
Letter of the 10th. instant.[1] The Returns of Vessels built in this District, within the periods therein mentioned, shall be forwarded as soon
as I can obtain a competent knowledge thereof. And should any Documents, relative to the Commerce, Manufactures &c. of this State, fall
into my hands, they shall be transmitted agreeable to his directions.
. . . I now enclose Seven . . . Drafts of the Treasurer, in favor of
Jabez Bowen Esquire, dated the 15th of Feby. last. . . ."

ADfS, Rhode Island Historical Society, Providence; copy, RG 56, Letters from
the Collector at Providence, National Archives.
   1. See Treasury Department Circular to the Collectors of the Customs, March
10, 1791, signed by Tench Coxe (LS, Hamilton Papers, Library of Congress).

To William Seton

[*Philadelphia, March 31, 1791.* On April 4, 1791, Seton wrote to
Hamilton concerning "the request expressed in your letter of the 31st."
Letter not found.]

To Otho H. Williams

Treasury Department
March 31st 1791

Sir.
   The device intimated to me in your letter of the 26th. of January,
I consider as a mere evasive expedient, which ought not to protect the
owner of the vessel from a prosecution for perjury. It is my desire

therefore that if any such case should occur you may direct proceedings on that ground against the offender.

I am, Sir,   Your obedt. Servant   Alexander Hamilton

Otho H Williams Esqr.
Collector.

LS, Columbia University Libraries.

To Richard Harison

Treasury Department
1 April 1791

Sir,

You will find in this inclosure two copies of a contract with John McComb junr, of New York, for building a light house on Cape Henry.[1] I request the favor of your sending for Mr McComb & procuring his execution of them. It will be necessary that the inclosed bond be also executed by Mr McComb, & two competent Sureties. The Persons offered to me were Messrs Nicholas Cruger & Peter Kemble,[2] whom I approve: but as Mr. Cruger is absent from New York, I must ask the favor of your selecting out of the names that may be offered by Mr. McComb one in lieu of Mr. Cruger; whom you shall deem sufficient.

The requisite provision for the first payment will be made at the Bank of New York; to obtain which Mr. McComb's exhibition of the contract executed by me will be sufficient. But this, of course, you will not deliver to him 'till the bond has been excuted to your Satisfaction.

I am, sir,   With great consideration,   Your Obed Servant
                                        Alexander Hamilton

Richard Harrison Esqr.
Atto. for the United States,
New York

LS, New-York Historical Society, New York City.
    1. For the background to this letter, see H to George Washington, January 5, 1791; "Agreement with John McComb, Junior," March 31, 1791.
    2. Cruger and Kemble were New York City merchants. As a boy H had worked for Cruger in St. Croix.

From Benjamin Lincoln

From the Collector of Boston
April 1st 1791

Sir,

Your instructions of the 18th ulto and the copy of a letter to Mr Appleton came by the last Post. I shall with the utmost cheerfulness attend to his applications and he may always depend on my best aid.

You have I hope before you several letters from me, one of Feby 23rd one of Feby 25th one of March 9th & one 18th. I wish to receive an answer to that of the 23rd Feby as early as it shall be convenient for you as the builder is at a loss to know what to do with his vessel.

I know that you are constantly crouded with business and that you cannot regularly answer all letters as they come to hand many may not require a speedy answer. It would however be a relief to me, if in cases where I am obliged to report, Mr Cox [1] when writing to me would just acknowledge the receipt of them for I have been anxious for some time past lest my letter of the 23rd had not reached you. Permit me to ask whether you have settled the question relative to the little Sloop Suffolk of Weymouth the owners have applied to me on the subject and seem anxious to know their fate, if she is to be given up, the Spring is the time for the owners to lay a plan for business for the season.

By the act making further provision for the collection of duties by law imposed on Teas it is enacted by the 4th Section that all teas which after the first day of April, then, next, which shall be imported into the United States from any foreign Port or place shall be landed under the care of the Inspectors of the Revenue.[2] No officer of that discription can act, I suppose untill the first day of July next. What practice will be adopted in the mean time.

To the Secy of the Treasury.

Copy, RG 56, Letters from the Collector at Boston, National Archives; LC, RG 36, Collector of Customs at Boston, Letter Book, 1790–1797, National Archives; copy, RG 56, Letters from the Collector at Boston, National Archives.

1. Tench Coxe, Assistant Secretary of the Treasury.
2. 1 *Stat.* 220–21 (March 3, 1791).

To John McComb, Junior

From the Collector of
April 1, 1791

Treasury Department
April 1. 1791

Sir

I have transmitted to Richard Harison Esq. two copies of the Contract for the lighthouse executed by me.[1] You will call upon him and execute them. I have also forwarded to Mr. Harison a bond to be executed by you, and Mr. Peter Kemble with some other sufficient surety in lieu of Mr. Cruger, who is absent. Mr. Harison will select one out of the persons you may offer to him.

On the execution of these papers one copy of the contract will be delivered to you with which you will apply to the Cashier of the Bank of New York, who will have my instructions to make you the first payment.

I do not approve of placing the oil vault within the lighthouse, nor of constructing the house in the form or of the size in your last proposition. I however should wish that the house and kitchen might be so varied as to be under one roof, and in one *square* building, the outlines of which would be of the exact size and of course of the exact value of the proposed building. The house would then have two rooms on the lower floor, one for a kitchen and one for a sitting room, and two chambers over them. A square shell is the most capacious and most firm, which last may be of consequence in so exposed a situation.

It is my wish that the house be of stone (instead of frame) with a cellar under it, and I shall be glad to know immediately what difference this will make in the Cost.

I am, Sir   Your obedt. servt.   A Hamilton

Mr. Jno. McComb Junr.
New York

LS, Lloyd W. Smith Collection, Morristown National Historical Park, Morristown, New Jersey.
    1. See H to Harison, April 1, 1791.

To William Seton

[*Philadelphia, April 1, 1791*. On April 11, 1791, Seton wrote to Hamilton: "I have to acknowledge the honor of your Letter of the 1st. instant." *Letter not found.*]

From Nathaniel Appleton

Boston, April 2, 1791. ". . . I have now to inform you that I began yesterday morning to pay Interest on the Public Debt agreeably to the Act of Congress making provision for the same.[1] I have compleated the Dividend book in which are Stated 863 Stockholders. The Duplicate Receipts are also prepared agreeably to the Instructions. . . ."[2]

LC, RG 53, Massachusetts State Loan Office, Letter Book, 1785–1791, Vol. "259–M," National Archives.
   1. "An Act making provision for the (payment of the) Debt of the United States" (1 *Stat.* 138–44 [August 4, 1790]).
   2. See H to Appleton, March 18, 1791.

To John Hopkins [1]

[*Philadelphia*] *April 2, 1791.* Authorizes Hopkins to send Thomas Williams to Hillsboro, North Carolina, to testify in a case concerning the alteration of North Carolina certificates. States "The expences of his Journey will be repaid to him."[2]

Extract, RG 217, Miscellaneous Treasury Accounts, 1790–1894, Account No. 4289, National Archives.
   1. Hopkins was commissioner of loans for Virginia.
   2. This letter was submitted in support of Williams's claim for the expenses of his journey to North Carolina. On June 19, 1793, Williams wrote to H requesting his aid in collecting the $77.50 due to him.

To Thomas Smith

[*Philadelphia, April 2, 1791*. On May 10, 1791, Smith wrote to Hamilton: "I am honored with your favor 2nd April." *Letter not found.*]

To Mathew Carey [1]

[*Philadelphia*] *April 4, 1791.* Presents his compliments to Carey and declines an invitation to a dinner of the Hibernian Society.

Copy, Historical Society of Pennsylvania, Philadelphia.
1. Carey, publisher of *The American Museum,* had emigrated to Philadelphia from Ireland in 1784. Early in the seventeen-nineties he organized the Hibernian Society for the relief of Irish immigrants.

From Edward Carrington

Richmond Apl. 4. 1791

Dr Sir

The private letter which you was so good as to accompany your Official communication with,[1] calls for and has my warmest acknowledgements. The point which I have mentioned in my Official letter,[2] as determining my acceptance of the Office of Supervisor, would have produced that issue, had the measure been less eligible in other respects than it really is, but had I upon any consideration been hesitating, your private letter would have turned the scale. I am well satisfied Sir of the truth of what you say as to the importance of the Office, and have no apprehension that the necessary compensations for the hazard and toils of the business, will be unattended to by you, or refused by Congress. This Office may doubtless with propriety embrace several duties more than now fall under it, and so long as I continue to hold it, any extension that may appear to you proper will be intirely agreable to me. I have heard no suggestions from any quarter that the Office of Marshal which I now hold is incompatible with it, and I am well assured I shall feel no difficulty in the execution of both. I will thank you for your ideas upon this point. Be pleased to present me to Mrs. Hamilton, and believe me to be, with the greatest, sincerity & truth   yr. Afft. Freind & Servt.   Ed Carrington

Colo. A. Hamilton.

ALS, Hamilton Papers, Library of Congress.
 1. Neither letter has been found, but see quoted extract from H's official letter to Carrington on March 21, 1791.
 2. Letter not found.

From William Seton

New York, April 4, 1791. "Agreeable to the request expressed in your letter of the 31st.[1] Mr. William Hill has been paid Five thousand Dollars. . . ."[2]

LC, Bank of New York, New York City.
 1. Letter not found.
 2. See Seton to H, March 28, 1791.

From George Washington

Mount Vernon April 4th. 1791

Dear Sir,

Your letter of the 27th. Ult. came duly to hand. For the information contained in it and for the notes which accompanied the same, I thank you.

Every expedient, as I believe you know, is in operation to avert a War with the hostile Indian tribes and to keep those who are in treaty with us in good temper;[1] but I am nearly thoroughly convinced that neither will be effected, or, if effected, will be of short duration while land jobbing and the disorderly conduct of our borders is suffered with impunity; and whilst the States individually are omitting no occasion to interfere in matters which belong to the general Government.

It is not more than four or five months since the Six Nations or part of them were assured (through the medium of Colo. Pickering)[2] that thence forward they would be spoken to by the Government of United States *only* and the same thing was repeated in strong terms to the Cornplanter at Philadelphia afterwards.[3] Now, as appears by the extract from Mr. King,[4] the Legislature of New York are going into some negotiations with these very people. What must this evince to them? Why, that we pursue no system, and that our declarations are not to be regard. To sum the whole up in a few words—the inter-

ferences of States, and the speculations of Individuals will be the bane
of all our public measures.

Sincerely & Affectionately   I am Yrs.   Go: Washington

Colo. Hamilton

ALS, George Washington Papers, Library of Congress; LC, George Washington Papers, Library of Congress.
    1. For an account of the measures undertaken by the Administration during
the spring of 1791 to conciliate the western Indians and to ensure the neutrality
of the Six Nations, see *ASP, Indian Affairs*, I, 139–71.
    2. Timothy Pickering met with the Seneca in November, 1790, to arrange
compensation for the murder of several Indians by white men.
    3. See "The reply of the President of the United States to the speech of the
Cornplanter, Half-Town, and Great-Tree, Chiefs and Councillors of the Seneca
nation of Indians," December 29, 1790 (*ASP, Indian Affairs*, I, 142–43). The
Seneca chiefs had met with Government officials in Philadelphia from December, 1790, to February, 1791, to consider Seneca complaints of land fraud and
encroachment.
    4. See Rufus King to H, March 24, 1791.

George Washington to Alexander Hamilton, Thomas Jefferson, and Henry Knox

Mount Vernon, April 4. 1791.

Gentlemen,

    As the public service may require that communications should be
made to me, during my absence from the seat of government, by the
most direct conveyances and as, in the event of any very extraordinary
occurrence, it will be necessary to know at what time I may be found
in any particular place, I have to inform you that unless the progress
of my journey to Savannah is retarded by unforeseen interruptions
it will be regulated (including days of halt) in the following manner.

    I shall be on the 8th. of April at Fredericksburg

11th. ———————	Richmond
14th ———————	Petersburg
16th ———————	Halifax
18th. ———————	Tarborough
20th. ———————	Newbern
24th. ———————	Wilmington
29th. ———————	Georgetown, south-Carolina
2nd. of May ——	Charleston, halting five days.
11th. ———————	Savannah, halting two days.

Hence, leaving the line of the mail, I shall proceed to Augusta, and, according to the information which I may receive there, my return, by an upper road will be regulated. The route of my return is at present uncertain, but in all probability, it will be through Columbia, Camden, Charlotte, Salisbury, Salem, Guilford, Hillsborough, Harrisburg, Williamsburg to Taylor's ferry on the Roanoke, and thence to Fredericksburg by the nearest and best road.

After thus explaining to you, as far as I am able at present, the direction and probable progress of my journey, I have to express my wish, if any serious and important cases should arise during my absence, (of which the probability is but too strong) that the Secretaries for the Departments of State, Treasury, and War may hold consultations thereon, to determine whether they are of such a nature as to require my personal attendance at the seat of government—and, if they should be so considered, I will return immediately from any place at which the information may reach me. Or should they determine that measures, relevant to the case, may be legally and properly pursued without the immediate agency of the President, I will approve and ratify the measures, which may be conformed to such determination.

Presuming that the Vice-President will have left the seat of government for Boston, I have not requested his opinion to be taken on the supposed emergency. Should it be otherwise I wish him also to be consulted.

I am, Gentlemen, Your most obedient Servant   Go: Washington

Thomas Jefferson, Alexander Hamilton, and
Henry Knox Esquires
Secretaries of the United States for the Departments of
State, Treasury, and War.

LS, Thomas Jefferson Papers, Library of Congress; copy, George Washington Papers, Library of Congress; copy, RG 59, Miscellaneous Letters, 1790–1799, National Archives.

From Joseph Whipple

Portsmouth, New Hampshire, April 4, 1791. Acknowledges receipt of Hamilton's "letter of the 18 Decr.[1] last together with Dycas's & Colles's Hydrometers." States that Colles's hydrometer may not be "truly graduated" and that there is a defect in the bulb of Dycas's hydrometer. Requests a new bulb.

LC, RG 36, Portsmouth Collector, Letters Sent, 1790–1791, Vol. 2, National Archives; copy, RG 56, Letters from the Collector at Portsmouth, National Archives.

1. "Treasury Department Circular to the Collectors of the Customs," December 18, 1790.

To Sharp Delany

Treasury Department,
5 April 1791

Sir,

The section of the collection law relative to the tares to be allowed at the Custom house upon the several species of goods therein mentioned [1] appears to require that the allowance ⅌ Centum upon

Coffee in bags ⎫
do.　　in bales ⎪
do.　　in casks ⎬ be computed upon the hundred pounds,
pepper in bales ⎪
do.　　in casks ⎭

and that the allowance ⅌ centum upon sugars (other than loaf) in hogsheads & boxes be computed on the 112 pounds.

You will perceive that the above arrangement applies to articles, sold universally by the pound, the tare ⅌ 100 lbs, and that it applies to articles sold ⅌ the hundred weight, the tare ⅌ 112 lbs.

As I find the customs in trade in various parts of the United States differ considerably, I think it necessary to inform you that the above is only my present idea. I shall take measures to obtain that accurate Statement of facts which will be necessary to a confirmed & settled construction of the act.

I am, sir,　Your obedt Servant　　　　　　　　Alex Hamilton

Sharp Delany Esqr.
Collr. Philadelphia

LS, Bureau of Customs, Philadelphia; copy, Office of the Secretary, United States Treasury Department; copy, RG 56, Circulars of the Office of the Secretary, "Set T," National Archives.

1. See Section 35 of "An Act to provide more effectually for the collection

of the duties imposed by law on goods, wares and merchandise imported into the United States, and on the tonnage of ships or vessels" (1 *Stat.* 166 [August 4, 1790]).

To Tobias Lear

[*Philadelphia*] *April 5, 1791.* Asks for commissions for seven inspectors of the revenue.

LC, George Washington Papers, Library of Congress.

From Tobias Lear

[*Philadelphia*] *April 5, 1791.* Sends commissions requested by Hamilton.

LC, George Washington Papers, Library of Congress.

From Francisco de Miranda [1]

[London, April 5, 1791]

mon Cher Tresorier Genèral.

Ayez la bonté d'agreer mes Complimens, et mes Respects, dans l'ocasion du depart de notre mutuel ami le Col: Smith,[2] qui a passé quelques Semaines dans cette Capitalle ici: qui m'a fait l'amitié de passer bien des moments ensamble; et a qui, J'ai êu le plaisir de voire parffaitement acueilir par tout le monde qui l'a connue antèrieurement, et vue dans l'ocasion actuelle.

Il pourrá vous dire l'etrange Sistheme Politique que l'Angleterre poursuit actuellement &c. et je peut vous assurer que vos *Plans* des finances; de Banc-nationalle; des colection des Taxes &c. non seulement ont merité l'admiration des gens de la plus grande consideration ici; mais ills ont donné aussi la plus haute idée du Nouveaux Gouvernement, qui se conduit a cet egard, par des principes *d'honeur*, et de *dignité* tres peu comuns dans les gouvernemens modernes! Je vous en felicite de tout mon Cœur, en atandant que les progres Repides des vos *institucions* produisent une prosperité general dans ce *Pais-fortuné*, et votre bonheur eternel qui est le prix immancable!

Portez-vous bien toujours, donnez moi des vos nouvelles (si vos ocupations vous le permetent), et croiez moi sincerement

Le votre,   F. de Miranda.

à Londres ce 5. Avril. 1791.
The Rig: Hon: Alexander Hamilton.

ALS, Hamilton Papers, Library of Congress.
    1. Miranda was a Venezuelan revolutionist who had become friendly with H during a visit to New York City in 1784. In 1789 he went to England to attempt to interest the British ministry in aiding his plans for a revolution in Spain's Latin American colonies. He apparently received some encouragement from the British government, especially during the Nootka Sound controversy in 1790. With the settlement of that dispute, however, British interest waned, and early in 1792 Miranda went to France to bring his proposals to the attention of the French Revolutionary government.
    2. William Stephens Smith, John Adams's son-in-law. In 1785 Smith had served as secretary of legation under Adams in London and later had been sent on a diplomatic mission to Portugal and Spain. During his stay in Europe he had accompanied Miranda on a tour of the Continent. In 1788 Smith returned to the United States where he engaged in various business enterprises. In 1789 he received an appointment as United States marshal for New York, and in March, 1791, he was appointed supervisor of the revenue for the District of New York. In December, 1790, Smith had applied for leave to go to Europe on private business.

To William Ellery

[*Philadelphia, April 6, 1791.* On April 19, 1791, Ellery wrote to Hamilton: "I have received your letter of the 6th. of this month." *Letter not found.*]

To William Duer

Treasury Department
April 7th 179[1] [1]

Sir
    In consideration of the moderate terms of Mr Fowler's contract with the public [2] and from a disposition to give all requisite aid to the Contractor in order that the public service may be effectually & certainly performed, I accede to the requests contained in your letter, [3] as explained in conversation—that is to say—I will advance immediately to you as Agent to Mr Fowler thirty thousand Dollars,

and a further sum of twenty thousand Dollars at the expiration of forty five days from the date of this letter.

If upon the first of October next there is a satisfactory evidence that the public service has called for supplies (which have been furnished) to an amount sufficient to entitle the Contractor to the additional sum of thirty thousand Dollars they shall be paid; though he should not be then ready to comply with the forms of the Treasury.

I am, Sir,   Your Obedt. Servt.   Alexander Hamilton
                                                    Secretary of the Treasury

William Duer Esqr.

Copy, New-York Historical Society, New York City.
    1. The copy of this letter is incorrectly dated "April 7, 1792."
    2. Theodosius Fowler was a New York City contractor and a speculator in securities and land.
    The contract, signed by Fowler with the Treasury Department on October 28, 1790, was transferred to Duer on January 3, 1791. A copy of the assignment is in the New-York Historical Society. For Fowler's statement on the contract, see "Contract for Army Rations," October 28, 1790, note 1. After the defeat of Major General Arthur St. Clair's expedition by the western Indians in November, 1791, congressional investigations stressed the fact that one of the principal causes for the debacle was the failure of the contractor to provide adequate supplies. At that time the terms of this contract and the circumstances under which it was issued became a major source of controversy. The May 8, 1792, report of the House committee appointed to inquire into the failure of the St. Clair expedition pointed out that the contract originally issued to Fowler had required a bond of one hundred thousand dollars, with Walter Livingston and John Cochran as securities. After the transfer of the contract to Duer, a second contract was entered into by Duer with the War Department for supplying the troops at Fort Pitt, and "a bond was at the same time entered into by the said William Duer for the due execution of the said contract, in the penalty of four thousand dollars, without any security whatsoever" (*ASP, Military Affairs*, I, 36). On February 15, 1793, the committee issued a supplementary report in which it was stated that "From documents received by the committee, since their last appointment, it appears, that the copy of the before mentioned transfer was not lodged in the office of the Secretary of the Treasury, until the seventh of April, one thousand seven hundred and ninety-one; at which time it was received by the Secretary of the Treasury, under cover of a letter from William Duer, informing him of the circumstance of the said transfer, and making requisitions for certain advances of money; that the Secretary of the Treasury, by a letter in reply of the same date, agrees to make the advances required to William Duer, *as the agent of Theodosius Fowler.*

    "It appears that all the warrants issued from the Treasury, for the purposes of this contract, were issued to William Duer, as the agent of Theodosius Fowler.

    "The Secretary of the Treasury has furnished the committee with the written opinions of the Attorney General of the United States, and several other lawyers of eminence, all of whom concur in opinion, that the securities to the bond, originally given by Theodosius Fowler, for the execution of this contract, are now responsible for all damages consequent upon any breach of that contract.

    "The Secretary of War, who alone appears to have been the agent, on the part of the United States, in all things relating to the execution of the contract has always corresponded with William Duer as the contractor, and his correspondence commences at a date prior to that of the copy of the contract lodged at the treasury." (*ASP, Military Affairs*, I, 42.)

Concerning the contract for four thousand dollars with the War Department, the committee reported: "The Secretary of War . . . states, that it was not the custom of the office to require other security than that of the contractor, for the due execution of contracts of small amount; and it appears, by a letter of the Secretary of the Treasury, written since the former report, that the Secretary of War consulted with him upon the occasion alluded to, and that he agreed in opinion, that farther security was not necessary" (*ASP, Military Affairs*, I, 42).

For the findings of the committee on the culpability of the contractor, see *ASP, Military Affairs*, I, 36–39, 41–44; *ASP, Claims*, 259–62.

3. Letter not found.

From Benjamin Lincoln

From the Collector of Boston
April 7th 1791

Sir,

I have the pleasure of enclosing a return of all the vessels built within this District from March 4th 1789 to March 4th 1791 collected & made agreeably to your wishes communicated by Mr Coxe your assistant the 10th ult.[1] You will find the number exceedingly small and is not I think, more than one third of what was built in the years 1784 and 1785. I will attempt to assign some reasons why the business has suffered so great a deminution. As in this statement I may suggest some *peices* of information as you have often requested.

In the first place, at the close of the war, we were destitute, almost of shipping of any kind especially of those suitable for the fishing business, we very soon increased our numbers and by 1787 or 1788 we were fully supplied with vessels of this kind & with a sufficient number for our other purposes had we no regard to the carrying trade. We early discovered that although our number of fishing vessels was far short of the number employed in that business before the war, yet that we had too many and that more fish were caught than

Copy, RG 56, Letters from the Collector at Boston, National Archives (incorrectly dated April 8, 1791); LC, incomplete copy, Massachusetts Historical Society, Boston; LC, RG 36, Collector of Customs at Boston, Letter Book, 1790–1797, National Archives; copy, RG 56, Letters from the Collector at Boston, National Archives.

1. Treasury Department Circular to the Collectors of the Customs, March 10, 1791, signed by Tench Coxe (LS, Hamilton Papers, Library of Congress).

could find a market at a price which would save the taken of them free from loss, this has induced many to quit the business, while others have lessened their capital employed in it. The embarrasment which we have experienced from the unfriendly disposition of the Algerines and the partiality which the French Nation discovered to their own fisheries have been checks upon the sale of our Cod Fish and induced many to employ these vessels in an-other channel, while our Mackrel business has been ruined, entirely, by a diversion in a great measure of those Fish from our coast. The state of our fisheries and the delay some of our vessels have experienced and the disappointment of others in obtaining freights in the Southern States damp our ardour for building and are among the causes which may be assigned that so few vessels have been built the last two years in this District. I say that these are among the causes, they are not the sole causes. The scarcity of Ship Timber near the Sea Coast in this District is a check upon our building, as in time it must unless some especial measures are adopted to prevent it, a circumstance which should it become general would be pregnant with the most dangerous consequences.

If we take a survey of the Eastern States we shall find that their timber trees are greatly reduced and totally gone in many parts from the shores to a line thirty miles perpendicular there to, and that through the Country in general they are destroyed as fast as it is for the interest of the husbandman to do it without regard to the exist-ance of a marine hereafter. If we reflect on the tenure by which our lands are held, that they cannot be secured in the same family, by the possessor of them for more than one or two lives at the most, that thereby is destroyed one of the greatest motives, which seems to have actuated mankind, who [2] have been seen when there was no prospect of their enjoying the fruit of their labours, while in old age tottering in the field aided by the staff and imploying their time in planting the achorn strengthened and ⟨animated⟩ [3] by a belief that they were lay-ing a foundation for the happiness & support of their offspring, if we consider that it requires a term from fifty to one hundred years from planting the Achorn to the tree becoming of sufficient size for planks & the largest timber and when we contrast the state of the timber now,

2. From this point the remainder of the text has been taken from Lincoln's letter book in the Massachusetts Historical Society.

3. Words within broken brackets have been taken from the first copy in RG 56, Letters from the Collector at Boston, National Archives.

with what it was only fifty years past, we cannot be at a loss to pronounce that unless some measures are adopted by the public & those immediately that the day will come and that many of the children now living will see it when we shall no longer command the means of commerce or defence; where then will be that jewel for which we have so long contended? I think it would not be more laughable to hear a man without hands boasting of his freedom and independence, than to see this country supposing itself on strong grounds among the nations of the earth while to others she owed the means of her defence.

If it may be said that we need not be anxious, that Britain has, long since, been deprived of most of her timber, but, that she always found a supply from the neighbouring nations, it is true that She has received a very ample supply from a broad, notwithstanding She would put nothing at hazard. She always cultivated with the utmost care a certain proportion of the Island with trees always sufficient at all times in cases of accident to have Kept up that force for which she has been so distinguished & which has been so necessary to her own safety. But where shall the United States look for ⟨supplies of Ship Timber,⟩ without their own limits? None ⟨can be found on this⟩ side of the atlantic. The whole Country Northward & Eastward of the State of New Hampshire, with a few exceptions only, where an indifferent Oak is to be found, is principally covered with what is called the black growth the pine, the spruce, the hemlock &c. In some parts will be found the maple, the beach, the white birch, & the yellow birch, with this timber some vessels have been built in this State and many by the British since the close of the war in the Province of New Brunswick. There has not been sufficient time since the war to ascertain the value of such timber; if however upon trial it should be found to answer the purpose we cannot promise our selves a supply of it long for when once cut off a different kind of wood generally springs up viz a growth of the black kind or the white birch which is a very indifferent wood. If on the whole we are convinced that the succeeding generations will have a demand for shipping and we cannot point out a source from which they will be able to draw a supply of timber for building other than by our attention, at this day, to the culture of trees and that measure suitable therefor when grown should be neglected by us we shall be highly reprehensible for the neglect and justly chargable with a criminal improviding.

We should not be in The same critical situation respecting this matter as we now are did we hold our land on the same tenure as are the estates held in England; there the grand sire who plants the achorn knows that his child or grand child will reap the benefits of his labours; but the case is very different here where there is no public security that lands shall remain any given time in the same line, hence a very different kind of improvement takes place and one the most unfriendly to the culture of trees for timber.

Secretary of the Treasury

To Jacob Cuyler [1]

[*Philadelphia, April 8, 1791.* On May 10, 1791, Richard Cuyler wrote to Hamilton: "My Father (Mr. Jacob Cuyler). has shewn me your polite Favor to him of 8th. Apl." *Letter not found.*]

1. Jacob and Richard Cuyler were Albany merchants.

From Richard Harison

New York 8 April 1791

Sir,

Immediately upon the Receipt of your Letter of the 1st. Instant, I sent for Mr. McComb, and proposed his executing the Contract transmitted to me, and that a proper Surety should be substituted in the Place of Mr. Cruger. Upon the latter Subject I am informed that no Difficulties will arise, but with Respect to the Contract itself Mr. McComb alledges that a Mistake has taken Place. The first Payment he says was to have been four thousand Dollars, and he does not think that a less Sum will furnish the requisite Materials. He proposes therefore, if it meets your Approbation, to give a Receipt for an additional Sum of One thousand Dollars in Part of the third Payment, which he supposes will be conformable to the original Agreement & enable him to complete the Undertaking. I find another small Mistake in the Contract as to Mr. McComb's Occupation, he being a Bricklayer, not a Carpenter; but I should think that Accuracy upon this Head is not essential.

In Consequence of the Communications which accompanied your Letter of the 15th of March & other information from New Jersey such Measures have been taken that Francis Crane and Israel Fuller, two of the supposed Criminals, have been apprehended and diligent Search is making for others who are accused of the same Offences. Unfortunately the Evidence which we were in Possession of was too loose in it's Nature to warrant even an Indictment by the Grand Jury. Crane, therefore, applied to the Circuit Court for his Discharge, but without Success. It will be absolutely necessary that before the next Sessions, I should either have sufficient Evidence upon which to proceed, or that the Prisoners should be sent to Places where the Crimes were committed and the Witnesses reside. I doubt whether any Crime cognizable by the national Courts can be fixed upon Fuller, and propose, if you do not object, to deliver him up to the Judicatories of the State.

During the last Circuit Court two Persons have been convicted upon Indictment for Offences against the Revenue Laws. One of them, Captn. Josiah Gorham Junr: had been guilty of false Swearing as well as smuggling. His Mate [1] was the principal Witness, whose Conduct in many Respects has been very meritorious. It appeared that the Captn. ordered him to land Goods upon the Arrival, & before the Entry of the Vessel. This from false Ideas of the Respect and Fidelity which he owed the Captain he was induced to comply with. In Consequence, an Action was commenced against him for the United States upon the [2] Section of the last Collection Law. Being Unable to find Bail He has been in Confinement upwards of six Months where his Health has suffered greatly and I fear that his Life may be lost, unless he is speedily released. Had he continued silent, it is beyond a Doubt that the Captain's Villainy would not have been brought to Light, and therefore it is much to be wished that some Plan may be devised for remitting the Penalty to which he is subject, & wh. at any Rate he is unable to pay.

I am, with the highest Respect &ca. Sir Your most obedt. & most humb. Servt.

Hon. A. Hamilton Esqr.
Secry Treasy. U. S.

LC, New-York Historical Society, New York City.

1. Charles Seely.
2. Space left blank in MS. Harison, however, may have been referring to Section 13 of "An Act to provide more effectually for the collection of the duties imposed by law on goods, wares and merchandise imported into the United States, and on the tonnage of ships or vessels" (1 *Stat.* 157–58 [August 4, 1790]). This section provided that goods that were unloaded without authority were to be forfeited.

From Pierre Charles L'Enfant [1]

George town [Maryland] April 8th 1791

It was my wish long before to gave you some Information about the particular local Intended for the seat of the federal City & I regreted much the Impossibility of seasing upon a moment, having had no leasure one since my arrival at this place where I have been constantly engaged in the most fatiguing work which I ever had to perform—that of surveying at so improper season of the year.

But now when you may probably have heard that I am finally charged with deliniating a plan for the City I feel a sort of embarassement how to speak to you as advantageously as I realy think of the situation determined upon. For as there is no doubt I must feel heighly interested in the succes of the undertaking, I become apprehensive of being charg with partiality when I assure you that no position in all america can be more suceptible of grand improvement, more capable of promoting the rapide Increases of a city nor Better situated to secure an Infinity of advantages to gouvernement as is that between the Eastern branch of the potowmack and George town—particularly since the cession just now made of all the territory comprehended between these tow points will allow the city to be plan on a surface of above six thousand acres of a most valuable land besides the adition of George town itself whose nature will before-long be suppressed and its whole district become a part of the cession in Increasing the mean of securing a revenu which must become very considerable and Incompatably more so that what might have been expected or even demanded of any of the States in competition with this. For I belive no cession would ever have been obtained from them to such an extant,

ALS, Hamilton Papers, Library of Congress.
1. L'Enfant, who had served as a major in the Corps of Engineers during the American Revolution, had been engaged to survey the site and draw up the plans for the new Federal capital on the Potomac.

it could at least not have been so valuable ones nor so readily made as has been the case here.

Tow parties of speculators first had rised thier expectations to that degree of extravagance which opposition and a self persuasion of each possessing the most of local advantages could not fail stimulating. They offered tow differents lots the one next to George town & the other contigous to the Eastern Branch both of which were much confined in thier limits as well as disadvantageous as to the terms stipulated and it remained when I arrived at this place to determine which of those tow differents position was the best, and most likely the scale was ready to draw on that side the less desirable but on the which of course the terms appeared to be the most generous.

How far I have contributed to over set that plotting business it would not do for me to tell, besides I am not wholy satisfied weather I would be tanked for by the people amongst whom you live. In Fact it was not my business; I was only to follow the direction given me to survey both those tow differents tracts of territory offered & I acknowlege I started from the line assigned to me but could not help when contemplating the whole local Feeling some concerned at seeing the advantages which it offered likely to be trample upon from a necessity of securing the Establishments by begoning it no matter were.

Niether of the tow offer singly taken appeared to me of a sufficient extant to enswer the grand object in view and how ever I might chance being charge *has I have been in a more northern latitude* of doing more than I am bid to do, I vantured the chance and gave imagination its full Scope in invading all the propriety of all, on a supposed more extansive location in which I comprehended the tow situations in competition and carring on my scheme further in extanding my ideas so as to lead the way to future and progressive improvement, I vantured some remarks thereon the which I submitted to the President on his arrival at this place and was fortunate enough to see meet with his approbation.

In pursuence of this new plan none of the tow offers made could be acceptable; nay more, the extant of the territory of the tow *taken together* appeared too contracted and the President resolving rather to delay than to part from the determination which he now had taken of securing what ever extant of territory may be wanting every one soon yielded to termes in fact, both just & equally advantageous to Individuals and the best calculated to secure to the publick a sufficiency of means to push on with vigour and succes the rasing of the Intended city.[2]

I need not assure you I shall do my best to contribut to this for besides what honor may reflect on me from the endeavour, I have to answer the confidence with which the President has been pleased to rest upon me, in directing I should delinate a grand and general plan for the local distribution of the city the which I have engaged to have got ready by the time when he return from his southern tour,[3] in about the 20 of jun next, at which time the lotts are to be laid out upon the ground agreable to the Scheme he shall have approved of & to be left at the choice of the advanturer in the purchase.

There is already a great competition of application made relative to the sale of these lots which can leave no doubt but they will be disposed off at a greater valu than has been rated. Indeed I would wish every unbeliver to be persuaded and this for thier own sake, for every thing will soon be here in a train as must overhelm all oposition—and I am sincerely of opinion that if the opposers to the measure would, in extanding thier considerations above the petit local of States Interest, view the matter in a proper light and honestly valu the merite of the position about to be deliniated in a city, they would agree with me that it is a most elligible one for to fix upon the capital of this extansive empire. And admitting that in the origine it was not a matter of choice but a result of party spirit and in a great measure of a collutation of local view it must be own that it is one of the most glaring Instances amongst the few when petit motives has prompted a grand Interest. And I dare assert that nothing could be more promoting of a general good as would a readily acquiessance on the part of the Eastern people manifested by Engaging of interest in the advancement of this business, in becoming at this early periode proprietor in this federal district were an acquisiton of lots or of ground undeliniated as such must in the end prove of infinit advantage to the purchasser. I earnestly wish all whom the eastern states can spare may

2. One group of land speculators was interested in Georgetown and the other in Carrollsburg. George Washington warned both groups that they might harm each other by their tactics. The warning had its effect, and on March 30, 1791, all the principal landholders accepted Washington's terms.

3. See Washington to H, Thomas Jefferson, and Henry Knox, April 4, 1791.

come this way and belive it would answer as good a purpose as that of thier emigrating to the west; it would deface that line of markation which will ever apose the south against the east for when objects are seen at a distance the Ideas we form of them is hapt to mislead us in to false conclusion and we fancy monstrous that object which from a nearer view would charm us with a well combination of formes and proportions—hence arrises a natural tho' unwarrantable prejudice of nation against nation, of state against state & so down to Individuals who often mistrust one another for want of being sufficiently acquainted with each other as I may vanture to say is the case with most of the people on this continant who are oppose to every thing they do not understand and for want of being made sensible of the benefice that may result to them from this or that measure withstand in opposition to thier one Interest.

I hope & beg your Indulgence for this long epistle which I will be happy if it is only intelligible as to direct your attention on the most important point. I veiw perhaps differently from many but I may say I consider thing as one whom nothing can Influence in favour of any particular state—& a federal men, while I stand as I do here upon my ground I may say without treason against any of them what I belive would be the Interest of all of them.

If I had not already intruded to long upon your patiance I should here tank you for the good disposition the president has manifested towards me but you do me I prom⟨ise⟩ that justice to rest assured I love to retrace to you what ever ⟨fate⟩ I wish to befal on me and therefore shall not weary you with usless acknowlegements for the prospect I have here, unless some under miner politick will come again to over sat the phyramide on the submit of which I rest my hope.

I have the Honor to be with respect sir   your most humble   most obedent servant   P.C. L'Enfant

allexander Amilton Secretary to the treasury

As I believe the baron [4] most be now near you I beg the favour of you to remember me to him & beg he will excuse my not writing for I realy have not that leasure at this moment. If will not stand upon Etiquette & let me heard from him I should be very happy.

4. Baron von Steuben.

To Benjamin Lincoln

Treasury Department
April 8th. 1791

Sir

In answer to your enquiry [1] whether you may exchange the certificates, purchased under the directions of the Trustees of the Sinking fund, for others which are desired to be given for them, I have to observe that it does not appear to me that such an exchange would be regular, or proper.

It is my wish that you subscribe the debt purchased by you on the books of the Commissioner of Loans for Massachusetts in conformity to the terms of the loan proposed by the funding Act,[2] in the names of the Trustees of the sinking fund, as expressed in the Act making provision for the reduction of the public debt.[3]

I request that you will as speedily as possible furnish me with an account of your purchases designating all the particulars which are required to be known by the law under which they are made.

I am, Sir,   Your obedt. servant   Alexander Hamilton

Benj. Lincoln Esq.
Boston

LS, RG 36, Collector of Customs at Boston, Letters from the Treasury, 1789–1808, National Archives; copy, RG 56, Letters to Collectors at Small Ports, "Set G," National Archives; copy, RG 56, Letters to the Collector at Boston, National Archives.

1. Letter not found.
2. "An Act making provision for the (payment of the) Debt of the United States" (1 *Stat.* 138–44 [August 4, 1790]).
3. 1 *Stat.* 186–87 (August 12, 1789).

Treasury Department Circular to the Commissioners of Loans

[*Philadelphia, April 8, 1791.* On May 3, 1791, Nathaniel Appleton wrote to Hamilton: "Your circular Letter 8th April is received." *Circular not found.*]

To John Adams

Treasury Department
April 9th. 1791.

Sir

I have just received a letter from Mr. Short [1] which I wish to submit, in order to certain measures being taken upon it, to yourself and the heads of the executive departments, in pursuance of the President's letter of the 4th. instant,[2] which I take it for granted has been communicated to you by the Secretary of State.

I request therefore that you will please to name a time and place for the meeting; and that it may be as early as will be convenient to you after tomorrow.

I have the honor to be   With the most respectful attachment,   Sir, Your Obedient servant   Alexander Hamilton

The Vice President of the United States.

LS, Adams Family Papers, deposited in the Massachusetts Historical Society, Boston.

    1. William Short to H, December 2, 1790.

    2. George Washington to H, Thomas Jefferson, and Henry Knox, April 4, 1791.

From John Adams

Philadelphia April 9. 1791

Sir

I have received the Letter you did me the honor to write me this morning and as the Secretary of State accidentally fell in before I had opportunity to answer it, we agreed to propose a meeting at his House at two o'Clock on Monday next. If that time and place are agreeable to you, and the Secretary at War, they will be particularly so to me who have the honor to be with great regard, Sir your most obedient and most humble Servt.   John Adams

The Secretary of the Treasury of the U.S.

LC, Adams Family Papers, deposited in the Massachusetts Historical Society, Boston.

From Nathaniel Appleton

Boston, April 9, 1791. Sends "Names of persons to whom some of the . . . [Treasury] drafts were directed." States that Hamilton's "special Letter 24th March [1] . . . and . . . Circular Letter 25th March [2] are this minute come to hand." Has complied with the instructions in Hamilton's letter of March 17, 1791.

LC, RG 53, Massachusetts State Loan Office, Letter Book, 1785–1791, Vol. "259-M," National Archives.
  1. Letter not found.
  2. Circular not found.

From Simon Gross [1]

[*April 9, 1791.* On April 20, 1791, Hamilton wrote to Gross: "I duly received your letter of the 9th. instant." *Letter not found.*]

  1. Gross was captain of the Maryland revenue cutter.

To Charles Lee

Treasury Department
April 9th. 1791

Sir
    Mr. Lowrey [1] a Merchant in your district presented at the Treasury some time ago the within certificate of your Deputy [2] when he was informed that the direction to refund at the office where the Tonnage was received had been given in a circular letter to the Collectors of the 20th. August 1790. To prevent further difficulty a memorandum of the date of the letter was made on the back of the certificate. Application has been again made at the Treasury for a settlement of the matter. I have therefore to enclose you a copy of my circular letter of August 20th. 1790, being entirely at a loss to know why the money is not repaid. If any other reason than what is expressed in the certificate obstructed the repayment, I presume it would have been communicated to me.

I am, Sir,   Your obedient servant   Alex Hamilton

Charles Lee Esqr.
Collector Alexandria

LS, RG 56, Letters to and from the Collector at Alexandria, National Archives; copy, RG 56, Letters to Collectors at Small Ports, "Set G," National Archives.
  1. Presumably William Lowry of Alexandria, Virginia.
  2. Vincent Gray.

From William Short

Paris April 9. 1791.

Sir

Since my return here questions have been from time to time asked me with respect to the appropriation of the loan lately made in Holland.[1] When asked by those to whom it was necessary to give an answer it was made conformable to that given to M. Caillard [2] at the Hague, as contained in my letter to him of the 6th of March, of which a copy was sent to you on the 11th from Amsterdam. The ministry of themselves would have said nothing because they are fully disposed to subscribe to the convenience of the US & because it is natural for them to await the decision of the President on the proposals of Schweizer & Jeanneret,[3] which they have adopted as far as depended on them. But the committee of finance urged probably by some of its members, who have views on the American debt, or by a patriotic zeal for recieving every thing as soon as possible into the public treasury, express their impatience with respect to this loan whenever an opportunity presents itself. As this has been hitherto done individually it has had no other effect than to shew the dispositions of the committee or some of its members. In the present situation of the assembly the committees & often a few members of a committee have it much in their power to pass a decree through the house. It could not but be disagreeable if a decree relative to the American debt

ALS, letterpress copy, William Short Papers, Library of Congress.
  1. See Short to H, February 17, 22, March 4, 1791. For a description of the Holland loan of March, 1791, see Short to H, February 17, 1791, note 1.
  2. Antoine Bernard Caillard. See Short to Caillard, March 6, 1791, enclosed in Short to H, March 11, 1791.
  3. See Short to H, December 18, 30, 1790; January 15, February 7, and March 11, 1791.

were hurried through the assembly by such means in a moment of impatience & ill humour. The surest means of avoiding it would be to be able to say something certain with respect to your intentions.

I mentioned to you in my letter of the 17th of February what had passed between Mr. G Morris & myself relative to proposals for a loan out of Holland. I learn from him here that the Austrian Netherlands were the place he had in view, & that he has recieved a letter from his correspondents there who urge the business being begun without delay, & that they are fully assured loans might be made successively to a considerable amount. Nothing more can be done in this business until I hear from you. I had always understood & it is the generally recieved opinion that foreign loans were not permitted there by the Imperial government. Still Mr Morris is absolutely certain that it is a mistake; & as he conversed with the bankers on the spot & has taken up his opinion from information collected there with a view to the subject it would seem that he was the least exposed to be misinformed.

I have had an opportunity also of collecting here further & more certain information with respect to Genoa. M. de Spinola,[4] the minister of that country at this court & personally interested in the concerns of speculation carried on there, told me that from the present abundance of money & the want of means of placing it he thought it highly probable the U.S. might make loans there if they should chuse it—he sent also to speak with me on the subject a person who is connected with the monied men of Genoa & who M. de Spinola told me was dependent on him—the meaning of which was that he, M. de Spinola, was concerned with him in business of this sort. I found immediately that this person was as ignorant of the present situation of the U.S. as Spinola himself, unacquainted with the change of their government, their commerce, & their revenues, he only had a general idea of a country whose debts had been formerly little attended to, but who began to think more about them at present & whose situation on the whole was ameliorating. I endeavoured to put him in possession of the present state of American affairs & the American government. I mentioned the amount of the last years revenue also—this of course he would consider as the conversation of a person interested in presenting the subject in its most favorable light. I ob-

4. Christoforo Vincenzo de Spinola.

served to him that it was not my intention to open a loan for the present, but that if after he had satisfied himself by his correspondents at Amsterdam or elsewhere of the present resources of the U.S. & particularly of the state of their credit at Amsterdam, where they were best known, he thought he could procure for them a loan on advantageous terms at Genoa, I would mention the subject to you. He seemed to be persuaded that a loan might be made there & observed that the Genoese would be guided in this business by the value of the American stock at Amsterdam. He observed that 5. p cent would of course be the rate of interest & talked of 5. or 6 p cent as the commission. I told him it was useless to talk about terms at present but that as to commission I could tell him beforehand that the U.S. would not give any thing like that. We separated in this manner a few days ago—he was to write to his correspondents & then to speak with me further on the subject. I have little doubt left that a loan might be made at Genoa for the U.S. at 5 p cent interest—there will be some difficulty perhaps with respect to the commission as the Genoese are remarkable for their avidity & craft in all money negociations.

The Empress of Russia has lately made a loan at Genoa for a million of dollars at 5 p. cent reimbursable I think in ten years. I know nothing of the rate of commission but have no doubt it was high—a second loan on the same terms is now open there. I understand it goes off slower than the first, but will be filled. They will be extended certainly if it can be done.

I understand that the monied men of Geneva have lately made a small loan to the Emperor. I am not acquainted with its conditions & suppose there must be some political view connected with the loan as it is unquestionable that he could have made loans at Amsterdam on as good & probably on better terms than I should imagine the Genevans would place their money with any power.

It is certain however that the present situation of the French government added to the immense reimbursements they are making must leave large sums unemployed as well at Genoa & Geneva. Under such circumstances there is little doubt that the U. S. if their resources were known might make loans there.

Besides the opportunity which is thus presented of making loans in order to pay off the arrears due to France there are other combinations which will necessarily take place & by which the debt due to France might be transferred to the one or other of these countries by means of the stock which they have in the funds here & which they are desirous of withdrawing somewhat on the principals proposed by Schweizer & Jeanneret & which have been submitted to you—or perhaps by waiting the two operations together viz. of a loan opened at Genoa for the money of that country & the translation of our debt from this country to that.

There is another circumstance also which may be found worthy of attention in future although it just now begins to develop itself. The immense quantities of assignats which are now in the hands of the monied people of Paris have reduced accordingly the interest of money. Individuals who were obliged last year to pay six per cent annual interest now borrow easily on the same security for four. They will always borrow cheaper than foreign states; but this fall of interest with them necessarily involves the same with other borrowers. It is possible then that there might be found some who would be disposed to make loans here to the U.S. & particularly on being secured against further depreciation—the government would probably not be opposed to such loans here as they would be for their use, & would take out of circulation the sums of assignats borrowed.

On the whole Sir I have no doubt of the U.S. being able to extend their loans immediately if they chuse it at Amsterdam. There is every reason to believe they might borrow also in the low countries, Genoa, or Geneva, or transfer their debt advantageously from France to one of these countries. It is possible also they might have an opportunity of making loans on good terms here & immediately paying off the arrears, or a part of those due this country.

It is useless to add that in order to derive the greatest advantages from this fortunate position of affairs it would be indispensable to give much latitude to those who have your confidence on this side of the Atlantic; I say those because I take it for granted that no individual would be rash enough to expose himself alone in a business of so much responsability, & particularly of so much delicacy, where there will be so many alternatives left for the exercising of the judgment & of course so much room for disapprobation & censure.

I cannot omit repeating also the necessity of unfolding the U.S. as much as possible to the view of those with whom it is desirable to raise their credit. The perfect ignorance in which all, except a few mercantile houses, are with respect to their present position & resources cannot but be greatly prejudicial. This would be easily removed by constant & authentic information & particularly the publication of authentic papers—such as the amount of duties collected the last year, your report for the establishment of a national bank, the proceedings of Congress thereon, the quantity of domestic debt purchased up &c.

The houses at Amsterdam [5] are regularly furnished with such information & papers, but my former letters will have shewn you how far it is from their interest to render them public.[6] The following extract of a letter which I recieved the day before yesterday from one of them will shew you to what length this information goes—"Mr Hamilton had received your letter to him of the day previous to our consenting to negotiate the future loans of Congress at 4. p. cent charges advising him you did not doubt of a loan being opened at 4 ½ p. cent charges or perhaps at 4. p. cent. We therefore expect soon his eventual orders for disposal of the monies of the March loan which being now more than half disposed of we shall be able to make a fine remittance immediately on the arrival of his directions, & we trust be able to conclude for a new loan on your first application to effect it, as well as to raise in a much shorter time than we formerly imagined the needful monies to pay off the arrears of interest & instalments of principal due to France by the U.S. so good is the credit actually enjoyed here by America." [7]

As it becomes every day more probable that Russia will be engaged in a war with England, it must necessarily render the lenders more difficult with respect to that country & more willing to lend to the U.S.—the progression of opinion mentioned in the above extract is probably connected with this circumstance.

I have the honor to be with sentiments of the most perfect respect & attachment   Sir,   Your most obedient humble servant   W. Short

The Honble Alexander Hamilton Secretary of the Treasury

5. Willink, Van Staphorst, and Hubbard.
6. See Short to H, February 22, March 11, 1791.
7. Van Staphorst and Hubbard to Short, April 4, 1791 (LS, Short Family Papers, Library of Congress).

To Richard Wylly [1]

Treasury Department, April 9, 1791.

Sir:

The acting Paymaster General of the Treasury [2] has reported to me the circumstances under which the certificate of the late Paymaster General,[3] for $123, 283 70/90, mentioned in your letter of the 1st ultimo, was issued.[4] I find that it is already passed to the credit of the State of Georgia, in the books of the Pay Office, and that it will be included in the statement of the general board of commissioners for settling the accounts of the several States with the United States. You cannot, therefore, receive that certificate in payment of subscription to the loan proposed by the act of Congress of the 4th of August, 1790.[5]

I am, sir, &c.   A. Hamilton, Secretary of the Treasury.

Richard Wylly, Esq.

ASP, Claims, 188.
1. Wylly was commissioner of loans for Georgia.
2. Joseph Howell.
3. John Pierce.
4. In 1785 Georgia had acquired from Pierce a certificate of credit in the account of the United States for the sum of $123,283 70/90 which the state had paid the officers of the Georgia line at the close of the American Revolution. For some years thereafter Georgia attempted unsuccessfully to collect interest on this certificate. In his letter of March 1, 1791, to the Treasury Department Wylly wrote:
"I was applied to, some years since, for interest on a certificate of Mr. Pierce's to this State, for $123,283 70/90, but as it was not noticed in his register, nor like his other certificates, I would not pay it. . . . I shall . . . be obliged to you to instruct me what I am to do with it, and at what time the interest is to commence, as that did not appear plain to me when I saw it." (*ASP, Claims,* 188.)
5. "An Act making provision for the (payment of the) Debt of the United States" (1 *Stat.* 138–44).

To James Greenleaf and James Watson [1]

Treasury Department
April 10th 1791

Gentlemen

I received on Saturday your letter of the   .[2]

I have, from a wish to accommodate, reconsidered my instruction with regard to the payment of *intire* dividends only; but I cannot satisfy myself that a department from it will be consistent with that exact order in the conduct of the business, which so complicated an operation as the payment of interest in thirteen different places accompanied with the continual possibility of a transfer from one to another, absolutely requires.

With regard to the refusal to pay interest, without the production of the certificates, this as far as regards the *funded* debt has been a misapprehension of the commissioner of loans of New York [3] which has been since rectified, as I presume you are by this time advised of.

I am with great consideration   Gentlemen   Your obed servant

A Hamilton

Messrs. Watson & Greenleaf
N York

ALS, Munson-Williams-Proctor Institute, Utica, New York.
    1. Greenleaf, a native of Massachusetts, was one of the largest land and security speculators in the United States. Watson was a New York City merchant. In 1788 the two men formed a partnership for a mercantile house in New York City.
    2. Space left blank in MS.   Letter not found.
    3. John Cochran.

To Samuel Henshaw

Philadelphia, April 10, 1791. "Your letter of the 15th of March duly came to hand. . . . I wish you not to consider it as mere compliment, when I say, that the light in which your character stands could not fail to have brought you into view in that arrangement. And could you be minutely acquainted with every circumstance that in the President's mind inclined the ballance a different way, you would find no reason to be dissatisfied with the estimation in which you have been held. You are well aware that in a comparison of the pretensions of men of merit collateral considerations may often be justly allowed to turn the scale. . . ."

ALS, Harvard College Library; ADf, Hamilton Papers, Library of Congress.

To Jedediah Huntington

Treasury Department
April 10th. 1791

Sir

It is certainly incumbent upon every master of a vessel to make report to the Collector of any district, into which he may go for whatever cause, within twenty four hours, and (if the vessel should remain so long in the district) to make an entry. The officers of the customs who do the duty consequently become entitled to a compensation. It is not however extraordinary that another opinion should have arisen with respect to the intention of the legislature, as different parts of the act [1] countenance a different inference. In such cases such construction must be adopted as will best reconcile them (prefering *express* directions to implied meanings) and such as will be most conducive to the security of the revenue without oppressing trade. The danger to the revenue would be excessive, if the first report and subsequent entry were dispensed with. But there is no inconvenience to trade as it is immaterial where the tonnage is paid, and the *cargo* may be carried to any other district without *paying or securing to pay* the duties in the first.

When it is decided by the vessel's departure, that she will not unlade in the district into which she has gone or in which she is detained, it is proper that the manifest be forwarded to the Collector of the District to which she is bound.

Should any vessel come within your [district from another] [2] which has not her name painted upon the fixed work of her stern, which is nailed or screwed to her, [it will I think be adviseable to demand] from her foreign tonnage [and if disputed to let it be persisted in to a judicial determination.]

If it appears necessary to you I shall be satisfied, that you procure for the Surveyor of Middletown a cheap boat fit for harbour service, and that you procure the necessary scales and weights.

I observe in your letter of the 16th. ultimo [3] you mention, that "the merchants have never failed so much in punctuality as at this period." The uncertainty that would arise in the operations of this department, and in the most momentous affairs of government from defaults at the custom house obliges me to refer you to my instructions [4] on this point which must be strictly executed. Should any bonds which are now due remain unpaid you will place them in the hands of the Attorney of the District.

I request to be informed how much lighter than their due weight were the dollars you mention, and whether there were any peculiar circumstances to which their lightness is to be attributed; as the dollars generally to be met with are of full weight.

I am, Sir,   Your obedient servant   A Hamilton

Jedediah Huntington Esqr
Collector New London

LS, with interlineations by H, MS Division, New York Public Library.
    1. H is referring to Section 16 of "An Act to provide more effectually for the collection of the duties imposed by law on goods, wares and merchandise imported into the United States, and on the tonnage of ships or vessels" (1 *Stat.* 158–59 [August 4, 1790]).
    2. Material within brackets in this letter is in the handwriting of H.
    3. Letter not found.
    4. See "Treasury Department Circular to the Collectors of the Customs," December 18, 1789.

From Thomas Jefferson

[Philadelphia, April 10, 1791]

Th. Jefferson has the honor to send to the Secretary of the Treasury a note just received from Mr. Otto [1] with copies of a correspondence between certain bankers desirous of lending 40 millions of livres to the U.S. the French ministers & mr Short.[2] He will ask the Secretary of the Treasury's consideration of these papers, & that he will be so good as to return them to him with the substance of the answer he would wish to have given to mr Otto. It is probable indeed we shall soon receive the same correspondence from mr Short with his observations on the offer made.

Apr. 10. 1791.

AL, Hamilton Papers, Library of Congress.
    1. Louis G. Otto was French chargé d'affaires in the United States.
    2. See William Short to H, December 18, 30, 1790; January 15, 1791.

To George Washington

[Philadelphia, April 10, 1791]

Sir,

I have duly received the private letter which you did me the honor to write me of the 4. instant.

It is to be lamented that our system is such as still to leave the public peace of the Union at the mercy of each state Government. This is not only the case as it regards direct interferences, but as it regards the *inability* of the National Government in many particulars to take those direct measures for carrying into execution its views and engagements which exigencies require. For example—A party comes from a County of Virginia into Pennsylvania and wantonly murders some friendly Indians. The National Government instead of having power to apprehend the murderers and bring them to justice, is obliged to make a representation to *that* of Pennsylvania: That of Pennsylvania again is to make a requisition of that of Virginia. And whether the murderers shall be brought to Justice at all must depend upon the particular policy and energy and good disposition of two state Governments, and the efficacy of the provisions of their respective laws. And the security of other States and the money of all is at the discretion of one.[1] These things require a remedy but when it will come—God knows.

From present appearances a pretty general Indian war is not a little to be apprehended. But there is now nothing for it, but to encounter it with vigour, and thus far in my Department the provisions are adequate.

I have the honor to remain with the truest & most respectful attachment   Sir   Your Obedt. servant   A Hamilton

Philada. April 10 1791.

LC, George Washington Papers, Library of Congress.
  1. See H to Washington, March 27, 1791, note 2.

To George Washington

Treasury Department
April 10 1791.

Sir

I have the honor of your letter of the 4th. instant addressed to the Secretary of State the Secretary at War and myself; to which due obedience shall be paid on my part.

A letter from Mr. Short dated at Amsterdam the 2d. of December has just come to hand giving me an account of his proceedings to that period; a copy of which will be forwarded by the tuesday's post. He informs me, among other things, that he had concluded with the Bankers of the United States [1] to open a loan in February for two millions and a half of Guilders, at five per Cent interest and four per Cent charges,[2] which is a half per Cent less than the last.[3] The term of reimbursement fifteen years, beginning at the end of ten, with liberty to the United States to reimburse at any time sooner.

You will recallect that by a particular instruction from you to me,[4] no succeeding *Loan* is to be opened, until *that* preceding has been submitted to you, and received your approbation. As it is very desireable that no delay may attend the progress of the business, both as it regards payments to France and the domestic operations, to which the loans may be applied, I have concluded to submit Mr. Shorts letter tomorrow to the Vice President, and the heads of Departments,[5] that they may consider, how far the case is within the purview of your letter; and whether it will not be expedient to authorise Mr. Short to proceed upon a further loan to the amount of three millions of guilders, which is the sum to which the money lenders have been accustomed, and *that* recommended by our Bankers as the most proper to consitute each Loan.

I request nevertheless to receive your instruction as soon as possible upon the subject. And I submit whether it will not be adviseable to change the restriction above mentioned so as to leave Mr. Short at liberty to open his loans successively for three millions of Dollars each; no new one to commence till after the preceding one has been filled; but without waiting for a ratification from this

Country; provided the terms be not in any case less advantageous than those now announced. There is always danger of considerable delay in waiting for approbation from hence, before a new loan can be undertaken; and favourable *moments* may be lost, for there are periods more or less favourable.

I think there is no probability for some time to come that loans can be obtained on better terms. And I may add that as far as I can judge, Mr. Short has conducted himself in the affair with judgment and discretion: and there will be safety in allowing him the latitude proposed. I believe also it will be adviseable to apply the present loan in the same manner as the former, that is to say one half, or perhaps 1,500,000 guilders to the use of France, and the residue to the purchase of the Debt here; on this point also I request your direction.

I have the honor to be   with the most perfect respect   Sir   Your most Obedient   & humble servant   Alex: Hamilton

LC, George Washington Papers, Library of Congress.
1. Willink, Van Staphorst, and Hubbard.
2. This is a reference to the Holland loan of March, 1791. For a description of this loan, see Short to H, February 17, 1791.
3. The "last" was the Holland loan of 1790. For a description of this loan, see Willink, Van Staphorst, and Hubbard to H, January 25, 1790; H to Willink, Van Staphorst, and Hubbard, November 29, 1790, note 1.
4. See Tobias Lear to H, August 26, 1790.
5. See H to John Adams, and Adams to H, April 9, 1791.

To William Ellery

Treasury Department
April 11th. 1791

Sir

The law has not provided for the payment of drawbacks, except the prescribed proofs of landing in some place, without the United States, be adduced. Goods exported for drawback cannot be landed again in the United States, without again paying the impost, under the existing laws,[1] though it ⟨is no⟩t improbable the legislature will provide a remedy in some future act for this inconvenience to trade.

Your proceeding in the case of the Charming Sally, Reed, is conformable with law, and I do not see fit to interfere. Her case must have a legal decision.[2]

The new act for registring vessels [3] will probably provide for the making American bottoms of vessels condemned and *actually sold* for breaches of the laws, but at present such a vessel cannot be registered. She may sail under her old papers, and the Marshall's certificate, but will be subject to foreign tonnage.

I am, Sir,   Your obedt. servant   Alex Hamilton

William Ellery Esq.
Collector Newport

LS, Newport Historical Society, Newport, Rhode Island.
   1. Ellery requested this information in a letter he wrote to H on January 31, 1791. This letter had not been found when Volume VII of *The Papers of Alexander Hamilton* was published; it will be published in a supplementary volume.
   The regulations governing the payment of drawbacks were contained in Sections 56, 57, 58, 59, 60, and 61 of "An Act to provide more effectually for the collection of the duties imposed by law on goods, wares and merchandise imported into the United States, and on the tonnage of ships or vessels" (1 *Stat.* 173–75 [August 4, 1790]).
   2. See Ellery to H, March 15, 1791.
   3. On July 22, 1790, a "bill for registering Ships or Vessels, for regulating those employed in the Coasting Trade and Fisheries, and for other purposes" was presented to the House of Representatives. On July 26, however, the House "*Ordered*, That the farther consideration of the bill . . . be postponed until the next session of Congress" (*Journal of the House*, I, 275–76, 282).

To Richard Harison

Treasury Department,
11 April 1791

Sir,

Mr. Abijah Hammond [1] has informed me that he delivered to the Grand Jury, before whom was brought the case of Christopher Bancker,[2] the certificate, on which the charge against him was founded.[3] I wish to know the present state of that affair.

I am, sir,   With great consideration,   Your Obedt Servant
                                                        Alex Hamilton

Richard Harison Esqr.
Atto. of the United States,
New York

LS, New-York Historical Society, New York City.
   1. Hammond was a New York City merchant.
   2. According to the New York City directory for 1792, Bancker was a "scrivener."

3. Bancker had apparently been charged with stealing Treasury certificates. See Harison to H, April 14, 1791.

To Benjamin Lincoln

Treasury Department,
11 April 1791

Sir,

The carriage of the Teas to Salem, as stated in your letter of the 9th Ultimo is a mere transportation & not an exportation of them. The outward entry must be made in due form at Salem *where the Ship America was lying*, and can only be made there. That outward entry is the *first* operation in the business of exportation, and as it will appear by the public books & papers that the goods were shipt from a district other than that into which they were imported, the drawback cannot be obtained. Nothing however in the law occurs to me, which will prevent the America from receiving part of her cargo in Salem, & proceeding to Boston to complete it. No tonnage will arise on an American Vessel trading in one district & proceeding to another, with Goods *not deliverable* in the latter. By means of this proceeding dutiable goods may be exported from Salem & Boston in the same Vessel so as to obtain the drawback on both.

I am, sir,   Your obedt Servant   Alex Hamilton

Benjamin Lincoln, Esqr.
Collr. Boston

LS, RG 36, Collector of Customs at Boston, Letters from the Treasury, 1789–1818, National Archives; copy, RG 56, Letters to the Collector at Boston, National Archives; copy, RG 56, Letters to Collectors at Small Ports, "Set G," National Archives.

To Jeremiah Olney

Treasury Department
April 11th. 1791

Sir

In answer to your letter of the 27th. of December I have to observe, that *under the existing laws*, I consider it as indispensible to an entry at any customhouse, that the vessel be actually within the district appertaining to it. The question has occurred in the port of Philadelphia, where cases of the nature you mention, frequently happen.

The legislature at a late stage of their session directed me to consider and make report upon the compensations and emoluments of the officers of the customs.[1] It was my wish to have done it, but the difficulty of making amidst so many other pressing objects a proper arrangement, and the shortness of the Session put it out of my power to form a satisfactory report. This business will however receive due attention the next Session, and I recommend to you not to think of a resignation till you have seen the issue of it.

In regard to the small articles mentioned in your letter of the 17th. January, the law does not contemplate the exemption of any dutiable goods, except sea stores and certain articles belonging to emigrants, and it will be most proper that you adhere to those two exemptions and make no other.

The deduction of 7½ per Cent from a Captain's or owner's account in lieu of due measurement is not a legal mode of ascertaining the duty on goods imported. Due examination into the case will be immediately made. In all cases of goods to be gauged, weighed, measured &c. to ascertain the duties no other mode can be legally adopted.

I am, Sir,   Your obedt. servant   A Hamilton

Jerh. Olney Esqr.
Collector Providence

LS, Rhode Island Historical Society, Providence; copy, RG 56, Letters from the Collector at Providence, National Archives; copy, RG 56, Letters to Collectors at Small Ports, "Set G," National Archives.
   1. On January 18, 1791, the House "*Ordered,* That the Secretary of the Treasury be directed to report to this House his opinion whether any, and what, further compensation ought to be made to the respective officers employed in the collection of the revenue" (*Journal of the House,* I, 357).

To Nathaniel Pendleton [1]

Treasury Department
11 April 1791

Sir,
   I return herewith the proceedings on the petition of Duncan Man-

son,[2] for the same reason, which has occasioned the remission of those in the case of Wm Backhouse.[3]

The circumstance of excuse, for not complying with the law,[4] is the change of Masters in the harbour of Charleston. The time of this change, and the time of departure ought to be known in order to a judgment whether any hurry or disconcertion on this account was the probable cause of omission.

As a general rule, the payment of the duties ought to be brought more to a point, by Shewing in what Vessel they were imported, and producing a certificate of their having been paid or secured, from the custom house. But as this may not always be practicable, it cannot always be regirously insisted upon.

I have the honor to be,   with very great consideration,   sir; Your Obed Hbe Servant   Alex Hamilton

Judge Pendleton

LS, United States District Court Case Files, District of Georgia, Federal Records Center, East Point, Georgia.

   1. Pendleton was Federal judge for the District of Georgia.
   2. Manson, a merchant of Frederica, Georgia, was the owner of a large quantity of goods which had been shipped on board the schooner *Swift* in the spring of 1790. In his statement Manson said that Christopher Hillary, collector of the customs at Brunswick, Georgia, had refused to let him claim his goods which had just arrived in St. Simons' Sound on board the *Swift* until the captain of the *Swift* produced a manifest. This the captain was unable to do, alleging he had been appointed master of the ship the day before it sailed from Charleston, South Carolina, and had assumed that the necessary papers had been secured by the previous captain. Manson pleaded that "no fraud was intended and that the duties were paid or secured to be paid in Charleston" (ADS, United States District Court Case Files, District of Georgia, Federal Records Center, East Point, Georgia).
   H eventually issued a warrant of remission in the case "upon the express condition, nevertheless that he the said Duncan M<anson> his Executors or Administrators do first satisfy all parties, other than the United States . . . [for claims connected with the forfeiture] and that he the said Duncan Manson do likewise pay all reasonable Costs and charges attending the proceedings touching the premises, to be assessed by the Judge. . . ." This warrant of remission and other papers connected with the case may be found in the United States District Court Case Files, District of Georgia, Federal Records Center, East Point, Georgia.
   3. No record of a case concerning William Backhouse has been found. H may be referring to the case of *United States* v *Christopher Backhouse*. On December 29, 1790, Pendleton ordered the clerk of the District Court to submit the facts of this case to H for his decision (United States District Court Docket Book, District of Georgia, Federal Records Center, East Point, Georgia). H's final decisions on Manson's and Backhouse's cases were referred to Venable Bond, the clerk of the District Court, on August 20, 1791 (LS, United States

District Court Case Files, District of Georgia, Federal Records Center, East Point, Georgia).

4. H is referring to Section 11 of "An Act to provide more effectually for the collection of the duties imposed by law on goods, wares and merchandise imported into the United States, and on the tonnage of ships or vessels" (1 *Stat.* 156–57 [August 4, 1790]), which reads in part as follows: "That every master or other person having the charge or command of any ship or vessel belonging in the whole or in part to a citizen or citizens, inhabitant or inhabitants of the United States, laden with goods as aforesaid, and bound to any port or place in the United States, shall on his arrival within four leagues of the coast thereof, or within any of the bays, harbors, ports, rivers, creeks or inlets thereof, upon demand, produce such manifest or manifests in writing, which such master or other person is herein before required to have on board his said ship or vessel, to such officer or officers of the customs, as shall first come on board his said ship or vessel, for his or their inspection, and shall deliver to such officer or officers a true copy or copies thereof (which copy or copies shall be provided and subscribed by the said master or other person having the command or charge of such ship or vessel)."

From William Seton

Bank of New York 11th Apl. 91

Sir

I have to acknowledge the honor of your Letter of the 1st. instant.[1] Whenever Mr. John McComb Junr. exhibits the contract signed by you & him the Three Thousand Dollars shall be paid to him as you desire and passed to the Debit of the United States in the Seperate Accounts.[2]

On the 16th. of Feby. agreeably to your desire we stopt the sale of the Treasurers Bills on the Collector then in Bank, as well those that had been Credited to his account as those that were not.[3] They have remained in this state of Suspence ever since. The Treasurer's last post has sent Bills on the Collectors for 18700 Dollars Desiring the Bank to give him immediate Credit for them, which is done. I must therefore request that you will honor me with instructions what I am to do with the former bills.

I am with great respect

LC, Bank of New York, New York City.
1. Letter not found.
2. See H to McComb, April 1, 1791.
3. See Seton to H, February 16, 1791.

To George Washington

Philada. April 11 1791.

Sir

I have just received a letter from Mr. King [1] in these words—
"Mr. Elliot,[2] who it has been said was appointed will not come to
America, owing say his friends here to a disinclination on his part
which has arisen from the death of his eldest or only son. Mr. Seaton [3]
yesterday read me an abstract of a letter from London dated February 2. & written, as he observed, by a man of information, which
says—'Mr. Frazer is appointed plenipotentiary to the United States
of America and will go out as soon as it is ascertained here that a
correspondent character is appointed in America'. Although Mr.
Elliot might not have been altogether adequate to the appointment,
yet he would not have been a bad choice; it is questionable whether
we can say even as much as that for Mr. Frazer, who is probably the
Gentleman lately resident with the Hans-towns, and formerly consul
at Algiers, and who is said to be a wrong headed impetuous man.[4]
Should this information be correct, the appointment is not only un-
promising but is also a pretty strong proof of the misguided opinions
of the British administration concerning this Country."

Nothing except the foregoing letter occurs worth communication
more than is contained in my official dispatch herewith.[5]

With the truest and most respectful attachment   I have the honor
to be   Sir   Your Obedt. Servant   A Hamilton

LC, George Washington Papers, Library of Congress.
  1. Rufus King. Letter not found.
  2. Samuel Flagg Bemis (*Jay's Treaty*, 62) suggests that the Elliot whose appointment as Minister to the United States was discussed by the British ministry
"might possibly have been Thomas Elliot who was seeking an appointment in
October, 1791" (see "Conversation with George Beckwith," January 19–20,
1791). In the correspondence of John Graves Simcoe, governor of Upper Canada, however, he is identified as Andrew Elliot (E. A. Cruikshank, *The Correspondence of John Graves Simcoe, with Allied Documents Relating to His
Administration of Upper Canada* [Toronto, 1923–1931], I, 21, 48; V, 163).
  3. William Seton.
  4. There were two Frasers who had served in the British diplomatic service,
each of whom partially fits H's description. Charles Henry Fraser was secretary
of the British legation in Russia in 1787 and 1788 and went to Madrid in 1790
as Minister Plenipotentiary. Recalled in November, 1790, he was made resident

of the Hanse towns. His credentials bore the date of April, 1791, and he reached Hamburg on May 13, 1791. Archibald C. Fraser was consul of Algiers from 1766 to 1774, but he held no other diplomatic position. A Scottish nobleman, he inherited the family estate in 1782 and was a member of Parliament for Invernesshire from 1782 to 1796.

   In any event, neither man received the appointment to the United States, for in 1791 George Hammond was named Minister Plenipotentiary.

   5. Letter not found.

To George Washington

[*Philadelphia, April 11, 1791.* On May 7, 1791, Washington wrote to Hamilton: "I have received . . . the opinions offered in your letters of the 11th." *Second letter of April 11 not found.*]

To Thomas Jefferson

Treasury Department
April 12th. 1791

Sir

   I have perused the papers communicated to you by the Chargé des Affaires of France.[1] The propositions to which they relate, as far as they are understood, appear to me inadmissible. The only advantage they offer to the United States is a prolongation of the time of reimbursement. The rate of interest is to remain the same, and the place of payment, according to the probable course of exchange, is to be altered for the worse, from Paris to Amsterdam. A premium of five ℈ Cent is also required, while the charges on the loans we make in Holland do not exceed four.

   There is however a proposition which is not understood. It is this, that the exchange on the sum to be paid at Paris and received at Amsterdam shall be regulated according to the *Tariff* announced in the law of Congress. Now there is nothing in the laws of the United States to which I can apply the term Tariff. It is possible however that Mr. Short's letters [2] when received may throw light on this point and some others, which may give a different complexion to the business.

   But there are various collateral considerations in relation to the transfer of the debt due from the United States to France, affecting the credit and financial operations of this country, which will make it in almost any form a delicate operation. It is desireable on every account to make expeditious payment to France; but this desire must be conciliated with that of invigorating and perfecting the system of public credit of the United States. And in adhering to this idea there is the additional inducement of a tolerable prospect of satisfying the claims of France in a manner perhaps as expeditious and probably more efficacious than would be incident to an acquiescence in the proposed plan.

I have the honor to be, with great respect and esteem   Sir   Your obedt. servant   Alexander Hamilton
                                                                    Secy of the Treasury

The honorable Thomas Jefferson Esqr.
Secretary of State

LS, James Madison Papers, Library of Congress.
    1. Louis G. Otto. See Jefferson to H, April 10, 1791.
    2. See William Short to H, December 18, 30, 1790, and January 15, 1791.

From Robert Troup

New York, April 12, 1791. "I recd. your last letter [1] with . . . your account [2] current with the Lees. . . ." [3]

ALS, Hamilton Papers, Library of Congress.
    1. Letter not found.
    2. The account is dated April 5, 1791 (ADS, Hamilton Papers, Library of Congress).
    3. Thomas and Richard Lee, English businessmen. H had served as their agent in America in the seventeen-eighties. See H's "Cash Book," March 1, 1782–1791, note 115.

To Jeremiah Wadsworth

[Philadelphia] April 12. 91

My Dear Sir
    I am sorry to learn that a certain heresy makes a progress. But there must be a portion of nonsense in human affairs—I bear in mind my promise to you.
    Pray send me a Memorandum without delay of the payments which you h⟨ave⟩ made me on Account of Mr Church [1] with their dates. I

am forwarding him my account,[2] and I want this memorandum to
Check my entries.

Yrs. sincerely   A Hamilton

J Wadsworth Esqr

ALS, Mr. Pierce W. Gaines, Fairfield, Connecticut.
    1. For Wadsworth's business connection with John B. Church, see H to Wads-
worth, March 12, 1791.
    2. See "Account with John B. Church," May 1, 1791.

From William Jackson [1]

Richmond, April 13, 1791. Encloses list of proposed inspectors of
revenue for Virginia. Asks Hamilton to "suspend issueing the commissions" until Edward Carrington indicates "the determinations of
the gentlemen who are appointed Inspectors."

LC, George Washington Papers, Library of Congress.
    1. Jackson, who had served as a major under Benjamin Lincoln during the
American Revolution, had been secretary of the Constitutional Convention in
1787. He became one of George Washington's secretaries in 1789.

From William Jackson

Richmond, April 13, 1791. "The President of the United States
commands me to request your attention to the enclosed memorandum. . . ."

LC, George Washington Papers, Library of Congress.

To William Short

Treasury Department
April 13th. 1791

Sir

I have recently received your letters of the 2d. December and
the 25th. of January. The others to which they refer have not yet
come to hand.

The manner in which you have proceeded, as detailed in your

letter of the 2d. of December, is entirely satisfactory to me and I doubt not will be equally so to the President, when known to him. He is now absent on a journey through the Southern States.

In consequence of the arrangement which has been made by the President relative to cases occurring in his absence,[1] I am at liberty to authorise you as soon as the loan you announce is filled, to cause another to be opened for three millions of guilders, which I accordingly do.

One million and a half of the loan you have set on foot [2] is destined as a payment to France, and you will please to take as early measures as possible to have the million remitted to Paris; the half million will wait for a further direction. I observe that the remittance of the million and a half of the last loan [3] has been effected with considerable advantage to the United States. I presume that a similar advantage will for some time to come attend succeeding remittances.

Though your letters, detailing the nature of the offers for a transfer of the debt due to France, are not arrived, a communication through the Chargé des affaires of France to the Secretary of State has given me the requisite information.[4] There is however one proposition of Messieurs Schweizer, Jeanneret & Co.[5] which I do not understand. It is the fourth, to this effect, "The difference of exchange upon the forty millions to be furnished at Paris, & upon the same sum to be received in contracts of the United States shall be regulated according to the *tariff* announced in the law of Congress." What is meant by this tariff I am wholly at a loss to determine, there being nothing in the law of Congress to which I can apply the term.

This being the case the propositions with the sole advantage of a prolonged period of reimbursement would leave the debt at the same rate of interest, and involve the disadvantage of making it payable at Amsterdam instead of Paris (subjecting the United States thereby to the loss arising from a less favourable course of exchange) together with the further disadvantage of a premium of five per Cent instead of four.

In this view of the matter the propositions are inadmissible. Your letter however by explaining the one I have quoted may possibly throw new light on the subject. But I do not despair that offers will be made better corresponding with the terms you are at liberty to accept.[6]

The domestic debt of the United States has reached the following prices in our market.

Six ⅌ Cent funded Stock bearing Interest from the 1st. instant 17/ ⅌ £ or 85 ⅌ Cent, and much in demand.

Defered Six ⅌ Cent Stock 9/ ⅌ £ or 45 ⅌ Cent

Three per Cents bearing Interest from the 1st. instant 9/ ⅌ £ or 45 ⅌ Cent, much in demand and rising.

I have the honor to be,   with perfect consideration & esteem,   Sir Your obedient servant   Alexander Hamilton
                                                       Secretary of the Treasury
Wm. Short Esq.
Amsterdam.

P.S. I omitted to make you my acknowledgments for the returns of exports from St Petersburg,[7] which I beg you now to accept. Such documents will always be most acceptable, and whenever they can be obtained without trouble or expence, I would request your transmitting to me copies of such as you may be able to procure. I have at present to ask of you the favor of obtaining for me the best information in your power concerning the establishment of the mint in the United Netherlands; the different offices, compensations to the persons engaged in it, the standards, weights, values &c. of the coins and such other particulars as are ever communicated, will all be desirable.

The situation of our East India trade renders it an object to obtain an account of the state of that branch of commerce in foreign countries. If you could with convenience furnish me with any thing relative to that of the United Netherlands it may be very useful at the present moment. I am particularly drawn to enquire about the affairs of the Dutch East India company by the circumstance of their borrowing money and at an high interest.

LS, William Short Papers, Library of Congress. A copy of this letter was enclosed in H's "Report on Foreign Loans," February 13, 1793.

1. See George Washington to H, Thomas Jefferson, and Henry Knox, April 4, 1791, and H to Washington, April 10, 14, 1791.

2. The Holland loan of March, 1791. For a description of this loan, see Short to H, February 17, 1791.

3. The Holland loan of 1790. For a description of this loan, see H to Willink, Van Staphorst, and Hubbard, November 29, 1790, note 1.

4. See Jefferson to H, April 10, 1791, and H to Jefferson, April 12, 1791.

5. See Short to H, December 18, 1790.

6. On April 25, 1791, Jefferson wrote to Short: "You know how strongly we desire to pay off our whole debt to France, and that for this purpose we will use our credit as far as it will hold good. You know also what may be the probability of our being able to borrow the whole sum. Under these dispositions and prospects it would grieve us extremely to see our debt pass into the hands of speculators, and be subjected ourselves to the chicaneries & vexations of private avarice. We desire you therefore to dissuade the government as far as you can prudently from listening to any overtures of that kind, and as to the speculators themselves, whether native or foreign, to inform them without reserve that our government condemns their projects, and reserves to itself the right of paying no where but in to the treasury of France, according to their contract" (ALS, letterpress copy, Thomas Jefferson Papers, Library of Congress).

7. See Short to H, January 25, 1791.

To Richard Harison [1]

Treasury Department
April 14th. 1791

Sir

It may prevent future trouble if the contract with Mr. McComb for the light house be redrawn; rectifying the error in regard to his occupation. He may execute two, and they may be sent to me, when I will duly execute them and transmit one to him. The first payment I find by his own propositions was to be as in the contract three thousand dollars, and it is not well that more is asked. I am content however that it be made four thousand in the new contract, and upon his executing the two copies you will be pleased to give him a certificate directed to the Cashier of the Bank of New-York, who will be instructed on the production of such certificate from you to pay him the money.

The other matters in your letter I will duly consider.

I am with great consideration   Sir   Your obedt. servant

Alex Hamilton

Richard Harison Esq.
Atty. of the U States
New York

LS, New-York Historical Society, New York City.
1. For background to this letter, see Harison to H, April 8, 1791.

From Richard Harison [1]

New York 14 April 1791

Sir

The Affair of Christopher Bancker having been previous to the Promulgation of the Law of the United States respecting Crimes, was not cognizable by any of the national Tribunals. It was therefore laid before a State Grand Jury which was sitting when Mr. Hardy [2] was in this Place, and both Mr. Hammond and that Gentleman were examined upon the Occasion. To my great Surprise no Indictment was found; & having taken an Oppy. to enquire the Reason, One of the Grand Jury informed me that Mr. Hardy could not identify the Certificate produced to be one of those stolen from the Treasury. His Evidence was, that the Number of the Certificates stolen was either the same as that of the one in the Hands of Mr. Hammond or another specific Number which he mentioned. This Testimony I am told was supposed to be too uncertain to afford Ground for a Prosecution of so serious a Nature & perhaps Sentiments of Pity for a respectable but unfortunate Family were suffered to mingle themselves with other Considerations upon this Subject.

I have the Honor to be with very great Deference, Sir

Honb. A. H. *Secy Treasy. U. S.*

LC, New-York Historical Society, New York City.
    1. This letter is in reply to H to Harison, April 11, 1791.
    2. Joseph Hardy, a clerk in the comptroller's office.

To Thomas Jefferson

Treasury Department 14th. April 1791

Sir

It was the intention of the President that you and myself should take such measures as appeared to us eligible towards carrying into execution the Resolution empowering him to procure Artists from Europe towards the establishment of a mint.[1]

It appears to me of great importance, if still practicable, to acquire

Mr. Droz,[2] And the terms mentioned in the enclosed note when applied to so preeminent an Artist do not seem extravagant. Mr. Droz however ought to be bound to give his service for not less than a year after his arrival in the United States. I should think it advisable too that some *determinate* allowance should be concerted with him as an equivalent for the expences of himself and servant. It may be per day.

With regard to instruments, such as are indispensable and *difficult* of execution ought to be procured in Paris.

The having a person who is *practically* and accurately skilled in the assaying of metals is of course an essential part of the establishment meditated. None such has hitherto been found in the United States. If one can be procured from France on terms not immoderate, I am of opinion that it will be expedient to procure him; unless it should appear upon inquiry that Mr. Droz is himself perfectly equal to this part of the business also. The requisite apparatus for making the assays ought in the first instance to be brought from Europe.

In the engagement of such a person it is highly important that no mistake should be made. He ought to be a man not only well skilled in the business, but altogether *trust worthy*.

If the payment of compensations could be deferred 'till after the services have been performed it would give security to the United States.

The requisite dispositions will be made to enable Mr. Short[3] to possess himself of the funds which the execution of this trust may require.

I have the honor to be, with great respect and esteem. Sir Your obedient humble Servant   Alexander Hamilton

The Honble. Thomas Jefferson.

Copy, William Short Papers, Library of Congress; letterpress copy, Thomas Jefferson Papers, Library of Congress; LC, Papers of the Continental Congress, National Archives.

1. On March 3, 1791, Congress adopted the following resolutions:

"Resolved *by the Senate and House of Representatives of the United States of America in Congress assembled,* That a mint shall be established under such regulations as shall be directed by law.

"*Resolved,* That the President of the United States be, and he is hereby authorized to cause to be engaged, such principal artists as shall be necessary to carry the preceding resolution into effect, and to stipulate the terms and conditions of their service, and also to cause to be procured such apparatus as shall be requisite for the same purpose." (1 *Stat.* 225.)

2. Jean Pierre Droz, a citizen of the canton of Neuchâtel, Switzerland, had

invented a machine that would strike the two faces and edge of a coin at a single stroke. Jefferson was not successful in his attempt to bring Droz to the United States; instead Droz was employed by the British government to set up the necessary machinery for coining copper halfpenny pieces in England.

3. William Short, chargé d'affaires at Paris.

To Benjamin Lincoln

Treasury Department
April 14. 1791.

Sir

On considering your letter [1] concerning the Revenue Cutter, I believe it will be on the whole best that the builder proceed with her, attending as far as possible to the other hints in my letter,[2] other than relative to her size. It seems now too late to make any alteration that would lessen her dimensions.

I am Sir   Your Obedt Serv

Benjamin Lincoln Esqr.
Collector of the Customs
Boston

L[S], RG 36, Collector of Customs at Boston, Letters from the Treasury and Others, 1790–1817, Vol. 10, National Archives; copy, RG 56, Letters to the Collector at Boston, National Archives; copy, RG 56, Letters to Collectors at Small Ports "Set G," National Archives; copy, RG 26, Lighthouse Letters Received, Revenue Cutter Service Letters Sent, Vol. "O," National Archives.

1. Lincoln to H. February 23, 1791.

2. Letter not found. This letter presumably was similar to the letters which H sent to other collectors of the customs on January 22 and 23, 1791. See also H to Lincoln, January 21, 1791.

To Daniel Ludlow [1]

[*Philadelphia, April 14, 1791.* On April 23, 1791, Ludlow wrote to Hamilton: "I am indebted to the Honor of your esteemed favor of the 14 Inst." *Letter not found.*]

1. Ludlow, a former Loyalist, was a prominent New York City merchant.

Receipt from Daniel Osborn

Philadelphia, April 14, 1791. Acknowledges payment by Hamilton of six shillings "for the freight of One box" from New York to Philadelphia.

ADS, New-York Historical Society, New York City.

Treasury Department Circular to the Collectors of the Customs

Treasury Department
April 14th. 1791.

Sir

The House of Representatives having been pleased to direct me to examine and report upon the emoluments of the several Officers of the Customs,[1] I find it necessary to enable me to form a satisfactory judgment upon the subject, that I be furnished with an accurate account, as much as possible in detail, of all the Monies received in the four quarters of the year 1790 by every Officer of the Customs, who, conceives himself to be insufficiently compensated. You will therefore, if you think it proper to have your case taken into consideration, transmit me such an Account, and you will exhibit in detail likewise in the same paper the expences of every kind, which you have actually paid during the same year. The sooner this information is received the more early I can enter upon the formation of a report. Should you think proper to make any observations, they will be acceptable. For the greater clearness I wish the letter inclosing the above account to be confined to the subject.

I am, Sir   Your Obedt. Servt.   A Hamilton

P.S. This letter will be accompanied by a letter from the principal Clerk in the Office of the Comptroller[2] to which you will be pleased to pay the same attention as if it had been signed by the Comptroller himself.

LS, to Sharp Delany, Bureau of Customs, Philadelphia; LS, to Benjamin Lincoln, RG 36, Letters from the Treasury, 1789–1818, Vol. 5, National Archives; LS, to Jeremiah Olney, Rhode Island Historical Society, Providence; LS, Chicago Historical Society; LS, Mr. William Dearborn, Nashville, Tennessee; LS, MS Division, New York Public Library; LS, Office of the Secretary, United States Treasury Department; copy, United States Finance Miscellany, Library of Congress; two copies, RG 56, Circulars of the Office of the Secretary, "Set T," National Archives.

1. On January 18, 1791, the House "*Ordered*, That the Secretary of the Treasury be directed to report to this House his opinion whether any, and what, further compensation ought to be made to the respective officers employed in the collection of the revenue" (*Journal of the House*, I, 357).

2. Joseph Hardy.

To George Washington

Treasury Department
April 14 1791

Sir

I have the honor to send herewith a copy of my letter of the 10 inst: and of that from Mr. Short of the 2d. of December to which it refers; and also the copy of another letter from Mr. Short of the 25 of January.

The result of my submission to the vice president and the heads of Departments [1] has been, that they have unanimously advised me to instruct Mr. Short to proceed to open a second loan as soon as the first shall be filled, and to extend this sum from two and a half to three millions of Guilders. I nevertheless request your direction concerning the alteration in his instruction, generally, which is proposed in my letter.

Finding on recurring to it, your instruction to me competent to the disposition of the sum borrowed; I have directed Mr. Short to apply one million and a half of the loan which was to commence in February, as payment to France.[2] The exchange between France & Holland afforded a benefit of more than ten ℔. Cent. to the United States on the last payment.

I thought it adviseable to dispose of a principal part of the loan to this object, not only from the general considerations which operate in the case, but from a desire to counteract the success of some Negotiations with the French Court for the purchase of the Debt due from us, which are not for the interests of the United States.[3]

I have the honor to be   with the most perfect respect   Sir   Your most Obedt.   & most hble servant   Alexander Hamilton

LC, George Washington Papers, Library of Congress.
  1. See H to John Adams, and Adams to H, April 9, 1791.
  2. H to William Short, April 13, 1791. For a description of this loan, see Short to H, February 17, 1791.
  3. See Thomas Jefferson to H, April 10, 1791, and H to Jefferson, April 12, 1791.

To Thomas Jefferson

Treasury Department,
15 April 1791

Sir,

The letter you sent me from Mr. Short & others which I have received,[1] since mine to you,[2] confirm the view of the subject therein taken. This you will perceive from the following passages extracted from one of them—"Since then (speaking of former overtures) another Company has presented itself for the same object, with a scheme by which the United States are to make the *sacrifices* on which *they count* for their profits." "The object of this company is, as you will see, to pay livres tournois in their present depreciated State & to receive from the United States florins at the usual exchange —by this means France would receive from them *as much as she is entitled to receive from us*, but we should be obliged to pay the Company *much more than we are obliged to pay France*." "Had I had powers competent to the purpose, I should not have thought myself justified to have opened such a negotiation where there was *all loss* and *no prospect of advantage* to the United States." "I must also add that the house which makes these propositions is *entirely unknown* here & that I never heared even their names at Paris, which proves that *it must be an inconsiderable one*." [3] Consequently the credit of the United States would be in imminent danger of suffering in their hands.

I have authorised Mr. Short to apply a million & a half of florins of the loan he has opened to the use of France,[4] and shall press as large payments, as may be practicable, to her.

I take it for granted that the Court of France will not attempt any operation with the debt, without the consent of the United States. Any thing of this sort, considering the efforts which are making on our part, to discharge the debt, would certainly be very exceptionable. Indeed I do not see how any valid disposition of the debt of a sovereign power can be made without its consent; but it would be disagreeable to have to use this argument. I trust it will never be rendered necessary.

I have the honor to be, With great respect, Sir, Your Obed Servant   Alexander Hamilton

Honble Thomas Jefferson

LS, James Madison Papers, Library of Congress.
1. See William Short to H, December 18, 30, 1790; January 15, 1791.
2. H to Jefferson, April 12, 1791.
3. These quotations are from Short to H, December 18, 1790.
4. H to Short, April 13, 1791. For a description of the Holland loan of March, 1791, see Short to H, February 17, 1791.

To Nathan Keais [1]

[*Philadelphia, April 15, 1791.* On May 6, 1791, Keais wrote to Hamilton: "Yours of the . . . 15th Ulto I have duly received." *Letter not found.*]

1. Keais was collector of customs at Washington, North Carolina.

Treasury Department Circular to the Commissioners of Loans

[*Philadelphia, April 16, 1791.* On April 27, 1791, Nathaniel Appleton wrote to Hamilton: "I am this minute favoured with your Circular Letter 16th instant." *Circular not found.*]

To George Washington

Treasury Department
April 17. 1791

Sir

I am very sorry to have to inform you, that the Comptroller of the Treasury [1] departed this life yesterday. His loss is sincerely to be regretted as that of a good officer & an honorable & amiable man.

With the most perfect   respect, I &

ADf, Connecticut Historical Society, Hartford; LC, George Washington Papers, Library of Congress.
1. Nicholas Eveleigh had been appointed the first comptroller of the Treasury on September 11, 1789.

To George Washington

Philadelphia April 17
1791

Private

Sir

You will probably recollect that previous to your departure from this place, anticipating the event which has taken place with regard to the death of Mr Eveleigh, I took the liberty to mention to you that Mr. Woolcott [1] the present Auditor would be in every respect worthy of your consideration as his successor in office.

Now that the event has happened, a concern as anxious as it is natural for the success of the department united with a sentiment of Justice towards Mr. Woolcott leads me to a repetition of that Idea. This Gentleman's conduct in the station he now fills has been that of an excellent officer. It has not only been good but distinguished. It has combined all the requisites which could be desired; moderation with firmness, liberality with exactness, indefatigable industry with an accurate & sound discernment a thorough knowlege of business & a remarkable spirit of order & arrangement. Indeed I ought to say that I owe very much of whatever success may have attented the merely executive operation of the department to Mr. Woolcott. And I do not fear to commit myself, when I add, that he possesses in an eminent degree all the qualifications desireable in a Comptroller of the Treasury—that it is scarcely possible to find a man in the United States more competent to the duties of that station than himself, *few* who would be equally so. It may truly be said of him that he is a man of *rare* merit. And I have good evidence that he has been viewed in this light by the members of Congress extensively from different quarters of

ADf, Connecticut Historical Society, Hartford; LC, George Washington Papers, Library of Congress; copy, Connecticut Historical Society.
1. Oliver Wolcott, Jr., who had served as auditor of the Treasury Department since September, 1789.

the Union, and is so considered by all that part of the public, who have had opportunities of witnessing his conduct.

The immediate relation too, which his present situation bears to that of Comptroller is a strong argument in his favour. Though a regular gradation of office is not admissible in a strict sense in regard to offices of a civil nature and is wholly inapplicable to those of the first rank (such as the heads of the great executive departments) yet a certain regard to the relation, which one situation bears to another is consonant with natural ideas of Justice and is recommended by powerful considerations of policy. The expectation of promotion in civil as in military life is a great stimulous to virtuous exertion: While examples of unrewarded exertion, supported by talent & qualification, are proportionable discouragements. Where they do not produce resignations, they leave men dissatisfied & a dissatisfied man seldom does his duty well.

In a government like ours, where pecuniary compensations are moderate, the principle of gradual advancement, as a reward for good conduct, is perhaps more necessary to be attended to than in others where offices are more lucrative. By due attention to it, it will operate as a mean to secure respectable men for offices of inferior emolument and consequence.

In addition to the rest, Mr. Woolcotts experience, in this particular line, pleads powerfully in his favour. This experience may be dated back to his office of Comptroller of the State of Connecticut [2] and has been perfected by practice in his present place.

A question may perhaps Sir arise in your mind whether some inconvenience may not attend his removal from his present office. I am of opinion that no sensible inconvenience will be felt on this score; since it will be easy for him as Comptroller, who is the immediate superior of the auditor to form any man of business for the office he will leave in a short period of time. More inconvenience would be felt by the introduction of a Comptroller, not in the immediate train of the business. Besides this it may be observed that a degree of inconvenience on this score cannot be deemed an obstacle, but upon a principle which would bar the progress of merit from one station to another. On this point of inconvenience a reflection occurs which I

2. Wolcott had served as comptroller of public accounts for Connecticut from May, 1788, until his appointment as auditor of the Treasury Department.

do not think I ought to suppress. Mr. Woolcott is a man of nice sensibility, not unconscious of his own value; and he doubtless must believe that he has pretensions from situation to the Office. Should another appointment take place & he resign, the derangement of the department would truly be distressing to the public service.

In suggesting thus particularly the reasons which in my mind operate in favour of Mr. Woolcott, I am influenced by information that other characters will be brought to your view by weighty advocates, and as I think it more than possible that Mr. Woolcott may not be mentioned to you by any other person than myself, I feel it a duty arising out of my situation in the department to bear my full & explicit testimony to his worth; confident that he will justify by every kind of *substantial* merit any mark of your approbation, which he may receive.

In contemplating the appointment of the Auditor as Comptroller, a question naturally arises concerning a substitute for the former. In forming your Judgment on this point you would probably desire to know what may be the pretensions of the next officer in the department below the Auditor namely the Register.[3] I say nothing of the Assistant Secretary [4] or the Treasurer,[5] because neither of them I presume would think the place of Auditor an eligible exchange for that which he now has & because I regard them both as distinct & irrelative branches of the department. The Register is a most excellent officer in his place. He has had a great deal of experience in the department, is a perfect accountant & a very upright man. But I cannot say that I am convinced he would make as good an Auditor as he does a Register. I fear he would fail on the score of firmness & I am not sure that his mind is formed for a systematic adherence to principle. I believe at the same time that he is perfectly content to remain where he is.

There will therefore be no difficulty in adjusting this matter to any collateral calculation which may be deemed requisite. A number of persons well qualified occur in this Quarter; but you probably will prefer directing your inquiries to the South on the principle of distribution. There is a circumstance which on this point I ought to mention. If I am rightly informed Mr. Nourse is originally from Virginia.

There is another circumstance which I ought not to conclude without mentioning to you. Mr. Coxe has signified to me his wish to be

3. Joseph Nourse.   4. Tench Coxe.   5. Samuel Meredith.

considered for the Office of Comptroller. On this point I have answered him & very sincerely to this effect "I am well convinced that the office under your direction would be in perfectly good hands. On the score of qualification my preference would not incline to any other man & you have every reason to believe that on personal accounts none would be more agreeable to me. But I am equally well satisfied on the other hand that no man ought to be preferred to Mr. Woolcott on the score of qualification for the office, and *this being the case,* I am of opinion that the relation which his present station bears to that in question gives him pretensions superior to any other person." He then asked me whether it would be disagreeable to me to make his wish known to you. To this my answer was in substance that I could have no possible objection to his doing it and that I would even do it myself [but that I apprised him it should be done in such a manner as would make it clearly understood to you that all circumstances considered, I thought, that Mr. Woolcott had a decidedly preferable claim.

I trust Sir that in thus freely disclosing my Sentiments to you, you will be persuaded that I only yeald to the suggestions of an honest zeal for the publick good, and of a firm conviction that the prosperity of the department under my particular care (one so interesting to the aggregate movements of the government) will be but promoted by transfering the present Auditor to the office of Comptroller of the Treasury.

I have the honor to remain   with the most respectfull Attachment Sir Your Most Obedient & humble   Servant   Alexander Hamilton

P.S. If you should be of opinion to appoint the Auditor as Comptroller and the Register as Auditor, There would be a choice of valuable characters in the department well qualified to take the Station of the register should you think it adviseable to persue that Course.] 6 That I may not be misapprehended, I beg leave to observe that though I do not think the Register well qualified for an Auditor in all respects, I do not think him so defective as to be a bad appointment.

[The President of the United States]

6. The bracketed material in this letter is not in H's handwriting.

From William Campbell, Thomas Withers, M. R. Willkings, Auly Macnaughten, George Hooper [1]

Wilmington [North Carolina] April 18, 1791. Ask for instructions concerning construction of the Cape Fear lighthouse.[2]

LS, RG 26, Lighthouse Letters Received, Early Lighthouse Letters, National Archives.

1. The men who signed this letter were the North Carolina commissioners to regulate shipping on the Cape Fear River.

2. North Carolina, which had begun construction of the Cape Fear lighthouse, subsequently ceded the site to the Federal Government in December, 1790, when the North Carolina state legislature ratified "An Act to cede and vest in the United States of America, the Lands therein mentioned, for the Purpose of building Light-Houses" (*Laws of North-Carolina. At a General Assembly, begun and held at Fayetteville on the First Day of November, in the Year of our Lord, One Thousand Seven Hundred and Ninety, and in the Fifteenth Year of the Independence of the said State: Being the First Session of the said Assembly* [n.p., n. d.], 2).

To Richard Harison [1]

Treasury Department,
18 April 1791

Sir,

As the confinement in which Charles Seely, the late Mate of Cap. Joseph Gorham junr.[2] now is, appears likely to affect his life, I request you to take such measures in regard to the case, as will certainly prevent a consequence so extreme. The President being absent, no relief can be derived from him. I am fully persuaded both his humanity & justice would induce him, as far as in his power, to prevent a Sacrifice of the life of even an ill intentioned Citizen in a case wherein the extremity of the law is limited by an inconsiderable pecuniary penalty.

I presume you concur in opinion with me that the case is not so far free from wilful negligence & intention of fraud, as to give him any chance of relief under the mitigating Act.[3]

I am, sir, with great consideration, Your Obedt. Servant

Alex Hamilton

Richard Harison Esqr.

LS, New-York Historical Society, New York City.

1. For background to this letter, see Harison to H, April 8, 1791.

2. H was referring to Captain Josiah Gorham, Jr., rather than to Joseph Gorham.

3. See "An Act to provide for mitigating or remitting the forfeitures and penalties accruing under the revenue laws, in certain cases therein mentioned" (1 *Stat.* 122–23 [May 26, 1790]). This act provided for mitigating or remitting forfeitures and penalties which had been "incurred without wilful negligence or any intention of fraud."

To Benjamin Lincoln

Treasury Department, April 18, 1791. States that it is impossible at this time to give a definitive answer to the questions raised by Lincoln's letter of March 18, 1791.

L[S], RG 36, Collector of Customs at Boston, Letters from the Treasury, 1789–1818, Vol. 5, National Archives; copy, RG 56, Letters to Collectors at Small Ports, "Set G," National Archives; copy, RG 56, Letters to the Collector at Boston, National Archives.

From Matthew Lyall

Wilmington, North Carolina, April 18, 1791. "It being conceived by the Commissioners of the Navigation of Cape Fear,[1] that since the Light House which I contracted to build here has been ceded to the United States, and the funds provided by the Assembly for that purpose having ceased, that the further prosecution of the business properly comes within the department of your Office, and therefore all applications relative to it should be made to you. . . . By reason of the insufficiency of the funds provided by the Assembly, together with the difficulty of procuring Brick, the building which ought to have been finished along time ago, is not yet completed, which has been attended with embarrassing consequences to me, and at this time I find myself in a very unhappy predicament not being able to quit the works with justice to myself nor, can the Commissioners proceed any further in the business nor yet, have they it in their power to make me compensation, so that untill some measures are effectually taken respecting it, I must remain in suspence and at a very considerable expence. . . ."

LS, RG 26, Lighthouse Letters Received, Vol. "A," Pennsylvania and Southern States, National Archives.

1. See William Campbell *et al.* to H, April 18, 1791.

From William Ellery

Custom House
Newport [Rhode Island] 19th. Apl. 1791

Sir,

I have received two pressing letters, one from the Surveyor of the Port of Warren & Barrington [1] and the other from the Surveyor of the Port of East-Greenwich [2] respecting boats for their Ports, extracts from which I now present to you.

"Agreeably to your request, (writes Mr. Phillips) I shall describe the Port of Warren and Barrington, and the parts adjoining. The Port of Warren lies on Palmer's river about two miles up its mouth, trending about NE and SW Warren laying on the Eastside & Barrington on the West. (NB. the Extracts referred to after I began to write this I thought it would be best to send inclosed in separate papers). It appears to me that a boat for each of these ports would be useful, a small two mast boat for Warren and Barrington, and a boat of one mast, to carry a sail occasionally for East-Greenwich. The two mast boat belonging to this Port is too small for it, and I think will suit Warren & Barrington, and may be from thence employed at times in the North part of this District to advantage. If you should approve of it, I will get a suitable boat built for this Port, station our present boat at Warren, and furnish East Greenwich with what I conceive would be a proper boat for that Port. The cost of both boats equipped will be about 160 dollars. I daily expect applications from Bristol, and Pawcatuck for boats, and perhaps from North Kingstown, neither of them having a Custom House boat.

I have received your letter of the 6th. of this month [3] respecting the Schooner Fly, and, when Mr. Brightman comes to town, if what you have written should not fully convince him I will, altho' I shall despair of success, endeavour to contribute to his conviction.[4] He desired me to write to you to obtain your consent that his goods might be excused from paying duties, and that his Schooner, altered, and enlarged as She was, might be Registered. I told him that convinced, as I was, that the duties had legally accrued, and that the vessel had not by the alterations and additions made to her become American I could not with any propriety comply with his request. What alterations and changes are required to metamorphose a foreign built vessel into an American built vessel the Laws of the United States do not inform me. I wish to know whether the purchaser of a foreign built vessel seized and legally condemned, being a citizen of the United States, would be entitled to a register for such vessel. The law is silent here; but if vessels so circumstanced are not admitted to the privileges of American built vessels, few if any citizens will bid for them.

You will receive with this a weekly return of monies on hand, the copy of an endorsement of the change of master on a Certife of Regr. No. 64. granted at this Port, Decr. 3. 1790 and the copy of a similar endorsement on Enrollment No. 19 granted at this port Sepr. 10 1790.[5]

I am Sir yr. most obedt. servt.   W Ellery Collr

Secry of the Treasury

LC, Newport Historical Society, Newport, Rhode Island.
   1. Nathaniel Phillips.
   2. Thomas Arnold.
   3. Letter not found.
   4. See Henry Marchant to H, December 20, 1790; H to Marchant, February 10, 1791.
   5. Ellery endorsed this letter "Answered Apl. 27th." H's reply has not been found.

From John Nicholson

Comptroler Generals Office [Philadelphia] April 19th 1791

Sir

Altho many of the Certificates the property of the State of Pennsylvania were not yet assigned thereto for which you have directed such provisions to be made as fully secures her interest therein, Yet there are also Certificates that appear to the Credit of the same State on the Treasury Books which *individuals* are intitled to on their delivering up the *New Loan* Certificates of Pennsylvania in their possession.[1] This business hath been done by my Power of Attorney to transfer to the Individual so much of this Registered Debt as they are severally intitled to and went on with great satisfaction to the Individuals, but since the late quarters Interest hath been payable on their species of Debt a difficulty arises, and I find that such as have since been transfered, will when they come to fund their paper notwithstanding the appearance of the Registered Certificate and commencement of Interest expressed thereon is the same as expressed in the former leaves One quarters Interest behind which remains to the Credit of and is receivable by the State of Pennsylvania, altho the whole Interest is in part their property. To Obviate this inconvenience if it can be Obviated is the design of my present application. From this information you will see our situation and alone can direct relief in the premises. The State of Pennsylvania have by a law thereof determined to fund their paper [2] according to the terms prescribed by Act of Congress, of August 1790.[3] It would therefore be to us the most agreeable to receive no Interest upon any of the Registered Debt in the shape it now is, and untill funded. If therefore all that appears to the Credit of the State were added to those contained in the List made to the Register and to the bank [4] and which are already excepted from the Quarters payment now making, it would at once remove the difficulty. The next practicable mode appears to me to be to frame my power of Attorney to transfer so as to include a power to receive also said Quarterly payment of Interest. However as I observed before, you are best Able to devise the method in which it should be done and I have great confidence that you will order it in such way as will accomodate the State and the individuals.[5]

I have the honor to be   with high respect.   Sir your most Obt. Very Hbl   Servant   J. N.

The Honorable Alexe Hamilton Esqr.
Secrety Treasury U States

Copy, Division of Public Records, Pennsylvania Historical and Museum Commission, Harrisburg; copy, Division of Public Records, Pennsylvania Historical and Museum Collection.

1. See Thomas Smith to H, February 14, 1791, and Nicholson to H, March 23, 25, 1791.
2. "An Act Authorizing and Directing the State Treasurer to Subscribe, in the Name of the Commonwealth, to the Loan Proposed by the United States, and for Other Purposes Therein Mentioned" (Pennsylvania Statutes, XIV, 39–41 [March 30, 1791]).
3. "An Act making provision for the (payment of the) Debt of the United States" (1 Stat. 138–44 [August 4, 1790]).
4. Nicholson is referring to the Bank of North America.
5. On May 13, 1791, Governor Thomas Mifflin of Pennsylvania wrote to Nicholson concerning the plan which H and Nicholson had agreed upon. Mifflin approved the plan, but warned Nicholson that in the future communications

between the Federal and state governments should take place only through the governor (LS, Division of Public Records, Pennsylvania Historical and Museum Commission, Harrisburg). On May 19, 1791, Mifflin advised Christian Febiger, treasurer of the Commonwealth of Pennsylvania, that he should pay to Nicholson, out of interest received from the United States on the registered debt, seven hundred dollars for the payment of interest to holders of "new loan" certificates registered at the Treasury (LC, Division of Public Records, Pennsylvania Historical and Museum Commission, Harrisburg).

To William Duer

[Philadelphia, April 20, 1791]

Dear Sir

I send you herewith a plan for a manufacturing Society [1] in conformity to the Ideas we have several times conversed about. It has occurred to me that Mr. Cazenove [2] might be willing to adventure in the project. The good sense and discernment, which he possesses, assure me that he will readily appreciate whatever of good there may be in the plan, and there has appeared to me in him a disposition very liberal and very favourable to whatever tends to advance the prosperity of the country. Besides the merit to which he is intitled on this score as an evidence of the beneficence of his temper, he Seems to have adopted the solid position that those things which tend to promote the developpement and amelioration of the means of this country tend also to render his speculations on its affairs more beneficial and to enlarge the sphere for future operations. He will not improbably regard the projected undertaking in this light and could he be induced to engage in it, it would have an encouraging effect.

I flatter myself that the subscription for the first 100,000, will rapidly fill. When completed, I will lose no time in taking measures in cooperation with the Attornies named in the instrument to obtain the desired sanction of the State of Jersey. The more I have considered the thing, the more I feel persuaded that it will equally promote the Interest of the adventurers & of the public and will have an excellent effect on the Debt.

With sincere regard   I remain Dr Sir   Your obdt. Servt.

A. Hamilton.

Philada. April 20, 1791.
to Wm. Duer Esqr.

Copy, Nederlandsch Economisch-Historisch Archief, Amsterdam.

1. This is, of course, a reference to what eventually became the Society for Establishing Useful Manufactures. Although this document has not been found, it may have been "A plan for a manufacturing establishment in the United States," which was enclosed in Tench Coxe to Thomas Jefferson, April 15, 1791. Both this document and the enclosing letter are in the Thomas Jefferson Papers, Library of Congress.

2. Théophile Cazenove, an Amsterdam entrepreneur, came to America in early 1790 as purchasing agent and correspondent for four large financial houses, Pieter Stadnitzki, Nicholaas and Jacob Van Staphorst, P. and C. Van Eeghen, and Ten Cate and Vollenhoven. When the Holland Land Company was formed in 1793, he became its agent in America. After his arrival in the United States Cazenove purchased considerable amounts of Federal and state debts, bought substantial shares in the Bank of the United States, and invested in a number of canal company promotions. H's objective was to obtain Dutch capital for the Society for Establishing Useful Manufactures, and Duer wrote to Cazenove, sending him both the plan and H's letter. In concluding his letter, Duer wrote: "If on Mature Consideration you Should determine to patronise our Infant Establishment, it will give Me great pleasure, to Signify your Intention to the Secretary. I have Embarked in it Myself, and will cooperate with you in all Measures which you Shall judge Adviseable for promoting the Interest of the Establishment." (Duer to Cazenove, April 30, 1791, Nederlandsch Economisch-Historisch Archief, Amsterdam.)

Cazenove persuaded his employers to subscribe twenty-five thousand dollars to the enterprise.

To Caleb Gibbs [1]

[*Philadelphia, April 20, 1791.* On May 16, 1791, Gibbs wrote to Hamilton: "I have been honored by your much esteemed favour of the 20th. Ulto." *Letter not found.*]

1. Gibbs and H had been close friends during the American Revolution when both had been aides-de-camp to George Washington.

To Simon Gross

Treasury Department:
20th. April 1791

Sir,

I duly received your letter of the 9th. instant [1] about which time I transmitted to you the Commissions of all the officers of the Maryland Revenue Cutter, whom the President has yet thought proper to appoint.

The provisions and necessary small articles of Ship Chandlery will be provided for you by the Collector.[2] I wish from him, after confering with you, a minute of the arms and ammunition that are thought necessary. You will be exceedingly careful not to proceed, without clear orders, in expenditures. I mention this the more particularly, because I perceive you mistook my request to have names sent me to submit to the President, for an authority to make the appointments. This is a power that I could not give you, and which can be exercised only by the president of the United States.

I presume from your manner of writing that the rigging and sails are prepared. If the latter are not, and Boston sail cloth cannot be procured in Baltimore as low as foreign I will immediately direct the necessary quantity to be Sent you from Boston.

I am, sir,   Your obedient Servant   Alexander Hamilton

Captain Simon Gross

Copy, Columbia University Libraries.
    1. Letter not found.
    2. The collector of the customs at Baltimore was Otho H. Williams.

To Otho H. Williams

Treasury Department,
20 April 1791.

Sir,

The remarks you propose to make upon the coasting law [1] will be very acceptable, as the new bill [2] stands postponed 'till the next Session of Congress. I shall at all times wish for such observations as may occur to the Collectors on the Subject of the Revenue & Trade laws.

I am of opinion that a consular certificate will not justify you, in paying a drawback.

The Agents for Mr. Stephen Zacharie [3] were put into the way of procuring a legal bill of sale for the Brigantine Hope, as I presume you were informed by them.

I am, sir,   Your Obedt. Servant.   Alexander Hamilton

Otho H Williams Esqr.

LS, Columbia University Libraries.
    1. "An Act for Registering and Clearing Vessels, Regulating the Coasting Trade, and for other purposes" (1 Stat. 55–65 [September 1, 1789]).

2. See H to William Ellery, April 11, 1791, note 3.

3. Zacharie was a member of the Baltimore merchant firm of Zacharie, Coopman, and Company. See Williams to H, December 29, 1790.

To Sharp Delany

Treasury Department,
21 April 1791

Sir,

I do not conceive the laws will admit of a Collectors receiving & certifying a Manifest of goods actually at the time *without his district;* nor could it be deemed safe so to frame a law that the certificates issued under it might be constantly applied to cover goods other than those for which they were intended as passports. I do not therefore deem myself justifiable in giving you the direction you suggest.

I am, sir; Your obedt Servant   Alexander Hamilton

Sharp Delany Esqr.
Collr. Philadelphia

LS, Bureau of Customs, Philadelphia; copy, RG 56, Letters to the Collector at Philadelphia, National Archives; copy, RG 56, Letters to Collectors at Small Ports, "Set G," National Archives.

From Jeremiah Olney

Providence, April 21, 1791. "I have been Honor'd with your favour of 11th Inst. . . . I am much obliged Sir, by your friendly communication and advice Respecting the Future prospect of a further Compensation to be made the Officers of the Customs. . . . I will Continue to execute the Duties of my Office, presuming, that it cannot be the Interest or Intention of the Legislature to appoint a person as principle in an Office of Considerable National importance, without annexing to it an adequate and decent support. . . ."

ADfS, Rhode Island Historical Society, Providence; copy, RG 56, Letters from the Collector at Providence, National Archives.

From William Allibone [1]

[*Philadelphia*] *April 22, 1791.* "I have herewith enclosed a Contract with Joseph Anthony & Son, for the supply of Oil for one years Consumption of the Lighthouse at Cape Henlopen. . . . I have also enclosed a Contract with John Wilson for Building a Beaconboat to replace the One used at Brown Shoal, it being in a State of decay as will not admit of its being depended upon for another year. . . ."

ALS, RG 26, Lighthouse Letters Received, Vol. "A," Pennsylvania and Southern States, National Archives.
    1. Allibone was master warden of the port of Philadelphia.

From Daniel Ludlow

New York, April 23, 1791. "I am indebted to the Honor of your esteemed favor of the 14 Inst [1] & though it was not in your Power, consistent with the Regulations, you had established to Accord to my Request, I am not the less Obliged to you for the favor of a Reply & ye pains you have taken, to prevent in future the like Inconvenience. . . . I have now taken my Passage for Europe & expect to embark by the 15th next month. . . . My Acquaintance in Europe not being sufficiently Extensive to Accord with my Views, induces me to trespass on your Friendship to Solicit . . . Letters of Introduction. . . ."

ALS, Hamilton Papers, Library of Congress.
    1. Letter not found.

To John M. Pintard [1]

Philadelphia April 23. 1791

Private
Dr Sir
    Your letters of the 7th of December & 19 of January have come duly to hand.
    What you mention concerning manifests and certificates of drawbacks certainly merits consideration. When the Collection law [2] originated consuls were not yet appointed. You will oblige me by freely

intimating whatever occurs to you for the benefit of our Trade and Revenue laws; whether arising from your observations on the practice of other countries, or from your own reflections.

I thank you for your attention in shipping me a pipe of Madeira, which I have received, and anticipate from its excellent quality, a regale in due time to my friends and myself. Mrs. Hamilton joins me in compliments to Mrs. Pintard.

I remain with much regard   Sir   Your Obed ser

ADf, Hamilton Papers, Library of Congress.
1. Pintard was United States consul in Madeira.
2. "An Act to regulate the Collection of the Duties imposed by law on the tonnage of ships or vessels, and on goods, wares and merchandises imported into the United States" (1 *Stat.* 29–49 [July 31, 1789]).

From Andrew Porter [1]

[*Philadelphia*] *April 23, 1791.* "I am desirous of having the evidence preserved of the Original Amount of a Debt, for money loaned the United states between septr. 1777 & March 1778 (6 ⅌ Cent per Ann. on the Amount of which is now payable) And at the same time of taking out a predicated Certificate on which to draw Interest as a Non Subscriber.[2] I am informed that you will, in case of Application for the purpose direct this evidence to be recorded on the Certificate to be given in lieu thereof. I have therefore to request that you will please to direct the Loan Officer in this State to make such indorsement on some Certificates the evidence of which I shall otherwise lose as they would be Merged in the Exchange."

LC, Division of Public Records, Pennsylvania Historical and Museum Commission, Harrisburg.
1. Porter was a Philadelphia broker.
2. "An Act making provision for the (payment of the) Debt of the United States" (1 *Stat.* 138–44 [August 4, 1790]) had prescribed the terms under which individuals holding certificates of debt issued under the Confederation might subscribe to the funded debt under the new government. Section 10, however, provided:
"That such of the creditors of the United States as may not subscribe to the said loan, shall nevertheless receive during the year one thousand seven hundred and ninety-one, a rate per centum on the respective amounts of their respective demands, including interest to the last day of December next, equal to the interest payable to subscribing creditors, to be paid as the same times, at the same places, and by the same persons as is herein before directed, concerning the interest on the stock which may be created in virtue of the said proposed loan. But as some of the certificates now in circulation have not hereto-

fore been liquidated to specie value, as most of them are greatly subject to counterfeit, and counterfeits have actually taken place in numerous instances, and as
embarrassment and imposition might, for these reasons, attend the payment of
interest on those certificates in their present form, it shall therefore be necessary to entitle the said creditors to the benefit of the said payment, that those
of them who do not possess certificates issued by the register of the treasury,
for the registered debt, should produce previous to the first day of June next,
their respective certificates, either at the treasury of the United States, or to some
one of the commissioners to be appointed as aforesaid, to the end that the same
may be cancelled, and other certificates issued in lieu thereof; which new certificates shall specify the specie amount of those in exchange for vhich they are
given, and shall be otherwise of the like tenor with those heretofore issued by the
said register of the treasury for the said registered debt, and shall be transfer-
able on the like principles with those directed to be issued on account of the
subscriptions to the loan hereby proposed."

During the operation of this act, one class of creditors, however, had consistently refused to surrender their certificates. These were the holders of certificates issued between September, 1777, and March, 1778, who believed the value
of their certificates superior to those the Treasury offered in exchange. For
background to these certificates, see Blair McClenachan et al. to H, March
16, 1791.

From Isaac Moses [1]

New York, April 24, 1791. "Whilst Congress was in Session I would
not disturb you, I now beg leave to Remind you of your promise, in
giving me a Deed for the House and I will execute a Mortage for
£ 800, you will greatly Oblige me by Condecending to this mode, as
I think all the Mony I have paid On a Very loose foundation. . . ."

ALS, Hamilton Papers, Library of Congress.
    1. Beginning in the seventeen-eighties H had acted for Moses, a New York
City merchant, in various legal affairs. See H's "Cash Book," March 1, 1782–1791.

From John Adams

Bush Hill [Philadelphia] April 25, 1791

Dear sir

I do my self the honour to transmit to you my Accounts which remain unsettled, for the last two years and Eight months of my Admin-
istrations abroad in the service of the United States.[1] I have left a

ADfS, Adams Family Papers, deposited in the Massachusetts Historical Society,
Boston.
    1. Adams was the United States Envoy to the Court of St. James's from
February, 1785, until his recall by Congress in February, 1788.

Blank for my Salary. In my own opinion it is but Justice that it should be filled up with the Sum of two thousand five hundred Pounds sterling a year, because this was the contract under which I accepted my Commission for the Peace in 1779 and that for their High Mightinesses in 1781 which last continued in force untill my Return home. The Resolution of Congress which Stated the Salary of a Minister abroad at 9000 Dollars,[2] could not reasonably be intended to operate upon Ministers and Commissioners which had been given and accepted upon different Conditions. Such an Interpretation of it would make it amount to a Breach of public faith. Moreover I have been well informed by Mr Gerry [3] who proposed the alteration that the Reason of this Resolution was a Supposition that in that time of Peace the Expences of living in Europe were reduced. This Motive was so far from being a just one, as applied to me, that I found the Expences of living in London about a quarter part dearer than I had ever known them in Paris or the Hague. This therefore was rather a Reason for raising my Salary to three thousand Pounds sterling a year, which I actually Spent than for reducing it to nine thousand Dollars. I have been informed by Mr Barclay [4] that Mr Franklin charged and has been allowed, two thousand five hundred Pounds sterling a year till his Return, and as I am in the same Predicament with him, it is at least as just that it should be allowed to me. Indeed it is more so because I certainly was obliged to spend more than that sum, and he undoubtedly spent less.

I have also requested an allowance for a private Secretary. As the Business of my Mission to Holland as well as that to England lay upon me, in Addition to my share in all the Negotiations with Prussia and the other Powers of Europe as well as the Barbary States, it may readily be conceived that I had a great deal of Business and Still more writing to do, as Copies of all such Correspondences must be preserved, and therefore I hope the Charge for a private Secretary will not be thought unreasonable.

An allowance is asked also for one Ministerial or Diplomatique Entertainment for each year. This is done for two Reasons 1. because it is

2. On May 7, 1784, Congress voted to set a maximum of nine thousand dollars on ministers' salaries (JCC, XXVI, 354).

3. Elbridge Gerry, member of the House of Representatives from Massachusetts.

4. Thomas Barclay, former commissioner for settling foreign accounts.

the Custom of the whole Corps Diplomatique. 2. because it seems to be a reasonable Custom and 3. because Mr Franklin has charged and been allowed for all Extraordinary Entertainments as I suppose, as he told me he had charged them or should charge them.

An outfit I have asked for, amounting to one years Salary. This will be but a very inadequate Compensation to me, for the extraordinary Expences I was put to by the Variety of services and multiplicity of Commissions, which were heaped upon me. My Case is Singular and distinguished from that of every other Gentleman who has ever been sent abroad in the service of the United States. In 1779 Congress sent me abroad, with two Commissions one to negotiate a Peace, and another to his Britannic Majesty to negotiate a Treaty of Commerce with that Power. Under these Commissions I went to Paris and resided there which obliged me to take an House or Appartement ready furnished, and establish an Household Equipage and sett of servants there. In 1780 Congress sent me a Commission to borrow Money in Holland to the amount of ten millions Dollars. This obliged me to live in Holland. In 1781 Congress sent me a Commission to treat with that Republick and a Letter of Credence to the states General. This obliged me to hire an House and completely furnish it, because there was no such thing to be hired in Holland as Furniture, as might be done and was done by Mr Deane Mr Franklin, Mr Jay and Myself at Paris. My Commission for the Peace obliged me to make Journeys to Versailles. My Commission for borrowing Money not only augmented my Expences, but gave me more trouble and occasioned more labour and perplexity than all the other services. The frequent Removals from one Country to another, the continual Change of servants and Liveries; the Wear and Tear of Baggage and Destruction of furniture; besides the perpetual plunder I was subjected to in my Absence from my house in one Country, while attending my duty in another, have wasted and consumed my salary in such a manner that my family must be deprived of that reward for my Time, Trouble, Risque and services which all of Us were intitled to and which some may have been happy enough honestly to secure. I say all of Us were intitled to it because Congress on the 28. sept. 1786 Resolved that their Ministers should live in such a stile and manner as they might find Suitable and necessary to support the Dignity of their public Character, and that besides their actual expences a handsome Allowance be made to each of them as a Compensation for their time Trouble Risque and Services.[5]

If the Articles I have Submitted are allowed me difficult as it will be to justify myself to my Family, I shall be content, but if not, I must crave an allowance of one half Per Cent, as Commissions on nine millions of Guilders, by me borrowed in holland for the United States.[6] When Congress allows four Per Cent to the Houses of Willinks and Vanstapherst and their Undertakers upon all these Loans, which has already amounted to an handsome fortune to each House it would be extreamly hard and unreasonable to oblige me, who had more trouble with every one of these Loans than those Houses had, nay who had more trouble with the first of them than they have had with the whole, not only to do this whole Business for nothing but live at my own Expence while I did it. This must be my hard fate if nothing can be allowed me as Commissions nor for extraordinary services. Considerable sums were Spent by me, at times for secret services and other sums to no small amount were Advanced to Americans in Distress, some of them in Prison and others escaped: but as I have no Vouchers for these and I suppose Congress would not be willing to set a Precedent I make no charge for them, although they were advanced out of my own Money Part of my salary. Let me ask the favour of you sir to look over these Accounts and then present them to the auditor, That they may be settled in some way or other, by the next sessions of Congress.

With great Esteem I have the honour   to be, Sir your most obedient and   most humble sert   John Adams

Alexander Hamilton
Secretary of the Treasury.

5. The resolution Adams is referring to was passed by Congress on September 26, 1776, rather than 1786. It reads in part as follows:

"*Resolved,* That the Commissioners should live in such stile and manner at the court of France, as they may find suitable and necessary to support the dignity of their public character, keeping an account of their expences, which shall be reimbursed by the Congress of the United States of America.

"That besides the actual expences of the commissioners, a handsome allowance be made to each of them as a compensation for their time, trouble, risque and services." (*JCC,* V, 833–34.)

6. These are the Holland loans of 1782, 1784, 1787, and 1788. See Willink, Van Staphorst, and Hubbard to H, January 25, 1790, note 15; H to William Short, September 1, 1790, notes 22, 24, and 25.

From William Ellery

Custom House
Newport [Rhode Island] Apl. 25th. 1791

Sir,

The 21st. of this month I received a thermometer which by your direction was sent to me from New york by Mr. Lamb.[1] By some accident the bulb was broken in its way from Philadelphia to this place. It came broken to me. As it was made at Philadelphia, and I suppose the maker is furnished with spare tubes I have remitted it to Mr. Lamb with a request that he would transmit it immediately to you. The graduated plate had I observed suffered some defacement.

I should be happy to receive your direction respecting a prosecution of the master of the Ship Warren, and on the case of William Almy a statement of which I transmitted to you on the 17th. of Jany. last,[2] and also on the case of James Munro junr. which I stated in my letter of the 28th. of March last.

This letter will be accompanied by my weekly return of Cash & by two Certifes. of Regy. the one No. 21 granted at Dighton, and dated Apl. 22nd. 1790, the other No. 15, granted at this Port, and dated Augt. 3d. 1790. The first was delivered up on account of a transfer of property, the last on account of the Sloop's being built upon.

I had the honour to receive your letter of the 11th. of this month, and am

Sir   Yr. most obedt. servt.   W Ellery Collr

A. Hamilton Esqr

LC, Newport Historical Society, Newport, Rhode Island.
    1. John Lamb, collector of customs at New York City.
    2. Ellery also wrote to H on the subject of the ship *Warren* on January 17, 1791. This letter had not been found when Volume VII of *The Papers of Alexander Hamilton* was published. It has since been located in the Newport Historical Society and will be published in a supplementary volume. See also Jeremiah Olney to H, November 29, December 24, 1790; H to Olney, December 13, 1790.

From William Jackson

Wilmington [*North Carolina*] *April 25, 1791.* States that the President [1] thinks that Joseph McDowell, Sr., "is perhaps, in all regards, the most proper person to be appointed Inspector of the survey No. 5" in North Carolina and that Captain William Cooke should be appointed captain of the revenue cutter at Wilmington.

ALS, The Huntington Library, San Marino, California; LC, George Washington Papers, Library of Congress.
    1. Jackson was with George Washington on a tour of the southern states.

From Jeremiah Olney

Providence, April 25, 1791. "From a difficulty which arises to git an old Millitary officer of Reputation to take Command of the Company to be raised in this State, I have been under the Necessity of Recommending Jeremiah Greenman to the Secretary of War, as a Gentleman that would do honor to the appointment. You will doubtless recollect that I Recommended this Gentleman as first mate of the Cutter Building in Connecticutt,[1] but his appointment not being made, and a Millitary life being more Congenial to his wishes, I have under these Circumstances taken the Liberty to name him to the Secretary of War. . . ."

ADfS, Rhode Island Historical Society, Providence.
    1. See Olney to H, February 17, 1791. During the American Revolution Greenman had served as lieutenant and regimental adjutant of the First Rhode Island Regiment.

From Jeremiah Olney

Providence, April 25, 1791. "Permit me to introduce to your acquaintance the Bearer. . . John S. Dexter, who has been honored by the President with the appointment of Supervisor of Excise for Rhode Island—he now goes forward as a Delegate from this State Society to attend the General meeting of the Cincinnati to be holden in the City of Philadelphia. . . ."

ADfS, Rhode Island Historical Society, Providence.

To Stephen Van Rensselaer [1]

[*Philadelphia, April 25, 1791.* The description of this letter in the dealer's catalogue reads: "Regarding 'several powers of attorney for the receipt of final settlement certificates' presented by Abijah Holbrook 'about whom reports of an unfavorable nature have been circulated;' the certificates being those of soldiers in Colonel Marinus Willet's regiment." [2] *Letter not found.*]

LS, sold at Parke-Bernet Galleries, December 3, 1957, Lot 104.
   1. Van Rensselaer was the patroon of Rensselaerwyck. In 1783 he married Hamilton's sister-in-law, Margaret Schuyler.
   2. Marinus Willett, who held several commands during the American Revolution, commanded two regiments of levies in 1781 and 1782.

To John Habersham

[*Philadelphia, April 26, 1791.* On May 20, 1791, Habersham wrote to Hamilton: "I have . . . received your letter of the 26th. ultimo." *Letter not found.*]

To Richard Harison

Treasury Department
April 26th. 1791.

Sir

You have been advised of the application of Samuel Dodge to the President for a Pardon.[1] You know also that he is convicted upon the 26th section of the last Collection Law.[2]

A question arises concerning the extent of the power to pardon. There is a general rule that a power to pardon cannot be exercised so as to divest Individuals of a right of action for their sole benefit, or of a *vested* right which they have in conjunction with the sovereign; as where there is a penalty part to the use of the Public and part to the use of an informer. The inquiry consequently is how far the penalties within the 26 Section are liable to the distribution contemplated by the 68 section of the same Act [3] and what difference the mode of proceeding by Indictment instead of a popular action [4] may make.

I wish your opinion after deliberate investigation on the points which arise out of the general question here made so as to exhibit principles which may guide in other cases as well as in this. I wish also your opinion whether the case of Dodge would be within the relief of the law concerning the Remission and Mitigation of Penalties.[5]

If it should appear that the Presidents pardon may remit a part and not the whole of the penalties incurred by Dodge, it will remain to inquire whether the pardon ought to be general leaving the Court to make the exception of what it cannot opererate upon or special remitting only so much as concerns the Public. What process of execution would be proper to enforce *part* of a penalty?

Another case has occured, concerning which, I also wish your opinion. It is whether the officers of the Customs are intitled under the 68th Section to a share of the penalty prescribed by the 65th for false swearing.[6] Distinctions on this point have been taken. If you should be of opinion, that the Officers of the Customs are intitled to nothing, it will be satisfactory to me to be informed of the ground of that opinion, or in other words, of the principle by which exceptions to the generality of the expression of the 68 section are to be governed.

With great consideration I have the honor to be, Sir Your Obedt servant.   Alexander Hamilton

Richard Harison Esqr.
New York

LS, New-York Historical Society, New York City.

1. See H to Harison, March 18, 1791.

2. "An Act to provide more effectually for the collection of the duties imposed by law on goods, wares and merchandise imported into the United States, and on the tonnage of ships or vessels" (1 *Stat.* 145–78 [August 4, 1790]). Although H refers to Section 26, it was Section 27 that he had in mind. The confusion arises from an error in the printing of the *Session Laws*. In the *Session Laws* Section 24 is incorrectly numbered 23. As a result all succeeding sections are misnumbered. Thus, in the *Session Laws* the final section of this statute is incorrectly numbered 74, while in all subsequent editions it is 75. Section 27 forbade unloading vessels in darkness without special permission of the collector and unloading at any time without a collector's permit. The penalty for such activity was a fine of four hundred dollars and ineligibility for Federal office for seven years (1 *Stat.* 163).

3. Section 69 rather than 68 is concerned with the distribution of the monies obtained from the sales (1 *Stat.* 177). See note 2.

4. An action for a statutory penalty or forfeiture given to a person who desires to claim the penalty or forfeiture.

5. "An Act to provide for mitigating or remitting the forfeitures and penalties accruing under the revenue laws, in certain cases therein mentioned" (1 *Stat.* 122–23 [May 26, 1790]).

6. These are references to Section 69 and Section 66 of the Collection Law. Section 66 provided that in cases where an oath was required of the captain of a ship or the owner or his agent "if the person so swearing shall swear falsely, such person shall, on indictment and conviction thereof, be punished by fine or imprisonment, or both, in the discretion of the court before whom the conviction shall be had, so as the fine shall not exceed one thousand dollars, and the term of imprisonment shall not exceed twelve months" (1 *Stat.* 175–76). Section 69 provided "That all penalties, fines and forfeitures, recovered by virtue of this act, (and not otherwise appropriated) shall, after deducting all proper costs and charges, be disposed of as follows: One moiety shall be for the use of the United States, and paid into the treasury thereof; the other moiety shall be divided into equal parts, and paid to the collector and naval officer of the district, and surveyor of the port wherein the same shall have been incurred, or to such of the said officers as there may be in the said district; and in districts where only one of the aforesaid officers shall have been established, the said moiety shall be given to such officer . . ." (1 *Stat.* 177).

To James McHenry [1]

[*Philadelphia, April 26, 1791.* On May 3, 1791, McHenry wrote to Hamilton: "I did not receive your letter of the 26th till the morning of the 2d." *Letter not found.*]

1. McHenry, who had served as George Washington's secretary during the American Revolution, had attended the Constitutional Convention and the Maryland Ratifying Convention. He was a member of the Maryland Assembly from 1788 to 1790.

From Nathaniel Appleton

Boston, April 27, 1791. "I wrote you 9th instant. I am this minute favoured with your Circular Letter 16th instant.[1] I have disposed of all the Treasury Drafts. . . ."

LC, RG 53, Massachusetts State Loan Office, Letter Book, 1785–1791, National Archives.
1. Circular not found.

To William Ellery

[*Philadelphia, April 27, 1791.* On May 9, 1791, Ellery wrote to Hamilton: "I have received your letter of the 27th. of last month." *Letter not found.*]

From Benjamin Lincoln

Boston Apl 27 1791

Sir

By the last post I was honoured by the receipt of your favours of the 8th. & 11th instant.

I have the pleasure to forward my account of the purchases I made of the public debt. You will find that a very high price was given for it though less than was the current price in Boston a few days before my return to it. The first offers I had were 6 ⅌ Cent Stock 19/6. I rejected all untill they fix at 18/9 Six ⅌ Cent & 9/9 3 ⅌ Cent & defered Stock, I could not delay longer in obedience to my instructions for these Sums appeared to be the general market price by which I was to regulate my self. I will in obedience to your wishes fund all I can with Mr Appleton.[1] There are some Loan office Certificates in my hands from different States. Shall I forward them to be funded in those states where they were issued without loss of time.

There is a ballance against me of One Hundred fifty four dollars & sixty eight Cents arising from interest received. How shall I discharge the Ballance by a purchase equal to that sum or by the cash?

Secy Hamilton

LC, Massachusetts Historical Society, Boston; LC, RG 36, Collector of Customs at Boston, National Archives; two copies, RG 56, Letters from the Collector at Boston, National Archives.
    1. Nathaniel Appleton, commissioner of loans for Massachusetts.

To Nathaniel Appleton

Treasury Department
28 April 1791

Sir,

The bills of the old emmissions enclosed in your letter of the 22d December [1] are now returned to you. Those which you have crossed are found to be counterfeit. That which remains unerassed is a true bill.

It will derange the established plan of operations to draw a warrant on you for your Salary & expenditures. It will be best that you appoint, as heretofore, an agent to receive your Salary at the Treasury. You have been directed by my letter of the 16th instant[2] to deposit any money which remains in your hands in the Massachusetts Bank.

I am, sir,   Your Obedt. Servant   Alexander Hamilton

Nathanl Appleton Esqr.

LS, Montague Collection, MS Division, New York Public Library.
    1. Letter not found. For background of the place of "old emissions" in the Continental debt and Federal funding plan, see Appleton to H, February 5, 1791, note 1.
    2. Circular not found. This was a Treasury Department circular to the commissioners of loans. See Appleton to H, April 27, 1791.

From Richard Harison

New York 29th. April 1791

Sir,

I had the Honor of receiving your Letter of the 26th. and shall pay due Attention to the Contents. The Questions proposed, are in themselves of great Importance & not free from Difficulties. They must therefore require mature and deliberate Consideration.

Inclosed you will find the Contract entered into with John McComb Junr.[1] & a Bond to secure the Performance of it. Mr. Cruger not having left proper Authority to execute an Obligation for him, I consented to accept of Messrs. Barrow and Boyd[2] in his Stead, both of whom I suppose possess some Property. Either of them with Mr. Kemble, would, I think, afford sufficient Security to the Public.

I did not judge it necessary to have the Contracts copied over as the Alterations were very minute, and a Vessel being on the Point of Sailing for Cape Henry a Delay would have been inexpedient.

I am, with great Respect,   Sir   Your most obedt. & most humb. Servt.

Hon. Alexr. Hamilton Esqr.

LC, New-York Historical Society, New York City.
    1. See H to Harison, April 1, 14, 1791; H to John McComb, Jr., April 1, 1791; Harison to H, April 8, 1791.

2. Thomas Barrow and William Boyd were both residents of New York City. Barrow was a Broad Street merchant and Boyd was a Wall Street broker.

From Benjamin Lincoln

Boston April 29th. [-May 3,] 1791

Sir

A few days since Captain Codman arrived here from the west indies. In his entery he returned one among other articles one bag of Coffee when the vessel appeared to be unladed all having been delivered agreeable to the entery & permit in consequence thereof. The officer after in examining the Vessel found under the Captains Cabbin four bags of Coffee which had not been entered on this the Captain came to the office & offered to enter it. I did not permit him to an entery of the articles. I did not suppose that the law meant an indulgence of the kind. The goods appeared to be secreted and we have teken them into custody.

May 3   Your favour of the 18 Ulto has been received as also your request respecting the Duck as mentioned by your assistant on the 20th.[1] That for Baltimore goes off this evening the other will follow as fast as vessels shall be found to take it on board.

Secy of the treasury

I received twenty nine Registers only the thirtieth was not signed by you. On signing it you will please to forward it to me.

LC, Massachusetts Historical Society, Boston; LC, RG 36, Collector of Customs at Boston, Letter Book, 1790–1797, National Archives; two copies, RG 56, Letters from the Collector at Boston, National Archives.

1. Tench Coxe, acting under H's direction, ordered canvas for the revenue cutters to be sent by Lincoln to the following collectors of the customs: George Wray, Hampton, Virginia; Otho H. Williams, Baltimore; Nathan Keais, Washington, North Carolina; and Joseph Whipple, Portsmouth, New Hampshire (Coxe to Lincoln, April 20, 1791, copy, RG 56, Letters to the Collector at Boston, National Archives).

From Charles Pettit [1]

Philadelphia 30th. April 1791

Sir

Pursuant to a Resolution of the House of Representatives of the

Commonwealth of Pennsylvania, concurred in by the Senate, and approved by the Governor,[2] I do myself the honor to apply to you for the balance remaining unissued of that part of the Bills of Credit which were directed to be issued on the credit of this State by the Act of Congress of the 18th. of March 1780.[3] By a statement which I have received from the Comptroller General of the State, the balance thus remaining unissued is supposed to be 78,642 dollars. In order to give you the more full information of the intention of the Legislature in directing this application to be made, and of the terms on which I am directed to receive, and to give a receipt for the money, I shall inclose herewith a copy of the Resolution on which the application is founded. I have the honor to be, sir

Your most obedt. & most humble servant

Charles Pettit Commissioner
for the State of Pennsylvania

The Honble. The Secretary of the Treasury of the United States.

Copy, Division of Public Records, Pennsylvania Historical and Museum Commission, Harrisburg.

1. On June 24, 1791, the Supreme Executive Council of Pennsylvania elected Pettit commissioner to settle the state's claims against the Federal Government.

2. This resolution, which was approved by Mifflin on April 13, 1791, reads as follows:

"*Resolved,* That the commissioner to be appointed, for the purpose of superintending the settlement of the accounts of the commonwealth with the United States, shall be empowered to apply to the Secretary of the Treasury for the balance of the emission of bills of credit, commonly called Dollar Money, which were to be issued by virtue of an act of the Legislature of *Pennsylvania,* entitled '*An Act for funding and redeeming the bills of credit of the United States of* America, *and for providing means to bring the present war to an happy conclusion,*' passed on the first day of *June,* one thousand seven hundred and eighty; that the respective claims of the United States and of this State on that head be left to be adjusted upon a final settlement of the accounts between the United States and this State; and that the aforesaid commissioner be empowered and directed to give a receipt accordingly to the Secretary of the Treasury of the United States, upon his receiving the aforesaid balance." (*Journal of the First Session of the House of Representatives of the Commonwealth of Pennsylvania, Which commenced at Philadelphia, on Tuesday, the Seventh Day of December, in the Year of our Lord One Thousand Seven Hundred and Ninety* [Philadelphia: Printed by Hall and Sellers—No. 51 Market-Street, 1790], 373.)

3. This resolution, which provided for the issue of bills of credit called "new emissions," reads in part as follows:

"*Resolved,* That the several states continue to bring into the continental treasury, by taxes or otherwise, their full quotas of fifteen million dollars monthly, as assigned them by the resolution of the 7th of October, 1779; a clause in the resolution of the 23d of February last, for relinquishing two-thirds of the said quotas, to the contrary notwithstanding; and that the states be further called on to make provision for continuing to bring into the said treasury their like quotas monthly, to the month of April, 1781, inclusive:

"That silver and gold be receivable in payment of the said quotas, at the rate of one Spanish milled dollar in lieu of 40 dollars of the bills now in circulation.

"That the said bills, as paid in, except for the months of January and February past, which may be necessary for the discharge of past contracts, be not re-issued, but destroyed.

"That as fast as the said bills shall be brought in to be destroyed, and funds shall be established, as hereafter mentioned, for other bills, other bills be issued, not to exceed, on any account, one-twentieth part of the nominal sum of the bills brought in to be destroyed.

"That the bills which shall be issued, be redeemable in specie, within six years after the present, and bear an interest at the rate of five per centum per annum, to be paid also in specie at the redemption of the bills, or, at the election of the holder, annually, at the respective continental loan offices, in sterling bills of exchange, drawn by the United States on their commissioners in Europe, at four shillings and six pence sterling per dollar.

"That the said new bills issue on the funds of individual states, for that purpose established, and be signed by persons appointed by them, and that the faith of the United States be also pledged for the payment of the said bills, in case any State on whose funds they shall be emitted, should, by the events of war, be rendered incapable to redeem them; which undertaking of the United States, and that of drawing bills of exchange, for payment of interest as aforesaid, shall be endorsed on the bills to be emitted, and signed by a commissioner to be appointed by Congress for that purpose. . . .

"That the said new bills shall be struck under the direction of the Board of Treasury, in due proportion for each State, according to their said monthly quotas, and lodged in the continental loan offices in the respective states, where the commissioner to be appointed by Congress, in conjunction with such persons as the respective states appoint, shall attend the signing of the said bills; which shall be compleated no faster than in the aforesaid proportion of one to twenty of the other bills brought in to be destroyed, and which shall be lodged for that purpose in the said loan offices.

"That as the said new bills are signed and compleated, the states respectively, on whose funds they issue, receive sixtenths of them, and that the remainder be subject to the orders of the United States, and credited to the states on whose funds they are issued, the accounts whereof shall be adjusted agreeably to the resolution of the 6th of October, 1779.

"That the said new bills be receivable in payment of the said monthly quotas, at the same rate as aforesaid of specie; the interest thereon to be computed to the respective states; to the day the payment becomes due.

"That the respective states be charged with such parts of the interest on their said bills, as shall be paid by the United States, in bills of exchange; and the accounts thereof shall be adjusted agreeably to the resolution aforesaid, of the 6th of October, 1779.

"That whenever interest on the bills to be emitted shall be paid prior to their redemption, such bills shall be thereupon exchanged for others of the like tenor, to bear date from the expiration of the year for which such interest is paid.

"That the several states be called on to provide funds for their quotas of the said new bills, to be so productive as to sink or redeem one sixth part of them annually, after the 1st. day of January next." (JCC, XVI, 263–66.)

"New emissions" were not considered a part of the debt of the United States under the funding system; on the other hand, they could not be considered a part of the assumable state debt, since the states had already been given credit when they were issued. If they had been assumed by the United States, the Federal Government would have been charged twice for the same debt.

Specie certificates of the Continental Congress were generally given preferential treatment under the Federal Government. Although "new emissions" had been underwritten by the Continental Congress as redeemable in specie equal to their face value, they had been issued by different states at different values. The Federal Government did not accept the claims made by holders of "new emissions" and relegated to the states the redemption of these certificates.

In this letter Pettit is requesting the "new emissions" of Pennsylvania remaining in the Treasury Department in order to give an estimate of the number of these certificates still in circulation. The redemption of the remaining certificates in Pennsylvania was carried out under Section II of "An Act to Provide for Paying and Redeeming Certain Public Debts, and for Defraying the Expenses of Government" (*Pennsylvania Statutes*, XIV, 307 [April 10, 1792]).

Account with John B. Church [1]

[*Philadelphia*] *May 1, 1791.* A record of Hamilton's administration of Church's affairs "as ℔ Account transmitted J B Church. . . . Dates not to be relied on. Entry having been subsequently made for memorandum."

ADS, Mr. Sol Feinstone, Washington Crossing, Pennsylvania.
  1. Church, who had come to the United States at the time of the American Revolution, had married Angelica Schuyler, Elizabeth Hamilton's older sister. During the Revolution, Church had acquired a fortune from his contracts for supplying the American army and from his activities with Jeremiah Wadsworth in supplying the French forces in America. When he returned to England after the Revolution, he left his American business concerns in the hands of H. This account is substantially the same as the accounts printed in H's "Cash Book," March 1, 1782–1791.

Treasury Department Circular to the Commissioners of Loans

[*Philadelphia, May 2, 1791.* On May 15, 1791, Nathaniel Appleton wrote to Hamilton: "I am favoured with your circular Letter 2d. instant. *Circular not found.*]

From Joseph Ward [1]

[*Boston, May 2, 1791.* On May 26, 1791, Hamilton wrote to Ward: "I duly received your letter of the 2d instant." *Letter not found.*]

  1. Ward was a Boston stockbroker and real estate dealer.

From Nathaniel Appleton

Boston, May 3, 1791. "Your circular Letter 8th April [1] is received. An Account agreably to the form sent shall be transmitted as soon as possible. I now inclose you a Statement of the United States Act Current as it stands in my Book the balance of 26385.83 is deposited in the Massachusetts Bank. . . ."

LC, RG 53, Massachusetts State Loan Office, Letter Book, 1785–1791, Vol. "259–M," National Archives.
    1. Circular not found.

From James McHenry

[Baltimore] 3 May 1791.

My dear Sir.

I did not receive your letter of the 26th [1] till the morning of the 2d. I immediately after saw Gen. Williams [2] and made such communication of your wishes as I thought most likely to be attended with success. You know his ambitious cast, and that he thinks he could be more serviceable at the head of a great department than collector of a district. I mentioned the death of the comptroller, [3] and the probability in *my opinion* that the President from the knowlege he had of the present auditors habits experience and capacities for business would fix upon him for a successor; in which case the auditorship which was a very important office would become vacant. I observed on the advantages of a residence at the seat of Congress if he still inclined to mount higher, that he knew your power and disposition, and said I would take upon myself to make the necessary suggestions. The idea of the auditors office being a step to a still more desirable one had its weight, but he finally declined, alledging his ill state of health, and the recent death of a brother in law Col. Stull [4] which has devolved upon him the care of his children and estate. In short he was not to be induced to be auditor, tho' I thought could I have said comptrouller he might, notwithstanding his present state of health would unfit him for discharging the duties of either.

I then called on Mr. Wm. Smith [5] who with less shew of talents

will make a much better auditor. He will have as little to learn as
the General; is as systematic, a more correct and perfect accountant,
of great respectability and of longer standing in society. I found also
here that the comptrollership was a more darling object. My first
conversation was yesterday, and it was not till about half an hour
ago I got him to consent to use my discretion, so you may use yours.
I was obliged to intimate, that from the opinion you had of him, I
could entertain no doubt but his appointment would be certain unless
the President got entangled to the Southward.

You judged right. Nay, should even what I once thought of take
place, and my present temper of mind continue, I would remain
where I am. My mind in the loss of a brother has received a severe
shock.[6] My wife like yours is every thing that is kind good and excellent, and was there only one man more in the world I should be
the happiest man in it.

Adieu and believe me yours most sincerely   and most affectionately   James McHenry

ALS, Hamilton Papers, Library of Congress.
    1. Letter not found.
    2. Otho H. Williams, collector of customs at Baltimore.
    3. Nicholas Eveleigh. See H to George Washington, April 17, 1791.
    4. Colonel John Stull was a prominent Maryland Federalist and a wealthy
landowner of Millsborough, Washington County. He married Mercy Williams,
one of Williams's sisters.
    5. Smith was a Baltimore merchant and Williams's father-in-law. He had
served as a Federalist member of the House of Representatives from 1789 to 1791.
    6. John McHenry, a Baltimore merchant, had died in May, 1790.

To Sharp Delany

Treasury Department
May 4th. 1791

Sir

I am informed, that a doubt has been made, whether in order to
obtain the Credit for *two years,* for the duties on Teas, according
to the Act making provision for the collection of the Duties by law,
imposed on Teas and to prolong the term for the payment of the
duties on Wines,[1] it is necessary that the Teas be deposited in conformity to the regulations prescribed in the Act—it being contended

that the parties will be intitled to the benefit of that Credit on giving Bond, *with surety*, as in other cases, conditioned for the payment of the duties in *two* years.

As I have no doubt that the true construction of the law makes the deposit of the Teas an *indispensable condition* to the allowance of that Credit, I am to desire that you will govern yourself accordingly.

I am, Sir,   Your Obedt. Servt.   Alexander Hamilton

Sharp Delany Esqr.
Collr. Philada.

LS, Bureau of Customs, Philadelphia; copy, RG 56, Letters to the Collector at Philadelphia, National Archives; copy, RG 56, Letters to Collectors at Small Ports, "Set G," National Archives.
    1. 1 *Stat.* 219–21 (March 3, 1791). The regulations for the deposit of teas may be found in Section 1.

To Benjamin Lincoln

Treasury Department,
4 May 1791

Sir,

Instructions relative to the collection of the Duties on Teas [1] are now preparing, and will be very soon transmitted.

The papers relative to the Suffolk of Weymouth were returned some time since to the District Court of Massachusetts, as they were not in such form as to enable me legally to decide upon the case.[2]

I am, sir,

B Lincoln Esqr.
Boston

L[S], RG 36, Collector of Customs at Boston, Letters from the Treasury, 1789–1807, Vol. 4, National Archives.
    1. "An Act making farther provision for the collection of the duties by law imposed on Teas, and to prolong the term of the payment of the Duties on Wines" (1 *Stat.* 219–21) had been passed on March 3, 1791.
    2. See Lincoln to H, April 1, 1791.

From William Short

Paris May 4 1791.

Sir

Since my last of April 9. I have received a letter from M. de Montmorin [1] in which he informs me that he had recieved a second letter from Schweizer & Jeanneret relative to the reimbursement of the American debt & their proposals respecting it, & that he had answered them that they must apply to me, being unable himself to interfere in the matter notwithstanding the favorable opinion he entertained of their proposals. They had previously applied to me to have something definitive done with respect to their terms, as not being willing or able to keep so large a sum unemployed upon an uncertainty & also as being limited as to time by the Genoese capitalists for whom they acted.[2] I told them that I had done all that I was authorized to do, which was to send you their proposals & that as soon as I was made acquainted with your sentiments I would communicate them. Since then & since their letter to M. de Montmorin I have heard nothing further from them.

The Genoese Minister [3] has as yet no answer from Genoa but he seems well persuaded that the U.S. may make loans advantageously there particularly since I have made him acquainted with the present situation of their debt, government, & revenue. In support of this it is indispensable that you should send here proofs of the amount of the taxes appropriated to foreign loans, properly authenticated. I have given him a copy of the act making this appropriation [4] & also the amount of the revenue to last October as taken from the newspapers. I have mentioned also the augmented duties to take place.[5] I think it highly probable by having a credit as well at Genoa as Amsterdam & by putting them in opposition with each other the U.S. may very soon reduce their rate of interest. The greatest obstacle to this would be the heavy arrears we owe France, & which it is supposed we shall immediately make loans to pay off. It is for this reason that it is doubly desirable to convert their arrears by some negotiation or other into a new form—or pay them off by loans made here which would of course not interfere with those to be made at Amsterdam or

Genoa. The depreciation of assignats continuing I think it probable the U.S. might make such loans & particularly by securing the lenders against further depreciation. It is possible also that it might be an agreeable circumstance to them to render them bonds for these loans or any part of them receivable in the land office of the U.S for the purchase of lands agreeable to the prices fixed by law. This is only an idea which occurs as being an additional security against depreciation.

I am promised an account in detail of the loans made at Genoa for twelve months past & will send it to you.

I have the honor to be with perfect respect & attachment   Sir, your most obedient   humble servant   W:Short

The Honble Alexander Hamilton Secretary of the Treasury

ALS, letterpress copy, William Short Papers, Library of Congress.
  1. Comte de Montmorin to Short, April 29, 1791 (LS, William Short Papers, Library of Congress).
  2. See Schweizer, Jeanneret, and Company to Short, December 14, 1790, enclosed in Short to H, January 15, 1791.
  3. Christoforo Vincenzo de Spinola.
  4. "An Act making provision for the (payment of the) Debt of the United States" (1 *Stat.* 138–44 [August 4, 1790]).
  5. Short is presumably referring to the duties on distilled spirits that were to go into effect on July 1, 1791. See "An Act repealing, after the last day of June next, the duties heretofore laid upon Distilled Spirits imported from abroad, and laying others in their stead; and also upon Spirits distilled within the United States, and for appropriating the same" (1 *Stat.* 199–214 [March 3, 1791]).

To Nathaniel Appleton

[*Philadelphia, May 5, 1791.* On May 15, 1791, Appleton wrote to Hamilton: "I am . . . favoured with your particular Letter 5th instant." *Letter not found.*]

From Thomas Mifflin

[Philadelphia, May 5, 1791]

Sir.

On the 28th. of Augt. 1788, the late Board of Treasury of the U.S. under the authority of a Resolution of Congress accepted the proposals which were made to them, on the 7th. of July preceding, by the Delegates in Congress from Pennsylvania on behalf of this State, for the purchase of a tract of Land, belonging to the U.S., contained in the interval betwixt a Meridian Line, run between Lake Erie and the state of Pennsylvania, and the boundaries of the States of New York and Massachusetts, at the rate of three fourths of a Dollar per Acre; payable in gold or silver, or in public securities of the U.S., bearing Interest.[1]

As I understand that the quantity of land contained in the above mentioned tract has been ascertained by actual survey, it is proper to inform you that I am ready, on the part of Pennsylvania, to comply with the terms of the contract. Permit me, therefore, to request that on the part of the U.S. you will be pleased to make the necessary arrangements, and to appoint an early day for closing the transaction. I am, sir, yr most obd   & hble serv   T. M.

5 May 1791
To Alexr Hamilton Esqr
S.T.U.S.

Df, in the writing of Alexander Dallas, Division of Public Records, Pennsylvania Historical and Museum Commission, Harrisburg; LC, Division of Public Records, Pennsylvania Historical and Museum Commission.
   1. On November 14, 1787, the Pennsylvania General Assembly "*Resolved,* That the Supreme Executive Council be authorized and requested to obtain, and lay before the General Assembly, a description of the lands lying between the northern boundary of this state and Lake *Erie,* with an estimate of the sum necessary to purchase such part thereof as may be thought necessary to accommodate this state" (*Minutes of the First Session of the Twelfth General Assembly of the Commonwealth of Pennsylvania, Which Commenced at Philadelphia, on Monday, the Twenty-second Day of October, in the Year of our Lord One Thousand Seven Hundred and Eighty-Seven* [Philadelphia: Printed by Hall and Sellers, in Market Street, 1787]). On February 5, 1788, the Council forwarded this resolution to the Pennsylvania delegates in Congress with a request that they forward to the Assembly "such information on the subject as may be in your power—especially on that part which relates to the Estimate of the sum necessary to purchase, and for what sum other Lands belonging to The United States in those parts were sold" (Hazard, *Pennsylvania Archives,* XI, 237).
   On June 6, 1788, the Continental Congress "*Resolved* That the geographer of the United States . . . or his deputy having run the meridian between lake Erie and the state of Pensylvania and marked and noted down in his field book proper land marks for perpetuating the same shall proceed to make a survey of the Land lying west of the said line between lake Erie and the state of Pensylvania so as to ascertain the quantity thereof and make return of such survey to the board of treasury, who are hereby authorised and empowered at any time before or after such survey to sell the said tract in whole at private sale for a

price not less than three fourths of a dollar per acre in specie or public securities drawing interest" (*JCC*, XXXIV, 203). On June 14, the Executive Council of Pennsylvania authorized the Pennsylvania delegates in Congress to purchase the tract. In response to this authorization, the following letter was sent to the Board of Treasury by the Pennsylvania delegates on July 7, 1788: "We the Delegates of the State of Pennsylvania, in compliance with instructions, and in virtue of powers, received from the said State, do hereby offer to contract (in behalf of the said State,) with the Honble Board of Treasury, for a tract of land belonging to the United States, contained in the interval betwixt a Meridian Line, run between Lake Erie and the state of Pennsylvania, and the Boundaries of the States of New York and Massachusetts, at the rate of three-fourth of a dollar per acre; payable in Gold or Silver, or in public securities of the United States, bearing interest; when the quantity ascertained by actual survey, in the manner prescribed by a Resolution of Congress of the . . . [6]th of June, 1788." On August 28, 1788, the Board of Treasury accepted Pennsylvania's proposal (Hazard, *Pennsylvania Archives*, XI, 382–83).

Congress approved the board's contract with Pennsylvania on September 4, 1788, and ceded title to the Triangle to that state (*JCC*, XXXIV, 499). The Continental Congress, however, went out of existence before the matter had been consummated.

From Jeremiah Olney

Providence, May 5, 1791. "It sometimes happens that Coasting Vessels, belonging to other Districts, arrive at this Port with Licenses which have been granted more than One Year; being at a loss to know precisely how to conduct, in such Cases, the Law being thereon silent; and as I am desirous in every Instance of doing my Duty entirely consonant to Law, I take the liberty Sir, to ask your Opinion and Direction on this Subject. . . ."

ADfS, Rhode Island Historical Society, Providence; copy, RG 56, Letters from the Collector at Providence, National Archives.

From Thomas Forrest, John Nicholson, and Others, Public Creditors [1]

[*Philadelphia, May 6, 1791.* In a letter dated May 27, 1791, and addressed to "Thomas Forrest, John Nicholson and others, Public Creditors," Hamilton wrote: "I have received your letter of the sixth instant." *Letter not found.*]

1. Forrest was "a purchaser of certificates and paper money" (Clement Biddle, *The Philadelphia Directory* [Philadelphia, 1791], 42). Nicholson was comptroller general of Pennsylvania.

From Joseph Hardy

Treasury Department, Comptroller's Office, May 6, 1791. "On examining the Accounts of John Halsted, Collector of the Customs, for the District of Perth Amboy, from 1st. October to 31st. December 1790, it appears, that he has collected duties on American coasting Vessels, under 20 Tons burthen, at the rate of 6 Cents per Ton, per annum, to the amount of 29 Ds. 04 Cts. with which he has credited the United States. As the Collection of those duties, seems to have been made, contrary to the intent of your circular Letter to the Collectors of the 30th. November 1789; I conceive it to be my duty to communicate the circumstance for your consideration."

LC, RG 217, First Comptroller's Office, Revenue Letters Sent, National Archives.

From Nathan Keais

Collectors Office
Port Washington [North Carolina] May 6th: 1791
Sir

Yours of the 14th [1] & 15th [2] Ulto I have duly received together with the last Acts of Congress. I shall as Soon as Possible and on the best terms I am able Contract with Some Person of Ability to build & Compleat the revenue Cutter. In your Letter of the 14th Ulto. you Say, on the receipt of this Letter you will Proceed to Contract with Suitable Persons for the erecting or fixing and Keeping up Setts of Stakes Which are Requisite to mark out the Several Channels that was formerly furnished with them. As no Particular Part of this Business is mentioned it has the appearance that you intended that I Should have the Management of all the sounds and Channels that was Ordered to be Stak'd by the Laws of this State.

Which I cannot think was your intentions, as the Waters of Cape Fear is so remote from all the Other Parts of this State the Legislature Gave them a Priviledge of Appointing Commissioners for that River alone. The Stakeage of the Swash and Royal Shoal in Pamplico Sound, was under the Directions of the Commissioners of Newbern Washington and Edenton; the Other Channels running into Pamplico & Albermarle Sounds under their Respective Commissioners.

This Method of Putting the Management of the Swash and Royal Shoal under the Care of three commissioners So remote from each Other was attended with Ill Consequences. I think this Business Ought to be put under the direction of One Person. I Shall Proceed to Hire Out the Stakeage of the Swash Royal Shoal and Pamplico Sound and All the Other Parts Within my District and Shall Wait your Instruction before I Proceed Further.

I am With Respect   Your Obedient Servant   Nath Keais

LS, RG 26, Lighthouse Letters Received, Vol. "A," Pennsylvania and Southern States, National Archives.
1. See "Treasury Department Circular to the Collectors of the Customs," April 14, 1791.
2. Letter not found.

To Benjamin Lincoln

Treasury Department,
6 May 1791

Sir,

I have transmitted the accounts enclosed in your letter of the 27 Ultimo to the Auditor of the Treasury. The stock which you fund in the Massachusetts office you will cause to be transferred to the Treasury, and for this purpose you will make application to Mr Appleton, the Commissioner of Loans. As the loan office certificates can be funded at the Treasury, it will be best that you transmit them hither for the purpose, taking great care to do it under such circumstances and with such precautions, that in case of accident you can clearly prove their transmission.

I am, sir, with great consideration,   Your Obedt Servant
A Hamilton

Benjamin Lincoln Esq.

LS, RG 36, Collector of Customs at Boston, Letters from the Treasury, 1789–1808, Vol. 4, National Archives; copy, RG 56, Letters to the Collectors at Small Ports, "Set G," National Archives; copy, RG 56, Letters to the Collector at Boston, National Archives.

To Thomas Jefferson [1]

Treasury Department
May the 7. 1791

The Secretary of the Treasury has the honor to inform the Secretary of State that there are in the bank of North America Bills at ten days sight for the sum of 32.175 Guilders, which the Cashier is directed to hold for him. A warrant is enclosed for the sum of 13000 dolls. in his favor, the money for which is intended to procure those bills for the purpose of obtaining a recognition of the treaty with the new Emperor of Morocco.

D, in unidentified handwriting, Thomas Jefferson Papers, Library of Congress.
1. For background to this letter, see Jefferson to H, March 12, 1791.

From George Washington

Charleston [South Carolina] May 7. 1791

Sir

I have received your letters of the 11 & 14 of last month. Concluding from Mr. Shorts statement of his negotiation in Amsterdam, and from the opinions offered in your letters of the 11th.,[1] that the loan has been obtained on the best terms practicable, and that its application in the manner you propose will be the most advantageous to the United States, I do hereby signify my approbation of what has been already done, as communicated in your letters of the 11th and 14th. of April. Assenting to the further progress of the loans as recommended by you in these letters, I request that instructions may be given for completing them agreeably thereto.

I am sir,   Your most Obedt. servt.   Geo: Washington

LC, George Washington Papers, Library of Congress.
1. Washington was presumably referring to H's letter to him of April 10, 1791.

To Joshua Wentworth [1]

[*Philadelphia, May 7, 1791.* On September 7, 1791, Wentworth wrote to Hamilton: "Your letters of the 7th May & 22d June were duly received." *Letter of May 7 not found.*]

1. Wentworth was supervisor of the revenue for the District of New Hampshire.

From George Washington

Charleston [South Carolina] May 8, 1791. "Mr. Cogdell,[1] the Collector of Georgetown appearing on enquiry a proper person to be appointed Inspector of Excise for that Survey, you will signify his appointment to that Office. . . . Capt. Robert Cochran [2] seems in all respects best qualified to command the revenue Cutter on this station, and I have in consequence appointed him to that Office. . . ."

LC, George Washington Papers, Library of Congress.
1. John Cogdell.
2. Cochran was formerly harbor master of Charleston, South Carolina.

To Nathaniel Appleton

[*Philadelphia, May 9, 1791.* Letter listed in dealer's catalogue. *Letter not found.*]

LS, sold by Stan V. Henkels, Jr., April 6, 1922, Lot 221.

To Pierpont Edwards [1]

Treasury Department
May 9th. 1791

Sir

Your account being allowed and *certified* by the District Judge must be forwarded to the Auditor of the Treasury, who will put it in a course of adjustment according to the forms of the Treasury.

You ought also to empower some person on the spot to receive and remit to you the amount of your account. The remittance can commonly be negotiated by a draught on one of your Collectors.

I am with great consideration   Sir   Your obed serv

⟨Alexander H⟩amilton

Pierpoint Edw⟨ards⟩

LS, The Huntington Library, San Marino, California.
1. Edwards was the United States attorney for the District of Connecticut.

From William Ellery

Custom House
Newport [Rhode Island] May 9th 1791

Sir,

I have received your letter of the 27th. of last month.[1] Always attentive to the business of the Cession of the Light-House &c I applied to leading members of the House,[2] a bill was preferred at the Session which began and finished last week. It passed the Lower House unanimously, but it was stopped in the Upper House; by the opposition made to it principally by the Governour, who as I am credibly informed declared against making any cession to the United States. I will see that this matter is revived at the next Session, which will commence on the 4th monday in June next.

The Surveyor of this port,[3] who is acquainted with Mr. Bowers, was at his house lately. Mr. Bowers shewed him his deed. The land on which the Light-House and Dwelling House stands are included in the grant. The Surveyor thinks that, when the Legislature shall have ceded their right & title, Mr. Bowers will not convey the fee to the United States, he is so tenacious of landed property; but that he may give them a long lease. His sentiments on this head will be more fully known after the State shall have relinquished their right.

I am obliged to you for your opinion relative to returned dutiable goods, and will attend to your direction respecting the disbursements for the Light-House.

The bulb of the Thermometer which Col. Lamb sent to me by your direction was broken before it came to my hands, and I remitted it, as I advised you in my letter of the 25th. of last month. I received a Dicas's Hydrometer by the last post, and I read the last paragraph touching the proof of each cask of Spirits to the Surveyor of this port, and shall communicate it to the Surveyors of the other ports. Several applications had been made to me for boats, before I wrote to you on that subject,[4] and you may depend upon it I shall never countenance any expence which I think is unnecessary. The trade of East Greenwich, and North Kingstown is very small. That of Warren and Barrington, and of Bristol is so large, as to render a boat for each necessary. The old sailing boat I shall place in the hands of the Surveyor of the Port of Warren & Barrington,[5] as soon as a new one can be provided for this, in the mean time I shall send him a small harbour boat, which, when he receives the old sailing boat, I shall order to be sent to the Surveyor.

Previous to the receipt of your letter I had conceived that no alterations were sufficient to convert a foreign built ship into an American bottom, and that foreign ships sold in consequence of forfeiture could not by law be made free bottoms. Your sentiments on these points have fully confirmed my opinion.[6] I have been advised of your determination respecting the cases of the Ushers.[7] It did not arrive until the District Court had risen, and it will not sit again until next August. The Goods were condemned at the preceeding Court, and will be sold. The Actions for the penalties are continued to August term.

This will be accompanied by a weekly return of Cash on hand, two Certifes. of Registry No. 36 and No. 62 both of which were granted at this Office and delivered up on account of transfer of property; also the copy of a memorandum of the change of master of the Sloop Favourite on a Certife. of Registry No. 47—Also three drafts of the Treasr. of the United States, No. 1223 for Five hundred Dolls. No. 1224 for Five hundred Dollars, and No. 1266 for one hundred Dollars, and a list of a post note amountg. to One hundred and ninety five Dollars, one moiety of which is now transmitted to Saml. Meredith, the other moiety was transmd. by the last post.

I am Sir   Yr. most obedt, servt.   W Ellery Collr

A Hamilton Esqr
Secry of Treasy.

LC, Newport Historical Society, Newport, Rhode Island.
   1. Letter not found.
   2. See Ellery to H, March 7, 1791.
   3. Daniel Lyman.

4. See Ellery to H, April 19, 1791.
5. Nathaniel Phillips.
6. See H to Ellery, April 11, 1791.
7. See Ellery to H, February 15, 1791.

To Andrew Porter

Treasury Department
May 9th. 1791

Sir

I have concluded to comply with the request contained in your Letter of the 23d of April last and have given directions Accordingly.

In doing this I merely yield to a disposition to Accomodate as much as may be in my power to the wishes of Individuals, convinced that what is directed to be done can make no difference in the legal effect of the Transaction.

I am Sir   Your Obedt Servant   A Hamilton

Mr. Andrew Porter

Copy, Division of Public Records, Pennsylvania Historical and Museum Commission, Harrisburg.

To William Seton

Treasury Department,
9 May 1791

Sir,

I am desirous of making a further payment to Mr William Hill,[1] of five thousand Dollars on account of his contract for cloathing for the Troops. The Bank of New York will oblige me by making him a payment of that sum, & taking his receipt for the same, as on that account. This sum will be charged, during the vacancy of the Comptroller's Office, to the seperate account for the United States, as in the former payment.

I am, sir   Your Most Obedt Servant   A Hamilton
                                            Secy of the Treasury

Wm Seton Esqr.
Cashier of the Bk of N Yk

PS. The Treasurer has been directed to send you for sale Two
hundred thousand Guilders to be disposed of on the same terms with
the last [2]—that is at 36$\frac{4}{11}$ ninetieths per Guilder payable in sixty
days, or in Ninety with the discount for thirty. Instead of two good
names or *two* firms, one *good* name and a deposit in any species of
the Stock of the United States, at its lowest current value, to an
amount equal to the sum purchased will suffice.[3]

A Hamilton

LS, Mr. William H. Thomas, Cleveland, Ohio.
   1. See Seton to H, March 28, 1791.
   2. See Seton to H, January 10, 1791.
   3. The postscript is in H's handwriting.

To William Short

Treasury Department
Philadelphia May 9th. 1791

Sir

Since mine to you of the 13th. of April, I have received your several letters of the eighteenth and thirtieth of December, the fifteenth
of January, the seventh, seventeenth and twenty second of february.

Thanking you for the copious information they contain, I assure
you, that the further developement of the business has increased my
satisfaction with the course you have pursued. The issue of the loan
set on foot by you, is too favourable to the credit of this Country
not to be particularly pleasing.[1]

I was apprehensive, that inconvenience might attend the restriction
by which you are required to defer opening a new loan, till the preceeding one has been communicated and approved.[2] And I doubt not,
that the President will readily consent to remove it on perceiving that
it has occasioned embarassment. He is expected to return to this place
by the middle of June; though as I have written to him on the subject,[3] it is probable that I shall, before his return, receive orders to
give you greater latitude.[4]

My letter of the 13th. of April will have enabled you to open a

second loan, either in Holland, or in the place to which Mr. Morris [5]
alludes—if the supposed opportunity shall have been found real and
shall not have passed by. It certainly would be very desireable to be
able to resort to more markets than one and if one of those markets
should happen to be England it would not be the worse on that
account. I think there is a train of good consequences involved in
the idea of opening the purses of monied men in that Country to the
Government of this. I suspect nevertheless, that it would not be long
tolerated.

My objections to the negotiation you announce for obtaining a
transfer of the debt due to France, have been confirmed by your
subsequent communications.[6]

You are informed that a million and a half of the last loan is
destined for France and authorised immediately to apply a million.[7]
I am now to inform you that directions have been given to the Treasurer to draw for Eight hundred thousand. Leaving funds for answering this sum, you are at liberty to complete the payment of the whole
sum destined for France, as speedily as you think fit.

When the President returns I shall take with him a definitive ar-
ragement, and give you a general view of the dispositions intended
to be made.

With great consideration and esteem   I have the honor to be   Sir
Your obedt. servt.   Alexander Hamilton

William Short Esquire
Chargé des affaires of the United States
at the Court of France

LS, William Short Papers, Library of Congress. A copy of this letter was enclosed in H's "Report on Foreign Loans," February 13, 1793.
    1. See Short to H, January 25, February 7, 17, 1791.
    2. See H to Short, September 1, 1790.
    3. H to George Washington, April 10, 14, 1791.
    4. Washington to H, May 7, 1791.
    5. See Short to H, February 17, 1791.
    6. H is referring to the proposals by Schweizer, Jeanneret, and Company con-
cerning the American debt due to France. See Short to H, December 18, 30,
1790; January 15, February 7, 1791.
    7. See H to Short, April 13, 1791.

To Thomas Smith

[*Philadelphia, May 9, 1791.* On June 8, 1791, Hamilton wrote to Smith: "You will perceive on reexamination that you have misconceived the instruction contained in my letter of the 9th Ulto." *Letter not found.*]

From Martha Walker [1]

[*Boston, May 9, 1791.* On July 2, 1791, Hamilton wrote to Martha Walker and referred to "your letter of the 9th of May." *Letter not found.*]

1. Martha Walker was a widow and a resident of Boston.

From Charles Weissenfels and George P. Weissenfels, Junior [1]

New York, May 9, 1791. Seek to obtain either a Government appointment or a pension for their father.[2]

LS, in writing of George P. Weissenfels, Hamilton Papers, Library of Congress.
  1. Charles Weissenfels is listed in the New York City directory for 1790 as living at "old Hobuck ferry house, Corporation dock." His brother George's occupation is given as "conveyancer" and his address as 24 King Street.
  2. Frederick Weissenfels, who had been a colonel of a New York regiment of levies during the American Revolution.

From Joseph Whipple

Portsmouth, New Hampshire, May 9, 1791. "I this day recd from the Collector Benj Lincoln Esqr. of Boston 12 ps Canvas which I presume are intended for Sails for the Cutter.[1] I had engaged the Canvas of the Mafactory here but have now Countermanded it. . . . Be pleased to advise what articles for equiping the Vessel or for Stores are to be forwarded that I may avoid making unnecessary purchases."

LC, RG 36, Collector of Customs at Portsmouth, Letters Sent, 1790–1791, Vol. 2, National Archives; copy, RG 56, Letters from the Collector at Portsmouth, National Archives.
1. See Benjamin Lincoln to H, April 29–May 3, 1791, note 1.

From Otho H. Williams

Baltimore, May 9, 1791. "I transmit you a copy of a report of the Surveyor of this district respecting a compari[s]on of Dycas's Hydrometer with the Substitute.[1] This is the first report which I have received upon the subject, and in consequence have directed the Surveyor to discontinue the use of the Substitute."

ADfS, RG 53, "Old Correspondence," Baltimore Collector, National Archives.
1. This report, which is a copy, is dated May 6, 1791, and was signed by Robert Ballard. It may be found in RG 53, "Old Correspondence," Baltimore Collector, National Archives. Ballard concludes: "By this trial I find that Dycas's Hydrometer on an average upon the Common West India Rum, makes the proof eight PCent higher than the Hydrometer given as a substitute."

From Nathaniel Appleton

Boston, May 10, 1791. "I had the honor to write you 3 instant & . . . I have receivd yours of 28 April in which you wish me to draw on the Treasury for the amount thereof agreably to which I have this day drawn on the Treasury two drafts . . . one for 375 Dollrs the amount of my last Quater's Salary & the other for 873 66/100 the amount of the Account of Expenditures for Clerkship & Stationary. . . ."

LC, RG 53, Massachusetts State Loan Office, Letter Book, 1785–1791, "Vol. 259-M," National Archives.

From Richard Cuyler

Albany, May 10, 1791. "My Father (Mr. Jacob Cuyler). has shewn me your polite Favor to him of 8th. Apl.[1] by which observe you continue to hold his Application in Veiw, but that nothing had yet Occurred. With Regard to an Office, of Collector of the Revenue, would with pleasure Accept, should I be so fortunate, as to be favored therewith. . . ."

ALS, Hamilton Papers, Library of Congress.
1. Letter not found.

From Jeremiah Olney

Providence, May 10, 1791. Encloses returns "of the Vessels built within this District." Acknowledges receipt of "One of Dicas's Hydrometers."

ADfS, Rhode Island Historical Society, Providence; copy, RG 56, Letters from the Collector at Providence, National Archives.

From Thomas Smith

[Philadelphia] May 10, 1791. ". . . I am nearly out of Indents,[1] the Comptroller of this State [2] informs me that about 300,000 Dolls. more will pay the Interest on the Certificates belonging to Individuals yet remaining in his Hands. I am honored with your favor 2nd April. . . ."[3]

LC, RG 53, Pennsylvania State Loan Office, Letter Book, 1790–1794, Vol. "615–P," National Archives.
1. For background to the issue of indents at the Pennsylvania loan office, see Smith to H, February 14, 1791, note 1.
2. John Nicholson.
3. Letter not found.

From Joseph Whipple

[Portsmouth, New Hampshire, May 10, 1791. On May 17, 1791, Whipple wrote to Hamilton and referred to "My last letter (May 10th)." *Letter not found.]*

From Jeremiah Olney

Providence, May 12, 1791. Encloses "weekly Return of Cash" and "Two Drafts of the Treasr." Acknowledges receipt of a "Thermometer, forwarded by the Collr. of New York."

ADfS, Rhode Island Historical Society, Providence; copy, RG 56, Letters from the Collector at Providence, National Archives.

Treasury Department Circular
to the Collectors of the Customs

Treasury Department,
May 13th, 1791.

Sir,

I find instances that have occurred in some of the Custom-houses, of receiving the duties on goods by estimates formed upon the invoices, or the statements of the Masters and Owners of the vessels, and by other means than actual gauging, weighing, measuring, &c. This, it is manifest, is not conformable to law, and may lead to practices very injurious to the revenue. Neither is it necessary to the accomodation of the Merchant, who, by the last Collection Act, is at liberty to carry his goods from one district to another, paying the duties in the districts for which they are destined, upon the goods only that are landed in each.[1] I have therefore to desire that the duties on goods may, in no instance, be ascertained but on the *actual landing* thereof, and by no means but by the measuring, weighing and gauging, in all cases wherein those operations are required by law. If vessels bound to other places put into your district, the mere securing there of the duties to be paid in the district for which the goods are destined, is to be done by estimation in the manner prescribed by law,[2] but no estimation is to be accepted when the duties are to be paid to you.

A question has also been stated for my determination, whether the Inspector put on board a vessel in one district to go to another, is to superintend the landing of the goods in the last district. I am of opinion that he is not, and that his authority on board the vessel terminates the moment she reports herself in the last district.

I find that a considerable difference, as well in the custom of Merchants as in the practice of the Custom-houses, in regard to the mode of calculating the Tare of goods, prevails through the Union: I have therefore to request that you will inform yourself accurately, what Tare is customary among Merchants in your district, upon the following goods—that is, whether they make their allowance per 112 lb or 100, and whether it be 2, 10, 12 or 15 per cent. viz—On sugars in hogsheads,—ditto in barrels—ditto in boxes; coffee in barrels—ditto in bags,—cocoa in ditto and ditto, and in hogsheads; piemento in bags and barrels,—pepper in ditto and ditto, and in bales; and so of any other goods, and in any kind of package usually imported.

I also request that you will inform me what has heretofore been your mode of allowing the Tares on the several kinds of goods above-mentioned, and in the several kinds of packages, under the Collection Law.

I am, Sir, ⟨your obedient Servant,⟩

L[S], to Benjamin Lincoln, RG 36, Collector of Customs at Boston, Letters from the Treasury, 1789–1807, Vol. 4, National Archives; LS, to Jeremiah Olney, Rhode Island Historical Society, Providence; LS, to Otho H. Williams, Office of the Secretary, United States Treasury Department; copy, to Jeremiah Olney, Rhode Island Historical Society, Providence; copy, United States Finance Miscellany, Treasury Circulars, Library of Congress; copy, RG 56, Circulars of the Office of the Secretary, "Set T," National Archives.

1. See Section 19 of "An Act to provide more effectually for the collection of the duties imposed by law on goods, wares and merchandise imported into the United States, and on the tonnage of ships or vessels" (1 *Stat.* 160 [August 4, 1790]).

2. Section 20 of the Collection Law provided "That the master or person having the charge or command of the said ship or vessel shall first give bond with one or more sureties to the satisfaction of the collector of the district within which the said ship or vessel shall first arrive, in a sum equal to the amount of the duties on the residue of the said goods, according to such estimate as the said collector shall form thereof, with condition that the said residue of the said goods shall be duly entered and delivered in such other district or districts of the United States, for which the same shall have been reported to be destined" (1 *Stat.* 160).

From Nathaniel Appleton

United States Loan Office
Boston 15 May 1791

Sr.

I wrote you 10 instant, at which time I drew on the Treasury for the amount of my last Quarters Salary & expenditures for the two first Quarters—Since which I am favoured with your circular Letter 2d. instant.[1] In answer I have to inform you that I have never issued a single Certificate to a nonsubscriber in exchang for Old Emisso. money or Indents of Interest. I have issued only one Certificate to a non subscriber for Certificates of public Debt which took place the present Quarter. I think there will not be another nonsubscriber in this State. I am also favoured with your particular Letter 5th instant.[2] I note your directions to the Treasury to transmit me Drafts for twenty thousand Dollars. When they are received I shall dispose of them agreably to your orders. The money arising from the Sale thereof shall be placed in the Massachusetts Bank as the former money was for its greater security &c. With great Respect   I have the honor to be Sr Y Servant   N A

LC, RG 53, Massachusetts State Loan Office, Letter Book, 1785–1791, Vol. "259–M," National Archives.
   1. Circular not found.
   2. Letter not found.

Conversation with George Beckwith [1]

[Philadelphia, May 15, 1791] [2]

7 [3]   "If the United States were at war with a great or respectable nation, the case would be different, a foreign mediation under certain circumstances might be desirable; in that case, the manner of the application would be official, and of course not to any public officer of that country abroad, but to the administration at home; on the present occasion, the thing in its existing shape is inadmissible, and I could not submit such a paper to the President's consideration—the objects of warfare are certain vagrant Indian Tribes who cannot be considered to be on the footing in which such a system as this would place them, however it may be our interest and policy to close hostilities, which are attended with trouble and expence, and which indeed may be excited by our frontier people, from interested motives: as an Indian war leads to the spending money in their country as well as to the gratification of their individual resentments."

   [Beckwith]   In suggesting the measure of an interference or rather of a pacific recommendation on the part of Lord Dorchester, I acted altogether as an individual, and my judgment led me to this from the sense of the thing, and from my conceiving the fomenting such a war could never be any object for such a government as yours. On the contrary I have concluded from those explanations which I have received by your means, of matters in the western Country, that your trading interests would be advanced, by the re-establishment of peace. We shall take occasion in the course of the summer to mark a pacific disposition to the Indians in general and to those hostile tribes in particular. We shall suggest to them the idea of a meeting to discuss the objects of difference, and if Lord Dorchester would suggest that a friendly accomodation and settlement would be a pleasing circumstance to your Government, it might have a tendency to promote it; in all this, I do not speak ministerially to you, although I am sure the thing is so, and that it would not only advance this object but tend to forward the establishment of those greater national points which I have frequently touched upon in our different conversations."

D, Public Archives of Canada, Ottawa, Ontario.

1. This document was enclosed in Lord Dorchester to Lord Grenville, June 14, 1791.

The background of this conversation was the ceaseless warfare on the western frontier between the Americans and several of the more hostile Indian tribes. After the failure of an expedition organized and commanded by Brigadier General Josiah Harmar in the fall of 1790, and with the continuing news of Indian depredations, Congress on March 3, 1791, in Section 15 of "An Act for raising and adding another Regiment to the Military Establishment of the United States, and for making farther provision for the protection of the frontiers," appropriated $312,686 for a new campaign (1 *Stat.* 224). Before the actual preparation for the campaign, Major General Arthur St. Clair, governor of the Northwest Territory, was to wait for the results of the negotiations of several agents who had been sent to the Indians to attempt to make peace (see "Conversation with George Beckwith," July 12, 1791).

H's remarks were in answer to Beckwith's "proposal that Lord Dorchester should intervene to effect peace between the United States and the Indians" (Brymner, *Canadian Archives*, 1890, 388).

2. Beckwith did not date this conversation. In a calendar of Canadian state papers Beckwith's communication is printed under the date of May 15, 1791 (Brymner, *Canadian Archives*, 1890, 288).

3. "7" was Beckwith's code number for H.

From Philip Schuyler

Albany May 15th 1791

Dear Sir

A few days after the receipt of your favor [1] covering letters for the Supervizor of Vermont [2] and Mr Jacob Cuyler [3] I wrote you [4] and my Eliza, but as I have not had a line from you since I fear my letters have not come to hand. I entreated Eliza to let me know when she would set out from Philadelphia for this place, that I might engage a good and discreet master of an Albany Sloop to bring her to this place, and begged her to bring all the children and their nurse with her. I fear If she remains where she is until the hot weather commences that her health may be much injured. Let me therefore intreat you to expedite her as soon as possible.

I have hardly enjoyed a day without pain since I left you, the Gout continues to torment me in feet & wrists. I impute much of It to the very ⟨rain⟩y weather we have hitherto experienced.

Mrs. Schuyler Joins me in love to all with you, adieu.

I am Dr Sir   Affectionately Yours &c &c   P Schuyler

Hone. Alexr Hamilton Esqr

ALS, Lloyd W. Smith Collection, Morristown National Historical Park, Morristown, New Jersey.
   1. Letter not found.
   2. Letter not found. The supervisor of the revenue for Vermont was Noah Smith, a prominent lawyer, politician, and landholder who had served in the Vermont Assembly, on the state Supreme Court, and as state's attorney. In January, 1791, he was an unsuccessful candidate for the United States Senate.
   3. Letter not found. See Richard Cuyler to H, May 10, 1791.
   4. Letter not found.

From Caleb Gibbs

Barre [Massachusetts] May 16th. 1791

My best friend

I have been honored by your much esteemed favour of the 20th. Ulto.[1]

With the most pungent greif did I read your Letter respecting Mr. Tracy's affair.[2] It is to much for me to relate. Nay My good Hamilton (excuse the freedom) it fairly unmanned me. And what is still more effecting to me, to see my amiable wife looking over the Letter and exclaiming is it possible, is it possible Mr. Gibbs that you have lost that hard earned money you friendly lent that wicked man. Indeed my friend it was too much for her to bear. And more particularly so, considering her situation we have been almost ever since in a state of dispair for I have all along held up to her the Idea, that there was hopes of recovering my property more especially as we thought it was in your hands—but now forever lost—not only so but *good money which I borrowed of you* to bear my expences thrown away in pursuit of what he owes me & god only knows when I shall ever be able to pay you.

Pray for gods sake my friend speak to the President for me. The Surveyorship of the Port of Boston is now vacant, cannot you befriend me. Every one who knows (& I know you do) that the great Oeconomy used in the Expenditures of the Generals family was in a very great degree owing to me. Speak peace to me. Drop but one drop of the balm of Comfort & Consolation. If I am worthy of another line from you, give me it as a Comforter.

I pray god to preserve you & believe me yours   devotedly

C Gibbs

P.S. Remember I am always ready to obey your Commands.

ALS, Hamilton Papers, Library of Congress.
    1. Letter not found.
    2. Nathaniel Tracy. See Gibbs to H, January 16, 1791.

From Jeremiah Olney

Providence, May 16, 1791. "There being but one Public Boat in this District and that Constantly employed by the Inspector at the Port of Pawtuxet [1] and so down the Bay, I find it Necessary that a Suitable one with Sails should be provided for the use of the Surveyor and Inspectors of this Port, to go on Board of Vessels, and particularly such as are frequently detained (by head winds &c.) for Several days, some miles below the Town. . . ."

ADfS, Rhode Island Historical Society, Providence; copy, RG 56, Letters from the Collector at Providence, National Archives.
    1. William Barton.

From William Seton

Bank of New York 16th May 1791

Sir.

Agreably to your desire [1] Mr Hill has been paid Five thousand Dollars for which enclosed you have his receipt. Of the Bills on Amsterdam 23,000 Guilders are sold; [2] and offer is made to take to the amount of 100,000 Dollars worth, for the one half of which a Deposit of Stocks would be made and for the other half Notes with sufficient Endorsers. To comply with this proposition, we shall want nearly 100,000 Guilders more, if agreeable to you to direct the Treasurer to send them on.

I have the honor to be with the greatest respect &c

LC, Bank of New York, New York City.
   1. See H to Seton, May 9, 1791.
   2. H had sent the bank two hundred thousand guilders early in May. See H to Seton, May 9, 1791.

From Stephen Van Rensselaer

Albany May 16 1791

Dear Sir

Your letter of the 25 of April [1] I received and have endeavoured to obtain the information you required. Respecting John Burk he was a Soldier in Col. Willets Regiment [2] & did on the 8 of March execute a power of Attorney to A. Holbrook but says that he received only two Dollars & wishes to revoke the power if possible.

With respect to E. Lewis [3] I could not learn whether he gave a similar power he being from Home but I know the man & that he was a Soldier.

I am D Sir Your Obt Servt   S. V. Rensselaer

ALS, Hamilton Papers, Library of Congress.
   1. Letter not found, but see dealer's catalogue quotation printed under this date.
   2. Marinus Willett, who held several commands during the American Revolution, commanded two regiments of levies in 1781 and 1782. John Burk served in these regiments.
   3. This is a reference to either Ebenezer or Elijah Lewis. Ebenezer Lewis served in the regiments under Marinus Willett's command mentioned in note 2. Elijah Lewis served in an unidentified regiment of levies.

From Benjamin Lincoln

Boston, May 17, 1791. "Your several favours of the 14th ulto & of the 4 & 6 instant have been received. Your first, the Circular, appears to be intended to those officers who conceive themselves insufficiently compensated. As I am not in that class I conclude no report will be expected from me. . . . The duck for the four Cutters has been forwarded agreeably to your directions. . . ." [1]

LC, Massachusetts Historical Society, Boston; LC, RG 36, Collector of Customs at Boston, Letter Book, 1790–1797, National Archives; copy, RG 56, Letters from the Collector at Boston, National Archives.
1. See Lincoln to H, April 29–May 3, 1791.

From Jeremiah Olney

Providence, May 17, 1791. "I was honored, by the last Post, with your circular Letter of the 14th of April, on the Subject of a Statement of the Monies received, and Expenses paid, by the Officers of the Revenue in this District, for the Four quarters in the Year 1790; but as a Year will not be compleated with us until the 21st of June next,[1] I beg leave respectfully to suggest the propriety of postponing my Account till that period. . . ."

ADfS, Rhode Island Historical Society, Providence; copy, RG 56, Letters from the Collector at Providence, National Archives.
1. Rhode Island did not ratify the Constitution until May 29, 1790.

From Joseph Whipple

Portsmouth, New Hampshire, May 17, 1791. ". . . My last letter (May 10th)[1] Stated the amount of the first moiety of Invalid Pensioners in New Hampshire at $1661\,98/100$ Dolls. This Should have been $1660\,9/100$ Dolls. which last mentioned Sum is the precise amount of the Said moiety deducting the Sum of $376\,35/100$ Dolls. paid by the State to those Pensioners."

LC, RG 36, Collector of Customs at Portsmouth, Letters Sent, 1789–1790, Vol. 1, National Archives.
1. Letter not found.

From Richard Wylly [1]

[*May 17, 1791.*] "I have the honor of enclosing you the affidavit of Mr. John Wereat, Auditor of this State, respecting the late Edward Davies, who issued sundry Loan Office certificates, without, I believe, any authority: as I can receive no answer from our Governor,[2] to whom I writ long since on this subject. . . ."

Copy, RG 233, Reports of the Treasury Department, 1792–1793, Vol. III, National Archives.

1. This letter was enclosed in "Report on the Petition of William Smith," March 28, 1792.

Wylly was commissioner of loans for Georgia. The Treasury Department had refused to accept loan office certificates countersigned by Davies which were presented under the provisions of "An Act making provision for the (payment of the) Debt of the United States" (1 *Stat.* 138–44 [August 4, 1790]).

2. Edward Telfair.

From John Habersham

Custom House,
Savannah, May 20th, 1791.

Sir,

I have to acknowledge the receipt of your letter of the 31st of March last.[1]

I shall observe what you have directed in regard to Captain Backhouse,[2] should the decision be against him.

When the Legislature have their next meeting, I shall use my best endeavors to obtain a Cession of the Light House to the United States.[3] In the mean time I have to inform you, that the additions and repairs to that building are compleated, and that as no Person had been appointed to take charge of it, I applied to the President of the United States on the 14th Inst., to authorize a temporary appointment, until I should hear from you on the subject, which he did, and I have accordingly given one to Mr. Ichabod Higgins, the Person who I recommended to you in my Letter of the 14th Novemr. 1789. Be pleased to inform me, whether it is agreeable to you that Mr. Higgins should be continued, and what compensation he is to receive; and also how I am to conduct myself with respect to obtaining the necessary supplies of Oil and Wick. For the present I shall lay in a small quantity of each to answer immediate purposes. It is with regret I inform you, that the expence of this business will considerably exceed what I mentioned in my letter of the 11th. of February last.[4] It became necessary to procure many Articles which I was not apprized of when that letter was written. I have had a survey of the work which has been done, and it is pronounced to be substantial and every way equal to the terms of the Contract.

I have also received your letter of the 26th. ultimo,[5] and shall lose no time in complying with the orders therein given, with respect to the transmission of all my Accounts to the 31st. of March last, and of Duplicates of my Weekly Returns, in the manner you have directed.

You will herewith receive a Weekly Return of monies received and paid by me, from the 8th. to the 14th. Instant, amount on hand being Twenty seven thousand two hundred & ninety nine Dollars and seventy nine and a half Cents, in Specie.

I am, Sir, very respectfully, Your Obedient Servant.

John Habersham
Collector of the Customs for Savh.

Alexr Hamilton, Esqr., Secry. of the Treasury.

ALS, RG 26, Lighthouse Letters Received, Vol. "A," Pennsylvania and Southern States, National Archives.
1. Letter not found.
2. See H to Nathaniel Pendleton, April 11, 1791.
3. Tybee Island lighthouse.
4. Letter not found.
5. Letter not found.

From John H. Livingston [1]

New York, May 20, 1791. "I am very sorry to be under the necessity of troubling you with inclosed paper to which your signature is necessary. Our Legislature broke up so soon after we recd. the necessary document for freeing you from this, that it was not in our power to get an Act for that purpose, but it shall be done at the next Sessions. In the mean while we will tresspass upon your time and friendship in this way as little as possible. . . ."

ALS, Hamilton Papers, Library of Congress.
1. For background to this letter, see John H. Livingston *et al.* to H, March 15, 1791.

From George Washington

Augusta [Georgia] May 20 1791.

Sir

While at Charleston I appointed Robert Cochran of that place to command the revenue cutter for the station of South Carolina,[1] & empowered him, with the approbation of the Governor [2] & general Moultrie,[3] to appoint his mates.

I have appointed John Howell Commander [4]—Hendricks Fisher, first mate, and John Wood second mate of the revenue cutter to be stationed on the coast of Georgia. You will transmit the commissions and your instructions to these Gentlemen.

I am, Sir,   Your most Obedt. Servt.   G: Washington

LC, George Washington Papers, Library of Congress.
   1. See Washington to H, May 8, 1791.
   2. Charles Pinckney.
   3. William Moultrie was a wealthy planter and a former governor of South Carolina. He served in the South Carolina Senate from 1787 to 1791.
   4. See James Gunn to H, November 11, 1790.

From William Ellery

[*Newport, Rhode Island*] *May 23, 1791.* "On the 16th. of this month I received your Circular letter of the 14th. of Aprl. last. . . . The Tare allowed in this District is calculated upon every One hundred and twelve pounds,[1] and this was the practice in this State before it adopted the new Constitution.[2] The merchants here have lately objected to this mode of taring, and say that the allowance ought to be made on every One hundred pounds, and that it is so allowed in New york. . . . Uniformity in this as well as every other respect should exist in the proceedings of the Custom Houses in the several States, and the merchants in each should be placed on the same foot. . . ."

LC, Newport Historical Society, Newport, Rhode Island.
   1. H requested information on tares in his "Treasury Department Circular to the Collectors of the Customs," May 13, 1791.
   2. Rhode Island ratified the Constitution on May 29, 1790.

From John McComb, Junior

[*May 23, 1791.* On June 8, 1791, Hamilton wrote to McComb and referred to "your letter of the 23rd of May." *Letter not found.*]

From Otho H. Williams

Baltimore 23d. May 1791

Sir

I have the honor, now, to enclose you an acct. of the emoluments and disbursements of my office for the year 1790. The compensation of the Collector, you will observe, is small; and, when compared to the multifarious duties required of him, disproportioned to his services. A general view of the laws respecting duties will show that the Collector is, in his district, principally responsible for the due execution of those laws, and whoever will take the trouble to examine the detail of the business must discover that an unreasonable portion of the labor is allotted him. The alternative, which the law allows the Collector, to receive the Naval officers fees, or to permit the Naval officer to receve the Collectors fees seems not founded in necessity, or convenience.[1] It has been and may again be a source of mutual dissatisfaction. Each should be at the trouble of receiving their own fees, which ought to be proportioned to the service required of them, and each should be responsible for his own conduct therein. The relative connections, duties, prerogatives and powers of the several officers of the customs seem not perfectly understood. They are certainly not understood by all alike. It would be painful to be making representations of misconduct resulting perhaps merely from error in judgment, if to be any how tolerated, or excused—But as I do not understand that it is in contemplation to revise the Collection law which is certainly susceptible of some improvement I need not to be more explicit at present.

I am, Sir, Your most obedient Humble Servant

O H Williams Collr.

[ENCLOSURE][2]

Account of Fees and Commission being "all the monies received in the four quarters of the Year 1790," by the Collector of Balte. District

Fees from the 1 January to the 31 March inclusive . . .	274.18	
Commission as allowed in a/c at the Treasury	90.30	
		364.48
Fees from 1st April to the 30 June inclusive	427.62	
Commission allowed in a/c at the Treasury	294.36	
		721.98
Fees from 1st July to the 30 Septr. inclusive	298.30	
Commission—in a/c at Treasury	62.15	
		360.45
Fees from 1st October to 31 Decemr. inclusive . . .	337.14	
Commission—in a/c at Treasury	544.93	
		882.07
		2.328.98

Disbursements.

Paid for records other Stationary & blanks   1st quarter   23.07
Ditto . . . . . ditto . . . . . 2d. quarter   28.53.
Ditto . . . . . ditto 3   quarter   30.52.
Ditto . . . . . ditto 4   quarter   9.83.

	91.95
Fuel and Chandlery for 1 year	40.00
Office rent, Collectors proportion	66.66⅔
One Servant hire and Subsistence	120.00
Deputy Collector, and Clerk's Wages	1,166.66⅔
	1,485.28⅓
Compensation to the Collector	843.69⅔
	2,328.98

O. H. Williams Collr

ADfS, RG 53, "Old Correspondence," Baltimore Collector, National Archives.
    1. H had requested information on the collectors' fees and emoluments in his "Treasury Department Circular to the Collectors of the Customs," April 14, 1791.
    2. ADfS, RG 53, "Old Correspondence," Baltimore Collector, National Archives.

From Richard Harison

New York 24th. May 1791

Sir,

Having attentively considered the Questions contained in your letter of the 26th. Ultimo, I am fully of opinion that the power to pardon which the Constitution has vested in the President of the United States cannot extend to affect the rights of Individuals. The principles of the Common Law of England upon this Subject appear to be founded in good sense and I think must govern where-ever they will apply. Nor do I think that a difference in the mere mode of proceeding can affect principles that are connected with substantial Justice. Altho' therefore the prosecution may be by indictment, or by suit in the name of the United States only, yet if a part of the fine or penalty is expressly given to any Individual, his right is to be respected, and I think cannot be disposed of without his own consent or a legislative provision.

I take it that by the 68th. Section of the last Collection Act,[1] the Officers of the Customs, & informer, where there is any, are entitled to a moiety of all fines inflicted by virtue of that act and not otherwise appropriated. I do not at present see any Ground of distinction upon this Subject, whether the prosecution is by indictment or otherwise. The words are general including *all fines* not otherwise appropriated; and tho' the word *recover* may be improper, when applied to this subject, yet it must receive a reasonable construction in furtherance of the intention of the act, which was to encourage vigilance in the officers by admitting them to participate in the emoluments derived from it.

I am sensible that exceptions might arise to the generality of the expressions used in the Act from the nature of the offence for which the fine is inflicted or forfeiture incurred; and perhaps some of the offences specified in the 65th: section [2] may be of this nature, where committed by a superior officer of the Customs, as it would be absurd that the party offending should be entitled to a share of the penalty which is the punishment of his offence.

I am very doubtful whether in the Case of Mr. Dodge,[3] any relief can be given under the act for remission of penalties [4] as besides the forfeiture a disability is incurred which the Secretary of the Treasury has no power to remit. At any rate the remission would not operate against this disability which would make it necessary to have recourse to the President.

The Question then naturally recurs, how is the constitutional power of pardoning to be exercis'd, so as not to interfere with the principles of Justice? Here the Laws of England can afford us no great light because I do not remember an instance where the prosecution is in the name of the Sovereign only, and yet a part of the penalty or fine given to individuals. I should suppose however that the pardon would be considered as a mere nullity, with respect to a moiety of the fine, and I do not see why execution might not go for the residue stating that part was satisfied or remitted. Neither do I see any objection to making the pardon conditional, "provided the offender satisfy the officers &c. for the one half of the fine or penalty & pay the expences of prosecution." A Practice somewhat analogous to this, has prevailed in England, where the Court frequently enquire whether the prosecutor is satisfied before they proceed to determine what fine shall be imposed upon the delinquent.

I am sensible that upon these subjects there must be great room for variety of opinion. The Questions depend upon the peculiar frame of Laws which in many instances have been drawn without attention to technical precision. Indeed, I am by no means assured that my own ideas are correct, with relation to these new & untried points. They, however, are the result of the best investigation which it has been in my power to make.

With the highest respect I remain, Sir. Your most obedt. & most humble. servt. Rich: Harison

Hon. A. Hamilton Esqr.
Secry of the Treasy.

LS, RG 59, Miscellaneous Letters, 1790–1799, National Archives; ADf, New-York Historical Society, New York City.
1. Actually Harison is referring to Section 69 (1 *Stat.* 177) rather than Section 68 of "An Act to provide more effectually for the collection of the duties imposed by law on goods, wares and merchandise imported into the United States, and on the tonnage of ships or vessels" (1 *Stat.* 145–78 [August 4, 1790]). For an explanation of the difference in the numbers of this act's sections, see H to Harison, April 26, 1791, note 2.
2. Harison is referring to Section 66 (1 *Stat.* 175–76).
3. Samuel Dodge. See H to Harison, March 18, April 26, 1791.
4. "An Act to provide for mitigating or remitting the forfeitures and penalties accruing under the revenue laws, in certain cases therein mentioned" (1 *Stat.* 122–23 [May 26, 1790]).

From Henry Knox

War Department, May 24, 1971. "I have the honor to inform you, that Messrs: Smith and Shepherd [1] have completed their contract of clothing for the levies, and that Mr: Hodgdon,[2] the quarter master, has receipted to them for the same. . . ."

Copy, RG 217, Miscellaneous Treasury Accounts, 1790–1894, Account No. 1339, National Archives.
1. The firm of Robert Smith and John Shepard had contracted on March 31, 1791, to supply the levies with clothing. The documents pertaining to this transaction may be found in RG 217, Miscellaneous Treasury Accounts, 1790–1894, Account No. 1339, National Archives.
2. Samuel Hodgdon had been appointed quartermaster general in March, 1791.

To Pierre Charles L'Enfant

[Philadelphia] May 24th. 1791

My Dear Sir

I received in due time your letter of the 8th. of April; an early acknowlegement of which has been prevented by the hurry of business.

I thank you much for the full communication you have made me concerning the intended seat of Government, and will be obliged by a continuance of your observations and such further information as the progress of your operations may render interesting.

You will not forget I hope the devices for the Coins. As soon as your imagination shall have fixed upon any thing I shall be glad to know it.

With very great regard   I remain always Yr. friend   & obed ser

A Hamilton

Major L'Enfant

ALS, Digges-L'Enfant-Morgan Collection, Library of Congress.

From Jeremiah Olney

Providence, May 24, 1791. "I have been favored with a Letter from Mr. Coxe of the 13th instant, covering a copy of a circular Letter, relative to Tare &c., intended to be transmitted to the several Collectors.[1] The Contents of which, tending to establish an uniform Practice in the collection of the Revenue, afford me much pleasure; and I shall speedily forward the Information required, respecting the Custom of the Merchants in this District, and my own practice, relative to the allowance for Tare on the several Articles therein mentioned. From repeated Experiments made by the Surveyor of this Port,[2] it appears that Dycas's Hydrometer makes the proof of Spirits about One quarter of a ℔. Cent lower than the Substitute: As the difference is so small, he purposes, in ascertaining the proof of Spirits, generally to use the latter, which is much more simple and convenient. . . ."

ADfS, Rhode Island Historical Society, Providence; copy, RG 56, Letters from the Collector at Providence, National Archives.
   1. "Treasury Department Circular to the Collectors of the Customs," May 13, 1791.
   2. William Barton.

To William Short

Treasury Department
May 24, 1791.

Sir,

The President of the United States has signified to me [1] his pleasure, that I should revoke that part of your instructions [2] which confines you to opening loans for no greater sum, at a time, than one million of dollars and which restrains you from opening a subsequent loan till the one preceding has received his approbation; and has also instructed me to *authorise* you to open each future loan for three millions of florins, and as soon as one loan shall be *filled* or *subscribed* to open another, till the sum necessary for fulfilling the act entitled, An Act making provision for the Reduction of the Public Debt [3] and for paying the arrears of interest and instalments of principal which shall have become due to France, to the end of the present year, shall have been completed. Provided however that the terms be not less advantageous than those upon which the last loan [4] has been effected.

With regard to the application of the monies that shall arise from the loans you may make subsequent to that, which has been already announced, it is to be as follows—Reserving in the hands of our Bankers [5] one million and a half of the next succeeding loan and a million of the one immediately succeeding that for completing the purpose of the Act abovementioned, the residue of each and the whole of the future loans are to be applied in payments to France; unless directions shall at any time be given to the contrary. The *first* monies which shall be *paid in* upon the two loans, out of which reservations are to be made to the extent contemplated, are, nevertheless, to be applied towards the payments to France; which you will accordingly cause to be done.

You will, doubtless continue to keep me punctually advised of your operations.

With very great consideration and the most cordial esteem,

I have the honor to be   Sir.   Your obedt. Servant

A Hamilton
Secy of the Treasury

Wm. Short Esqr.
Chargé des Affaires &ca
Amsterdam

LS, William Short Papers, Library of Congress. A copy of this letter was enclosed in H's "Report on Foreign Loans," February 13, 1793.

1. George Washington to H, May 7, 1791.
2. See H to Short, September 1, 1790.
3. 1 *Stat.* 186–87 (August 12, 1790).
4. For a description of this loan, see Short to H, February 17, 1791.
5. Willink, Van Staphorst, and Hubbard.

To Jabez Bowen

Treasury Department,
May 25, 1791

Sir,

I have directed the Treasurer to forward to you drafts payable to you or your order for six thousand Dollars towards paying the ensuing Quarters Interest.

These drafts, which will be transmitted with proper blanks, may be directed either to Tench Francis Esquire, Cashier of the Bank of North America, or to William Seton Esquire, Cashier of the Bank of New York or to the respective Collectors of New Port [1] & Providence.[2]

There are at this time in the hands of the Collector of New Port seventeen hundred Dollars, and in the hands of the Collector of Providence two thousand two hundred Dollars, ready to answer the Drafts which are to be sent to you. You will do well to open a communication with those Collectors to obtain information of the sums they shall have received subsequent to the date of this letter to the end of the quarter; which, in addition to the above-mentioned sums will be left in their hands to answer your drafts.

But it will be equally agreeable to me that you negotiate the drafts sent you, upon the two banks or either of them, if you find a demand for them.

The Directions given to you [3] in other respects in relation to the drafts transmitted for the last quarter's interest are of course to be observed in the disposition of those of which you are now advised.

You will give me as soon as possible your opinion whether any greater sum is likely to be called for, in order that provision may be made accordingly. And you will send me a summary of the Stock standing on your Books when they are closed for the ensuing quarter at the same time, & in the same manner as was done in relation to the last.

Exact punctuality being essential to the support of public credit, I shall rely that you will always take your arrangements so as to be ready at the day, and that in the detail of your payments you will give all possible facility & dispatch as far as shall consist with your instructions.

I shall be glad to be advised weekly of the disposition of the drafts.

I am, sir,   Your Obed Servant   A Hamilton

Jabez Bowen Esqr.
Commr of Loans for Rhode Island & Providence &c
Providence.

LS, Harvard College Library.
  1. William Ellery.
  2. Jeremiah Olney.
  3. See "Treasury Department Circular to the Commissioners of Loans," February 14, 1791.

To Tobias Lear

                                               Treasury Department
                                               May 25. 1791.

Sir
    Pursuant to instructions from the President of the United States, I am to request that you will cause some of the blank commissions left with you to be filled as follows: one with the name of John Whitaker as Inspector of the revenue for Survey No. 4. in the District of North Carolina, one with the name of Joseph McDowell the elder, as inspector of the revenue for survey No. 5. in the same District, one with the name of William Cooke, as Master of a revenue Cutter in the service of the United States.[1]

I have the honor to be, with great consideration & regard Sir   Your
Obt. Servant   Alex. Hamilton

LC, George Washington Papers, Library of Congress.
1. See William Jackson to H, April 25, 1791.

From Benjamin Lincoln

Boston, May 25, 1791. "By an act made to explain and amend 'an act making farther provision for the payment of the Debts of the United States' It is enacted that the duty of 7½ ℔ Ct ad valorem laid by the act aforesaid on chintses and coloured calicoes shall be deemed and taken to extend to all printed stained & coloured goods, or manufactures of cotton, or of linen, or of both, which hereafter shall be brought into the United States from any foreign port or place.[1] When I read the law I supposed that all goods of Cotton &c painted stained and *coloured*, (coloured by painting or staining) should be subject to a duty of 7½ ℔ Cent but the law is read differently by others; Mr. Ames [2] and the District Atty [3] are of opinion that all cotton good all linen goods & goods of Cotton & Linen united which have but a stripe in them are embraced by this act, such as bed ticks, checked linings for shirtings &c. These they consider as coloured goods. I pay, as I ought, great respect to the opinion of these Gentm. yet as I am the only responsible person I wish your sentiments on the Law. . . ."

LC, Massachusetts Historical Society, Boston; LC, RG 36, Collector of Customs at Boston, Letter Book, 1790–1797, National Archives; two copies, RG 56, Letters from the Collector at Boston, National Archives.
1. See Section 2 of this act (1 *Stat.* 198 [March 2, 1791]).
2. Fisher Ames, Federalist member of the House of Representatives from Massachusetts.
3. Christopher Gore, United States attorney for the District of Massachusetts.

To Jeremiah Olney

Treasury Department,
May 25 1791

Sir,
It will be agreeable to me that the Officers of the Customs in the District of Providence make return of the emoluments of their respec-

tive Offices for one year following the time of their entering upon their duty instead of the year mentioned in my circular letter of the 14 of April.[1] You will be pleased to give them an early intimation of this.

I shall not object to a small boat fit for harbour service for the Port of Providence,[2] but as your district will then be as well provided as some of much greater extent and trade I hope it will not be necessary to go to greater expence.

I am, sir,   Your Most Obed Servant   A Hamilton

Jerh Olney Esqr.
Collr Providence.

LS, Rhode Island Historical Society, Providence.
  1. See also Olney to H, May 17, 1791.
  2. See Olney to H, May 16, 1791.

From Arthur St. Clair

Fort Washington [1] [Northwest Territory] May 25th. 1791

Sir

A few days ago Mr. Ludlow presented to me the Instructions he had received from you [2] for compleating the Surveys of certain Tracts of Land in this Territory contracted for with the late Board of Treasury and requested an Escort of Troops to enable him to comply with those Instructions. The situation of Affairs, and the present weakness of this Garrison put it out of my power to furnish him with the necessary Escort; but, on perusing the Instructions, to my astonishment, I found that the purchase made by Judge Symmes [3] did not extend farther up the Ohio than twenty Miles from the mouth of the Great Miami River.[4] He had given out and published indeed to the World, that he had contracted for all the Lands, to a certain distance northerly, which were contained between the little and the great Miamies as eastern and western Boundaries. On my first arrival in this part of the Territory I found the Judge here, and a number of People settled already, to whom he had sold Lands far to the eastward of the twenty Miles.[5] It never could have entered into my Head that any person, much less one invested with a respectable public Character, had published a falsehood, was persisting in it, and availing himself of the pecuniary advantages flowing from it. The Settlement therefore met with all the Countenance which I could give it, which I conceived to be a duty I then owed to the adventurers and to the united States; but I see I was wrong, and find myself in a very disagreeable predicament, having cloathed many Persons with civil and military authority, whom it was more properly my duty to have removed, and so far sanctioned their intrusion on the Lands of the united States. As soon as possible after this discovery I wrote a Letter to Judge Symmes of which the enclosure No 1 [6] is a copy and No. 2 [7] his Answer, which I received this day. The Answer does not appear in any wise satisfactory, for it is clear that, tho' there had been a proposal for a Contract different from that entered into, it had never been more than a proposal, and he has been selling the Lands of the united States upon the little Miami, which he had not Contracted for, to pay for Lands his Agents had contracted for in his name upon the great Miami. As soon as it is practicable Mr. Ludlow shall be enabled to fulfill your Orders. In the mean time I am much at a loss what Course I ought to hold with those Settlers, neither do I know very well where to address myself for Directions. If it is a Business that falls within the Sphere of your Office I shall be happy to receive, and carry into execution any which you may think proper to give. If it does not fall within your Office, may I request the favour of your friendly Advice. It seems to me that all I can do at present, and it may be proper to do it, is to publish a Proclamation warning all Persons against further intrusion, and permitting the occupancy of the present Settlers until the Pleasure of Congress shall be known.[8] To remove those if it could be done, would be ruin to them, and they are innocent not wilful trespassers; and to revoke the Commissions that have been granted would leave them in a State of Anarchy. Excuse I entreat you the Liberty I have taken to trouble you with the Dilemma I am caught in and believe me with every Sentiment of Respect and Esteem   Sir   Your very humble Servant   Ar. St. Clair

The honorable Alexander Hamilton
Secretary of the Treasury.

ALS, RG 59, Territorial Papers: Northwest Territory, Vol. I, National Archives; ADf, Public Archives of Canada, Ottawa, Ontario. This letter was enclosed in St. Clair to H, July 21, 1791.
    1. Fort Washington was at Cincinnati.

2. H's letter of instruction to Israel Ludlow, a New Jersey surveyor and land speculator, dated November 20, 1790, had not been found when Volume VII of *The Papers of Alexander Hamilton* was published. It has subsequently been located and reads as follows:

"Sir

"I have concluded to commit to y⟨ou⟩ the making of the Surveys which still remain to be made towards a complete demarkation of the boundaries of the several Tracts of land which have been contracted for with the persons respectively denominated The Ohio Company, The Scioto Company, and the Miami Company.

"You have already had from the late Geographer a description of the external boundary of the two Tracts contracted for with the two first mentioned companies, and you have already completed the Survey of that external boundary. But *the lines of division* between them are still to be surveyed. This forms a part of the business you are to execute. The following is the description of the boundary of the Ohio tract.

" 'All the certain tract or parcel of Land beginning at the place where the Western boundary line of the seventh range of Townships laid out by the authority of Congress intersects the Ohio and extending hence along that River South Westerly to the place where the Western line of the seventeenth range of Townships to be laid out according to the Land Ordinance of the twentieth day of May in the year of our Lord One thousand seven hundred and eighty five would intersect the said river and extending thence northerly on the western boundary line of the said seventeenth range of Townships so far that a line drawn due east to the Western boundary line of the Said seventeenth range of Townships will with the other lines of this tract include One Million and a half of Acres of land ⟨b⟩esides the several Townships Lots and parcels of Land herein after mentioned to be reserved or appropriated to specific purposes, thence running east to the Western bounds of the seventh range of townships and thence southerly along those bounds to the place of beginning.'

"The lines of division alluded to, as those requiring to be surveyed are—First, that which *begins* at the point of intersection of the Western line of the seventeenth range of Townships with the Ohio *and* extends along that Western line Northerly so *far that* a *line* drawn due East to the Western boundary line of the seventh range of Townships will with the other lines of the above described tract include a Million and a half of Acres, and secondly the last mentioned *line* vizt. the one to be drawn from the Northerly termination of the first line to the Western boundary of the seventh range of Townships.

"The survey and demarkation of these two lines will complete the survey of the external boundaries of the two tracts of the Scioto and Ohio Companies." (Extract, RG 217, Miscellaneous Treasury Accounts, 1790–1894, Account No. 2472, National Archives.)

Ludlow's appointment was made in obedience to the following congressional resolution of August 12, 1790:

"*Resolved by the Senate and House of Representatives of the United States of America in Congress assembled,* That all surveys of lands in the Western Territory, made under the direction of the late geographer, Thomas Hutchins, agreeable to contracts for part of the said lands made with the late board of treasury, be returned to, and perfected by, the Secretary of the Treasury, so as to complete the said contracts: and that the said secretary be, and is hereby, authorized to direct the making and completing any other surveys that remain to be made, so as to comply on the part of the United States with the several contracts aforesaid, in conformity to the terms thereof." (1 *Stat.* 187.)

3. John Cleves Symmes was appointed judge in the Northwest Territory in 1788.

4. This was the Miami Company Purchase. See Jonathan Dayton to H, May 29, 1790. The eastern and northern limits of the grant became a matter of conflicting claims and extended dispute.

5. Although Symmes had proposed to buy the whole Ohio River frontage between the two Miami Rivers, the Treasury Board in 1788 placed the eastern boundary of his purchase about fourteen miles west of the Little Miami River. Being unaware of this limitation, Symmes regarded the area as his property and sold twenty thousand acres of it in 1788 to Benjamin Stites, who founded the first settlement in the Miami country.

6. St. Clair to Symmes, May 23, 1791 (Carter, *Territorial Papers*, II, 342–43). In this letter St. Clair wrote that he had learned from Ludlow's instructions that the Miami Purchase did not include the land east of a point twenty miles from the Great Miami River and that he intended to carry out his instructions to reserve part of the land in dispute for a military reservation.

7. Symmes to St. Clair, May 23, 1791 (Carter, *Territorial Papers*, II, 343–47). In this letter Symmes, while admitting that there was some confusion concerning the eastern boundary of his purchase, based his claim to the disputed area on his original proposal to buy one million acres. Symmes alleged that part of the confusion arose from the Treasury Board's ignorance of Ohio geography and that the board would never have limited him to a twenty-mile frontage on the Ohio if it had had any knowledge of the country. He asked that no steps be taken until he could return to North Bend and consult his papers. Finally, he offered to the Government the unsold land at Fort Washington.

8. St. Clair's proclamation is dated July 19, 1791. It is printed in Smith, *St. Clair Papers*, II, 211–12.

Treasury Department Circular
to the Collectors of the Customs

[*Philadelphia, May 25, 1791.* On June 7, 1791, Jeremiah Olney wrote to Hamilton: "I have received your two circular letters of the 25th. and 26th of May." *Circular of May 25 not found.*] [1]

1. On May 25, 1791, H wrote a letter to Olney marked "circular," but as the information in this letter was clearly not intended for the other collectors of the customs it has not been printed as a Treasury Department circular. Olney may be referring to this letter as the circular of May 25.

To Otho H. Williams

Treasury Department
May 25th. 1791.

Sir,

It is necessary for the Government of the Commissioner of loans [1] in the disposition of some Treasury drafts which have been sent him that he should be informed weekly of the monies which you shall have received subsequent to the date of your last return namely the 20th instant.

Fourteen hundred Dollars of the ballance then in your hands together with the amount of your subsequent receipts, to the extent in the whole of 8000 Dollars, will be left to answer the drafts sent him towards paying the ensuing Quarters interest; though he is at liberty to negociate them upon the two banks of North America & New York if a demand occurs.

I am   Sir   Your most Obedt Servant   Alexander Hamilton

Otho H. Williams
Collector
Baltimore

LS, Columbia University Libraries.
    1. The commissioner of loans for Maryland was Thomas Harwood.

From Jeremiah Olney

Providence, May 26, 1791. "I have received Mr. Coxe's circular Letter of the 12th instt.,[1] accompanying the Form of a Return of outward Tonnage: The directions respecting which shall be attended to, and the Return completed and transmitted as soon as possible. . . ."

ADfS, Rhode Island Historical Society, Providence; copy, RG 56, Letters from the Collector at Providence, National Archives.
    1. Tench Coxe's circular transmitted a "form of a return of outward tonnage" to be made up by the collectors of the customs for the period April 1, 1790, to March 31, 1791 (LS, to Jeremiah Olney, Rhode Island Historical Society; copy, to Charles Lee, RG 56, Circulars of the Office of the Secretary, "Set T," National Archives).

From James Rivington [1]

[New York, May 26, 1791]

Sir

I have now the Satisfaction to announce the Arrival of the first Volume of Hawkesworths Narrative,[2] and the three last Volumes of Cooks Voyages,[3] together with a large folio Volume of Charts & Copper Plates applying to them; these, I trust, will serve to perfect the incomplete Set You had from me, previous to your Removal to Philadelphia. They are all safely packed in a Box directed to You, I hope they will reach your hands in good order by the Borderden town [4] Stage which departed this day; I am, Sir, with sincere orisons for your health, felicity and ascention to still higher eminence, Your faithfull and much obliged humble servant   Jas Rivington.

New York May 26th. 1791.

ALS, Hamilton Papers, Library of Congress.
    1. Rivington, who had published a newspaper in New York City before and during the American Revolution, was at this time a New York City bookseller.
    2. John Hawkesworth, *An Account of the Voyages undertaken by the order of his present Majesty for making discoveries in the Southern Hemisphere, and successively performed by Commodore Byron, Captain Wallis, Captain Carteret, and Captain Cooke, in the Dolphin, the Swallow, and the Endeavour: drawn up from the journals which were kept by the several commanders, and from the papers of Joseph Banks*, 3 Vols. (London, 1773).
    3. James Cooke, *A Voyage to the Pacific Ocean undertaken . . . for making discoveries in the Northern Hemispheres*, 3 Vols. (London, 1784).
    4. Bordentown, New Jersey.

Treasury Department Circular to the Collectors of the Customs

Treasury Department,
May 26 1791

Sir,

Inclosed you will find for your information, generally, and Government, in certain particulars, certain explanations & instructions concerning the two Acts, severally entitled "An Act repealing after the last day of June next, the duties heretofore laid upon distilled spirits imported from abroad, and laying others in their stead; and also upon spirits distilled within the United States and for appropriating the same," [1] and "An Act making further provision for the col-

LS, to Jeremiah Olney, Rhode Island Historical Society, Providence; L[S], to Otho H. Williams, Office of the Secretary, United States Treasury Department; LS, Mr. Roger Barrett, Kenilworth, Illinois; L[S], RG 36, Collector of Customs at Boston, Letters from the Treasury, 1789–1807, Vol. 4, National Archives; copy, RG 56, Circulars of the Office of the Secretary, "Set T," National Archives; copy, United States Finance Miscellany, Treasury Circulars, Library of Congress.
    1. 1 *Stat.* 199–214 (March 3, 1791).

lection of the duties by law imposed on Teas, and to prolong the term for the payment of the duties on Wines." [2]

I am, sir, your Obedt Servant.   Alexander Hamilton

[E N C L O S U R E] [3]

Explanations and Instructions Concerning The Act, Entitled, "An ACT repealing after the last day of June next, the duties heretofore laid upon distilled SPIRITS imported from abroad, and laying others in their stead; and also upon spirits distilled within the United States; and for appropriating the same:" Passed In the third Session of CONGRESS, On the 2d of March 1791.

Explanations, &c.

SECT. 2. It appears by this section,[4] that in regard to spirits imported from foreign countries, the same proceedings are to be had at the respective custom-houses, as if the present act had not passed; the provisions of which are to be considered as supplementary to those heretofore established (except as to particular alterations specified in it) as well as auxiliary to the other parts of the system introduced by this act. It is not doubted that the officers of the customs, and those appointed under this act,[5] will zealously co-operate to facilitate its execution, and obviate any little embarrassments which may ensue. This co-operation has been rendered more easy and simple by ap-

2. 1 *Stat.* 219–21 (March 3, 1791).

3. Copy, New-York Historical Society, New York City.

4. Section 2 of this act reads as follows: "*And be it further enacted,* That the said duties shall be collected in the same manner, by the same persons, under the same regulations, and subject to the same forfeitures and other penalties, as those heretofore laid; the act concerning which shall be deemed to be in full force for the collection of the duties herein before imposed, except as to the alterations contained in this act" (1 *Stat.* 199).

5. Section 4 of this act provided "That the President be authorized to appoint, with the advice and consent of the Senate, a supervisor to each district, and as many inspectors to each survey therein as he shall judge necessary, placing the latter under the direction of the former. *Provided always,* That it shall and may be lawful for the President, with the advice and consent of the Senate, in his discretion to appoint, such and so many officers of the customs to be inspectors in any survey of inspection as he shall deem advisable to employ in the execution of this act" (1 *Stat.* 200).

pointing in some instances the Collectors, in others the Surveyors of the customs Inspectors of the Revenue.

SECT. 5. The forms of accounts contemplated by this section,[6] are now in preparation, and will be transmitted with proper directions *before* the first day of July next.

SECT. 6. The following shall be the form of the oath or affirmation to be taken pursuant to this section: [7] "I [insert here name and office of the person] do swear [or if of a *religious denomination*, conscientiously scrupulous of swearing—*do solemnly, sincerely and truly affirm and declare*] that I will diligently and faithfully execute the duties of my said office, and will use my best endeavours to prevent and detect frauds, in relation to the duties laid by the act, entitled, "An Act repealing, after the last day of June next, the duties heretofore laid upon distilled spirits imported from abroad, and laying others in their stead; and also upon spirits distilled within the United States, and for appropriating the same."

SECT. 7. Every Inspector of the Revenue for a port or ports, and every deputy of such Inspector, at a port different from that

6. Section 5 reads as follows: "*And be it further enacted*, That the supervisors, inspectors and officers to be appointed by virtue of this act, and who shall be charged to take bonds for securing the payment of the duties upon spirits distilled within the United States, and with the receipt of monies in discharge of such duties, shall keep fair and true accounts and records of their transactions in their respective offices, in such manner and form as may be directed by the proper department or officer having the superintendence of the collection of the revenue, and shall at all times submit their books, papers and accounts to the inspection of such persons as are or may be appointed for that purpose, and shall at all times pay to the order of the officer, who is or shall be authorized to direct the payment thereof, the whole of the monies which they may respectively receive by virtue of this act, and shall also once in every three months, or oftener if they shall be required, transmit their accounts for settlement to the officer or officers whose duty it is, or shall be to make such settlement" (1 *Stat.* 200).

7. Section 6 reads as follows: "*And be it further enacted*, That all officers and persons to be appointed pursuant to this act, before they enter on the duties of their respective offices, shall take an oath or affirmation diligently and faithfully to execute the duties of their said offices respectively, and to use their best endeavours to prevent and detect frauds, in relation to the duties on spirits imposed by this act, which oath or affirmation may be taken before any magistrate authorized to administer oaths within the district or survey to which he belongs, and being certified under the hand and seal of the magistrate by whom the same shall have been administered, shall within three months thereafter be transmitted to the comptroller of the treasury, in default of taking which oath or affirmation, the party failing shall forfeit and pay two hundred dollars for the use of the United States, to be recovered with costs of suit" (1 *Stat.* 200).

where the Inspector resides, must have an office in conformity to this section.[8] Every Collector of the Revenue charged with the collection of the duties on stills, must also have such an office. And in every city, town or village, there must be such an office, kept either by the Supervisor himself, or by some one of the Inspectors of *surveys*, or Collectors of the Revenue whom the Supervisor may think fit to nominate. It is desireable to have an office accessible (within the distance of ten miles) to every owner of a still, in order that the entry contemplated by the law may be made by each. With this view in the appointment of Collectors, an eye ought to be had to place of residence. But as the *qualities* of the person, rather than his place of residence, ought to decide each choice; and as it may not always be practicable to reconcile a due regard to *them* with the *circumstance* of residence, it may be found expedient, in some counties, to establish auxiliary offices under the care, and at the houses of discreet persons, who are willing for some small consideration by way of rent, to undertake the thing. The total expence of these auxiliary offices, must not exceed, in either of the districts of Virginia, Pennsylvania and North-Carolina, two hundred dollars in a year; in either of the districts of South-Carolina and Maryland, one hundred dollars in a year, nor in any other district fifty dollars in a year. Indeed this idea is not considered as applicable to those districts where there are only distilleries from foreign materials. Each of these auxiliary offices must be placed under the superintendence of a Collector of the Revenue within the county in which it may be established. This regulation, nevertheless, concerning auxiliary offices, is not intended to be enjoined, but is left to the discretion of each Supervisor, to be adopted or not as he shall judge adviseable; assigning his reasons for not having recourse to it, to the Secretary of the Treasury.

SECT. 8.   This and the eleventh section [9] contemplate an Inspec-

8. Section 7 reads as follows: "*And be it further enacted*, That the supervisor of the revenue for each district, shall establish one or more offices within the same, as may be necessary; and in order that the said offices may be publicly known, there shall be painted or written in large legible characters upon some conspicuous part outside and in front of each house, building or place in which any such office shall be kept, these words, "OFFICE OF INSPECTION;" and if any person shall paint or write, or cause to be painted or written, the said words, upon any other than such house or building, he or she shall forfeit and pay for so doing, one hundred dollars" (1 *Stat.* 200–01).

9. These two sections read as follows:

"Sec. 8. *And be it further enacted*, That within forty-eight hours after any

tor of the Revenue at each port. To obtain this object of the law, the
following arrangement appears the most convenient. The present collection law,[10] section sixth, empowers the Collector of each district
occasionally, and from time to time, to employ a person to perform
the duties of Surveyor at every port of delivery to which no Surveyor is assigned by the law, and to allow him a compensation similar
to that of Inspectors of the Customs; which compensation by the 52d
section of the same law, may be any sum not exceeding a dollar and
a quarter for each day of his employment. This provision, it is presumed, was introduced for two reasons—one a general supposition
that there ought to be some officer to take care of the revenue at every
port at which deliveries from abroad were allowed and *practiced*—
another that it might conduce to facilitate to coasters a compliance
with the coasting act,[11] by not rendering it necessary for them to go
too great a distance for their outward entries: While at the same time
it was not thought eligible to provide affirmatively that there should
be such an officer at each, as it was supposed that the expence might
be saved at such where no deliveries from foreign countries were ever
made. Hence (it may be inferred) the matter has been left to discretion, and is not enjoined in every case.

---

ship or vessel, having on board any distilled spirits brought in such ship or vessel
from any foreign port or place, shall arrive within any port of the United States,
whether the same be the first port of arrival of such ship or vessel, or not, the
master or person having the command or charge thereof, shall report to one of
the inspectors of the port at which she shall so arrive, the place from which she
last sailed, with her name and burthen, and the quantity and kinds of the said
spirits on board of her, and the casks, vessels or cases containing them, with
their marks and numbers; on pain of forfeiting the sum of five hundred dollars"
(1 *Stat.* 201).

"Sec. 11. *And be it further enacted,* That all spirits which shall be imported
as aforesaid, shall be landed under the inspection of the officer or officers of inspection for the place where the same shall be landed, and not otherwise, on
pain of forfeiture thereof; for which purpose the said officer or officers shall,
at all reasonable times, attend: *Provided,* that this shall not be construed to exclude the inspection of the officers of the customs as now established and
practised" (1 *Stat.* 202).

10. "An Act to provide more effectually for the collection of the duties imposed by law on goods, wares and merchandise imported into the United States,
and on the tonnage of ships or vessels" (1 *Stat.* 145–78 [August 4, 1790]).

11. "An Act for Registering and Clearing Vessels, Regulating the Coasting
Trade, and for other purposes" (1 *Stat.* 55–65 [September 1, 1789]). The Coasting Act was amended by "An Act to explain and amend an Act, intituled 'An
Act for registering and clearing Vessels, regulating the Coasting Trade, and for
other purposes' " (1 *Stat.* 94–95 [September 29, 1789]).

It is conceived, that this provision of the collection law may be made auxiliary to the execution of the act, which is the object of these instructions, till experience shall point out a course which it may be eligible to define and fix by legislative authority.

Let the Collector of each district, then, appoint one of these persons for every port, where deliveries from foreign countries are *practiced*, and at which there is no other officer of the CUSTOMS, or of the REVENUE, and let the Inspector of the Revenue within whose jurisdiction such port is included, depute the same person to act on his behalf. With a view to this arrangement, the Collector of each district in which there is no Surveyor at the port of entry, and the Surveyor at each port of entry, has been constituted Inspector not only of such port, but of all other ports, within the district of the Customs to which he may belong, to *which* there is no Surveyor assigned.

The appointment of each of these persons, to fulfil the law, ought to be periodical, that is "from time to time," and may be renewed at the expiration of each period. It would not however be proper, that the allowance to them per day should extend to a dollar and a quarter. A far less allowance, it is not doubted, under this modification of the thing, and for the kind of service, will command characters deserving of the trust, and œconomy in every item of expence is indispensable: A return to the Treasury from each Collector will be expected of the number of these persons by him appointed, the places for which they are respectively appointed, and the compensation allowed by him to each.

SECT. 8.   The report directed to be made by this section, must be in writing signed by the Master; and must be compared with that which he makes to the Collector of the Customs.

SECT. 9.   The entry to be certified pursuant to this section [12] is

12. Section 9 reads as follows: "*And be it further enacted,* That the collector or other officer, or person acting as collector, with whom entry shall have been made of any of the said spirits, pursuant to the act intituled 'An act to provide more effectually for the collection of the duties imposed by law on goods, wares and merchandises imported into the United States, and on the tonnage of ships or vessels,' shall forthwith after such entry certify and transmit the same, as particularly as it shall have been made with him, to the proper officer of inspection, of the port where it shall be intended to commence the delivery of the spirits so entered, or any part thereof: for which purpose, every proprietor, importer or consignee, making such entry, shall deliver two manifests of the contents (upon one of which the said certificate shall be given) and shall at the time thereof declare the port at which the said delivery shall be so intended to

that, not of the Master, but of the owner or consignee, according to the twenty-first section of the present collection law.[13]

SECT. 10. For the CERTIFICATES to be issued pursuant to this section,[14] forms will be transmitted to each Supervisor, who will provide printed certificates with proper blanks, and issue them from time to time to the Inspectors of Ports; and an account is to be kept with each Inspector, of the expenditure of these certificates.

SECT. 12. The Inspectors of the Customs may be *deputed* by the

---

be commenced, to the collector or officer with whom the same shall be made. And every permit granted by such collector, for the landing of any of the said spirits, shall previous to such landing, be produced to the said officer of inspection, who shall make a minute in some proper book, of the contents thereof, and shall endorse thereupon the word "INSPECTED," the time when, and his own name: after which he shall return it to the person by whom it shall have been produced; and then, and not otherwise it shall be lawful to land the spirits therein specified; and if the said spirits shall be landed without such endorsement upon the permit for that purpose granted, the master or person having charge of the ship or vessel from which the same shall have been so landed, shall for every such offence forfeit the sum of five hundred dollars" (1 *Stat.* 201).

13. Section 21 of the Collection Law provided that "the owner or owners, consignee or consignees of any goods, wares or merchandise on board of any such ship or vessel, or in case of his, her or their absence or sickness, his, her or their known factor or agent, in his, her or their names, within fifteen days after report of the master or person having the charge or command of such ship or vessel to the collector of the district for which such goods, wares or merchandise shall be destined, shall make entry thereof with the said collector" (1 *Stat.* 160-61).

14. Section 10 reads as follows: "*And be it further enacted,* That whenever it shall be intended that any ship or vessel shall proceed with the whole or any part of the spirits which shall have been brought in such ship or vessel from any foreign port or place, from one port in the United States to another port in the said United States, whether in the same or in different districts, the master or person having the command or charge of such ship or vessel, shall previous to her departure, apply to the officer of inspection, to whom report was made, for the port from which she is about to depart, for a certificate of the quantity and particulars of such of the said spirits as shall have been certified or reported to him to have been entered as imported in such ship or vessel, and of so much thereof as shall appear to him to have been landed out of her at such port; which certificate the said officer shall forthwith grant. And the master or person having the command or charge of such ship or vessel, shall within twenty-four hours after her arrival at the port to which she shall be bound, deliver the said certificate to the proper officer of inspection of such last mentioned port. And if such ship or vessel shall proceed from one port to another within the United States, with the whole or any part of the spirits brought in her as aforesaid, without having first obtained such certificate; or if within twenty-four hours after her arrival at such other port, the said certificate shall not be delivered to the proper officer of inspection there, the master or person having the command or charge of the said ship or vessel, shall in either case forfeit the sum of five hundred dollars; and the spirits on board of her at her said arrival, shall be forfeited, and may be seized by any officer of inspection" (1 *Stat.* 201-02).

Inspector of the Revenue for the port, to perform the duties enjoined by this section.[15] The marks may be abbreviated according to the following example.

No. 1. Sh: —— Betsey,
Philadelphia,
First proof, 100 G: ——

Here Sh: —— would signify ship. If the vessel should be a brigantine, B: would be a sufficient designator; if a sloop, Sl: —— if a schooner, Sc: —— &c. G: —— is designed for gallons. The Supervisor is to provide and furnish the instruments for marking, to the several officers. Where the *vessels* are of a kind, that they cannot themselves be marked, the marks may be set on small pieces of strong paper, vellum or parchment, and sealed to the vessels.

Forms for the books here required to be kept, will be transmitted from the Treasury.

SECT. 13.   Forms for the Certificates directed by this section,[16]

15. Section 12 reads as follows: "*And be it further enacted,* That the officers of inspection under whose survey any of the said spirits shall be landed, shall upon landing thereof, and as soon as the casks, vessels and cases containing the same shall be gauged or measured, brand or otherwise mark in durable characters the several casks, vessels or cases containing the same, with progressive numbers; and also with the name of the ship or vessel wherein the same was or were imported, and of the port of entry, and with the proof and quantity thereof; together with such other marks, if any shall be deemed needful, as the respective supervisors of the revenue may direct. And the said officer shall keep a book, wherein he shall enter the name of each vessel in which any of the said spirits shall be so imported, and of the port of entry and of delivery, and of the master of such vessel, and of each importer, and the several casks, vessels and cases containing the same, and the marks of each: and if such officer is not the chief inspector within the survey, he shall as soon as may be thereafter, make an exact transcript of each entry, and deliver the same to such chief officer, who shall keep a like book for recording the said transcript" (1 *Stat.* 202).

16. Section 13 reads as follows: "*And be it further enacted,* That the chief officer of inspection within whose survey any of the said spirits shall be landed, shall give to the proprietor, importer or consignee thereof, or his or her agent, a certificate to remain with him or her, of the whole quantity of the said spirits which shall have been so landed; which certificate, besides the said quantity, shall specify the name of such proprietor, importer or consignee, and of the vessel from on board which the said spirits shall have been landed, and of the marks of each cask, vessel or case containing the same. And the said officer shall deliver to the said proprietor, importer or consignee, or to his or her agent, a like certificate for each cask, vessel or case; which shall accompany the same wheresoever it shall be sent, as evidence of its being lawfully imported. And the officer granting the said certificates, shall make regular and exact entries in the book to be by him kept as aforesaid, of all spirits for which the same shall be granted, as particularly as therein described. And the said proprietor, importer or consignee, or his or her agent, upon the sale and delivery of any of

will be transmitted from the Treasury. Printed certificates, with proper blanks, are to be provided by the Supervisor of each district, and furnished from time to time by him to the several Inspectors of the Revenue for ports; keeping an account with each, of the expenditure of the said certificates. As a security against Counterfeits, an instrument for stamping these certificates with some proper impression, will be sent from the Treasury to each Supervisor, who will consequently cause the certificates to be stamped before they are issued. These certificates must be *signed by the Inspector* of the Revenue, for *the port* where they are granted. At such ports, where there are deputy Inspectors according to the instruction upon the 8th section, blank certificates *so signed*, must be furnished by the Inspector, to each deputy, with whom a regular account of the expenditure of the certificates must be kept. Before any deputy Inspector issues a certificate, he must countersign it.

SECT. 15. This section [17] distinguishes distilleries of domestic materials in cities, towns and villages, from those in other places; it is therefore necessary to form an idea of what is to be understood by a city, town or village. In some States it is presumed the local institutions will conform to and designate the sense of this part of the act; but in others, they may lead rather to misapprehension. Some explanation consequently may be requisite. But this explanation can rather furnish some leading circumstances of distinction than afford a precise definition.

It is plain that the separation intended by the act is in the main the same with that, which in common and popular parlance separates *town* from *country*. In this sense the different duties are to apply. The *town* distilleries are to be rated by the gallon of the spirits produced, the *country* distilleries by the gallon of the capacity of each still. In those States therefore where the laws have divided the whole country into *townships* or *towns*, the *legal* idea of a Town must be exchanged for the popular and common one, which last must govern.

---

the said spirits, shall deliver to the purchaser or purchasers thereof, the certificate or certificates which ought to accompany the same; on pain of forfeiting the sum of fifty dollars, for each cask, vessel or case with which such certificate shall not be delivered" (1 *Stat.* 202).

17. Section 15 prescribed the duties upon "all spirits which after the said last day of June next, shall be distilled within the United States, from any article of the growth or produce of the United States, in any city, town or village" (1 *Stat.* 203).

What constitutes a city, will be readily understood in each State.

By a town or village must be intended a collection of houses in close neighbourhood. The limits of each must be determined by the common understanding of the neighbourhood. Where there are any forms of magistracy particularly attached to these *collections*, exclusive of the surrounding country, the limits of their jurisdictions may serve as guides.

SECT. 17. This section [18] relates to the distilleries, in respect to which the duty is rated by the gallon. It is conceived, that it will be a good rule for regulating the penalty of the bond in each case, to multiply the number of gallons, English wine measure, of the capacity of each still, or the aggregate of the capacities of the stills, if more than one, at any distillery, by two, and to take the product for the amount of the penalty in dollars. This proceeds on the idea that a still of any given dimensions, worked once a day for three months, would yield such a quantity of spirits, as computed at the rate of eleven cents per gallon, the lowest rate of duty on spirits distilled from foreign materials, would be equal to one dollar per gallon of the capacity of the still, to which adding one hundred per cent. for the greater security to the public, the result would be two dollars per gallon nearly, the rate, which it is supposed ought to govern the penalty. This rule however is only suggested, not enjoined. Each Supervisor may prescribe any other rule, assigning his reasons for it to the Secretary of the Treasury. The object must be to cover the public, by an adequate penalty, without giving it an immoderate or excessive appearance.

SECT. 18. A general idea has heretofore been given, with regard to the number of officers which it is deemed expedient should be appointed pursuant to this section.[19] And their *denomination* has been

18. Section 17 reads as follows: "*And be it further enacted*, That the said duties on spirits distilled within the United States, shall be paid or secured previous to the removal thereof from the distilleries at which they are respectively made. And it shall be at the option of the proprietor or proprietors of each distillery, or of his, her or their agent having the superintendence thereof, either to pay the said duties previous to such removal, with an abatement at the rate of two cents for every ten gallons, or to secure the payment of the same, by giving bond quarter-yearly, with one or more sureties, to the satisfaction of the chief officer of inspection within whose survey such distillery shall be, and in such sum as the said officer shall direct, with condition for the payment of the duties upon all such of the said spirits as shall be removed from such distillery, within three months next ensuing the date of the bond, at the expiration of nine months from the said date" (1 *Stat.* 203).

19. Section 18 reads as follows: "*And be it further enacted*, That the super-

prescribed by the President of the United States. The distilleries of spirits from foreign materials, and those from domestic materials in a city, town or village, must be visited by the Collector of the Revenue, under whose immediate survey they are *at least* twice a day, in order to observe the progress of the work, and take an account from day to day of what has been done; of which a weekly return ought to be made to the Inspector of the Revenue, under whose jurisdiction he is, distinguishing the product of each day. The Inspector from these returns ought to make and transmit a weekly abstract to the Supervisor, distinguishing the quantity made at each distillery during each week. For these returns forms will be transmitted.

Each Collector of the Revenue, having the care of one or more of these distilleries, must hold himself constantly ready to attend deliveries; so that no delay may embarrass the business of the Distiller. It may, *in the progress of the thing*, be found necessary to have an officer continually attending each distillery.

SECT. 19. The marks here contemplated [20] may be abbreviated according to the following example:

No. 1. J——n Wilson,

Philadelphia,

First Proof, 100 G:——

J——n will here signify JOHN, and any other Christian name may be abbreviated in like manner. Forms for the Certificates here directed will be sent from the Treasury. They are to be *provided, stamped* and

---

visor of each district shall appoint proper officers to have the charge and survey of the distilleries within the same, assigning to each, one or more distilleries as he may think proper, who shall attend such distillery at all reasonable times, for the execution of the duties by this act enjoined on him" (1 *Stat.* 203).

20. Section 19 reads in part as follows: "*And be it further enacted,* That previous to the removal of the said spirits from any distillery, the officer within whose charge and survey the same may be, shall brand or otherwise mark each cask containing the same, in durable characters, and with progressive numbers, and with the name of the acting owner or other manager of such distillery, and of the place where the same was situate, and with the quantity therein, to be ascertained by actual gauging, and with the proof thereof. And the duties thereupon having been first paid, or secured, as above provided, the said officer shall grant a certificate for each cask of the said spirits, to accompany the same wheresoever it shall be sent, purporting that the duty thereon hath been paid or secured, as the case may be, and describing each cask by its marks; and shall enter in a book for that purpose to be kept, all the spirits distilled at such distillery, and removed from the same: and the marks of each cask, and the persons for whose use, and the places to which removed and the time of each removal, and the amount of the duties on the spirits so removed" (1 *Stat.* 203-04).

issued by the respective Supervisors to the several Inspectors upon the like terms, and under the like regulations as those herein before mentioned concerning the certificates to be issued pursuant to the thirteenth section.[21] Each Inspector, after signing those furnished to him, is to distribute them to the respective Collectors, each of whom is to countersign those which shall be issued by him. Accounts of the issuing and expenditure of these certificates must be kept between the respective officers.

SECT. 21.[22] *The several Collectors of the Revenue must lose no time in visiting and measuring the stills under their surveys respectively;* of which they must make exact returns under their hands to their respective Inspectors, specifying in these returns the name of each owner or manager of a distillery, the city, town or village, and if not in a city, town or village, the parish, precinct, township or other district (constituting the smallest sub-division of a county) and the county in which such distillery is situate, the number of stills at each, and their capacity in gallons English wine measure, the materials from which they usually distil, and the time for which they are usually employed. The Inspectors must make similar returns abstracted from those of the Collectors, and shewing the like particulars to their respective Supervisors; who on their part must make like returns to the Treasury. These *different* returns must be continued half yearly, so as that those to be made to the Treasury, may be *received* in the months of May and November.

SECT. 23. This section [23] contemplates that each Collector of the Revenue is to be charged with the *superintendance* of a certain number of stills. This intent of the law, it is conceived, may easily be fulfilled by assigning to each the *charge* of all the stills within *certain defined* limits; as within a particular county by name, &c.

21. See note 16.

22. Section 21 reads as follows: "*And be it further enacted*, That upon such stills which after the last day of June next, shall be employed in distilling spirits from materials of the growth or production of the United States, in any other place than a city, town or village, there shall be paid for the use of the United States, the yearly duty of sixty cents for every gallon, English wine-measure, of the capacity or content of each and every such still, including the head thereof" (1 *Stat.* 204).

23. Section 23 provided that "the said duties on stills shall be collected under the management of the supervisor in each district, who shall appoint and assign proper officers for the surveys of the said stills" (1 *Stat.* 204).

SECT. 24.   Any book which may be kept pursuant to this section,[24] or a copy thereof, must be left by the party wishing to avail himself of the provision therein contained, with the Collector of the Revenue under whose *charge* his distillery may be, who must administer the oath or affirmation prescribed to the party applying. This oath must be in writing, annexed to the book or the copy thereof, in the following form:

I [name of person] of [place of abode, occupation] do swear [or if of a religious denomination conscientiously scrupulous of oaths, do solemnly, sincerely and truly affirm and declare] that the Book [or copy of the book, as the case may be] now by me produced and shewn, doth contain, to the best of my knowledge and belief, true entries made in the said Book, at their respective dates, of all the spirits distilled from the stills therein referred to, from the   day of   to the   day of   both days inclusive, amounting to   gallons, and also of the disposition thereof; and further, that there are   gallons of the said spirits now remaining on hand.

A—— B——

Sworn [or affirmed, as the case may be]
the   day of   17
before me
C—— D——
Collector of the Revenue.

The two days, referred to in the above form, for which blanks are left, must be the first and last of the dates of the entries in the book. The next succeding blank must be filled with the number of gallons made, and the one next after that with the number of gallons undisposed of. A—— B—— is designed to denote the place of the signature of the party swearing or affirming, and C—— D—— that of the signature of the officer. The blanks are to be filled in words at length, not figures. If the entries shall have been made by a person

24. Section 24 provided that "the proprietor of any such still, finding himself or herself aggrieved by the said rates, shall enter or cause to be entered in a book to be kept for that purpose, from day to day when such still shall be employed, the quantity of spirits distilled therefrom, and the quantity from time to time sold or otherwise disposed of, and to whom and when, and shall produce the said book to the officer of inspection within whose survey such still shall be, and shall make oath or affirmation that the same doth contain to the best of his or her knowledge and belief, true entries" (1 *Stat.* 204).

other than the proprietor, a similar oath or affirmation, in writing, to be taken by him, must *likewise* be annexed to the book, or copy thereof. These books or copies will be vouchers to the accounts of the respective Collectors. Forms for them to be furnished to the owners of stills, will be transmitted.

SECT. 25. The provisions in this section,[25] in regard to stills (not worked together with other stills and) not exceeding in capacity fifty gallons, seem to be, in a great measure, abandoned by the 36th [26] section; at least the penalty specified in this section for not complying with these provisions, is in respect to such stills superseded. It does not however follow, that they are to be exempted from the duty. And a compliance with that provision which regards the entry of the stills, is of great importance to the complete execution of the law.

It is understood that the entries required by this section (except in the case of those who shall be distillers of spirits on the first day of July next) will only be necessary when any person first sets up a still or distillery, in or at any particular house, building or place, or first begins to make use of such house, building or place, as a depository of the spirits by him or her distilled. It will not require the giving notice of any particular process of distillation intended to be begun in any house, building or place before entered. But those who are distillers of spirits from foreign materials wheresoever, or from domestic materials in any city, town or village, on the first day of July next, must on that day, or within three days after, that is *before* the *fifth* of July, make the entry herein required—subject on and after that day, in case of omission, to the pains and penalties specified.

SECT. 26. It is conceived that this section [27] is only applicable to distilleries from foreign materials, and to distilleries from domestic materials in cities, towns and villages—not to stills, which are rated according to their respective capacities. The visitation and inspection contemplated, will probably be most conveniently done by the Col-

25. Section 25 concerned the regulations for establishing distilleries (1 *Stat.* 205).

26. Section 36 exempted "any person who shall employ one still only, and that of a capacity not exceeding fifty gallons" from penalties arising from failure to obey the regulations prescribed in Section 25 (1 *Stat.* 208).

27. Section 26 concerned the procedures for inspection by the excise officers (1 *Stat.* 205).

lectors of the Revenue. Forms for the account directed to be taken will be transmitted. The marking may be according to the following example:

No. 1, J——n Jones,

First Proof R 20 G:——

Old Stock.

R—— signifies Rum, by which is meant spirits distilled from molasses or sugar. Whiskey or spirits distilled from grain may be expressed by W. Brandy or spirits distilled from fruits and other vegetables except grain, by B——. The account taken, or a copy thereof must be returned by each Collector to his Inspector; who must enter them in the book which he is directed to keep according to the form which will be prescribed. The certificates must be prepared, stamped, furnished, issued and accounted for in the same manner, and under the same regulations as with regard to the certificates directed by the 19th section.[28]

SECT. 27. Each Inspector to record in a book to be kept by him, according to a form to be prescribed, the entries directed by this section.[29] The certificates herein mentioned, to be prepared, stamped, furnished, issued and accounted for in the same manner, and under the same regulations as those directed by the 19th and 26th sections.[30]

SECT. 28. Seizures under this section [31] will require circumspec-

28. See note 20.

29. Section 27 reads in part as follows: "*And be it further enacted*, That every importer of distilled spirits, who, on the first day of July next, shall have in his or her possession any distilled spirits, shall, within three days thereafter, make due entry thereof with the officer of inspection within whose survey the same shall then be; who shall mark the casks, vessels or cases containing such spirits, in like manner as is herein before directed touching such spirits as shall be in the possession of distillers on the first day of July next, and shall grant the like certificates therefor as for such spirits, which certificates shall accompany the respective casks, cases and vessels to which they shall relate, wheresoever they shall be sent, and such importer, his or her agent, upon the sale and delivery of any of the said spirits, shall deliver to the purchaser or purchasers thereof the certificate or certificates which ought to accompany the same, on pain of forfeiting fifty dollars for each cask, case or vessel with which such certificate shall not be delivered" (1 *Stat.* 206).

30. See notes 20 and 27.

31. Section 28 provided "That if any cask, case, or vessel containing distilled spirits, which by the foregoing provisions of this act, ought to be marked and accompanied with a certificate, shall be found in the possession of any person unaccompanied with such marks and certificate, it shall be presumptive evidence that the same are liable to forfeiture, and it shall be lawful for any officer of inspection to seize them as forfeited" (1 *Stat.* 206).

tion. Those made from foreign materials may be seized with greater confidence, if found without the proper certificates; the seizure of those made from domestic materials, would require other circumstances of suspicion than the mere want of a certificate, because a certificate is not in all cases a necessary appendage.

SECT. 29. This section [32] is conceived to be applicable only to distilleries from foreign materials, and to those from domestic materials in cities, towns and villages; not to those in respect to which the duty is payable according to the capacity of the still.

SECT. 35. Forms for the Books contemplated by this section [33] will be transmitted. The oath or affirmation, in support of them, must be in writing annexed to each book, and will be administered by the Collector of the Revenue, to whom such book is delivered. The following form is deemed eligible.

I [name of party swearing or affirming] of [name of city, town, village, parish, precinct or other district] do swear [or if of a religious denomination conscientiously scrupulous of swearing, do solemnly, sincerely and truly affirm and declare] that the entries in the Book now by me delivered and hereunto annexed, were by me made at the respective days of the dates thereof, and that they were intended by

32. Section 29 reads as follows: "*And be it further enacted,* That it shall be lawful for the officers of inspection of each survey at all times in the daytime, upon request, to enter into all and every the houses, store-houses, ware-houses, buildings and places which shall have been entered in manner aforesaid, and by tasting, gauging or otherwise, to take an account of the quantity, kinds and proofs of the said spirits therein contained; and also to take samples thereof, paying for the same the usual price" (1 *Stat.* 206).

33. Section 35 reads in part as follows: "*And be it further enacted,* That every distiller of spirits, on which the duty is hereby charged by the gallon, shall keep or cause to be kept, an exact account of the said spirits, which he or she shall sell, send out, or distil, distinguishing their several kinds and proofs, and shall every day make a just and true entry in a book, to be kept for that purpose, of the quantities and particulars of the said spirits by him or her sold, sent out or distilled on the preceding day; specifying the marks of the several casks in which they shall be so sold or sent out, and the person to whom and for whose use they shall be so sold or sent out: which said books shall be prepared for the making such entries, and shall be delivered upon demand, to the said distillers, by the supervisors of the revenue of the several districts, or by such person or persons as they shall respectively for that purpose appoint, and shall be severally returned or delivered at the end of each year, or when the same shall be respectively filled up, (which shall first happen) to the proper officers of inspection; and the truth of the entries made therein shall be verified, upon the oath or affirmation of the person by whom those entries shall have been made, and as often as the said books shall be furnished upon like demand by the proper officers of inspection, to the said distillers respectively" (1 *Stat.* 207).

me to be, and according to the best of my knowledge, recollection and belief, are true and exact, and do verify and truly shew the whole quantity of spirits distilled at   and also the whole quantity of spirits sold and sent out from the distillery, to which they are therein alleged to relate, from the   day of   to the   day of   including both the said days, the quantity so distilled during the said time, amounting to   gallons and no more.

A—— B——

Sworn [or affirmed, as the case may be]

the   day of   17

C—— D——

Collector of the Revenue.

The explanations concerning the form of the oath or affirmation, given in a preceding place, apply to this. The blanks are to be filled in like manner.

The books delivered to the Collectors of the Revenue are to be by them forwarded to the Inspectors of the surveys to which they respectively belong, who after comparing them with the returns and accounts received from the Collectors, shall write at foot of the oath, the word "compared," and shall each subscribe his name and stile of office, and shall transmit the same to the respective Supervisors, who after making the like comparison thereof with the accounts and returns which shall have been rendered to them, shall certify the same in like manner as the Inspectors are required to do, and shall forward the books so certified, to the Secretary of the Treasury.

SECT. 37.[34] Hydrometers for ascertaining the proofs of spirits imported, have in most cases been forwarded, and the deficiency will soon be completed. Others for ascertaining the proofs of spirits distilled within the United States, will be furnished as speedily as they can be prepared. In the mean time, the lowest rate of duty only is to be demanded; that is 9 cents on spirits distilled from domestic materials, and 11 cents for those distilled from foreign materials.

SECT. 50. This section[35] empowers the Supervisors, or their *lawful deputies*, to administer any oath or affirmation prescribed by the law. These instructions contemplate that certain oaths or affirma-

34. Section 37 concerned proof marks for "casks, vessels, and cases containing any distilled spirits" (1 *Stat.* 208).
35. 1 *Stat.* 210.

tions are to be administered by the Collectors of the Revenue. It will certainly be most convenient that it should be done by them in the cases in which it is proposed; and it is hoped that characters will be found for Collectors, fit for so delicate a trust. In some cases it would almost seem a matter of course that they should administer the oath or affirmation prescribed; and their power may be put out of all question by a deputation from the Supervisor, which must be made under his hand and seal, and may be in the following form:

Know all men, that I   Supervisor of the Revenue for the district of   have made and appointed, and by these presents do make and appoint   my lawful Deputy, for the purpose of administering and taking oaths and affirmations, pursuant to the act entitled, "An Act repealing, after the last day of June next, the duties heretofore laid upon distilled spirits imported from abroad, and laying others in their stead, and also upon spirits distilled within the United States, and for appropriating the same." And I do hereby give to my said Deputy, all the power and authority which I myself have or might exercise for that purpose by virtue of the act aforesaid. In witness whereof I have hereunto subscribed and set my hand and seal, the   day of   in the year one thousand, &c.

  Sealed and delivered
     in the presence of

It will probably be found convenient that a like power be given to each Inspector of the Revenue.

This point being one of considerable delicacy, it is wished that the Supervisors may consider well the safety and expediency of the arrangement suggested concerning it, and communicate as soon as may, their ideas. The prompt execution of the service in a convenient and safe mode is by all means to be aimed at.

The cost of stationary, printing, procuring marking instruments, and every other incidental charge, will be to be defrayed out of the product of the duties; and being supported by proper vouchers, will be allowed in account.

In every case in which any act is herein directed to be done *to* an Inspector of the Revenue, it is to be understood that it is to be done *to* the Supervisor, in those cases and within those surveys in which he is required to perform the duties of Inspector.

INSTRUCTIONS concerning the ACT, entitled, *"An Act making further provision for the collection of the duties by law imposed on Teas, and to prolong the term for the payment of the duties on Wines."*

SECT. 1. THE store-houses contemplated by this section,[36] may either be those of the importers themselves, or others to be agreed upon between them and the Inspector of the Revenue for the port. Where the importers have *proper* store-houses of their own, which they are desirous of having made use of for the purpose, these for the accommodation of trade are to be preferred: But they must be such as are capable of being secured by the locks mentioned in the section, so as to be inaccessible without the knowledge of the Inspector. The locks to be affixed upon each store-house must be provided by the Inspector; and to save expence, must be such as will fix and unfix. Care must be taken to provide such locks as are of the securest kind, and the two upon each store-house must be different from each other, so that the key of either lock will not *open* the other. Indeed it will deserve particular attention that the keys of none of the custom-house locks may fit any other than those for which they are respectively

36. Section 1 reads in part as follows: "The teas, for the duties whereof the said bond shall be accepted, shall be deposited at the expense and risk of the said importer, in one or more storehouse or storehouses, as the case may require, to be agreed upon between the said importer and the inspector, or other officer of inspection of the revenue, for the port where the said teas shall be landed; and upon every such storehouse, the said inspector or officer of inspection shall cause to be affixed two locks, the key of one of which locks shall be kept by such importer, his or her agent, and the key of the other of which locks shall be kept by the said inspector, or by such other person as he shall depute and appoint in that behalf; whose duty it shall be to attend at all reasonable times, for the purpose of delivering the said teas out of the said storehouse or storehouses. But no delivery shall be made of any of the said teas without a permit in writing, under the hand of the said inspector or officer of inspection. And in order to the obtaining of such permit, it shall be necessary that the duties upon the teas, for which the same shall be required, be first paid, or, at the option of the party or parties applying for the same, secured to be paid in manner following; that is to say: The said party or parties shall give bond with one or more surety or sureties to the satisfaction of the said inspector, in double the amount of the duties upon the quantity of teas in each case to be delivered, with condition for the payment of the said duties, if the same shall not exceed one hundred dollars, in four months; or, if the same shall exceed one hundred dollars, and shall not exceed five hundred dollars, in eight months; or, if the same shall exceed five hundred dollars, in twelve months; *Provided always,* That the time to be allowed for the payment of the duties upon any parcel of teas to be delivered, shall not be such as to extend the credit for such duties beyond the term of two years originally allowed upon the depositing of the said teas" (1 *Stat.* 219-20).

designed. In many (if not in most) cases however, it will be unnecessary to provide more than one lock, as there will be already one on the door of the building which will satisfy the importer.

The Inspectors of the Customs may be deputed in aid of the Inspector of the Revenue, for the charge of these store-houses.

These Inspectors must keep an exact account in some proper book, of the Teas of each importer, distinguishing the several kinds of boxes, chests and cases, and their respective marks.

When the importer, or his agent has occasion to remove from any store-house, the whole or any part of the Teas therein deposited, he must make application to the Inspector of the Revenue, deliver him a note in writing, of the chests, boxes or packages desired to be removed, specifying their several marks and numbers, and must pay, or *secure* to the satisfaction of the Inspector, the duties thereupon: Which being done—the Inspector must grant a permit for the delivery, in the following form:

1	No. 1, W. M. S. Canton.	PORT of [*Philadelphia*] permit [*Willing, Morris and Swanwick*] or bearer, to remove [*ten chests*] of Tea, imported in the [*ship Canton*] marked as per margin, the duties upon which amounting to [*four hundred dollars,*] have been [*paid or secured.*]
3	W. M. S. No. 1 to 3, Canton.	
4	No. 5 to 8, W. M. S. Canton.	
2	W. M. S. Canton. No. 10 12.	
10		

[*May* 1, 1791.]

William McPherson,
[*Inspector of the Revenue.*]

To [*John James*] Inspector

Printed permits, with proper blanks formed by leaving out the words which above stand between [   ] ought to be provided. The name or firm to be inserted is always to be that of the Importer or Importers, in conformity to the third section.[37] A sufficient margin must

---

37. Section 3 provided that "the permits which shall have been granted by such inspector, for the delivery of any teas, out of any storehouse wherein they shall have been deposited, shall be received by such collector towards satisfying any bond, which shall have been, in the first instance, taken by the said collector, touching the said teas; which permits shall therefore specify the amount of the duties which shall have been paid or secured upon the teas to be delivered in virtue thereof; and the name of the ship or vessel in which they shall have been imported, and of the importer or importers thereof" (1 *Stat.* 220).

be left for the marks, the nature of which will be explained in another place.

The proviso to this section is to be thus understood. Suppose *eighteen* months to have elapsed from the time the whole parcel of Teas was first deposited. Suppose the duties on the quantity to be removed, to amount to one thousand dollars. The credit in this case would only be six months, which added to eighteen, would complete the original term of credit.

SECT. 3.   This section renders it necessary that the permits to be granted by each Inspector of the Revenue, should remain with the Importer or his Agent. A duplicate, however, ought in each case to be furnished by him, to be left with the officer or person by whom the delivery is made, as his voucher. This officer or person when a delivery is made, ought to indorse on the permit (which is to be retained by the Importer) the word *delivered*, and *the day*, and *year*, and *his own name.*

SECT. 4.   The Inspector of the Revenue for each port, must *depute* the Inspectors of the Customs to aid in the performance of the duty required by this section.[38] The indorsement required to be made on the permit of the Collector, must be thus—"Produced this first day of May 1791," to which must be *subjoined* the signature of the Inspector of the Revenue. It will be found convenient that the marks to be set on the respective chests, boxes and packages, should besides expressing a number and the name of the vessel, designate the *Importers,* and the *qualities* of the Teas, as classed in the law. How this

38. Section 4 reads in part as follows: "*And be it further enacted,* That all teas which, after the first day of April next, shall be imported into the United States from any foreign port or place, shall be landed under the care of the inspectors of the revenue for the ports where the same shall be respectively landed; and for that purpose every permit which shall be granted by any collector, for landing the same, shall, prior to such landing, be produced to the said inspector, who by an endorsement thereupon under his hand, shall signify the production thereof to him, and the time when; after which, and not otherwise, it shall be lawful to land the teas mentioned in such permit. And the said inspector shall make an entry of all such permits, and of the contents thereof; and each chest, box or package containing any teas, shall be marked by the officer under whose immediate inspection the same shall be landed, in legible and durable characters, with progressive numbers, and with the name of the vessel in which the same shall have been imported. And the said officer shall grant a certificate for each such chest, box or package, specifying therein the name or names of the importer or importers, the ship or vessel in which the same shall have been imported, and the number thereof to accompany the same wheresoever it shall be sent" (1 *Stat.* 220).

may be done with brevity, will be understood by an explanation of the marks in the preceding example. Willing, Morris and Swanwick, are there supposed to be the importers of the Teas. The initials of their names are therefore taken W. M. S.—which letters may serve instead of the names at length. The first of the four marks is intended to denote the first class of teas, namely Bohea, which is done by placing the number of the chest or package *first*, on the left hand, on a line with the initials of the Importers names. Thus No. 1. W. M. S.

=====   Canton.

The second of the four marks is intended to denote the second class of teas, namely Souchong and other black teas, which is done by placing the number of the chest or package after the initials of the name, on the right hand and in a line with them, thus—W. M. S. No. 1.

Canton =====

The third of the four marks is intended to denote the third class of teas, namely Hyson, which is done by placing the number of the chest or package above the initials and the name of the ship, thus—No. 5.

=====

W. M. S. Canton.

The fourth of the four marks is intended to denote the fourth class of teas, namely Green Teas other than Hyson, which is done by placing the number of the chest or package below the initials and the name of the ship, thus—W. M. S. Canton.

=====

No. 10.

The progression of the numbers ought to begin and terminate with each class. Thus if there should be eight chests of Bohea, and six chests of Souchong, the Bohea should be numbered 1 to 8, and the Souchong 1 to 6, etc. Where the packages containing teas are of a kind not capable of being marked to advantage, the marks may be set on small pieces of vellum or parchment, and sealed or glued to the packages.

Let the following be the form of the Certificate to be granted for each chest, box or other package:

No. 1. W. M. S.
    Canton.

PORT of [*Philadelphia*] I certify that [*Willing, Morris and Swanwick*] have imported according to law, in the [*ship Canton*] from [*Canton*] one chest of Tea marked as per margin. [*May first*] one thousand seven hundred [*ninety-one.*]

[*William McPherson*]
Inspector of the Revenue.

Printed Certificates with proper blanks for this purpose, will be indispensable.

The expence of Stationary, Printing and providing instruments for marking, must be defrayed by the Collector, and charged to the United States.

☞ It has been made a question whether the credit for *two* years allowed by the Act,[39] may not be obtained by giving bond *with* sureties, but without a deposit of the teas. A construction of this kind is unfounded and inadmissible. The despoiting of the Teas is an *indispensable* condition of the allowance of the credit for the above mentioned term.

FINIS.

39. See note 36.

To Joseph Ward [1]

Treasury Department,
May 26 1791

Sir,

I duly received your letter of the 2d instant.[2] The species of paper you mention presents an embarrassing question.[3] Being issued upon the funds of individual states with a stipulation for the payment of interest by the United States, and a contingent guarantee of the principal, it is not easy to pronounce under what denomination of public debt it properly falls. It is however not in my opinion provided for by the Act making provision for the debt of the United States.[4] It is not comprehended within the enumeration of the kinds of certificates receivable upon loan as debt of the United States; and if it is to be considered as on state foundation, it seems to come under the description of paper *money*, which has not been understood as within the meaning of the words *certificates* or *notes* which "were issued by the respective states as *acknowlegements* or *evidences* of *debt* by them respectively owing."

This question has been rendered the more embarrassing by some steps taken in the house of Representatives during the last session concerning it which however did not issue in any provision.

It is with regret I find myself thus circumstanced on the subject; as there is nothing more my wish than to see the interest of every class of public creditors equitably embraced.

I am, sir   with consideration,   Your obdt Servant   A Hamilton

Joseph Ward Esqr.
Boston.

LS, Chicago Historical Society.
    1. On February 11, 1791, "A memorial of Thomas Walley, William Smith, and Joseph Ward, was presented to the House and read, praying that certain bills issued under the authority of the former Congress, of which the petitioners are possessed, the interest whereof was payable in sterling bills of exchange in Europe, may be liquidated, and the arrears of interest paid, or the principal and interest of the said bills funded in like manner with loan office certificates" (*Journal of the House,* I, 376).
    2. Letter not found.
    3. Presumably H is referring to the "new emission" certificates authorized by the Continental Congress under a resolution of March 18, 1780. See Charles Pettit to H, April 30, 1791, note 3.
    4. Sections 3 and 13 of "An Act making provision for the (payment of the) Debt of the United States" stipulated certificates receivable upon loan (1 *Stat.* 139–40, 142 [August 4, 1790]). For Section 3, see Nathaniel Appleton to H, February 5, 1791, note 1. For Section 13, see Thomas Smith to H, June 6, 1791, note 1.

From Otho H. Williams

Collectors Office Baltimore 26th May 1791

Sir

Your circular letter came to hand last evening.[1]

I do not apprehend, Sir, that you allude to any illegal, or improper receiving of duties in this office. The laws of Congress, according to my comprehension of their meaning, have always been adhered to here, with the utmost possible exactness; But as my conception of some parts of the "act to provide more effectually for the Collection

ADfS, RG 53, "Old Correspondence," Baltimore Collector, National Archives.
    1. "Treasury Department Circular to the Collectors of the Customs," May 13, 1791.

of the duties" [2] &c differs very much from the literal meaning of your circular letter of the 13th, it is proper for me to reply particularly to that part.

You "desire that the duties on goods may *in no instance* be ascertained but on the *actual landing* thereof, and by no means, but by the measuring, weighing, and gauging in all cases wherein those operations are required by Law."

Altho' it is impracticable to perform those operations without landing the goods, the act prohibits the landing *any* goods *before* the duties are paid, or secured to be paid: and that upon "a gross estimate of their amount" (see s. 25.)[3] "and then, and *not otherwise* it shall be lawful to land" &c. which gross estimate, after further process, according to the directions of the act, is to be revised, and the duties finally adjusted—section 28.[4]

Why Congress thought proper to require this double labor of the Collector, the advantages of the mode do not well explain, and possibly some, who think it might as well be omitted, may consider your instructions as intending to dispence with the previously securing the duties according to "a gross estimate," and may give permission to land goods, which I think contrary to the obvious direction of the act.

Your decision, respecting the service of Inspectors going from one district to another, is a confirmation of the propriety of the instructions heretofore given by me in such cases.

The custom of Merchants here has been very much governed by the customs of those places from whence they import. The general rule of allowing tare on a Hogshead of Sugar, or on a Cargo of Casks &c is twelve pounds per *hundred weight* (12 ℔ l cwt or 12 ℔ 112 lbs.) But they have had some few instances of clean Hhds, with cane hoops, from port au Prince containing 18 cwt, to 20 cwt. where the tare did not exceed ten per Centum, or one tenth part of the whole nett pounds weight. Sugar Barrels are always tared according to their make, to wit, French flour barrels, used for Sugar, 28 lbs tare— American flour barrels, most in use for this markett, 20 lbs—and the

2. 1 *Stat.* 145–78 (August 4, 1790).
3. Actually Williams is referring to Section 26 (1 *Stat.* 163). For an explanation of the confusion over the section numbers of this act, see H to Richard Harison, April 26, 1791, note 2.
4. Williams is referring to Section 29 (1 *Stat.* 164).

same distinction is applied to barrels containing Coffee Cocoa, Pimento, Pepper &c. Casks containing Rice, or Casks or boxes containing Indigo are always tared according to their actual weight, ascertained before the commodity is put in them; where it happens otherwise ten perCent, or 1/10th of the nett hundred is usually allowed.

Merchants very seldom allow tare for baggs unless damaged, and then not exceeding three pounds ⅌ bagg. This is the general practice, but in many cases the merchants in selling, as well as in buying, abide by the tare expressed in the invoice. The practice at the Custom House is Similar, except where the law directs otherwise; where the law is explicit it is implicitly followed. But as the term ⅌ *Cent* is some times used in referrence to the nett sum of one hundred, and some times to the gross weight, or One hundred and twelve, doubts arise whether Congress mean that the allowance shall be from the nett weight, uniformly, or from the gross as the case may be. The duties are imposed ⅌ *pound* upon Sugars, Coffees, Tea, Coccoa, Candles, Cheese, Cotton, Indigo, Lead & Shott, Nails, Pepper, Pimento, Soaps. and Manufactured Tobacco and ⅌ *cwt.* on Cables, Cordage, Hemp, Steel & Twine. There is no tare allowed from articles taxed ⅌ Cwt. And the tare which is allowed from articles taxed ⅌ pound is ⅌ *Centum*. The terms made use of in the law raises a doubt whether Congress intended the tare to be analagous to the duty or merely an abatement from the gross hundred, some of the articles taxed ⅌ lb. being invoiced and sold by the gross, and some by the nett hundred. All, however, are weighed and returned to the Customs House by the Gross and the tare calculated accordingly. This mode was induced by the custom of Merchants here; But I am not confident that I have not thereby done them injustice in allowing less tare than the law entitles them to. Any given quantity of Sugars or other Article will, no doubt, have the same certain abatement for tare ⅌ *centum*— whether the operation of the numbers allowed for ⅌ Centage be upon the gross weight (that is ⟨either⟩ cwts grs & lbs) or upon the same given quantity reduced to nett pounds. But the doubt is whether by the term ⅌ *Centum* is meant 100 or 112. It is variously used, or applied, in the acts of Congress and makes a real difference in calculations.[5]

5. In MS a table of figures is superimposed on this paragraph.

I understand, by Merchants that the Spanish 100 lbs is equal to the U States 104 lbs; that the French 100 lbs is Equal to the United States 108 lbs; and we differ in calculation almost from every other Nation, except the British. Yet the term *one hundred* pounds weight, is used to express all alike. Congress make use of the words *per centum* to signify by the hundred and merchants and public Officers some times differ in making the application of that term. So long as a *definite* number, as ten, or twelve, is allowed as a discount from an *indefinite* number (Centum, as it may be understood to signify 100—104—108—112 &c &c) so long there will be various modes of calculation, and different conclusions, in respect to relative numbers.

Would it not render the business extremely simple, and each deduction more certain, if a proportional part of an Article, or of any given quantity of an Article and its package were allowed for tare? Say *one tenth* instead of ten ℔ Cent; which, on a nett hundred, is the same thing, but more on 1 cwt., or 112 lbs; *One twentieth* instead of 5 ℔ Cent; *One thirty three and a third part* instead of three ℔ Cent; One fiftieth part instead of two ℔ Cent. The rule of proportion would operate invariably upon Invoices, actual weights, or tale of Merchandize, or money, whereas a *definite* number must have a contrary effect when applied indiscriminately, as a scale of abatement, to *indefinite* sums, or quantities, agreeing in denomination only.

But to reply more particularly to your request respecting the mode of allowing tare, heretofore, at this office, I am to add, that upon Sugars (other than Loaf) in Hogsheads, Tierces, Barrels, I have allowed twelve pounds out of the *hundred weight*, or one hundred and twelve pds,

Same in Boxes, fifteen pounds out of the hundred weight;

Coffee in Casks, twelve pounds out of the hundred weight;

Same in Bags, two pounds . . . . .Same . . . .;

Same in Bales, three pounds . . . . .Same . . . .;

Pepper in Casks . . twelve pounds . . .Same . . . .;

Same in Bales . . five pounds . . . . . . .Same . . . .;

Tea in Chests, and boxes, according to the Specific directions of the Act, section 34.[6]

Loaf Sugar, and on all other goods according to Invoice

6. Williams is referring to Section 35 (1 *Stat.* 166),

Saving to the importer, or consignee, the privilege of estimating the tare by Invoice in all cases.

I am, Sir,   Your most Obedient and Most Humble Servant

O. H. Williams Collr.

Alexander Hamilton Esqr.
Secretary of the Treasury

To Thomas Forrest, John Nicholson, and Others, Public Creditors

Treasury Department
May 27. 1791.

Gentn

I have received your letter of the sixth instant [1] and have paid careful attention to the contents of it. But notwithstanding my earnest desire to meet the wishes of every class of the public Creditors, my judgment of the true construction of the law in the point in question remains as disclosed in my first letter.[2]

The fact is, that the Certificates issued by the Register of the Treasury do express a certain principal sum of *specie*, though without calling it so, and stipulate an interest of six per Centum per annum on that *precise sum*. The Certificates requested would express a certain principal sum, of *nominal* not *specie* value, and though they would also express, incidentally, the *specie sum* due, they would stipulate interest not on *that* sum but on the *nominal* sum. In the first case the rate of six per cent would be payable on the *specie* value, in the last on the *nominal* value; though in both cases the principal sum to be redeemed by the Public would be the specie value only. Here then are contracts of a nature substantially different; and certificates, which should import such different contracts, would necessarily be of *tenors* substantially different from each other.[3]

Allow me to add Gentlemen that the very application you make to me, with an earnestness which in your situation is not unnatural, is itself an illustration of the truth of the construction given to the law by the officers of the Treasury. They are willing to give you certificates precisely of the tenor of those which have been accustomed to be issued by the Register of the Treasury. You demand others, and consider those offered as a violation of your rights. Can those you require be substantially of a like tenor with those you reject? If they were, your good sense would have restrained you from making a serious question of the matter. You certainly would never have been so strenuous for a difference merely formal and immaterial, in the tenor of a certificate.

Admitting, as you contend, that the construction insisted upon by me is not conformable to the main or general intent of the Act it will not follow that it is eroneous. It is no uncommon case for the general design of a law to fail of its full effect by some particular provisions in it. The inference would only be in the present case that there has been an omission in regard to the Species of public debt in which you are interested. This inference will I apprehend be far more agreeable to rules of legal interpretation, than a construction, which would annul the effect of so important a directory clause, as that which declares that the "new certificates shall specify the *specie amount* of those in exchange for which they are given and shall be *otherwise* of the *like tenor* with those theretofore issued by the Register of the Treasury for the Registered Debt." [4]

I remain with great consideration　Gentn.　Your obedt Servant

Alexander Hamilton
Secy of the Treasury

Messrs Thomas Forrest
John Nicholson
and others, Public Creditors

LS, Hamilton Papers, Library of Congress.
1. Letter not found.
2. Letter not found.
3. For the provision for "non-subscribers" made by the funding system and the special case of the certificates to which H is referring, see Andrew Porter to H, April 23, 1791, note 2.
4. This is not an exact quotation. See 1 *Stat.* 141.

From Tobias Lear

Philadelphia, May 27, 1791. Encloses "two commissions for the inspectors of Surveys No. 4 and 5 in the District of North Carolina."

LC, George Washington Papers, Library of Congress.

To Charles Pettit

Treasury Department May 27. 1791.

Sir

I have enquired into the subject of your letter of the 30th. of April, and according to the reports made to me by the proper Officers, it appears that the State of Pennsylvania has received its full proportion, namely, six tenths of the whole sum struck upon the security of its funds being 1495000 Dollars.

The balance of 78642 Dollars stated by the Comptroller General of the State, as unissued, arises on the 4/10 of the above sum, reserved for the use of the United States.

I have the honor to be, Sir,   Your Obedt. & humble Servant

Alexander Hamilton Secy. of the Treasury

Charles Pettit Esqr.

Philadelphia

Copy, Division of Public Records, Pennsylvania Historical and Museum Commission, Harrisburg.

Treasury Department Circular to the Commissioners of Loans

Treasury Department,
May 27 1791

Sir,

By the 18th Section of the Act, making provision for the debt of the United States, it is declared that the payment of interest, whether to States or to Individuals, in respect to the debt of any State which may have exchanged its own securities for those of the United States, shall be suspended until a reexchange shall have taken place or a surrender be made of the *last mentioned* securities.[1]

I request therefore that you will inform me whether any thing of the above kind has been transacted in your State. If it has, due attention must be paid to the restriction concerning it.

You will not, I presume, have failed to advert to that part of the

10th section of the same act which limits to the first of June the exchanges of certificates in the case of non-Subscribers.[2] The issuing of new certificates to non-Subscribe[r]s for old ones, not produced previous to that day, will, of course, be forborne.

I am, sir,   with due consideration,   Your Obed Servant

A Hamilton

LS, to Jabez Bowen, Massachusetts Historical Society, Boston; copy, to Thomas Smith, Division of Public Records, Pennsylvania Historical and Museum Commission, Harrisburg.

1. Sections 17 and 18 of the act read in part as follows:

"But as certain states have respectively issued their own certificates, in exchange for those of the United States, whereby it might happen that interest might be twice payable on the same sums:

"*Be it further enacted,* That the payment of interest whether to states or to individuals, in respect to the debt of any state, by which such exchange shall have been made, shall be suspended, until it shall appear to the satisfaction of the secretary of the treasury, that certificates issued for that purpose by such state, have been re-exchanged or redeemed, or until those which shall not have been re-exchanged or redeemed, shall be surrendered to the United States." (1 *Stat.* 144 [August 4, 1790].)

2. 1 *Stat.* 141.

From Tobias Lear

Philadelphia, May 29, 1791. Encloses a proposal for a mint which had been sent to President Washington by John H. Mitchell.[1]

LC, George Washington Papers, Library of Congress.

1. Mitchell's interest in a mint was of some standing, for an entry in the *Journal of the House* for April 7, 1790, reads: "A Member from South Carolina presented to the House a letter addressed to him from John H. Mitchel, of the said State, reciting certain proposals of Matthew Boulton, of the kingdom of Great Britain, for supplying the United States with copper coinage to any amount that Government shall think fit to contract with him for, upon the terms therein mentioned" (*Journal of the House,* I, 190).

To Benjamin Lincoln

[Philadelphia, May 29, 1791]

Private
Dr Sir

I have written to the Directors of the Bank of Massachusettes, a letter of which the inclosed is a copy.[1] Be so good as to aid in diffusing the knowledge of the arrangement.

You need not mention the transmission of the letter lest it should be misinterpreted.

I remain very truly   Your friend & serv   A Hamilton

May the 29. 1791
General Lincoln

ALS, Maine Historical Society, Portland.
   1. H to the President and Directors of the Massachusetts Bank, May 30, 1791.

To William Ellery

[*Philadelphia, May 30, 1791.* On June 13, 1791, Ellery wrote to Hamilton: "I have received your letters of the 26th. and the 30th. of May last." *Letter of May 30 not found.*]

To the President and Directors of the Massachusetts Bank [1]

Treasury Department
May 30th. 1791.

Gentn.

With a view to the accommodation of those in your quarter, who may incline to become subscribers to the Bank of the United States, I have concluded on the following arrangement.

That for any sums which shall be deposited in the Bank of Massachusetts to the Credit of the United States, to an amount not exceeding in the whole sixty thousand Dollars, I will cause equal sums to be paid in the City of Philadelphia towards the subscriptions which such persons respectively, or their respective representatives shall make to the Bank of the United States.[2]

In order that this arrangement may be carried into execution it will be necessary that the sums paid in be duly passed to the Credit of the United States; and that the parties or their Agents produce certificates from the Cashier of the Bank specifying the sums paid in and that they have been passed to the Credit of the United States.

And it is to be clearly understood that the operation to be for the sole purpose of subscriptions to the Bank as no money will be paid here in lieu of that deposited but on account of such subscriptions.

I take it for granted that your Direction will chearfully cooperate in a measure, so exclusively dictated by a desire to accommod⟨ate⟩ and so convenient to all concerned.

I have not thought fit to make any public annunciation of this arrangement, but it is my wish that it be informally communicated as extensively as may be.

I have the honor to be　Gentn.　Your obedt Servant

The President and Directors
of the Bank of Massachusetts.

Copy, RG 36, Collector of Customs at Boston, Letters from the Treasury, 1772–1818, Vol. 6, National Archives.

1. A copy of this letter was enclosed in H to Benjamin Lincoln, May 29, 1791.

2. The statute of incorporation of the Bank of the United States stipulated that a subscriber could deposit one-fourth of the purchase price of each share and then pay the balance over a period of eighteen months. Since the shares were four hundred dollars each, the down payment was one hundred dollars. The law, however, required that only one-fourth of the first payment be in specie and payable immediately; as a result the investor needed only twenty-five dollars in gold or silver for each share. The remaining seventy-five dollars might be in three or six percent Government stocks which were not payable until January, 1792. See "An Act to incorporate the subscribers to the Bank of the United States" (1 *Stat.* 191–96 [February 25, 1791]) and "An Act supplementary to the act intituled 'An Act to incorporate the subscribers to the Bank of the United States'" (1 *Stat.* 196–97 [March 2, 1791]). By offering the Massachusetts Bank a credit of sixty thousand dollars H guaranteed to Massachusetts investors twenty-four hundred shares of bank stock.

H's proposal was of major importance not only to the Boston investors but also to the New York subscribers, for he included the New Yorkers in his plan. By this procedure H ensured Boston and New York influence in the bank. Inasmuch as the law set Philadelphia as the place of subscription, purchasers in distant regions were at a disadvantage. Nonresidents had to travel to Philadelphia with their specie or employ agents to act for them.

To the President and Directors of the Bank of New York

[*Philadelphia, May 30, 1791.* On June 7, 1791, William Seton wrote to Hamilton: "I . . . acknowledge the honor of your letter of the 30 May." [1] *Letter not found.*]

1. This letter was presumably the same as H to the President and Directors of the Massachusetts Bank, May 30, 1791.

To Jeremiah Olney

Treasury Department
May 30th. 1791.

Sir,

Having considered the case of the Ship Warren, Capt Smith belonging to Messr. Brown & Francis,[1] I find it necessary to communicate to you some remarks concerning it.

I find from the letters of the Collector of Newport [2] that this ship
had departed from his district for India before my letter directing
him [3] to proceed against the Captain was received: and I learn from
the papers that several days after her departure from Providence
when the warren was out of the limits of your district the owners
obtained from you a licence, a certified manifest, and a permit to proceed to Newport in which district she then actually was. The ac-
quisition of these papers arms the Captain & vessel so strongly, that
they render the issue of any legal proceedings, which otherwise it
might have been proper to institute, too uncertain to risque. I have
not therefore hitherto directed any proceedings to be commenced
against the Ship or Captain on the Warren's return. You will perceive, that a certified manifest of the Cargo with which the ship left
your district could not be given with certainty requisite to satisfy
your own mind nor with safety to the revenue. Similar observations
occur in regard to the licence and permit. It is fit that you pay more
than ordinary attention to the vessels of Messr. Brown & Francis and
particularly to that commanded by Captain Smith, since a disposition
to disregard the revenue laws has manifested itself in them on this
occasion.

I do not find that Mr Jeremiah Greenman is appointed to a *military* command.[4] If therefore he is willing to accept the station of
second mate of the revenue cutter building in Connecticut, I will
submit his name to the President for that place, which, as well as that
of the third mate, yet remains unfilled. The Captain and chief mate
have been appointed some time. I wish to know whether you think
Mr. Daniel Bucklin Junr. would take the birth of third mate.[5] The
President will be at Mount Vernon the last week in June when at

soonest he might consider the fitness of these two appointments.

Coasting Vessels arriving in your district whose licences have expired, are to be treated precisely as if they had never been licenced, for those official papers are of no force after the expiration of the year for which they were granted. The nature of the Cargo's and the places from whence they came are to determine the fees &c to which they are subject, exactly as in the cases of Vessels never having been Coasters.[6]

I have already taken measures for the regulation of the tares of various kinds of goods of which you have been informed.[7]

I am, Sir,   Your obed. Servant   Alexander Hamilton

Jeremh. Olney Esqr.
Collector of Providence

LS, Rhode Island Historical Society, Providence; copy, RG 56, Letters to the Collector at Providence, National Archives; copy, RG 56, Letters to Collectors at Small Ports, "Set G," National Archives.
    1. The Providence merchant firm of John Brown and John Francis. See Olney to H, November 29, 1790.
    2. See William Ellery to H, April 25, 1791. Ellery also wrote to H on the subject of the *Warren* on January 17, 1791. This letter had not been found when Volume VII of *The Papers of Alexander Hamilton* was published. It has since been located in the Newport Historical Society, Newport, Rhode Island, and will be printed in a supplementary volume.
    3. According to Ellery's endorsement on the letter book copy of his letter to H of January 17, 1791, H's reply is dated May 30, 1791. This letter has not been found.
    4. See Olney to H, April 25, 1791.
    5. See Olney to H, February 17, 1791.
    6. See Olney to H, May 5, 1791.
    7. See Olney to H, May 24, 1791.

From Joseph Hardy

Treasury Department, Comptroller's Office, May 31, 1791. "The enclosed Letter from William Benson, containing his resignation of the Office of Surveyor of the Customs, at the Port of Windsor, in the district of Edenton and state of North Carolina, was just now received at this Office; and I consider it, to be my duty, immediately to transmit it, for your consideration."

LC, RG 217, First Comptroller's Office, Revenue Letters Sent (Customs), National Archives.

From Charles Pettit

Philadelphia 31st. May 1791.

Sir.

I have this morning had the honor to receive your letter of the 27th instant. The application of the 30th. of April was made on a supposition of the facts being as you state them. But the Legislature having made provision for the redemption of the whole sum of 1,495,000 dollars, it is supposed that the State is credited by the United States for the whole of the 4/10ths which were reserved in their hands, and that whatever part thereof shall be delivered up as unissued, will be debited in return so as to make a fair liquidation. Having nearly collected all that was in circulation, and wishing to know with precision what remains to be collected, the Legislature have directed this application to be made, with a view as well to ascertain the amount of this kind of money which remains to be redeemed from the channels of circulation, as to become fairly possessed of such part of the proportion reserved by the United States, as yet remains unissued, and which it is supposed must hereafter remain useless.

Considering the Application I had the honor to present to you the 30th. of April, in this point of view, you will perceive it is not yet fully answered.

I have the honor to be, sir, Your most obedt. and most humble servant   Charles Pettit

Alexander Hamilton Esqr.
Secretary of the Treasury

Copy, Division of Public Records, Pennsylvania Historical and Museum Commission, Harrisburg.

To Otho H. Williams

Treasury Department
May 31st. 1791

Sir,

It is my wish that you make the Bank of Maryland, which is

established in the Town of Baltimore the place of depositing the Cash belonging to the United States which may be from time to time in your hands as collector of the District of Baltimore.

I shall transmit a circular letter with respect to the receipt of its Notes, to which I must refer you on that point.[1]

I am, Sir   Your most Obedt Servant   Alexandr Hamilton
                                                        Secy of the Treasy

Otho. H. Williams Esqr
Collr.
Baltimore

LS, Columbia University Libraries.
    1. See "Treasury Department Circular to the Collectors of the Customs," June 1, 1791.

From James Blanchard [1]

Philadelphia May 1791

Gentlemen

I enclose you a Letter [2] Similar to a Number that have been Sent to the Officers of the Late Continental army and I beg Leave to give you the reason of its being done.

When Government under the new Constitution was making arrangements for the payment of the public debt the officers from the Massachusetts Line prefered a Memorial to Congress [3] praying some mode might be adopted to ascertain the value of the Certificates they received for their pay and Subsistence at the Conclusion of the war (as other depretiated Curency heretofore had been done) and they be debeted on the public Books for what they had received and the residue be Still due to them.

The representatives of the Southern States Urged the Justice of the Claim and the impropriety of one Class of men accumelating such Large sums for so Small Considerations from the failure and delay of the public to the distress and ruin of another Class of men to whom they were so much indebted for the Freedom and Independence they then Enjoyed.

But the Gentlemen from the Northern States having been purchasers of Final Settlements were of a different opinion and their petition was rejected [4] and a Funding Law passed [5] which ascertained a Note given for £70.18 that had in Seven year accumelated £29.12. to be worth £82. or there abouts.

The Massachusetts officers waited on their representatives on their return to the State, who Informed them that a Funding Law had passed by a *Majority* and the value of their Certificates were Ascertained by the said Law, but if the public paid their debts to Individuals on the Same principles that one Individual was compelled by the Laws of the Country to pay to another, there was a residue that could be paid to the original Creditor.

The Officers wishing for Tranquility & every possible means of Justice, observed that notwithstanding they had alienated their Certificates Similar to all other Bills of public Credit that had been reduced by a scale of depreciation to the Current value and their assigns had received a Retribution from 200. to 500. perCent in Specie by a Law on their purchase, they would be Contented with the residue at it Stood on the public books.

But Last Sessions a remonstrance was presented to Congress under the fictitious Signiture of Original Creditors against the Injustice of the Funding Law in delaying to pay the said residue to the present possessors of Certificates.[6]

This representation come forward at an Unseasonable Time and in such Indecent & Illiberal Terms that Only Mr Morris from the Senate and three Gentlemen from the House of representatives voted for the adoption of it.[7]

And as it was declared by Mr Sedgwick in Congress the 12th. of February 1790 and Confirmed by a Majority of the members that the Army had been fully paid Exclusive of the final Settlements [8]—and that Justice could not be done to other public Creditors, because the greatest part of the public debt was in fictitious Certificates and Mr Beudinot [9] and Other members of Congress had Large Sums of that Species of paper—and it was declared and placed upon record that the Army were a description of men that any farther payment would do them an Injury.

The Officers from different States and at different meetings Signifying their uneasiness from a different Opinion requested the Letter might be Circulated and by the Advice and direction of a Number of respectable Officers I have done it.

I am Gent Your Humble servt

James Blanchard

N.B. I beg leave to refer you to the Journals of Congress Feby. 12. & 16. & 19. &c &c.[10]

Copy, Hamilton Papers, Library of Congress.

1. On a note attached to this letter is written: "Copy of a Letter directed to the Officers of the Lat[e] C[ontinental] Army."

Blanchard addressed a similar, but not identical, letter, dated June 1, 1791, to the officers of the New Hampshire line. This letter is printed in the New Hampshire State Papers (Albert Stillman Batchellor, ed., *Early State Papers of New Hampshire* [Concord, 1893], XXII, 814–15).

Blanchard had served as quartermaster and regimental paymaster of the Third New Hampshire Regiment during the American Revolution. In 1791–1792 he was a persistent opponent of the funding system and an advocate of discrimination in favor of those Revolutionary War soldiers who through necessity had alienated their certificates. Although he was not a member of the New Hampshire Society of the Cincinnati, the published records of that organization include letters written by him to officers of the society and to Samuel Livermore, Representative in Congress from New Hampshire. Blanchard's letters suggest that he was a self-appointed delegate to persuade the soldiers of the Revolutionary Army in the various states to demand from the United States Congress a settlement of their claims. See *The Institution and Records of the New Hampshire Society of the Cincinnati* (Concord, 1893), 58–63.

2. Blanchard is presumably referring to a circular letter dated April 19, 1791, which has not been found. He refers to this circular in his June 1, 1791, letter to the officers of the New Hampshire line as follows: "You will receive a Circular Letter of my Signature of the 19 of April Similar to a Number that have been sent to the Officers of the Late American Army. . . ."

3. An entry in the *Journal of the House* for August 3, 1790, reads:

"A petition of the Officers of the late Massachusetts line of the American Army, in behalf of themselves and the Soldiers of the said line, was presented to the House, and read, praying that further and adequate compensation may be made for military services rendered during the late war.

"*Ordered,* That the said petition do lie on the table." (*Journal of the House,* I, 287.)

4. In the June 1, 1791, letter to the officers of the New Hampshire line, this sentence reads: "But the Representatives from the Northern States being purchasers of Certificates. . . ."

5. "An Act making provision for the (payment of the) Debt of the United States" (1 *Stat.* 138–44 [August 4, 1790]).

6. On December 20, 1790, in the Senate Robert Morris presented "The memorial and remonstrance of the public creditors who are citizens of the commonwealth of Pennsylvania" petitioning for a revision of the Funding Act.

On December 23, 1790, the Senate "*Resolved,* That it would be inexpedient to alter the system for funding the public debt established during the last session of Congress, and that the petition of Thomas M'Kean and others, styling themselves a committee of the public creditors of the Commonwealth of Pennsylvania, cannot be granted" (*Annals of Congress,* II, 1781). This resolution was passed with one dissenting vote from Robert Morris.

7. According to the *Journal of the House,* I, 390, only Elbridge Gerry of Massachusetts and Thomas Scott of Pennsylvania voted in favor of the petition.

8. There is no record in the *Annals of Congress* of this statement by Theodore Sedgwick of Massachusetts on February 12. In the Hamilton Papers, Library of Congress, however, there is a document entitled "For the American daily advertiser," which is written in the same handwriting as the Blanchard letter printed

above. Signed "A Continental," it contains the following "Extract from Mr. Sedgwicks Speech in Congress Feby. 12. 1790: That with regard to discovering who was the original Holder, except so far as respected the army debt it was declared there was no document by which the necessary fact could be discovered.

"That it was Stated as a fact with regard to much the greatest part of the public debt any fictitious name was Inserted.

"That with regard to the army Debt the Soldiers who were in Service at the end of the war received ample Sattisfaction at the time of their Inlistment."

9. Elias Boudinot of New Jersey.

10. On these dates the House considered H's "Report Relative to a Provision for the Support of Public Credit," January 9, 1790. See *Journal of the House*, I, 158, 160, 161; *Annals of Congess*, I, 1267–84; II, 1338–42.

From John Berrien [1]

Savannah, June 1, 1791. "I have the honor to acknowledge the receipt of my appointment as Inspector of the Revenue for the port of Savannah. . . . I take the liberty to inform you, that the excise [2] is by no means a popular measure in this Country—people urge a variety of arguments against it—and it will require propriety & stability in the execution of the several Offices, to carry the Law into effect. Our Supervisor, Mr. Matthews [3] is a gentleman whom I never saw. I presume he is not acquainted with the nature of the business to wh: he is appointed. From its being intirely new to him & as he resides in the upper Country, One hundred & Seventy or Eighty miles from this City (and in this District I imagin nine tenths of the business of the whole State will be transacted) I shall not have an opportunity of geting his advice or support when occasions may require. I shall therefore Sir, if you will permit me, take the Liberty of asking your direction & advice very frequently, wh. I trust you will excuse, when you view my responsibility to the public, & to the individual. . . . I perceive, that my Commission expresses, that I am appointed for the port of Savannah. I presume the district is intended to be included, Yet as there are several ports in the district an explanation will be necessary. . . . I further beg leave to inform you, that in the use & trial of Dycas's & Colles's hydrometers, they appear to exceed the true proof of Spirituous liquors. . . ."

ALS, RG 58, General Records, 1791–1803, National Archives.

1. Having held a post in the Georgia customs service, Berrien applied in 1789 for the position of collector of customs at Savannah. Although he was not named collector, he was appointed surveyor of the port of Savannah in August, 1789.

2. "An Act repealing, after the last day of June next, the duties heretofore laid upon Distilled Spirits imported from abroad, and laying others in their stead; and also upon Spirits distilled within the United States, and for appropriating the same" (1 *Stat.* 199–214 [March 3, 1791]).

3. John Mathews.

Circular Letter from the Officers of the Massachusetts Line of the Late Army [1]

[*Boston, June 1, 1791.* On February 28, 1792, a committee appointed by the "Officers of the Massachusetts line of the late Army" wrote to Hamilton: "By a letter bearing date June 1, 1791, you were informed of the measures adopted in persuing that object." *Letter not found.*]

1. For background to this document, see James Blanchard to H, May, 1791.

From Jonathan Dayton [1]

[*June 1, 1791.* In a letter to Dayton on June 6, 1791, Hamilton referred to "your letter of the first instant." *Letter not found.*]

1. Dayton, a New Jersey lawyer, had been a member of the New Jersey Council in 1789 and speaker of that state's Assembly in 1790. He was associated with John Cleves Symmes in the Miami Purchase.

To Tobias Lear

Treasury Department, June 1, 1791. Requests the commissions for the Virginia inspectors of the revenue.

LC, George Washington Papers, Library of Congress.

From Tobias Lear

[*Philadelphia*] *June 1, 1791.* "In compliance with your request, I . . . transmit the commissions filled with the names as you directed. . . ."

LC, George Washington Papers, Library of Congress.

To Jeremiah Olney

Treasury Department, June 1, 1791. "Your letter of the 24th Ultimo has been received. I approve the intention of the Surveyor to use generally the substitute for Dycas's Hydrometer, the difference being so small. Yet, in any case, where that difference would convert one class of proof into another, Dycas's must govern; unless it should appear by any imported Hydrometer of Dycas's, which you may be able to borrow, that the other is more accurate, or unless it should better correspond with what is stated in the instructions for using those instruments, to be the usual proofs of spirits from different Islands. . . ."

LS, Rhode Island Historical Society, Providence; copy, RG 56, Letters to the Collector at Providence, National Archives; copy, RG 56, Letters to Collectors at Small Ports, "Set G," National Archives.

Treasury Department Circular to the Captains of the Revenue Cutters

Treasury Department
June 1, 1791

Sir,

I have already communicated to you some general instructions [1] to govern you in the execution of your duty as the Commander of the revenue cutter for the [Massachusetts] [2] Station. I have now to inform you that your vessel will be under the management of the Collector of [Boston] as to supplies of provisions, stores, and occasional repairs, and I shall write [3] him to that effect this day. You will on receipt of this letter, communicate to him such information relative to these objects as it would be necessary to give your vessel's owner, were you in the merchants service, with due attention to such variations as the nature of the cutters employment will require. I shall send him a list of what was allowed in one instance and shall be particular otherwise in my instructions to him. I will therefore only add to you that while I am disposed to have the cutter supplied with all real necessaries of such kinds as are requisite to the safety and comfort of the Officers & Men, and the execution of the service, I am very solicitous that the public money may in no instance, nor in any, the smallest degree, be expended for superfluous articles, or such as are extravagant by being shewy or more costly than is necessary.

I am, sir,   Your Obed Servant   Alexander Hamilton

LS, to John Foster Williams, Essex Institute, Salem, Massachusetts; copy, to Simon Gross, Circulars of the Secretary, "Set T," National Archives; copy, to Simon Gross, Office of the Secretary, United States Treasury Department.
  1. Letter not found, but see "Treasury Department Circular to the Captains of the Revenue Cutters," June 4, 1791.
  2. The bracketed material in this document varies according to the captain to whom the circular was addressed.
  3. "Treasury Department Circular to the Collectors of the Customs," June 1, 1791.

Treasury Department Circular to the Collectors of the Customs

Treasury Department
June 1st. 1791

Sir

I have this day written to the Captain of the revenue cutter [1] building for the [Pennsya.] [2] station and I enclose you the letter unsealed which you will deliver to him open after you have caused a copy of it to be made and kept for your own information. It will also be proper that you retain a copy of my circular instructions to him,[3] which are likewise transmitted unsealed.

You will perceive that I have for the present thought it expedient to commit the business of the supplies, and repairs of the cutters to the Collectors of the ports most convenient to their station. In executing this Duty I shall hope for the strictest œconomy in the disbursments which may be found consistent with the safety and comfort of the officers and men, and the effectual execution of the public Service. The establishment not being entirely agreeable to many Members of the community, it will require uncommon care that it be not rendered more exceptionable by any unnecessary expence. A list was transmitted to me by the commander of one of the cutters and after some correction was returned to him with permission to procure the Articles. You may supply [Capt. Montgomery] with such of them as appear necessary. I request that they may be bought on the lowest terms for cash. The discounts on most goods purchased for ready money are considerable, and I wish the public to enjoy the benefit of that kind of dealing. As this letter is circular and some of the Collectors to whom it is addressed may not be experienced in the supplying and equipping of Vessels, I recommend occasional consultations with some suitable person of known Judgment and œconomy who has been or is a Merchant or Master of a Ship or both.

In regard to provisions you will take care that the Cutter be properly supplied with them. Fresh provisions will often be the cheapest, and therefore the supplies may be in a sufficient degree made up of them while in port, but as Cruizes on the coast subject Vessels to be blown off to a great distance sometimes even to the West Indies, it will be always proper that they have salted meat with biscuit and water on board sufficient to subsist them in Case of such an accident.

As public Vessels cannot be registered or recorded agreeably to the act of the 1st. of Septr. 1789 [4] it will be proper that a description of the Cutter be transmitted to the Treasury in order that a proper instrument in lieu of a register be furnished. This description must be in every particular as in the Case of a Merchantship.

The act of Congress [5] extends the hands that may be employed on board to four men and two boys, but as it is very desireable to observe all possible œconomy, which the service will admit, you will ship only such Number as on consideration may be found really necessary.

  I am Sir Your most Obedt Servt.   Alexander Hamilton

LS, to Sharp Delany, Columbia University Libraries; L[S], to Benjamin Lincoln, RG 36, Collector of Customs at Boston, Letters from the Treasury and Others, 1790–1817, Vol. 10, National Archives; LS, Office of the Secretary, United States Treasury Department; copy, United States Finance Miscellany, Treasury Circulars, Library of Congress; copy, RG 56, Circulars of the Office of the Secretary, "Set T," National Archives.

 1. See "Treasury Department Circular to the Captains of the Revenue Cutters," June 1, 1791.

 2. Bracketed material in this document varies according to the collector to whom the circular was addressed.

 3. Letter not found, but see "Treasury Department Circular to the Captains of the Revenue Cutters," June 4, 1791.

 4. "An Act for Registering and Clearing Vessels, Regulating the Coasting Trade, and for other purposes" (1 Stat. 55–65).

 5. Sections 62, 63, and 64 of "An Act to provide more effectually for the collection of the duties imposed by law on goods, wares and merchandise im-

ported into the United States, and on the tonnage of ships or vessels" provided for the construction and operation of the revenue cutters (1 *Stat.* 175 [August 4, 1790]).

Treasury Department Circular to the Collectors of the Customs

Treasury Department
June 1. 1791

Sir,

The Bank of Maryland being in operation,[1] and its paper having gone into circulation, it is my desire, that the cash notes (that is those payable in specie on demand) be received by you in discharge of all duties of impost and tonnage, arrising in your district under the laws of the United States, and that you will exchange whatever specie you may at any time have in your hands for those notes. In order to guard you against counterfeits in this instance, I shall request the directors of that Bank to send you the signatures of the President and Cashier, together with a description of the marks of their notes.

You will also remit, from time to time, whatever money may come to your hands, in specie or the notes of the Bank of Maryland, to that Bank, taking duplicate receipts from its cashier for each deposit, specifying that it is on account of the United States, one of which you will transmit to this office, and retain the other yourself. These receipts will discharge you at the Treasury, for what sums you shall remit. It is my wish, that whenever you have a sum amounting to one hundred dollars, over and above what may be requisite for current expences, that you forward it by the first ⟨safe⟩ conveyance to the Bank. Your weekly returns must specify your remittances.

These measures are intended to enable me as far as possible to avail the public of the revenues arising in your state, without drawing the money out of it, by facilitating the negotiation of draughts, for which there is rarely any demand up⟨on⟩ your place.

I am, Sir,   Your obedt Servant   Alexander Hamilton
                                          Secy of the Treasury

LS, to Otho H. Williams, Office of the Secretary, United States Treasury Department; copy, to Otho H. Williams, Circulars of the Office of the Secretary, "Set T," National Archives.

1. The Maryland legislature chartered the Bank of Maryland in November, 1790, authorizing a capital of three hundred thousand dollars. The organizers opened subscriptions in Baltimore in December, 1790, and acquired two-thirds of their capital within two weeks. Banking operations apparently did not begin until April or May, 1791.

From Thomas Mifflin

[Philadelphia, June 2, 1791]

Sir,

Inclosed I transmit a copy of a letter from the Register General of Pennsylvania,[1] proposing an arrangement relative to the subscription of the State Certificates to the loan of the United States; in which, as it will expedite the business, and furnish the proper checks to the State Officer, I hope it will not be inconvenient to acquiesce at the Treasury of the Union.

I am, Sir   Your most obed Hble Servt.

Phila. 2d. June 1791.
To Alex Hamilton

[E N C L O S U R E]

John Donnaldson to Thomas Mifflin [2]

[Philadelphia, June 1, 1791]

Sir

As the time for subscribing the State Certificates to the loan of the United States has arrived, I think it my duty to submit to the consideration of your Excellency a plan of arrangement that may probably expedite the business & furnish the proper checks to the State Officer with but little trouble to the Creditors of this State intitled to the benefit of the Act of the 9th April last.[3]

The form already prescribed by the Treasury of the United States requires that such State Certificates proposed to be loaned shall be particularly described as to number, date, payee, period to which interest hath been paid & by whom loaned.

In addition to which I beg leave to propose:

That the Secretary to the Treasury be requested to direct That the Certificates to be issued for the proportional part of said loan in 3 ℔ Cent & deferred debt, express by endorsement or otherwise the number of the receipt given at the time of subscribing.

That the Creditors holding said receipts to enable them to receive the compensation proposed by the Act of the 9th of April must produce the said receipt to this office where they shall be credited (in Books to be kept for the purpose) with the proportion of 3 ℔ Cent & deferred debt on which they will be entitled to receive a further allowance from the State & on presenting the Certificates of the United States for the same they shall receive by themselves or their Attornies a Certificate or Certificates payable at the Treasury agreeably to said Act.[4]

I am with great respect &c.   J.D.

Reg. Gen. Office

June 1st. 1791

Tho. Mifflin Esq.
Governor

Df, in writing of Alexander Dallas, Division of Public Records, Pennsylvania Historical and Museum Commission, Harrisburg; LC, Division of Public Records, Pennsylvania Historical and Museum Commission.

1. See enclosure.

2. LC, Division of Public Records, Pennsylvania Historical and Museum Commission.

3. "An Act Granting Relief to Certain Creditors of the State and for Repealing Part of an Act, Entituled 'An Act for Furnishing the Quota of This State Toward Paying the Annual Interest of the Debts of the United States, and for Funding and Paying the Interest of the Public Debts of This State'" (*Pennsylvania Statutes*, XIV, 76–79).

4. The Pennsylvania act of April 9, 1791, provided in part "That every creditor of this state, who shall subscribe to the said loan, proposed by congress . . . shall, besides the certificate or certificates which such creditor is thereupon entitled to have and receive from the United States, . . . be also entitled to have and receive from the comptroller-general and register-general, or other proper officers, who are by law authorized to issue certificates for claims against the commonwealth, certificates [pur]porting that the state stands pledged, from the first of January next, to pay six per cent. interest, annually, on that part of the subscribed debt which is termed the deferred debt, until the United States shall make provision for the payment of the said interest, and also that the state stands further pledged to pay an additional interest of three per cent. annually, from the first day of January next, on that part of the subscribed debt which bears an interest of three per cent., which said three per cent. shall continue to be paid, half yearly, by the state treasurer, unless the United States shall at any time, hereafter, increase the rate of interest of the said three per cent. stock; in which case the interest to be paid by the state shall be proportionately reduced, and the said six per cent. interest on that part termed the deferred debt, shall continue to be paid, half yearly, until the United States shall provide for the payment of

the interest on the said deferred debt; and the said last mentioned certificate or certificates the said comptroller and register-general, or other proper officers aforesaid, are hereby authorized and directed to issue in like form and manner as other public certificates are issued, upon the application of every such creditor, and satisfactory proof being given, that the subscription to the said loan, proposed by congress as aforesaid, has been made and effected according to the provisions, true intent and meaning of this act" (*Pennsylvania Statutes*, XIV, 76–77).

To Thomas Mifflin

[*Philadelphia, June 3, 1791*. The catalogue description of this letter reads "Letter concerning a proposition made by the Register General of Pennsylvania." [1] *Letter not found.*]

LS, sold at American Art Association, April 10, 1929, Lot 255.
    1. See Mifflin to H, June 2, 1791.
    An entry in the executive minutes of Pennsylvania for June 6, 1791, reads: "Copies of a Letter from the Secretary of the Treasury of the United States declaring his acquiescence in the proposition of the Register General relative to the subscription to the loan proposed by the United States were transmitted to the Comptroller General and Register General" (*Pennsylvania Archives*, 9th ser., I, 124–25).

To Thomas Mifflin

[*Philadelphia, June 3, 1791*. "The want of the return of survey of the tract on Lake Erie purchased by Pennsy, from the United States, has hitherto prevented my adopting the measures you have desired [1] for the completion of that business." [2] *Letter not found.*]

LS, sold at Parke-Bernet Galleries, March 26, 1957, Lot 87.
    1. See Mifflin to H, May 5, 1791.
    2. Text taken from dealer's catalogue.

From William Short

Paris June 3. 1791

Sir

I have had the honor of recieving a few days ago, the 3d & 4th. of your letter of April 13th.—one by the way of England, the other by the way of Holland. This is the only letter I have recieved from

ALS, letterpress copy, William Short Papers, Library of Congress.

you since that of Sep. 1. 90. The 1st. & 2nd. have not yet arrived.

It gives me infinite pleasure Sir to find that the manner in which I proceeded in the business you confided to me, has met your approbation. It is the strongest & most agreeable presumption I can have that it will meet also that of the President.

I have the honor of inclosing you Sir, the copy of the letter of the bankers of the U.S. to me [1] covering your 4th. of April 13 mentioned above. This will shew you the present situation of the loan lately opened there, the present value of American stock, & their hope of being soon able to reduce the rate of interest on loans there. I have written to them to inform me with as much precision as they can when they think a loan at a reduced rate of interest may be proposed.[2] It may be proper to observe that I understand they mean 4½ p. cent as the reduced rate. Until I recieve their answer then it is impossible for me to say what measures I shall take in consequence of your authorisation to open a new loan.[3] To proceed immediately to make a loan at 5. p. cent, after the opinion of the bankers that by postponing it it might be done at 4½ would seem highly improper, & yet I must own to you that I do not enter fully into the opinion of the bankers, notwithstanding the desire I shall have to see it realized. I think it necessary to mention this circumstance as well as the following considerations that you may not be misled by the enclosed letter of the bankers.

When I was at Amsterdam the 5. p. cent obligations of the Emperor sold at 2 or 3. p. cent above par, & still I never heard it supposed & am sure it was not supposed by any body that he could borrow at a lower rate of interest. If he could have done it he certainly would in order to have redeemed such as he had a right to reimburse.

The United States are in a less favorable situation than the Emperor for reducing their rate of interest because it is known at Amsterdam that they have a large debt to France of which a considerable part is already due & must be paid without regard to terms & that the price & interest of their domestic debt is such as to present them great advantages in purchasing it up by loans made abroad at 5. p. cent.

1. See enclosure.
2. Short to Willink, Van Staphorst, and Hubbard, May 26, 29, June 3, 1791 (ALS, letterpress copies, William Short Papers, Library of Congress). The letter of May 26 is printed as an enclosure to Short to H, June 10, 1791.
3. See H to Short, April 13, 1791.

But it may be asked why have the bankers, to whom these considerations must have presented themselves, held out an opinion that the rate of interest might be reduced by postponing future loans? 1. It is possible that it may be their real opinion, & if so it is useless to search for any other reason for their holding out. 2. But if it was not their opinion or if they had doubts respecting it, still there are reasons which may have induced them to wish that we should be persuaded of it. They are acquainted with attempts which have been made to purchase our debt to France. They know that the consent of the U.S. will be necessary to the success of any of these attempts. The better the terms on which we suppose we can make new loans, the less we shall be disposed to consent to those which are asked by the persons wishing to purchase. It is possible also that they may be informed by means of the Genoese correspondents at Amsterdam of some disposition in them to make loans to the U.S. A hope that we could borrow at Amsterdam at a lower rate of interest would be the most effectual means of preventing us from giving the present rate at Genoa. Besides the business of loaning on the domestic debt of the U.S. is still carried on at Amsterdam. The house of V. Staphorst is immediately & ostensibly interested in them—that of Willink also indirectly in all probability. It is desirable therefore for them to postpone the loans of Congress as long as this business lasts, provided however that they should ultimately be made there. (It was calculated when I was in Amsterdam that this business would cease when the domestic debt rose to 75. p. cent, but as they alienated them proportionably higher in these loans, they were continued notwithstanding the rise in the domestic debt as mentioned in my letter to you of Jan 15.) Further the bankers contemplate a rise in the commission in proportion as the rate of interest is lowered. This rise in the commission they mentioned to me as being altogether in favor of the undertakers—whether so or not I cannot say, but I have no doubt they would prefer making a loan at an increased rate of commission & decreased rate of interest, to the inverse.

Thus enabled to appreciate fully the circumstances attending the opinion of the bankers you will not be surprized if the reduced interest should not take place as soon as they seem to hope. Still you may be persuaded Sir, that I shall cherish the idea & do whatever depends on me to have its realisation accelerated.

I shall have the less difficulty in delaying the proposition for a new loan also in order to see whether the rate of interest can be reduced, because I find that you use more delay in employing the money borrowed than I had supposed you would. It would have been an advantage if the last loan [4] had been opened two or three months later, since the interest paid on a great part of it for four months viz from Feb. 1. till now might have been avoided, as well as that which has accrued on the rest from the time of the bonds being delivered. Such losses may be avoided on future loans if you were to give more early directions for the employment of the money as recieved. If on the contrary you do not give directions until you have notice of the loan being opened there will be always three or four months interest at least, as in the last instance, unnecessarily paid. I have already mentioned to you that when a loan is opened, constant usage obliges the bankers to recieve the money immediately, if the undertakers chuse to deposit it, & to allow interest from the first of the month. Three months after that, must be allowed for the notice going to America & orders being recieved thereon; so that four months interest, on a moderate calculation, will always be paid before the money is used. In the last loan 600,000 florins, I think, were recieved in the latter part of February— of course interest paid on them from the 1st. of that month although employed only now.

There is another inconvenience also with respect to the part which is intended to be paid this country. As they are always acquainted with the loans opened at Amsterdam & of course know that the U.S. have money there at their disposition, they cannot account for its not being paid them. They take up various ideas with respect to the delay & some of them far from being favorable to the U.S. As the exchange is becoming every day more disadvantageous in proportion as the *assignats* depreciate, many of them suppose it is a speculation, to hold back the payment as much as possible in order to take advantage of this depreciation. You will easily see how impossible it would be to convince of the contrary those who know that the U.S. have had at their disposition large sums for three months past during which time the assignats have gone on regularly depreciating.

If only the ministry meddled with this matter there would be much less inconvenience in it, but in the new organisation of affairs a great

4. For a description of this loan, see Short to H, February 17, 1791.

number of new people are brought into action, all of whom cast themselves to become as conspicuous as possible in clamouring for the public interest. The American debt has particularly excited the attention of a number of them & above all of the six new commissioners of the treasury.[5] They have made several visits to M. de la fayette respecting it. They have sent me several messages through him, & one of them, M. de Condorcet,[6] lately wrote him the letter inclosed No 1.[7] which he sent me. He added that as an American, he could not help telling me how much he wished that the U.S. should do whatever they could to satisfy these exclamations. This was eight or ten days before I recieved your orders to pay the million of florins.[8]

From this letter & some other circumstances I feared there would be difficulty made by the new commissioners of the treasury in recieving their payment at the present rate of exchange, particularly as they desire it to be put into the hands of their bankers at Amsterdam, & as a part of it is to be applied to the loan made there by France for the U.S.[9] On recieving your orders I informed M. de Montmorin [10] that I was now ready to have another payment made. He desired I would take arrangements with the Director of the treasury; [11] who without hesitation requested that it should be made in the same manner as the last & He will of course send his reciept to the bankers for the sum in livres equal to the million of florins according to the present rate of exchange which is much more favorable than it was at the time of the former payment, & which you are informed was highly advantageous to the U.S.

With respect to the ½ million of florins which you destine ultimately for this country & which are to wait for further directions, as I am not acquainted with the reasons which induced you to postpone these directions, I cannot conjecture when they will be given, & of course shall avoid being questioned about them here as much as pos-

5. In March, 1791, the Assembly reorganized the public treasury. It placed authority in the hands of a committee of six commissioners appointed by the King.

6. Marie Jean Antoine Nicholas Caritat, Marquis de Condorcet, one of the Encyclopedists.

7. Enclosure not found.   8. See H to Short, April 13, 1791.

9. For a description of this loan, see Willink, Van Staphorst, and Hubbard to H, January 25, 1790, note 3.

10. At this time the Comte de Montmorin was French Minister for Foreign Affairs.

11. Bertrand Dufresne.

sible. It is tautology to add that as this sum is already in the hands of the bankers the U.S. will be paying an unnecessary interest on it until employed.

There is another consideration also which is worthy of being taken into the account. The depreciation of the assignats so long as they continue to be a circulating medium is an advantage to those who have debts to pay to France by remittances from abroad. But this depreciation has been such for some time past as to give serious apprehensions that the time may come & that ere long, when it must be forced out of circulation. In that case the exchange would unavoidably turn in favor of France on account of the immense sums of specie which have been sent out of the country & the effort which would be then made to restore the equilibrium by their return. In such an event you will readily see the loss which the U.S. will sustain from having not extended to the utmost their payments under present circumstances.

It is impossible to give as certain any conjecture respecting these assignats & of course what I have said must be understood with that limitation. You will be able to form a more satisfactory opinion yourself perhaps from the following observations. The lands by which they are to be redeemed are selling every where without opposition. It becomes every day more evident that their mass exceeds the highest estimation—the assignats arising on those sales are entering regularly into the treasury & are publicly burnt. Upward of 120. millions (one tenth of the whole emission) have already gone through this process, & yet the depreciation continues regularly. There was one extraordinary moment when the difference between this paper & specie was 19. p. cent. It was brought back to ten & is now at twelve p. cent, with the probability of continuing to encrease. It is to be observed that this takes place in a time when they have not war either foreign or domestic, & before the experiment is made on the new system of taxation. To those who think with me, that the greater part of the taxes proposed would not be paid soon under any system of perception, & that the system adopted is the one the least likely to raise taxes of any kind whatever, the experiment when made cannot be considered as favorable to the credit of the assignats. There seems no doubt now that there will be a necessity for a new emission of assignats before the taxes voted some days ago (as you will see by the Journals sent to the Secretary of State) can be collected under the most favorable supposition. If to this cause of discredit should be added intestine dissensions & civil war which in the present state of parties & weakness of the government, cannot be considered improbable, it is impossible to say that the assignats will not so far depreciate as to be no longer capable of answering the purposes of a circulating medium.

I have thought it my duty to mention these circumstances to you as they may serve instead of a better guide, in examining the French debt & the mode of repaying it under the several aspects to which it will be presented to you. I gave you several ideas on this subject in my letter of April 9. As they consisted in transferring the debt from the French government to individuals either in France or Genoa, or some other foreign country, & as the assignats would be the necessary vehicle for that operation it is essential that you should be made acquainted with their present, & as far as can be done, their future situation. So long as they continue in circulation, the fall in their value & the rise of American credit will necessarily facilitate any such translation & render it more advantageous for the U.S. But should any disaster, or any of the circumstances mentioned above throw them out of circulation, before orders could be recieved from you, it of course would defeat any plan formed on them. It will be necessary therefore I think, if you should judge proper to make use of any of the ideas suggested to you either in this or a former letter, & adopt any system in consequence of them, to do it with a view to the possibility of the assignats ceasing to be a medium of circulation before your orders could be recieved & executed.

I have spoken to Mr. Grand the son (one of the house of that name which has always acted for the U.S., & which perhaps has as little confidence in their credit as any house in Paris) with respect to the plan of making loans in assignats here in order to pay off the French debt, & giving bonds to secure the lenders against further depreciation. He took time to consider of it. We have since spoken of it & he seems fully persuaded it might be done. I mentioned to him that I had no authority to set such a plan on foot—of course that I did not chuse it to become a matter of public consideration here—but that if after a proper examination he considered there was a probability of carrying such a scheme into effect for the advantage of the U.S., I would recommend it to your consideration. The caution he considered himself bound to use in his enqueries, has prevented his consulting with as many of the monied people as he would have chosen; still the opinion he seems to have founded on his own observations & those of a few others, induces me to renew to you my wishes that you would take the subject into consideration.

It is useless to mention that the advantages resulting from this plan would be to relieve the U.S. in a short period from the part of their debt already due to France—the placing it probably in a more advantageous rate of interest & the leaving the loans to be made in Holland free to be employed in the sinking of the domestic debt. In that case Congress would certainly find it advantageous to extend the operation beyond the two million of dollars already embraced by their act.[12]

Such foreigners, Dutch, Genoese, or others as are reimbursed here by this country in assignats, would probably prefer recieving the bonds of the U.S. payable either at Amsterdam or Genoa. In that case the assignats they would lend the U.S. would be estimated according to the existing rate of exchange & of course would be an advantageous operation for the U.S. The instructions you give must necessarily be such as to authorize the embracing the several combinations which may take place so as to sieze the most favorable. This will require that your instructions should be very full & very much in detail with respect to each contingent. It will be necessary also that your views with respect to the necessity of discharging without delay the foreign debt due & the propriety of changing that to become due & that this may [be] judged of, your ideas with respect to the operation of purchasing up the domestic debt, should be known. And after all the latitude which must still be left is such as no individual probably would be bold enough to act in. I mention this because I feel as to myself a total incapacity to act alone in a case of so much delicacy & where there would be so much room for censure, as that of changing entirely the nature of the foreign debt. It would seem to me essential in order that every advantage under every change of circumstances should be made use of, that those to whom this business may be confided should be at least two. They will be more likely in proportion to their number, to lose no opportunity of acting for the advantage of the U.S., from the timidity which every individual must unavoidably be influenced by in such a case. The several ministers which the U.S. have or may have

12. See "An Act making Provision for the Reduction of the Public Debt" (1 *Stat.* 186–87 [August 12, 1790]).

at the courts of Europe might very well act together in this business either by assembling at Paris if it was thought necessary or by correspondence. The latter mode would most probably suffice; as after having decided on a view of the circumstances of the moment, which might be done by letter, what measures were proper to be taken, their execution might be left to the person who may reside here.

The following alternatives will probably present themselves to their examination & choice. 1. To pay off the French debt due or to become due, by loans made here in assignats, giving the bonds of the U.S. payable here for a certain sum of specie, either in weight or in crowns of six livres. 2. By loans made here giving bonds payable either at Amsterdam, Genoa, or elsewhere as may be agreed on with the lenders, & expressed in the money of that country agreeably to the value of the livre Tournois according to the then rate of exchange. 3. To open loans at Amsterdam Genoa or elsewhere & to recieve bills on Paris, or French stock such as the Government should agree to recieve, the bonds of the U.S. being expressed in the money of the country agreeably to the value of the bills or stock recieved. 4. To open such loans recieving part in cash, to be transmitted to you, & part in bills or stock of the above kind. Other alternatives may also present themselves; but these I think you may consider as sufficiently probable to merit your examination & instructions thereon. The circumstances of this country however are necessarily so unsettled & so subject to change, that it is impossible to say how long they will continue thus favorable for an operation much to be desired & highly beneficial for the U.S. It is for that reason Sir that I have taken the liberty of thus urging it on your consideration. You would no doubt regard it as an abuse of your time if I were to detain you longer by adding the propriety of discharging without delay, at least that part of the debt to France which has become due & the advantages of employing the loans made in Holland at 5. p. cent or lower, to the purchase of the domestic debt. The certainty that so long as money can be placed in the domestic funds at an high rate of interest by purchasing them under par, considerable sums will be diverted from the productive operations of agriculture & commerce to that kind of barren speculation, suffices alone to demonstrate the public benefit which would result from raising them at least to that point.

My letters which you mention having not recieved will not change

your determination with respect to the offers of Schweizer & Jeanneret. The *tariff* to which they allude & of which you desire the explanation [13] is that fixed by Congress for the rate at which foreign
coin is to be recieved in the collection of the duties.[14]

Since my return to Paris I have been obliged to see these people because they were referred to me by the Minister [15] as mentioned in my
letter of May 4 although their character and reputation could not but
render such interviews disagreeable. I told them at once that I did not
think their propositions would be accepted. They urged me much to
treat with them adding they had been informed that I had sufficient
powers to treat conditionally subject to the ratification of the President. They offered in that case to change their terms for the advantage of the U.S. As I had every reason to believe that they were not
in a condition to fulfill their engagements, & that they were made the
ostensible persons merely that if the bargain turned out a bad one, it
might be avoided on their part & further that they meant to make use
of any conditional agreement they might induce me to sign, in order
to draw after them those people on whom they counted for support,
I declined any kind of treaty, adhering to what I had previously told
them, that I would communicate to you any terms they might offer,
& that if I thought them acceptable I would add my recommendation
for their acceptance.

I observed to them however the propriety of their employing M.
de Ternant who was about to embark for America,[16] & who might recieve instructions from the minister to take definitive arrangements
on this subject. I added that in order to insure the success of the operation it would be necessary 1. That M. de Ternant should be authorized
to say that it was desired by the ministry. 2. That he should be fully
satisfied that they (Schweizer & Jeanneret) had sufficient powers & a
sufficient capital either of themselves or of those for whom they
acted, to fulfill such engagements, & should be able to say so to the
government of the U.S. 3. that the terms they offered should be ac-

13. See H to Short, April 13, 1791.
14. For the rates of exchange for foreign coins and currency, see Section 40
of "An Act to provide more effectually for the collection of the duties imposed
by law on goods, wares and merchandises imported into the United States, and
on the tonnage of ships or vessels" (1 *Stat.* 167–68 [August 4, 1790]).
15. Comte de Montmorin.
16. Jean Baptiste de Ternant had been appointed French Minister Plenipotentiary to the United States.

ceptable, & therefore that a considerable latitude should be left to M. de Ternant in fixing them.

They had told me that they were willing now to change their former offers so as to give up entirely the commission asked & to diminish the number of florins to be recieved so as to give up to the profit of the U.S. one million on the whole operation provided the debt of the U.S. amounted to 40. million of livres, or at that rate for a smaller sum. I added that I would recommend to your acceptance, such proposals provided the conditions abovementioned with respect to M. de Ternant were fulfilled by them.

They accordingly sent me a supplement to their former offers accompanied by the papers marked No. 2.[17] & herewith enclosed. On my observing to them that they mistated in their supplement their conference with me, they abolished that statement & sent me a new supplement together with the papers marked No. 3.[18] This supplement therefore is to be considered as containing the terms they offer at present. They are 1. to obtain from the French government the bonds of the U.S. & to recieve from the U.S. in lieu of them at the rate of 18 millions of florins for 40 millions of livres, for the part already due & at the rate of f. 7,000,000, for 40,000,000 ₶, for the part to become due.

By the standard fixed by Congress the calculation of these people makes 40,000,000 livres equal to f. 18,974,359—of course in fixing their demand at 18 millions they state this sacrifice at nearly a million, whereas in truth according to the par between Paris & Amsterdam 18,-000,000 florins are equal to 40,000,000 ₶.

I saw M. de Ternant after they had written to me that they had satisfied him with regard to their powers & their ability to perform their engagements, & he told me they had given him no such satisfaction. M. de Montmorin told me also that he had recommended the plan [19] of these people because M. Lambert [20] the then Comptroller general approved it, but he seemed to think now that M. Lambert had adopted the opinion without examination, that these people had the funds to make good their engagements.

17. Enclosure not found.   18. Enclosure not found.
19. See Short to H, December 18, 1790.
20. Charles Guillaume Lambert had succeeded Jacques Necker as French Controller General of Finances in September, 1790, and was removed from office one month later by the Assembly.

On the whole I believe myself, that they are two adventurers who have gone on this principle; that if they could engage the ministry to bind themselves to recieve assignats & the U.S. to give their bonds at par there would be such a gain that the Capitalists of Genoa, Paris or elsewhere would gladly support them as the fall in the value of the assignats would leave an immense profit, that if on the contrary they entered into a contract which should turn out ill, they having nothing to lose had nothing to fear. You will be able to learn from M. de Ternant how far these powers & abilities extend & to him alone I must refer you as they have given me no other proof of them than the letter of M. Lambert written last fall & forwarded to you from Amsterdam.[21]

This affair will after all present itself to you under the following conditions. 1. M. de Ternant will not undertake to answer for the abilities of Schweizer & Jeanneret, which I think will certainly be the case, & of course, it must end there. Or 2. he will answer for them & offer to enter into negotiation with you, & in that case, he will be authorized to give more advantageous terms than those proposed in the supplement. The exchange between Paris & Amsterdam is now more than 20. p. cent in favor of the latter. This is the real standard by which you should be guided. The expences of commission & the profit which the lenders of such a mass would have a right to expect must of course be taken into the account. In such a case I should think it highly advantageous for the U.S. to accept the terms, as it would be effecting at once a measure of which I have stated the benefit above. You may insist also on a part of the bonds being made payable at Genoa or elsewhere than Amsterdam, wch. you will certainly consider as desirable for the U.S.

I mentioned to you in my letter of Feb. 17. what had passed between Mr. Morris & myself respecting a loan for the U.S. in the low countries. I have lately satisfied myself that I had been mistaken in supposing that foreign powers were not allowed to borrow there. I am waiting now therefore with much impatience for your sentiments on that subject, which I may now expect without delay. I have no doubt myself that it would be advantageous for the U.S. to open a loan there for the money to be remitted to France, even if the terms were the same with those at Amsterdam, on account of having a credit at more than one place. Still as I may so soon expect to hear from you

21. See Short to H, December 18, 1790.

on that subject I have determined not to make the experiment there until then, unless I find that a loan can be obtained at an inferior rate of interest; which however is not to be hoped. As soon as I recieve an answer from the bankers therefore to whom I have written to know when they think the U.S. could with propriety propose the loan at the reduced rate they mention, I shall take measures for informing myself if I could now make a loan in the low countries at 4½ p. cent & in that case I shall think myself warranted to set it on foot. Should I find however that this could not be done at less than 5. p. cent, & should no answer come from you, I shall not think myself fully authorized to transfer your loans thither, as I am sure of being able to obtain the one ordered by you, at that rate at Amsterdam.

I have not for some time seen the Genoese minister [22] who is now in the country. I imagine his constituents are making the proper inquiries with respect to the present situation of the credit of the U.S. & I take it for granted they will be fond of making them loans.

The information which you desire respecting the establishment of the mint in the United Netherlands,[23] I fear it will be difficult to acquire with exactitude without being on the spot. The time of my being there will depend of course on the time of a new loan being made. Still I shall endeavour to collect the best information I can from thence whilst absent & will forward it, as also that which you desire concerning their E. India company. When I was there it was considered that their affairs were in the most declining posture, & since I have left that place, they have authorized individuals to partake in that commerce with them except only I think as to gun powder, arms, & some other articles, which is a proof that they do not consider the company's resources as adequate to it. With respect to the present situation of the affairs of the Eng. East-India company you will see the most authentic details in their present Parliamentary debates which you recieve of course.

I inclose you an *Appercu* of the revenue & expences of this country for the present year & also a plan of *Tontine* which I have not yet read & of course know not whether it is worthy of your attention.

My former letters have said so much of the advantage of recieving from you authenticated copies of the revenues of the U.S., the state

22. Christoforo Vincenzo de Spinola.
23. See H to Short, April 13, 1701

of their commerce & other papers of the kind,[24] that I will not repeat it at present, as I do not doubt you will be fully convinced of it.

I have the honor to be with sentiments of the most perfect esteem & respect   Sir   your most obedient & most humble servant

W: Short

P.S. The letters which I have written to you since those mentioned in that of Jan. 25. of which last you acknowlege the reciet are as follows: Feb. 7, 17, 22. March 4, 11. from Amsterdam—April 9, May 4. from Paris.

The Honble. Alexander Hamilton Secretary of the Treasury.

[E N C L O S U R E]

Wilhem and Jan Willink, Nicholaas and Jacob Van Staphorst, and Nicholas Hubbard to William Short[25]

Amsterdam 23 May 1791

Sir

We have the honor to inclose a Letter We received for you this Morning ℔ the English Mail, which brought us late Intelligence from America.

It is with satisfaction We inform you, that We have delivered near all the Bonds of the Loan of March, and that the actual Price for them is ¾ ℔ Cent above Par. They will probably still rise, and We flatter ourselves sufficiently high, by postponing yet some time any proposals for a new Loan, to enable us to obtain the Subscription for the next Loan for the United States at a reduced rate of Interest. Every thing promises fair to bring about this desirable Point, and You know You can rely upon our utmost Exertions, to improve, the favorable Circumstances to the benefit of the United States.

We are respectfully   Sir   Your most obdedient and very humble servants.   Wilhem & Jan Willink

N & J. Van Staphorst & Hubbard

Willm. Short Esqr. Paris

24. See Short to H, February 22, March 11, and April 9, 1791.
25. LS, Short Family Papers, Library of Congress.

From Nathaniel Appleton

Boston, June 4, 1791. ". . . Your Circular Letter 27th May is received. It has not been in my power to see the Treasury of this State since your Letter came to hand but I am very confident that this State never redeemed a Continental public security by issuing their own obligation. This State has loaned considerable Sums of Old paper money which was recd. for taxes & public Securities which were received for the Sale of Lands which I presume was not contrary to the Act of Congress.[1] I duely noticed the first of June as it respected nonscribers & it has turned out as I expected. I have only one of that discription & I don't know but he will recant before the Quarter Closes."

LC, RG 53, Massachusetts State Loan Office, Letter Book, 1785–1791, Vol. "259–M," National Archives.
   1. "An Act making provision for the (payment of the) Debt of the United States" (1 *Stat.* 138–44 [August 4, 1790]). For background to "old emissions" to which Appleton is referring, see Appleton to H, February 5, 1791, note 1.

Treasury Department Circular to the Captains of the Revenue Cutters

Treasury Department
June 4 1791.

Sir

As you are speedily to enter upon the Duties of your Station, it becomes proper briefly to point them out to you. Accordingly I send you a copy of the Act [1] under which you have been appointed & in which are contained your powers, & the objects to which you are to attend & I shall add such observations as appear to me requisite to guide you in fulfilling the intent of that Act.

LC, to John Foster Williams, RG 36, Collector of Customs at Boston, Letters from the Treasury and Others, 1790–1817, Vol. 10, National Archives; copy, to Simon Gross, Office of the Secretary of the Treasury, United States Treasury Department; copy, to Simon Gross, RG 56, Circulars of the Office of the Secretary, "Set T," National Archives.
   1. Sections 62, 63, and 64 of "An Act to provide more effectually for the collection of the duties imposed by law on goods, wares and merchandise imported into the United States, and on the tonnage of ships or vessels" (1 *Stat.* 145–78 [August 4, 1790]) deal with the construction and operation of the revenue cutters.

It may be observed generally that it will be, in a particular manner, the province of the Revenue Cutters to guard the Revenue Laws from all infractions or ⟨br⟩eaches either upon the Coasts or within the Bays, or ⟨up⟩on the Rivers & other Waters of the United States, pre⟨vi⟩ous to the anchoring of Vessels within the *harbours* ⟨for⟩ which they are respectively destined.

Hence it will be necessary for you from time to time to ply along the Coasts in the neighbourhood of your Station, & to traverse the different parts of the Waters which it comprehends. To fix yourself constantly or even generally at one position would in a great measure defeat the purpose of the establishment. It would confine your vigilance to a particular Spot, & allow full Scope to fraudulent practices every where else.

The 63d. section of the Act herewith transmitted declares that the Officers of the Revenue Cutters are to be deemed Officers of the Customs & enumerates certain powers with which they are to be invested.[2] The 30th. section specifying two of the same powers that of demanding Manifests & that of Searching Vessels, enters into some details concerning them.[3] These two sections require particular attention as

2. Actually H is referring to Section 64 (1 *Stat.* 175). For an explanation of the discrepancy in numbering, see H to Richard Harison, April 26, 1791, note 2. Section 64 reads as follows: "*And be it further enacted,* That the officers of the said boats or cutters, shall be appointed by the President of the United States, and shall respectively be deemed officers of the customs, and shall have power and authority to go on board of every ship or vessel which shall arrive within the United States, or within four leagues of the coast thereof, if bound for the United States, and to search and examine the same and every part thereof, and to demand, receive and certify the manifests herein before required to be on board of certain ships or vessels, and to affix and put proper fastenings on the hatches and other communications with the holds of ships or vessels, and to remain on board the said ships or vessels until they arrive at their places of destination."

3. Actually H is referring to Section 31 (1 *Stat.* 164–65), which reads as follows: "*And be it further enacted,* That it shall be lawful for all collectors, naval officers, surveyors, inspectors, and the officers of the revenue cutters herein after mentioned, to go on board of ships or vessels in any part of the United States, or within four leagues of the coast thereof, if bound to the United States, whether in or out of their respective districts, for the purposes of demanding the manifests aforesaid, and of examining and searching the said ships or vessels; and the said officers respectively shall have free access to the cabin, and every other part of a ship or vessel; and if any box, trunk, chest, cask, or other package, shall be found in the cabin, steerage or forecastle of such ship or vessel, or in any other place separate from the residue of the cargo, it shall be the duty of the said officer to take a particular account of every such box, trunk, cask or package, and the marks, if any there be, and a description thereof; and if he shall judge proper to put a seal or seals on every such box, chest, trunk, cask or pack-

marking the outline of your authority & duty. But in the capacity of Officers of Customs you will possess some other powers & be bound to perform some other duties which are not mentioned in these sections. You will have a right for example & it will be your duty to seize Vessels & Goods in the cases in which they are liable to seizure for breaches of the Revenue Laws, when they come under your notice. But all the powers you can exercise will be found in some provisions of the Law, & it must be a rule with you to exercise none with which you are not clearly invested. In every case of doubt you will follow the advice of the Officer to whom you will be refered in a separ⟨ate⟩ Letter. On points of importance which admit of delay, you may correspond with the Secretary ⟨of⟩ the Treasury.

The 9th. 10th. 11th. & 12th. sections which re⟨late⟩ to manifests will also require your particular attention.[4] The due observance of the provisions of these sections is considered as of material consequence to the security of the Revenue, & ample time having been allowed for them to be generally known & complied with, it is now indispensible that they should be strictly enforced.

You will perceive that they are only required in respect to Vessels belonging wholly or in part to a "Citizen or Citizens, Inhabitant or Inhabitants of the United States." [5] It is understood that by Inhabitant is intended every person *residing* in the United States whether *Citizen* or *Foreigner*. The reason of this limitation is, that Citizens & *resident* Foreigners are supposed to be acquainted with the Laws of the Country; but that foreign Citizens residing in foreign Countries have not

---

age; and such account and description shall be by him forwarded to the collector of the district to which such ship or vessel is bound. And if upon her arrival at the port of her entry, the boxes, trunks, chests, casks or packages so described, or any of them shall be missing, or if the seals put thereon be broken, the master or commander of such ship or vessel shall forfeit and pay for every such box, trunk, chest, cask or package so missing, or of which the seals shall be broken, two hundred dollars. And it shall also be lawful for the inspectors who may be put on board of any ship or vessel, to secure after sunset in each evening, the hatches and other communications with the hold of such ship or vessel, with locks or other proper fastenings, which fastenings shall not be opened, broken or removed, until the morning following, or after the rising of the sun, and in presence of the inspector or inspectors by whom the same shall have been affixed, except by special license from the chief officer of the port. And if the said locks or other fastenings, or any of them, shall be broken or removed during the night, or before the said rising of the sun, or without the presence of the said inspector or inspectors, the master or person having the charge or command of such ship or vessel, shall forfeit and pay the sum of two hundred dollars."

4. 1 *Stat.* 155–57.   5. Section 9 (1 *Stat.* 155).

the same knowledge & consequently ought not to be subjected to penalties in regard to a thing which they might not know to be necessary.

But since you cannot be presumed to know before hand what Vessels are owned in whole or in part by Citizens or Inhabitants, it will of course be your duty to demand the Manifests of all indiscriminately, & to report those from which you do not receive them, to the Collectors of the Districts for which they are respectively first destined. You will also keep a record of all the Vessels from which you demand Manifests, not only of those from which you receive them, but of those from which you do not receive them, & of the Districts for which they are bound, & you will at the end of every month (pursuing the division of the year by the Calendar) send me an abstract of your Record.

Careful attention is likewise due to the 13th. & 14th. sections of the Act.[6] It is of importance that Vessels should not break bulk, or put

6. Section 13 reads as follows: "*And be it further enacted,* That if after the arrival of any ship or vessel so laden with goods as aforesaid, and bound to the United States, within the limits of any of the districts of the United States, or within four leagues of the coast thereof, any part of the cargo of such ship or vessel shall be unladen for any purpose whatever, from out of such ship or vessel as aforesaid, within the limits or distance aforesaid, before such ship or vessel shall come to the proper place for the discharge of her cargo or some part thereof, and shall be there duly authorized by the proper officer or officers of the customs to unlade the same, the master or other person having the charge or command of such ship or vessel, and the mate or other person next in command, shall respectively forfeit and pay the sum of one thousand dollars; and the goods, wares and merchandise so unladen and unshipped, shall be forfeited and lost, except in the case of some unavoidable accident, necessity or distress of weather; of which unavoidable accident, necessity or distress, the master or other person having the charge or command of such ship or vessel, shall give notice to, and together with two or more of the mariners on board such ship or vessel, shall make proof upon oath before the collector or other chief officer of the customs of the district, within the limits of which such accident, necessity or distress shall happen, or before the collector or other chief officer of the first district of the United States within the limits of which such ship or vessel shall afterwards arrive, if the said accident, necessity or distress shall have happened not within the limits of any district, but within four leagues of the coast of the United States, (which oath the said collector or other chief officer is hereby authorized and required to administer)" (1 *Stat.* 157–58).

Section 14 reads as follows: "*And be it further enacted,* That if any goods, wares or merchandise so unladen from on board of any such ship or vessel, shall be put or received into any other ship, vessel or boat, except in the case of such accident, necessity or distress as aforesaid, to be notified and proved as aforesaid, the said master or other person having the charge or command of the ship, vessel or boat into which the said goods shall be so put and received, and every other person aiding and assisting therein, shall forfeit treble the value of the said out any part of their cargoes, even temporarily, previous to a regular entry & permission obtained, except in cases of real necessity to be duly reported & proved. You will observe that besides the penalties on the Master & Mate of the Vessels from on board of which any Goods shall have been illegally removed, the Master or Commander of the Vessel or boat into which they may be received, & all Persons aiding in the removal, are liable to a forfeiture of treble the value of the Goods removed, & the Vessel or boat into which they may be received is also subject to forfeiture. It is well known that one of the most extensive cases of illicit trade is that which is here intended to be guarded against, that of unlading Goods before the arrival of a Vessel into Port in Coasters & other small Vessels which convey them clandestinely to land. Hence the bare removal of Goods from one Vessel to another is made penal, though they may not have been landed. Nor will the pretext of their being intended to be replaced avail any thing. The provisions of these sections admonish you to keep a very careful eye upon the motions of coasting Vessels without however interrupting or embarassing them unless where some strong ground of suspicion requires that they should be visited & examined.

The execution of the 15th. section of the Act [7] must essentially depend on the Revenue Cutters. It is easy to see that it would be dangerous to the Revenue for Vessels to be permitted to go at pleasure from one part of the United States to another, without announcing themselves to some proper Office. Hence though each *may proceed on her voyage* from a more *exterior* to a more *interior* District to which she may be bound, yet none can go back from a more interior to more exterior District or from one part of the United states to another, without first reporting herself to the Collector of the District

---

goods; and the said ship, boat or vessel shall also be forfeited and lost" (1 *Stat.* 158).

7. Section 15 reads in part as follows: "*And be it further enacted,* That if any ship or vessel which shall have arrived within the limits of any district of the United States from any foreign port or place, shall depart or attempt to depart from the same, unless to proceed on her way to some more interior district to which she may be bound, before report or entry shall have been made by the master or other person having the charge or command of such ship or vessel, with the collector of some district of the United States, the said master or other person having such charge or command shall forfeit and pay the sum of four hundred dollars. And it shall be lawful for any collector, naval officer, surveyor, or commander of any of the cutters herein after mentioned, to arrest and bring back, or cause to be arrested and brought back, such ship or vessel, to such port of the United States to which it may be most conveniently done" (1 *Stat.* 158).

in order that she may come under the notice & precautions of the Law. Nor can this be deemed a hardship seeing her report will not oblige her to unlade any part of her cargo, but she may afterwards proceed with it wheresoever she pleases.

I have now noticed to you the principal parts of the Law which immediately relate to the execution of your duty. It will however be incumbent upon you to make yourself acquainted with all the Revenue Laws which concern foreign Commerce or the Coasting Trade, a knowledge of the whole spirit & tendency of which cannot but be a useful Guide to you in your particular sphere. You will observe that the Law contemplates the Officers of Cutters in certain Cases remaining on board of Vessels until they arrive at their places of destination,[8] & with a view to this it is, that so many Officers have been assigned to each Cutter. It is not however expected that this will be done in every case, & it must be left to the discretion of the commanding Officer when it shall be done. Where there is a Vessel, the lading of which is of very great value or which has any considerable quantity of Goods on deck or in other situations from which they can readily be removed, or where the nature of the Cargo is such as to admit more easily a clandestine landing, or from the highness of the duty to afford a more than ordinary temptation or where any suspicious circumstances appear; in these & the like cases it will be well to let an Officer accompany the Vessel to her place of destination. The want of a Manifest will be a circumstance in favour of so doing. It will not however be adviseable to make known the circumstances under which it is deemed most peculiarly proper to use these precautions; as it might sometimes unnecessarily give offence. It may be always left to be understood that it is the practice whenever the *state* of the Cutter renders it convenient. You are empowered among other things to affix seals on packages found in certain situations. For this purpose proper seals will be prepared & transmitted. Till they are received any others may be made use of. The principal design of this provision is to identify the packages found in such situations.

It will be expected that a regular journal be kept in each Cutter in the same manner as far as circumstances are applicable, as is practised in Sea voyages; & that all occurences relative to the execution of the Laws & to the conduct of all Vessels which come under their notice be

8. Section 64 (1 *Stat.* 175).

summarily noted therein, & that a copy of this journal to the end of each month be regularly forwarded to the Treasury.

It has also occurred that the Cutters may be rendered an Instrument of useful information concerning the Coast, inlets, bays, & rivers of the United States & it will be particularly acceptable if the Officers improve the opportunities they will have (as far as shall consist with the Duties they are to perform) in making such observations & experiments in respect to these objects as may be useful in the business of navigation communicating the result from time to time to the Treasury.

While I recommend in the strongest terms to the respective Officers, activity, vigilance & firmness, I feel no less solicitude that their deportment may be marked with prudence, moderation & good temper. Upon these last qualities not less than upon the former must depend the success, usefulness, & consequently *continuance* of the establishment in which they are included. They cannot be insensible that there are some prepossessions against it, that the charge with which they are entrusted is a delicate one, & that it is easy by mismanagement to produce serious & extensive clamour, disgust & odium.

They will always keep in mind that their Countrymen are Freemen & as such are impatient of every thing that bears the least mark of a domineering Spirit. They will therefore refrain with the most guarded circumspection from whatever has the semblance of haughtiness, rudeness or insult. If obstacles occur they will remember they are under the particular protection of the Laws, & that they can meet with nothing disagreeable in the execution of their duty which these will not severely reprehend. This reflection & a regard to the good of the service will prevent at all times a spirit of irritation or resentment. They will endeavour to overcome difficulties, if any are experienced, by a cool and temperate perseverance in their duty, by address & moderation rather than by vehemence or violence. The former stile of conduct will recommend them to the particular approbation of the president of the United states, while the reverse of it, even a single instance of outrage, or intemperate or improper treatment of any person with whom they have any thing to do in the course of their duty, will meet with his pointed displeasure, & will be attended with correspondent consequences.

The foregoing observations are not dictated by any doubt of the prudence of any of those to whom they are addressed. These have been selected with so careful an attention to character as to afford the strongest assurance that their conduct will be that of good Officers & good Citizens. But in an Affair so delicate & important it has been judged most advisable to listen to the suggestions of caution rather than of confidence & to put all concerned on their guard against those sallies to which even good & prudent men are occasionally subject. It is not doubted the instruction will be received as it ought to be, & will have its due effect. & that all may be apprised of what is expected, you will communicate this part of your orders, particularly, to all your Officers & you will inculcate upon your Men a correspondent disposition.

The 5th. Section of the act [9] transmitted you requires that all Officers appointed pursuant to that Act should take a certain Oath therein specified. The act of the 1st. day of June 1789 [10] requires that you should also take the oath to support the Constitution of the United states. These oaths each of your Officers must take before some Judge of the United States, if access can conveniently be had to one, if not before some other Magistrate, duly empowered to administer oaths, & a certificate from him of the taking it must be transmitted to the Comptroller of the Treasury.

I am Sir your obedient servant. Alexander Hamilton.

9. 1 *Stat.* 153–54.
10. "An Act to regulate the Time and Manner of administering certain Oaths" (1 *Stat.* 23–24 [June 1, 1789]).

Treasury Department Circular
to the Commissioners of Loans

Treasury Department
June 4. 1791.

Sir

You will by the post *immediately* succeeding the closing of your books, preparatorily to the payment of interest, in *each* quarter, transmit to the Treasury a summary of the amount of each kind of stock then standing on your books, in order to the requisite provisions for making such payment.

I am, Sir,   Your obedt. servant   Alex. Hamilton

LS, to James Tilton, Delaware Historical Society, Wilmington.

From Joseph Whipple

Portsmth. New Hamp. June 4. 1791

Sir

In consequence of a Circular letter of the Asistant Secretary dated the 10th. of March last [1] a few weeks since received, I herewith inclose you Returns of the decked Vessels built in the District of Portsmouth N. H. for two Succeeding years, the first commencing the 4th. of March 1789.

The Same letter Signifid to me your wish to have forwarded from time to time as they may come into my hands "any documents that have relation to the Commerce, Navigation, Fisheries, Manufactures, or Productions of the State, either in the time of the province, or in that of the Commonwealth." This request shall be carefully attended to, & such documents forwarded, should any come to my hands. In the meantime, conceiving that such circumstances respecting those objects, which may have fallen under my own observation, or that have otherwise come to my knowledge would be acceptable, in lieu of such documents, I will now mention them generally.

Commerce & Navigation commenced at the earliest period of the Settlements on the River Piscataqua increasing gradually till the year 1775. From the year 1720 to 1760 there was a Considerable trade with Spain to which Nation were Shiped large quantities of Fish, Oak Timber, plank & Staves. From 1760 to 1775 Shipbuilding had so much greatly increased & there were annually built 30 to 40 Sail of two decked Vessels of 180 to 350 tons, besides Smaller ones, with one deck. The two decked Vessels were principally employed in supplying the English West India Islands with Sundries whence they proceeded to

LC, Collector of Customs at Portsmouth, Letters Sent, 1790–1791, Vol. 2, National Archives; copy, RG 56, Letters from the Collector at Portsmouth, National Archives.

1. Treasury Department Circular to the Collectors of the Customs, March 10, 1791, signed by Tench Coxe (LS, Hamilton Papers, Library of Congress).

England freighted with the produce of the Islands & were sold in England. Many Vessels also going directly to different ports in England loaded with Lumber were there sold. A great Number of Ships were also built on acct of British merchants residing in England & Scotland. The Single decked Vessels (rigged Sloops, Schrs. & Brigs) were employed also in supplying the Islands with Lumber & Fish, which Supp[ly] voyages extended to the Dainish & Dutch Islands & Settlements on the main & also to those of France & Spain when they could get admittance into their ports. The Vessels taking freight for England remitted the proceeds of their Lumber Cargoes to Europe in Bills or to America in produce, & those returning bringing with them the different productions of those Islands & Settlements which were vended partly at home, & the residue exported to the neighbouring provinces, chiefly to the Carolinas, Virginia & Maryland in exchange for Corn & other provisions. Agriculture was little attended to, the Settlemts. being circumscribed to the limits of 30 or 40 Miles from the Sea Coast & the Settlers employed in procuring lumber, neglected their attention to Farming.

The Productions of New Hampshire in provisions was not Sufficient to Support the inhabitants till after the peace between France & England which took place in the Year 1762.[2] Since that period, the Settlements have been extended to the Western boundaries of the State, & so far, that the procuring of Lumber on account of the distance for its transportation has ceased to be an object with the Settlers, they have therefore been confined in that article to the amount of their own consumption for building their Houses &c, & have bent their attention to the cultivation of their Lands.

The Manufactures of New Hampshire tho' considerable, are without System * or Patronage.† More or less has been done in Linnen,

---

* Among our Manufactures however may be enumerated, Several Forges, Works for Manufacturing Bar Iron, One Furnace, One Rolling & Slitting Mill, 4 or 5 Oyl Mills, A Number of Fulling Mills & one Manufactory of Sail Cloth.

† In exception [to] these remarks, it must be Noted that the Sail Cloth Manufactory is a well regulated undertaking of a Single proprietor & the Rolling & Slitting Mill had the Assistance of the Legislature [3] by a generous grant.

2. This was the preliminary peace treaty of the Seven Years' War.

3. "An Act to encourage the erecting of Mills for Slitting, Rolling and Plating Iron, and to encourage and promote the Manufacturing of Nails within this State," passed by the New Hampshire legislature on September 22, 1787, provided a seven-year abatement of taxes for the owners of slitting or rolling mills and a premium of one hundred pounds on the first slitting mill erected (*Acts and Laws of the State of New-Hampshire* [Exeter, n.d.], 453–54).

Woolen & Cotten for many years. This is principally performed in private families in the Country, every Farmhouse having its Utensels for manufacturing the wool & flax produced by its proprietor together with a proportion of imported Cotton. These manufactures are of great use in the families where they are carried on, Serving in part for their cloathing; but too much of them are exchanged for foreign Superfuities. About the Year   [4] a number of families from the North of Ireland came into the State & settled about 40 miles from the Sea, who being acquainted with the Manufacture of Linen have carried it on in a greater degree of perfection than any other in the State, which their descendents continue to this day. These people were very usefull & had the emigrations continued, great benefit would have derived to the Country from their example of Industry & Economy, but the ill judged policy of the day, founded on Superstitious opinions, put a Stop to the migration of all foreigners to the State.

The productions of New Hampshire had been almost confined to its Lumber & its Fisheries till since the peace of 1762 above mentioned. The produce of Beef, Wheat, Rye, Indian Corn & Pulse have since that period increased with the Settlement of the inland Townships & are now produced in great quantities; but wheat is produced only in the more distant Towns from the Sea Coast. Pot & Pearl Ashes is now also become an article in our Manufactures of great importance.

The greater part of the produce of the new Townships are transported by Land to Massachusetts, whence many of the Settlers emigrated. The Situation of the Roads admitting of a conveyance equally eligible & the Seat of government or rather the Sessions of the Legislature shifting from place to place & not being confined to, or indeed scarcely ever held in the Capital of the State, but little commercial intercourse is formed between it & the back Country. Hence the productions of the State are carried to & exported from Massachusetts & the Foreign Articles here consumed imported into & purchased from the Importers in that State, a Circumstance greatly prejudicial of our own State though probably of no national consequence.

The present State of Commerce & Navigation being perfectly known to you from the Returns continually making, no observations there on are necessary. I have the Hn to be &c

4. Space left blank in MS.

To Otho H. Williams [1]

Treasury Department
June 4th. 1791.

Sir,

I send you herewith sundry papers, relating to applicatons of John MacRae and John Morrison to the Judge of the District Court of Virginia, upon the Act for the remission or mitigation of penalties. This transaction appears to me thus far in an *extremely questionable* shape, so that I am very far from being satisfied, that there has not been more than inadvertence in the case. Unwilling nevertheless to precipitate a forfieture as long as there is a chance of new light to evince innocence, I have concluded to give you the trouble of a further investigation. To this I am led by the additional consideration that if any fraud has been committed, these documents and the circumstances which have been brought into view may serve as a clue to it.

It appears extraordinary that the omission which took place should have happened at Baltimore where it could have been attended with no trouble to comply with the law—that the business should have been permitted to proceed to condemnation before any step was taken—that the evidence of the due importation of the goods should not have been rendered more precise and certain.

You will observe that even the last affidavit of Mr. Fraser, *that* taken before the Justice, is extremely vague and loose. It does not specify where the goods were imported nor when nor in what vessel or vessels.

I request therefore that you will send for Mr. Fraser, and, if willing, examine him concerning the above particulars, and such others as may occur to you calculated to elucidate the affair. When this is done, you will examine the entries and documents in your office to ascertain whether any goods of the description of those mentioned in the papers, as to marks Numbers &ca. have been entered with you. You will cause Mr. Frasers examination to be put in writing and get him to swear to it before some proper Magistrate, and you will officially certify whatever may appear to you from the records and documents in your office. When this is done you will forward the examination and your certificate to the Judge before whom the proceedings were had, in order that he may transmit them to me as a supplement; and you will return to this office the papers herewith transmitted.

In executing this business you will I doubt not probe the case with all the care which its suspicious appearance calls for, and if you discover any fraud that has been committed you will take the proper steps to enforce the penalties of the law.

I am, with great consideration   Sir,   Your obedt Servant.

Alexander Hamilton

Otho H. Williams Esqr
Collr.
Baltimore

LS, Columbia University Libraries.
    1. For background to this letter, see H to Cyrus Griffin, February 15, 1791.

From Otho H. Williams

Baltimore 4th. June 1791

Sir

I have, this day, received, under cover, a letter from you to Messrs. Elliot & Williams,[1] which I shall forward by the first opportunity.

This day, also, I have received a letter from Mr. E. Williams, dated "Fort Washington May 3d. 1791." informing that he was preparing to leave that Country, and expected to be in Hagarstown in all this month, June.

He also informs that he will forward in the month of May, and that he will bring with him the vouchers necessary for closing the accounts of Elliot and Williams in the Treasury.

I am, Sir, Your most Obedient   Humble Servant   O. H. Williams

Alexander Hamilton Esqr.
Secretary of the Treasury

ADfS, Maryland Historical Society, Baltimore.
    1. Letter not found. Robert Elliot and Elie Williams had contracted to supply the western posts in 1789.

From William Short

Paris June 5. 1791

Sir

Since my letter of the day before yesterday I have procured the inclosed works on the fabrication of money. Supposing they may be useful to you on the question at present under your consideration I have the honor of forwarding them. One is a report of the committee of money made to the national assembly,[1] another the speech of Mirabeau on the subject,[2] & a third the observations of an artist of merit presented to the committee. I am promised also by one of the directors of the mint, their *Reglemento,* & other articles which he says will be useful. It has been impossible to get them for this opportunity, by a person who goes to join M. de Ternant,[3] but they shall be sent by the next together with an additional work of Mirabeau, which it is said will appear in ten or fifteen days. I must observe that M. de Condorcet,[4] who is considered as a man of knowlege in these matters, though I think too theoretical in all, told me that the inclosed papers as well of Mirabeau as of the committee were exceedingly defective & contained false principles. This is submitted to your examination.

The Honble.
Alexander Hamilton Secretary of the Treasury

AL, letterpress copy, William Short Papers, Library of Congress.
1. Since there were three reports by the Committee on Coinage, it is not apparent to which one Short is referring. The committee reported to the National Assembly on November 2, December 9, and December 12, 1790. The Assembly discussed the merits of bimetallism, the ratio of gold to silver, recoinage, composition and fineness of coins, denominational units, and costs of coinage. See Charles Gomel, *Histoire Financière de L'Assemblee Constituante* (Paris, 1896–1897), II, 470–79.
2. Honoré Gabriel Riquetti, Comte de Mirabeau, a liberal nobleman, had been elected president of the National Assembly in January, 1791. He died in April, 1791.
3. Jean Baptiste de Ternant.
4. Marie Jean Antoine Nicholas Caritat, Marquis de Condorcet.

To Jonathan Dayton

[*Philadelphia, June 6, 1791.* "My determination on the subject mentioned in your letter of the first instant [1] is still suspended on the answer of the Attorney General, which has not yet been given." [2] *Letter not found.*]

ALS, sold at Anderson Galleries, April 28, 1915, Lot 162.
   1. Letter not found.
   2. Text taken from extract of letter in Adrian H. Joline, *Catalogue of Autographs and Portraits of Members of the Continental Congress Including Signers of the Declaration of Independence* (New York, 1897).

From William Ellery

Custom-House
Newport [Rhode Island] June 6 1791

Sir,

   I received a letter from the Surveyor of the Port of Warren [1] some time ago inclosing a letter from you of the 13th. of Decr. 1790. relative to the lawful portion of the compensations the Surveyors are respectively to receive for their services.[2] It is I am sensible my duty to pay them their lawful portions of fees received by me; but a dispute has arisen between the Surveyors of Warren & Barrington and the Surveyor of this Port [3] respecting their rights to the fees arising on Registers, Enrollments and Licenses which they wish you would decide. The dispute seems to turn upon the meaning of the *expression such fees as shall arise*, in the 31 Sec: of the Coasting Act. The distributory part of the Sec: which relates to this question runs thus "and where there is more than one Surveyor in any District, each of them shall receive his *proportionable part* of *such fees as shall arise* in the port for which he is appointed." [4] The Surveyor of the Port of Warren & Barrington claims a right to a proportionable part of the fees for Registers, Enrollments and Licenses of Vessels *belonging to the Port* of which he is Surveyor, and the Surveyor of this port says that he alone is entitled to them; because all vessels belonging to this District are registered, enrolled and licensed in this port, and of consequence the fees *arise* in this port. The Surveyor of

Warren &c e contra says that the *fees arise* in the port where the vessel belongs, that he doth not consider the Surveyors as entitled to any part of the fees for registering, enrolling and licensing vessels on account of any services they perform relative to those acts; especially since an allowance has been made to them for the admeasurement of vessels; but as intended as a part of their compensation for services in general.

This letter was framed some time ago, and would have been sent to you, if the Surveyor of this Port had not informed me that he had written to you on the subject.[5]

I have lately received a letter from the Surveyor of North Kingstown,[6] in which he writes thus "it will be necessary for me to come to Newport as there are some monies in your office that I am interested in vizt for Enrollments, Clearances &c of vessels belonging to this Port, as thereby I shall be able to make a complete Statement of the Emoluments of my office." The other Surveyors in this District may make similar claims.

It is not only the wish of the Surveyors, but mine also that you would be pleased, as early as may be convenient, to communicate your sentiments on this matter; for until this dispute is decided by you there will be an uneasiness, and the Surveyors will not be able it seems to exhibit complete accounts of their Emoluments.[7]

I am Sir   Yr. most obedt. servant   W Ellery Collr.

A Hamilton Esqr
Secry of the U. S.

LC, Newport Historical Society, Newport, Rhode Island.
  1. Nathaniel Phillips.
  2. No letter from H to Phillips on this date has been found, but see H to Thomas Arnold, December 13, 1790.
  3. Daniel Lyman.
  4. "An Act for Registering and Clearing Vessels, Regulating the Coasting Trade, and for other purposes" (1 *Stat.* 64 [September 1, 1789]).
  5. Letter not found.
  6. Daniel Eldridge Updike.
  7. Ellery endorsed the letter book copy of this letter "Answered Sepr. 16 1791." H's reply has not been found.

From William Ellery

Custom House
Newport [Rhode Island] June 6th 1791

Sir,

On the 3d. instant I recd. your circular letters of the 13th. & 25th of May last. I do not recollect that in any instance duties on goods brought into this district have been ascertained otherwise than on the *actual landing* thereof, and by the measuring, weighg. & gauging, where those operations are required by law. A particular attention will be paid to your direction in that respect.

Your opinion relative to the termination of the authority of Inspectors put on board of vessels in one district to go to another I am happy to know, because the law is not explicit on that head.

I will inform myself as accurately as I can what tare is customary among merchants in this District &c and will communicate such information by the next Post. Before the receipt of your letter on the preceding subjects, I wrote a letter to you dated May 23. 1791 in which I mentioned generally the custom of merchants here, and the practice of the Custom-house in regard to the mode of calculating the tare of goods, requesting your opinion on that part of the Collection Law.[1]

I have delivered your letters directed to the Navl. Officer and Surveyor of this Port,[2] and intimated to them that it would be agreeable to you that their returns of the emoluments of their respective offices should be for one year following the time of their entering upon their duty, instead of the year mentioned in your circular letter of the 14th of April; and have given the same intimation to the Surveyors of the other ports in this District in letters [3] in which I have inclosed your letter to them respectively. This letter will be accompanied with a weekly return of monies received and paid and a monthly schedule of bonds, with a draft upon me by the Treasr. in favour of the Cashr. of the bank of N. A. No. 1460 for Five Hund. dolls., and the copy of an Endorsment of the change of Master, on a Certif: of Reg. No 2, granted at this Port.

I am, Sir, yr. most obedt. servt.

W Ellery Collr

Secry of Treasy.

LC, Newport Historical Society, Newport, Rhode Island.

1. Section 35 of "An Act to provide more effectually for the collection of the duties imposed by law on goods, wares and merchandise imported into the United States, and on the tonnage of ships or vessels" provided for the drafts and tares on imported articles (1 *Stat.* 166 [August 4, 1790]).

2. Robert Crooke and Daniel Lyman. Neither of these letters has been found.

3. Ellery's circular to the Rhode Island surveyors, dated June 3, 1791, may be found in the Newport Historical Society.

From Thomas Smith

Loan Office [Philadelphia] Pennsa: June 6th 1791.

Sir

As the holders of Certificates in the Debt of this State are now presenting them at this Office for deposit agreable to the Act of the 4th Augt. 1790 [1] I think it my duty to apply to you for any farther

LC, RG 53, Pennsylvania State Loan Office, Letter Book, 1790–1794, Vol. "615-P," National Archives.

1. Sections 13, 14, 15, 16, and 17 of "An Act making provision for the (payment of the) Debt of the United States" outlined the program for assumption by the Federal Government of state debts incurred during the American Revolution. These sections read as follows:

"Sec. 13. *Be it therefore further enacted,* That a loan be proposed to the amount of twenty-one million and five hundred thousand dollars, and that subscriptions to the said loan be received at the same times and places, and by the same persons, as in respect to the loan herein before proposed concerning the domestic debt of the United States. And that the sums which shall be subscribed to the said loan, shall be payable in the principal and interest of the certificates or notes, which prior to the first day of January last, were issued by the respective states, as acknowledgements or evidences of debts by them respectively owing, except certificates issued by the commissioners of army accounts in the state of North Carolina, in the year one thousand seven hundred and eighty six.

"*Provided,* That no greater sum shall be received in the certificates of any state than as follows; that is to say:

"In those of New Hampshire, three hundred thousand dollars.

"In those of Massachusetts, four million dollars.

"In those of Rhode Island and Providence Plantations, two hundred thousand dollars.

"In those of Connecticut, one million six hundred thousand dollars.

"In those of New York, one million two hundred thousand dollars.

"In those of New Jersey, eight hundred thousand dollars.

"In those of Pennsylvania, two million two hundred thousand dollars.

"In those of Delaware, two hundred thousand dollars.

"In those of Maryland, eight hundred thousand dollars.

"In those of Virginia, three million five hundred thousand dollars.

"In those of North Carolina, two million four hundred thousand dollars.

"In those of South Carolina, four million dollars.

"In those of Georgia, three hundred thousand dollars.

Instructions you may judge necessary in the execution of this business the situation of which appears as follows. This State has been Issuing consolodated certificates for a number of small ones but as some of those Certificates are dated since the first of Jany. 1790, altho' the holders of them say they were prior to that Date, I have

"*And provided,* That no such certificate shall be received, which from the tenor thereof, or from any public record, act, or document, shall appear or can be ascertained to have been issued for any purpose, other than compensations and expenditures for services or supplies towards the prosecution of the late war, and the defence of the United States, or of some part thereof during the same.

"Sec. 14. *Provided also, and be it further enacted,* That if the total amount of the sums which shall be subscribed to the said loan in the debt of any state, within the time limited for receiving subscriptions thereto, shall exceed the sum by this act allowed to be subscribed within such state, the certificates and credits granted to the respective subscribers, shall bear such proportion to the sums by them respectively subscribed, as the total amount of the said sums shall bear to the whole sum so allowed to be subscribed in the debt of such state within the same. And every subscriber to the said loan shall, at the time of subscribing, deposit with the commissioner the certificates or notes to be loaned by him.

"Sec. 15. *And be it further enacted,* That for two thirds of any sum subscribed to the said loan, by any person or persons, or body politic, which shall be paid in the principal and interest of the certificates or notes issued as aforesaid by the respective states, the subscriber or subscribers shall be entitled to a certificate, purporting that the United States owe to the holder or holders thereof, or his, her or their assigns, a sum to be expressed therein, equal to two thirds of the aforesaid two thirds, bearing an interest of six per centum per annum, payable quarter yearly, and subject to redemption by payments, not exceeding in one year, on account both of principal and interest, the proportion of eight dollars upon a hundred of the sum mentioned in such certificate; and to another certificate, purporting that the United States owe to the holder or holders thereof, his, her or their assigns, a sum to be expressed therein, equal to the proportion of thirty-three dollars and one third of a dollar upon a hundred of the said two thirds of such sum so subscribed, which after the year one thousand eight hundred shall bear an interest of six per centum per annum, payable quarter yearly, and subject to redemption by payments, not exceeding in one year, on account both of principal and interest, the proportion of eight dollars upon a hundred of the sum mentioned in such certificate; and that for the remaining third of any sum so subscribed, the subscriber or subscribers shall be entitled to a certificate, purporting that the United States owe to the holder or holders thereof, his, her or their assigns, a sum to be expressed therein, equal to the said remaining third, bearing an interest of three per cent. per annum, payable quarter yearly, and subject to redemption by payment of the sum specified therein whenever provision shall be made by law for that purpose.

"Sec. 16. *And be it further enacted,* That the interest upon the certificates which shall be received in payment of the sums subscribed towards the said loan, shall be computed to the last day of the year one thousand seven hundred and ninety-one, inclusively; and the interest upon the stock which shall be created by virtue of the said loan, shall commence or begin to accrue on the first day of the year one thousand seven hundred and ninety-two, and shall be payable quarter yearly, at the same time, and in like manner as the interest on the stock to be created by virtue of the loan above proposed in the domestic debt of the United States.

refused them as I think the Act of Congress precludes them.[2]

The Interest is endorsed on those Certificates paid to Jany. 1st 1792.[3] at the State Treasury but no signature. The method I have taken with what has been presented has been to send them to the Comptroller of this State [4] for examination. He declares them right but puts no mark of Approbation on them. The Checks he says are necessary in his Office and Cannot therefore be spared. This method is attended with great loss of Time and risque which at this time is particularly inconvenient.

If a method could be devised for the holders of them to present their accounts of them to the Comptroller of this State & he would certify they were genuine & assumable it would be safe & convenient.

I wish for the Safety of the Office I could be permitted to make an Office mark on each Certificate of State Debt received such as striking a mark thro' with a sharp Iron thus ⚓ which it would make without taking a piece out. As the people are possessed of Certificates Issued by this State under the late funding law [5] in lieu of Certificates Issued by the United States have it in their power to possess themselves of their original Certificates on refunding the Interest they

"Sec. 17. *And be it further enacted,* That if the whole sum allowed to be subscribed in the debt or certificates of any state as aforesaid, shall not be subscribed within the time for that purpose limited, such state shall be entitled to receive, and shall receive from the United States, an interest per centum per annum, upon so much of the said sum as shall not have been so subscribed, equal to that which would have accrued on the deficiency, had the same been subscribed in trust for the non-subscribing creditors of such state, who are holders of certificates or notes issued on account of services or supplies towards the prosecution of the late war, and the defence of the United States or of some part thereof, to be paid in like manner as the interest on the stock which may be created by virtue of the said loan, and to continue until there shall be a settlement of accounts between the United States and the individual states; and in case a balance shall then appear in favour of such state, until provision shall be made for the said balance." (1 *Stat.* 142–44 [August 4, 1790].)

2. Smith is referring to Section 13 of "An Act making provision for the (payment of the) Debt of the United States." See note 1. See also "Report on Certificates of Debt Issued After January 1, 1790," February 25, 1791, note 1.

3. Section III of "An Act Granting Relief to Certain Creditors of the State and for Repealing Part of an Act, Entitled 'An Act for Furnishing the Quota of This State Toward Paying the Annual Interest of the Debts of the United States, and for Funding and Paying the Interest of the Public Debts of This State'" provided in part that interest to January 1, 1792, be marked on the back of the certificates of state debt and paid to the holder before the certificates should be subscribed to the Federal loan (*Pennsylvania Statutes,* XIV, 77–78 [April 9, 1791]).

4. John Nicholson was comptroller general of Pennsylvania.

5. "An Act for the Further Relief of the Public Creditors who are Citizens of This State by Receiving on Loan Certain Debts of the United States of

have received from the State by returning Indents in Lieu thereof, I have therefore received no such state Certificates on Loan to the U states. People who had Loaned before your orders 9th May [6] for making endorsement on the back of their Certificates if required viz. Issued in Lieu of Certain Loan office Certificates which were issued between 1st Septr. 1777. & the 1st of March 1778 are applying for similar endorsements.[7] Is it proper I should make them if required?

Mr. Tench Francis Cashier of the Bank [8] has applied to me for a form similar to that furnished by the register of the Treasury for payment of Interest at the Bank. I informed him of my readiness to accomodate and comply with any orders I might receive from you but did not think myself authorized to make any Alterations of the present forms without express orders. If Sir you chuse to gratify him I shall most chearfully execute any form in the power of Sir   Your &c.

Honble. Alex. Hamilton Esqr. Secy of Treasy. U. S.

America and for Funding the Same and for Paying the Annual Interest of Such Loans and the Interest of Certain Debts of This State Every Six Months" (*Pennsylvania Statutes*, XII, 158–64 [March 1, 1786]). For the provision concerning the return of "new loan" certificates to which Smith is referring, see Smith to H, February 14, 1791, note 1.

6. Letter not found.

7. In a resolution of September 9, 1777, Congress had provided that interest on loan office certificates issued after the date of the resolution should be paid in bills of exchange (*JCC*, VIII, 725). This offer expired on March 1, 1778. Certificates issued under the resolution, however, continued to receive preferential treatment. On June 28, 1790, Congress resolved that interest on these certificates be paid on the nominal value and the depreciated value be used only for purposes of redemption (*JCC*, XVII, 568).

8. Francis was cashier of the Bank of North America from November 26, 1781, until January 12, 1792.

Treasury Department Circular
to the Commissioners of Loans

Treasury Department
June 6th. 1791

Sir,

In consequence of an enquiry made of me, I think it necessary to inform you that I consider the holders of Certificates received from the Government of any State in lieu of certificates of the federal debt, as having a right to *subscribe* those State Certificates to the Loan of the Assumed debt, and I consider the State as having a right to subscribe the continental Certificates which they have obtained by the exchange to the Loan proposed by the Act of the 4th. August 1790;[1] but *no interest* is to be paid on the Assumed debt of the State either to the State or to individuals, until you shall be informed, that I am satisfied, that all the certificates so issued by the State have been re-exchanged or redeemed, or that all those, which shall not be re-exchanged or redeemed, have been surrendered to the United States.

To distinguish in a clear and striking manner this description of New Loan Certificates from all others, I have determined to have a hole, of about one fifth of an inch, cut through a part near the centre, being at the end of the blank left for the creditors name immediately before the word "*is*" and directly over the letter "*t*" in the word "*amount*".

When the Stock represented in these certificates shall be transferred from and to the Loan Offices or the Treasury, the transfer certificates must have this central hole cut or punched through them in like manner.

In order to full information, on this subject, I request you to transmit to me a copy or sufficient extract from any laws passed by the Legislature of the State in which you reside, relative to the exchange of federal Certificates for those of the State, and to the re-exchange of those of the State for federal Certificates, in doing which you will be careful to collect whatever there may be.

You will also communicate such observations as may appear necessary for the perfect understanding of the course, which the business has taken.

I am Sir   Your Obedt. servt.   Alexander Hamilton

Copy, to Thomas Smith, Division of Public Records, Pennsylvania Historical and Museum Commission, Harrisburg.

1. "An Act making provision for the (payment of the) Debt of the United States" proposed "a loan to the full amount of the said domestic debt" (1 *Stat.* 139). See "Treasury Department Circular to the Commissioners of Loans," May 27, 1791.

To Benjamin Lincoln

Treasury Department
June 7th. 1791

Sir

Before the receipt of your letter of the 25th. of May the question concerning the true intent and meaning of the Act to amend and explain the last impost law, relative to printed, stained, and coloured goods [1] had arisen from another quarter.

In determining the articles to which the amendatory act will apply the defect alledged to exist in the original law seems proper to be had fully in view. The clause to be explained and amended [2] was that which laid a duty upon chintzes and coloured calicoes, which are *printed* goods, and it should therefore seem, that it was intended for the purpose of including all those goods, which are of the nature and resemblance of calicoes and chintzes, and which belong to the printing branch, some of which being of *linen,* and of *cotton and linen* mixed were not deemed within the letter of the original clause. Those goods, which are fabricated out of different coloured linen or cotton yarns such as Haerlem stripes, British checks &c. and which are not appurtenant to the *printing* branch do not appear to me to be included.

There is manifestly considerable doubt concerning the true meaning of this clause from the two respectable opinions, which you mention in your letter. This circumstance alone is sufficient to justify you in not requiring the duty of 7½ from the importers of striped and checked goods not appurtenant to the printing branch, for it is conformable with law, and with sound policy that dubious clauses should be construed favorably to the importer.

I am, Sir,

Ben. Lincoln Esq.
Boston.

L[S], RG 36, Collector of Customs at Boston, Letters from the Treasury, 1789–1807, Vol. 4, National Archives; copy, RG 56, Letters to the Collector at Boston, National Archives; copy, RG 56, Letters to Collectors at Small Ports, "Set G," National Archives.

1. Section 2 of "An Act to explain and amend an act intituled 'An Act making further provision for the payment of the debts of the United States'" provided for a duty of seven and one-half percent ad valorem for "printed, stained, and coloured goods" (1 *Stat.* 198 [March 2, 1791]).

2. This was the first section of "An Act making further provision for the payment of the debts of the United States" (1 *Stat.* 181 [August 10, 1790]).

From Jeremiah Olney

Providence, June 7, 1791. "I have received your Two circular Letters of the 25th and 26th of May.[1] The information contained in the first, relative to the Emoluments of the Officers of the Customs, I have communicated to the Naval Officer and Surveyors of this District, agreeable to your request. I shall attend to what you say in providing for the Boat wanted for the Service of this Harbour. . . ."

ADfS, Rhode Island Historical Society, Providence; copy, RG 56, Letters from the Collector at Providence, National Archives.

1. Circular of May 25 not found. On May 25, 1791, H wrote a letter to Olney marked "circular" which has not been printed as a Treasury Department circular to the collectors of the customs because the contents were clearly intended only for Olney. This letter may, however, be the Treasury Department circular of May 25 to which Olney is referring.

From William Seton

New York 7 June 1791

Sir

I am desired by the President & Directors to acknowledge the honor of your letter of the 30 May;[1] this having been the first board day since its reception. The President & Directors of this Bank will chearfully Co-operate in the measures you point out for the reception of subscriptions to the National Bank; and have given me Orders to comply with the tenor and spirit of your Letter, which shall be done with the greatest pleasure conforming myself to the pointed observations you make on the subject and as extensive a communication of the arrangement shall be made as will cope with the object.

I have the honor to be. &c.

LC, Bank of New York, New York City.

1. Letter not found, but see H to the President and Directors of the Bank of Massachusetts, May 30, 1791.

To Thomas Jefferson [1]

Treasury Department
June 8th 1791.

Sir

It has occurred to me that it would be productive of very useful information if some Officer of the United States in each foreign Country, where there is one, were instructed to transmit, occasionally, a state of the coins of the Country specifying their respective standards weights, and values, and, periodically, a state of the market prices of gold and silver in coin and bullion, and of the rates of foreign exchange, and of the rates of the different kinds of labour as well that employed in manufactures as in tillage.

I would beg leave to request if there appears to you no inconvenience in the thing that an instruction may be sent for the above purpose and that copies of the statements which shall from time to time be received in consequence of it may be furnished to the Treasury.

I have the honor to be with great respect   Sir,   your obedient servt.   Alexander Hamilton

The Secretary of State.

LS, James Madison Papers, Library of Congress.
1. In *HCLW*, IV, 58–59, and *JCHW*, IV, 162, this letter is dated June 21, 1791.

To John McComb, Junior

Treasury Department
June 8. 1791

Sir

I have this day written to Col. Thomas Newton [1] of Norfolk in Virginia on the subject of your letter of the 23rd of May.[2] It is my wish that you may proceed without delay upon the terms mentioned to him. I doubt not you will carefully and justly estimate the extra work in the foundation (should it prove necessary to go deeper than is stipulated in the contract) but as the matter is placed by law under the ultimate direction of the President, your charge with the contract you make must be submitted to him. In case your demand should appear too high in the judgement of the President a condition will be admitted that the value of that extra work may be determined by three indifferent persons.

I am sir   Your Obed. servant   Alexander Hamilton

Mr. John McComb Jun.
Princess Ann County
Virginia

LS, Miss Elizabeth Ball, Oakhurst, Indiana.
  1. Letter not found.
  2. Letter not found.

To Thomas Newton, Junior

[*Philadelphia, June 8, 1791.* On June 8, 1791, Hamilton wrote to John McComb, Jr.: "I have this day written to Col. Thomas Newton." *Letter not found.*]

To Charles Pettit

Treasury Department June 8th. 1791.

Sir

I have received your letter of the 31st. of May. Inclosed are two statements shewing the *precise sums* of New Emission money, which have been paid over to the State of Pennsylvania, those which have been disposed of as on account of the United States, and the sum which is understood to be now in the Treasury.

These statements will, I presume, answer every purpose, which can be desired, in regard to the settlement of accounts between the United States and the State of Pennsylvania.

It is not perceived in what manner the surrender of the sum now in the Treasury can contribute to that end; and while such a surrender is not required by the original form of the business, it would be wholly inexpedient, as involving the possibility of an encrease of the mass of floating paper; and this without necessity, or utility.

Pennsylvania is not the only state which might make a similar claim, if a precedent for it were furnished. Measures are now in train for cancelling all paper of this kind.

I have the honor to be   Sir,   Your most obedt. Servt.

Alexander Hamilton

Charles Pettit Esquire.

[ENCLOSURE] [1]

[Philadelphia, June 4, 1791]

Memorandum of monies specified in a warrant No. 35 dated 30th. July 1790 drawn on Thomas Smith Esquire. Vizt.

for Pennsylvania bills of credit of the new Emissions struck
in pursuance of the Act of Congress of the 18th
March 1780 [2] 74,100
loose money in ditto 544
Amount of new Emission of Pennsylvania of 18th March
1780 74,644
ditto............... of Maryland 27
ditto............... of New Jersey 347
ditto............... of Massachusetts 140
ditto............... State Money of Pennsylvania .... 2 ⅔

Dollars 75,160 ⅔

Statement of the United States quota of 4/10ths. of bills emitted on the Funds of the State of Pennsylvania in March 1780. Vizt.

Quota of 4/10ths. of 1.495.000 Dollars 598.000
On account of which Thomas Smith Esqr. Commis-
sioner of Loans has made the following charges. Vizt.
Warrants drawn by the Board of Treasury, the Super-
intendant of Finance, and the Presidents of Congress 519.682.54
Commissions 1.940.70
Contingent Charges 593.45
Carried to the United States Account Current for
which the Commissioner is to Account 622.41
Remitted to the Secretary of the Treasury in July 1790 75.160.60

Dollars 598.000

Extracted from the books of Thomas Smith Esqr. Commissioner for Pennsylvania.

Auditors Office June 4th. 1791.
Ezekl. Freeman Clk.

Copy, Division of Public Records, Pennsylvania Historical and Museum Commission, Harrisburg.
  1. Copy, Division of Public Records, Pennsylvania Historical and Museum Commission.
  2. JCC, XVI, 263–64. See Pettit to H, April 30, 1791, note 3.

From Richard Platt [1]

New York June 8th. 1791.

Colonel Hamilton
Dear Sir

    When I had last the pleasure of seeing you in Philada.; I told you, that our mutual friend Col Smith, had gone to Europe on his & my business,[2] in order to try the experiment of borrowing money on the principles or plan of Cassineux [3] & others—our Six ⅌ Cents being then at 14/ & the other parts bearing a ratio thereto—but the sudden rise so instantaneously succeeded his departure,[4] as to leave no room for Speculation on our intended Operation & my friend took his departure wisely for America & is now on the spot to embrace his appointment. Altho' we have been foiled in our Object as we had projected, yet I am persuaded that public good as well as private emolument will flow from his voyage. To these conclusions I am led by Documents in his possession as well as concurring facts & Circumstances from Sources of good Information—the former of which, will no doubt be opened to your view, & the latter daily unfolding themselves in Confirmation.[5] If then my good friend such impressions should be made on your enlightened mind on this subject, as it's importance requires, his merits in my opinion justly entitle, & the seeming partiality of some leading Characters in the British Administration apparently warrants, I ask whether our friend might not be named among the Candidates who will probably soon be exhibited, for Employ at Foreign Courts. But as I am told that England intends very soon to send an Ambassador to this Country, & in fact has for some time past, delayed it only with a view to find out, what man will be most agreeable to us in that Capacity; common civility and propriety would require a similar attention to that Country and this is the focal Point, I wish Smith to be seen at, being persuaded that he is perfectly agreeable, & in my partial view, very superior to most of our Countrymen for such a mission. I wish you will give the thing a fair revolution in your mind & contrast a patriotic polish'd man, with others who may be led astray by contracted habits, fatuous prejudices & party views, however celebrated they may be for science & Literature. I apprehend Chancellor Livingston,[6] Bingham [7] Governeur Morris & such kind of men will pit themselves on this occasion & if so I am certain you will agree with me that neither of them can do any National Good abroad. I know well your friendship for both of us & assure myself that as far as policy & justice authorise so ⟨far⟩ you will heartily cherish & support his favorite wish. I am Dr. Sir

affectionately yours,

Richd: Platt

P.S. Your wishes respecting the wine shall very soon be realized and I believe it will not be inferior to any in Philada.

ALS, Hamilton Papers, Library of Congress.

1. Platt was a New York City broker, speculator, and business associate of William Duer.

2. See Francisco de Miranda to H, April 5, 1791, note 2. William S. Smith attempted to secure a loan based on deposit of United States six percent stocks.

3. This is apparently a reference to Théophile Cazenove, the agent in America for several Dutch banking houses. See H to Duer, April 20, 1791.

4. In December, 1790, the market price of the six percent stocks rose from 15s.10d. to 17s.6d., and at the end of the year they had reached as high as 18s.6d.

5. Smith was used by Lord Grenville, the British Secretary of State for the Home Department, as a means of informing United States officials that Great Britain desired a settlement of outstanding issues and that the government would shortly send a minister to the United States. Smith, departing for America immediately after his conversation with Grenville, reached New York City on June 5, 1791.

6. Robert R. Livingston.

7. William Bingham.

To Thomas Smith

Treasury Department
June 8th. 1791

Sir

You are right in considering yourself not authorized by Law to accept on the Loan of the assumed debt Certificates of the State of Pennsa. dated on or after the 1st day of January 1790.[1] It is however my wish that you minute in a Book to be kept for that purpose the amount of such Certificates offered by any person together with the name of the person offering them.

It will not be proper that you commit the examination & checking of the Certificates of the assumed debt to any person who does not actually belong to your Office. It cannot be deemed a legal execution of your duty to rely upon any person not duly authorised. You will receive these Certificates and give, on the delivery of them to you and before comparision with the checks, a descriptive receipt for them, which will amount to no more than an acknowledgment, that such Certificates are placed in your hands with a view to the Loan. The subscribers will be sensible that the receipt cannot be deemed final because the subscriptions may exceed the Assumption and the Certificates may prove counterfeit or forged. Having recd. them in the manner above mentioned you will commit to some person competent to so nice and important a business the comparison of the Certificates with the registers & checks in the offices of the State, to which no doubt the easiest access will be given, should however any unexpected impediment occur you will make it known to me.

I do not perceive any objection to your striking a Mark in the form you have exhibited ⌐⌐ , upon all the Certificates deposited with you towards the Loan of the assumed debt, which however should be done in such manner as not to obliterate the printed or manuscript Words. You will be careful to select a proper place for the Mark, which as far as possible should be uniformly made that the eye may instantly perceive it. I do not consider you as justifiable in refusing the Certificates of the State of Pennsa. (which are in all other respects assumable) because they have been recd. of the State in lieu of Continental Certificates. It will not however be improper to use your endeavours to persuade the holders to exchange them, but you cannot if they persist to offer refuse to receive them.

You will perceive on reexamination that you have misconceived the instruction contained in my letter of the 9th Ulto.[2] in regard to Loan office Certificates issued prior to March 1778. It applied to those only pointed out in the 10th. section,[3] that is to the *Nonsubscribed* & not to those that should be Loaned. You will discontinue the practice of marking such indorsements on those *Loaned,* and you will, when transfers take place of such Stock as has arisen from Loans of those Certificates take care not to make a similar endorsement on the new Certificate to be given. I do not think any person making a Loan has a right to do it in any other manner than that which is deemed perfectly conformable to Law. In regard to such *Nonsubscribers* Certificates as have not that endorsement on them I have no objection to your making it if desired, but great care must be taken to be correct.

   I am sir   Yr Most Ob servt   Alexander Hamilton

Thos. Smith Esqr
Commr. of Loans
Pennsa.

Copy, Division of Public Records, Pennsylvania Historical and Museum Commission, Harrisburg; copy, Chicago Historical Society.
   1. See Smith to H, June 6, 1791.
   2. Letter not found.
   3. This is Section 10 of "An Act making provision for the (payment of the) Debt of the United States" (1 *Stat.* 141–42 [August 4, 1790]).

From Thomas Smith

[*Philadelphia*] *June 8, 1791.* ". . . Abstract of Certificates Indents & old Emission money received on the loan proposed by the act of Congress of 4th Augt. 1790 [1] from the 1st to 31st May inclusive the Certificates old emission money and Indents are this day forwarded to Oliver Wolcott Esqr Auditor. . . ."

LC, RG 53, Pennsylvania State Loan Office, Letter Book, 1790–1794, Vol. "615–P," National Archives.
   1. "An Act making provision for the (payment of the) Debt of the United States" (1 *Stat.* 138–44).

From Joseph Whipple

Portsmh. New Hamp. 9 June 1791

Sir

Your Circular letter of the 14th. of April came to my hands the 20th Ultimo. Availing myself of the indulgence of the house of Representatives in committing to your examination and report, the emoluments of the Officers of the Customs I do myself the honor to transmit you here with a Statement of the emoluments of my office as Collector of the Customs District of Portsmouth for the four quarters of the Year 1790: not having a doubt but your report will be founded in the Strictest Justice, & that it will have the approbation & confidence of the Legislature.

In this Statement the Article of fees is precisely the Amount received taken from an accurate account kept of them. The Amount of Commission is taken by Calculation on the foot of each quarterly account, tho' not half the Sum Stated has yet been received. In the account of expenses the charge of office Rent is the result of an accommodation between the Naval Officer & myself, & the building occupied which belongs to him, is stated at the rate for which it would Rent & the charge for Clerks Service is the amount of payments made in Money together with the value of gratuitous compensations not equal to the amount of the Services performed according to the usual Rate of Clerks wages.

By this Statement it will appear that   [1] Dolls. is the Net Amount of my emoluments for the year, a Sum not equal to one third the real value of the Services incumbent on the Office, inclusive of its responsibility. Conceiving of the impossibility of prejudging of an equitable reward for every officer of the Revenue under the circumstances of its Sudden establishment, I have presumed on the justice which I flatter myself will be the result of a candid enquiry, Such as I am persuaded will be made, for a reasonable reward, as well for the past as the future Services. It will naturally occur that the first who are in the exercise of these offices will have the greatest difficulties to encounter—having unbeaten paths to explore & to reconcile a people accustom'd almost to no law but their will, to strict observance of

Revenue Laws, which are generally in their nature obnoxious to Such a people & I have the Satisfaction to believe the fewest Successfull attempts have been made to evade the Revenue Laws in this district of any in the United States that are so conveniently situated for that purpose.

I have the honor to be   Sir   very respectfully   Your Mo Obt. servt.

Hon. Alex. Hamilton Esqr.

LC, Collector of Customs at Portsmouth, Letters Sent, 1790–1791, Vol. 2, National Archives.
1. Space left blank in MS.

To Thomas Mifflin [1]

Treasury Department
June 10th 1791

Sir

Having received the return the want of which delayed a definitive answer to yours Letter of the fifth of May; I have now the honor to inform you that this department is ready to proceed in the business which is the Subject of it.

According to the course of Proceedings at the Treasury the adjustment will begin with the Auditor and be completed by the Comptroller. The Auditor will accordingly be ready at any time to enter upon the matter with any person whom you shall be pleased to authorize for the purpose, on behalf of the State.

I have the honor to be   Sir   Your Most Obedient Servant
Alexander Hamilton
Secry of the Treasury of the United States
His Excellency Thomas Mifflin
Governor of Pennsylvania

Copy, Division of Public Records, Pennsylvania Historical and Museum Commission, Harrisburg.
1. For background to this letter, see Mifflin to H, May 5, 1791.

From William Short

Paris June 10. 1791

Sir

Since my last letters of the 3d & 5th. inst. I have recieved a letter from the commissioners at Amsterdam of which I have the honor of inclosing a copy [1] as well as of mine to them which occasioned it.[2] I have not yet recieved their answer to mine [3] written in consequence of theirs of which I inclosed you a copy in my letter of the 3d.[4] but this letter serves as an answer as you will see by the contents. I am taking measures therefore to know whether the U.S. can now make a loan in the low countries at $4\frac{1}{2}$ p cent interest. In that case I shall suppose there can be no doubt as to the propriety of making there that which your letter of April 13 authorizes me to open. I have hopes that whilst acquiring this information I shall be happy enough to hear from you as to the propriety of obtaining a credit for the U.S. somewhere out of Holland. Until then I cannot know whether you consider the subject in the same light that I do, nor whether it has presented itself to me in all the aspects in which you may think it should be examined; & of course I shall postpone for that purpose making the experiment unless tempted to it by being offered better terms than can be procured at Amsterdam.

You will observe also that the commissioners added to the opinion which I mentioned to you of the necessity of augmenting the commission if the rate of interest is diminished. It is possible this may be found necessary but I am not fully convinced of it. Of course it would not be done without a further conviction of the necessity. If the elimination of the interest cannot be effected on any other terms, a very little calculation will shew the advantage of adopting them.

ALS, letterpress copy, William Short Papers, Library of Congress.
  1. See enclosure.
  2. See enclosure.
  3. Short to Willink, Van Staphorst, and Hubbard, May 29, 1791 (ALS, letterpress copy, William Short Papers, Library of Congress).
  4. See Willink, Van Staphorst, and Hubbard to Short, May 23, 1791 (LS, Short Family Papers, Library of Congress). This letter is printed as an enclosure to Short to H, June 3, 1791.

In anxious expectation of hearing from you fully on these subjects I have the honor to be Sir, your most obedient humble servant.

W: Short

P.S. I have just learned that the Dutch E. India company, have recalled the Governor of the Cape of Good-hope & determined to send there commissaries in order to examine into the state of affairs & restore order in them. This confirms the opinion of their extreme disorder.

The Honble. Alexander Hamilton Secretary of the Treasury Philadelphia

[ENCLOSURE]

William Short to Wilhem and Jan Willink, Nicholaas and Jacob Van Staphorst, and Nicholas Hubbard [5]

Paris May 26. 1791.

Gentlemen

The departure of the post leaves me barely time to inform you that I have at length recieved a letter from the Secretary of the Treasury which renders it necessary that I should know the present situation of the loan opened at Amsterdam & with as much precision as you can have, the time when you think another could be set on foot there. [6] I will thank you to give me the information by the return of the post & to let me know also the price of American bonds on your market. A million of florins of the late loan will be to be paid to France immediately. I will not mention it to the minister [7] unless it becomes necessary until I shall have recieved your answer—if necessary however I shall not hesitate to do it as I suppose it cannot possibly be attended with inconvenience. He will of course desire it to be paid to Hogguer & Co. [8] It is possible you may recieve the order before your answer. In the mean time I have the honor to be.

Messrs. W & J. Willink, Nas. & Jab. V. Staphorst & Hubbard—Amsterdam

5. AL, letterpress copy, William Short Papers, Library of Congress.
6. See H to Short, April 13, 1791.
7. Comte de Montmorin, Minister of Foreign Affairs.
8. The firm of Hogguer, Grand, and Company. The partners were Paul Iwan Hogguer and George Le Grand.

[ENCLOSURE]

Wilhem and Jan Willink, Nicholaas and Jacob Van Staphorst, and Nicholas Hubbard to William Short [9]

Amsterdam 3 June 1791

Sir

In reply to your respected favor of 26 Ultimo,[10] We acquaint you, that the Order You purpose giving us to pay One Million of Florins unto the Director-General of the Finances of France,[11] shall be punctually complied with, in the Mode that Minister will desire.

All the Bonds of the Loan of March last are now delivered; And We do not doubt, We should be able in the present Moment, to procure a New Loan for the United States, at the usual rate of Interest.

But, having cherished the Idea, of improving the present favorable Circumstances of the United States and their consequent growing Credit, to operate a Reduction of Interest on their future Loans, and exerted ourselves to accomplish it, We have the pleasure to see our Efforts so far succeed, as that the actual Price of their Bonds is Three Quarters to One per Cent above par, with the probability of going still higher; so that if the Proposal for a New Loan was postponed for Two, Three or Four Months, and no unfavorable Events should intervene, We have good ground to flatter ourselves, We might obtain the next Loan to an Amount not exceeding Three Million of Florins, at the rate of Four and an half per Cent Interest per Annum: To effect it, an Augmentation of One per Cent in the Charges would be necessary; but this is an Object of no Moment, compared with the annual saving of One half per Cent on the Interest, and the honor accruing from such an Increase of Credit and Confidence.

We shall take care to advise you, when We think a Loan at 4½ per Cent, might be offered to our Undertakers, with the probability of succeeding; And in the mean time We hold ourselves ready, for the execution of what you may judge most conducive to the Interest and Conveniency of the United-States.

9. LS, Short Family Papers, Library of Congress.
10. See first enclosure.
11. Claude Antoine de Valdec de Lessart.

We are respectfully   Sir   Your most obedient and very humble servants

Wilhem & Jan Willink

N. & J. Van Staphorst & Hubbard

Willm. Short Esqr.

From Otho H. Williams

Frederick Town [Maryland] 10 June 1791

Sir

According to the advice of Physicians, and the importunity of some of my friends, I left Baltimore and business with an intention of going to the Sweet Springs for the recovery of my health, which is much impaired and am thus far on my Journey.

I have here the honor of recieving your letter of the 4th instant with the papers relating to the seizure of Messrs. McRea and Morrisons goods.[1] I regret that they did not come to hand time enough for me to have executed personally your particular instructions respecting the case. I will however, refer them to Mr. Delozier [2] Deputy Collector of the district, with such directions in the business as will, I hope, fully answer your expectation and the object intended; At present I can only say that from such circumstances as have come to my knowledge I am very far from entertaining any suspicion of fraud by any of the parties, yet inad⟨ver⟩tence is an indifferent apology for risquing so considerable an amount of property.

Permit me to explain what I mean by circumstances within my own knowledge. I know that Mr. Fraser [3] is an importer of goods, and that in all his transactions with the Custom House he has conducted himself, in every instance within my notice, with correctness and a due respect for the laws and which is all of Mr. Frazer that I do know. I know that it is customary for merchants in Baltimore to open packages of merchandize to oblige their customers, and that in making up parcels for the retailers in the different districts, they sometimes compose a parcel with pices, and perhaps parts of pieces, of goods imported at different times and in different Vessels. It is not necessary, to transport goods, from district to district that they be contained in the same trunk, package &c. If the Master of a Coasting Vessel, having on board goods, Wares &c. above the value of &c, bound to another district, will deliver to the Collector of the port from whence he is about to depart a Manifest of such goods &c and will make Oath that *he* doth not know and hath no reason to believe that the revenue of the United States hath been defrauded by the illegal importation thereof the Collector must certify the same and the law is satisfied.[4] Now I know from observation, and it might be conceived from the nature of the business, that not one Master of a Coaster in fifty can possibly have any *knowledge* of the importation of goods in Sea Vessels, or any about the payment of the duties. If the intention were to prevent small vessels from receiving goods from large ones, and if the Oath were to be administered at the place of delivery, it might affect the consciences of some so as to prevent direct Smuggling. But as the Oath is required to be administered at the place where the Goods are laden on board there can be nothing more negative, or nugatory, than such testimony of their having been legally entered. The individual circumstance of the goods being within a district is in my opinion a stronger evidence of the legality of their introduction into the United States, than the Oaths of ever so many skippers who swear only to their ignorance of the matter. But when to the first circumstancial evidence be added the positive testimony of one respectable merchant (altho the forms of Law be not strictly complied with) I should be much inclined to admit the equity of exonorating such goods from condemnation, more especially if that merchant having disposed of his property in them, were no longer interested in their fate.

I have ventured to obtrude these observations from an apprehension that multiplicity of more important business prevents your marking the minute imperfections of the coasting law. They will have no influence on the further investigation of the case referred to. Your instructions shall be followed as well in the manner of interrogating Mr. Fraser as in transmitting the respective papers to the Judge and to the department of the Treasury. Mr. Delozier will examine the matter with all the attention, care and precaution that the most suspicious circumstances would justify.

I am neither well enough, nor prepared here to make a fair transcript of my letter. You will therefore have the goodness to excuse its being done for me by Mr. Delozier who will subscribe my name.

I am, with very great respect,   Sir, Your most Obedient and Most
Humble Servant   O. H. Williams Collr.

Alexr. Hamilton Esqr.
Secy Treasury

ADfS, RG 53, "Old Correspondence," Baltimore Collector, National Archives.
    1. John McRae and John Morrison. See H to Cyrus Griffin, February 15,
1791; H to Williams, June 4, 1791.
    2. Before 1789, Daniel Delozier of Annapolis had been Williams's assistant
in the Maryland state customs service.
    3. Thomas Fraser. See Delozier to H, September 3, 1791.
    4. This is a paraphrase of Section 25 of "An Act for Registering and Clearing
Vessels, Regulating the Coasting Trade, and for other purposes" (1 *Stat.* 61–62
[September 1, 1789]).

To William Campbell, Thomas Withers, M. R. Willkings, Auly Macnaughten, and George Hooper

Treasury Department
June 11. 1791

Gentlemen,

I have received your letter of the 18th. of April relative to the lighthouse which was begun by the government of North Carolina on Cape
Island, near the mouth of Cape Fear River. The general provisions
made by Congress with respect to light houses do not extend further
than repairing and maintaining them. Nothing therefore can at this
moment be done in this case, though it is probable earlier information,
or an application to the legislature in any of their past sessions would
have been attended with a compliance with your wishes. Similar applications were followed by grants to build a lighthouse on Cape Henry,
and to finish one, which was commenced by the government of Massachusetts on Portland head. I shall bear this subject in mind when the
next session commences, and I would advise your recommending it to
the attention of the gentlemen from your district in the house of representatives.

An indispensible requisite to a grant of money to finish the building
will be the completion of the instruments of cession to the United
States. I therefore request that you will favour me with copies of such

laws as have been enacted by the state legislature (as *the extracts* sent
may not be deemed sufficient) and with a copy of Mr. Smith's deed
for the ten acres of land. I also recommend your procuring from the
Governnor of your state a deed in pursuance of the act of December
1790.[1] The early receipt of these is desirable, as it will afford time to
obviate difficulties, if any should arise before the meeting of Congress.

In the mean time I find it necessary to request of you answers to
the following questions relative to the business.

When was the building commenced? Is there any the least appearance of its suffering from the winter or winters it has sustained since
it was built, and in what parts? What parts of the building are of
stone, and particularly as to the foundation, water table, cills of the
doors and windows, and the curbs? Is the lime used *stone lime,* or
oyster shell lime? Are the frame and sashes of the lanthorn to be of
iron, or wood? What is the thickness of the base in *feet* and *inches:*
the plan calls it seven bricks thick, but it is not known whether it is
seven times the *length,* the *breadth* or the *thickness* of a brick. Was
there a solid bottom in the earth, on digging down for the foundation?
Is the spot an eminence, or is it level with the land for 100 or 200
yards around it? Is it in any degree a drifted sandhill, and if it is did
the workmen take care to go down through it to the solid earth? Is
there any frame work laid under the foundation as proposed, and what
are its construction, and the kinds of timber used? What are the several thicknesses of the wall of the pyramid in *feet* and *inches,* in those
parts above the foundation, which are represented to be *six* bricks,
five Bricks thick, and *four and an half* bricks thick? Is the diameter
the same at the top of the story in which the doors are as at the bottom
of that story, and what is that diameter from outside to outside? What
is the diameter at the top of the masonry, immediately under the lanthorn, proposed to be? What are the diameter and height of the lanthorn, exclusive of the dome-roof and what is the height of the dome
on roof? What is the height of the building from the earth to the ball
on the top of the lanthorn? It appears by the plan to be near 112 feet.
Will the thickness of two bricks, which as I suppose, cannot be
seventeen inches, be sufficiently strong at the height of 75 to 90 feet
from the earth and will the thickness of six bricks (or 4½ to 5 feet)
be thick enough for the lower part of a building of so great a height?

I have been the more particular in these enquiries, because time admits of your giving me the requisite answers, and it is necessary that a building of so great expence to the United States, and of so much importance to its commerce, should be œconomically and solidly executed.

I am, Gentlemen,   with great consideration,   Your obedt. servant

The Commissioners of the Navigation of Cape Fear.

Copy, RG 26, Lighthouse Letters Received, Early Lighthouse Letters, National Archives.

1. For this law, see William Campbell *et al.* to H, April 18, 1791, note 2. According to this statute, Benjamin Smith of Brunswick County had deeded "for the use of the state and the security of the navigation of Cape-Fear . . . ten acres of land situated on the Cape-Island, for the purpose of erecting thereon a lighthouse."

From Jeremiah Olney

Providence 11th. June 1791.

Sir

I Have been honored with your Letter of 30th Ulto. & in reply to that part of it respecting the appointment of the Second and Third mate of the Cutter building in Connecticutt I beg leave to remark that Mr. Jeremiah Greenman is exceedingly mortified (after throwing himself out of the best Imploy in this Town and waiting four or five months with a reasonable expectation of Receiving an appointment to the office of first mate of the Cutter, to which he was Early recommended) [1] to find that he must now accept the Station of Second mate, or continue out of business. Since the late *expected* millitary appointment [2] Seems to be delaid and remains uncertain, (which I regret exceedingly as I know he was an officer of Excellent Character *in the late army* & is the most Suitable for the present command, of any that can be obtained in the State,) he is therefore *from the necessity of the case* induced to accept the Appointment of Second mate of the Cutter, presuming that his rank and pay will commence as early as that of the Gentlemen already appointed, having for nearly five months held himself in constant readiness for public Service. From a Consideration of the merits of this Gentleman and the agency I have been called upon to take in this Business, I feel a particular Interest in his favour, I therefore take the Liberty Sir, to request your powerfull influence in his behalf. Mr. Daniel Bucklin Junr. having waited now four months with an Expectation of receiving the appointment of Second mate to the Cutter,[3] & a Vessell offering a few Weeks past he accepted the Command of her to Virginia and is expected to return in Ten days when I will consult him on his acceptance of the Station of Third mate of the Cutter and acquaint you with the Result.

I have the honor to be Respectfully   Sir   Your Most Obed. & Most Hum serv.   Jereh. Olney

Alexander Hamilton Esqr.
Secretary of the Treasury

ADfS, Rhode Island Historical Society, Providence.
  1. See Olney to H, February 17, 1791.
  2. See Olney to H, April 25, 1791.
  3. See Olney to H, February 17, 1791.

From Thomas Smith

[*Philadelphia*] *June 11, 1791.* "This accompanys abstract of Certificates received by me from non subscribers [1] to the Loan proposed by act of Congress of the 4th of Augt 1790 [2] from 1st to 31st May 1791 which closes the whole of the non-subscription business. . . ."

LC, RG 53, Pennsylvania State Loan Office, Letter Book, 1790–1794, Vol. "615–P," National Archives.
  1. For the provisions made for "non-subscribers" to whom Smith is referring, see Andrew Porter to H, April 23, 1791, note 2.
  2. "An Act making provision for the (payment of the) Debt of the United States" (1 *Stat.* 138–44).

From William Ellery

Custom-House [Newport, Rhode Island]
June 13th. 1791

Sir

I have received your letters of the 26th.[1] & the 30th. of May last.[2] To the explanations and instructions, and the act respecting further

LC, Newport Historical Society, Newport, Rhode Island.
  1. "Treasury Department Circular to the Collectors of the Customs," May 26, 1791.
  2. Letter not found.

provisn. for collecting the duties on Teas, and for prolonging the term for the payment of the duties on Wines inclosed in the first I shall pay attention. In answer to the last, Capt. Smith left his coasting papers with me agreeably to law, and his license was remitted to the Collector of the District of Providence.[3]

A Disposition to disregard the Revenue laws, will, and it is natural that it should, excite a jealous attention to the vessels of those in whom it is discovered. Be assured, Sir, that it is my wish, and the wish of the other Offrs. of this port, by a faithful discharge of their duty, to merit your approbation and the approbation of their Constituents.

Agreeably to my letter of the 6th. of this month I will now give you the best information I have been able to obtain of the tare customary among merchants in this District.[4]

Tare on Sugars in hogsheads is .... 12 lb on each 112 lb.
ditto on barrels (if in American flour
    barrels) is .... 11 lb on each 112 lb
if in French bbls. .... 14 lb on   ditto
There has been only one importn. of
    Sugars in boxes since this Office was
    opened.

The mode of Taring coffee in barrels is the same as that used in taring sugar in barrels; but the deduction is made from each 100 lb. (Coffee being sold by the pound and not by the hundred). No tare is allowed on coffee in bags.

The same mode is pursued in taring barrels of Cocoa, but Cocoa is sold by the long hundred as it is called here or 112 lb. and not by the pound and the tare is taken out of each 112 lb. No tare allowed on Cocoa in bags.

It is not usual to import Cocoa in hogsheads, nor has there been a single hogshead of that article imported since this Office was opened. Neither has there been any importation of Piemento, or Pepper.

Our mode of allowing tare before and since the New Collection Law,[5] has been,

    3. Jeremiah Olney.
    4. H had requested this information in his "Treasury Department Circular to the Collectors of the Customs," May 13, 1791.
    5. For the tares prescribed by Federal law, see Section 35 of "An Act to provide more effectually for the collection of the duties imposed by law on goods, wares and merchandise imported into the United States, and on the tonnage of ships or vessels" (1 *Stat.* 166 [August 4, 1790]).

On Sugar in Hogsheads .... 12 lb on 112 lb

ditto in barrels, if American flour barrels, be-
    fore the Law took place was   22 lb on each bbl
    if French .... 28 lb on ditto

since the new Law it has been   12 lb on each 112 lb.

The mode of taring Coffee in bbls before the
    New Law was the same as that used with
    regard to Sugar in barrels; since that time
    it has been .... 12 lb on each 112

ditto in bags before the new Law was from
    2 to 3 lb upon 112 lb according to the
    quantity of the stuff of which the bag was
    made. Since that time it has been .... 2 lb on each 112 lb

Ditto of Cocoa in barrels and in bags, has
    been the same both before & since the New
    Law, as in the case of Coffee in barrels and
    in bags.

No Cocoa has been imported in hogsheads;
    nor Piemento, nor Pepper since this office
    was opened.

On Cotton in bales or bags we allow a tare of ... 3 lb on each 112 lb

There has been only two importations of
    powdered Sugars, the first was in Augt.
    1790 in white Oak Hogsheads fully
    hooped—the tare allowed on each hogs-
    head was   136 lb on each Hhd.

The last was in boxes and the tare allowed
    was   15 lb on each 112 lb.

The information I have given of the tare *customary* among merchants in this District can hardly be called *customary*. No Commercial Society is established here. The merchants proceed on separate
ground. Each consults his particular interest, and makes the best
bargain he can with regard to the tare as well as the price of his goods.
The Grocers frequently insist upon goods being started and weigh the
cask, case or box to determine the tare.

Inclosed is a weekly return of monies received and paid. A list of
a Ten dollar note of the North American bank No. 7573, one moiety
thereof is now transmitted to the Treasr., a Certife. of Regy No. 32.

issued at the Port of Dighton May 24th 1790 and delivered up on account of transfer of property, Copy of a memorandum of the change of master of the Sloop Industry endorsed on Rege. No. 11, issued at this Port, a like copy endorsed on Cert. No. 37. dated 24th. Sept. 1790; a like copy on Cert. No. 45 dated Oct. 12 1790, & a like copy on Certif. No. 5 dated 1791.

I am, Sir,   Yr. most obedt. servt.   Wm Ellery Collr

A Hamilton Esqr.
Secry of Treasy.

From George Washington

(private)

Mount Vernon, June 13. 1791.

My Dr. sir

I am arrived at this place and just in time to acknowledge (in a hasty manner by this days post—the first opportunity that has offered of writing to Philada. since I left Savanna)—the receipt of your private letter of the 17th. of April by Mr. Smith [1] who lodged it at Cambden,[2] through which it was known my rout would be on my return to the seat of the Government.

Mr. Wolcott [3] may be informed that it is my intention to appoint him to the office of Comptroller. With respect to his successor, as auditor, I shall suspend any determination, (if no manifest inconvenience will result from it) until my arrival in Philadelphia, which however is not likely to happen before the 5. or 6 of July as (by appointment at the last meeting) I am to meet the Commissioners,[4] undr the residence Act [5] on Monday the 27th. inst: at Georgetown, and may, for aught I know to the contrary, be detained there several days, and afterwards must move slowly, on account of the exhausted condition of my horses.

No letters from the Northward or Eastward of this, bearing date between the 15th. & 30th. of May have come to my hands—and having abundant evidence before I reached Charleston of the slow movements of the mail through the three Southernmost States, I did, before I left that place on the 9th. of that month direct that all letters which might be for'd following me to be returned to Fredericksburgh as the first place I should touch the post line upon my return. But these directions not arriving in Richmond in time (as I conjecture) the letters of that interval, agreeably to the superscriptions which I am informed were on them, were forwarded from that place to Taylors Ferry, in expectation of meeting me there, but to this circumstance, which was unknown to me, and to finding from better information than I set out with, that it would be more convenient to cross James river higher up than at Taylors; is to be ascribed my missing the communications which were made between the 15 & 30. of May as mentioned before. These dispatches I may be long without, & perhaps never get; for there are no cross posts in those parts and the letters, which will have to pass through *many* hands, may find *some* who are not deficient in curiosity.

My return to this place is sooner than I expected; owing to the uninterruptedness of my journey by sickness, from bad weather, or accidents of any kind whatsoever. Having obtained before I left Philadelphia the most accurate account, I could get there, of the places & roads through, & by which I was to perform my tour; and the distances between the former; I formed my line of march accordingly; fixed each days journey & the day to halt; from neither of which have I departed in a single instance, except staying, from a particular circumstance, two days in Columbia, and none at Charlotte, instead of one at each and crossing James river at Carters ferry in place of Taylors, as was the original intention. But the improbability of performing a tour of 1700 miles (I have already rode more), with the same set of horses without encountering any accident by which a deviation would be rendered unavoidable appeared so great that I allowed eight days for casualties, and six to refresh at this place when I should have returned to it. None of the former having happened, account for the 14 days I shall remain here before the meeting with the Commrs.; one of whom Mr. Johnston chief Justice of the State of Maryland, & living at a pretty considerable distance from Georgetown; having made his arrangements agreeably thereto, would not be able to meet me sooner.

I mention this matter, that if there is anything pressing in either of the Departments it may be known where I am.

with affectionate regard   I am sincerely yours   G: Washington

LC, George Washington Papers, Library of Congress.
  1. Presumably William L. Smith of South Carolina.
  2. Washington was at Camden, South Carolina, on May 25.
  3. Oliver Wolcott, Jr.

4. These were the commissioners for the Federal District. They were Thomas Johnson, chief justice of Maryland, Daniel Carroll, member of the House of Representatives from Maryland, and Dr. David Stuart of Fairfax County, Virginia.

5. "An Act for establishing the temporary and permanent seat of the Government of the United States" (1 *Stat.* 130 [July 16, 1790]).

To Otho H. Williams

Trasury Department
June 13. 1791

Sir,

On the receipt of this letter you will be pleased to pay to Mr. Stodder [1] the balance due upon his contract with you for the building and outfit of the revenue cutter, provided you find he has duly complied with the Terms of his engagement.

It is requisite that you transmit to the Treasury a copy of your Contract with Mr. Stodder.

I am   Sir,   Your most Obedt Servant   Alexander Hamilton

Otho H. Williams Esqr

LS, Columbia University Libraries.
    1. David Stodder, a Baltimore shipbuilder.

From Richard Wylly [1]

[*June 13, 1791.*] "I have, without success, applied a second time to the Governor, to know, by what authority Mr. Davies acted as Loan Officer. I am well assured, he had none."

Copy, RG 233, Reports of the Treasury Department, 1792–1793, Vol. III, National Archives.
    1. For background to this letter, see Wylly to H, May 17, 1791.

From Benjamin Lincoln

[*Boston, June 14, 1791.* On June 23, 1791, Hamilton wrote to Lincoln: "I have received your letter of the 14th instant." *Letter not found.*]

From Jeremiah Olney

Custom House,
Providence 14th June 1791.

Sir.

I have recd. your Two Letters of the 30th. of May and First in-stant. The Surveyor will attend to your directions in the use of the Hydrometers.

All the Papers furnished by me for the Ship Warren [1] were *dated* Four Days after She had committed a breach of the Law by proceed-ing to Newport without them, of which particular, perhaps, you have not been apprised. Misconstruction of the Tonnage Act,[2] (an ac-knowledgemt. of which I have since made, by repaying the Duty) and Mr. Brown's [3] expectation, signified to me by him, of her return-ing to this Port, induced me to grant the Licence; and a desire to ob-tain an Accot. of her Cargo, which I no other way could, and which I then thought essential, prompted me to give the Certified Manifest and Permit. Tho' these might as well have been omitted, yet I should suppose, they could not affect the Penalty incurred by a previous transaction. I wish not however, to Criminate Messrs. Brown & Fran-cis, but to justify myself; for this purpose, I beg leave further to ob-serve, that the Manifest, presented and sworn to by the Master, is the only Evidence I can have of the Cargo on board any *outward*bound Vessel, excepting the Articles which may have been Entered for Ex-portation: the one therefore, delivered and sworn to by Captain Smith, tho' the Warren was then at Newport, possessed all the requisites towards the satisfaction of my Mind, that it would had it been pre-sented before She sailed from this District. I shall not relax, in my attention, to the Vessels of Messrs. Brown & Francis, nor to those of any other Person's; I may err in Judgement, but my *Intention* shall always be right.

I do not Sir, comprehend your meaning, when you say, that "the nature of the Cargoes and the places from whence Coasting Vessels come, with expired Licences, are to determine their Fees &c. exactly as in the cases of Vessels never having been Licenced." The former have generally arrived here from adjoining States without any kind of Clearances; but the latter, when from any of the United States, always with such as the Law requires, which exempts the Cargoes from Duty, tho' the Fees, excepting to the Surveyor, are the same as if they were from foreign Ports. Now if the former are to be viewed in the same light as Vessels never Licenced, should they have any Goods on board subject to Duty, it must be demanded, & the Surveyor's Fees be in proportion to the size of the Vessels. I have never taken any more Fees on the Entry of such Vessels than the Law allows for Coasters; but before they departed from the Port, I have obliged the Masters to renew their Licences, and pay the Tonnage Duty; this Practice, not being pointed out in the Law, I was doubtful of its propriety, and therefore wished to have your opinion on the Subject.

I enclose copy of a Certificate endorsed on Register No. 5, granted by me in 1790.

I have the Honor to be, Very Respectfully Sir, Your Most Obedt. & Most Huml. Servt.   Jereh. Olney Collr.

Alexander Hamilton Esqr.
Secretary of the Treasury.

ADfS, Rhode Island Historical Society, Providence; copy, RG 56, Letters from the Collector at Providence, National Archives.
   1. See Olney to H, November 29, December 24, 1790; H to Olney, December 13, 1790.
   2. "An Act imposing duties on the tonnage of ships or vessels" (1 Stat. 135–36 [July 20, 1790]).
   3. John Brown, Providence merchant and business partner of John Francis.

To John Cochran

Treasury Department,
June 15, 1791.

Sir,

I am of opinion that the law under which you act [1] does not justify the Commissioners in the payment of interest on any new loan certificate issued for the certificates of any state, which certificates were issued by that state in exchange for those of the federal debt, until the whole of the identical state certificates, so issued, have been exchanged or redeemed, or the continental certificates shall be surrendered to the United States. It does not appear to satisfy the law that an equal sum of state certificates have been redeemed. Those that went forth, by means of the exchange, are to be redeemed or re-exchanged, or the continental certificates, received for them, are to be surrendered.

The Treasurer of New York [2] is right in the opinion that the certificates for claims on forfeited Estates are not included in the assumption.

I am sir,   Your Most Obedt. Servant   Alexander Hamilton

John Cochran Esqr.
Commr. of Loans,
New York.

LS, from the original in the New York State Library, Albany.
1. For the provisions of "An Act making provision for the (payment of the) Debt of the United States" (1 *Stat.* 138–44 [August 4, 1790]) to which H is referring, see "Treasury Department Circular to the Commissioners of Loans," May 27, 1791.
2. Gerard Bancker.

Conversation with George Beckwith [1]

Philadelphia
June 15th. 1791.

Conversations with a gentleman in Office

Mr. ———— I believe I told you during the winter, that Colonel Smith went to England on private business altogether, in part for his Father in Law the Vice President, and he had other personal objects in respect to our funds.[2] Whether it was conceived in London that Mr. Smith had political objects there or not, I cannot say, but after certain explanations, he had a conversation of some length with Lord Grenville,[3] the general scope of which was pleasing and promising; it placed in a decided light, its being the determination of your Cabinet to enter on the consideration of Commercial subjects between the two Countries, and after declaring that Mr. Elliot had declined his appointment as Minister to this Country,[4] his Lordship informed Colonel Smith, that it was the determination of Administration to have a Minister here at a very early period; his Lordship then asked Colonel Smith what sort of Minister would be most pleasing to America? who replied,   [5] One part only of this conversation was of a nature to excite some regret, or rather of doubt on our part; Lord Grenville turned the conversation on our present war with the Savages in the Western Country; his Lordship said he was sorry to find from our newspapers, it was more than insinuated that Great Britain indirectly encouraged those depredations; his Lordship disclaimed this in its utmost extent, observing that it had already proved injurious to your Commerce, and if protracted would become infinitely more so; that he hoped the idea of totally extirpating those nations was not seriously entertained in the States as Great Britain could not view this with indifference. Colonel Smith said to this, that those Savages had committed a variety of depredations, and that The States were compelled to make War on them, in their own defence or words to that effect; to which his Lordship replied, he hoped The States would consider of it.

This part of his Lordship's conversation, is liable to two interpretations; the one, conveys the idea of its being merely the wish of your government, that those hostilities should be brought to a close, as they injure your trade, to a certain extent; the other, goes further and suggests its being your intention to take a certain part in the progress of this business.

I feel no difficulty in declaring it to be my opinion, that it is our interest to make peace with the hostile Indians, whenever we can do it on proper terms, but in the present condition of affairs, we have no other part to take but to proceed, our very safety requires it, and I should feel extremely concerned, if a fair prospect of a happy settlement of the affairs of the Two Countries, should be prevented by a consideration of this comparitively trivial nature.

The conversation [6] then turned on a late application from Mr. Key, the Collector of the Customs at Alburgh; [7] Mr. ——— said, I have received a letter from Mr. Key,[8] he had no authority whatever for the application You mention, and I have reason to consider him as one of those busy characters, who are anxious to shew their own consequence; [9] I have written to him [10] in such terms, as will I trust obviate any sort of inconvenience in the discharge of his duty. I understand that the place fixed upon by law for the Custom house is at least thirty miles from Pointe au fer,[11] being situated at the mouth of Onion river; I am not acquainted with the country myself, not have I any plans of it; I expect to hear from Mr. Key in a few days.

Some circumstances relating to the conduct of persons in the neighbourhood of Pointe au fer were then mentioned to Mr. ———— [12]

D, PRO: F.O., Series 4, Vol. 12, Part II.

1. This document was enclosed in a letter Beckwith wrote to Lord Grenville, July 31, 1791. An account of the same conversation was forwarded by Lord Dorchester to Grenville on July 27, 1791 (Public Archives of Canada, Ottawa, Ontario). The two records of the conversation are the same with the exceptions indicated in notes 5 and 6. Although in his letter to Grenville Beckwith identified his informant only as "a gentleman in office," Dorchester wrote in the margin opposite the remarks of Beckwith's informant "supposed 7," the code number for H.

Beckwith also enclosed in his letter to Grenville of July 31, 1791, an account of a conversation which he held with H on July 12. This account has been printed under that date.

2. See Francisco de Miranda to H, April 5, 1791; Richard Platt to H, June 8, 1791.

3. See Platt to H, June 8, 1791, note 5.

4. Presumably Andrew Elliot. See H to George Washington, April 11, 1791.

5. Beckwith left the space blank in his letter. The account of this conversation which Lord Dorchester forwarded to Grenville on July 27, 1791, supplied the missing words as follows: "His Lordship then asked Colonel Smith, what sort of minister would be most pleasing to this country, who replied, that an English gentleman would be preferred, or words to that effect" (Public Archives of Canada, Ottawa).

6. Although the remainder of Beckwith's conversation with H on this date was not reported by Beckwith in his letter to Grenville, it was included in the account of July 27 which Dorchester forwarded to Grenville (Public Archives of Canada, Ottawa).

7. The Senate, meeting in special session in March, 1791, had appointed Stephen Keyes collector of customs at Alburg in northwestern Vermont.

8. Letter not found.

9. The application mentioned by Beckwith must have been that mentioned in the following summary of a letter from an English official:

"Sends letter from Mr. Keyes, living at Burlington Bay, to which he has deferred giving an answer until he is directed by Lord Dorchester. The place called "Port of Alburgh" is on Caldwell's Manor and within the post at Dutchman's Point. Letter enclosed from Keyes, that he had received a commission from the President of the United States as officer of Customs with directions to establish the office at the Port of Alburgh, which is within the British garrison." (Brymner, *Canadian Archives*, 1890, 288.)

10. Letter not found.

11. Section 8 of "An Act giving effect to the laws of the United States within the state of Vermont" (1 *Stat.* 198 [March 2, 1791]) specified that Alburg was to be the site of the custom house in Vermont.

The post at Pointe-Au-Fer, one of the western posts held by the British in violation of the treaty of peace of 1783, was on Lake Champlain.

12. The British were disturbed not only by the establishment of the United States customs house at Alburg but also by the fact that Vermonters had settled on the Chazy River, only eight miles from the post of Pointe-Au-Fer.

From Robert Troup

[New York] 15 June 1791

My dear friend

Your bill for 200 dollars was presented to me about half an hour ago & I paid it upon being presented. You need make no arrangements for the repayment of this money. I shall as soon as I can rid myself of a little business which now presses me write you concerning the state of our accounts. I entreat you at all times without the least hesitation to make use of me as you please. It is amongst the pleasures I value most for me to contribute to your convenience, to your fame, or to your happiness. Thank God I am happy to an extreme in my wife & children & have as little reason as any of my neighbours to complain of business. I devote myself to retirement & have abandoned the field of politics. I am mortally disgusted with the weakness of some of our associates & with the treachery of others of them.[1] I never shall be indifferent to the interests of the Government or the wishes *of those in our circle* who have proved themselves worthy of confidence. This number is exceedingly small & of course it cannot break in materially upon my fixed & irrevocable design of collecting a little modiecum to enable me to quit the drudgery of the law & pursue my plan of ease and quietude. I do not see what the enemies of the Government can at present do or what is likely in future to be within the sphere of their power. Their barkings therefore I am determined to disregard.

King [2] & I have availed ourselves of every opportunity of impressing Laurence [3] with the necessity of his continuing amongst us. I fear the impressions we have made are but slight. We are without materials to make a proper sucessor of and I have resolved to distress myself no more about it. I suspect M. Smith [4] is in keeping for the office. He is now one of our motley City representation.

There was every appearance of a pasionate courtship between the Chancellor,[5] Burr, Jefferson & Madison when the two latter were in Town.[6] Delenda est Carthago I suppose is the Maxim adopted with respect to you. They had better be quiet, for if they suceed they will tumble the fabric of the government in ruins to the ground. Upon this subject however I cannot say that I have the smallest uneasiness. You are too well seated in the hearts of the citizens of the Northern

& Middle States to be hunted down by them. That your foes may be confounded & that your administration may encrease in sucess & lustre is the cordial wish of

My dear friend   Your affectionate   Rob. Troup

A Hamilton Esqr

ALS, Hamilton Papers, Library of Congress.
   1. See Troup to H, January 19, 1791.
   2. Rufus King, Federalist Senator from New York.
   3. John Laurance, a New York City lawyer, was a Federalist Representative in Congress.
   4. Melancton Smith, a merchant, speculator, and lawyer, was a leading New York Antifederalist. In the spring of 1791 he won election to the New York Assembly.
   5. Robert R. Livingston.
   6. This observation by Troup fostered the suspicion of the Federalists that Jefferson and Madison were utilizing their journey in May and June, 1791, through New York, Vermont, and Connecticut to build a political alliance with the New Yorkers. See Dumas Malone, *Jefferson and the Rights of Man* (Boston, 1951), 361–63.

From Joseph Whipple

Portsmouth New Hamp. June 15. 1791

Sir

I have recd. the assistant Secretarys letter of the 12th. Ulto.[1] inclosing a form of a Return of Outward Tonnage which I now return inclosed, filled up, except the Fishing Tonnage which is left blank being in doubt whether it might not have been intended to include the Smaller Vessels. This blank may be filled up by your direction from the Mem. that Accompaneys the Return in which a discrimination is made between them. The Additional Memo. respecting the Coasting Vessels may also be of use.

I have taken it for granted that the Tonnage on the Coasting and Fishing Vessels should be taken once only in the year and that the Tons of every Vessel performing a foreign Voyage should be taken at each clearance, some of which were cleared twice & others three times within the year.

If this was not the intention I have proceeded on wrong principles, & it will be necessary to make a new return, of which I request that you will be pleased to advise me.

I would observe that the Vessels cleared for the "West Indies generally" go to the Dutch Danish & French West Indies, but chiefly to the French. I have the honor to be &c

Hon. Alex. Hamilton Esqr.

LS, RG 36, Collector of Customs at Portsmouth, Letters Sent, 1790–1791, Vol. 2, National Archives; copy, RG 56, Letters from the Collector at Portsmouth, National Archives.

1. This is a Treasury Department circular signed by Tench Coxe which gave directions for completing Treasury Department forms for the returns of outward tonnage (LS, to Jeremiah Olney, Rhode Island Historical Society, Providence; copy, to Charles Lee, RG 56, Circulars of the Office of the Secretary, "Set T," National Archives).

To Nathaniel Appleton

[*Philadelphia, June 16, 1791*. On June 24, 1791, Appleton wrote to Hamilton: "Your favour 16th instant is received." *Letter not found.*]

From Joseph Hardy

Treasury Department
Comptroller's Office
16th. June 1791.

Sir,

On examining the Accounts of George Bush, Collector of the Customs, for the District of Delaware, from the 1st. of January, to 31st. March last; it appears, that he has collected duties on American Coasting Vessels, under twenty Tons burthen, at the rate of six Cents per annum, to the Amount of Five dollars, and twenty two Cents.

As the Collection of those duties, seem to have been made, contrary to the intent of your Circular Letter to the Collectors of 30th. November 1789, I conceive it to be my duty to submit the circumstance to your consideration.

I have the honor to be &c.   J H. P. Clk.

LC, RG 217, First Comptroller's Office, Revenue Letters Sent (Customs), National Archives.

From Joseph Hardy

Treasury Department, Comptroller's Office, June 16, 1791. "On examining the Accounts of John Davidson Collector of the Customs for the District of Annapolis in the state of Maryland, from 1st October to 31 December 1790; it appears, that he has collected duties on American Coasting Vessels under twenty Tons burthen, at the rate of six Cents per Ton per Annum, to the Amount of two Dollars and Forty Cents. . . ."

LC, RG 217, First Comptroller's Office, Revenue Letters Sent (Customs), National Archives.

From William Heth

Collectors Office
Bermuda Hundred [Virginia] 16th June 1791

Dr Sir
(Private)

This will be accompanied with a public letter,[1] enclosing a statement of outward tonnage.[2]

Having readily complyed with your wishes in this instance; and as I ever shall be, to furnish you with any information in my power, or which the books or files in this office can afford, you will not I trust be displeased at my asking yr private opinion of the *legality* of such requests. Is it not requiring *extra services* of Collectors wch. are quite independent of the defined duties of their offices, such as are not contemplated in the law under which they were appointed, and for which, consequently, no compensation is provided? Ought the labor or time of any man to be ask'd by the public for nothing? The Collectors, not having, like the favorite officers of Congress, the Loan Officers, who were on handsome salaries; any thing allowed them for Clerks wages, office rent, or extra services & expences, I consider every thing required of them, which is not defined, or comprehended in the latter part of the 6th. sectn. of the Collection law,[3] as unjustifiable and oppressive, and with which, they are not *obliged* to comply. "They are to keep their books agreeably to forms prescribed &c."

This we do. "They are also to *submit* their books &c. to the *Inspection* of such persons as may be appointed." Very different this, from being called upon to *furnish* such returns or statements from time to time, as those books & papers *might* afford to such Officers of Inspection and which, are no ways connected with the accounts, which are to be transmitted as often as required *for settlement*. They have no emoluments whatsoever, but what arises from business actually performed (for much of which, they are mainly paid) and are subject to all expences incidental to their Offices. How unjust then, that they should be liable, to be called upon to do *something* for *nothing?*

These questions and observations are now, with great respect and humility, submitted to you, in order to enforce the propriety & equity, nay, the absolute Justice, of allowing the Collectors something in the way of Salary, as a compensation for extra services rendered to government, and for extra expences. For tho' I am well convinced that *your* duty has & will frequently oblige you to call upon the Collectors to do things out of the line of their current, or defined duty (and in wch. I trust you will never be disappointed), yet, I am as well assured that, if you think me right, you have too much candor not to confirm my opinions, and too much Justice to withhold you endeavors to obtain proper & equitable provisions. If I am wrong, I feel a persuasion, that your friendship for me, will not suffer me to remain so. And you know the great respect wch. I have, and ever shall be, disposed to pay to your opinions.

Being with the most sincere esteem, respect and friendship   Dr sir Yr obt Srt   W Heth

The Hnble Alex Hamilton Esqr.[4]

ALS, Hamilton Papers, Library of Congress.
    1. Letter not found.
    2. This was in reply to a Treasury Department circular signed by Tench Coxe. See Joseph Whipple to H, June 15, 1791, note 1.
    3. "An Act to provide more effectually for the collection of the duties imposed by law on goods, wares and merchandise imported into the United States, and on the tonnage of ships or vessels" (1 *Stat.* 154–55 [August 4, 1790]).
    4. On the back of this letter H wrote:
    "Answered June 23.
    "Bound to perform the duty
    "Laws could not define all particulars.
    "Relative if these required to *specified* objects of duty to determine what is matter of obligation what not.
    "It is *fairly relative* to give all information which arise out of official documents & transactions, &c &c."

From William Heth

[*Bermuda Hundred, Virginia, June 16, 1791.* On June 16, 1791, Heth wrote to Hamilton: "This will be accompanied with a public letter, enclosing a statement of outward tonnage." *Letter not found.*]

From Nathan Keais

Washington [*North Carolina*] *June 16, 1791.* States that the contract for "erecting and Keeping up the Stakes" has been let for two hundred and twenty-five dollars, which was the lowest bid submitted.

ALS, RG 26, Lighthouse Letters Received, Vol. "A," Pennsylvania and Southern States, National Archives.

From Joseph Whipple

Portsmouth N H. June 16th. 1791.

Sir

Your Circular letter of the 13th. Ulto. respecting duties having been received on estimates of Cargoes &c, and respecting the Custom of Merchants & practice of Custom Houses in calculating the tare on goods was received the 3rd. instant.

It has been my invariable practice to receive duties only on actual weighing, gauging & measuring, when the articles were of a Nature, which rendered it in my opinion necessary, that is all kinds of West India goods which pay duty on the weight, Liquors & Salt; but on goods arriving from England accompanied with regular and unsuspected Invoices, I have taken duties on the weight charged in Such Invoices to avoid an expence of weighing which appeard unnecessary, Such as Nails, Lead Shot, Bar & Sheet Lead, China, twine & in some instances Hemp, & there can be much greater dependence on the truth of the weight of those articles from the Size of the package, than on the Value of goods contained in Trunks, Bales &c which are never examined but under circumstances of Suspicion. When Nails,

Cheese, Cordage, Hemp &c have been purchased by Masters of Vessels & not accompanied with a proper Invoice or when Imported from other Countries than England whose weights were not so well known I have caused them to be weighed also. Altho' I conceive your directions to *weigh* has referrence to such goods only as I have *weighed*, yet as the direction is expressed in positive terms, I could wish to know your further opinion respecting the weighing of goods not subject to waste & accompanied with Invoices that can be relied on.

The Custom of Merchants for allowing tare on the kinds of goods enumerated in your letter is nearly as follows

on Sugar in   hhds ⎫
              bbls ⎭ 10 pr.Cent (that is 10 pr. 100)
              Boxes—none imported

Coffee in hhds ⎫
          bbls ⎬ tare generally marked on the Cask
          bags—nothing, on common thin bags

Cocoa in hhds ⎫
          bbls ⎬ tare marked
          bags—on thin bags nothing

Piemento none imported

Pepper in bbls, brot. from other Am. States, tare marked in Bags none imported, but from London, where the tare allowed is 4 lb. pr. bag—& trett is also allowed by the Seller in Londn. 4 lb pr 104, but this trett is not allowed by the Seller here in any instance that I have known.

My practice in allowing tare under the present Collection law has been precisely as designated by the   [1] Section of that Law. Under the first collection law [2] in which no rate was established my allowance for tare of Sugar in hhds was 12 lb pr. 112, on bbls 10 pr.Ct. This difference was made to give Satisfaction to merchts. as well as to do more equal Justice as there was a manifest difference between a clumsy French hhd, & barrels, often American flour bbls & I conceived 10 pr.Ct. on hhds was not equal to the tare. When barrels were full hooped & appeared heavy, I allowed 12 pr. 112 on them also. My allowance for tare on Coffee in hhds was 12 ℔ Ct., on

Cocoa 15 ⅌ Ct. When this was not satisfactory to the importer, I gave him the option of taking the tare allowd, or to determine it by shifting & weighing the Cask.

I have the Honor to be &c

The Hon. Alex. Hamilton Esq.

LC, RG 36, Collector of Customs at Portsmouth, Letters Sent, 1790–1791, Vol. 2, National Archives; copy, RG 56, Letters from the Collector at Portsmouth, National Archives.

　1. Space left blank in MS. Whipple is referring to Section 35 of "An Act to provide more effectually for the collection of the duties imposed by law on goods, wares and merchandise imported into the United States, and on the tonnage of ships or vessels" (1 *Stat.* 166 [August 4, 1790]).

　2. "An Act to regulate the Collection of the Duties imposed by law on the tonnage of ships or vessels, and on goods, wares and merchandises imported into the United States" (1 *Stat.* 29–49 [July 31, 1789]).

From David Wolfe [1]

[*New York, June 16, 1791.* On July 12, 1791, Hamilton wrote to Wolfe: "I received your letter of the 16th. Ultimo." *Letter not found.*]

　1. Wolfe had been assistant deputy quartermaster general at Claverack, New York, during the American Revolution.

To William Seton

[Philadelphia, June 17, 1791]

Dr Sir

　A considerable time since Mr. Francis Cashier of the Bank of North America delivered me the inclosed piece of Metal which has Mr. Brasiers [1] stamp and is alleged to be less valuable than the Stampt piece of equal weight to which it was intended to correspond by 8/10 Pa. Currency.

　This estimate is formed according to the specific gravity of the piece as ascertained by the Hydrostatic Ballance.

　In the hurry of business I misplaced the piece and it has only turned up within a few days. As the circumstance is worthy of attention I now send it forward with what has been alleged. When you have made the proper investigation you will please to return it.

With great regard   I remain   Your Obed Servamt   A Hamilton

Philadelphia June 17 '91
Wm. Seton Esqr Cashier

ALS, Mr. Broadus Mitchell, New York City.
   1. Ephraim Brasher, goldsmith, of Queen Street, New York City.

To John Davidson

Treasury Department
June 18th 1791

Sir

It has been stated to me by the principal clerk of the Comptrollers Office,[1] that on examining your accounts from October 1st to December 31st 1790 it appears that you have collected from American coasting vessels under twenty tons burthen the sum of two Dollars and forty cents.

The collection of this sum being as I conceive unauthorized by law, and contrary to my circular instruction of Nov 30 1789, it will be proper that you refund the same to the owners of the several vessels from whom you may have collected it.

I am Sir   Your Obedt Servant   Alexander Hamilton

John Davidson Esqr
Collector
Annapolis

Copy, RG 56, Letters to and from the Collectors at Bridgetown and Annapolis, National Archives; copy, RG 56, Letters to Collectors at Small Ports, "Set G," National Archives.
   1. See Joseph Hardy to H, June 16, 1791.

From Abishai Thomas [1]

[Philadelphia, June 18, 1791]

Sir

Congress having appropriated Money for payment of the Invalid pensioners commencing with the 4th March 1789,[2] and payment for the whole of that year having been made by the State of North Carolina to all the pensioners on the returns of that State,[3] prior to the appropriation aforesaid, or at least prior to the knowledge thereof being obtained within the State, it follows that the money sent pursuant to the appropriation remains in the hands of Mr. Haywood [4] the Gentleman who was appointed to make the payments for account of the United States. As Agent for the said State in settlement of her accounts with the United States, the documents and vouchers of the aforesaid payments by the State will necessarily pass through my hands, and I conceive it would be neither proper nor just to exhibit them as charges against the union on the same principles with those for services and supplies rendered during the late war, but rather that as actual money has been paid by the State for the purpose for which the appropriation was made by the U, S, She ought to be reimbursed in actual money, under this impression I take the liberty to solicit that instead of withdrawing the money from the hands of Mr Haywood and appropriating it to other purpose, you cause it to be paid into the hands of the Treasurer of the State [5] on his producing proper vouchers that payment has been made to the invalids by the State aforesaid.

I have the honor to be &c

ADf, North Carolina Department of Archives and History, Raleigh; copy, North Carolina Department of Archives and History.

1. Hugh Williamson and Thomas were appointed as "Agents to Superintend the Settlement of the accounts of this State" with the United States by the North Carolina House of Commons on December 4, 1788 (Clark, *State Records of North Carolina*, XXI, 160).

2. "An Act providing for the payment of Invalid Pensioners of the United States" (1 *Stat.* 95 [September 29, 1789]) had been continued by "An Act further to provide for the Payment of the Invalid Pensioners of the United States" (1 *Stat.* 129–30 [July 16, 1790]) and "An Act to continue in force the act therein mentioned, and to make further provision for the payment of Pensions to Invalids, and for the support of lighthouses, beacons, buoys, and public piers" (1 *Stat.* 218 [March 3, 1791]).

3. On December 29, 1785, in accordance with a recommendation of the Continental Congress, the legislature of North Carolina had passed "An Act for the Relief of the Officers, Soldiers and Seamen, Who Have Been Disabled in the Service of the United States During the Late War" (Clark, *State Records of North Carolina*, XXIV, 735–37).

4. John Haywood had been appointed treasurer of North Carolina early in 1787. See H to Haywood, February 2, 1790.

5. John Haywood.

To Joseph Whipple

Treasury Department
June 18, 1791.

Sir

I have received your letter of the 4th. instant and am much obliged by the historical Statement of the Trade of the State of New hampshire contained it.

I consider a Coasting Licence as rendered void as to the remainder of the year, whenever a vessel departs from the United States upon a foreign Voyage.

The Act of Congress of the 20th day of July 1790 [1] intitles the owner of the Vessel you mention to restitution of the Foreign Tonnage (reserving however the six Cents) altho it may have a bad effect in this Case wherein it appears that the Master shewed a very unbecoming disposition.

It will be proper that you return the defective Hydrometer on Dicas's construction to the Collector of New York or Mr. Christopher Colles of that place, informing them of the reason and advising me of it. The last of Dicas's I presume you have received.

I am, Sir,   Your Obedt. & Hble. servant   Alexander Hamilton

Joseph Whipple Esqr.
Collector of the Customs,
Portsmouth N. Hampshire.

LS, RG 56, Letters to the Collector at Portsmouth, National Archives; copy, RG 56, Letters to Collectors at Small Ports, "Set G," National Archives.
  1. "An Act imposing duties on the tonnage of ships or vessels" (1 *Stat.* 135–36).

From William Short

Paris June 19. 1791

Sir

I had the honor of addressing you by M. de Ternant [1] three letters dated June 3. 5 & 10. In the first of them I informed you that the

ALS, letterpress copy, William Short Papers, Library of Congress.
  1. Jean Baptiste de Ternant, French Minister Plenipotentiary to the United States.

million of florins you had destined for this country would be paid immediately by the desire of this government to their bankers at Amsterdam.[2] A difficulty has since arisen between them & the commissioners of the U. S.[3] which it is necessary to explain to you, as well as what has led to it.

You will recollect that last fall a part of the reimbursement made to this country was by bills of exchange, & that the government had written to request that the rest should be paid to their bankers at Amsterdam. M. du Fresne's letter [4] went further & requested that in future the commissioners of the U. S. would pay such sums as might be destined for France, to the same bankers instead of remitting it by bills of exchange. The rate as you know was settled agreeably to that which was then current. It was evident that the commissioners were not pleased with this mode of payment & desired to have the remitting of the sums by bills. Still it appears to me so especially just & proper to comply with the request of the French government & so impossible to refuse it, the rate of exchange being settled agreeably to the common course that I did not hesitate to have the payment made in that manner. The commissioners made no other observations than that by remitting these sums gradually, the U. S. might derive advantages which they could not have by paying the whole sum at once at Amsterdam. I was not of the same opinion with respect to the advantage accruing to the U. S. because large remittances though made gradually must effect the exchange somewhat (as happened on the small part they remitted last fall) before completed, whereas if paid on the spot it may be regulated according to the rate of the moment. Besides even if this mode exposed the U. S. to the loss of small advantages, I am persuaded they would not think themselves justified truly in refusing this request of the French government, since the payment is of sums which became due long ago & at a time when the exchange was very different from what it is at present.

In order however that there might be no risk of disadvantage to the U. S. by any time elapsing between the moment of this re-imbursement being made known & that of its being effected (as artificial

2. Hogguer, Grand, and Company.
3. Willink, Van Staphorst, and Hubbard, the United States bankers in Amsterdam.
4. Bertrand Dufresne to Short, November 26, 1790 (LS, William Short Papers, Library of Congress). See Short to H, December 18, 1790.

means might be used for giving a momentary rise to the exchange) I thought it advisable to give previous notice to the commissioners that they might take the precautions which should appear to them proper if any were judged necessary. Accordingly on the 26th. of May I wrote to give them [5] notice of this intended payment, adding that I should not mention it to the minister unless it became necessary, before recieving their answer; but if necessary I should do it supposing it could not possibly be attended with inconvenience. Having found it necessary & proper to mention this reimbursement to the minister, I wrote to the commissioners on the 29th [6] informing them of it, authorizing them at the same time if they found it proper, to make the payment to the French bankers at Amsterdam, which they had a right to do under M. Dufresne's letter of last year.[7] M. de Montmorin had desired I would concert the present payment with him also. His absence in the country prevented his sending me his answer [8] to my letter [9] on this subject until the day after (the 30th.) in which he renewed his request to have this payment made to the French bankers at Amsterdam. By the next post therefore I wrote to the commissioners to make this payment.[10] They recieved my letter on the evening of the 7th. of June at the same time that the French bankers recieved that of M. Dufresne. The rate of exchange had undergone a precipitate fall which had astonished every body, the more so as it far exceeded the progressive depreciation of assignats. The commissioners inform me in their letter of the 9th [11] that on the day before they recieved my letter it had been 42½. The post from London bringing an account of a rise in the exchange between that place & Paris, it rose immediately at Amsterdam to 44. When the commissioners offered this money to the French bankers it was from 45 to 46, as quoted on

5. Short to Willink, Van Staphorst, and Hubbard, May 26, 1791 (ALS, William Short Papers, Library of Congress). This letter is printed as an enclosure to Short to H, June 10, 1791.

6. Short to Willink, Van Staphorst, and Hubbard, May 29, 1791 (ALS, letterpress copy, William Short Papers, Library of Congress).

7. See note 4.

8. Comte de Montmorin to Short, May 30, 1791 (LS, William Short Papers, Library of Congress).

9. Short to Montmorin, May 29, 1791 (ALS, letterpress copy, William Short Papers, Library of Congress).

10. See Short to Willink, Van Staphorst, and Hubbard, June 3, 1791 (ALS, letterpress copy, William Short Papers, Library of Congress).

11. Willink, Van Staphorst, and Hubbard to Short, June 9, 1791 (LS, Short Family Papers, Library of Congress).

the certified rate of exchange. Still the bankers refused recieving the money at less than 46. The commissioners refused paying it at that rate without express orders from me & wrote to me on the 9th. desiring instructions. In that letter they hint that this rise was owing in some measure to artificial measures. Probably they thought it in consequence of the intended re-imbursement & they had no doubt it would immediately fall again. They add that they are determined not to make the payment without my orders & *hope I may settle the matter so that they may remit it to Paris, not doubting but that in a very few posts the whole would be placed in the public treasury.* On the 10th. they wrote me "After the departure of our respects of yesterday for the ordinary post Messrs. Hogguer Grand & Co. proposed to furnish us their draught for one million of guilders hence, leaving the course of exchange to be settled between you & M. Dufresne, which obviating all objection on our part we this evening remit this bill for that amount on the public treasury to M. Dufresne, with whom you will please adjust the sum the United States are to be credited for the same." [12]

I was much mortified to learn the difficulty which had taken place at Amsterdam & still more so to find that the commissioners had thus thrown it on me. They must have been sensible that it was much less proper for me to litigate the rate of exchange with M. Dufresne, than for them with Messrs Hogguer, & also that I had much fewer data than they for ascertaining what the usages of the exchange of Amsterdam would entitle us to insist on in such cases.

In consequence of their letters to me & those of the French bankers to M. Dufresne we have had a meeting. He insists on 46. being taken as the rate of exchange, & thinks there can be no doubt that should be rate since it is certified as current at the time of the draught being dated. As the payment was not made as soon as it might have been on account of the difficulty between the American & French bankers & as the former protested formally against the rate being fixed at 46 I told him it was impossible for me to take on myself to fix it having no data for that purpose—that I know not what was the usage of the exchange of Amsterdam in such cases, but that it appeared to me there was no other way of settling the difficulty than by having the

12. Willink, Van Staphorst, and Hubbard to Short, June 10, 1791 (LS, Short Family Papers, Library of Congress).

rate ascertained by indifferent persons on the spot, & that therefore we should refer it to the American & French bankers to be settled in that manner. He neither rejected or accepted this proposition but said he would write to Messrs Hogguer & Co. for further information & in this manner we separated. I have written to Messers Willink &c to make them acquainted with this circumstance & to express to them my mortification at their having thought it advisable to force me to dispute a matter of this sort with the French ministry.

M. Dufresne gave me his word that he had not used any means for having this momentary rise in the exchange effected in consequence of our intended payment to them & agreed it would have been unfair & beneath the dignity of government. It is evident also that the rise cannot be owing entirely to this circumstance since the letter of Messers. Willink &c of the 9th. informs me that the first start took place in consequence of the exchange of London on Paris coming quoted to Amsterdam at ¾ d Stlg per crown higher than the preceding post; & this was before our intended payment was known. It is possible however that the French bankers who recieved M. dufresne's letter at the same time that my second one arrived for Messrs Willink &c may have made it known before the order was made for the purpose of contributing to the rise. If it is found that this was the case I have no doubt the French ministry will agree that the rise occasioned thereby should not be used to the disadvantage of the U.S. & you will certainly think that as far as the use was independent of that circumstance the U. S. should in justice submit to it. The more so as it is evident that the fall of the exchange at Amsterdam to 42½. was artificial & local since the exchange at Paris on Amsterdam did not fall to the same point but remained I think always above 44. I should mention also that one of the principal causes of the sudden fall of exchange caused at that time, viz the large sums that this government found it necessary to have brought from abroad in Specie. I suppose it useless to add that the exchange has gone on regularly declining for some time so that 46, the rate which M. Dufresne insists on for this payment is much below that at which the payment was made last fall & which you considered with reason as highly advantageous—it having been if I do not mistake about 50.

I hope you will excuse these minute details, Sir & that you will be of opinion with me; first that I ought not to have refused making this payment at Amsterdam being requested thereto by the French government, they agreeing to the current rate of exchange—2: that I take all reasonable precautions for avoiding the disadvantage of a sudden rise in the exchange on account of this payment—& 3. that if finally the French ministry agree that the rate should be settled at what impartial people may think it would have been independent of this payment, as I am persuaded they will, you will consider that the U. S. deserve all the advantages from it to which they are entitled. I will take care that for future payments there shall not be the pretext of a difficulty.

Having said so much in explanation of what concerns myself, it is but justice that I should add with respect the bankers of the U. S., that although they were certainly not satisfied with the mode of payment which I thought myself obliged to prescribe, still I am persuaded they have in this instance acted agreeably to what they considered the interest of the U. S. in making the difficulty. Considering the rise as artificial & momentary on the day after recieving the order for payment, they refused to make it at the rate Messrs Hogguer & Co. insisted on—this was the 8th.—finding that the rise continued on the 9th. & 10th. & not knowing where it would stop, they determined to make the payment, thus extricating themselves from the embarrassment & leaving me to dispute the rate at which it should be settled. I have the honor to be with perfect respect Sir your most obedt. humble servt.

Wm. Short

The Honble Alexander Hamilton Secretary of the Treasury

To George Washington

Philadelphia June 19th. 1791.

Sir

I have been duly honored with your letter of the 13 inst: from Mt. Vernon; and, according to your desire, have informed Mr. Wolcott of your intention to appoint him Comptroller. This appointment gives me particular pleasure, as I am confident it will be a *great* & *real* improvement in the state of the Treasury Department. There can no material inconvenience attend the postponing a decision concerning the future Auditor, till your arrival in this city.

I am very happy to learn that the circumstances of your journey have been in all respects so favourable. It has certainly been a particularly fortunate one, and I doubt not it will have been of real utility.

There is nothing which can be said to be new here worth communicating, except generally that all my Accounts from *Europe,* both private & official, concur in proving that the impressions now entertained of our government and its affairs (I may say) *throughout* that quarter of the Globe are of a nature the most flattering & pleasing.

With my best & warmest wishes for your health & happiness, and the most cordial & respectful attachment,

I have the honor to be,   Sir,   Your most Obedient   & most hble Servant   Alex: Hamilton

LC, George Washington Papers, Library of Congress.

From John Fitzgerald [1]

[*Alexandria, Virginia, June 20, 1791.* On June 30, 1791, Hamilton wrote to Fitzgerald: "Yours of the 20th of June came duly to hand." *Letter not found.*]

1. Fitzgerald, a neighbor of George Washington, had served as one of his aides during the American Revolution. In 1793 he succeeded Charles Lee as collector of customs at Alexandria.

From William Seton

Bank of New York 20th June
1791

Sir

I have the honor to inform you that in the course of half an hour this day, deposits were offered & received at this Bank for the entire Sum of Sixty thousand Dollars towards the Subscriptions to the Bank of the United States agreably to the latitude given in your Letter of the 30th May.[1] Further Deposits on the same principle have already been offered to the amount of Twenty thousand Dollars more, and if it is agreable to you to extend the Sum to be received here to Sixty Thousand Dollars more, am convinced it would be immediately filled up.

I have the honor to be with the greatest respect   Sir, Your Obedt. Hum Sert.   Wm Seton Casr.

Alexr. Hamilton Esqr
Secy. of the Treasury of the U.S.

ALS, Hamilton Papers, Library of Congress; LC, Bank of New York, New York City.
1. Letter not found, but see Seton to H, June 7, 1791.

From Jeremiah Olney

Providence, June 21, 1791. "Mr. Daniel Bucklin Junior has now retd. from Virginia: he having again reassumed the Command of a Coasting Vessel in good employ, and being disappointed in his first expectation of *second*, he declines accepting the station of *Third* Mate, onboard the Cutter building in Connecticut. . . ." [1]

ADfS, Rhode Island Historical Society, Providence; copy, RG 56, Letters from the Collector at Providence, National Archives.
1. See Olney to H, February 17, June 11, 1791.

From Jeremiah Olney

Custom-House,
Providence 21st. June 1791.

Sir.

Mr. Welcome Arnold [1] of this Town imported in the Ship Genl. Washington, which arrived and Entered here from Canton on the 7th instant, a quantity of Teas, which were deposited, and a Bond taken according to Law, [2] for about 1,700 Dollars: Since which, on the 13th. instant, a Bond of his for upwards of 1,000 Dollars became payable, it was not discharged, and the next Day transmitted to the District Attorney, [3] who has put it in Suit. A question now arrises, whether the Bonds directed to be taken by the Inspector of the Revenue for the ascertained Duties on Mr. Arnold's Teas, are to be considered as an *after* Credit, or only a completion of the Bond first taken by me?

He has applied to remove some of the Teas; as the point appeared doubtful, and as refusing Credit to a Merchant of considerable Eminence was a delicate Matter, I have advised the Inspector to permit him, for the present, to take out a small quantity, securing the Duties to his satisfaction. As he will probably wish to take out more in a short time, I beg leave Sir, to intreat your speedy reply to this Letter, with your Opinion upon the subject, and directions for the conduct of the Inspector relative to the remainder of Mr. Arnold's Teas until his Bond shall be satisfied; which was put in Suit at the *stated* District Court in August, and the Execution returnable in November next.

I have the honor to be, With great Respect, Sir, Your Most Obedt. & Most Huml. Servt. Jereh. Olney Collr.

Alexandr. Hamilton Esqr.
Secretary of the Treasury.

ADfS, Rhode Island Historical Society, Providence; copy, RG 56, Letters from the Collector at Providence, National Archives.
1. Arnold was a wealthy merchant and Federalist politician.
2. Olney is referring to Section 42 of "An Act to provide more effectually for the collection of the duties imposed by law on goods, wares and merchandise imported into the United States, and on the tonnage of ships or vessels" (1 *Stat.* 168 [August 4, 1790]), which governed the importation of tea from China.
3. William Channing.

From Jeremiah Olney

Custom House,
Providence 21st. June 1791.

Sir.

In conformity to your circular Letters of the 14th. of April and 25th of May,[1] I now enclose an Account of all the Fees and Commissions received, and the Expences paid, by the Officers of the Customs in this District, the latter in detail, and the former as much so as, I hope, will prove satisfactory. By the Statement in the Tenth page, it will appear how the Account stands at the end of the Year with myself, the Naval Officer,[2] and the Surveyor[3] of this Port: the balance of mine, you will perceive, is 56 Dollars and 8½ Cents against me! *You* Sir, I am convinced, *do* not, and I flatter myself that *Congress will* not, expect me to execute the disagreeable Duties of my Office without an adequate Compensation, much less for Nothing. I have therefore no doubt but my Case will, at the next Session, be taken into consideration, and a handsome Provision made for me in future, and an equitable allowance for the Year past.

In what way this can best be done, must be left to your superior Judgement to Report, and the Wisdom of the Legislature to determine.

The Naval Officer and Surveyor, will address you in their own behalf, by this Post.[4]

I have the Honor to be, With great Respect and Esteem, Sir, Your Most Obedt. & Most Huml. Servt.

Jereh. Olney
Collector.

Alexr. Hamilton Esqr.
Secretary of the Treasury.

ADfS, Rhode Island Historical Society, Providence; copy, RG 56, Letters from the Collector at Providence, National Archives.
   1. Circular of May 25, 1791, not found, but see H to Olney, May 25, 1791.
   2. Ebenezer Thompson.
   3. William Barton.
   4. No letter on this subject from Thompson or Barton has been found.

Treasury Department Circular to the Supervisors of the Revenue

Treasury Department,
June 22, 1791.

Sir,

Having been directed by the House of Representatives to report a Plan for *promoting Manufactures* in the United States,[1] I am desirous of obtaining as accurate Information as possible of the actual State of Manufactures in the several States.

Conceiving that this Information is not likely to be obtained in any Way so complete, full and systematic, as by a resort to the Supervisors of the respective Districts, I do not permit myself to be diverted from an Application to you by the Reflection that the Trouble it will give you does not fall within the particular Line of your official Duty. I count on your readiness to cooperate in whatever may promote the public Service.

I request therefore that you will give me as accurate Information as it shall be in your Power to obtain, *of the Manufactures of every Kind carried on within the Limits of your District, whether incidentally in the domestic Way, or as regular Trades—of the respective Times of their first Establishment—of the Degree of Maturity they have obtained—of the Quantities periodically made—of the Prices at which they are sold—of their respective Qualities—of the impediments, if any, under which they labour—of the Encouragements, if any, which they enjoy under the Laws of the State—whether they are carried on by Societies, Companies, or Individuals.*

It would also be acceptable to me, to have Samples in Cases in which it could be done with Convenience, and without Expence.

It is my Wish that this Information, be transmitted progressively, that is, as fast as it can be obtained. And where you receive any Communications by Letter, it will fully answer my Purpose to receive the Letter, instead of a transmission of its Substance, in a Letter from Yourself.

It is unnecessary for me to observe, that there is nothing so urgent in the Object of this request as to require that you should, in the least, interfere, with your other Engagements.

I am, with great Consideration,   Sir, Your Obl. Sert.

A. Hamilton

Copy, to John Dexter, Rhode Island Historical Society, Providence.

1. On January 15, 1790, the House "*Ordered,* That it be referred to the Secretary of the Treasury to prepare and report to this House, a proper plan or plans, conformably to the recommendation of the President of the United States, in his speech to both Houses of Congress, for the encouragement and promotion of such manufactories as will tend to render the United States independent of other nations for essential, particularly for military supplies" (*Journal of the House,* I, 141–42).

For a similar request for information on manufactures, see H to Benjamin Lincoln, January 25, 1790.

To Joshua Wentworth [1]

[*Philadelphia, June 22, 1791.* On September 7, 1791, Wentworth wrote to Hamilton: "Your letters of the 7th of May & 22nd June were duly received." *Letter of June 22 not found.*]

1. As Wentworth was the supervisor of the revenue for the District of New Hampshire, this letter may have been the Treasury Department circular which H sent to the supervisors of the revenue on this date.

To John Adams

[Philadelphia, June 23, 1791–1794]

Mr. Hamilton will have the honor of Dineing with the Vice President on the 30th. of June agreeably to his Obliging invitation.

June 23th

D, in unidentified handwriting, Hull Collection, Smithsonian Institution.

To William Heth

Philadelphia
June 23 [–24] 1791

My Dear Sir

I have before me your letter of the 16th instant.

My opinion is that there is and necessarily must be a great number of undefined particulars incident to the general duty of every officer, for the requiring of which no special warrant is to be found in any law. The test of what he is obliged to do and what he is not must be the relation which the thing required bears to his *prescribed* or *specified* duties. Thus it is the duty (for instance) of every officer employed in every department of the Revenue to give the Treasury all the information which arises out of his official documents and opportunities, though it is not his duty to furnish dissertations on midwifry or witchcraft.

What law could ever define the details of the duty of a Secretary of the Treasury? It is evident these must be an endless variety of things unexpressed which are incident to the nature of his station & which he is bound in duty to perform at the call of the President. One of these duties is to give information concerning all matters which are ascertainable by the course of proceedings at the custom houses relating to the Trade of the Country. And how is he to perform this duty if he has not a right to call on each officer of the customs for the materials in his possession?

If it be said the law should then require this, I answer that the detail would be endless. And surely it would not answer to say in respect to any officer that he must do *whatever* he is required to do. And if all that he is to do is to be defined the Statutes of the United States must be more voluminous than those of any Country in the world.

There is a large chapter of duties *between Executive Officers* which grow out of the Nature of Executive power and which the natural relations of things can alone determine.

Consult, my Dear Sir, the Code of any nation whatever and examine the practice in relation to the point in question and you will find there is no law providing for a thousandth part of the duties which each officer performs in the great political machine & which unless performed would arrest its motions.

The mode of compensation can make no difference whether by salary Commission fees some or all. In whatever shape each of them is only a compensation for performing the duties of a *certain office* and what the officer is bound to perform must be tested by the nature of the Office not by the nature of the reward.

I am aware that I have in different instances called for services which were not incident to the nature of the offices of the persons from whom they were asked. But I have been pretty careful to the best of my judgment to distinguish them from those which were incident to the Office & even in cases which would justify it to procure for them some special emolument. The instance which produced your letter is in my opinion fairly within the line of office.

I acknowlege however that it is possible even to make duties which are applicable to offices oppressive by calling for too much. Whether I have done this, I will not undertake to say. It is certain that it has not been my intention. That I have required nothing which has not been of real importance.

There is no doubt that the compensations whatever shape they assume ought to be adequate. It is to be admitted that though in some instances those allowed under the National Government are ample, in others they are deficient. They have in most cases however in regard to the Officers of the Customs been progressive & a further progress is in the nature of the thing.

Do not mistake any thing I have said. I am not dissatisfied with your appeal nor unfriendly to its object, though my judgment in the particular case is decidedly against yours.

You will I doubt not on your part receive what I have said as I intend it & believe me always to be as I truly am

Your real friend & humble ser   A Hamilton

June 24. 1791
Col W Heth

ALS, Mr. Hall Park McCullough, North Bennington, Vermont.

To Benjamin Lincoln

Treasury Department, June 23, 1791. "I have received your letter of the 14th instant,[1] inclosing three certificates of public debt in the names of the Trustees of the sinking fund. Two of them are herewith returned, that they may be cancelled, and certificates of Transfer to the books of the Treasury, issued in lieu of them. . . ."

LS, RG 36, Collector of Customs at Boston, Letters from the Treasury, 1789–1808, National Archives; copy, RG 56, Letters to the Collector at Boston, National Archives; copy, RG 56, Letters to Collectors at Small Ports, "Set G," National Archives.

1. Letter not found.

To William Seton

[*Philadelphia, June 23, 1791.* On June 24, 1791, Seton wrote to Hamilton: "I am this moment favored with your Letter of the 23rd." *Letter not found.*]

From Nathaniel Appleton

United States Loan Office
Boston 24th June 1791

Sr.

Circular Letter 6th instant is received. The Treasurer of this State [1] informs me that this State never issued any of their own Obligations in exchange for Continental Securities, all the Federal securities which they are, or have been possessed of, were received either by Taxes or by the Sale of Lands &c. so that I presume the precautions which you point out will not be necessary in this State. Your favour 16th instant [2] is received as also the Treasurer's of same date inclosing his draft on the Cashier of the Massachusetts Bank for 40,000 Dollars. I believe this sum with the 20,000 recd. before will be sufficient for the Interest due next Quarter. If it should appear otherwise when the Books are ballanced I shall give you the earliest notice.

 with great respect I have the honor to be Sr. y most humble Servant   N A

LC, RG 53, Massachusetts State Loan Office, Letter Book, 1785–1791, Vol. "259–M," National Archives.
 1. Alexander Hodgdon.
 2. Letter not found.

From John Berrien [1]

District of Savannah June 24th.
1791

Sir

 I observe in the Excise Law, that all Casks & other Vessels containing spirituous liquors imported into the United States &c. are to be mark'd with the Number, Quantity, proof, name of the Vessel in wh. it is imported, & Port of Entry.[2] I will thank you to direct me whether the idea extends to each Jug of Ginn wh: contains only one quart, or every basket of Annisseed wh. contains only one Gallon. The law does not except them in the clause wh. directs that all spirits shall be marked & yet I conceive that it cannot be the intention to include them. I shall be much oblig'd by your direction on the subject, & am Sir very Obediently Your Most hume Servt.

               John Berrien
               I. R.

Alexr. Hamilton Esqr.

ALS, RG 58, General Records, 1791–1803, National Archives.
 1. Berrien was inspector of the revenue for Savannah.
 2. For Section 12 of "An Act repealing, after the last day of June next, the duties heretofore laid upon Distilled Spirits imported from abroad, and laying others in their stead; and also upon Spirits distilled within the United States, and for appropriating the same" (1 *Stat.* 202 [March 3, 1791]), see "Treasury Department Circular to the Collectors of the Customs," May 26, 1791.

From William Seton [1]

Bank of New York 24 June [1791]

Sir

I am this moment favored with your Letter of the 23rd,[2] saying it will be agreable to you that deposits be received towards subscriptions to the Bank of the United States to the extent of Forty thousand Dollars more upon the same principals with those for the Sixty thousand.

This extention of Forty thousand Dollars is already all engaged, and I have applicants names set down for Thirty three thousand seven hundred Dollars more, that I have not the least doubt Sixty thousand beyond the Forty thousand would be immediately taken up. If it is agreable to you to grant this extention it will be doing a favor to the Citizens of the State.

I have the honor to be.

LC, Bank of New York, New York City.
   1. For background to this letter, see H to the President and Directors of the Bank of Massachusetts, May 30, 1791, and Seton to H, June 7, 20, 1791.
   2. Letter not found.

From Thomas Jefferson

Philadelphia June 25, 1791.

Sir

Your favour of the 8th. inst. could only be recieved on my return here, and I have this morning been considering of it's contents. I think with you that it will be interesting to recieve from different countries the details it enumerates. Some of these I am already in a regular course of recieving. Others when once well executed, will scarcely need to be repeated. As to these I already possess what may answer your views in part. ⟨I⟩[1] must therefore give you the trouble to call on me in some ⟨of your walks⟩, in order that after seeing what I possess, ⟨we⟩ may decide on the proper supplement. I think it advi⟨seable⟩ not to trouble gentlemen abroad with sending what we have already, because the less we give them to do the more secure we shall be of having it done.

I am with the most respectful esteem Dr. Sir   Your most obedt &
most humble servt   Th: Jefferson

The Secretary of the Treasury

ALS, letterpress copy, Thomas Jefferson Papers, Library of Congress; LC, Papers
of the Continental Congress, National Archives.
    1. The words within broken brackets have been taken from the letter book
copy.

To William Seton

Treasury Department June 25th 1791.

Sir,

    You will find from my Letter of the 23rd instant [1] that I have ex-
tended the sum that may be received by the Bank of New York of
persons intending to become subscribers to the Bank of the United
States as far as 100,000 Dollars, which supercedes in a degree the
requisition with regard to the Notes of your institution.

    I could not engage in the arrangement proposed by means of that
paper because I [should] [2] not [be] able to limit the extent [of the
operation.]

    I am, Sir,   Your most obedt servant   Alexander Hamilton

Willm Seton Esqr

LS, The Andre deCoppet Collection, Princeton University Library.
    1. Letter not found.
    2. Bracketed words are in H's handwriting.

To William Short

(Duplicate)   Treasury Department
                                              June 25th. 1791

Sir,

    I received two days since your letter of the 11th. of March last.

    Mine to you of the 13th. of April & of the 9th & 24th of May (of
which copies are herewith sent) will have informed you of my
opinion, concerning the negotiation for the transfer of the debt due
to France, will have removed the impediments to your progress on

the business committed to you, and will have apprised you of my views generally.

You will readily imagine, that it must have been in a great degree necessary to let the devellopement of our prospects at home precede a definitive arrangement with regard to the disposition of foreign resources; and you will, from this, account for your not having been earlier apprized of what was to be done.

It is not impossible, that the return of the President to this place which is expected to be on the 4th. or 5th of next month will give you still greater latitude than has been yet given.

I observe with some surprize the application which has been made by Mr. Grand.[1] Surely the naming of a place in any contract for the payment of monies can have reference only to the contracting parties, and may at pleasure be changed by their joint consent.

Your suggestion of the expediency of diffusing in Holland a knowledge of the affairs of the United States is evidently well founded.

It would however be of some delicacy to select such things as might make a favourable impression from those which might have a contrary tendency, which cannot well be judged of but by a person on or near the spot. And unless there were an *American* character stationary in the scene itself, there would be little certainty of a disinterested or judicious selection.

With great consideration and esteem   I have the honor to be   Sir
Your obedient Servant   Alexander Hamilton

William Short Esqr.
Chargé des Affairs

LS, William Short Papers, Library of Congress.
  1. Ferdinand Le Grand. See Short to H, March 11, 1791.

Treasury Department Circular to the Supervisors of the Revenue

Treasury Department
June 25 1791

Sir,

It appears proper that a notification to the *distillers* and *importers* of distilled spirits be published in the Gazettes, containing information of the Office of inspection in which they are (in the three first days of July) to make entry of the spirits by them respectively distilled or imported, which shall be on hand on the 1st day of July next.[1]

I am, sir, Your Most Obedt Servant   Alexander Hamilton

LS, to John Chester, MS Division, New York Public Library.
  1. This was a requirement of Section 25 of "An Act repealing, after the last day of June next, the duties heretofore laid upon Distilled Spirits imported from abroad, and laying others in their stead; and also upon Spirits distilled within the United States, and for appropriating the same" (1 *Stat.* 205 [March 3, 1791]).

To Otho H. Williams

Treasury Department,
June 25 1791

Sir,

The Commissioner of Loans for the state of Maryland,[1] after allowing for the Eight thousand dollars with which you furnished him,[2] and a sum of five thousand dollars remitted him, in notes of the Bank of Maryland, would be deficient about five thousand five hundred Dollars of the sum requisite for the payment of the interest which will be payable in your state, upon the public debt on the first of next month; unless he should have been able to dispose of some drafts sent him upon the Banks of North America & New York.

I have desired him, in case of deficiency, to apply to the Bank of Maryland on the presumption, that funds will be there on the public account to meet the demand. But there is a possibility that this may not be the case, to the extent of about four thousand dollars. Deducting the amount of all the drafts, which have been drawn upon you from the Treasury, it appeared by your return of the 18th instant, that you would have a surplus of seven thousand one hundred & sixty six Dollars, ninety four cents, to be applied to the purposes of the Commissioner of Loans. The eight thousand Dollars, with which you have furnished him, somewhat exceeds that surplus; but whatever you *shall have received after the date* of the above mentioned return, *over and above the difference* between the then surplus and the eight thousand dollars furnished to the Commissioner is open to a disposition. This, therefore, to an amount not exceeding four thousand Dollars, you will pay into the Bank of Maryland to be passed to the Credit of the Treasurer of the United States; taking duplicate receipts for what you shall pay, and forwarding one of them to this Office. And I shall be glad to be immediately advised how much of this sum you will be able to pay into the Bank by the first of July.

I am, sir, Your Obed Servant. Alex Hamilton

Otho H Williams Esqr.

LS, Columbia University Libraries.
1. Thomas Harwood.
2. See H to Williams, May 25, 1791.

From William Ellery

Newport [Rhode Island] June 26, 1791. Encloses weekly return and requests Hamilton "Please to inform me for what ports or places Consuls are appointed, and of the names of the Consuls for the respective places."

LC, Newport Historical Society, Newport, Rhode Island.

Alexander Dallas to Alexander Hamilton, Henry Knox, and Thomas Jefferson

Philadelphia, June 27, 1791. "In Obedience to the directions of the Governor, I have the honor to present to you, a Copy of the Laws of this Commonwealth, passed at the last Sessions of the General Assembly."

LC, Division of Public Records, Pennsylvania Historical and Museum Commission, Harrisburg.

From Thomas Smith

June 27th 1791 Loan Office [Philadelphia] Penna.

Sir,

The Ballance of Stock remaining on the Books of this Office are as follows viz—

6 ℔ Ct Stock
Dollrs.

393.386 .. 9	Interest from January 1791	11801 .. 58
773.051 .. 57	Ditto April ditto	11595 .. 77
		23397 .. 35

3 ℔ Ct Stock

162421 .. 82	Interest from Jany 1. 1791	2436 .. 32
363317.49	Do April 1. 1791	2724. 88
		5161 .. 20

Unfunded Stock

82221 .. 63	Int from Jan 1st 1791	1644.43
29573 .. 77	Int from April 1. 1791	295.73
	Arearages of Int	269.86
		2210 .. 2
		30768 .. 57.

There therefore appears to be thirty thousand seven hundred & sixty eight Dollars & 57/100 necessary for the payment of Int. to the quarter ending the 30th. June Inst. There may be some small deviations as it has been impossible for me yet to finish the Examination of the Books &c. but I hope to compleat it by to morrow night when if any material alterations should happen, I shall immediately inform you thereof.

I am &c.

Honble. Alexander Hamilton Secy Treasury

LC, RG 53, Pennsylvania State Loan Office, Letter Book, 1790–1794, Vol. "615-P," National Archives.

From James Taylor and Abishai Thomas [1]

[Philadelphia, June 27, 1791]

Sir

As there are sundry Credits to the State of N. Carolina existing on the books of the Treasury of the U.S. The vouchers of which the undersigned Agents of said State are not in possession of whereon to Support the claims of said State for such credits, We take the liberty to solicit that you will be so good as to direct the proper Officer to furnish us on or before the 30th instant with an authenticated Account of all such credits. We are

With great respect, Sir Yr. Most Obt Servts.

27th June 1791
The honle A Hamilton
Sec of the Treasury

Df, in the writing of Abishai Thomas, North Carolina Department of Archives and History, Raleigh; copy, North Carolina Department of Archives and History.
1. In the recess of the North Carolina legislature Taylor had been appointed by Governor Alexander Martin as a second state agent to superintend the settlement of the accounts of North Carolina with the United States. Taylor replaced Hugh Williamson, who was prohibited from serving both as agent and as member of the House of Representatives from North Carolina. Taylor served until January 19, 1792.
For a discussion of the general problem of adjusting the accounts between the states and the United States in which Taylor and Thomas were involved as agents of North Carolina, see Ferguson, *Power of the Purse*, 203–19.

Treasury Department Circular to the Governors of the States

Treasury Department
June 27. 1791

Sir,

The legislature of the United States have directed in the 18th. Section of the Act making provision for the public debt [1] that the payment of interest should be suspended in respect to the debt of any State which may have issued its own certificates for those of the ⟨U⟩nited States "until it shall appear to the satisfaction of the Secretary of the Treasury that certificates issued for that purpose by such state have been reexchanged or redeemed or until those which shall not have been reexchanged or redeemed, shall be surrendered to the United States." I find it necessary therefore to request your attention to the subject. If the state of Maryland [2] has issued any such certificates as are contemplated by the above recited Section, it will give certainty to the operations of the Treasury and may prevent delays inconvenient to the public creditors if you will direct the proper officers to cause the state of the fact as it regards Maryland to be made to appear to me. Should this general suggestion be less explicit than you desire, I shall on being notified that it is your wish, point out more particularly the documents that would appear to satisfy the law.

I have the honor to be with perfect respect   Sir   Your most obedient and most humble Servant

Alexander Hamilton
Secy of the Treasury

LS, to George Clinton, Virginia Historical Society, Richmond; LS, to Samuel Huntington, Yale University Library; copy, to Samuel Huntington, Massachusetts Historical Society, Boston; LS, to Alexander Martin, North Carolina Department of Archives and History, Raleigh; LC, to Alexander Martin, North Carolina Department of Archives and History, Raleigh; LS, to Beverley Randolph, Archives Division, Virginia State Library, Richmond; copy, to Thomas Mifflin, Division of Public Records, Pennsylvania Historical and Museum Commission, Harrisburg.

1. "An Act making provision for the (payment of the) Debt of the United States" (1 *Stat.* 138–44 [August 4, 1790]). See "Treasury Department Circular to the Commissioners of Loans," May 27, June 6, 1791.

2. The name of the state varies in each circular, but there was apparently some confusion on the part of the clerk. In the circular addressed to Randolph the state inserted is Connecticut. In the circular sent to Mifflin "Delaware" is inserted, but at the bottom of the page the following note signed by Alexander Dallas appears: "say 'Pensylvania.' Error in the original."

Treasury Department Circular
to the Supervisors of the Revenue

Treasury Department
June 27 1791

Sir,

Inconveniencies have been apprehended by some of the *holders* of distilled spirits, *other than importers and distillers,* from the want of the Mark of "Old Stock" on the spirits they may have in store on the first day of July next.[1] It appears advisable to let it be understood among the holders of spirits that if they desire their stock on hand to be examined and marked, their wishes will be complied with. At the same time it may be well to observe to them that it was within the original plan, to apply the safeguard, of thus marking the Old Stock as well to that held by purchasers, as to the stock of importers and distillers. This and other parts of the law wherein the alterations it underwent might, without circumspection, give rise to hardships and inconveniencies, may be so noticed to the dealers in spirits, and will recommend ⟨to⟩ all the Officers of the Revenue great prudence in their operations under it, particularly in respect to seizures *merely* for want of certificates. An early opportuni⟨ty⟩ may be taken to correct some parts of it, and others, like that respecting Old Stock, will be merely occasional.

I am, Sir,   Your Most Obedt Servant   Alexander Hamilton

LS, to John Chester, New Jersey Historical Society, Newark.
    1. The new excise law went into effect on July 1, 1791. See "An Act repealing, after the last day of June next, the duties heretofore laid upon Distilled Spirits imported from abroad, and laying others in their stead; and also upon Spirits distilled within the United States, and for appropriating the same" (1 *Stat.* 199–214 [March 3, 1791]).

From William Allibone

[*Philadelphia, June 28, 1791.*] Reports on the condition of navigational aids in the Delaware River in the vicinity of Philadelphia.

ALS, RG 26, Lighthouse Letters Received, Vol. "A," Pennsylvania and Southern States, National Archives.

From Clement Biddle [1]

[Philadelphia] June 28. 1791

I have on your behalf engaged the House & Lot in Market street of Mr. stein [2] for One Year. The House to be furnished in about six weeks from this Date & he is to erect a frame stable for Six Horses & Coach House for the Rent of Two hundred & fifty pounds for the year.   C B

LC, Historical Society of Pennsylvania, Philadelphia.
    1. Biddle was a prominent Philadelphia merchant and Federal marshal of Pennsylvania.
    2. Philip Stein, a Philadelphia merchant

From Richard Harison

New York, June 28, 1791. "Inclosed is my Account against the United States as far as the same has been audited. There are some services relating to Persons still in Confinement which will be included in my future Accounts when *their* Fate is ascertained. . . ."

LC, New-York Historical Society, New York City.

From Gouverneur Morris [1]

London 28 June 1791.

My dear Sir

I have lately been compelled to take some of your three per Cent Stocks in order to cover Part of a large Debt very disagreably circumstanced and to replace a Portion of heavy Advances have sold it again and am bound in heavy Penalties to have the Transfer immediately made. This Stock consists of the Arrearage of Interest to the last Day of the last Year on $382.878. .60 Cts of liquidated Debt standing in the Treasury Books at the Credit of Messrs. Francis Baring, Edmund Boehm and Thomas Henchman of this City; which Arrearage amounts to $68918 .. 15 Cts. I have some Reason to believe that Difficulties have arisen in the Treasury Offices upon this Subject heretofore and that they have objected to seperating the three perCents from the omnium unless the whole were subscribed to the new Loan. But this which is a Kind of compulsory Proceeding will have a very bad Effect on our Credit which is still exposed to many Attacks every one of which is more or less injurious. But as to these Things in general I will not pretend to judge leaving them entirely to you and applying only to my own particular Affair which will prove exceedingly injurious should I be disappointed in the Hope that this Transfer may immediately take Place. The Attorney appointed to transact the Business is Mr. George Fox of Philadelphia and I have requested my friend Mr Morris [2] who will deliver you this Letter to attend to it.

LC, Gouverneur Morris Papers, Library of Congress.

1. The transaction described in this letter apparently involved Morris's association with Daniel Parker in an attempt to purchase into the United States domestic debt. E. James Ferguson has described this enterprise as follows:

"In 1789 Parker's negotiations involved Gouverneur Morris. Morris had gone abroad early that year to restore the badly deteriorated affairs of his friend Robert Morris. . . . He soon became engrossed in securities speculation and in efforts to refinance the American debt to France. Upon his arrival, he met Parker. . . . He and Parker talked of organizing an international syndicate which would combine all European investors in a single company and purchase virtually the entire domestic debt of the United States. . . . Morris [went] to

London where he gained the ear of several English capitalists, including the Barings, who had already begun to invest in American securities. Morris, in company with Parker and an English merchant, Samuel Rogers, agreed with Francis Baring, Edmund Boehm, and Thomas Hinchman to deliver $600,000 in securities before the end of the year." (*Power of the Purse*, 264–65.)

2. Presumably Robert Morris. The firm of Willing, Morris, and Swanwick, of which Robert Morris was a member, was also involved in the transfer of securities. See George Fox to H, September 14, 1791.

To William Seton

[*Philadelphia, June 28, 1791*. On June 30, 1791, Seton wrote to Hamilton: "I have been honored . . . with your Letter of the 28th." *Letter not found.*]

From William Seton

[New York] 28 June 1791

Sir

I am just honored with your Letter of the 25th and hope tomorrow to hear from you in answer to mine of the 24th as the applications to pay in Money towards the Subscriptions to the Bank of the United States have now increased to the sum of 41775 Dollars beyond the last extention of forty thousand.

I have the honor to be with great respect   Sir   Your Obed. Humb Ser

LC, Bank of New York, New York City.

From James Taylor and Abishai Thomas

[Philadelphia, June 28, 1791]

Sir

On the 18th. Instant Mr. Thomas had the Honor to address you on the Subject of the pensions paid to invalids by the state of N. Carolina, since which we have found that payments made by that State to Widows & orphans of deceased officers are in the same predicament.[1] We therefore respectfully request that with your answer to Mr. Thomas's letter you will favour us with your sentiments on the propriety of presenting all claims for payment under the latter head subsequent to the fourth March 1789, at the Treasury of the United States for reimbursment in money.

We are &c

A. T.⎱
J. T.⎰ Agents

28th June 1791
Hone A Hamilton
Sec. Treasury

Df, in the writing of Abishai Thomas, North Carolina Department of Archives and History, Raleigh; copy, North Carolina Department of Archives and History.
  1. On December 29, 1785, the North Carolina legislature had passed "An Act for the Relief of the Widows or Children of Officers Who Have Died in the Service of the United States" (Clark, *State Records of North Carolina*, XXIV, 744). Governor Alexander Martin had suggested in a letter read in the North Carolina House of Commons on November 12, 1790, that the North Carolina pension acts for Revolutionary War invalids, widows, and orphans should be repealed in view of Federal legislation. On December 11, 1790, however, a resolution continuing payments was passed by the House of Commons and approved by the Senate (*Journal of the House of Commons. North Carolina. At a General Assembly begun and held at Fayetteville, on the first day of November, in the year of our Lord one thousand seven hundred and ninety, and in the fifteenth year of the independence of the United States of America: Being the first session of this Assembly* [Edenton: Printed by Hodge & Wills, n.d.], 17, 71).

From Joseph Whipple

Portsmouth New Hampe. 28 June 1791

Sir

The Carpenter who undertook the Hull of the Revenue Cutter building in this port having been Sick Several Weeks the Work was unavoidably delay'd. She will be launched in 8 or 10 days. The Station of 3rd Mate being Still vacant I would beg leave to name Samuel Hobert,[1] a young man of whom I have heard a good Character, & the Nomination of him is made by Capt Yeaton.[2]

I now transmit you An Act lately enclosed to me by the President of the State [3] making a Conditional Cession to the United States of the Lighthouse together with 1¾ Acre of Ground which takes in the Old Fort on the eastern point of the Island of New Castle.[4] There is Still half an acre of land remaining, claimed by the State, which would be a useful addition should any fortification on this Spot be thought necessary hereafter. It has been customary heretofore to hoist Colours on the approach of any Vessels, the expence of which having been supported under the Military establishment continued at this Fort more than a Century past, has now ceased, on the Cession of the Fort & discharge of its keepers, & it cannot be continued without a small additional expence to the Lighthouse to which it was before connected. It would be a gratifying conveniency to the Trade to have these Signals continued.

If any particular form is required in the Statement of the Lighthouse Accounts & the introduction of them into my Account Current be pleased to advise me. I shall compleat my payments to the Contracter on the last day of this Month & form a new Contract. I shall be obliged to increase the Sum given in order to enable the Contractor to furnish the best quality of Oil which could not be done under the first contract.

The first years pensions of Invalids directed to be paid by me, is discharged except the pensions of 4 Invalids who have not yet appeared, & who are probably removed out of the State, or dead. Your directions to retain monies in my hands for these payments and also the Secretary for the Department of War's ⟨warrant⟩ [5] specifies a larger Sum than I have, or shall pay. I wish to be informed to whom the vouchers of payment shall be transmitted, & how the charge is to be Introduced into my general Account with the United States.

I have the honor to be   Sir,   very respectfully   Your Most Obedt servt.   Joseph Whipple

Honble. Alexander Hamilton Esquire

ALS, RG 26, Lighthouse Letters Received, Vol. "B," New Hampshire and Massachusetts, National Archives; LC, Collector of Customs at Portsmouth, Letters Sent, 1790–1791, Vol. 2, National Archives; copy, RG 56, Letters from the Collector at Portsmouth, National Archives.

  1. Samuel Hobart.

  2. Hopley Yeaton was the master of the Federal revenue cutter in Portsmouth harbor.

  3. John Sullivan.

  4. Whipple is referring to Fort William and Mary and the Portsmouth lighthouse on New Castle Island. The New Hampshire legislature voted the cession in February, 1791.

  5. This word has been taken from the letter book copy.

To John Fitzgerald

Philadelphia
June 30. 1791

My Dear Sir

Yours of the 20th of June [1] came duly to hand. The inclosed for our friend Lee [2] was immediately forwarded to him. I was happy in the occasion of hearing from you.

Are you doing any thing at Alexandria about the Bank of the United States? Tis to be wished the interest in it may be as much diffused as possible. Nor will this disserve your local views. The prospect is that in a week the subscriptions will be full.

Afecty Yrs   A Hamilton

John Fitzgerald Esqr.

ALS, Mr. William N. Dearborn, Nashville, Tennessee.
   1. Letter not found.
   2. Charles Lee.

To Benjamin Goodhue [1]

Philadelphia June 30. 1791

My Dear Sir

As Mr. Coxe,[2] who I think informed me he had a letter from you on the same subject undertook to say all that could be said in relation to Mr. Gray's affair; I permitted the hurry of business to keep me silent. Nothing further concerning the affair has since come to me; so that I am wholly ignorant what turn it may have taken.

It must have given you pleasure to learn how much the constitution of the United States & the measures under it, in which you have had so considerable an agency have contributed to raise this Country in the estimation of Europe. According to the accounts received here, the change which has been wrought in the opinion of that part of the world respecting the U States is almost wonderful.

The British Cabinet wish to be thought disposed to enter into amicable & liberal arrangements with us. They had appointed Mr Elliot [3]

who on private considerations had declined & it is affirmed from pretty good though not *decisive* authority, that they have substituted a Mr. Hammond,[4] & that his arrival may shortly be expected.

I would not warrant the issue; but if some liberal arrangement with Great Britain should ensue, it will have a prodigious effect upon the Conduct of some other parts of Europe. Tis however most wise for us to depend as little as possible upon European Caprice & to exert ourselves to the utmost to unfold and improve every domestic resource.

In all appearance the subscriptions to the Bank of the United States will proceed with astonishing rapidity. Twill not be surprising if a week completes them.

With very great esteem & regard   I remain D Sir   Your Obed serv   A Hamilton

B Goodhue Esqr

ALS, New York Society Library, New York City.
1. Goodhue was a member of the House of Representatives from Massachusetts.
2. Tench Coxe, Assistant Secretary of the Treasury.
3. Presumably Andrew Elliot. See H to George Washington, April 11, 1791.
4. George Hammond, who had served as chargé d'affaires at Vienna from 1788 to 1790. In 1791 he served as Minister Plenipotentiary at Madrid. In September, 1791, he was appointed British Minister Plenipotentiary to the United States.

To John Haywood

Treasury Department
June 30th. 1791

Sir,

I duly received your letter [1] relative to the payment of the invalid pensioners of the State of North Carolina, and the two remittances, which have been made to you for the purpose of discharging the same.[2] On receipt of this letter it is my desire that you pay to William Skinner Esqr. the Commr. of Loans or to his order the specie in your hands, and that you deliver to him the Treasurers draft on the Collector of Newbern, endorsed by you payable to him or his order. You will also furnish him, if you please with the original or copies of the letters of instruction, and the originals of any other papers ⟨you⟩ may have received from this department or that of War relative to this business. If you will take the trouble to procure duplicate receipts for the Cash draft and papers and will transmit one of them ⟨to⟩ this office, its reception here shall be duly acknowledged.

I am, Sir with great consideration   Your most Obedt Servant

Alexander Hamilton

⟨John Hay⟩ward Esqr
⟨Treasurer⟩of the State of No Carolina
Hillsborough

LS, Southern Historical Collection, University of North Carolina Library.
   1. Letter not found.
   2. For background concerning the payment of invalid pensioners in North Carolina, see Abishai Thomas to H, June 18, 1791; James Taylor and Thomas to H, June 28, 1791; H to Taylor and Thomas, June 30, 1791.

From William Seton

[New York] 30th. June 1791

Sir

I have been honored this afternoon with your Letter of the 28th.[1] authorising the receipt at this Bank of the further Sum of 60,000 Dollars in addition to the 100,000 towards the Subscriptions to the Bank of the United States.

I have the pleasure to say the whole and entire Sum of 160,000 Dollars is engaged and I expect will be actually deposited in the course of tomorrow & Certificates granted for the same.

This Money I have carried to the credit of the United States in a Separate Account in our Books, and wish to receive your instructions whether it is to remain so, or be passed to the Treasurers Account.

I have the honor to be with great respect   Sir   Your Obed Hue Serv

LC, Bank of New York, New York City.
   1. Letter not found, but see Seton to H, June 24, 1791, and H to Seton, June 25, 1791.

To William Short

(Duplicate)   Treasury Department
                                               June 30th. 1791.

Sir,

Since closing my letter,[1] herewith transmitted, yours of the 4th. of March transmitting a copy of the contract for the last loan has been delivered to me.

A ratification of that contract by the President will be forwarded as speedily as possible after his return to the seat of Government which is expected to be in the first week of the next month.

There is in a late letter from Messrs. Willinks & Van Staphorst[2] something like a hope expressed of a possibility ere long to obtain money for the United States, at a lower rate of interest than heretofore; if a competent discretion be allowed to watch and improve favourable moments. There is no disinclination here to your allowing those Gentlemen such a discretion as you may judge requisite to the accomplishment of so valuable an end, within the limits of your own.

Lest any misapprehension should arise from the mode of expression in my letter of the 24th. of May, you will please to understand that you are at liberty to set on foot a new loan, upon the amount of the first being *taken up* or *contracted* for. I observe that the word *subscribed* is used in different letters from Holland as synonimous with the *payment* of the money *contracted for,* or as we should say here *subscribed.*

With very great consideration & esteem   I have the honor to be Sir   Your most obedt Servant   Alexander Hamilton

Willm. Short Esqr
Charges des Affairs

LS, William Short Papers, Library of Congress.
  1. H to Short, June 25, 1791.
  2. Letter not found.

To James Taylor and Abishai Thomas

Treasury Department
June 30th. 1791.

Gentlemen:

I have to acknowledge the receipt of your letters of the 18th. and 28th. instant as agents for the state of North Carolina.

Altho the laws relative to the payment of the invalid pensioners [1] fully authorize the payment of the money to those individuals, I do not consider them as warranting a payment to the State of North Carolina whose Executive appears to have discharged a part of the demands of those persons upon the public. It has moreover not been the practice to pay to a state the amount of any claims upon the United States they may have discharged, tho' such state is intitled to introduce a corresponding charge into the accounts to be rendered to the general board of Commissioners.[2]

As I conceive the payments made by North Carolina to the widows and orphans of deceased officers [3] to depend on the same principles, which I have mentioned in the case of the invalids, I can only recommend that those payments also be introduced into the accounts to be rendered to the Commissioners in behalf of that state.

I am, with due Consideration Gentlemen Your most obedt Servant
Alexander Hamilton

A. Thomas & James Taylor
Esqrs., Agents for the
State of North Carolina

LS, Pierpont Morgan Library, New York City.
1. See Thomas to H, June 18, 1791, note 2.
2. H is referring to the board of commissioners for settling accounts between the United States and the individual states.
3. See Taylor and Thomas to H, June 28, 1791.

To Wilhem and Jan Willink, Nicholaas and Jacob Van Staphorst, and Nicholas Hubbard

Treasury Department,
June 30th. 1791.

Gentlemen,

You will please to consider it as a standing instruction, that you are to apply whatever monies may be, at any time, in your hands, of which no different application has been specially directed, to the payment of the interest and premiums, which shall, from time to time, become payable on the loans, which have been or shall be made, for the United States in Holland.

I am &c. Alexander Hamilton.

Messrs. Willink, Van Staphorst and Hubbard.

Copy, RG 233, Reports of the Treasury Department, 1792–1793, Vol. III, National Archives. This letter was enclosed in H's "Report on Foreign Loans," February 13, 1793.

Agreement with Titus Salter [1]

Portsmouth, New Hampshire, July 1, 1791. Salter agrees to "support, maintain and attend the Lighthouse at New Castle" from July 1 to December 31, 1791, for $158.60.

DS, RG 26, Lighthouse Letters Received, "Segregated" Lighthouse Records, Lear, National Archives; copy RG 26, Lighthouse Letters Received, Lighthouse Deeds and Contracts, National Archives.

1. This document is signed by Salter and by Joseph Whipple for H.

From Meletiah Jordan

Frenchman's Bay [District of Maine] July 1, 1791. ". . . Your letter of March the 10th [1] enclosed a copy of Return of Vessels built in this District. There has been no business of that sort. . . . Your Letter (Circular) of the 21st March [2] observes I should inform you what Post Office would be most convenient for me to get my Letters from. I could wish to have them left at the Post Office at Beverly &

if it is proper to address them to the care of Captain Robert Haskell of that Place who generally trades to this and the neighbouring District. The Boat I had your sanction to procure for the use of the Office I expect in a few days. The detached situation of the District interspersed with waters and abounding with a Number of Islands which afford commodious harbours and some of them as far distant as thirty miles from the Office will occasion my sending a Boat sometimes to visit the District throughout for I not only have reason to supsect that defrauding the Revenue is practised among the Island part of the District but have been informed of many little parcels of Goods landed on the Coast part of the District, it was impossible for me to prevent, all which difficulties a Boat will in a great measure remedy. The harbour of Cranberry Island particularly is distant from the Office about 25 Miles & is a standing thoroughfare & anchorage for British Vessels bound to & from St. Johns & other parts of the British Provinces of New Brunswick which I have great reason to suspect at times carries on the smuggling Trade. In my letter of the 1st Jany. 1791 I requested you would inform me whether my salary commenced with the date of my Commission or the passing of the Law [3] respecting it. If it should occur to your mind in your first letter to this Office Sir I will be particularly obliged."

LC, RG 56, Letters to Collectors at Gloucester, Machias, and Frenchman's Bay, National Archives.
1. Letter not found.
2. Circular not found.
3. Section 54 of the Collection Law (1 *Stat.* 172–73 [August 4, 1790]).

To Mercy Warren [1]

Philadelphia, July 1, 1791

Madam,—In making you, thus late, my acknowledgements for the honor you did me, by presenting me with a volume of your poems, I dare not attempt an apology for the delay. I can only throw myself upon your clemency for a pardon.

I have not however been equally delinquent towards the work itself, which I have read, more than once, with great interest. It is certain that in the Ladies of Castille, the sex will find a new occasion of triumph. Not being a poet myself, I am in the less danger of feeling mortification at the idea, that in the career of dramatic composition at least, female genius in the United States has outstripped the Male. With great consideration and esteem I have the honor to be, Madam, Your most obedt and humble Servant,   **A. Hamilton**

"Warren-Adams Letters, Being Chiefly a Correspondence Among John Adams, Samuel Adams, and James Warren," II, *Massachusetts Historical Society Collections*, LXXIII (Cambridge, 1925), 326.
   1. Mercy Warren, the sister of James Otis and the wife of James Warren of Plymouth and Milton, Massachusetts, was a well-known poet, dramatist, and historian.

To Fisher Ames

[*Philadelphia, July 2, 1791.* On July 31, 1791, Ames wrote to Hamilton and referred to "your favor of the 2 July." *Letter not found.*]

From William Heth

Private
Dear Sir

Shillelah [1] [Virginia] 2. July 1791

The close application which I have been obliged to pay to the duties of my office, added to the unhealthyness of the place, has confined me at home some days, with a bilious intermittent fever. To this circumstance it is owing, that I have so soon received your very friendly answer of the 23d. Ulto.

Believe me Dear Sir, had you been less frank in delivering your Sentiments and opinions—tho they might have been more flattering perhaps—they would not have been recd as such strong proofs of your friendship for me. I feel myself much indebted to you, for your condescension in replying to me so fully, & for treating me with so much candor & familiarly.

I fear that, I must have expressed myself very illy, in my private letter of the 16th. Ulto or you never could have supposed that, I lookd for laws to define *minutely*, or even *particularly*, the duties of any officer of government; much less, could I possibly question the propriety, necessity, and, consequently the *Right*—in one sense of

ALS, Hamilton Papers, Library of Congress.
   1. Shillelah was one of three Virginia estates owned by Heth.

the word—of *your* calling upon the Officers of the Customs for such information as—to comply with *your* duty—was essential to obtain. The propriety of every syllable which you have said on this subject, never formed any doubt in my mind. I have little doubt also, but I used the word "*right*" improperly, without duly considering the construction it would give to the Sentence, of which it was a member. The *object* of my suggestions, you readily, & clearly enough comprehended. And, my true meaning was this. It appeard to me, to be inconsistent with Justice, & the Spirit of Freedom, for any Legislative Body, to enact such laws, as must in their operation, draw *services* from the free Citizen, without *compensation* and therefore it was, and is still my opinion, that Congress had no *right* to do so. Do I receive any thing from the U States as a compensation for a single Sheet of paper, used out of the current, & clear line of Duty? Commissions & fees of Office, are recd for special services actually performed, & clearly defind. To the aforegoing opinion, I do not find a single remark in your address repugnant. Indeed—so far from it—that I am convinced you think every Collector ought to receive an annual allowance—equal to his stationary at least—if not for such extra Services, as the nature of his Office, and the business which he does, must necessarily subject him to. To obtain such provision, a provision, which Justice & equity demands, was the objct of my address, and to which, you are pleased to say, you are not unfriendly. Sure I am then, you will—being the most proper person—ask it of Congress.

However widely you may have misunderstood me in one respect, persuaded I am, you could not in another. The promptitude with which I have complyd with every request from you, within the scope of my abilities and secluded situation—whether *immediately* in the line of my duty, connected therewith, or independent thereof, must have convinced you, that I never thought you calld for "*too much*" or, "*unimportant information*." Could I for a moment suppose, my Dear Sir, that my zeal, pride, & ambition on this Score, had not been long perceived by you, the mortification which I should feel, would be great indeed!

The indisposition of which I flatter myself I have so far recovered, as to be able to go to the office on Monday to engage in making up my quarterly accounts, urges me to make an observation here, which ought to have been noted in my letter accompanying a statement of the emoluments of my office for the year 1790.[2] Viz—that my emoluments ought to be such, as to enable me to employ a Clerk qualified to do the business of the office in every respect, in case of *sickness or absence.* You will have perceived that the charge for the wages of a clerk, his board &c in *that* Statement, is very low. He is an honest, faithful servant, of great integrity and application, but is possessed of so little genius, or capacity, that he is totally lost whenever a case occurs, in the least deviating from the current business—nor could he post up & close the accounts in the Ledger, & render the present quarterly returns, if his salvation depended upon it. Had my present indisposition happend in April or May or Sept. Oct. or Novr. last, I question whether my office would not have been protested against. You are the best Judge, whether the importance of this District to the revenue is such, as that I ought to be enabled to guard against such casualties. Suppose I was obliged to give 400 Dlls ℔ ann to a Clerk, instead of 250—and which must have been the case, if I had not been able to pay such close attention, & to perform the greatest part of the duty myself—what a pittance I should have had left, for my own labor, responsibility &c, the aforesaid statement will shew.

I had thoughts of, and still wish to pay my respects to you in person, some time this month or next—being vacation season—to consult with you on the eligibility of continuing in my present office, in hopes of Superintendents of the revenue being appointed, on the propriety of the office being moved to a place more healthy, & more desireable to the Merchants of the District, or on the prudence of my offering my services to fill an office more immediately under your eye. On these subjects, I wrote a letter to you some time in May last, but concluding that I might be thought too impatient as to the first, Doubting of the propriety of the second to Richmond, or to any other place in the District but Broadway,[3] And being diffident of my qualifications as to the latter, I declined to forward it, And I should not now, have hinted at them, if I had not formed a resolution to resign my office after next session of Congress, should it not prove so productive as to enable me to settle nearer to it or to pay me better than it has done, for the great sacrifice which I make of my domestic enjoyments; and

2. See Heth to H, January 25, 1791.
3. Broadway or Broadway Landing, which was on the south bank of the Appomattox River about one-half mile west of that river's junction with the James River.

for my own labor, responsibility and risque. Persuaded that you will receive these communications, as made in confidence by a friend, I remain Dear Sir, with the greatest esteem & respect,

Most truly & sincerely Your obliged friend and Very hble servant　　　　　　　　　　　　　　　　　　　　　Wm Heth

The Honble Col Alex Hamilton

To William Seton

[*Philadelphia, July 2, 1791.* Letter listed in dealer's catalogue. *Letter not found.*]

ALS, sold at Parke-Bernet Galleries, May 2–12, 1947, Lot 257.

To Martha Walker [1]

Pha July 2d. 1791

Madam

Mr. Ames [2] has conveyed to me your letter of the 9th of May.[3]

Hitherto it has not been in my power to consider the merits of your application to Congress but you may be assured of its being done so as to admit of a Report at the Commencement of the ensuing session.[4]

While I do not encourage any expectation & while my conduct must be determined by my view of official propriety & duty I may with great truth say that I shall enter upon the Examination with every profession which can be inspired by favorable impression of personal merit & by a sympathetic participation in the distresses of a Lady as deserving as unfortunate. With great consideration I am Madam your obednt Sert　　　　　　　　　　　　　　　　　　　　　A H.

Copy, Hamilton Papers, Library of Congress.

1. An entry in the *Journal of the House* for May 4, 1789, mentions a "petition of Martha Walker, of Boston . . . praying that some relief may be granted her, as the distressed widow of Thomas Walker, Esq. late of Boston, who, at the commencement of the late Revolution, abandoned a very considerable property in the province of Quebec, and attached himself to the interests and fortunes of the United States" (*Journal of the House,* I, 27).

2. Fisher Ames, Federalist Representative from Massachusetts in the House of Representatives.

3. Letter not found.

4. On May 4, 1789, the House tabled Mrs. Walker's petition, and on September 25, 1789, referred it "to the Secretary of the Treasury, to report thereupon . . . to the next session of Congress" (*Journal of the House*, I, 27, 123). No record that H ever made a report on this petition has been found.

From Charles Lee

Alexandria [Virginia] July 3, 1791. "In answer to your letter of the 13th of May,[1] I shall make the following observations. Within this District the practice has been to ascertain the Duties, by Guaging, Weighing and Measuring in all cases where those operations are required by Law. The Authority of an Inspector put on board a vessel coming from an other District into this, has been considered as ceasing with the report of the Vessel at my Office, when another Inspector has been placed in the room of him who attended the Vessel into this District. The Customary Tare allowed by the Merchants here is upon 100 lbs and not 112 lb. . . ."

Copy, RG 56, Letters to and from the Collector at Alexandria, National Archives.
  1. "Treasury Department Circular to the Collectors of the Customs," May 13, 1791.

From Baron de Rottenbourg [1]

London, July 3, 1791. ". . . J'ai pris la liberté de vous ecrire il y a environ 6. Semaines. . . .[2] Aujourdhui je m'emancipe de Vous importuner une Seconde fois à la Sollicitation de ma femme . . . pour obtenir à la cour Federale une entiere reparation des Abus cruels que MMrs. Burr & Cutting [3] ont fait de ma trop grande confiance et credulité. . . . Je vous demande mille pardons de mes importunités, mais persuadé comme je suis de la bonté de votre cœur vis à vis des infortunés innocents, et le de votre droitures, je ne puis que me flatter que vous ne voudrés pas lui refuser cette faveur. . . ."

ALS, Hamilton Papers, Library of Congress.
  1. This letter concerns the claim of Rottenbourg's wife, the former Louisa Henriette Williamos, to the estate of her brother, Charles Williamos of New York, who died in Paris in the seventeen-eighties. In August, 1787, Rottenbourg applied to James Beekman, a New York importer and businessman, for an account of the estate claimed by his wife. Beekman gave Rottenbourg the following account of the estate and Williamos's relationship with Aaron Burr:
  ". . . Your Letter of the 26th August last we duly received respecting the Affairs of the late Mr. Charles Williamos, requesting our Information as to the

State of the Property he possessed in these Parts and whom he might have authorized to administer on his Possessions.

"Although we had the Pleasure of that Gentleman's Acquaintance while in this City, Still our Intimacy was not so great as to be acquainted with the Situation of his Concerns. However heard that he had purchased a Farm at a Place called Paramus (about 20 Miles from hence) in the State of New Jersey of Aaron Burr Esquire of this City.

"Accordingly applied to that Gentleman for Intelligence on the Subject, who informs that Mr. Williamos bought that Farm of him, containing about 300 Acres, Mills etc. for £1200 Currency on which he had paid but a small part of the purchase Money. Says there is due him thereon and for Services done in his Law Profession about £1100. That the Deceased owned in the Township of Stratton 24000 Acres, Value unknown. Likewise in the Patent of Gatehouse in the County of Ulster and State of New York 650 Acres, valued at £1800, though if sold at public Vendue, it would not fetch any thing near that Sum. That the late Mr. Williamos owed on Bond to Mr. P. Allaire £300. Also to Messrs. [W]all and Tardy of Hispaniola a considerable unsettled account as their Attorney has informed Colonel A. Burr, forbidding him to dispose of any of the Property untill their Demand is fully satisfied. And that his personal Effects were valued and sold for £60. . . ." (Philip L. White, ed., *The Beekman Mercantile Papers* [New York, 1956], III, 1245–46.)

In the Hamilton Papers, Library of Congress, there is an undated detailed account in Rottenbourg's handwriting of Williamos's estate and a statement, dated September 3, 1787, of the account with Wall and Tardy, both of which were presumably forwarded to H by Rottenbourg.

2. Letter not found.

3. Leonard M. Cutting, a New York City lawyer.

From William Ellery

Custom House
Newport [Rhode Island] July 4th. 1791

Sir,

Inclosed is my weekly return of monies received and paid, and a monthly return of bonds a certife of Regy. No. 66 granted at this port, & a Cerf. on account of transfer of propy., the copy of an endorsment of the change of master on Regy. No. 4 and a like copy on Enrollment No. 9, also four draughts made on me by the Treasr. of the U. S. in favour of Jabez Bowen Commr. of Loans viz No 1616, & No 1617, for four hund. and fifty dollars each, and No 1624 & 1625 for three hundred dollars each.

Permit me to ask the following question and to request your answer to it. Should not every vessel receive her first Certificate of Registry &c from the Collector of the District where She is built? What hath given rise to this question is this, a vessel built in this District for and to be delivered to citizens residing in the District of Providence was moved thither without papers, and there was first Registered.

It was convenient for them it seems to move her there a hull before she was masted and rigged.

The denomination of vessels is I believe commonly fixed before, and their names given at the time of launching; yet in the case stated the Surveyor of the Port where She was built might find a difficulty in certifying the number of her masts; and the advantages which merchants may find in moving new vessels unmasted & unrigged from one district to another in the same State or from one adjoining State to another, especially in bays & rivers, may be greater than the disadvantages which might possibly result to the Revenue from such vessels passing from one adjoining district and from one adjoining State to another.

The General Assembly of this State sat and rose the last Week, but nothing was done respecting the Light-house.[1] I spoke to some members of both houses, and to a gentleman who is near the Governor, on the subject. They were of opinion that as the United States had Enacted that the expences for the support &c of all Light houses &c shall continue to be defrayed by them until the first day of July 1792, and allowed to the States respectively which had not ceded them, that time to make cessions,[2] a revival of the former motion would prove unsuccessful at present, and that it was best to let it rest.

The Keeper of the Light House informs me that the top of the Light House leaks very much. I shall enquire further into this matter, and give you the necessary information.[3]

I am   Sir   Yr. most obed servt.   Wm Ellery Collr

A Hamilton Esqr
Secry of Treasy

LC, Newport Historical Society, Newport, Rhode Island.
  1. See Ellery to H, March 7, May 9, 1791.
  2. "An Act for the establishment and support of Lighthouses, Beacons, Buoys, and Public Piers" provided that the expenses of such aids to navigation would be paid by the Government for one year upon establishments not yet ceded to the Federal Government by the states (1 *Stat.* 53–54 [August 7, 1789]). "An Act to amend the act for the establishment and support of Lighthouses, beacons, buoys, and public piers" (1 *Stat.* 137 [July 22, 1790]) extended for one year the payment by the Government of the expenses of unceded lighthouses, and by "An Act to continue in force the act therein mentioned, and to make further provision for the payment of Pensions to Invalids, and for the support of light-

houses, beacons, buoys, and public piers" (1 *Stat.* 218–19 [March 3, 1791]) the time limit was extended to July 1, 1792.

3. Ellery endorsed the letter book copy of this letter "Answered Sepr. 16 1791." H's reply has not been found.

From Benjamin Lincoln

Boston, July 5, 1791. "Your letter covering instructions to Cap Williams [1] has been received. I have caused a copy of them to be made. I will attend particularly to his supplies. . . ."

LC, Massachusetts Historical Society, Boston; LC, RG 36, Letters from the Collector at Boston, Letter Book, 1790–1797, National Archives; two copies, RG 56, Letters from the Collector at Boston, National Archives.

1. John Foster Williams. See "Treasury Department Circular to the Captains of the Revenue Cutters," June 1, 4, 1791.

To Jeremiah Olney

Treasury Department
July 6th. 1791

Sir,

It is with regret I feel myself restrained by my sense of the meaning of the law from directing the refusal of Credit to Mr. Arnold [1] on the removal of the teas which have been lately deposited by him; in consequence of the non payment of his Bond as mentioned by you.

But I consider the allowance of subsequent credits upon teas deposited as no more than a continuation of a Credit already given upon the first Bond and which cannot afterwards be revoked. The consideration, which decides my opinion on that point, is, that a different construction might affect third persons who might have purchased the teas and contracted to pay the duties themselves, and who under the law would I conceive have acquired a right to the Credit upon the Teas purchased.

It is proper you should give immediate notice to the Collector of Newport [2] of the delinquency of Mr. Arnold, and a similar notice ought to be extended to the Collectors of Ports in the neighbouring states from Boston to New York lest a credit should be sought elsewhere in evasion of the law. I have no objection however, before you take these steps, which could hardly fail to affect Mr. Arnolds credit as a Merchant, that you apprise him of your instruction to do so; in order that he may have an opportunity to avoid the inconvenience by the payment of his bond.

I am   Sir   Your most obedt Servant   Alexander Hamilton

Jeremh. Olney Esqr.
Collector of Providence

LS, Rhode Island Historical Society, Providence; copy, RG 56, Letters to the Collector at Providence, National Archives; copy, RG 56, Letters to the Collectors at Small Ports, "Set G," National Archives.
    1. Welcome Arnold. For background to this letter, see Olney to H, June 21, 1791.
    2. William Ellery.

From Tobias Lear

[*Philadelphia*] *July* 7, *1791.* "By the Presidents command T. Lear has the honor to transmit to the Secretary of the Treasury a letter from Capt. Cochran [1] of Charleston (S. C.) respecting the building of a cutter at that place. . . ."

LC, George Washington Papers, Library of Congress.
    1. Robert Cochran had been appointed master of the revenue cutter for South Carolina.

To Rufus King

[Philadelphia] July 8. 1791

My Dear Sir

I received your letter [1] on a certain subject and was obliged by it. But there was nothing practicable by way of remedy.

The thing, as it has turned out, though good in the main, has certainly some ill sides. There have also been faults in the detail, which are not favourable to complete satisfaction. But what shall we do? 'Tis the lot of every thing human to mingle a portion of ill with the good.

The President as you will have seen has returned. His journey has done good, as it regards his own impressions. He is persuaded that the dispositions of the Southern people are good; and that certain pictures which have been drawn have been strongly colored by the imaginations of the Drawers.

We have just heared from the Westward; but of no *event* of importance. Things are said to have been in good preparation; The People
of Kentuke wonderfully pleased with the Government: And *Scot*
with a Corps of ardent Volunteers, on their route to demolish every
savage man, woman and Child.[2]

On Tuesday next, I expect to leave this for New York with Mrs.
Hamilton.

Sincerely Yrs.   A Hamilton

R King Esqr.

ALS, New-York Historical Society, New York City.
    1. This letter has not been found. It may, however, be the extract quoted by
H in his letter to George Washington of March 27, 1791. For this extract see
King to H, March 24, 1791.
    2. Indian relations had deteriorated steadily in the Northwest Territory, and
Congress in March, 1791, voted money for a major campaign against the Indians
of the Maumee and Wabash valleys. As part of this campaign Governor Arthur
St. Clair approved a march on the Wabash by Brigadier General Charles Scott,
Virginia commandant of Kentucky, with three thousand mounted Kentucky
militiamen.

From Thomas Mifflin

Philadelphia, July 8, 1791. "Upon the receipt of your circular Letter, of the twenty seventh Ultimo, I directed the Comptroller General of this State,[1] to furnish me with the information which you requested; and I have now inclosed his answer upon the subject. . . ."

[E N C L O S U R E] [2]

John Nicholson to Thomas Mifflin

[Philadelphia, July 2, 1791]

sir,

Through the secretary of The Commonwealth I have received a
copy of a letter circular from the secretary of the Treasury of The
United States addressed to your Excellency on the subject of Certificates of state debt issued for Certificates of Continental debt and relative to the assumption thereof.[3] As the regulations and provisions of
this state enable such creditors to repossess themselves of the Conti-

nental Certificates received for them by the state [4] I apprehend that the case of such creditors of penna. is fully provided for. However in case the secretary of the Treasury wishes to be informed of The quantity Issued by Penna. and now out of this kind, and your Excellency should chuse to lay the same before him; I beg leave to represent that the whole quantity so issued was 5.167 695 33/90 Dollars of which 316,864 30/90 Dolls. were redeemed by The state, and upwards of ⅔ ds. of the remainder have been returned in exchange for the Continental Certificates, and, that the residuary sum is diminishing Daily by farther applications and exchanges thereof.

I have the honor to be   sir   your Most Obed servant

Jno Nicholson
Compt Genls Office
July 2d 1791.

His Excellency Thos Mifflin Esqr Governor of Penna.

LC, Division of Public Records, Pennsylvania Historical and Museum Commission, Harrisburg.

1. On July 1, 1791, Alexander Dallas, secretary of the Commonwealth of Pennsylvania, wrote to John Nicholson, comptroller general of Pennsylvania, requesting a report of the "new loan" certificates (Edmund Hogan, *The Pennsylvania State Trials: Containing the Impeachment, Trial, and Acquittal of Francis Hopkinson and John Nicholson, Esquires* . . . [Philadelphia, 1794], I, 276).

2. ALS, Division of Public Records, Pennsylvania Historical and Museum Commission, Harrisburg.

3. "Treasury Department Circular to the Governors of the States," June 27, 1791.

4. See Thomas Smith to H, February 14, 1791, note 1.

From Thomas Newton, Junior

Norfolk [*Virginia*] *July 8, 1791.* "A long absence from home has been the cause of your letter of the 8th Ulto [1] not being answered sooner. The business shall be attended to as you requested. . . . The business has not been in the least retarded, Mr McComb [2] is ingaged in getting up the stone formerly lodged there, for the same purpose, to make the foundation with. . . ."

ALS, RG 26, Lighthouse Letters Received, Vol. "A," Pennsylvania and Southern States, National Archives.

1. Letter not found.

2. John McComb, Jr., had contracted for the construction of the lighthouse at Cape Henry.

From William Short

Paris July 8. 1791.

Sir

In my last of the 19th. of June I mentioned to you a difficulty which had arisen between the French & American bankers at Amsterdam [1] relative to the payment of the million of florins ordered by your letter of the 13th. of April. I have now the satisfaction to inform you that it is removed & that the payment is probably completed agreeably to the basis proposed by our bankers viz. at the rate of exchange existing at Paris before the sudden rise at Amsterdam. This was 44½—a rate much more advantageous for the U. S. than that at which the payment was made last fall. I was glad that the French ministry came to these terms as well because I was sure it was all the U. S. could have any shadow of right to claim, since it was the proposition of our own bankers as because it spared the disagreeable circumstance of appearing difficult with so just, & patient a creditor as France has been.

I had the pleasure of recieving yesterday Sir, your letter of the 9th of May & am rendered extremely happy by finding that you continue to be satisfied with the course I have pursued in the business confided to me. My late letters will have given you further information with respect to the rising credit of the U. S. & the additional resources which might probably be made use of for exonerating them from their debt to France.[2] I shall add nothing on the subject at present except that the opportunities formerly mentioned continue equally promising.

I have made no direct application for a loan at Genoa & have recieved as yet no direct answer or information with respect to the subject from the minister of Genoa.[3] Still he seems persuaded that a loan might be made there & expects greater lights from his friends to whom he has written & who are the most powerful & richest people of the Republic—the first loan being made would remove all other difficulties. I think it probable they have written to the Genoese consul [4] lately sent to America, for particular information with respect to our

ALS, letterpress copy, William Short Papers, Library of Congress.
  1. The French bankers were Hogguer, Grand, and Company. Willink, Van Staphorst, and Hubbard were the American bankers.
  2. See Short to H, April 9, May 4, June 3, 10, 1791.
  3. Christoforo Vincenzo de Spinola.   4. Joseph Ravard.

situation, government & present resources. Their perfect ignorance of us is certainly the greatest obstacle we should meet with. It is for that reason Sir that I cannot help repeating to you how essential it is that constant, if possible, weekly details should be sent here of the progress of the U. S. in whatever concerns their revenue, commerce, manufactures or agriculture—such things being frequently presented to the public eye would make them acquainted with the U. S. & what is much to be desired make them forget their distance.

I have not yet proposed the loan authorized by your letter of the 13th. of April, because not knowing when your disposition of it would arrive I supposed a short delay could not be disadvantageous, & also because our bankers holding out the idea that by it the rate of interest might possibly be reduced, I could not think myself authorized to neglect such an idea although I did not consider it absolutely to be relied on. This was fully developed in my letters by M. de Ternant.[5] I am now waiting for their explicit answer to my enquiries contained in my letter to them of the 24th. of June, & of which I inclose you a copy.[6] I may now expect this answer daily which will decide what steps I shall take.

Mr. Morris[7] has just returned here from London. He tells me he expects daily an answer from his friends in the low countries to his enquiries made at my request whether they would engage to obtain a loan for the U. S. at $4\frac{1}{2}$ p. cent interest. He seems now to think that they will insist on 5. p cent but adds that he can say nothing certain. As soon as I recieve the information expected from these two places I shall communicate it, & in the mean time shall proceed according as circumstances may dictate relative to the loan.

If I were acquainted with the proportion which you intend for this country I should find it advisable perhaps to open the loan on the condition of recieving that part payable in assignats or such of the French effects as the ministry should be willing to accept. Such a measure could not fail to facilitate a loan whether opened at Amsterdam, Antwerp or Genoa. It is understood that the bonds of the U. S. given in such a loan should be calculated agreeably to the present advantageous rate of exchange on Paris.

5. Jean Baptiste de Ternant, French Minister Plenipotentiary to the United States. See Short to H, June 3, 5, 10, 1791.

6. See enclosure.   7. Gouverneur Morris.

In my researches on the subject of American loans I shall not lose sight of London particularly as I find that you contemplate a credit there as promissory of good consequences.[8]

I shall take measures for having the additional payment of f500,000 made as speedily & as advantageously as possible for the U. S.

I beg you to be persuaded of the sentiments with which I have the honor to be   Sir,   Your most obedient servant   W: Short

The Honble.
Alexander Hamilton, Secretary of the Treasury, Philadelphia.

[E N C L O S U R E]

William Short to Wilhem and Jan Willink, Nicholaas and Jacob Van Staphorst, and Nicholas Hubbard [9]

Paris June 24. 1791.

Gentlemen

Since my last I have not seen M. Dufresne [10] & of course have nothing new to say to you concerning the disagreeable affair of the rate of exchange for the million of florins paid by you. I fear he will not consent to any other mode of settling it than that of the current rate ascertained by sworn brokers agreeably to the data of Messrs. Hogguers & Co's draught furnished you. I hope you will furnish me with proper grounds for contesting this matter since you have thought it proper to throw it on my hands—these can only be by ascertaining the moment of your tender of the million of florins & the then rate of exchange. It would be however much more agreeable & more suitable to the interests of the U. S. if you & Messrs. Hogguer & Co. settle this matter agreeably to the usages of the exchange of Amsterdam.

I will thank you to let me know also the progress of your opinion with respect to the loan at 4½. p. cent—the present price of the 5. p. cent bonds—& also whether it will be *absolutely indispensable* to augment the commission as you say. As it may become essential for the U. S. to make a new loan before the time may arrive when one at 4½. p. cent can be insured—or rather as it may under certain circum-

8. See H to Short, May 9, 1791.
9. ALS, letterpress copy, William Short Papers, Library of Congress.
10. Bertrand Dufresne, director of the Public Treasury of France.

stances be judged proper to open a loan at 5. p. cent instead of await-
ing the contingency of one at 4½. p. cent, it becomes proper to have
your ideas with respect to the commission in that case. Supposing the
value of the bonds had continued as when the last loan [11] was opened
I should have been of opinion that it would have been most for the
advantage of the U. S. to have put the commission of the undertakers
on the former footing viz 1½. p. cent instead of 2 p. cent given on the
last loan, as this would have been an economy of ½. p. cent, for the
U. S. without risking the success of the loan, & would have been the
same thing for you. As the value of these bonds has now risen above
par, I suppose you will consider it perfectly just that the commission
should be paid out of this incident value; & particularly as this value
is increasing I suppose it will be still more agreeable for the undertakers. The current value of the bonds I think was 99½ p. cent at the
opening of the last loan. The commission was then 4. p. cent of which
2. p. cent went to the undertakers—reducing this 2. p. cent to its
former standard of 1½.—it would be equally advantageous for you
to open the next loan at 3½. p. cent commission provided the bonds
had remained at 99½. I suppose then that the U. S. have a right to expect to open their next 5 p. cent. loan at 3½. p. cent commission,
estimating the value of the bonds at 99½. so that whatever their value
may be above that at the opening of the loan will be diminished on the
3½. p. cent—thus if they are at 101.—1½. p. cent will be diminished,
so that the U. S. will have to pay only 2. p. cent commission, although
you receive 3½.—& so in proportion. I suppose there will be no difficulty in this matter as your profits will remain the same as in the last
loan. I shall wait for your answer & hope to recieve it by the return of
post that I may decide according as circumstances may arise here
whether to wait for the contingency of the 4½. p. cent loan or directions (if it becomes indispensable) at 5. p. cent. The former will of
course be waited for as long as possible & would be much prefered as
being much for the interest & credit of the U. S. I am with the utmost
sincerity, Gentlemen, your most obedt. servt.   W: Short

Messers. W & J. Willink &c Nas. & Job. Van Staphorst & Hubbard.
Amsterdam

11. For a description of this loan, see Short to H, February 17, 1791.

Treasury Department Circular
to the Collectors of the Customs

Treasury Department
July 8th. 1791.

Sir,

I have already written to you in regard to the disbursements of the Revenue Cutter on your station,[1] except the pay of the officers and men, and have now to request that you will duly attend to that business also, so as to have in your hands the entire agency. A form will be transmitted to you, in which you will make your quarterly returns at the same periods (though distinctly) as in the Custom house department; and in the mean time, as some arrears of pay are due, you will discharge the demands of the officers from the dates of their commissions and of the seamen from the time when they were shipt, taking sufficient vouchers for your payments.

I am, Sir,   Your most obedt. servant   Alexander Hamilton

LS, to Benjamin Lincoln, RG 36, Collector of Customs at Boston, Letters from the Treasury and Others, 1790–1817, Vol. 10, National Archives; L[S], Office of the Secretary, United States Treasury Department; copy, United States Finance Miscellany, Treasury Circulars, Library of Congress; copy, RG 56, Circulars of the Office of the Secretary, "Set T," National Archives.
1. See "Treasury Department Circular to the Collectors of the Customs," June 1, 1791.

Treasury Department Circular
to the Collectors of the Customs

Treasury Department
July [8–12] [1] 1791.

Sir,

In consequence of two questions lately proposed to me, the first upon the impost Act.,[2] and the 2nd. upon the 41 section of the Collection law,[3] I signify to you my opinion on the following points.

1st. That the teas called "*Young Hyson*" and "*Hyson skin*," are not subject to the duties which, in the several cases are laid on Hyson, but to those only which are imposed on other Green teas; namely twenty Cents, if from China and India in Ships or vessels of the United States. Upon inquiry it appears to me that those teas are not in mercantile language comprehended under the denomination of Hyson; and from inferiority of quality & lowness of price they are not within the spirit of the duties on Hyson.

2ndly. That any merchant who imported teas during the year 1790, and prior to the 4th of August in that year and whose bonds for the duties upon such teas have not expired on paying the duties upon such as have been sold may deposit the residue, with an allowance of further credit not exceeding in the whole eighteen months, pursuant to the 41st. section of the Collection Law. In order to this the identity of the teas ought to be ascertained to the satisfaction of the Collector; In some cases, perhaps, this may be done by comparing the marks of the Chests &ca. with documents in the Office. Where this fails, the Oaths of the parties may be received and it is reasonable and proper that they should be required, as well as the production of such original documents, invoices &ca. as may be in their power.

This being an indulgence susceptible of abuse, it is confided that it will not be allowed without due caution and competent evidence.

I am, Sir,   Your obedt. servant

L[S], to Benjamin Lincoln, RG 36, Collector of Customs at Boston, Letters from the Treasury, 1789–1807, Vol. 4, National Archives; LS, to Jeremiah Olney, Rhode Island Historical Society, Providence; L[S], to Otho H. Williams, Office of the Secretary, United States Treasury Department; copy, United States Finance Miscellany, Treasury Circulars, Library of Congress; copy, RG 56, Circulars of the Office of the Secretary, "Set "T," National Archives.

1. The copy of this circular addressed to Jeremiah Olney was dated July 8, 1791. The other circulars were dated July 12, 1791.

2. "An Act making further provision for the payment of the debts of the United States" (1 Stat. 180–82 [August 10, 1790]).

3. H is actually referring to Section 42, rather than Section 41, of "An Act to provide more effectually for the collection of the duties imposed by law on goods, wares and merchandise imported into the United States, and on the tonnage of ships or vessels" (1 Stat. 168 [August 4, 1790]). This section governed the collection of duties on the importation of tea from China. For an explanation of the discrepancy in the numbering of this act, see H to Richard Harison, April 26, 1791, note 2.

To George Washington

[Philadelphia, July 8, 1791]

The Secretary of the Treasury presents his respects to the president of the United States, and has the honor to enclose a Dispatch which he has just received from Georgia.

July 8. 1791.

LC, George Washington Papers, Library of Congress.

To George Washington

Treasury Department July 8. 1791.

The Secretary of the Treasury has the honor respectfully to submit to the president of the United States, a contract made between the superintendant of the Delaware lighthouse, and Joseph Anthony & Son for oil, the terms of which he humbly conceives to be as favourable to the United States, as could have been effected with any other person for an equal quantity.   Alexander Hamilton

LC, George Washington Papers, Library of Congress.

To George Washington

Treasury Department
July 8, 1791.

The Secretary of the Treasury has the honor respectfully to submit to the President of the United States, a contract between the superintendant of the establishments on Delaware river, & John Wilson, for building a Beacon-boat to be anchored on the shoals of the said river. On a comparison of the estimate of the said Wilson with that of Warwick Hale herein enclosed, and after due enquiry into the proportional value of a similar Beacon-boat heretofore built for the same purpose, as also into the present rates of building vessels in Philadelphia—the Secretary is humbly of opinion, that a contract, more beneficial to the United States with a workman of competent ability would be difficult to effect.   Alexander Hamilton

LC, George Washington Papers, Library of Congress.

From Tobias Lear

[*Philadelphia*] *July 9, 1791.* ". . . the President has received a letter from Mr. Rue,[1] who was appointed second mate of the revenue Cutter on the Delaware station, declining his appointment & returning his commission."

LC, George Washington Papers, Library of Congress.
  1. Benjamin Rue was a Philadelphia sea captain.

To the President and Directors of the Bank of New York

[*Philadelphia, July 9, 1791.* On July 14, 1791, William Seton wrote to Hamilton: "The President & Directors desire me to acknowledge the receipt of your Letter of the 9th instant." *Letter not found.*]

From Edmund Randolph [1]

Philadelphia July 9. 1791

Sir

In answering your communication of the 10th. of december last,[2] I cannot do better, than acknowledge my conviction from the reasoning of Mr. Dayton. That reasoning being in your possession, I beg leave to refer to it, as the groundwork of my opinion, that military rights to land ought to be received on account of his that is Judge Symmes's contract in the manner, contended for by him.

I have the honor, sir,   to be with real esteem   and respect   yr. mo. ob. serv.   Edm: Randolph

The Secretary of the Treasury

ALS, University of Virginia.
  1. For background to this letter, see Jonathan Dayton to H, May 29, 1790.
  2. Letter not found.

From John Daves [1]

New Bern [*North Carolina*] *July 10, 1791.* "Last year when the Law passed laying duties on imported Spirits to be ascertained by Dycas's Hydrometer,[2] not knowing I should be furnished with that Instrument, I sent by a gentleman to London, for one of Dycas's patent Hydrometer's complete which I received in December last just before the law took place requiring the use of that instrument, which one I have made use of ever since. The Hydrometer sent me from your Office I received some time in February last and Fahrenheits Thermometer I never received until the last of March following. That Hydrometer being incomplete when received I never made use of it until the other day I made a tryal with that & the pattent one, and to my very great surprise found a variation of ten degrees between the two. The pattent Hydrometer appears to be a very complete one and corrisponds as near as may be with the different kinds of spirits agreeing with the different rates of proof contained in your letter accompanying the Hydrometer. . . .[3] Should the pattent Hydrometer meet with your approbation, would be glad of your permission to charge it in my account, it cost three and half Guineas in London, which I paid no more than the first cost & charges. It is incumbent on me to acquaint you of the difficulty some of the Officers of the Customs labour under in this District, that is, there are two ports of delivery on the sea board, being each about forty miles from this town, and about twenty-five miles distant from each other, where trade is carried on, there being a Surveyor and Inspector at each port, they not having any Hydrometer to ascertain the Spirits by as yet, I have directed a bottle to be sealed up and sent me of each Cargo, which appears to be a very precarious mode. . . . These Officers are also without Scales & weights or even a very large pair of Steelyards, nor is there any to be borrowed in either place. . . ."

Copy, RG 56, Letters from the Collector at New Bern, National Archives.
    1. Daves was collector of customs at New Bern.
    2. See Section 1 of "An Act making further provision for the payment of the debts of the United States (1 *Stat.* 180–81 [August 10, 1790]).
    3. "Treasury Department Circular to the Collectors of the Customs," December 18, 1790.

From Sharp Delany

[*Philadelphia, July 11, 1791.* On September 8, 1791, Hamilton wrote to Delany: "I have considered the case proposed to me in your letter of the 11th. July." *Letter not found.*]

From William Ellery

Newport [*Rhode Island*] *July 11, 1791.* ". . . Inclosed is a statement of the case of the Brig Seven Brothers, and of the case of Joseph Finch late master of her. I have applied to the Carpenter who covered the Light-House to examine the condition of it.[1] He could not attend this business the last week, but said he will attend it this and make report."

LC, Newport Historical Society, Newport, Rhode Island.
  1. See Ellery to H, July 4, 1791.

From Beverley Randolph

Council Chamber, Richmond
July 11th. 1791.

Sir,

I have had the Honour to receive your Favour of the 27th. of the last month.[1] In answer to which I have to inform you, that this State never issued her own Certificates in exchange for those of the United States. And am respectfully &c.   Beverley Randolph.

LC, Archives Division, Virginia State Library, Richmond.
  1. "Treasury Department Circular to the Governors of the States," June 27, 1791.

From Nathaniel Appleton

Boston, July 12, 1791. ". . . I improve the first oppo. to inform you of the amount of the dividend of Interest made up to 30th June last, it appears at present to be 55.768 $^{80}/_{100}$. . . ."

LC, RG 53, Massachusetts State Loan Office, Letter Book, 1785–1791, Vol. "259-M," National Archives.

Conversation with George Beckwith [1]

Philadelphia
July 12th. [–30] 1791

Lieutenant Colonel Beckwith. The gazette of the United States, published this morning gives us a detailed account of certain recent proceedings in the Western territory and at Detroit, communicated at Pittsburgh, by a person of the name of Ray, who had been made prisoner by the Savages, and having, as it is stated been purchased by an officer in The King's Service, obtained his freedom, was conveyed to Niagara, and from thence, returned to Fort Pitt; [2] the whole account is so improbable, so incompatible with our system, and so diametrically opposite to my communications from Lord Dorchester, that I feel it incumbent on me to declare, I consider the information to be little better than a fable.

Mr. _____ I have not seen the Newspaper account, but I am acquainted with the communications to which you refer; from those, Ray appears to be a very illiterate man, and his intelligence is very improbable in many respects; he is however extremely particular; he says he saw a Colonel or Mr. McGee in the Indian Country, a Mr. Elliot and some others whose names he mentions, and he goes into details respecting these gentlemen and their objects at the Indian Towns; [3] no decisive opinions can be formed from his communications but of course they attract attention.

Lt. Colonel Beckwith Insofar as Ray's declarations may have a tendency to excite any suspicions of an unfriendly nature on the part of the King's government, they are totally devoid of truth, and as such, I trust will not be credited.

There are accounts from different parts of the Indian Country within these few days; they mention, that your treaty with the Five Nations is concluded, that you have made a peace with them and that they are determined to maintain a strict neutrality. [4]

Mr. _____ Yes, it is so stated; Colonel Pickering however is not yet arrived in Town; he is expected daily with the particulars of the Treaty, which are not yet fully known. [5]

Lt. Colonel Beckwith   Colonel Procter was sent to these Tribes, about the end of last March; it was reported at that time, that this gentleman's message was to induce them to join your forces, against the hostile Indians; I never took particular notice of this, as it did not seem well authenticated.[6]

Mr. _____ Colonel Proctor was sent about the time you mention, but not with that object. You may recollect some of our frontier people, committed a murder on certain Indians of the Five Nations, and this gentleman was sent to those Tribes by The President, to dissuade them from joining the hostile Indians, in consequence of that atrocious proceeding, individuals might have wished them to have taken a part in The War, but Colonel Proctor was not charged with any such message by our government.

I have read the speech of one of the Indian Chiefs, at the late treaty with the Five Nations respecting the political conduct of your government in relation to them; this speech is replete with sound sense, and carries with it the most convincing proofs of your influence being extended to promote pacific purposes.

Lt. Colonel Beckwith   It is precisely in the spirit of the declarations I have uniformly made you, and the same views are extended to all the other Tribes in the Western Territory.

I have read General Scott's report of his expedition against The Wabash Tribes,[7] and his message to them, subsequent to the destruction of their Towns; from the general aspect of things at present, I am inclined to hope a peace may take place during the Autumn.

Mr. _____ We are disposed to pacific measures with those Indians, and if they shew any symptoms of such being their wish, we shall be ready to meet them on fair terms of accomodation.

D, PRO: F.O., Series 4, Vol. 12, Part II.

1. This document was enclosed in a letter Beckwith wrote to Lord Grenville, July 31, 1791. Beckwith also enclosed in this letter an account of a conversation which he held with H on June 15, 1791.

Beckwith identifies his informant only as "a gentleman in office." In the account of this conversation which Lord Dorchester sent to Grenville, however, the first of the two conversations recorded in this letter—that of June 15, 1791—was attributed to "Supposed 7," Beckwith's code number for H. As Beckwith in his letter of July 31 to Grenville attributed the conversation of July 12, 1791, to the same person who conversed with him on June 15, H must have been his informant.

2. The "Narrative of Mr. Thomas Rhea, who arrived at Pittsburg, from

captivity, the 30th of June 1791" is printed in *ASP, Indian Affairs*, I, 196–97. The "Narrative" was sent to Henry Knox, Secretary of War, by Major General Richard Butler, second in command under Governor Arthur St. Clair. Knox, in turn, submitted it to George Washington.

3. Colonel Alexander McKee was the British deputy Indian superintendent at Detroit; Captain Matthew Elliott was McKee's assistant. The Indians, Thomas Rhea reported, came to McKee's headquarters on the Miami River "in parties of one, two, four, and five hundred at a time, from different quarters, and received from Mr. McKee, and the Indian officers, clothing, arms, ammunition, provision, &c. and set out immediately for the Upper Miami towns, where they understood the forces of the United States were bending their course, and in order to supply the Indians from other quarters collected there" (*ASP, Indian Affairs*, I, 196).

4. At the beginning of this paragraph Beckwith wrote: "In continuation." In the margin opposite the paragraph he dated this portion of the conversation "July 30th. 1791."

On May 2, 1791, Colonel Timothy Pickering had been authorized by the Secretary of War to assure the "Six Nations of Indians, so termed" that the United States Government wished to treat them "with entire justice and humanity" (*ASP, Indian Affairs*, I, 165).

5. Pickering concluded his negotiations with the Indians on July 15. They are described in his letter to the Secretary of War dated August 16, 1791 (*ASP, Indian Affairs*, I, 170), and in Pickering's "Journal of the Council and Treaty Held at Newtown Point, June 1791," Timothy Pickering Papers, Massachusetts Historical Society, Boston.

6. In March, 1791, Colonel Thomas Procter was sent as commissioner from the United States to negotiate with the Miami and Wabash Indians. The Secretary of War's instructions to Procter, which are printed in *ASP, Indian Affairs*, I, 145–46, do not include the orders mentioned by Beckwith.

7. Brigadier General Charles Scott was authorized by Knox in March, 1791, to command the Kentucky militia in an expedition against Indian towns on the Wabash River. The results of the expedition were reported to Knox on June 28, 1791 (*ASP, Indian Affairs*, I, 131–32). Scott, leading some seven hundred Kentuckians, destroyed four or five Indian towns on the upper Wabash.

To Joseph Whipple

Treasury Department
July 12. 1791

Sir,

The Act of the legislature of New Hampshire, inclosed in your letter of the 28th June, is received. The name of Mr Samuel Hubert [1] will be placed before the President when he is filling the Station of the 3d Mate of the Cutter.

You will be pleased to inform in what particulars the hoisting of the flag at the fort [2] is convenient or useful to the trade and navigation, and the annual expence which will attend the continuance of it. Your account, as Superintendant of the light house, must be kept distinctly and rendered separately from that in your capacity, as Collector of the Customs, as also must be that as paymaster of the invalids. They are to be transmitted with the vouchers to this departm⟨ent⟩.

Joseph Whipple Esqr.
Portsmouth.

L[S], RG 56, Letters to the Collector at Portsmouth, National Archives; copy, RG 56, Letters to Collectors at Small Ports, "Set G," National Archives.
  1. Samuel Hobart.
  2. See Whipple to H, June 28, 1791.

To David Wolfe

Treasury Department
July 12. 1791.

Sir,

I received your letter of the 16th. Ultimo,[1] on the subject of the certificates of the late Quartermaster general.[2]

The observations you make have been duly communicated to the Comptroller and will receive a proper consideration, but you will perceive that in adjusting the affairs of the Quartermaster Generals department, under the late Government, the information of the gentleman [3] who was charged with the superintendence of it, can not fail to have considerable weight with the officers of the Treasury.

I am   Sir   Your obedient Servant   Alex Hamilton

Mr. David Wolfe
New York

LS. The Andre deCoppet Collection, Princeton University Library.
  1. Letter not found.
  2. During the American Revolution the quartermaster general issued certificates in lieu of money for goods and services.
  3. Timothy Pickering had served as quartermaster general during the American Revolution.

To Richard Harison

Treasury Department
July 13, 1791.

Sir,

The account taxed by the Judge of the District Court and rendered by you, on the 28th Ultimo, against the United States has been transmitted to the Auditors office, and when passed by that Officer & the Comptroller, will be discharged by the Treasurer on my warrant. That which relates to the opinions given by you on cases arising in this office will be paid to you when there shall be an appropriation for those objects. This however will not be until the next session of Congress.

I am, sir, with great consideration [1]   Your Most Obedt Servt.

Alex Hamilton

Richd Harison Esqr.
Atto of the U States,
New York.

LS, New-York Historical Society, New York City.
1. The words "with great consideration" are in H's handwriting.

From Benjamin Lincoln

[Boston] 13 July 1791

Sir

A short time since we had a vessel entered here with about one hundred quarter chests of tea. It was entered by the importer as Camphu. H since informs me that his papers also describe it as *Bohea Congo*. As it was entered as a black tea other than Bohea, tho~ it appears to me to be of the same kind, and the importer says it cannot be sold for more, I hardly know what to do with it. If I receive the duty as a Black Tea other than Bohea the ods in duty will probably prevent it's being sold here. I have inclosed a sample for your inspection. I wish your after opinion.

No distilled Spirits can be imported into the United States in casks less than 50 Gals:, excepting gin &c.[1] A number of vessels have arrived since the first of July with ardent Spirits. Some were out of the country when the law passed. By law all such spirits as are found in casks less than 50 Gals are forfeited, & The Vessel. I was always in hopes that as an executive officer I should not be obliged to hesitate one moment respecting the propriety of my executing, fully, the law or not, but here I find a keg of rum on board one vessel, a qtr Cask on board an other &c, put on board without a knowledge of the law; as an evidence there of they have been reported without reserve. Matters thus circumstanced have induced me to pauses. To detain the vessels would I think operate injuriously to the revenue & sour many of our best merchants & friends to the government. I think it probable that such cases must have taken place with you & some mode of conduct must have been established, which may operate as a general rule. I shall be much obliged by your sentiments on the subject by the very first opportunity.

LC, Massachusetts Historical Society, Boston; LC, RG 36, Collector of Customs at Boston, Letter Book, 1790–1797, National Archives; copy, RG 56, Letters from the Collector at Boston, National Archives.

1. Section 33 of "An Act repealing, after the last day of June next, the duties heretofore laid upon Distilled Spirits imported from abroad, and laying others in their stead; and also upon Spirits distilled within the United States, and for appropriating the same" (1 *Stat.* 207 [March 3, 1791]) provided: "That after the last day of June next, no spirituous liquors except gin or cordials in cases, jugs or bottles, shall be brought from any foreign port or place, in casks of less capacity than fifty gallons at the least, on pain of forfeiting of the said spirits, and of the ship or vessel in which they shall be brought. . . ."

From William Lowder for the Board of Assessors of the Town of Boston [1]

Boston, July 14, 1791.

Sir,

The assessors of the town of Boston are now apportioning a large tax on the inhabitants. Their duty obliges them to take every measure in order to ascertain the quantum of taxable property each citizen holds, that the assessment may be just, and the burthen equal. They have already ascertained the full amount of the property in trade, in such a manner as can scarcely fail of being right, by appealing to the public impost-office; this class of citizens, together with the industrious mechanics, have so long born the burthen of public taxes, without an equal aid, from the new funded interest, that they have become clamorous, and indeed unless the taxes are more equally distributed in future, will not be able to discharge their several assessments.

In relief, therefore, to this useful part of the community, we are called upon by every principle, to use every means to come to a true knowledge of the property of those citizens who live upon the interest of their monies in the public funds. For that purpose the committee of the assessors have officially waited upon Mr. Appleton [2] here, and desired him to suffer them to inspect his books of loans: he has hitherto declined a compliance (or rather doubted his authority to comply) with their request. The object of the board in this request is as much with a design to do justice to the stock-holders, as the community at large; for should we be refused this reasonable request for the purpose of doing public equity, it will throw us into the disagreeable necessity of taxing the stock-holders according to their reputed property in the funds, which in very many instances may be greater than they really possess. We therefore should esteem it a particular favor in the Secretary of the Treasury to direct the loan commissioner here to expose the public books of loan to the inspection of the assessors of the town of Boston, whenever they shall officially think it necessary. Not doubting that so reasonable a request will be readily complied with. In behalf and by order of the assessors,

I have the honor to subscribe myself your most obedient and very humble servant,   William Lowder, Chairman.

P.S. Shall esteem it a favor to have an answer to this as soon as may be, as the business of this office must necessarily be at a stand until we hear from you.

To the hon. Alexander Hamilton, esquire, Secretary of the Treasury of the United States, Philadelphia.

The Federal Gazette and Philadelphia Daily Advertiser, August 30, 1791.
  1. The assessors explained the publication of this letter in these words: "From the various applications made to the assessors of the town of Boston, relative to the correspondence between them and the Secretary of the Treasury on the subject of taxation, they find themselves necessitated, in order to prevent any misrepresentations, as well as to gratify their fellow citizens, to furnish them with a copy of what has passed on the subject" (*The Federal Gazette*, August 30, 1791).
  2. Nathaniel Appleton was commissioner of loans for Massachusetts.

From William Seton

[New York] 14 July 1791

Sir.

The President & Directors desire me to acknowledge the receipt of your Letter of the 9th instant [1] inclosing a List of the Certificates for money deposited at this Bank towards the Subscriptions to the Bank of the United states which have been paid at the Treasury amg. to 159675 Dolls.

This List exactly agrees with the record of the Certificates granted at this Bank—excepting

One to Bernard Hart [2] of _____ Doll __ 75
& one to Peter Kemble [3] of _____ 250
which would compleat the sum of 160,000 Dollars directed by you to be received.

When these two Certificates appear the money shall be refunded & the remaining 159675 Dolls. passed to the credit of the Treasurer of the United States agreably to your Letter of the 2d. instant.[4]

There was but one Certificate granted for each Deposit.

I have the honor to be with the greatest respect   Sir   &ca.

LC, Bank of New York, New York City.
1. Letter not found.
2. Hart was a New York City broker.
3. Kemble was a New York City merchant.
4. Letter not found.

From Welcome Arnold [1]

Providence 15th July 1791

Sir

The Collector of this district has this day Furnished me with an Extract of your letter to him requiring notice to be transmitted to the Collectors from Boston to New York of my delinquency in the payment of a Bond given in his Office, to Prevent my obtaining Credit Elsewhere "*in Evasion of the Law.*" This official Direction Sir, to the

Collectors of this port I presume could not be given without coming to a Judgment in the dispute Subsisting between him & myself.

I cannot believe Sir that you would knowingly countenance a Public Office under your department, being used as an Engine of Pique, or Resentment; and being Ignorant of the facts & Circumstances Stated to you (except that they were Ex parte)—I was no less Astonished, then wounded, at the order from the Secretary of the Treasury f⟨or⟩ an official Stab at my reputation without any Conditional referrence to the Circumstances of the Case. Is it not possible Sir that a Collector may Err? That he may put a bond in Suit when it is not due? That he may demand a Greater Sum than is due?

When he is convinced of this last, and offers to remit the Surplussage shall he be justified in demanding the cost which may have arisen on the Suit? This cost I take to be the only Obstacle which prevents the duties your letter Alludes to being paid—and Convinced as I am Sir, of the unjustifiable Motives from which it has been Incurred; of my own uprightness towards the public revenue, actually, and Intentionally, and from which No Ill-treatment by the Collector shall provoke me to depart ⟨there⟩ is no Consequence of Property or Reputation, that it can Involve, which I shall not hazard with Chearfulness; in Preference to a Voluntary Complyance with what I deam so Injurious to the rights of a Citizen. Colo. Olney has this moment acquainted me that 127 dol will be deducted from the bond on which I am Sued. The Remainder is ready for him, and has been, I shall pay him no Cost except by Execution. What the Law will determine I know Not, but I am at no loss what will be the feelings of my fellow Citizens. Shall a merchant be placed in the disagreeable Alternative of having his credit destroyd, or of paying every demand which a Collector thro' mistake, or Design shall Exhibit against him? No Sir, I ask your pardon ⟨then⟩ for offering, thus late, some Reasons for my Conduct in a case in which it may Seem, to Some, you have given your opinion; But it is the first moment of my knowledge it was before you in judgment; And I rely with Confidence upon your known Character both in Public & ⟨in⟩ Private life, that the moment you are apprised it was a disputable Case, you will no Sooner decree a Severe penalty upon one party, unheard, in a case between a Citizen and a public Officer, than between Citizen, & Citizen.

I have the Honour to be With all due Respect Sir your most
obt Ser   W A

Hon. Alexander Hamilton Esq.
Secretary of the Treasury
Philadelphia

ADfS, The John Carter Brown Library, Providence, Rhode Island.
    1. For background to this letter, see Jeremiah Olney to H, June 21, 1791; H
to Olney, July 6, 1791.

From William Ellery

Custom House
Newport [Rhode Island] July 18 1791

Sir,

Inclosed is my Statement of fees &c. on which I beg leave to make
a few remarks.

The number of Certifs. of Regy. and Enrollments issued in this,
will probably be less than in the last year, and for the following
reasons. Upon adopting the Constitution by this State the last year [1]
a number of vessels belonging to it were without those papers, which
will not want them this; and the property of several vessels, which,
before that event, had, in order to obtain them, been transferred to
citizens in Massachusetts, have been since transferred and registered
and enrolled anew in this District. The number of first and subsequent
Registers, will therefore, in my opinion, be lessened, and my fees along
with them. And if the fees for coasting vessels should be reduced by
the alterations proposed to be made in the Coasting Act,[2] as it is said
they will be, the balance this year will be against me.

I have not in my Statement credited 29 dolls. 18½ cents received
for my proportion of forfeitures; because I conceive it was not intended that the Officers of the Customs should, in any degree depend
for their support on such precarious a ground; but that a proportion
of fines, penalties and forfeitures is allowed them as some reward for
their vigilance, and the vexation and ill-will which will always accompany prosecutions for transgressions of the Revenue Law.

Permit me, Sir, to refer you to my letter of the 31st. of Jany. last which inclosed my Statement of receipts and Expenditures for the first six months and a third of a month, in which I mentioned there was no prospect, that the nett income of my Office in the succeding six months, would be much encreased.[3] By comparing that with the inclosed Statement it will appear that my opinion was well founded; and it is not probable that the emoluments of my office will be augmented this year.

I have spent a year of great perplexity in the public Service, and unless an allowance is made for my services, it will, on my part, have been spent for naught and in vain. Justice to myself and my family will not admit of such sacrifices, and I am sure, the justice of Congress cannot expect them. It doth not become me to suggest means by which I might receive a sufficient compensation. In you, Sir, I confide for that attention to my case, the influence of which will I trust procure me an allowance for my past, and an adequate compensation for my future services. On this hope and confidence I rest, and am with great esteem

Sir   Yr most obedt servant   W Ellery Collr

A Hamilton Esqr
Secry of Treasy

LC, Newport Historical Society, Newport, Rhode Island.
   1. Rhode Island ratified the Constitution on May 29, 1790.
   2. See H to Ellery, April 11, 1791, note 3.
   3. This letter had not been found when Volume VII of *The Papers of Alexander Hamilton* was published. It has since been located in the Newport Historical Society and will be printed in a supplementary volume.

From William Ellery

Newport [*Rhode Island*] *July 18, 1791.* ". . . The Light-House has been examined by the Carpenter,[1] who covered it, accompanied by the Surveyor of this Port,[2] and the former reports that the Lead upon the Platform in which the Lanthorn stands, is cracked in several places, that the water passes through the crack and falls upon the Wall and inside Wooden work, & that fifteen pieces of sheet lead three feet long & six Inches wide with necessary nails will secure the platform, and some paint & putty the Lanthorn against rain & snow, and that the whole expence of repairs will amount to about thirty dollars. Please to give me your directions whether the repairs shall be made or not."

LC, Newport Historical Society, Newport, Rhode Island.
1. See Ellery to H, July 4, 1791.
2. Daniel Lyman.

From Thomas Newton, Junior

Norfolk [Virginia] July 18th. 1791

Sir

Since I wrote you of the 8th I have been to Cape Henry & took a veiw of the place for fixing the Light house. The Sands are much shifted since laying of the two acres. I had some conversation with Mr. McComb [1] on the subject of going deeper; it is not yet certain that it will be necessary. I will attend to the business & do all in my power for the best, but shall be at a loss, how to act without a copy of the agreement or some instructions, to know in what manner the work is to be done, which you'l please to send on as soon as possible as Mr McComb thinks of beginning the foundation in a fortnight. He mentiond that sheds were to be built for holding of oil, I am apprehensive that they wou'd be coverd with sand in a short time, one gale of wind might effectually prevent the keepers getting at oil, if cesterns were fixed in the Light house they wou'd be safer & more convenient & I suppose no extra charge wou'd attend it, they should be lined with lead. Mr. McComb also mentiond a wooden cornice; if it is the case I am afraid it will soon want repairs, the exposed situation of the place woud soon destroy any wood that cou'd be fixed there & shou'd it want repairing, the scaffolding alone will cost more than the differance between a stone & wooden Cornice.

In what manner is the pavement to be laid? If it is to be done on the loose sand without a wall to keep it up, it will be of little use, but if a wall is run about three feet deep and ten feet from the light house, it wou'd add greatly to the safety of the house & the pavement. I thought it my duty to give these informations; but shall follow whatever directions you shall give. I am

Respectfully   Yr. Obt Servt   Thos. Newton Jr.

ALS, RG 26, Lighthouse Letters Received, Vol. "A," Pennsylvania and Southern States, National Archives.
    1. John McComb, Jr., who had the contract for the construction of the lighthouse at Cape Henry.

From Thomas Marshall [1]

[New York] July 19th. 1791

Sir

Having for a Considerable time entertaind an Opinion that proper Encouragement wou'd be given in this Country, to the Cotton Spinning Manufactory if constructed upon the Genuine Principles of Sir Richard Arkwright the Inventor and Patentee of the Machinery; I form'd the resolution of Visiting America, but previous to my departure from England, I was Introduced, by a friend, to Mr. H. Crugar [2] of this Town: and in April last to Col: Smith,[3] and by the Advice of the latter Gentleman, I took my departure for New York where I arrived on Tuesday last the 12th Inst. and in Consequence of the Interviews I have been favour'd with from Mr. Duer, Mr. Crugar and Mr. Sands [4] on the Business, I have respectfully taken the Liberty of addressing you on the Subject.

The Laws of England being very severe against the Emigration of Mechanic's,[5] I am deprived of every Testimony or Document of my Capability in the Manufactory, which if I had fortunately possest wou'd in all probability have recommended me to your particular Notice, and I flatter myself Sir, you'll join me in opinion, that no branch is so difficult to be Explain'd or Elucidated by Words, as Mechanism. As I am thus debar'd of every Exterior recommendation, I have only to solicit your perusal of the following Narrative of facts, which if my Oath wou'd enforce, I shou'd be exceeding happy in giving the proof.

Were I weak enough to be vain of any Occurrence in Life, that of my Immediate Tuition under Sir Richd. Arkwright wou'd make me so, a Man whom *all* attempt to Imitate in the Business, but few or none can Equal. I enter'd into this Gentlemans employ in 1786, and thus derived my Knowledge of the Manufactory upon his Principles and that his method claims a very decided Seperiority over every other Competitor needs no Comment. I Superintended the very last work

Sir Richard Erected, at Marsden, Opposite Matlock Bath, Derbyshire, and so late as November last I was all over his Works, and am Consequently fully acquainted with every modern Improvement, some of which are of material Consequence. I last Winter Erected the Cotton Mill in all its branches for a Mr. Callaway [6] of Canterbury, Kent. This Gentleman was the Inventor of the Muslins that bear the Name of the above Town, and which there is such a rappid demand for now all over England. The foreman of his Weaving business I am in treaty with and only waits my Letter for to join me, so that the whole Business of Carding, Drawing, Roving, Spinning, Bleaching, and Weaving, can be conducted under one firm, and this, Sir, I pledge myself equal to, and Capable of, and shou'd I be fortunate enough to be honor'd with your Confidence in the Undertaking, nothing shall be wanting to Estabish and Speedily bring to its utmost perfection in its fullest Extent the whole of the above Business's, and entertain no doubts but I can quickly Accomplish it. I shou'd prefer a share of the Nett produce, which I willingly leave to your honor & Determination, and will pay legal Interest for any Sums which on my own Account I may draw during the Mills Completion, or the Undertaking of the Business, but as particulars cannot be Stated here, I most respectfully wait your Commands, which shall be immediatly attended to by Sir   Your Most Obedient   Humble Servant,

T Marshall

ALS, Hamilton Papers, Library of Congress.

1. In December, 1791, H appointed Marshall superintendent of the cotton mill for the Society for Establishing Useful Manufactures.

2. Although Henry Cruger spent much of his life in England, he was a New Yorker by birth. A successful merchant of Bristol, England, he served in the House of Commons from 1784 to 1790, when he declined renomination and returned to New York.

3. William S. Smith, John Adams's son-in-law, was a prominent New York speculator.

4. William Duer and Comfort Sands were leading American entrepreneurs and, like Cruger, were interested in the promotion of American manufactures.

5. For these restrictive statutes, see 5 Geo. I, C. 27 (1718); 23 Geo. II, C. 13 (1750); 14 Geo. III, C. 71 (1774); 22 Geo. III, C. 60 (1782).

6. John Callaway. By 1789 the silk manufacture of Canterbury was becoming increasingly less prosperous and Callaway introduced the manufacture of piece goods called Canterbury (or Chamberry) muslins using silk and cotton twist to revive the industry.

From Jeremiah Olney

Providence, July 19, 1791. "I have received your Letter of the 6th. Instant,[1] relative to Mr. Arnold's Teas &c. and it affords me pleasure to inform you, that I have reason to expect he will discharge his Bond tomorrow; if he does, it will prevent the transmission of the Notice you mention. I enclose my quarterly Return of Exports, amounting to One Hundred and Twelve Thousand Five Hundred and Ninety-three Dollars & 14 Cents. . . ."

ADfS, Rhode Island Historical Society, Providence; copy, RG 56, Letters from the Collector at Providence, National Archives.
1. See also Olney to H, June 21, 1791.

From William Short

Paris July 19. 1791

Sir

I had the honor of writing to you on the 8th. of this month by the French packet & of acknowleging the reciept of your letter of the 9th. of May.

The commissioners at Amsterdam have since then informed me [1] that all difficulties being removed they have consummated the payment of the million of florins to the French bankers there & recieved their bill on this government for its amount 2,696,629 ₶. 4. This you will find a much more advantageous rate of exchange than that of the payment made last fall, which was also advantageous.

In consequence of your letter of the 9th. of May which authorized me after leaving f800,000 in the hands of the commissioners, to complete the payment of the million & an half of florins of the last loan destined for France I wrote to them [2] informing them of this disposition—adding that before the intended payment was made known I would settle with the present commissioners of the treasury (who

AL, letterpress copy, William Short Papers, Library of Congress.
1. Willink, Van Staphorst, and Hubbard to Short, July 11, 1791 (LS, Short Family Papers, Library of Congress).
2. Short to Willink, Van Staphorst, and Hubbard, July 8, 1791 (ALS, letterpress copy, William Short Papers, Library of Congress).

have succeeded to the Director general) [3] a basis for fixing the rate of exchange. I had no knowlege of the late loan being otherwise disposed of than as to the f800,000. mentioned in your letter. In answer to mine I have just recieved one from them of which I send you an extract. It is dated Amsterdam July 14. 1791.

"Your calculation of our having funds in hand to discharge this order of f800,000 is erroneous, the disposals of the Secretary of the Treasury having absorbed the balance of the U.S. up to about f350,000. Thus we shall be in advance about f150,000—besides which there will be due for interest in February next on loan of 2. mills   80,000

do.	do.	3	150,000
March	do.	2½	125.000

so that the U.S. will have to provide here in a few months f505,000— which considering the employ there appears to be yet in America for monies negotiated here, we presume the Secretary would desire to face by a loan, preferably to making us remittances for it." [4]

As it appears to me from your letter [5] that you expected the payment of f500,000 to be made out of the loan I shall write to the commissioners that such appears to me to be your wish & of course that I do not direct a payment beyond what the loan furnishes viz. about f350,000. I have not fixed any term of payment or any sum with the commissioners of the treasury but have desired them to authorize their bankers to recieve such sums as may be offered them by the commissioners in proportion as they may have monies in their hands & to fix the rate of exchange agreeably to that which prevails at the time of payment. The commissioners of the treasury like M: Dufresne [6] desire the payment to be made at Amsterdam, but proposed that the exchange should be fixed according to a mean rate taken on eight days prior & eight days posterior to the payment. I have told them that this was inadmissible because it subjected us to the loss accruing from any artificial rise which might be occasioned in consequence of such payments & remittances being made known. They have agreed individually that the observation was just & have promised to settle it otherwise at their first meeting. I am waiting only for the result in order to give orders to our commissioners.

3. See Short to H, June 3, 1791.
4. LS, Short Family Papers, Library of Congress.
5. See H to Short, May 9, 1791.
6. Bertrand Dufresne, director of the Public Treasury of France.

In answer to my letters with respect to a loan at 4½. p. cent interest & also a diminution of the charges in case of the interest being continued at 5.p.cent, they [7] continue to say that the reduced interest can be hoped for only from delaying the loan & augmenting the commission. And as to the loan on the same interest they persist in assuring that no diminution of the charges can take place. They say that the bonds will inevitably fall to par on such a loan being proposed, the rise to 101 having taken place only from its having been believed that no other 5. p. cent loans would be proposed & that the bonds may be now had [at] 100½ in parcels. They add that it would be highly impolitic to sink the goodwill of the undertakers by reducing them ½ p.cent on their commission as I proposed. I own I am not of the same opinion & am persuaded that if they pleased, they might carry through a loan at 3½ p.cent commission. I have not informed them of my intention to open soon a loan either there or elsewhere, but only have given them to understand, which they know however full as well as I do, that Congress will soon have occasion for further loans: & so the matter stands with respect to them.

Mr. Morris is in correspondence with his friends at Antwerp respecting a loan as mentioned to you in a former letter.[8] He shewed me a letter from them in which they say that they think a small sum might be raised at 4½. p. cent by allowing sufficient time, but that the commission must be 6. p. cent. I have authorized Mr. Morris to propose to them a commission of 4. p.cent. & to say that in that case I would contract with them. He is now waiting for their answer though I have little hopes they will take so low a commission. As it would be highly advantageous however to make such a loan even as they offer, I may perhaps be tempted to accept it if nothing better can be done—but in that case, as the solidity of the house would be much less known to me than that of the houses at Amsterdam I should think it most advisable to have the sums remitted here in proportion as they recieve them, taking it for granted you would approve such precaution although you have not given orders for the payment. By it the U.S. will reduce the interest of their debt & will also gain considerably by the advantage of the exchange on making the payment.

7. Willink, Van Staphorst, and Hubbard.
8. Short had written to H frequently about Gouverneur Morris's investigation of the possibility of an Antwerp loan. See Short to H, February 17, April 9, June 3, July 8, 1791.

I have had a further conversation with Mr Grand on the subject of paying off a part of the French debt by loans here.[9] He thinks now that it will be necessary to fix the interest at 5. p. cent & also to recieve the assignats at 10. p. cent depreciation, although in fact it is 14. He has taken up this opinion from an idea that the holders of assignats think they will appreciate & of course would not place them for eight or ten years at their full depreciation. If so it will be much more advantageous to make loans abroad for the payment of the French debt, as the exchange which in that case operates as depreciation is much more considerable.

Under these circumstances I shall wait somewhat before opening a loan unless it should be that at Antwerp at 4½ p. cent interest. The probability of peace taking place to the north increases: should it be realized it may perhaps enable the U.S. to make a loan also at Amsterdam at a reduced rate of interest. If however I were authorized to complete the payment of the whole sum due France I should prefer the certainty of doing it immediately by 5. p. cent loans abroad to waiting for the smaller sums to be raised by degrees at 4½. p. cent, because the present advantageous rate of exchange would counterbalance the ½. p. cent interest.

The bankers at Amsterdam have written to me that they have no doubt that a loan opened there the middle of next month might be pushed to six millions of florins, at 5. p. cent.[10] The same interest would unquestionably procure loans also at Antwerp & perhaps at Genoa. These resources being used, the French debt as far as due might be immediately paid & large sums remitted you for purchasing up the American funds, which bearing an higher interest & selling considerably below par present great advantages for the public credit. The benefit of such measures depending on a general combination of your plans, no steps of course can be taken towards it but by your orders. The view however in which this subject has long presented itself to me makes me regret that such advantages should be lost or delayed. It is useless to mention to you the effect which our domestic funds being at par would have on the credit abroad.

I have never known the reason why the Senate threw out the bill

9. See Short to H, June 3, 1791.
10. Willink, Van Staphorst, and Hubbard to Short, July 8, 1791 (LS, Short Family Papers, Library of Congress).

for paying off the foreign officers.[11] It would certainly have had an happy influence on our credit & particularly here. Its not being done could thwart much any design of borrowing money in Paris to pay off the French debt or at least would render the terms less advantageous.

I have thus made you acquainted Sir with the present position of affairs & shall take care to inform you of every step that is taken respecting them.

Various circumstances have prevented the directors of the mint here giving me as yet the information they promised. As soon as obtained it shall be forwarded to you.[12]

In the mean time I beg you to be fully persuaded of the [13]

11. On February 11, 1791, the House passed a bill "authorizing the President of the United States to cause the debt due to foreign officers to be paid and discharged" (*Journal of the House,* I, 375). On February 23 this bill was rejected by the Senate (*Annals of Congress,* II, 1807). See also Short to H, August 3, 1790.
12. H had asked Short to send information on foreign mints. See H to Short, April 13, 1791.
13. The remainder of this letter has not been found.

From Arthur St. Clair [1]

Fort Washington [Northwest Territory] July 21st 1791

Sir,

On the 26th. of May last I had the honour to address you on the Subject of the purchase which Judge Symmes had made of the public Lands and enclosed Copies of Some Correspondence between him and me relative thereto. The Boat by which those papers were Sent was Attacked by the Indians on the Ohio River and defeated, and the dispatches were thrown over Board. I have now taken the Liberty to forward Duplicates.

The Letter I mention to the judge, has been the fruitful Mother of Thousand more, and produced a Lengthy Correspondence which must be laid, I believe, before you, or the Secretary of State; but it could not be got ready for the present Occasion. It has Issued in the publication of the Proclamation I alluded to, in which the Boundaries of the Contract are set forth, and a piece of Land round the Fort is laid out for the Use of the Garrison—notwithstanding, that I Shewed him the Orders for laying out that Ground, he has gone on Selling it every Since; and there is very little that has not been Appropriated: whatever may be done with the rest of what is without his Bounds, which he has laid Claim to, and sold, this round the Fort will I hope be reserved: I have not now ground to form a Battalion upon nor can I pay so much attention to the health of the few Troops that are here, as to change the ground of their encampment, for they are not enough to take a position at any distance in the Woods.

General Butler (nor any of the levies) has not yet arrived, and three Companies only of the recruits.[2] I am at my Wits end about it, for much will be to be done after they do arrive and the Season is passing—from every appearance it will be September at Soonest before it will be possible to move, and then there is not much time left for the operations of the Campaign.

Mr. Duer [3] has not put the affairs of his department in that Certain State they ought to be with respect to the transportation; Mr. Laidlow [4] has some agency in it but he tells me he has not sufficient authority to procure Horses. In hopes of hearing from Mr. Duer I directed him a fortnight ago to make conditional Agreements which if neither he nor me had information, in a Short time, that might render it improper, I would direct him to make final—if that information does not reach me I must take it upon myself.

I have the Honour to be   Sir   Your most obedient Servant

Ar. St. Clair

The honorable Alexander Hamilton
Secretary of the Treasury

Copy, Public Archives of Canada, Ottawa, Ontario.

1. For background to this document, see St. Clair to H, May 26, 1791.

2. At this time preparations were under way for a new campaign against the western Indians under St. Clair's command. His second-in-command, Major General Richard Butler, was in Pittsburgh, engaged in recruiting and arranging for supplies.

3. William Duer was contractor of the Army for the St. Clair campaign.

4. In addition to his surveying duties, Israel Ludlow was acting as Duer's agent on the frontier.

To Welcome Arnold

New York, July 22. 1791

Sir

I have before me your letter of the 15 instant, which first apprised me of any controversy between the Collector and yourself, about the validity of any part of the demand on you.

From the *simple* statement of the fact to me, I had been led to conclude that there had been a delay of payment of an acknowleged and undisputed debt, and as I had understood that your situation precluded the supposition of want of resource, I was left to suppose, that there was a voluntary delinquency, on some mere motive of convenience. Hence the instructions I gave.

Being now informed that there is a controverted demand, I write to the Collector of Providence [1] to suspend, if not too late, the notifications he was directed to give, and to state particularly to me the circumstances. I shall be glad also to receive them from you; as it is my earnest wish to see the laws executed with equity and moderation, as well as exactness.

I am Sir with all due consideration   Your obedient servt.

Alexander Hamilton

Welcome Arnold Esquire

ALS, The Andre deCoppet Collection, Princeton University Library; copy, The John Carter Brown Library, Providence, Rhode Island.
 1. See H to Olney, July 22, 1791.

From Jedediah Huntington

[*New London, Connecticut, July 22, 1791.* On August 25, 1791, Hamilton wrote to Huntington: "I have considered the case you State in your letter of the 22nd July." *Letter not found.*]

To Jeremiah Olney

New York July 22d. 1791

Sir

Having received a letter from Mr. Arnold [1] informing me that the delay of payment of his bond had proceeded from a part of the demand being controverted, I am to desire that, if not already given, you will suspend the notifications you were required to give to the Collectors out of your state, and that you will inform me particularly of the nature and circumstances of the controversy. I have requested Mr. Arnold to do the same, and I shall be glad if possible, that there may be no disagreement in the statement of facts.

You will also forbear any further proceeding upon the bond until you hear again from me.

I am with consideration   Sir   Your Obed ser   Alex Hamilton

Jeremiah Olney Esqr
&c

ALS, Rhode Island Historical Society, Providence; copy, RG 56, Letters to the Collector at Providence, National Archives; copy, RG 56, Letters to the Collectors at Small Ports, "Set G," National Archives.

1. Welcome Arnold to H, July 15, 1791.

From William Skinner [1]

United States Loan Office [Hillsboro]
North Carolina, July 22nd. 1791.

Sir,

The Governor of this State [2] with the advice of his Council two days past, Entered into a Resolution directing the Comptroller [3] to subscribe for; and Deposite in my Office in behalf of the State, all the Certificates of this States Debt, which are in the Comptroller's office, as well those punched as unpunched; This I consider to be in direct opposition to a paragraph in your circular Letter of the first of November last which says that it is an Erroneous Idea that a State can become a Subscriber for a proportion of that part of the Debt which has been Assumed; from the construction which I put on this part of your Letter. I think I can by no means admit of such a Subscription; I therefore wish your imediate direction how I am to govern myself in this matter.

I am most respectfully   Your most Obedient Servant.   W Skinner.

The Honble. Alexander Hamilton Esqre.

Copy, North Carolina Department of Archives and History, Raleigh. This letter was enclosed in H's "Report to the Governor of North Carolina," July 31, 1794.

1. Skinner was appointed commissioner of loans for North Carolina on August 7, 1790. He had served in the same capacity under the Continental Congress from December 13, 1785, until December, 1789.
2. Alexander Martin.
3. Francis Child.

From William Skinner

The 22nd. of July 1791. from Hillsbo. [North Carolina]

Sir,

Since writing you on the Subject of the States becoming a Subscriber,[1] the inclosed. was handed me by the Governor Private Secretary[2] which I do myself the Honour of inclosing you to which please to give me an imediate answer.

I am most Respectfully   Your most obedient Servant

W Skinner.

[ENCLOSURE][3]

State of North Carolina
In Council July 20th. 1791.

A Proposition of His Excellency the Governor. Having received information that the States of New York[4] and South Carolina[5] have funded their Public securities by Subscribing them on Loan to the United States, pursuant to an Act of Congress passed in their second Session intituled an Act "for making provision for the debt of the United States," I consider it the duty of the Executive as the General Assembly will not meet till after the time limited by said Act for taking in Subscriptions to said Loan[6] to lay this important subject before you on so urgent an occasion. I submit to your deliberations and advice the propriety of Subscribing at this time all the State Certificates and Public Securities thereof fundable by said Act now in the possession of the Treasurer[7] Comptroller[8] or other Public Officers of the State as a Loan in the Office of the Commissioner of Loans of the United States for this State. Please to signify your advice accordingly and should the measure meet your approbation the manner and by whom the same is to be effected. As these Certificates are of a negoceable nature and the property of the State acquired by taxation and purchace it appears that she has a right to dispose of them as she pleases. Should the public accounts be never settled as is suggested by some [9] a saving of the interest will be made to the State by subscribing these Certificates as aforesaid. Should a Settlement take place which is ardently wished for this State it is presumed will be a large Creditor State. She will have it in her power to deduct from the ballance due her the sum subscribed or so much thereof as will be an equivalent to said Ballance and the residue if any will be on Loan to the United States. Should the State contrary to all expectations be a debtor,[10] she will still have it in her power to transfer the Subscription by her made in payment of part or in full of the Ballance that may be due the United States.

Alex: Martin

The Council taking the proposition of his Excellency the Governor under consideration conceive it a subject of great magnitude in which the State is much interested having maturely considered the fourth Section of the Act of Congress for making provision for the debt of the United States [11] are of opinion that the words "Body Politic" mentioned therein give this State, being the first Political corporate Body by which we are governed in a State capacity a right to Subscribe to the United States a Loan of its Public Securities equal to a person or persons therein mentioned. And as the reasons set forth in the Governor's pro[po]sition together with the emergency of the occasion seem to call for the immediate interposition of the Executive Resolved they do recommend and advise that His Excellency the Governor authorize and empower Francis Child Esquire Comptroller of the public accounts of this State to subscribe or cause to be Subscribed on or before the last day of September next for and in behalf of this State in the Office of the Commissioner of Loans of the United States for this State all Certificates and other Public Securities the property of this State fundable by said Act now in his possession or that may come into his possession before that time: And that the said Comptrollor obtain a Certificate or Certificates or a receipt or receipts for the same from the said Commissioner of Loans and make return thereof to the Governor by him to be laid before the next

General Assembly [12] that the State be enabled to derive from the said Loan the advantages mentioned in said act.

Extract from the Journals of the Council of State.

Test.   Tho. Rogers C C.

Copy, North Carolina Department of Archives and History, Raleigh. This letter was enclosed in H's "Report to the Governor of North Carolina," July 31, 1794.

1. Skinner is referring to the first letter that he wrote to H on July 22, 1791.

2. Thomas Rogers at this time was serving both as private secretary to Governor Alexander Martin of North Carolina and as clerk of the council of state.

3. Copy, North Carolina Department of Archives and History, Raleigh. This document was enclosed in H's "Report to the Governor of North Carolina," July 31, 1794.

4. See Skinner to H, August 29, 1791.

5. On February 19, 1791, the South Carolina legislature passed "An Act for loaning to the United States, a Sum of the Indents of this State under certain Limitations therein mentioned." The act provided in part as follows:

"That the commissioners of the treasury, or any of them, be authorized, required and directed to subscribe in behalf of this state, on loan to the United States, on the last day of September next, so many of the fundable indents of this state as may then be in their possession, which, when added to the amount of private subscriptions, will make in the whole four millions of dollars, or as near thereto as may be, but in no case to exceed that sum, and to receive in lieu thereof, in behalf of the state, from the commissioner of loans, the funded certificates of the United States, in such sums as they may deem most convenient. . . .

"That the commissioners of the treasury take forthwith an account of all indents in their possession, distinguishing those which are fundable from those which are not, and those which are cancelled from those which are not, and report the same to the legislature when sitting, or in their recess, to his excellency the governor; and the commissioners of the treasury, and all other officers of the state, who have received, or who may receive fundable indents on behalf of the state, are hereby required to forbear from cancelling the same till the last day of September next, any law, usage or custom to the contrary notwithstanding." (*State of South-Carolina. At a General Assembly, begun and holden at Columbia, on Monday the third day of January, in the year of our Lord one thousand seven hundred and ninety-one, and from thence continued by divers adjournments, to the fourteenth day of February, in the same year, and in the fifteenth year of the Independence of the United States of America* [n.p., n.d], 72–74.)

6. "An Act making provision for the (payment of the) Debt of the United States" had provided that subscriptions to the new Federal loan could be received until October 1, 1791 (1 *Stat.* 138–44 [August 4, 1790]).

7. John Haywood.

8. Francis Child.

9. This is a reference to the widespread belief in the southern states that the final settlement of the accounts between the states and the Federal Government, from which the southern states expected to obtain substantial benefits, would in fact never be completed.

10. In actuality, North Carolina turned out to be a debtor rather than a creditor. In the final settlement of accounts that appears in the report of the commissioners of accounts for June 29, 1793, North Carolina is listed as one of the debtor states (*ASP, Miscellaneous*, I, 69).

11. 1 *Stat.* 140.

12. In a speech on December 7, 1791, the governor laid the journal of the council of state before the North Carolina legislature. On December 12, 1791, Francis Child, the comptroller, notified the legislature that he had "funded as a loan to the United States" the certificates in his possession and noted that Skinner's receipt would be produced on request (*Journal of the House of Commons. North-Carolina. At a General Assembly begun and held in the town of Newbern, on the fifth day of December, in the year of our Lord one thousand seven hundred and ninety-one, and of the independence of the United States of America the sixteenth: Being the first session of this Assembly* [Edenton: Printed by Hodge & Wills, Printers to the State, n. d.], 4, 9). A more complete report of a committee of finance appears in the *Journal of the Senate* for December 22, 1791. The report reads in part as follows: "the . . . certificates . . . [in the North Carolina treasury] were delivered to the Comptroller unpunched, in consequence of its having been in contemplation to fund them; they have therefore called on the Comptroller, and find that he, pursuant to instructions from the Governor and Council, hath placed in the office of the Commissioner of Loans for the United States in North-Carolina, . . . to amount of one hundred and seventy-two thousand seven hundred and ninety-four pounds two shillings and three pence, including interest . . ." (*Journal of the Senate. North-Carolina. At a General Assembly begun and held in the town of Newbern, on the fifth day of December, in the year of our Lord one thousand seven hundred and ninety-one, and of the independence of the United States of America the sixteenth: Being the first session of this Assembly* [n.p., n.d.], 14–15).

From Theodore Foster [1]

[*July 23, 1791.* On September 1, 1791, Hamilton wrote to Foster: "I have had the pleasure of receiving your two letters of the 23rd July & 4th of August." *Letter of July 23 not found.*]

1. Foster, a Providence, Rhode Island, lawyer, had served in the Rhode Island House of Representatives from 1776 to 1782, as town clerk of Providence from 1775 to 1787, and was appointed judge of the Court of Admiralty in 1785. In 1790 he was elected United States Senator from Rhode Island.

From Benjamin Lincoln

Boston July 23d: 1791

Sir

Agreeably to your orders [1] I here send you a description of the Cutter Massachusetts built at Newbury port in the Commonwealth of Massachusetts in the year 1791. She has on deck two masts her length is sixty feet above her upper deck her depth is seven feet Eight inches her breadth seventeen feet Eight inches she measures seventy tons $\frac{43}{95}$. She is a square sterned schooner has quarter badges & an Indian head she has a long quarter deck & a deep waist.

You will Observe that the Cutter is much biger than I contracted to have her. This is caused by her being much deeper than is mentioned in the contract. When Captain Williams [2] went to inspect her I wrote to the builders and permitted them to make any little alterations in finishing her, diverse from the plan, given them which Captain Williams should direct but so as never to augment the price of the vessel. The first wish Captain Williams Expressed was to lay the deck eight inches higher than in the original plan with this request the Carpenters complied hence the vessel is much biger than was expected or wished for.

The builders notwithstanding my letter to them, directing that they might not do any thing which should increase the price of the vessel, had hopes as they now say that an allowance would be made them now finding this to be inadmissible they propose to build an other vessel of the size first contracted for & receive this back when the other shall be fitted for the Sea. I hope they will pursue their present intentions for this vessel is biger than is necessary.

I find that the Masters of the Cutters are allowed three rations ⅌ day & the mates two. The officers will take care & supply themselves & receive the money of me. What must they receive for each ration? I have allowed them twelve cents a ration, the same price which is given for the supply of the Soldiers here, for time back.

The officers complain that while at Newbury fixing the vessel they were involved in an expence much above the value of twenty four Cents ⅌ day. Can I make them any allowance & can they be allowed any thing besides their pay while working on board the vessel before fitted for the Sea?

Is it expected that the Sailors be confined to the same ration to which the soldiers are? If they are to have rations in manner of land troops by whom are they daily to be issued?

I have the pleasure to return the two certificates in a form which I hope will be agreeable.

Secretary of the Treasury

LC, Massachusetts Historical Society, Boston; two copies, RG 56, Letters from the Collector at Boston, National Archives.
   1. "Treasury Department Circular to the Collectors of the Customs," June 1, 1791.
   2. John Foster Williams, captain of the Massachusetts revenue cutter.

From Jeremiah Olney

Providence, July 23, 1791. "I have recd. your circular Letter of the 8th instant, relative to Teas. The Duties on the Hyson-Skin, imported in the Ship Genl. Washington, were ascertained at 20 Cents a pound; it appearing from all accounts, to be less costly than even Souchong and inferior in quality, I judged it could not properly be classed higher than 'other green Teas'. . . ."

ADfS, Rhode Island Historical Society, Providence; copy, RG 56, Letters from the Collector at Providence, National Archives.

From Joseph Whipple

Portsmouth, New Hampshire, July 23, 1791. Acknowledges receipt of the "Commissions of the three first officers of the Revenue Cutter."

LC, RG 36, Collector of Customs at Portsmouth, Letters Sent, 1790–1791, Vol. 2, National Archives; copy, RG 56, Letters from the Collector at Portsmouth, National Archives.

From Thomas Marshall

[New York, July 24-31, 1791] [1]

Sir

From the Nature of your enquiries on Saturday I have ventured to presume so far on your time and Candour as to Solicit your perusal of the following lines.

After you have made choice, Sir, of a person for the Directorship, the first Necessary Consideration may be that of obtaining Mechanics from England, (if they cannot be got here) for the purpose of making Machinery and assisting in the Conducting of the Manufactory. A Man for the Brass Work, or fileing up business will be very Necessary; a Person Accustom'd to Superintend the Drawing in the Capacity of "Master of the Room" will be of infinite Utility; a Man who is Master of his business in the weaving branch, and in possession of all or most of the Fashionable Patterns now worn in England will be very Useful. If the Bleaching business is not intended to be confin'd solely to the Cotton Manufactory, a person Competent to the Undertaking, wou'd

I doubt not, well answer the Expence of Importation. If any of these men shou'd have Children Accustom'd to work in the Mill their Utility wou'd be greatly Increased.

If the above steps are approved, Sir, it may next be proper to direct the attention towards an Eligible Spot for Erecting the Manufactory upon, in the Judicious choice of which very much indeed depends. The grand Object in this point is Water, and too much precaution and Circumspection in this particular is Impossible, especially upon the very Extensive scale at present Contemplated; for if there is not a regular and constant Supply of Water in the driest of Seasons Sufficient to work the Mill 23 hours pr Day, the Interest of the Subscribers will severely suffer. To prevent this, Sir, it will be Necessary to be Acquainted with the Scource (if easily possible) of the River, the Situation of the Country through which it runs, the Number of other streams that empty themselves into it, and from whence or by what means they are supplied. From these and Similar Observations together with the best Information that can be obtained from those who have long known the River & its particularities, a Judgment may be form'd what Effect a Dry or Wet Season has on it; that is, Sir, wether in a drought there will be a Sufficiency of Water to Supply the Works, and when heavy or continued rains happen, what Effects are to be Apprehended either from its Overflowing, or the Accumulated Impetuosity of its Current, which if not known and guarded against may prove totally destructive to the Buildings. Next fixing on a place where the Natural Current, (within a reasonable distance) is not impeded by Mills, Bridges, Projections or Eddies: the *Speed* of the Water must be taken (by which the Interior heavy Wheels are regulated) together with the Quantity of Water it is capable of delivering in a given time: the *Fall* must likewise be measured.

If the Person employ'd in this Business is satisfied about the above particulars, the next Object is the Exact Spot for the Building, and he shou'd consider that not only the common requisites which belong to Mills in General, such as the Convenience of good head Water, Tumbling Bays, and a Sufficient clearance or decent for the purpose of carrying off the back Water & preventing the Wheel from Sludging, is Necessary; but also that particular regard be paid to the Natural Foundation on which he is about to Build. An Amazing Weight stands on the Ground, therefore it is absolutely Necessary that the Strata to a Considerable Depth Shou'd be of a disposition proper to sustain the Burden, such as Stone Gravel or hard Clays; without this precaution, however Judicious ⟨ever⟩y other step, the building must Inevitably be in Imminent danger of having its foundation undermined by the Water, or giving way and falling to pieces.

If the above Obstacles are done away, Sir, the next Step may be that of entering into Agreement with the most able and Experienced Mill Wright to be met with, but as the Nature and Extent of his Employ depends much upon the particular Situation of the Spot &c no decisive rule can at present be laid down. The Building follows next, and perhaps, Sir, you might approve of the Smiths & Carpenters Shops being run up first, which wou'd enable the Machine makers to have some parts ready for setting up by the time the Mill was finish'd. The last thing is the market for the raw Material of Cotton.

If, Sir, I have mistaken the Information you wish'd to Obtain, I have humbly to Solicit your pardon for the truble I have here given you, and beg leave to remain,

Your Most Obedient Humble Servant   Thos: Marshall

ALS, Hamilton Papers, Library of Congress.
1. This letter is undated, but presumably it was written after Marshall's letter to H of July 19, 1791. The reference in the first paragraph of the letter to an interview with H would indicate it was written after July 23, the Saturday before H's return to Philadelphia.

From William Short

Paris July 24. [–25] 1791

Sir

Since my last of the 19th inst. in which I gave you an account of the then prospects with respect to loans at Amsterdam or Antwerp, Mr. Morris has recieved an answer from his correspondent at the latter place.[1] He still assures that a loan for the U.S. being opened there for a million of florins at 4½. p. cent might successively be carried to

ALS, letterpress copy, William Short Papers, Library of Congress.
1. Gouverneur Morris had been corresponding with Charles John Michael de Wolf, an Antwerp banker, concerning the possibility of raising an American loan in Antwerp.

greater amount. He insists however on the commission of 6. p. cent: as he seemed to do this more fully in his last letter I have authorized Mr. Morris to offer him 5. p. cent commission, & to tell him that if he would accept it he might set on foot immediately a loan for any sum not less than a million of florins & might extend it as far as three million—taking care however not to commence it without having full certainty of its success.

Mr. Morris assures me that the house with which he corresponds (Wolfe of Antwerp) may be relied on for solidity and prudence, & is particularly regarded as having the best influence among the money lenders. It was formerly employed by Russia in loans made there. At present Hope [2] obliges that power to concentrate its loans at Amsterdam.

Should this loan succeed I shall go to Antwerp to sign the bonds if thought necessary. Hitherto I have thought it best to let Mr. Morris negotiate this business by his correspondence so that the U.S. might not appear in it unless it should be brought to effect.

It is easy to see that such an event would be attended with a variety of good consequences for the credit & interest of the U.S. If they are able to make loans at this reduced rate of interest at Antwerp there is no doubt that that will enable them to do the same at Amsterdam in a very short time.

There is however one aspect in which this subject may be considered differently. Should the U.S. be able to borrow a small sum only a 4½. p. cent, as it is certain they might immediately make large loans at 5 p. cent, it may be questioned whether the advantages arising from paying off the French debt with the present immense profit of exchange, or from purchasing up the domestic debt at its present price, would not more than counter-balance the ½. p. cent additional interest. The privilege which the U.S. reserve to themselves of re-imbursing their loans would have weight in deciding that large sums at 5. p. cent were more for their advantage at present than a small one at 4½. Still it would be necessary to be much better acquainted with your general plan & views on these subjects than I am, not to make this experiment of a loan at a reduced rate of interest. You shall be kept regularly informed of its progress.

2. Henry Hope of the House of Hope.

M. Durezzo of Genoa,[3] one of the richest & most influential citizens of the Republic, is now here. I have put him fully in possession of the present situation of the government and resources of the U.S. He seems highly satisfied with them & in the present situation of affairs in Europe considers the U.S. as a new treasure found for the capitalists of Genoa: viz. for all the men of property of the country. He does not return to Genoa before October or November next, & he thinks that the information which he shall carry there & the zeal which he should use in person would insure loans for the U.S., particularly if in the beginning by the way of inducement they would recieve a part in the French funds to be set off by the ministry here against the American debt. He says the months of October & November are favorable also for loans. I rather think however he has fixed on that season because he expects before that time to recieve further information from the Genoese Consul [4] in America to whom he has written on the subject. It is natural that information coming from that source should be more relied on by the Genoese & for that reason I am happy that M. Durezzo has taken measures for collecting it. Should the Consul shew any desire to resort to administration in his researches I don't doubt you will consider it proper to give him every facility, as it is certain the more the real situation of the U.S. is exposed to the Genoese the greater will be their confidence. I think it highly probable that the U.S. will in time find considerable resources at Genoa & that these will be followed by commercial advantages also.

The commissaries of the treasury having not yet changed the principle on which they had desired the payment at Amsterdam to be made, it is probable I shall find it necessary to desire our commissioners [5] to remit the balance in their hands to Paris, as otherwise we should be exposed to the artificial rise in the exchange which our payments would enable the French bankers or other persons interested, to make.

I have the honor to renew the assurances of attachment & respect with which I shall ever remain   Sir   Your most obedient humble servant   W: Short

3. Presumably Girolamo D. Durazzo, member of a famous Genoese family and last Doge of the Republic.
4. Joseph Ravard.   5. Willink, Van Staphorst, and Hubbard.

P.S. July 25. The commissaries of the treasury have just come to desire I would have the payment made at Amsterdam & have agreed to fix the rate of exchange according to what it may be to day at that place. The exchange has been rather on the rise for some time viz from 44½ to 44⅞. I shall desire our bankers to comply with this request.

The Honble. Alexander Hamilton, Secretary of the Treasury. Philadelphia

From William Ellery

Newport [*Rhode Island*] *July 25, 1791.* ". . . A person usually residing in this District, is in the District of Boston & Charlestown and there purchases a vessel; is he obliged to take the Oath or Affirmation, required by law previous to the making a Registry or granting a Certificate, before the Collector of this District omitting in said oath or affirmation and inserting what is to be omitted and inserted according to the Proviso in the 7th. Sec. of the Coasting Act,[1] and to produce a Certificate thereof to the Collector of the District in which he and the vessel are, in order to obtain from him a Certificate of Registry for such vessel? Please to favour me with an answer to this question. . . ."

LC, Newport Historical Society, Newport, Rhode Island.

1. Section 7 of "An Act for Registering and Clearing Vessels, Regulating the Coasting Trade, and for other purposes" reads as follows: "*Provided always, and be it further enacted,* That whenever the owner or owners of such ship or vessel, usually resides or reside out of the district within which such ship or vessel may be at the time of granting the certificate of registry, that such owner, or where there are two or more owners, any one of them may take and subscribe the said oath or affirmation, before the collector of the district within which he usually resides, omitting in the said oath or affirmation the description of such ship or vessel, as expressed in the certificate of the surveyor, and inserting in lieu thereof, the name of the port and district within which such ship or vessel may then be; and the collector before whom such oath or affirmation may be taken and subscribed, shall transmit the same to the collector of the district where such ship or vessel may be, upon the receipt whereof the said collector shall proceed to register such ship or vessel, in like manner as though the usual and regular oath or affirmation had been taken and subscribed before him" (1 *Stat.* 56–57 [September 1, 1789]).

To William Martin [1]

[*Philadelphia, July 25, 1791*. On March 14, 1794, Hamilton wrote to Martin: "Since mine to you of the 25 of July 1791." *Letter not found*.]

1. Martin was a resident of North Yarmouth, District of Maine.

From William Short

Paris July 26. 1791.

Sir

After closing & forwarding my letter to you yesterday I recieved one from the bankers at Amsterdam of which I think it necessary to send you a copy.[1] It is for the most part in answer to one from me [2] in which I had repeated the arguments, already communicated to you,[3] in favor of our right to reduce the rate of commission in the case of a new loan being opened at 5. p. cent. You will see that the bonds of the U.S. instead of rising have taken a considerable fall. This is so different from the expectation of every body that it is to me quite unaccountable unless indeed it should be intended as a means of removing all grounds for reducing the charges of loans in future.

It is possible also they may have had at Amsterdam some hint of the intended experiment at Antwerp [4] & may wish to make it fail. It would be unjust to adopt suspicions of this kind & to propagate them. Still taking it for granted that the present fall in the price of the bonds is not in the actual course of things, & searching for what may be the artificial cause, I own I see none so probable as the desire of those interested in the American loans at Amsterdam to prevent their being carried elsewhere & to keep the charges from being reduced. I had hoped the loan would be published at Antwerp before it were known at Amsterdam (& I am not yet certain that it is known there) as I feared a coalition at that place among the bankers, brokers & undertakers might be formed in order to counteract if possible our designs elsewhere.

I shall be anxious to know what effect this fall will produce at Antwerp & it seems highly probable that it will render impossible the reduction of interest there. If so & a loan can be effected at 5. p. cent I shall suppose it better to make it there than at Amsterdam for the sake of having a credit in two places & of course being less dependent on the speculations of those employed in the loans. I hasten to send this letter in hopes of its overtaking that sent yesterday to Havre. I have the honor to assure you of the attachment & respect with which I am,

Sir,   Your most obedient, humble servant   W: Short

The Honble. Alexander Hamilton Secretary of the Treasury—Philadelphia

[ENCLOSURE]

Wilhem and Jan Willink, Nicholaas and Jacob Van Staphorst, and Nicholas Hubbard to William Short [5]

Amsterdam 21 July 1791

Sir

We have your respected favor of 15 Instant, in consequence of which We have confirmed to Messr. Hogguer Grand & Co. our having received your Order to pay them f500,000.—.—. on account of the U.S. and our readiness to fulfill it. They will apply to us for the Money so soon as they shall be authorized by the Commissaries of the Treasury; When We will endeavor to fix the Exchange at a just and equitable rate.

There are some Truths difficult to be seized and especially at a Distance: This is the case, with the American Bonds being at present only at par in very small Quantities, and obtainable in Numbers at 99½ per Cent; Such a State of Things, while far from having any bad We have none but the best and most encouraging News of the Government and Finances of that Country, baffles all reasoning, entirely overturns your Hypotheses grounded upon the Price of Bonds at 100 per Cent, and is almost impossible to be impressed unto the Conviction of any Persons not well acquainted with our Local, altho' It is perfectly visible and feelingly experienced by the Holders of these Effects. In these Circumstances, to secure a Loan at any rate would be an hard Task, We however hope It will still be possible to have one undertaken after the Middle of next Month; But We cannot consent to any Reduction in the Charges, after their having been reduced by you to the very lowest pitch, below what they ought to have been in reason & Justice, or than the Custom of this Place has sanctioned to Transactions of this Nature.

As any thing interesting will occur, We shall not fail communicating it to you, in the Interim We are with great Esteem and Respect

   Sir   Your most obedient and very humble Servants

Wilhem & Jan Willink

N & J. Van Staphorst & Hubbard

Les Obligations sur le Liquidated debt ont emalemt. decliné, ceux de 5½ ℔ C d'interêt j'achettent a 99½ ℔ Ct.

Willm. Short Esqr. Paris.

ALS, letterpress copy, William Short Papers, Library of Congress.
  1. See enclosure.
  2. Short to Willink, Van Staphorst, and Hubbard, July 15, 1791 (ALS, letterpress copy, William Short Papers, Library of Congress).
  3. See Short to H, June 3, 1791.
  4. See Short to H, July 24-25, 1791.
  5. LS, Short Family Papers, Library of Congress.

From Joseph Whipple

Portsmouth [New Hampshire] July 26, 1791. Describes the case of "the Brig Polly Wentworth R. Miller Master," which arrived from France on October 1, 1790. States that "a quantity of plaister of Paris which is exempted from duty was inserted in the Manifest," but that the manifest did not include "a quantity of Bur Stone." Points out that Miller did not appear "to be acquainted with the exemption of duty on Plaister of Paris & could not therefore . . . have any intention to conceal the Bur Stone."

LS, RG 36, Collector of Customs at Portsmouth, Letters Sent, 1790–1791, Vol. 2, National Archives; copy, RG 56, Letters from the Collector at Portsmouth, National Archives.

To the Board of Assessors of the Town of Boston

Treasury Department, July 27th, 1791.

Gentlemen,

A Temporary absence from the seat of government has delayed an answer to your letter of the 14th instant.

It is an established rule at the treasury not to disclose the amount of the stock which stands to the credit of any person on the public books, to any but the proprietor himself, or his regular representative; and the reasons of the rule extend it, of course to the respective loan-offices. One of those reasons is, that as property in the public funds, constitutes an useful and a considerable portion of mercantile capital, wherever public credit is well supported, the permitting an inspection into the stock account of individuals, to others than the parties respectively interested, would have a tendency to lay open the affairs and operations of merchants more than is consistent with the spirit of trade. Indeed not only merchants but other classes of citizens may often have fair and valid reasons for being disinclined to such an inspection. And it may be even conceived that it would not at all times be expedient to allow access to the secret emissaries of a foreign power to discover the quantum of interest which its own citizens might have in the fund of a nation.

In thus assigning some of the reasons, which have given occasion to the rule that has been mentioned, I yield to a desire of satisfying the board, that it is not unsupported by considerations of weight, and that a relaxation of it, in compliance with their request, could not with propriety be acceded to on my part. At the same time I feel myself called upon by the occasion, to express an opinion, that every thing, in the nature of a direct tax on property in the funds of the United States, is contrary to the true principles of public credit, and tends to disparage the value of the public stock. If any law of the state of Massachusetts, therefore, gives sanction to such a tax, it is presumed that it must have been passed without an advertence to this important idea, and it is not doubted that in the execution of it, there will be all the care and moderation which the delicacy of the operation requires. It is desirable on every account, that no occasion should be given to a discussion concerning the regularity of the proceeding.

With very great respect and consideration I have the honor to be, Gentlemen, Your obedient servant, Alexander Hamilton.

The Board of Assessors of the Town of Boston.

The Federal Gazette and Philadelphia Daily Advertiser, August 30, 1791.

To Elizabeth Hamilton

[Philadelphia] July 27. 91

I am again My beloved Betsey in the hot City of Philadelphia; but in good health. And you may depend I shall take all the care in my power to continue so. Will you my Angel do the same? Consider how much our happiness depends upon it; and I pray you do not relax in attention.

I have been to see your new house & like it better than I expected to do.[1] Twill soon be ready and I shall obey your orders about papering &c.

Adieu My Precious Wife Blessings without number on you & my little ones A Hamilton

Mrs. Hamilton

ALS, Hamilton Papers, Library of Congress.
  1. See Clement Biddle to H, June 28, 1791.

From William Short

Paris July 27. 1791.

Sir

Mr. Morris has just recieved a letter from his correspondent at Antwerp in which he informs him that since his last of which I mentioned to you [1] the subject he had recieved an express from the Russian ministry authorizing him to open a loan for the Empress at 5. p. cent interest with a considerable advantage in the exchange. He of course declines undertaking the American business for the present (he had not then recieved Mr. Morris's letter in which I propose 5. p. cent commission & 4½. p cent interest) & begs Mr. Morris to endeavour to secure it for him when he shall have completed this loan for Russia. The matter will rest in status quo for the present & consequently not become public. The reduction of interest at Antwerp will be impossible to be effected so long as Russia keeps a loan open there at 5. p. cent with the high commission she gives, & until the obligations of the U. S. at Amsterdam shall have taken a rise. Under present circumstances therefore it will be necessary to give still 5. p. cent interest & probably without a diminution of the charges—still however I shall use every endeavour to effect it.

Russia having ordered a loan at Antwerp shews that she is endeavouring to extricate herself from the house of Hope; [2] unless indeed it should be with their consent. As there is no longer any probability of a rupture with England I rather think the Russian ministry will continue to place their whole confidence in that house.

I write to-day to the Secretary of State by the way of the English packet but I think it best to send this letter by the way of Havre in order to avoid its being read in the English port, as it is possible it may still arrive in time for a vessel that sails from thence.

I beg you to be assured of the sentiments of attachment with which I have the honor to be

   Sir,   Your most obedient & very humble servant   W: Short

The Honble. Alexander Hamilton Secretary of the Treasury Philadelphia

ALS, letterpress copy, William Short Papers, Library of Congress.
   1. See Short to H, July 24–25, 1791.
   2. This was an Amsterdam banking firm whose head was Henry Hope.

From Tobias Lear

United States July 29. 1791.

By the Presidents command T. Lear has the honor respectfully to transmit to the secretary of the Treasury the enclosed obligation of J. G. Blount & Chas. Cook for the stakage of certain shoals & channels within North Carolina [1] which has been approved of by the

President. Also a letter from Mr. Short to the Secretary of the Treasury, & instructions for Mr. Short on certain points relative to Loans.[2]

Tobias Lear

S.P.U.S.

LC, George Washington Papers, Library of Congress.
1. See H to George Washington, July 29, 1791.
2. See Washington to H, July 29, 1791, and H to William Short, August 1-2, 1791.

From Benjamin Lincoln

Boston July 29 1791

Sir

I have been honoured with the receipt of your circular letter of the 8th. instant. I will aim at that discharge of the duties therein required which shall give satisfaction.

A few days since I had a hint that a vessel from the Bahama Islands had touched into tarpaulin cove, in one of the Elizabeth Islands, and had there landed a few bags of Cotton. The same vessel came into this port and entered without reserve. The surveyor [1] afterwards mentioned to the master [2] the hint we had received. At first he absolutely denied the fact, but afterwards finding us possessed of certain facts he acknowledged his error. Thereon we brought an action against him & his mate for the fine of one thousand dollars as directed in the Statute.[3] The Captain gave bond, & the mate was committed. The Captain, I suppose, has been advised to attempt a justification on the ground of distress. To this purpose he yesterday took the depositions of all his men & a passenger or two. Of this the Captain in the first place made no mention. How far a Jury may carry the necessity of landing two bags of Cotton weighing both about five hundred after making almost her whole passage I know not. At the time of taking these depositions the Attorney of the district [4] was present & it so fully turned up in the course of this business that the Cotton was landed and as the master had not made any mention of it at the time of entery but swore to the contrary Mr. Gore thought it his duty to prosecute the Captain & have him bound over to answer to the Circuit Court for false swearing.

I wrote immediately to the officer at Martha Vineyard [5] in whose district is tarpaulin cove that he might put hand on the cotton so landed. Since I have received the following answer. "On the receipt of yours of the 12th. inst. I immediately went to tarpaulian cove and applied to Mr: Nye who informed me that about a fortenight before there was a Schooner came in there the Master of which asked of him the favour to leave two bags which he granted. He thereupon landed two bags which he took to be cotton containing as near as he could guess 200 each. The bags were in his Garrot where they remained five or six and were carried off unbeknown to him. Neither did he know the man that landed the same. The foregoing is the whole of the information which I could obtain respecting the cotton."

I am &c

Mr. Secretary Hamilton

LC, Massachusetts Historical Society, Boston; two copies, RG 56, Letters from the Collector at Boston, National Archives.
1. Thomas Melville (or Melvill).
2. Samuel Davis.
3. This is a reference to Section 13 of "An Act to provide more effectually for the collection of the duties imposed by law on goods, wares and merchandise imported into the United States, and on the tonnage of ships or vessels" (1 *Stat.* 157–58 [August 4, 1790]), which prescribed the penalties incurred by the unlawful landing of cargoes before a ship was reported to the customs officers.
4. Christopher Gore, United States attorney for the District of Massachusetts.
5. John Pease was collector of customs at Edgartown on Martha's Vineyard.

From Jeremiah Olney [1]

Custom-House
Providence 29th. July 1791.

Sir.

I am astonished that Mr. Arnold, to excuse the non-payment of his Bond, should have recourse to a subterfuge so wholly unfounded, as "that the delay was occasioned by part of the demand's being controverted"! Permit me Sir, to assure you, upon my honor, that no Controversy ever existed between Mr. Arnold and me, relative to this Bond, after its amount was first ascertained; before which, indeed, he disputed the value of the Rix Dollar of Denmark, as stated by Law.[2] But on my receipt of the Act repealing that Law,[3] which was about

Six Weeks before his Bond became due, application was made to him for Documents to ascertain the real value of the Rix Dollar, that a Statement might be made, and the difference in the amot. of Duties allowed in payment of the Bond; which, in this case, was the only proper mode of refunding, and to which Mr. Arnold never lisped an Objection, *until after the Suit was commenced.* The *delay*, therefore, could not proceed from this cause; and in fact, the only one he pretended to aledge here, was a disappointment in a Remittance he expected from Philadelphia. This, if necessary, can be proved by a number of Witnesses. In short Sir, it appears, upon reflection, to be my Duty to inform you, that Mr. Arnold has said, in the presence of several Persons, that he had made a Calculation, and found it would be no disadvantage to let the law take its course; and that he did not mean to pay the Money until he was obliged to. And I have no doubt but your Instructions [4] to notify his delinquency, was the sole cause of his discharging the Bond on the 20th instant, to which Day I had limitted the payment, as the only condition that would prevent a compliance with your directions. That Mr. Arnold should have no shadow of complaint, the Money to be refunded on account of the Rix Dollar, was repeatedly offered to him, first on the Day his Bond was transmitted to the District Attorney, and about a Week afterwards, in my Office, before the Naval Officer and Surveyor; but he refused it, and threatned a Prosecution; which, however, he thought proper to omit. Upon his refusing the Money, I acquainted Mr. Channing [5] with the amount, requesting him to see that Judgement should be made up for so much less. I also not only gave him the usual Ten Days notice, but on the Evening of the Day his Bond became due, I called at his Store, and he being out, desired his Clerk to request him to send the Money on opening my Office the next Morning. Hearing nothing from him in the Morning, and being extremely unwilling to commence a Prosecution, I requested the Surveyor to call on him and let him know, that if the Bond was not discharged before a Packet sailed for Newport, I should be under the necessity of sending it to the District Attorney; but there appearing from his reply no probably of his paying the Money that Day, I conceived it to be my Duty, in compliance with the Law and your possitive Instructions, to transmit the Bond by the Packet, which departed about an hour after; but it was not put in Suit until Four Days had elapsed, which afforded him abundant Time, had he been so disposed, to have stopped the Process by Payment of the Money.

If Mr. Arnold should represent any other Matters unfavorable to the rectitude of my Conduct, in the execution of my Office, I have no doubt you will, by a communication thereof, afford me an opportunity of justifying myself.

I have the honor to be,   Very respectfully, Sir,   Your Most Obedt. & Most Huml. Servant   Jereh. Olney Collr.

Alexr Hamilton Esqr.
Secy. of the Treasury.

ADfS, Rhode Island Historical Society, Providence; copy, RG 56, Letters from the Collector at Providence, National Archives.

    1. For background to this letter, see Welcome Arnold to H, July 15, 1791; H to Arnold, July 22, 1791; H to Olney, July 22, 1791.

    2. Section 40 of "An Act to provide more effectually for the collection of the duties imposed by law on goods, wares and merchandise imported into the United States, and on the tonnage of ships or vessels" set the value of the rix dollar of Denmark at 100 cents (1 *Stat.* 167–68 [August 4, 1790]).

    3. "An Act relative to the Rix-Dollar of Denmark" (1 *Stat.* 215–16 [March 3, 1791]).

    4. See H to Olney, July 6, 1791.

    5. William Channing, United States attorney for the District of Rhode Island.

To George Washington

Treasury Department
July 29th. 1791

The Secretary of the Treasury has the honor respectfully to submit to the President of the United States, a contract made by the Collector of the District of Washington in North Carolina,[1] for the stakage of all the shoals & channels of the State to the Northward of the District of Wilmington, which have been heretofore thus designated. The former stakes having generally to decay, or being washed away for want of attention, the expence will be necessarily greater in the reestablishment than it probably will be in the future preservation of the stakeage now intended to be executed. It is stated by the collector that the contract for the renewal of the stakes on these waters shortly after the late war, was made at the rate of 250 Dollars pr. annum, & that tho' the expiration of so considerable a part of the current year had given rise to an expectation that he should be able to contract for less money, yet he found it impracticable to provide for the execution of the business on more favourable terms. Tho' there does not appear to be anything particularly advantageous in this agreement, the Secretary begs leave to suggest an idea that the interests of the United States may be more advanced by the immediate accommodation to the navigation, than it might be, by an uncertain experiment of forming a more reasonable contract.

All which is humbly submitted   Alexander Hamilton
                                                 Secy. of the Treasury.

LC, George Washington Papers, Library of Congress.
  1. Nathan Keais.

To George Washington

Treasury Department
July 29. 1791.

The Secretary of the Treasury having had the honor to lay before the president of the United States, the correspondence of Mr. Short respecting the loans made, & to be made, pursuant to the several Acts of Congress for that purpose,[1] begs leave to note particularly for his consideration two circumstances which appear in that correspondence.

First, that there are moments when large sums may be borrowed in Holland with more facility & advantage than small sums at other times.

Secondly, that there is some prospect of opening loans with success in other countries than the United Netherlands.

These circumstances appearing, the Secretary respectfully requests the consideration & instruction of the President of the United States; whether it may not be expedient to remove the present restrictions upon Mr. Short,[2] so as to enable him to embrace favourable moments, and open at his discretion, loans at such times & places and for such sums, as he may find adviseable, within the limitations of the respective laws authorising the Loans.

which is respectfully submitted by   Alexander Hamilton
                                                 Secy. of the Treasury.

LC, George Washington Papers, Library of Congress.
1. See "An Act making provision for the (payment of the) Debt of the United States" (1 *Stat.* 138–44 [August 4, 1790]) and "An Act making Provision for the Reduction of the Public Dept" (1 *Stat.* 186–87 [August 12, 1790]).
2. See H to William Short, September 1, 1790.

From George Washington

United States July 29. 1791.

Upon a full consideration of the reasons offered by Mr. Short,[1] in his correspondence with you, for removing the restrictions laid upon him by his present instructions, so far as relates to his not opening a loan for more than a certain sum and not being allowed to open a new Loan until the terms of the preceding one shall have been ratified here, I have thought it expedient, & for the interest of the United States that those restrictions should be removed. And I do hereby authorise you to inform Mr. Short that he may open at his discretion loans for the United States, at such times & places, & for such sums as he may find adviseable within the limitations of the respective Laws authorising these Loans.   Go. Washington

LC, George Washington Papers, Library of Congress.
1. See H to Washington, July 29, 1791.

Receipt from George Parkinson [1]

Philadelphia July 30th. 1791

Received from Alexander Hamilton Esquire Forty eight Dollars, being for three months subsistence to wit; from the 20th April 1791 to the 20th instant.   Geo: Parkinson
Dollars 48.

DS, Hamilton Papers, Library of Congress.
1. Parkinson, an English mechanic, came to America in 1790. With the support of Tench Coxe he drew up plans for a flax-spinning machine and secured a patent for it. In December, 1791, H appointed him a foreman for the Society for Establishing Useful Manufactures.

From Fisher Ames

Boston July 31. 1791

Dear Sir

I gave your letter addressed to Mrs Warren [1] into the hands of her husband, and tho, you inform me, something pretty was in it, I cannot believe it was a love letter. I told him that I was desired to subscribe for you to her poetical work. I shall take half a dozen Books, which, I presume, will be as much poetry as you will consume, and will carry the compliment as far as it will bear with any appearance of sincerity.

Mrs Walker lives in the country. I have sent your Letter [2] to her. I hope your enquiries will find proper ground to allow her petition.

You make mention of the Bank in your favor of the 2 July.[3] The eagerness to subscribe is a proof of the wealth and resources of the country and of the perfect confidence reposed by our opulent men in the Govt. People here are full of exultation and gratitude. They know who merits the praise of it, and they are not loth to bestow it. But with all this good temper, many lament that the Philadelphians have engrossed so much of the stock, & have so divided the shares as to multiply *their* votes.[4] They believe that there was management and partiality in the commissioners. They wonder that of the five, the three Philadelphians only attended.[5] Suffer me to write unreservedly.

Mr Willing's [6] name is mentioned for Prest. It is said that he is Prest. of the N. Ama. Bank, that his name will be useful to the circulation, that his appointment would quiet, perhaps destroy, a faction in the city &c. Allow me to state the other side of the question.

They urge here, that the Prest. ought to be free from all suspicion of management—above the influence of favorites—that Mr Morris, whom they fear as a man of talents & intrigue, with his connections, will make a property of this man & govern him at their pleasure.[7] I

ALS, Hamilton Papers, Library of Congress.
1. See H to Mercy Warren, July 1, 1791.
2. H to Martha Walker, July 2, 1791.   3. Letter not found.
4. See H to the President and Directors of the Massachusetts Bank, May 30, 1791.
5. See H to Tobias Lear, March 23, 1791.   6. Thomas Willing.
7. Willing and Robert Morris were business partners.

fear that his appointment would create a faction here. His friends will not pretend that he has talents to make him worth forcing upon the stockholders in the eastern quarter. An idea that the Bank will be hazarded by partiality to men who will make desperate speculations would be a bad one to get a currency. The Prest. & Directors should be solid and fair. I only wish to have you possessed of the fact that our prudent and respectable stockholders will entertain the opinions I have suggested, and I leave it to your judgment whether Mr Willing is a proper man for Prest.

If the Bank would do business for five per Cent, they would do a great deal more & with safer people. They would overpower the state Banks by giving borrowers better terms. I have had my fears that the state Banks will become unfriendly to that of the U.S. Causes of hatred & rivalry will abound. The state banks will narrow the business of the U.S. Bank & may become dangerous instruments in the hands of state partizans who may have bad points to carry. I will not expatiate. The occasion is a favorable one. The Bank & the U.S Govt. at this moment possess more popularity than any institution or Govt. can maintain for a long time. Perhaps no act of power can be done to destroy the state banks, but if they are willing to become interested individually, I mean the state stockholders, and to establish Sub Banks so as to absorb the funds & contract the business of the local Banks, why should any measures be adopted to support the local Banks to the prejudice of my hypothesis? Or why should cold water be thrown upon the plan of Sub Banks? Mr Willing & the Philadelphians are thought unfriendly to this idea. Perhaps it may be attended with some hazard. But if it must fail, let it not be charged to local prejudice, but to solid reason.

I have lately conversed with a judicious respectable friend on the subject of the Bank in this town. The justness of his sentiments or their coincidence with my own induced me to request his ideas in writing. He has complied and I inclose them. They are the offspring of a moment & were intended for me only. You will read them with due allowance for the manner of their production.

The success of the Govt. of the U.S and especially of the measures proceeding from your department has astonished the multitude & while it has shut the mouths it has stung the envious hearts of the state leaders. All the influence of the monied men ought to be wrap'd up in the union and in one Bank. The State Banks may become the favorites of the States. They, the latter, will be proud to emulate the example of the union & to shew their sovereignty by a parade of institutions like those of the nation. I intended to be concise, & by writing in haste I have been lengthy.

The Distillers here have answer'd a letter from New York, desiring them to shut up their Distilleries &c, with proper disapprobation. Some increase of the duty on W. I. Spirits & some amendment of the excise system, I presume would be proper. It is what they expect & their late conduct has a claim to merit.

Your plan relating to Manufactures is not yet generally known here.[8] I think it will be popular. Have you any objection to a similar incorporation in New England? Some object that agriculture better merits encouragement, & that domestic manufactures will be injured by the company. I do not think these topics unanswerable.

I regret it that when the funding Act [9] passed, the Stock had not been declared free from tax. Some inconvenience & vexation I fear will spring from this neglect. The Assessors are, in some places, disposed to pry into the entries at the Custom House, and the Loan Office Books.[10]

I write meaning that you only should read but I am not sure that the sentiments deserve your perusal. I will not desire an answer. I know your time is occupied sufficiently. I am, dear Sir, with sentiments of esteem and regard

Your very Obedt. hble servant   Fisher Ames

Mr Hamilton

8. Ames is referring to the proposed Society for Establishing Useful Manufactures.
9. "An Act making provision for the (payment of the) Debt of the United States" (1 *Stat.* 138–44 [August 4, 1790]).
10. See William Lowder for the Board of Assessors of the Town of Boston to H, July 14, 1791, and H to the Board of Assessors of the Town of Boston, July 27, 1791.

From Elizabeth Hamilton

[*Albany, July 31, 1791.* On August 10, 1791, Hamilton wrote to Elizabeth Hamilton: "I received your precious letters of the 31 of July & 3d. of August." *Letter of July 31 not found.*]

INDEX

COMPILED BY JEAN G. COOKE

Abbeville County, S.C., 190
Adams, John: claim of, 306-9; *letters from*, 258, 306-9; *letters to*, 258, 499; and the vice presidency, 243, 246, 270, 288, 475, 557
Agriculture, 219, 222, 420, 535; in New Hampshire, 435; and shipbuilding, 249
Albany, N.Y., 5, 213, 251, 338, 343, 346
Albemarle Sound, 329
Alburg, Vt., 166, 476-77
Alexandria, Va., 260, 494, 527; and Bank of the U.S., 516; collector of customs at, *see* Fitzgerald, John, *and* Lee, Charles; deputy collector of customs at, *see* Gray, Vincent; tare on goods at, 527
Algiers, 249; British consul at, 277-78
Alienage: laws of, 77-78, 107-8, 109
Allaire, P., 528
Allegheny County, Pa., 189
Allibone, William, 540-41; *letters from*, 304, 511
Almy, William, 310
America, 273
The American Museum, 167-68, 240
American Philosophical Society, 29
American Revolution, 5, 9, 10, 21, 22, 136, 157-58, 165-66, 180, 181, 193, 248, 250, 253, 265, 280, 301, 311, 312, 314, 320, 337, 346, 365, 403, 444, 445, 446, 485, 487, 494, 514, 526, 547, 586; and Continental Congress, 65; and invalid pensions, 13
Ames, Fisher, 359, 562; *letter from*, 589-91; *letter to*, 523
Amsterdam, 10, 51, 52, 58, 152, 158, 170, 171, 177, 179, 226, 262, 282, 301, 324, 330, 423, 424, 425, 461, 491, 492, 493, 559; bank of, 172; banking houses at, 560; French bankers at,

see Hogguer, Grand, and Co.; loans in, 172, by Holy Roman Empire, 413, by Russia, 171-72, 574, and Russo-British relations, 264, tax on foreign, 173; payment of U.S. debt to France at, 281, 575-76; rate of exchange with Paris, 423, 534, 536; sale of bills on, 345-46; U.S. stock and bonds in, 419, 460-61, 582. *See also* Loans; Short, William; United Netherlands; Willink, Van Staphorst, and Hubbard
Annapolis, Md., 464, 481; collector of customs at, *see* Davidson, John
Anson County, N.C., 190
Anthony, Joseph, and Son, 540
Antifederalists, 135, 162, 479
Antwerp: proposed U.S. loans at, 261, 336, 423-24, 459, 535, 560, 561, 573-74, 577-78, 581-82; Russian loans at, 574, 581-82
Appleton, Nathaniel, 32, 153-54, 203-4, 237, 257, 290, 315, 329; and Boston tax, 549-50; *letters from*, 7-9, 15, 29, 41, 61, 154, 182, 191-92, 192-93, 207, 227, 239, 259, 314, 321, 338, 341-42, 426, 501-2, 543; *letters to*, 13-14, 146, 153, 161-62, 199-200, 212, 315-16, 325, 331, 480; Treasury Department circulars to, 34-35, 198
Appomattox River, 525
Arkwright, Sir Richard, 556-57
Arnold, Thomas, 297-98
Arnold, Welcome: *letter from*, 551-53; *letter to*, 564; and Jeremiah Olney, 495-96, 530-31, 558, 564-65, 584-86
Assignats, *see* France
Assistant Postmaster General, *see* Burrall, Jonathan
Assistant Secretary of the Treasury, *see* Coxe, Tench

Assumption of state debts, 2, 33, 60, 144-45, 202, 443-46, 446-47, 455-56; and Continental certificates, 532-33; and forfeited estates, 475; and North Carolina, 443, 508-9, 565-66; and Virginia, 443, 543. *See also* Congress of U.S., acts of; Loans; Pennsylvania
Attorney General, *see* Randolph, Edmund
Auditor of the Treasury Department, 548. *See also* Wolcott, Oliver, Jr.
Augusta, Ga., 243, 349

Backhouse, William, 274-75, 348-49
Bahama Islands, 583
Ballard, Robert, 338
Baltimore, Md., 15, 25, 28, 35, 39, 151, 302, 303, 317, 321, 338, 350, 388, 401, 437, 438, 462; and Bank of Maryland, 410; collector of customs at, *see* Williams, Otho H.; customs officers at, 35-37; deputy collector of customs at, *see* Delozier, Daniel; surveyor of port of, *see* Ballard, Robert
Bancker, Christopher, 272, 284
Bancker, Gerard, 212-13, 475
Bankers of U.S. in Amsterdam, *see* Willink, Van Staphorst, and Hubbard
Banknotes: advantages of, 133-34
Bank of Boston, *see* Massachusetts Bank
Bank of England, 220
Bank of Maryland, 400-1; and collector of customs, 409-10; and commissioner of loans, 506-7; notes of, 506
Bank of New York, 4-5, 34, 49, 57, 61, 120, 208, 223, 226, 334-45, 345, 357, 364, 494, 503; and Bank of the U.S., 92, 449, 494-95, 503, 504, 513, 518, 551; bills of, 93; cashier of, *see* Seton, William; drafts on, 192, 506; incorporation of, 212-13; and lighthouse on Cape Henry, Va., 236; and payment of interest on public debt, 34-35; president and directors of, 449, 551, *letters to,* 397, 541; and treasurer of the U.S., 276
Bank of North America, 102, 121, 219, 299, 330, 357, 364, 442, 444, 446, 485, 589-90; bills of, 93; cashier of, *see* Francis, Tench; drafts on, 192, 506; notes of, 1-2, 3, 38, 201, 469; and payment of interest on public debt, 34-

35; and Pennsylvania, 215; president of, *see* Willing, Thomas
Bank of the U.S., 61, 94, 264; and Alexandria, Va., 516; and Bank of Massachusetts, 396-97; and Bank of New York, 92, 449, 494-95, 503, 504, 513; and borrowing of money, 92, 96-97, 124; branches of, 222, 223, 590; and collection of taxes, 92-96, 121-23; and commerce, 92, 126-27; commissioners to receive subscriptions of, 210-11, 214, 589; constitutionality of, 50-51, 57-58, 63-134; duration of, 220-21; Federal ownership of stock of, 134; and general welfare, 91; Hamilton's notes on Edmund Randolph's opinion on, 46-49; Hamilton's opinion on constitutionality of act to establish, 63-135, 218-23; incorporation of, 397; and loans, 91-92, 96-97; and media of exchange, 92-93; and monopoly, 110; and national defense, 92, 127; and necessary and proper clause, 94, 95; and New York State, 213; organization of, 92, 120-21; president of, 589-90; and property of U.S., 92, 127-28; and public debt, 221-22; purpose of, 91-97; Edmund Randolph's opinion on constitutionality of, 46-49; reasons for establishing, 219-23; seat of, 221; and specified powers, 91-97; and state banks, 590-91; and the states, 110, 222, 223; subscriptions to, 210-11, 396-97, 449, 494-95, 503, 504, 513, 517, 518, 551, 589; superiority to state banks, 219-20. *See also* Congress of U.S., acts of; Jefferson, Thomas; Randolph, Edmund
Bankruptcy: laws on, 79, 109
Banks: advantages of, 218-23; and agriculture, 218-19; of Amsterdam, 220; and augmentation of capital of a nation, 218; credit of, 122; and frontier defense, 219; of Genoa, 220; and government, 219; and Great Britain's prosperity, 19; of Hamburg, 220; and loans, 219; and manufactures, 218-19; and merchants, 219; notes, as money, 218; and Scotland's prosperity, 19; and specie, 218; state, 102, 219-20, and Bank of the U.S., 223; and taxes, payment of, 219; and trade, 218-19; in U.S., 71; of Vienna, 220
Barbary States: and John Adams, 307

Barclay, Thomas, 307
Baring, Sir Francis, 512-13
Barlow, Joel, 227-33
Barre, Mass., 344
Barrington, R.I.: customs boat for, 297, 333; surveyor of port of, *see* Phillips, Nathaniel
Barrow, Thomas, 316-17
Bartholomew, Edward: *letter from*, 193-97
Bartholomew County, S.C., 190
Barton, William, 345, 355, 406, 473, 496-97, 585
Bayard, William, 146
Bayley, Rafael A.: *The National Loans of the United States from July 4, 1776, to June 30, 1880*, 52
Baylis, Hodijah, 163-64, 183
Beatty, Ercurius, 136
Beaufort County, N.C., 190
Beckwith, George: Hamilton's conversations with, 41-45, 342-43, 475-77, 544-46; *letter from*, 51
Bedford County, Pa., 189
Beekman, James, 527
Bell, William: *letter from*, 193-97
Benbury, Thomas, 190
Benson, William, 399
Berkeley County, S.C., 190
Berks County, Pa., 189
Berkshire County, Mass., 189
Bermuda Hundred, Va., 481-83; collector of customs at, *see* Heth, William
Berrien, John: *letters from*, 404-5, 502
Betsy, 225-26
Beverly, Mass., 522
Biddeford, District of Maine, 234
Biddle, Clement: *letter from*, 511
Big Beaver Creek, Pa., 213, 218
Big Bottom: Indian attacks on, 124
Bimetallism, *see* Coins
Bingham, William, 454
Blackden, Samuel (Col.), 228
Bladen County, N.C., 190
Blanchard, James: *letter from*, 401-4
Blount, J. G., 582
Board of Treasury, 150, 205, 216, 325-27; and new emissions, 319; and Northwest Territory, 360, 363; and Scioto Co., 229-30; warrants of, 452
Boehm, Edmund, 512-13
Bond, Venable, 275
Bordentown, N.J., 365

Bordley, John Beale, 210-11; *letter from*, 214; *letter to*, 210
Boston, Mass., 7, 15, 27, 29, 34, 41, 61, 144, 146, 150, 154, 162, 163, 167, 168, 182, 185, 191, 192, 204, 207, 227, 239, 243, 248, 259, 273, 302, 314, 315, 320, 321, 337, 338, 341, 346, 359, 397, 405, 426, 472, 501, 526, 530, 543, 548, 569, 576, 589; Board of Assessors of, 591, *letter from*, 549-50; *letter to*, 580-81; collector of customs at, *see* Lincoln, Benjamin; duck, 317; sailcloth, 302; shipbuilding in, 248-51; surveyor of port of, 345 (*see also* Melville, Thomas); tax, 580-81
Boudinot, Elias, 402, 404
Boulton, Matthew, 395
Bounty, 88; and emigration from Europe, 18-19
Bowen, Jabez, 197, 208, 224-25, 235, 528; *letter to*, 357-58; Treasury Department circulars to, 34-35, 394-95
Bowen, Thomas B. (Maj.), 136
Bowers, Jerathmeel, 163-64, 332
Boyd, William, 316-17
Brackett, James, 201-2
Brady, Samuel, 218
Brasher, Ephraim, 485-86
Breweries, 166-68
Brightman, William, 297-98; petition of, 16
Bristol, England, 557
Bristol, R.I.: customs boat for, 297, 333; inspector of port of, *see* Munro, William
British East India Co., 424
British West Indies: trade with, 434-35
Broadway Landing, Va., 525
Brown, John (Ky.): *letter to*, 164-65
Brown, John (R.I.), 398, 473-74
Brunswick, Ga., 275
Brunswick County, N.C., 190, 466
Bucklin, Daniel, Jr., 51, 398, 467, 495
Bucks County, Pa., 189
Burk, John, 346
Burke, Ædanus, 152
Burke County, N.C., 190
Burlington, Vt., 166
Burlington Bay, Vt., 477
Burr, Aaron: and Baron de Rottenbourg, 527-28; U.S. Senator from N.Y., 4-5, 478
Burrall, Jonathan: *letter from*, 215-16
Bush, George, 154-55, 480
Butler, Pierce, 151; *letter from*, 152

Butler, Richard (Maj. Gen.), 546, 563

Cadwalader, Lambert, 210-11
Caillard, Antoine Bernard, 170-71, 260; *letters from* William Short, 177, 177-78; *letters to* William Short, 170, 177
Caldwell, Andrew: *letter from,* 193-97
Caldwell's Manor, 477
Calico, *see* Duties
Callaway, John, 557
Camden, S.C., 470, 472
Camden (Cambden) County, N.C., 190
Campbell, Robert, 17
Campbell, William: *letter from,* 295; *letter to,* 464-66
Canals, 19, 301, 436; Federal construction of, 82-83, 110-11
Candles, *see* Duties
Canton, China, 495
Cape Fear, N.C.: commissioners of navigation of, 296-97; lighthouse at, 295, 296-97, 464-66
Cape Fear River, 328, 464, 466
Cape Henlopen, Del.: lighthouse at, 181, 304, 540
Cape Henry, Va.: lighthouse at, 46, 234, 236, 238, 251, 276, 283, 316, 450-51, 464, 533-34, 555-56
Carey, Mathew: and *The American Museum,* 167-68; *letter to,* 240
Carmichael, William, 205
Carrington, Edward, 187, 188, 280; *letter from,* 240-41; *letter to,* 207
Carroll, Charles, of Carrollton, 142-43
Carroll, Daniel, 472
Carrollsburg, Md.: and Federal District, 255
Carrying trade: and shipbuilding, 248
Carteret County, N.C., 190
Carters Ferry, Va., 471
Caswell County, N.C., 190
Cazenove, Théophile, 453-54; and a manufacturing society, 300-1
Certificates of public debt, *see* Public debt, certificates of
Chaloner, John, 180-81
Channing, William, 184, 495-96, 585-86
Charleston, S.C., 225-26, 242, 275-76, 330, 331, 349, 470; collector of customs at, *see* Hall, George Abbot; harbor master of, *see* Cochran, Robert; lighthouse at, 181, 183
Charleston County, S.C., 190

Charlestown, Mass., 576
Charlotte, N.C., 243, 471
Charming Sally, 183-84, 271
Chatham County, N.C., 190
Chazy River, 477
Cheese, *see* Duties
Cheever, Abijah, 27, 62, 148
Chesapeake Bay, 25
Chester, John, 187, 188; Treasury Department circular to, 506
Chester County, Pa., 189
Chester County, S.C., 190
Chesterfield County, S.C., 190
Child, Francis, 565-66, 567, 568, 569
Childs, Francis: *The* [New York] *Daily Advertiser,* 167-68
China: tea, 539; trade with, 20-21
China, *see* Duties
Chintz, *see* Duties
Chowan County, N.C., 190
Church, Angelica Schuyler (Mrs. John B.), 320
Church, John B., 180-81, 279-80; account with Hamilton, 320
Cincinnati, 361
Cincinnati, Society of the, 311; New Hampshire Society of the, 403
Claims: by widows and orphans, 513-14, 520
Clarendon County, S.C., 190
Claverack, N.Y., 485
Clermont County, S.C., 190
Clinton, George, 4-5, 213; Treasury Department circular to, 509-10
Clymer, George, 187, 188
Coal, 36-37
Coasting trade, 273, 327, 462-64, 479; and duties, 328, 462-64; and fees, 473-74; and licenses, 473-74; and revenue laws, 431; ships in, 399, 430, 479, 480, 481, 486, 488, 553; and the surveyor of the port, 474
Cobb, Samuel, 27, 62, 148
Cochran, John (Dr.), 32, 247, 266; *letter from,* 212; *letters to,* 223-24, 474-75
Cochran, Robert, 331, 349, 531
Cocoa, *see* Duties; Tare on goods
Codfish, 249
Codman, ——— (Capt.), 317
Codwise, George, 226-27
Coffee, 317. *See also* Duties; Tare on goods
Cogdell, John, 190, 331
Coins, 282, 355; assay of, 57; bimetal-

lism, 439; composition and fineness of, 439; copper, 205, 395; dollars, weight of, 268; in England, 286; foreign, 450; recoinage, 439; regulation of, 79, 109

Collectors of customs, 81, 358, 371, 429, 430-31; at Alburg, Vt., *see* Keyes, Stephen; at Alexandria, Va., *see* Fitzgerald, John, *and* Lee, Charles; at Annapolis, Md., *see* Davidson, John; at Baltimore, Md., *see* Williams, Otho H.; at Bermuda Hundred, Va., *see* Heth, William; at Biddeford, District of Maine, *see* Hill, Jeremiah; at Boston and Charlestown, Mass., *see* Lincoln, Benjamin; at Brunswick, Ga., *see* Hillary, Christopher; at Charleston, S.C., *see* Hall, George Abbot; at Dighton, Mass., *see* Baylis, Hodijah; at Edenton, N.C., *see* Benbury, Thomas; at Edgartown, Mass., *see* Pease, John; at Frenchman's Bay, District of Maine, *see* Jordan, Meletiah; at Georgetown, S.C., *see* Cogdell, John; at Hampton, Va., *see* Wray, George; at New Bern, N.C., *see* Daves, John; at New London, Conn., *see* Huntington, Jedediah; at Newport, R.I., *see* Ellery, William; at New York City, *see* Lamb, John; at Pepperellborough, District of Maine, *see* Hill, Jeremiah; at Perth Amboy, N.J., *see* Halsted, John; at Philadelphia, Pa., *see* Delany, Sharp; at Portsmouth, N.H., *see* Whipple, Joseph; at Providence, R.I., *see* Olney, Jeremiah; at Savannah, Ga., *see* Habersham, John; at Washington, N.C., *see* Keais, Nathan; at Wilmington, Del., *see* Bush, George; at Wilmington, N.C., *see* Read, James; and administration of oaths, 38-39; and Bank of Maryland, 409-10; and certificates of registry, 163, 183, 224, 298, 310, 333, 442, 469, 528-29, 553, 576; clerk for, 525; and coasting trade, 16, 462-63, 553; and commissioners of loans, 162-63, 197, 506-7; compensation and expenditures of, 10, 267, 274, 287-88, 303, 346-47, 350-52, 449, 457-58, 481-82, 496-97, 522, 523-24, 554; and condemned merchandise, 15; and customs boats, 297-98, 522; and drawbacks, 168-69,

271, 273; and duties, 297-98, 442-43, 538-39; duties of, 351, 481-83, 499-501, 523-24; and entry of ships, 147-48, 267, 273-74; fees of, 553-54; and forfeitures, 15, 16, 295-96, 333, 437-38, 553; and frauds, 437-38; and hydrometers, 158; as inspector of the revenue, 191, 370; and inspectors of the port, 340; and libels, 184; and manifests, 303, 427, 462-63; and Massachusetts Bank, 199-200; monthly schedule of bonds, 158, 528; and payment of interest on public debt, 162-63; and payments of invalid pensions, 25-26; quarterly returns of, 145-46, 524-25, 538, 558; and refund of tonnage duty, 259-60; and remission of penalties, 38-39; and report on exports, 145-46; and revenue, 267; and revenue laws, 302, 553; and seizures, 16, 38-39, 184, 204, 297-98; and shipbuilding, 248-51; and smuggling, 204; and supervisors of the revenue, 366, 525; and surveyors of the port, 369; and tares, 244-45, 340-41; and tonnage, 364; and trade laws, 302; treasurer's bills on, 49-50; weekly return of money received and paid, 15, 38, 158, 163, 183, 201, 208, 224, 298, 310, 333, 339, 348-49, 442, 469, 507, 528; and wharves and warehouses, 35. *See also* Colles's hydrometer; Distilled spirits; Dycas's hydrometer; "Excise Law"; Revenue cutters; Ship registers; Tare on goods; Treasury Department circulars to the collectors of the customs

Collectors of the revenue, 191, 368; and distilleries, 375, 377-78, 380-81; duties of, 376, 378-79; and inspectors of revenue, 379; and oaths, 381-82

Colles, Christopher, 488. *See also* Colles's hydrometer

Colles's hydrometer, 243-44, 404

Colleton County, S.C., 190

Collins, James, 189

Columbia, S.C., 243, 471

Columbian Magazine, 135

Commerce, 420; and Bank of the U.S., 126-27; in New Hampshire, 434-36; regulation of, by Congress, 70-71, 74, 75, 79, 87-88, 109; request for information on, by Hamilton, 224-25, 235, 434; and revenue laws, 431; and

Commerce (*Continued*)
shipbuilding, 250; treaty with Great Britain, 41-45; of U.S., 535. *See also* Trade and industry; Trading companies

Commissioners of loans: for Delaware, *see* Tilton, James; for Georgia, *see* Wylly, Richard; for Maryland, *see* Harwood, Thomas; for Massachusetts, 32 (*see also* Appleton, Nathaniel); for New Hampshire, *see* Gardner, William; for New York, 32 (*see also* Cochran, John); for North Carolina, *see* Skinner, William; for Pennsylvania, 32 (*see also* Smith, Thomas); for Rhode Island, *see* Bowen, Jabez; for Virginia, 32 (*see also*, Hopkins, John); books of, 549-50; and Boston tax, 549-50, 580-81; certificates of, 193-97; and certificates of debt, 144-45; and certificates of register of the Treasury, 198; clerks of, 8, 31-32, 224; and collectors of customs, 162-63, 197, 506-7; compensation of, 31-32, 207, 481; and comptroller of the Treasury, 169; and counterfeits, 198; and extraordinary expenditures, 31-32; and nonsubscribers, 341-42; and old emissions, 341-42; and public debt, 7-9; stationery for, 31-32, 224; and stocks, 192-93, 227; and treasurer's drafts, 161-62. *See* Invalid pensions, payment of; Public debt, payment of interest on; Treasury Department circulars to the commissioners of loans

Commissioners of the U.S., *see* Willink, Van Staphorst, and Hubbard

Commissioners to settle the accounts: of the Army, 8; of the commissary department, 8; of the marine, clothing, and hospital departments, 8; of Pennsylvania line, 135-36; of the quartermaster department, 8; between U.S. and individual states, 8, 265, 520. *See also* Gilman, John T.; North Carolina; Pennsylvania

Common defense: and Bank of the U.S., 92, 127; and shipbuilding, 250; and taxes, 90

Common law, 352; and corporations, 77-78, 79, 109

Comptroller of the Treasury, 458. *See also* Eveleigh, Nicholas; Wolcott, Oliver, Jr.

Condorcet, Marie Jean Antoine Nicholas Caritat, marquis de, 416, 439

Confederation: debt of, 305, 316; defects of, 22; finance of, 8-9; and Pennsylvania certificates, 455-56. *See also* Board of Treasury; Continental loan officers

Congress of U.S., 66, 194, 240, 264, 281, 302, 306, 321, 421, 525; adjournment of, 165; and Bank of the U.S., 113-14, 135; and bankruptcy laws, 79, 109; "bill for registering Ships or Vessels, for regulating those employed in the Coasting Trade and Fisheries, and for other purposes," 272; and canal construction, 82-83, 110-11; and commercial treaty with Great Britain, 41-45; and commissioners of loans, 8, 31-32; and compensation of clerks, 141-42; and compensation of customs officers, 10, 274, 287-88, 303, 496-97, 554; and customs officers, 523-24; and Federal District, 76, 112-13; funding program, 9; and general welfare clause, 90, 91, 129; and Holland loans, 55, 177-78; and Indians, 247, 343, 532; and invalid pensions, 486-87; and Ferdinand Le Grand, 178-79; and lighthouses, 464-65, 529-30; and loans, 87, 125, 560; and mint, 168, 285; and Gouverneur Morris's mission to Great Britain, 41-45; and Northwest Territory, 361, 362; and payment of interest on public debt, 509-10; and Pennsylvania, 23-24; and post roads, 81-82; and power to create corporations, 63-134, debate on, 113-14; and power to erect a government, 91; powers of, *see* "Opinion on the Constitutionality of an Act to Establish a Bank"; and proposed purchase of U.S. debt to France, 176; and regulation of coins, 79, 109; and regulation of trade, 70-71, 74, 79, 87-88, 109; resolves of, 284-86, 362, 446 (June 28, 1790), 209 (September 23, 1789); and ship registers, 5-7; on ship's legal classification, 16; and sovereignty, 67; and taxes, 85-87, 128-29; and territories of U.S., 89, 128; and trading companies, 75, 89; and George Washington's message (December 8, 1790), 137-38; and Oliver Wolcott, Jr., 291-92. *See also* Bank of the U.S.; House of Representatives; Loans; Petitions; Senate

Congress of U.S., acts of: "An Act to continue in force the act therein mentioned, and to make further provision for the payment of Pensions of Invalids, and for the support of lighthouses, beacons, buoys, and public piers," March 3, 1791, 14, 487; "An Act to establish an Executive Department, to be denominated the Department of War," August 7, 1789, 107; "An Act to establish the Treasury Department," September 2, 1789, 107; "An Act for establishing an Executive Department, to be denominated the Department of Foreign Affairs," July 27, 1789, 107; "An Act for establishing the Salaries of the Executive Officers of Government, with their Assistants and Clerks," September 11, 1789, 141-42; "An Act for establishing the temporary and permanent seat of the Government of the United States," July 16, 1790, 470, 472; "An Act for the establishment and support of Lighthouses, Beacons, Buoys, and Public Piers," August 7, 1789, 70, 104, 106, 163-64, 529; "An Act to explain and amend an act intituled 'An Act making further provision for the payment of the debts of the United States,' " March 2, 1791, 359, 448-49; "An Act to explain and amend an Act intituled 'An Act for registering and clearing Vessels, regulating the Coasting Trade, and for other purposes,' " September 29, 1789, 127, 369; "An Act further to provide for the Payment of the Invalid Pensioners of the United States," July 16, 1790, 13-14, 487; "An Act for the government and regulation of Seamen in the merchants service," July 20, 1790, 88, 118; "An Act for the Government of the Territory of the United States, south of the river Ohio," May 26, 1790, 77, 120; "An Act imposing duties on the tonnage of ships or vessels," July 20, 1790, 473-74, 488; "An Act to incorporate the subscribers to the Bank of the United States," February 25, 1791, 50-51, 57-58, 63-135, 142-43, 397; "An Act for laying a Duty on Goods, Wares and Merchandises imported into the United States," July 4, 1789, 25; "An Act making an appropriation for the purpose therein mentioned," March 3, 1791, 180, 186; "An Act making farther provision for the collection of the duties by law imposed on Teas, and to prolong the term for the payment of the Duties on Wines," March 3, 1791, 156, 237, 322-23, 365, 383-87; "An Act making further provision for the payment of the debts of the United States," August 10, 1790, 14-15, 21, 25, 52, 118, 448-49, 538-39, 542; "An Act making provision for the (payment of the) Debt of the United States," August 4, 1790, 8-9, 31-32, 32-33, 52, 177, 194, 195, 196, 239, 257, 265, 299, 305-6, 324-35, 348, 387-88, 392-93, 394-95, 401, 402, 403, 426, 443-46, 446-47, 456, 467, 474-75, 509-10, 566, 567, 568, 587-88, 591; "An Act making Provision for the Reduction of the Public Debt," August 12, 1790, 1-2, 137-38, 177, 257, 356-57, 419, 587-88; "An Act to provide for the Government of the Territory Northwest of the river Ohio," August 7, 1789, 107, 120; "An Act to provide for mitigating or remitting the forfeitures and penalties accruing under the revenue laws, in certain cases therein mentioned," May 26, 1790, 16, 38-39, 203, 295-96, 313-14, 353-54, 437-38; "An Act to provide more effectually for the collection of the duties imposed by law on goods, wares and merchandise imported into the United States, and on the tonnage of ships or vessels," August 4, 1790, 36-37, 93, 121, 130, 147-48, 154-55, 168-69, 184, 204, 225-26, 244-45, 252-53, 267-68, 271-72, 276, 312-13, 313-14, 340-41, 352-54, 369, 370, 371, 389, 391, 408-9, 421, 426-31, 433, 442-43, 468-69, 481-82, 484-85, 495-96, 538-39, 583-84, 586; "An Act providing the means of intercourse between the United States

Congress of U.S., acts of (*Continued*) and foreign nations," July 1, 1790, 205-6; "An Act providing for the payment of the Invalid Pensioners of the United States," September 29, 1789, 13, 487; "An Act for raising and adding another Regiment to the Military Establishment of the United States, and for making farther provision for the protection of the frontiers," March 3, 1791, 96, 124, 186, 343; "An Act for Registering and Clearing Vessels, Regulating the Coasting Trade, and for other purposes," September 1, 1789, 5-7, 127, 302, 369, 408, 440-41, 462-64, 553-54, 576; "An Act to regulate the Collection of the Duties imposed by law on the tonnage of ships or vessels, and on goods, wares and merchandises imported into the United States," July 31, 1789, 168-69, 304-5, 485; "An Act to regulate the Time and Manner of administering certain Oaths," June 1, 1789, 433; "An Act relative to the Rix-Dollar of Denmark," March 3, 1791, 584-86; "An Act repealing, after the last day of June next, the duties heretofore laid upon Distilled Spirits imported from abroad, and laying others in their stead; and also upon Spirits distilled within the United States, and for appropriating the same," March 3, 1791, 23, 96, 124, 187-91, 207, 325, 365-82, 502, 506, 510-11, 548-49; "An Act supplemental to the 'act establishing the Treasury Department,' and for a farther compensation to certain officers," March 3, 1791, 142; "An Act supplementary to the act intituled 'An Act to incorporate the subscribers to the Bank of the United States,'" March 2, 1791, 397; "An Act supplementary to the act making provision for the reduction of the Public Debt," March 3, 1791, 137-38, 529-30

Connecticut, 9, 37, 51, 112, 180, 311, 398, 435, 466, 479, 495; and assumption of state debts, 443; collectors of customs of, 332; comptroller of, *see* Wolcott, Oliver, Jr.; governor of, *see* Huntington, Samuel, *and*

Trumbull, Jonathan; supervisor of revenue for, *see* Chester, John; survey of inspection of, 189; U.S. attorney for District of, *see* Edwards, Pierpont; U.S. judge for the District of, *see* Law, Richard

Constituent Assembly, *see* France, National Assembly

Constitution (U.S.), 45, 141, 350, 401; adopted by Rhode Island, 347, 350, 553; Article IV, Section 2, 218; Article IV, Section 3, 77; Article X, 98, 99, 108; broad construction of, 63-134; and canal construction by Federal Government, 82-83, 110-11; and constitutionality of Bank of the U.S., 63-134, 135; criterion of constitutionality, 107; design of, 132; and enumerated powers, 68, 69, 72, 73-74, 99-100, 112-13, 120; and Europe, 516; and Federal District, 76, 112-13; framers of, 83; general welfare clause, 90, 91, 129; Hamilton's "Notes on Edmund Randolph's Opinion on the Constitutionality of an Act to Establish a Bank," 46-49; and Holland loans, 53; and implied powers, *see* "Opinion on the Constitutionality of an Act to Establish a Bank"; and liberty, 22; limitations and exceptions in, 67; "means and ends," 67, 70, 73, 74, 82, 98, 101, 104, 107, 110, 114, 121, 131; necessary and proper clause, 68-72, 74, 92, 94, 95, 101-7, 119; oath to support, 201, 433; and pardons, 352-54; and powers of incorporation, 63-134; ratification of, 347; and resulting powers, 100; and rights of individuals, 73; and rights of states, 73; and states, 22; strict construction of, 66; supremacy clause, 67, 99; and taxes, 89-90, 115-16, 128-29

Constitutional Convention, 314; and canal construction by Federal Government, 82-83, 111-12; and corporations, 82-83, 85, 110-11; debates in, 70; interpretation of intention of, 111; and necessary and proper clause, 103; secretary of, *see* Jackson, William

"A Continental" (anonymous), 404

Continental Army, 466; accounts of, and North Carolina, 444, and Rhode Island, 3-4; claims of, 401-4; commissary general of purchases, *see* Wadsworth, Jeremiah; Corps of Engineers, 253; officers of, 401-4; paymaster general, *see* Pierce, John; quartermaster department, 547; quartermaster general, *see* Pickering, Timothy; supplies for, 164-65

Continental Congress, 228, 306, 566; acts of, 194, act of March 18, 1780, 318-20, 388, 452-53; bills of exchange of, 319, 387-88; certificates of, 320; and claims, 138-41; comptroller of treasury, *see* Milligan, James; and Holland loan, 158; member from Delaware, *see* Rodney, Thomas; ministers of, 307; and new emissions, 9, 387-88; and North Carolina, 487; old emissions, 7-9; ordinance of October 18, 1782, 216; and paymaster general, 8; petition to, 138-39; powers of, 65; presidents of, 452 (*see also* Lee, Richard Henry); resolutions of, 308-9 (September 28, 1776), 446 (September 9, 1777), 319 (October 6, 1779), 318 (October 7, 1779), 307 (May 7, 1784), 139-40 (June 27, 1785), 139 (November 4, 1785), 326-27 (June 6, 1788), 325-27 (August 28, 1788); and Scioto Co., 230; secretary of, *see* Thomson, Charles; securities of, 426; treasury of, 318-19. *See also* Board of Treasury

Continental debt, *see* Confederation

Continental loan officers, 216, 319; for North Carolina, *see* Skinner, William; for Rhode Island, *see* Ellery, William

Contracts: for Army supplies, 226-27, 246-48, 334, 354; for beacon boats, 304, 540-41; for lighthouse construction, 234, 236, 238, 251, 276, 283, 316, 450-51, 555-56, supplies, 181-82, 183, 304, 521, 540; and loan office certificates, 194-95; to purchase western lands, 326-27; for quartermaster department supplies, 164-65; for stakage, 483, 586-87; for western posts' supply, 438; for West Point supply, 138-41

Conyngham, David, 155

Cook, Charles, 582

Cooke, James: *A Voyage to the Pacific Ocean undertaken . . . for making discoveries in the Northern Hemisphere,* 364-65

Cooke, William, 311, 358

Copper coins, *see* Coins, copper

Cordage, *see* Duties

Cornplanter, 241, 242

Corporations: and Constitutional Convention, 82-83, 85, 110; definition of, 77, 81, 89, 123; examples of Federal, 130-31; and monopoly, 75, 131; nature of, 77-78, 108-9; right of U.S. to charter, 63-134; and the states, 77-80, 103, 109; trading companies as examples of, 89, 131, 132

Cotton: manufacturing, 556-57, in New Hampshire, 436, and Society for Establishing Useful Manufactures, 571-73; mills, 556-57. *See also* Duties; Tare on goods

Counterfeiting, 185, 197, 198, 252, 315, 409, 455; and payment of invalid pensions, 26; and public debt, 149-50, 306; and supervisor of revenue, 373

Cowper, —— (Miss), 4

Coxe, Paul: *letter from,* 193-97

Coxe, Tench, 40, 146, 152, 224-25, 237, 293-94, 355, 364, 516-17, 588; circular letters of, 235, 248, 434-36, 479-80; and revenue cutters, 317

Cranberry Island, District of Maine, 522

Crane, Francis, 252

Craven County, N.C., 190

Crawford, James, 154-55

Creditors, *see* Public creditors

Crooke, Robert, 442-43

Cruger, Henry, 556-57

Cruger, Nicholas, 227, 236, 238, 251, 316

Cumberland County, N.C., 190

Cumberland County, Pa., 189

Currituck County, N.C., 190

Customhouses: defaults at, 268; receipts of, 199; returns of, 39-40; and tare, 350

Customs boats, *see* Collectors of customs

Customs officers, 86; compensations of, 36, 287-88, 346, 347, 350-52, 359-60, 449, 457-58, 496-97, 499-501, 523-25; and distilled spirits, 365-82; duties of, 351, 499-501, 523-24; expenses of, 496-97; and forfeitures, 553; and informers, 353; and moiety of fines, 353; and wines and teas, 383-87

Customs service, see Collectors of customs; Customhouses; Customs officers; Duties; Revenue cutters; Ships
Cutler, Manasseh, 228-30
Cutting, Leonard M., 527-28
Cutts, Thomas, 234
Cuyler, Jacob, 338, 343-44; letter to, 251
Cuyler, Richard, 251; letter from, 338-39

Dallas, Alexander, 532-33; letters from, 135-36, 209, 507; letter to Thomas Jefferson, 507; letter to Henry Knox, 507
Danish West Indies, 435, 480
Darlington County, S.C., 190
Dauphin County, Pa., 189
Daves, John, 190, 517; letter from, 542; letter to, 201; Treasury Department circular to, 162-63
Davidson, John, 480; letter to, 486
Davies, Edward, 215-16, 347-48, 472
Davis, Samuel, 583-84
Dayton, Jonathan, 440, 541; letter from, 405
Deane, Silas, 308
Debt: certificates of, 193; deferred, 411-12; to foreign officers, 561-62; and stock, 41, 144, 233. See also Assumption of state debts; Public credit; Public debt; Speculation; States
Declared powers, see Constitution (U.S.), enumerated powers
Deferred payment, see Public debt
Delany, Sharp: letter from, 543; letters to, 14-15, 147-48, 244-45, 303, 322-23; Treasury Department circular to, 407-9
Delaware, 112, 155, 489; capes of, 147; commissioner of loans for, see Tilton, James; militia, 21; revenue cutter for, 541; supervisor of revenue for, see Latimer, Henry; survey of inspection of, 189
Delaware Bay, 14
Delaware County, Pa., 189
Delaware River, 511, 540
Delozier, Daniel, 38-39, 352, 462-64
Denmark: rix dollars of, 584-85
Department of State, see State Department

Department of the Treasury, see Treasury Department
Department of War, see War Department
Derby, Elias Hasket: petition of, 155-56
Dericks, J. G., 158
Descent: laws of, 77-78, 107-8, 109
Detroit, 544. See also McKee, Alexander
Dexter, John S. (Maj.), 3-4, 187-88, 311, 495-96; Treasury Department circular to, 497-98
Dighton, Mass., 163-64, 183, 224, 310, 470
Diplomatic service: money for, 204-5, 205-6
Distilled spirits: and collectors of the customs, 548-49; and collectors of the revenue, 380-81; and distillers, 366-82; importation of, 548-49; in Massachusetts, 591; in New York, 591; regulation of, 502, 505-6, 510-11; seizures of, 379-80. See also Duties; "Excise Law"
Distilleries, see Distilled spirits
Distribution: laws of, 77, 107-8, 109
District of Maine, see Maine
Dobbs County, N.C., 190
Dodge, Samuel: petition of, 202-3, 312-13, 353-54
Domestic debt, see Public debt
Donnaldson, John: letter to Thomas Mifflin, 410-12
Dorchester, Lord, 44, 342-43, 477, 544, 545
Drawbacks, 168-69, 271, 273, 302, 304-5
Droz, Jean Pierre: and mint, 285-86
Duane, James, 548
Duer, William, 4-5, 138, 454, 556-57, 563; letters to, 246-48, 300-1; and Scioto Co., 228-33
Dufresne, Bertrand, 179, 416, 489-93, 536, 558-59
Dumas, Charles William Frederick, 205
Dunham, Aaron, 187, 188
Duplin County, N.C., 190
Durazzo, Girolamo D., 575
Dutch, see United Netherlands
Dutch East India Co., 282, 424, 460
Dutch loans, see Loans, Holland
Dutchman's Point, Vt., 477
Dutch West Indies, 435, 480

Duties, 23-24, 264; "additional," 14-15, 25, 28 (*see also* Congress of U.S., acts of, "An Act making further provision for the payment of the debts of the United States" [August 10, 1790]); on burrstone, 579; on cables, 390; on candles, 390; on cheese, 390, 484; on china, 483; on chintzes and calicoes, 359, 448-49; and coasting vessels, 328, 462-64, 480, 481, 486; on cocoa, 390; on coffee, 390; collection of, 81, 388-89; and collectors of customs, 442-43; on cordage, 390, 484; on cotton, 222, 359, 390, 448-49; on distilled spirits, 23-24, 191, 324-25, 483 (*see also* Supervisors of the revenue); and drawbacks, 271-72; exemptions from, 274; French, on oil, 11-13, 160, 173-74, 175, on tobacco, 11-13, 60-61, 160-61, 174; on hemp, 390, 483, 484; how determined, 274, 340, 483-84, 527; on indigo, 390; and inspectors of the port, 340; on lead and shot, 390, 483; on linen, 359, 448-49; on nails, 390, 483; payment of, 38-39, 275-76, 297-98, 340, 388-89; on pepper, 390; on pimento, 390; on plaster of Paris, 579; on porter, 167; repayment of, 473; return of, 155; on salt, 483; on snuff, 167; on soap, 390; on steel, 167, 390; on sugar, 390; on tea, 20-21, 155-56, 237, 273, 322-23, 390, 467-68, 495-96, 530-31, 538-39, 548, 558, 571; on tobacco, 390; on twine, 390, 483; on wines, 322-23, 467-68. *See also* Tonnage duty
Dycas's hydrometer, 158, 243-44, 332-33, 338, 339, 355, 381, 404, 406, 488, 542

Eastern states: and Federal District, 255-56; and ship timber, 249-50
East Greenwich, R.I., 163, 297; customs boat for, 297, 333; surveyor of the port of, *see* Arnold, Thomas
East India trade, 282
Edenton, N.C., 49, 329, 399; collector of customs at, *see* Benbury, Thomas
Edgartown, Mass., 584
Edgecombe County, N.C., 190
Edgefield County, S.C., 190
Edinburgh, 17
Edwards, Pierpont, 268; *letter to*, 331-32

Edwards, Thomas, 138
Edwards, Timothy, 138
Elizabeth Islands, 583
Ellery, William, 34, 357-58, 398-99, 530-31; *letters from*, 37-38, 57, 163-64, 183-84, 208, 224-25, 225-26, 297-98, 310, 332-34, 350, 440-41, 442-43, 467-70, 507, 528-30, 543, 553-54, 554-55, 576; *letters to*, 246, 271-72, 314, 396
Elliot, Robert, 164-65, 438
Elliot, Thomas, 277
Elliot and Williams, 164-65
Elliott, Andrew, 277, 475, 477, 516-17
Elliott, Matthew (Capt.), 544-46
Emigrants, 18; and duties, 274; proposal to encourage, 17-19
Encyclopedists, 416
"Ends and means," *see* Constitution (U.S.), "Means and ends"
England, *see* Great Britain
Enumerated powers, *see* Constitution (U.S.)
Erkelens, Gosuinus, 157-58
Essex County, Mass., 189
Europe, 21, 181, 246, 285, 304, 307, 388, 420, 453, 494, 516-17; and Scioto Co., 230
Eveleigh, Nicholas, 35-37, 140, 149, 225; death of, 290-91, 321-22; illness, 169
Ewing, John, 29
"Excise Law": and Massachusetts distillers, 591; and New York distillers, 591; and North Carolina, 45-46; Thomas Rodney on, 23-24; and Savannah, Ga., 404-5. *See also* Congress of U.S., acts of, "An Act repealing, after the last day of June next, the duties heretofore laid upon Distilled Spirits imported from abroad, and laying others in their stead; and also upon Spirits distilled within the United States, and for appropriating the same"
Executive departments: heads of, 292; instructions to, by George Washington, 243; meeting of, 258
Executive power: nature of, 500
Exports: report on, 39-40, 145-46; from St. Petersburg, 282
Express powers, *see* Constitution (U.S.), enumerated powers

Fahrenheit's thermometer, 542
Fairfax County, Va., 472

Fairfield County, S.C., 190

Favourite, 333

Fayette County, Pa., 189

Febiger, Christian, 300, 411

Federal District, 253-56, 355, 470, 471, 472; commissioners of, *see* Carroll, Daniel, *and* Johnson, Thomas, *and* Stuart, David; and Constitution (U.S.), 76, 112-13

The Federal Gazette and Philadelphia Daily Advertiser, 550, 581

Federalists, 61, 135, 322, 359, 479, 496

Feliechj (Feliechy), Philip, 4-5

Fenner, Arthur, 332, 529; *letter from,* 3-4

Finch, Joseph, 543

"First Report on the Further Provision Necessary for Establishing Public Credit" (December 13, 1790), 155-56

Fisher, Hendricks, 349-50

Fisheries, 434; in New Hampshire, 436; request for information on, 224-26; and shipbuilding, 248-49

Fishing ships: tonnage on, 479

Fitzgerald, John: *letter from,* 494; *letter to,* 516

Five Nations: murder of members, 218, 269, 545. *See also* Six Nations

Flax: in New Hampshire, 436; spinning machine, 588

Fly, 16, 297

Foreign officers: debt to, 561-62

Forfeiture and escheat: laws of, 77-78, 107-8, 109

Forfeitures, 252-53, 295-96, 313-14, 333, 353

Forrest, Thomas: *letter from,* 327; *letter to,* 392-93

Fort Harmar, 124

Fort Pitt, 247, 544

Fort Washington, 360-61, 363, 438, 562

Fort William and Mary, 514

Foster, Theodore, 158; *letter from,* 569

Fowler, Theodosius, 246-48

Fox, George, 512

France, 69, 233, 246, 285, 288, 579; assignats, depreciation of, 263, 325, 415, 417-18, 535, 561, and Genoa, 419, and Holland, 419, and payment of U.S. debt to France, 418, 420, 423, 490; bankers at Amsterdam, *see* Hogguer, Grand, and Co.; and banks, 221; chargé d'affaires at The Hague, *see* Caillard, Antoine Bernard;

chargé d'affaires at Philadelphia, *see* Otto, Louis G.; commissioners of the treasury, 416, 558-59, 575-76, 578; Committee on Coinage, 439; Committee on Finance, and purchase of U.S. debt to France, 170-71, 260-61; Comptroller General of Finances of, *see* Lambert, Charles Guillaume, *and* Necker, Jacques; Directeur du Trésor Royal, *see* Dufresne, Bertrand; Director General of Finances, *see* Lessart, Claude Antoine de Valdec de; duties, on oil, 11-13, 160, 173-74, 175, on tobacco, 11-13, 60-61, 160-61, 174; expenses of, 424; fisheries, 13, 249; foreign invasion of, 175-76; Garde Nationale, 174; government, 262; and Holland loans, 260-61; king of, 174, 176, 178, 416; loans, possibility of, 535, 561, to U.S. (July 16, 1782), 416; meaning of "percent," 391; Minister from Genoa to, *see* Spinola, Christoforo Vincenzo de; Minister of Foreign Affairs, *see* Montmorin Saint-Herem, Armand Marc, comte de; Minister Plenipotentiary to U.S., *see* Ternant, Jean Baptiste de; mint, 439, 562; National Assembly, 11-13, 60-61, 260-61, 422, 439, decrees on navigation and commerce, 173-76, and Holland loans, 159, president of, *see* Mirabeau, Honoré Gabriel Riquetti, comte de, and purchase of U.S. debt to France, 171; plan of tontine, 424; public treasury, 283, 416; queen of, 176; revenue of, 424; revolution and riots in, 173-76, 228; and Schweizer, Jeanneret, and Co., 11-13; and Scioto Co., 227-33; as source of private loans, 263; tax system, 417; treaties of, 13, 41-44, 178; U.S. chargé d'affaires at Paris, *see* Short, William; U.S. debt to, 11-13, 177-78, 262-63, 271, 278-79, 423, payment of, 137-38, 178-79, 264, 281, 283, 288, 289-90, 324-35, 336, 356-57, 413, 415-17, 418-23, 460-61, 488-93, 534, 536, 558, 559, 560, 562, 574, 575-76, 578, proposed purchase and transfer of, 12-13, 170-71, 176, 281, 288, 289-90, 324-25, 336, 414, 418, 421-23, 504-5, 512-13, and western lands, 325

Francis, John, 398

Francis, Tench, 4-5, 34-35, 138, 139,

146, 206, 330, 357, 442, 444, 473-74, 485

Frankfort, Ky., 164-65

Franklin, Benjamin, 111, 178, 307, 308

Franklin County, N.C., 190

Franklin County, Pa., 189

Fraser, Archibald C., 278

Fraser, Charles Henry, 277

Fraser, Thomas, 38-39, 437-38, 462-64

Frauds, 295-96; and ship registers, 5-7

Frederica, Ga., 275

Frederick (Town), Md., 462

Fredericksburg, Va., 242, 243, 470

Freeman, Ezekiel, 453

French and Indian War, 436

Frenchman's Bay, District of Maine, 169; collector of customs at, see Jordan, Meletiah; customs boat for, 522; shipbuilding at, 521

French West Indies, 435, 480

Frontier: defense of, and banks, 219

Fuller, Israel, 252

Funded debt, 305-6, 316, 392-93; certificates of, 7-9, 29, 41; and new emissions, 319-20; payment of interest on, 266; stock of, 161-62, 233. See also Public debt

Funding, 33. See also Public debt

Gallipolis settlement, 230

Gardner, William, 200; letter to, 201-2

Gates County, N.C., 190

General Washington, 495, 571

General welfare clause, see Constitution (U.S.)

Geneva: and foreign loans, 262

Genoa, 324-25; consul to U.S., see Ravard, Joseph; doge of, see Durazzo, Girolamo D.; and foreign loans, 261-62; and French assignats, 419; Minister to France, see Spinola, Christoforo Vincenzo de; possibility of U.S. loan at, 263, 324-25, 414, 420, 424, 534-35, 575, 561; and U.S. bonds, 419; and U.S. debt to France, 418, 423

Geographer of U.S., see Hutchins, Thomas

Georgetown, Md., 207, 253-54, 470, 471; and Federal District, 255

Georgetown, S.C., 242; collector of customs at, see Cogdell, John

Georgia, 112, 347-48, 540; and assumption of state debts, 443; auditor of, see Wereat, John; and cession of

lighthouse on Tybee Island, 348-49; commissioner of loans for, see Wylly, Richard; governor of, see Telfair, Edward; line, 265; revenue cutter for, 349-50, captain of, see Howell, John, mates for, see Fisher, Hendricks, and Wood, John; state customs service, 404; supervisor of revenue for, see Mathews, John; survey of inspection, 189; U.S. judge for the District of, see Pendleton, Nathaniel; U.S. Senator from, see Gunn, James

Germans: and emigration, 18-19

Gerry, Elbridge, 139, 307, 402-3

Gibbs, Caleb: letter from, 344-45; letter to, 301

Gibbs, —— (Mrs. Caleb), 344

Gilford, see Guilford

Gilman, John T., 201-2

Glasgow, 18

Godwin, Charles, 214

Gold, 439; British standard, 4

Goldsmiths, 57

Goodhue, Benjamin: letter to, 516-17

Gore, Christopher, 359, 583-84

Gorham, Josiah, Jr., 252, 295-96

Gorham, Nathaniel, 187, 188

Government: as a corporation, 89; and general good, 65; nature of, 65, 83-84; objects and powers of, 65; principles of, 98; and taxation, 24

Grand, see Le Grand

Granville County, N.C., 190

Granville County, S.C., 190

Gray, —— (Mr.), 516

Gray, Vincent, 259-60

Great Britain, 7, 11, 51, 52, 69, 82, 87, 117, 159, 170, 175, 245-46, 320, 395, 412, 484, 556; and banks, 19, 221; chargé d'affaires at Vienna, see Hammond, George; common law, 352; cotton mills in, 556-57; Court of St. James's, 306-7; customhouse duties, 17; diplomatic service of, 277-78; and excise laws, 23; House of Commons, 17, 557; and indented emigrants, 18; and Indian policy, 544-45; and Indian war, 342-43; king of, 43; and land tenure, 251; laws of trade, 5-7; mechanics from, 571, 588; and Minister to U.S., 453-54, 516-17 (see also Hammond, George); Minister Plenipotentiary at Madrid, see Hammond, George; ministry of, 246;

Great Britain (*Continued*)
and national debt, 19; Navigation Act of 1660, 5-7; pardons in, 352-54; Parliament, 17, 278; possibility of loan in, 336, 536; power to erect corporations, 76, 81, 101; products of, 483; queen of, 45; representative in U.S., *see* Beckwith, George: revenue of, 17; and rights of individuals, 23; and Russia, 264, 582; Secretary of State for the Home Department, *see* Grenville, Lord; and ship timber, 250; and Spain, 42; special U.S. agent to, *see* Humphreys, David; statutes of, 5-7 (12 Car. II, C. 18 [1660]), 557 (5 Geo. I, C. 27 [1718]), 557 (23 Geo. II, C. 13 [1750]), 557 (14 Geo. III, C. 71 [1774]), 557 (22 Geo. III, C. 60 [1782]), 5-7 (26 Geo. III, C. 60 [1786]); and taxes, 17, 23; trade with, 434, 435; treaties, of alliance, 43, commercial, 43, 308; and U.S. commerce, 43; U.S. Envoy to, *see* Adams, John; and U.S. relations, 453-54

Great Miami River, 360, 361, 363

Great-Tree, 242

Greene, Catharine (Mrs. Nathanael): *letter to*, 165-66

Greene, Nathanael (Maj. Gen.), 165-66

Greenleaf, James: *letter to*, 265-66

Greenman, Jeremiah, 51, 311, 398-99, 466-67

Greenville County, S.C., 190

Grenville, Lord, 41, 343, 454, 475-77, 545; *letter from* George Beckwith, 41, 45

Griffin, Cyrus, 437-38, 463; *letter to*, 38-39

Gross, Simon: *letter from*, 259; *letter to*, 301-2; Treasury Department circulars to, 406-7, 426-33

Guilford, N.C., 243

Guilford (Gilford) County, N.C., 190

Gunn, James, 143

Habersham, John, 312, 404; *letters from*, 26, 348-49; *letter to*, 234

Hagerstown, Md., 438

The Hague, 177, 178, 260, 307; French chargé d'affaires at, *see* Caillard, Antoine Bernard

Haines, Caspar, 167-68

Hale, Warwick, 540

Half-Town, 242

Halifax, N.C., 242

Halifax County, N.C., 190

Hall, George Abbot, 225-26

Halsted, John, 328

Hamilton, Alexander: Army, retirement from, 181; and Bank of the U.S., notes on Edmund Randolph's opinion on, 46-49, opinion on, 57-58, 63-134, 218-23, request by George Washington for opinion on, 50-51; and George Beckwith, conversations with, 41-45, 342-43, 475-77, 544-46; and John B. Church's affairs, 180-81, 320; on commercial treaty with Great Britain, 43-44; Continental Congress member, 139-40; election to American Philosophical Society, 29; on France, 43-44; house for, 511, 581; on legal classification of ships, 16; opinion on forfeiture, 16; on power to borrow, 186; on promotion in office, 292; on William Short, 271; on Oliver Wolcott, Jr., 291-94

Hamilton, Elizabeth, 240, 305, 320, 343, 532, 581; *letter to*, 591

Hammond, Abijah, 272, 284

Hammond, George, 278, 517

Hampshire County, Mass., 189

Hampton, Va., 317

Hand, Edward, 189, 217

Hanse towns, 277-78

Hardy, Joseph, 141-42, 169, 284, 287-88, 486; *letters from*, 328, 399, 480, 481

Harison, Richard, 251-53, 312-14; *letters from*, 5-7, 197, 284, 316-17, 352-54, 511-12; *letters to*, 184-85, 202-3, 236, 272-73, 283, 295-96, 548; and lighthouse contracts, 238

Harmar, Josiah (Brig. Gen.), 164-65, 213, 343

Harrisburg, N.C., 243

Hart, Bernard, 551

Hartford, Conn., 166

Hartford County, N.C., *see* Hertford County, N.C.

Harvard College, 147

Harwood, Thomas, 206-7, 363-64, 506-7

Haskell, Robert, 522

Hawkesworth, John: *An Account of the Voyages undertaken by the order of his present Majesty for mak-*

ing discoveries in the Southern Hemisphere . . . , 364-65

Hawkins, Benjamin: *letter from,* 45-46

Haywood, John, 487, 566, 568; *letter to,* 517-18

Hazard, Ebenezer, 215-16

Hazard, Nathaniel: *letter from,* 166-68

Hemp, *see* Duties

Henchman, Thomas, 512-13

Henderson, James, 14-15

Henshaw, Samuel: *letter from,* 185; *letter to,* 265

Hertford County, N.C., 190

Heth, William, 3; *letters from,* 481-83, 483, 523-26; *letter to,* 499-501

Hibernian Society, 240

Higgins, Ichabod, 348

Higginson, Stephen, 146, 153, 182, 191-92, 227; *letter from,* 61

Hill, James, 201-2

Hill, Jeremiah, 234

Hill, William, 226, 241, 334-35, 345

Hillary, Christopher, 275

Hillsboro, N.C., 239, 243, 518, 565, 566

Hilton County, S.C., 190

Hispaniola, 528

Hobart, Samuel, 514-15, 546

Hodgdon, Alexander, 501

Hodgdon, Samuel, 354

Hogguer, Paul Iwan, 460. *See also* Hogguer, Grand, and Co.

Hogguer, Grand, and Co., 171, 179, 416, 460, 489-93, 536, 559; and payment of U.S. debt to France, 534, 558, 578

Holbrook, Abijah, 312, 346

Holker, John, 138

Holland, *see* United Netherlands

Holland Land Co., 301

Holland loans, *see* Loans, Holland

Hollins, John: petition of, 25, 28

Holy Roman Empire, 52, 58; loans of, 261, 262, 413

Hooper, George: *letter from,* 295; *letter to,* 464-66

Hope, Henry, 171, 574, 582

Hope, 302

Hopkins, John, 32; *letter to,* 239

Hospital department, 27

House of Hope, 171, 574, 582

House of Representatives, 124, 359, 464; Bank of the U.S., debate on, 80-81, 113, subscribers to, 142-43; and certificates of debt, 144-45; and compensation of customs officers, 31-32,

457-58; and debt due foreign officers, 562; and Theodosius Fowler, 247-48; "Funding Act," 402; and manufactures, 497-98; message of President to, 41-42; orders of, 20-21, 28, 39-40, 138, 141, 145-46, 154-55, 155-56, 157-58, 272, 274, 287-88, 403, 497-98; petitions to, 25, 388, 403 (*see also* Petitions); reports to, 20-21, 28, 31, 39-40, 136-38, 138-41, 141-42, 144, 145-46, 154-55, 155-56, 157-58; and state paper money, 388

Howell, John, 349-50

Howell, Joseph, 265

Howell, Samuel, 210-11

Huger, Isaac, 151, 152

Humphreys, David (Lt. Col.), 179-80, 205

Huntington, Jedediah, 181-82; *letters from,* 193, 564; *letter to,* 267-68

Huntington, Samuel: Treasury Department circular to, 509-10

Huntington County, Pa., 189

Hutchins, Thomas, 362

Hutchinson, James, 29

Hyde County, N.C., 190

Hydrometers, 473. *See also* Colles's hydrometer; Dycas's hydrometer

Immigration, 18

Implied powers, *see* Constitution (U.S.)

Import duties, *see* Duties

Importers: and inspectors of revenue, 383-87

Impost, *see* Duties

Incorporation: Federal power of, 63-134

Indents of public debt, *see* Public debt, indents of

Independence: and Federal Government, 22

India, 398; tea, 539; trade with, 20-21

Indians: depredations of, 343, 476, 562; expedition against, 96, 124, 164-65, 213, 247, 343, 532, 563; and Great Britain, 544-46; murder of, 218, 269, 545; and New York State, 213; in Northwest Territory, 544-46; and powers of Congress, 115-16; treaty with, 241-42, 545, 546; wars, 42, 124, 241-42, 269, 342-43, 476. *See also* Five Nations; Maumee Indians; Miami Indians; Seneca Indians; Six Nations; Wabash Indians

Indigo, 390
Indirect taxes, *see* Taxes
Individual rights, 352; and Constitution
   (U.S.), 73
Industry, 470
Inspection laws, 70
Inspectors of the ports (customs), 369,
   389, 428, 542; authority of, 442; for
   Bristol, R.I., *see* Munro, William;
   and duties, 340, 527; and inspectors
   of revenue, 371-72, 384, 385-86; for
   New York, *see* Dodge, Samuel; for
   Pawtuxet, R.I., 345; and ship manifests, 427; and supervisors of the rev-
   enue, 371
Inspectors of the revenue, 151, 207, 237,
   280, 366-82; appointment of, 189-90;
   and certificates, 375-76; and collectors of customs, 370; commissions
   for, 245; compensation of, 189-91;
   and distilled spirits, 372-73, 379;
   duties of, 188-91; and inspectors of
   the ports, 371-72, 384, 385-86; for
   Massachusetts, 185 (*see also* Jackson,
   Jonathan; Jarvis, Leonard); for
   North Carolina, 311 (*see also* Benbury, Thomas; Daves, John; Mc-
   Dowell, Joseph; Read, James; Whitaker, John); and oaths, 382; for
   Pennsylvania, *see* Collins, James, *and*
   Hand, Edward, *and* Neville, John;
   and permits to importers, 385; for
   South Carolina, 190, 331; and store-
   houses, 383; and supervisors of the
   revenue, 382; and tea, 383-87, duties
   on, 495-96; for Virginia, 405 (*see
   also* Newton, Thomas, Jr.)
Invalid pensions: and North Carolina,
   486-87, 513-14; payment of, 8, 13-14,
   25-26, 154, 182, 192, 347, 486-87, 515,
   517-18, 520, 547. *See also* Congress of
   U.S., acts of
Iredell County, N.C., 190
Ireland, 7, 219, 240; and emigrants, 18,
   436

Jackson, Jonathan, 109
Jackson, William: *letters from*, 280,
   311
Jacobins, 175
James River, 471, 525
Jarvis, James: *letter from*, 205
Jarvis, Leonard, 189
Jay, John, 308
Jeanneret, François: proposals for pur-
chase of U.S. debt to France, 11-13.
   See also Schweizer, Jeanneret, and
   Co.
Jefferson, Thomas, 12, 29, 204-5, 233,
   258, 270, 281, 417, 582; appropriation
   for Department of State, 205-6; *letters from*, 26, 179-80, 234-35, 268, 503-
   4; *letter from* Alexander Dallas, 507;
   letters from William Short, 11-13,
   60-61, 160-61, 173-76; *letter from*
   George Washington, 242-43; *letters
   to*, 278-79, 284-86, 289-90, 330, 450;
   letter to William Short, 282; and
   New York politics, 478-79; opinion
   on constitutionality of an act to establish a bank, 50-51, 64-65, 68-69,
   70-72, 74, 76-77, 79, 82-83, 91, 97, 99,
   101-2, 103-4, 107-8, 110-11, 113, 120,
   126-27, 128-29, 133; and Schweizer,
   Jeanneret, and Co., 12; and John C.
   Symmes's land purchase, 562-63
John, 25
Johnson, Thomas, 471, 472
Johnston (Johnson) County, N.C., 190
Jones, Margaret Livingston (Mrs.
   Thomas), 185-86
Jones, Thomas: *letter from*, 185-86;
   letter to, 210
Jones County, N.C., 190
Jordan, Meletiah, 209; *letter from*, 521-
   22; *letter to*, 169

Kanawha River, 230
Keais, Nathan, 290, 317, 586-87; *letters
   from*, 328-29, 483; *letter to*, 290
Kearsley (Kearsly), G.: *Kearsley's
   Tax Tables & Stamp Duties*, 17
Kemble, Peter, 236, 238, 316, 551
Kentucky, 228; and Federal Govern-
   ment, 532; and Indians, 213; militia,
   546; U.S. representative from, *see*
   Brown, John; and Virginia, 532
Kentucky District, *see* Kentucky
Keppele, Catherine: *letter from*, 193-97
Kershaw County, S.C., 190
Keyes, Stephen, 166, 476-77
King, Rufus, 112, 217, 227, 241-42, 478-
   79; *letter from*, 212-13; *letter to*, 531-
   32
Kingston County, S.C., 190
Kitty, 14
Knox, David, 14-15
Knox, Henry, 8, 33, 218, 247-48, 270,
   311, 515, 546; *letter from*, 354; *letter*

from Alexander Dallas, 507; *letter from* George Washington, 242-43
Kurrituck County, N.C., *see* Currituck County, N.C.

Ladies of Castille, 522-23
Lafayette, Marie Joseph du Motier, marquis de, 175; and U.S. debt to France, 416
Laidlow, *see* Ludlow
Lake Champlain, 477
Lake Erie, 326, 327, 412; and Pennsylvania, 458
Lamb, John, 276, 310, 332, 339, 488, 530, 551
Lambert, Charles Guillaume, 422-23
Lancaster County, Pa., 189
Lancaster County, S.C., 190
Land: office, 325; purchase by John Cleves Symmes, 562-63; tenure, 249-51
Latimer, Henry, 187, 188
Latin America, 246
Laurence, John, 478-79
Laurens County, S.C., 190
Law, Richard, 331-32
Lawrence, Jonathan, 138
Laws of U.S.: publication of, 234-35
Lead and shot, *see* Duties
Lear, Tobias, 203; *letters from,* 146-47, 158, 164, 166, 183, 211, 217, 245, 393, 395, 405, 531, 541, 582-83; *letters to,* 210, 217, 245, 358-59, 405
Lee, Charles, 494, 516; *letter from,* 527; *letters to,* 3, 203, 259-60; Treasury Department circular from Tench Coxe, 364
Lee, Richard, 279
Lee, Richard Henry: *letter from* Thomas Willing, Robert Morris, and John Swanwick, 150
Lee, Thomas, 279
Leghorn: U.S. consul at, 4-5
Le Grand, ——— (son), 418
Le Grand, Ferdinand, 171, 505, 561; *letters from* William Short, 171, 179; *letters to* William Short, 171, 178
Le Grand, George (brother), 171, 460
Le Havre, 578, 582
L'Enfant, Pierre Charles: *letter from,* 253-56; *letter to,* 354-55
Le Roy, Herman, 146
Le Roy and Bayard, 146, 153, 191-92, 227
Leslie, Robert: *letter from,* 168

Lessart, Claude Antoine de Valdec de, 461
Lewis, Ebenezer, 346
Lewis, Elijah, 346
Lewis, William, 148-49, 185; *letter from,* 62; *letter to,* 27
Lewisburgh County, S.C., 190
Lexington County, S.C., 190
Liberty County, S.C., 190
Lighthouses, 14; on Cape Fear, N.C., 295, 296-97, 464-66; on Cape Henlopen, Del., 181, 304, 540; on Cape Henry, Va., 226, 236, 238, 251, 283, 316, 450-51, 464, 533-34, 555-56; at Charleston, S.C., 181, 183; on New Castle Island, Portsmouth, N.H., 514-15, 521, 546-47; at New London, Conn., 181-82, 183; at Newport, R.I., 163-64, 332, 529, 543, 554-55; superintendent of, *see* Ellery, William; at Portland, District of Maine, 464; on Tybee Island, Ga., 348-49. *See also* Congress of U.S., acts of; Contracts
Lincoln, Benjamin, 34-35, 192, 199-200, 280, 337, 530, 551; drafts on, 154; *letters from,* 61-62, 144, 168-69, 204, 237, 248-51, 315, 317, 346-47, 359, 472, 530, 548-49, 569-70, 583-84; *letters to,* 1-2, 203-4, 257, 273, 286, 296, 323, 329, 395-96, 448-49, 501; and purchases of the public debt, 1-2; Treasury Department circulars to, 340-41, 407-9, 538, 538-39
Lincoln County, N.C., 190
Lincoln County, S.C., 190
Linen, *see* Duties
Lisbon, 179-80
Lispenard, Anthony, 167-68
Little Miami River, 360, 361, 363
Livermore, Samuel, 403
Livingston, Brockholst: *letter from,* 185-86; *letter to,* 210
Livingston, John H.: *letters from,* 185-86, 210, 349
Livingston, Margaret, *see* Jones, Margaret Livingston
Livingston, Maria, *see* Livingston, Maria Livingston
Livingston, Maria Livingston (Mrs. Philip), 186
Livingston, Philip Henry, 185-86
Livingston, Philip Philip, 185-86
Livingston, Robert R., 4-5, 454, 478-79
Livingston, Sarah, *see* Livingston, Sarah Livingston

Livingston, Sarah Livingston (Mrs. John H.), 186
Livingston, Walter, 138, 185-86, 247
Livingston, William, 139, 157-58, 185-86
Loan office debt, *see* Public debt
Loan offices, 447; business of, *see* Commissioners of loans; certificates of, 193-97, 315, 329, 348, 446, 456
Loans: Antwerp, possibility of U.S. loan at, 55-56, 336, 423-24, 459, 535, 560, 561, 573-74, 577-78, 581-82; authorizations for, 183, 186, 335-36, 356-57, 459, 519, 535, 587-88 (*see also* Short, William); and Bank of the U.S., 91-92, 96-97; and banks, 219; domestic loan of 1790, 455-56, 467, and assumption of state debts, 443-46, 455, certificates of, 447, certificates of debt, 144-45, New York as a subscriber, 566, 568, and nonsubscribers, 161-62, 194-95, 202, 207, 211, 233, 305-6, 341, 392-93, 394-95, 426, 446, 456, 467, North Carolina as a subscriber, 566, 568, and Pennsylvania, 410-12, 443-46, proposed, 32-33, 265, 443-46, 455-56, South Carolina as a subscriber, 566, 568, stock of, 41, 59, 144, 193, 282, 315, 397, 411, 454, 508, 512-13, subscribers to, 202, 411, 443-46, 446-47, 455, 566-69 (*see also* Assumption of state debts; North Carolina; Pennsylvania; Public debt); French, of July 16, 1782, 416, possibility of new U.S. loan, 535, 561, 562; Genoa, possibility of U.S. loan in, 324-25, 534-35, 561, 571; Great Britain, possibility of U.S. loan in, 336, 536; Holland, 51-57, 87, 157-58, 172, 177-78, 260-61, 281, 414, 415, 459, 573, 577-79, 309 (of September 14, 1782), 58, 309 (of February 1, 1785), 309 (of 1787), 309 (of July, 1788), 52, 59, 136-48, 159-66, 182, 270-71, 281 (of August, 1790), 11-13, 52, 54-55, 58-59, 158-60, 170, 177-78, 260, 270-71, 278-79, 281, 288, 289-90, 330, 335-36, 356-57, 413, 415, 425, 460-61, 519, 537, 558-59 (of March, 1791), commission on, 152-53, 159-60, 270, 414, 459-61, 536-37, 560, by individual states, 59, interest due on, 521, 559, and payment of U.S. debt to France, 271, 420, possibility of new U.S. loan, 264, 415, 425, 459-61, 536-37, 560, 561, and Russo-

British relations, 264, and U.S. domestic debt, 271, 413-14, 420 (*see also* "Report on the Holland Loan of Three Million Florins," February 24-25, 1791; Willink, Van Staphorst, and Hubbard); and lotteries, 87, 117; and powers of Congress, 87, 125; and taxes, 324; in wartime, 96, 124
London, 14, 17, 42, 226, 245, 246, 277, 307, 475, 484, 490, 492, 512, 527, 535, 542
Lotteries: and loans, 87, 117
Lowder, William: *letter from*, 549-50
Lowrey, Thomas, 138
Lowry, William, 259-60
Loyalists, 286
Ludlow, Daniel: *letter from*, 304; *letter to*, 286
Ludlow, Israel, 360-63, 563; *letter to*, 362
Luzerne County, Pa., 189
Lyall, Matthew: *letter from*, 296-97
Lyman, Daniel, 163-64, 184, 332-34, 440-41, 554-55
Lyning, Samuel, 150

McClenachan, Blair: *letter from*, 193-97
McComb, John, Jr.: agreement with, 234; *letters to*, 238, 450-51; and lighthouse at Cape Henry, Va., 236, 251, 276, 283, 316, 350, 533-34, 555-56
McDowel, John (Pa.), 189
McDowell, John (N.C.), 190
McDowell, Joseph, Sr., 190, 311, 358, 393
McDowell, Joseph, Jr., 190
McGree, *see* McKee
McGuire, Francis, 218
McHenry, James: *letter from*, 321-22; *letter to*, 314
McHenry, John, 322
McKean, Thomas: petition of, 403
McKee, Alexander (Col.), 544-46
Macnaughten, Auly: *letter from*, 295; *letter to*, 464-66
McRae, John, 38-39, 437-38, 462-64
McRea, *see* McRae
Madeira: U.S. consul at, *see* Pintard, John M.
Madison, James: and Federal power of incorporation, 80, 112, 133; and New York politics, 478-79
Madrid, 277; British Minister Plenipotentiary at, *see* Hammond, George

Magaw, Samuel, 29
Maine, 189; U.S. Representative from, see Thatcher, George
Malcolm, William, 139
Manson, Duncan: petition of, 274-75
Manufactures, 222, 434; and banks, 218-19, 221; encouragement of, 126; and House of Representatives, 497-98; information on, 235; in New Hampshire, 435-36; request for information on, 224-25, 497-98; textile, in Great Britain, 556-57; of U.S., 535. *See also* Manufacturing society; Society for Establishing Useful Manufactures
Manufacturing society: plan for, 300-1
Marchant, Henry, 37-38, 272; *letter from*, 30; *letter to*, 16
Marietta, 124
Marion County, S.C., 190
Marlboro County, S.C., 190
Marsden, England, 557
Marshall, Thomas: *letters from*, 556-57, 571-73
Martha's Vineyard, Mass., 584
Martin, Alexander, 45, 465, 509, 514, 520, 565-66, 566-69; speech to legislature, 569; Treasury Department circular to, 509-10
Martin, William: *letter to*, 577
Martin County, N.C., 190
Maryland, 112, 322, 506; Assembly of, 314; and assumption of state debts, 443; and Bank of Maryland, 410; chief justice of, *see* Johnson, Thomas; commissioner of loans for, *see* Harwood, Thomas; and commissioners to receive subscriptions of Bank of the U.S., 210-11; Eastern Shore of, 210; and foreign loans, 59; inspector of the revenue for, 151; legislature of, 410; new emissions of, 452; and payment of interest on public debt, 509-10; Ratifying Convention of, 314; revenue cutter for, 301-2, 472, captain of, *see* Gross, Simon; state customs service, 464; survey of inspection in, 189, 368; and trade, 435; U.S. Representatives from, *see* Carroll, Daniel, *and* Smith, William; U.S. Senator from, *see* Carroll, Charles, of Carrollton
Mason, George, 112
Massachusetts, 27, 112, 121, 146, 228, 266, 326, 327; and assumption of state debts, 443; commissioner of loans

for, *see* Appleton, Nathaniel; and Continental Congress certificates, 426; District Court of, 323; and Federal securities, 501-2; fisheries in, 248; General Court of, 163; House of Representatives of, 307; inspector of the revenue for, 185 (*see also* Jackson, Jonathan; Jarvis, Leonard); line, and funding law, 401-4, *letter from*, 405; new emissions of, 452; and New Hampshire trade, 436; old emissions of, 426; revenue cutter for, 61-62, 237, 286, 406-7, 569-70, canvas for, 317, captain of, *see* Williams, John Foster, sailcloth for, 346; and Rhode Island ships, 553; state collector of customs, *see* Henshaw, Samuel; supervisor of the revenue for, *see* Gorham, Nathaniel; survey of inspection, 189; treasurer of, *see* Hodgdon, Alexander; treasury of, 426; U.S. attorney for the District of, *see* Gore, Christopher; U.S. Representatives from, *see* Ames, Fisher, *and* Gerry, Elbridge, *and* Goodhue, Benjamin, *and* Sedgwick, Theodore. *See also* Maine
Massachusetts, 569-70
Massachusetts Bank, 34, 61, 161-62, 192, 199-200, 316, 321, 342; and Bank of the U.S., 396-97; bills of, 93; cashier of, 396, 502; directors of, 395, *letter to*, 396-97; drafts on, 154
Mathews (Matthews), John, 187, 188, 404-5
Matlack, White, 166-67
Matlock Bath, Derbyshire, England, 557
Matthews, *see also* Mathews
Matthews, Joseph, 151
Matthews, William, 151
Maumee Indians, 532
Maxwell, William, 167
Mecklenburg (Mecklenbergh) County, N.C., 190
Melville (Melvill), Thomas, 583-84
Merchants: and banks, 219; and laws of U.S., 126
Mercier, John D., 139
Meredith, Samuel, 1-2, 25-26, 34-35, 38, 223, 225, 276, 293-94, 335, 469, 501, 507, 548, 551; account of, 518; bills of, 49-50, 146, 200, 346; drafts of, 161-62, 191-92, 208, 227, 235, 333, 339, 357, 442, 517, 528; and Holland loan

Meredith, Samuel (*Continued*)
of March, 1791, 336; and Willink,
Van Staphorst, and Hubbard, 204-5
Metals: assay of, 285
Miami Co. Purchase, 360, 362, 363, 405
Miami Indians, 546
Miami River, 546
Middlesex County, Mass., 189
Middletown, Conn., 267
Mifflin, Thomas, 209, 218, 299-300, 318,
507; *letters from*, 325-27, 410-12, 532;
letter from John Donnaldson, 410-
12; *letter from* John Nicholson, 532-
33; *letters to*, 412, 458; Treasury De-
partment circular to, 509-10
Mifflin County, Pa., 189
Miller, Wentworth R., 579
Milligan, James, 139, 149-50
Millsborough, Md., 322
Milton, Mass., 523
Mint, 168; establishment of, 284-86;
French, 562; proposal for, 395; in
United Netherlands, 282, 424
Mirabeau, Honoré Gabriel Riquetti,
comte de, 439
Miranda, Francisco de: *letter from*,
245-46
Mitchell, John H., 395
Money: and Bank of the U.S., 92-93;
and banks, 218; and commerce, 126;
deposit of, 94; increase of circula-
tion of, and banks, 218; manufacture
of, 439; and state paper, 202; and
taxes, 89-90
"Monied interest": and banks, 239
Monopoly: and government corpora-
tions, 75, 131; laws of, 77, 79-80; of
U.S. banks, 110
Monroe, James, 143
Montgomery, James, 407
Montgomery County, N.C., 190
Montgomery County, Pa., 189
Montmorin Saint-Herem, Armand
Marc, comte de, 11-13, 179, 324-25,
416, 421, 422, 460, 490; *letter to*
Louis G. Otto, 12; *letters to* Wil-
liam Short, 170, 176
Moore County, N.C., 190
Morocco, 205; emperor of, 180, 330;
mission to, 186; treaty with, 180
Morris, Gouverneur, 454; and Ant-
werp loan, 261, 336, 423-24, 535, 560,
573-74, 581-82; and foreign loans, 55-
56; *letter from*, 512-13; and Scioto

Co., 231; U.S. representative in
Great Britain, 42-45
Morris, Robert, 136, 149-50, 402, 403,
512-13, 589-90; Superintendent of
Finance, 138-39, 452
Morrison, John, 38-39, 437-38, 462-64
Mortmain: laws of, 77, 108
Moses, Isaac: *letter from*, 306
Moultrie, William, 349-50
Mount Vernon, 241, 242, 398, 470, 493
Munro, James, Jr., 225-26, 310
Munro, William, 37-38

Nails, *see* Duties
Nantucket, Mass., 11-13
Nash County, N.C., 190
National Bank, 245. *See also* Bank of
the U.S.
Naval officers, 427, 430; compensation
of, 351-52, 449, 457, 496-97; for New-
port, R.I., *see* Crooke, Robert; for
Providence, R.I., *see* Thompson,
Ebenezer
Navigation: encouragement of, 126;
in New Hampshire, 434-36; request
for information on, 224-25; of U.S.,
222
Necessary and proper clause, *see* Con-
stitution (U.S.)
Necker, Jacques, 422
Nesbitt, John M., 155
Neuchâtel, Switzerland, 285
Neville, John, 189
New Bern, N.C., 49, 242, 328, 517, 542;
collector of customs at, *see* Daves,
John
New Brunswick, Canada, 250
Newbury County, S.C., 190
Newburyport, Mass., 61, 569
New Castle, Del., 154
New Castle Island, N.H., 514, 521
New emissions, *see* Paper money
New Hampshire, 112, 146, 202, 250,
436, 498; acts of, 202, 514, 546, "An
Act to encourage the erecting of
Mills for Slitting, Rolling and Plat-
ing Iron, and to encourage and pro-
mote the Manufacture of Nails with-
in this State" (Sept. 22, 1787), 435;
agriculture in, 435; and assumption
of state debts, 443; "Colony bills,"
202; commerce of, 434-36, 488; commissioner of loans for, *see* Gardner,
William; debt of, 202; legislature of,

435, 436, 514-15; line, 403; manufacturing in, 435; navigation in, 434-36; paper money, 202; president of, *see* Sullivan, John; revenue cutter for, 514, captain of, *see* Yeaton, Hopley, officers of, 546-47, 571; shipbuilding in, 434-36; supervisor of revenue for, *see* Wentworth, Joshua; survey of inspection, 188-89; Third Regiment, 403; U.S. attorney for the District of, *see* Sherburne, Samuel; U.S. Representative from, *see* Livermore, Samuel

New Hanover, N.C., 189

New Jersey, 112, 362, 404; Assembly of, 405; and assumption of state debts, 443; and commissioners to receive subscriptions of Bank of the U.S., 210-11; Council of, 405; counterfeiters in, 252; governor of, *see* Livingston, William; new emissions of, 452; and Society for Establishing Useful Manufactures, 300-1; supervisor of the revenue for, *see* Dunham, Aaron; survey of inspection, 189; U.S. Representative from, *see* Boudinot, Elias

New London, Conn., 193, 564; customs boat for, 267; lighthouse at, 181-82, 183

Newport, R.I., 3, 30, 34, 37-38, 57, 163, 183, 208, 224, 297, 310, 332, 350, 398, 440, 441, 467, 473, 507, 528, 543, 553, 554, 576, 585; collector of customs at, *see* Ellery, William; customs boat for, 297; lighthouse at, 332, 529, 543, 554-55; naval officer for the port of, *see* Crooke, Robert; surveyor of the port of, *see* Lyman, Daniel; tare in, 468-70

Newton, Thomas, Jr., 162, 450; *letters from*, 46, 533-34, 555-56; *letter to*, 451

Newtown Point, N.Y.: treaty at, 546

New York City, 4, 5, 61, 112, 166, 167, 183, 185, 205, 212, 227, 229, 236, 241, 246, 247, 251, 266, 279, 286, 304, 306, 310, 316, 317, 337, 349, 350, 352, 364-65, 453, 454, 478, 479, 511, 513, 518, 527, 528, 530, 532, 551, 556, 564, 571; and Bank of the U.S., 397; collector of customs for, *see* Lamb, John; inspector of the port of, *see* Dodge, Samuel

The [New York] *Daily Advertiser*, 167-68

New York State, 121, 241, 326, 327; acts of, "An Act directing the treasurer of this State to subscribe to the bank of the United States" (March 24, 1791), 213, "An Act to incorporate the stockholders of the Bank of New York" (March 21, 1791), 212-13, "An Act for the relief of the creditors of this State" (February 23, 1791), 213; Assembly, member of, *see* Smith, Melancton; and assumption of state debts, 443; and Bank of New York, 212-13; and Bank of the U.S., 213; chancellor of, *see* Livingston, Robert R.; commissioner of loans for, *see* Cochran, John; and Continental paper, 212-13; distillers and "Excise Law," 591; election in, 4-5; and foreign loans, 59; frontier of, 213; governor of, *see* Clinton, George; and Indians, 213, 241-42; legislature of, 185-86, 241-42, 349; and the public debt, 213; Ratifying Convention, 6; regiment of levies, 337; and speculation in western lands, 213; as subscriber to domestic loan of 1790, 566, 568; supervisor of revenue for, *see* Smith, William S.; survey of inspection, 189; treasurer of, *see* Bancker, Gerard; U.S. attorney for the District of, *see* Harison, Richard; U.S. judge for the District of, *see* Duane, James; and U.S. loans, 212-13; U.S. marshal for the District of, *see* Smith, William S.; U.S. Representative from, *see* Laurence, John; U.S. Senators from, *see* King, Rufus, *and* Schuyler, Philip

Niagara, 544

Nicholson, John, 33, 135-36, 318, 339, 394, 411-12, 443; *letters from*, 193-97, 211-12, 214-15, 298-300, 327; *letters to*, 214, 392-93; *letter to* Thomas Mifflin, 532-33

Nixon, John: *letter from*, 193-97

Nonsubscribers, *see* Loans

Nootka Sound controversy, 246

Norfolk, Va., 46, 450, 533, 555

Northampton, Mass., 185

Northampton County, N.C., 190

Northampton County, Pa., 189

North Bend, 363

North Carolina, 45, 112; and accounts with U.S., 486-87, 508-9; acts of, "An Act to Cede and Vest in the United States of America, the Lands therein mentioned, for the Purpose of building Light-Houses" (December, 1790), 295, 465-66, "An Act for the Relief of the Officers, Soldiers, and Seamen, Who Have Been Disabled in the Service of the United States During the Late War" (December 29, 1785), 487, "An Act for the Relief of the Widows or Children of Officers Who Have Died in the Service of the United States" (December 29, 1785), 513-14; agents to settle accounts with U.S., see Taylor, James, and Thomas, Abishai, and Williamson, Hugh; Army accounts in, 443; and assumption of state debts, 443, 508-9, 565-66; and Cape Fear River, 328-29; certificates of, 239; and claims of widows and orphans, 513-14, 520; commissioner of loans for, see Skinner, William; comptroller of, see Child, Francis; Council of State of, 565, 566-69, clerk of, see Rogers, Thomas; and "Excise Law," 45-46; General Assembly, 45-46, 296, 566, 568; governor of, see Martin, Alexander, secretary of, see Rogers, Thomas; House of Commons of, 487, 514; inspectors of revenue for, 311, 358-59 (see also Benbury, Thomas; Daves, John; McDowell, Joseph; Read, James; Whitaker, John); legislature of, 295, 509, 514; and lighthouse on Cape Fear, 295, 296-97; and payment of invalid pensions, 486-87, 513-14, 517-18, 520; revenue cutter for, 311, 358, captain of, see Cooke, William; Senate of, 514; as subscriber to domestic loan of 1790, 566-69; supervisor of the revenue for, see Polk, William; surveys of inspection, 189-90, 368, 393; trade of, 435; treasurer of, see Haywood, John; U.S. Representative from, see Williamson, Hugh; U.S. Senator from, see Hawkins, Benjamin

North Kingston, R.I.: customs boat for, 297, 333

Northumberland County, Pa., 189

Northwest Territory, 120, 124, 228, 343; governor of, see St. Clair, Arthur; Indians in, 164-65, depredations of, 532, 544-46; judge of, see Symmes, John Cleves; land speculations in, 360-63; secretary of, see Sargent, Winthrop; surveyor of, see Sherman, Isaac

North Yarmouth, District of Maine, 577

Nourse, Joseph: register of the Treasury, 7, 293-94, 446; books of, 153, 211; certificates of, 8, 9, 15, 41, 61, 150, 198, 227, 306, 392-93; and Pennsylvania, 299-300

Nova Scotia, 204

Nye, —— (Mr.), 584

Oaths: and collectors of customs, 38-39

Office of inspection, 368, 380; and distilled spirits, 505-6. See also Collectors of the revenue; Inspectors of the revenue; Supervisors of the revenue

Ohio: and Indians, 213

Ohio Co., 228, 362; and Scioto Co., 230

Ohio River, 229, 230, 360, 362, 363, 562

Oil: French duty on, 11-13, 160, 173-74, 175

Olney, Jeremiah, 34, 224-25, 357-58, 363, 468, 551-52; letters from, 30, 51, 147, 158, 197, 235, 303, 311, 327, 339, 345, 347, 355, 364, 449, 466-67, 473-74, 495, 495-96, 496-97, 558, 571, 584-86; letters to, 273-74, 359-60, 398-99, 406, 530-31, 564-65; Treasury Department circular from Tench Coxe, 364; Treasury Department circulars to, 162-63, 340-41, 538-39

Onion River, 476

Onslow County, N.C., 189

"Opinion on the Constitutionality of an Act to Establish a Bank" (February 23, 1791), 63-134

Orange County, N.C., 190

Orange County, S.C., 190

Osborn, Daniel, 287

Osgood, Samuel, 215-16

Otis, James, 523

Otto, Louis G., 11-13, 170, 176, 268, 278, 281

Page, John, 27, 62, 148

Page, Margaret Scott (Mrs. John), 27, 62, 148

Palmers River, 297

Pamplico Sound, 328-29

Paper money, 126; certificates, 7-9; and funded debt, 319-20; indents, 7-9; in Maryland, 452; in Massachusetts, 426, 452; new emissions, 318-20, 387-88, 451-53; in New Hampshire, 202; in New Jersey, 452; old emissions, 7-9, 32-33, 315-16, 341, 426, 456; in Pennsylvania, 317-20, 451-53; state, 387-89

Paramus, N.J., 528

Pardoning power, 312-14, 352-54

Paris, 12, 13, 55, 159, 160, 161, 170, 171, 173-76, 177, 178, 179, 227, 228, 260, 263, 278, 281, 285, 289, 307, 308, 324, 412, 420, 421, 423, 425, 439, 459, 460, 490, 491, 492, 527, 534, 558, 573, 575, 577, 581; payment of U.S. debt to France at, 281; possibility of U.S. loan at, 562; riots in, 174, 175; U.S. chargé d'affaires at, *see* Short, William; U.S. money exchange with Amsterdam, 423, 534, 536

Parker, Daniel, 138

Parker, Josiah: *letter from*, 162

Parkinson, George, 588

Pasquotank County, N.C., 190

Paterson, Samuel: *letter from*, 17-19

Patterson, R., 29

Pawcatuck River, 297

Pawtucket (Pawtuxet), R.I., 345

Pease, John, 584

Pendleton, Nathaniel: *letter to*, 274-76

Pendleton County, S.C., 190

Pennsylvania, 22, 34, 112, 269; and accounts with U.S., 211-12, 214-15, 317-20, 339, 394, 400, 451-53; acts of, 209, 507, "An Act Authorizing and Directing the State Treasurer to Subscribe, in the Name of the Commonwealth, to the Loan Proposed by the United States and for Other Purposes Therein Mentioned" (March 30, 1791), 299; "An Act for funding and redeeming the bills of credit of the United States of America, and for providing means to bring the present war to an happy conclusion" (June 1, 1780), 318, "An Act for the Further Relief of the Public Creditors Who are Citizens of This State by Receiving on Loan

Certain Debts of the United States of America and for Funding the Same and For Paying the Annual Interest of Such Loans and the Interest of Certain Debts of This State Every Six Months" (March 1, 1786), 195-96, 211-12, 443-46, "An Act Granting Relief to Certain Creditors of the State and for Repealing Part of an Act, Entituled 'An Act for Furnishing the Quota of This State Toward Paying the Annual Interest of the Debts of the United States, and for Funding and Paying the Interest of the Public Debts of This State'" (April 9, 1791), 410-12, 443, 446, "An Act to Provide for Paying and Redeeming Certain Public Debts, and for Defraying the Expenses of Government" (April 10, 1792), 320, "An Act to Repeal So Much of Any Act or Acts of Assembly of the Commonwealth as Directs the Payment of the New Loan Debt or the Interest Thereof Beyond the First Day of April Next, and for Other Purposes Therein Mentioned" (March 27, 1789), 33; and assumption of state debts, 33, 211-12, 214-15, 298-300, 317-20, 339, 394, 400, 410-12, 443-46, 455-56, 532-33; commissioner of loans for, *see* Smith, Thomas; and commissioners to receive subscriptions to Bank of the U.S., 210-11; commissioner to settle state claims, *see* Pettit, Charles; comptroller general of, *see* Nicholson, John; delegate to Continental Congress, 326-27; and "Excise Law," 22-23; and foreign loans, 59; General Assembly of, 326-27, 507; governor of, *see* Mifflin, Thomas; House of Representatives of, 23, 136, 317-18; inspectors of the revenue for, *see* Collins, James, *and* Hand, Edward, *and* Neville, John; land purchase on Lake Erie, 412, 458; legislature of, 209; line, 135-36; "The memorial and remonstrance of the public creditors who are citizens of the commonwealth of Pennsylvania," 403; and new emissions, 317-20, 451-53; public creditors of, 403, 410-12; Ratifying Convention of, 135; register general of, *see* Donnaldson, John; revenue cutter for, 164, cap-

Pennsylvania (Continued)
tain of, see Montgomery, James;
secretary of, see Dallas, Alexander;
Senate of, 23, 318; supervisor of revenue for, see Clymer, George; Supreme Executive Council of, 136,
318, 326-27; surveys of inspection,
189, 368; treasurer of, see Febiger,
Christian; treasury of, 443; U.S. at-
torney for the District of, see Lewis,
William; U.S. marshal for the Dis-
trict of, see Biddle, Clement; U.S.
Representative from, see Scott,
Thomas; U.S. Senators from, 23
(see also Morris, Robert); and west-
ern lands, 326-27
Pensions: application for, 337. See also
Invalid pensions
Pepper, see Duties; Tare on goods
Pepperellborough, District of Maine,
234
Perquimans County, N.C., 190
Perth Amboy, N.J., 328
Petersburg, Va., 242
Petitions, 138-39, 401, 403; of merchants
of Philadelphia trading to India and
China, 20-21; of widows and orphans,
513-14, 520. See also Conyngham,
David; Crawford, James; Derby,
Elias Hasket; Dodge, Samuel; Erke-
lens, Gosuinus; Greene, Catharine;
Hollins, John; McKean, Thomas;
Manson, Duncan; Massachusetts,
line; Nesbitt, John M.; Saddler,
Christopher; Sands, Comfort; Simmons, William; Smith, William;
Walker, Martha; Walley, Thomas;
Ward, Joseph
Pettit, Charles: letters from, 317-20,
400; letters to, 394, 451-53
Philadelphia, 2, 15, 17-18, 26, 28-29, 32,
38, 41, 46, 50-51, 57, 61-62, 73, 100,
112, 134-35, 142-44, 146-48, 150-52,
154-55, 158, 164-69, 179-81, 183, 186-
87, 189, 205-8, 210-12, 214, 217, 233-
35, 239-42, 245-46, 251, 257, 266, 269,
274, 277-79, 286-87, 290-91, 300-1, 304,
310-12, 314, 317, 320, 323, 325, 327,
331, 335, 337, 339, 342-43, 354, 363,
365, 393, 395-97, 400, 410, 412, 440,
443, 451-54, 456, 467, 470-71, 475, 480,
485-86, 493, 495, 498-99, 501, 507, 511-
13, 516, 522-23, 526, 531-32, 540-41,
543-44, 573, 577, 581-82, 585, 588; and
Bank of the U.S., 221, subscriptions

to, 589-90; collector of customs at,
see Delany, Sharp; French chargé
d'affaires at, see Otto, Louis G.;
master warden of port of, see Al-
libone, William; merchants of, and
trade with India and China, 20-21;
prison of, 201
[Philadelphia] Gazette of the United
States, 544
Phillips, Nathaniel, 297-98, 333, 440-41
Philps, Oliver, 138
Pickens, Andrew, 190
Pickering, Timothy, 241-42, 544, 546,
547
Pierce, John, 150, 265
Pimento, see Duties; Tare on goods
Pinckney, Charles, 349-50
Pintard, John M.: letter to, 304-5
Pintard, —— (Mrs. John M.), 305
Piscataqua River, 434
Pitt, William, 43
Pitt County, N.C., 190
Pittsburgh, Pa., 213, 544, 545, 563
Platt, Richard: letter from, 453-54
Playfair, William: letter from, 227-33
Plymouth, Mass., 523
Pointe-Au-Fer, Vt., 476-77
Polk, William, 187-88
Poll tax, see Taxes
Polly, 579
Poplar Grove, Del., 21
Porter, Andrew: letter from, 305-6;
letter to, 334
Porter, Daniel, 138, 512-13
Porter and beer, see Duties
Portland, District of Maine: lighthouse
at, 464
Portsmouth, N.H., 16, 40, 147, 243, 317,
337, 339, 347, 434, 457, 488, 514-15,
521, 571, 579; collector of customs at,
see Whipple, Joseph; lighthouse at,
514-15, superintendent of, see Whip-
ple, Joseph
Portugal, 246; special agent to, see
Humphreys, David; U.S. Minister
Resident of, see Humphreys, David
Postmaster General: powers of, 216.
See also Hazard, Ebenezer; Osgood,
Samuel
Post Office of U.S., 209
Post roads, 81-82
Potomac River, 253-54
Potter, James, 14-15
Potter, Richard, 14-15
Powers: of U.S. Government, 63-134

Premiums: in New Hampshire, 435
President of U.S., *see* Washington, George
Price, Richard, 17
Princess Ann County, Va., 451
Prisoners: payment of expenses of, 209
Proctor, Thomas (Col.), 545-46
Property, 89-90; and Bank of the U.S., 92
Providence, R.I., 3, 30, 34, 147, 158, 184, 197, 225-26, 235, 303, 311, 327, 339, 345, 347, 355, 359, 364, 398, 449, 466, 495, 496-97, 529, 551, 558, 569, 571, 584; collector of customs at, *see* Olney, Jeremiah; customs boat for, 345, 360, 449; naval officer for the port of, *see* Thompson, Ebenezer; shipbuilding at, 339; surveyor of port of, *see* Barton, William
Prussia: and John Adams, 307
Public credit: and Bank of the U.S., 221-22; and Boston tax, 580-81; and commissioners of loans, 358; need for publicity of, 172-73; of U.S. in Amsterdam, 172; and U.S. debt to France, 279-561; in wartime, 96, 124. *See also* Public debt
Public creditors, 7-9, 34-35, 150, 194-97, 224, 392-93, 401-4; and nonsubscribers, 305-6; and payment of interest on public debt, 161-62, 162-63, 199-200; of Pennsylvania, 410-12. *See also* Public credit; Public debt
Public debt, 128, 324, 393-94; and Army officers, 401-4; and Bank of the U.S., 221-22; and Boston tax, 549-51; certificates of, 15, 149-50, 214-15, 305-6, 341-42, 501; and counterfeits, 306; domestic, 282, 443-46, and domestic loan of 1790, 446-47, and Holland loans, 413-14, 419, 420, purchase of, by Dutch in America, 59, 264, 301, 315, 512-13, sinking of, 419; to France, 177-79, 279-80, 324-25, and assignats, 418, 423, payment of, 178-79, 283, 288, 289-90, 336, 356-57, 413, 415-17, 418-23, 460-61, 488-93, 534, 536, 558, 559, 561, 562, 574, 575-76, 578, proposed purchase and transfer of, 170-71, 176, 263, 268, 281, 288, 289-90, 324-25, 336, 414, 418, 421-23, 504-5, 512-13; funded debt, 8-9, 401-4; indents of, 7-9, 15, 32-33, 456; interest on, 305-6, 445, 502, payment of, 8, 34-35, 153, 161-62, 162-63, 182,

199-200, 202, 206, 211-12, 214-15, 224-25, 239, 266, 298-300, 357-58, 364, 394-95, 410-12, 433-34, 474-75, 506-7, 508, 509-10; liquidated, 172; and New York State, 213; and North, 401, 403; and Pennsylvania, 317-20, 339, 394, 400, 410-12, 443-46, 452; purchases of, 1-2, 144, 257, and Amsterdam loans, 271; registered, 298-300, 306, 393; and revenue, 90; sale of, 9; and sinking fund, 1-2, trustees of, 501; and Society for Establishing Useful Manufactures, 300; and South, 401; speculation in, 171-72; and states, bills of credit, 387-89, certificates, 474-75; stock of, 8-9; transfers of, 9; and western lands, 82. *See also* Amsterdam; Assumption of state debts; Congress of U.S., acts of; France; Loans; "Report Relative to a Provision for the Support of Public Credit" (January 9, 1790); Short, William

Quebec, 526

Randolph, Beverley, 59-60, 218; *letter from*, 543; Treasury Department circular to, 509-10
Randolph, Edmund, 203, 247, 440; Hamilton's "Notes on Edmund Randolph's Opinion on the Constitutionality of an Act to Establish a Bank," 46-49; *letters from*, 148-50, 541; *letters to*, 28, 30; opinion of constitutionality of an act to establish a bank, 46-49, 50-51, 64-66, 70, 72, 74, 80, 83, 84-91, 97, 98-99, 105-6, 107, 111-20, 133
Randolph County, N.C., 190
Ravard, Joseph, 534-35, 575
Ray, *see* Rhea, Thomas
Read, James, 190
Rebecca, 226
Reed, James, 183, 271
Reforestation, 249-51
Remsen, Henry, 139
Rensselaerwyck, 312
"Report on Certificates of Debt Issued After January 1, 1790" (February 25, 1791), 144-45
"Report on Compensation to the Commissioners of Loans" (February 14-15, 1791), 31-32

"Report on the Establishment of a Mint" (January 28, 1791), 57

"Report on the Holland Loan of Three Million Florins" (February 24-25, 1791), 136-38

"Report on the Petition of Conyngham, Nesbitt and Company, and James Crawford" (March 2, 1791), 154-55

"Report on the Petition of Elias Hasket Derby" (March 2, 1791), 155-56

"Report on the Petition of Gosuinus Erkelens" (March 2, 1791), 157-58

"Report on the Petition of John Hollins" (February 12, 1791), 28

"Report on the Petition of the Merchants of Philadelphia Trading to India and China" (February 10, 1791), 20-21

"Report on the Petition of Comfort Sands and Others" (February 24-25, 1791), 138-41

"Report on the Petition of William Simmons" (February 29, 1791), 141-42

"Report on the Petition of William Smith (March 28, 1792), 348

"Report Relative to a Provision for the Support of Public Credit" (January 9, 1790), 9, 404

"Reports on Exports for the Year Ending September 20, 1790" (February 15, 1791), 39-40

Republicans, 136

Reserved powers, see States

Revenue, 324; officers of the, 511; of U.S., 535. See also Collectors of customs; Duties; "Excise Law"

Revenue cutters, 164, 317, 358; captains, and collectors of customs, 428, 429, 430-31, duties of, 426-33, and forfeitures, 430, and revenue laws, 427-33, and Secretary of Treasury, 429; and collectors of customs, 286, 406-7, 407-9, 428, 429, 430-31, 538; for Delaware, 541; for Georgia, 349-50; journals of, 431-32; for Maryland, 259, 301-2, 472, captain of, see Gross, Simon; for Massachusetts, 61-62, 237, 286, 569-70, captain of, see Williams, John Foster; for New Hampshire, 40, 337, 514, 546-47, 571; for North Carolina, 311, 328, captain of, see Cooke, William; officers, instructions to, 406-7, qualities of, 432-33; for Pennsylvania, captain of, see Montgomery, James; purpose of, to gather coastal information, 431; rations for, 302, 570; registration of, 408; for Rhode Island, 30, 37-38, 51, 57, 311, 398-99, 466-67, 495; sailcloth for, 346; for South Carolina, 331, 349-50, 531, captain of, see Cochran, Robert. See also Treasury Department circulars to the captains of the revenue cutters

Revenue laws: breaches of, 252, 428, 553; and collectors of customs, 267-68, 302; Congress's power to regulate trade, 74; disregarded, 398, 468; enforcement of, 457-58; evasion of, 457-58; and revenue cutter captains, 427-33; and U.S. consuls, 304-5

Revolutionary War, see American Revolution

Rhea, Thomas, 544-46

Rhine River, 175

Rhode Island: and assumption of state debts, 443; commissioner of loans for, see Bowen, Jabez; and Constitution (U.S.), 347, 350, 553; Continental loan officer, see Ellery, William; District Court of, 333; First Regiment, 311; General Assembly of, 163, 529, "Report of the Committee appointed by the General Assembly relative to the services of Major John S. Dexter, as agent of the Rhode Island regiment," 3-4; governor of, see Fenner, Arthur; House of Representatives of, 569; legislature of, 3-4, 332; lighthouse in, 163-64, 529, 543; superintendent of, see Ellery, William; line of, agent for, see Dexter, John S.; revenue cutter for, 30, 37-38, 50, 57, 311, 398-99, 466-67, 495; Society of Cincinnati of, 311; supervisor of revenue for, 158 (see also Dexter, John S.); survey of inspection, 188-89; treasurer of, 3; treasury of, 3-4; U.S. attorney for the District of, see Channing, William; U.S. judge for the District of, see Marchant, Henry; U.S. Senators from, 158 (see also Foster, Theodore; Stanton, Joseph)

Rice: tare on, 390

Richards, Nathaniel, 181

Richland County, S.C., 190

Richmond, Va., 207, 240, 242, 280, 471, 525

Richmond County, N.C., 190
Rittenhouse, David, 29, 210-11
Rivington, James: *letter from*, 364-65
Roads and canals, 436; and tax on tobacco, 19
Roan County, N.C., *see* Rowan County, N.C.
Roanoke River, 243
Robertson County, N.C., *see* Robeson County, N.C.
Robeson County, N.C., 190
Rockingham County, N.C., 190
Rodney, Thomas: *letter from*, 21-24
Rogers, Samuel, 513
Rogers, Thomas, 566, 568
Roman law: and incorporation, 76, 101
Roosevelt (Rosevelt), Isaac, 137
Rottenbourg, Baron de: *letter from*, 527-28
Rottenbourg, Baroness de, 527-28
Rowan County, N.C., 190
Rue, Benjamin, 541
Russell, Thomas, 150
Russia, 277; and Great Britain, 264, 582; loans, 171, at Amsterdam, 172, at Antwerp, 574, 581-82, at Genoa, 262; stock in Holland, 58
Ruth, 30
Rutherford County, N.C., 190
Rutledge, Edward, 165-66
Rutledge, John, 166

Saddler, Christopher: petition of, 204
Sage, Comfort, 267
Sailcloth, 435
St. Clair, Arthur (Maj. Gen.), 247, 343, 532, 546; *letters from*, 360-63, 562-63; *letter from* John Cleves Symmes, 363; *letter to* John Cleves Symmes, 363; proclamation of, 361, 363
St. Croix, 227, 236
St. Johns, New Brunswick, 183, 522
St. Petersburg, Russia, 172, 282
St. Simon's Sound, 275
Salem, Mass., 155, 168-69, 273
Salem, N.C., 243
Salisbury, N.C., 243
Salt, 36-37; duties on, 483
Salter, Titus, 521
Sampson County, N.C., 190
Sands, Comfort, 556-57; report on petition of, 138-41
Sands, Joshua, 138

Sands, Richardson, 138
Sargent, Winthrop, 228-30
Savannah, Ga., 49, 167, 242, 348, 470, 502; collector of customs at, *see* Habersham, John; deputy postmaster at, *see* Davies, Edward; and "Excise Law," 404-5; postmaster at, *see* Watt, Alexander; surveyor of the port of, *see* Berrien, John
Schuyler, Angelica, *see* Church, Angelica Schuyler
Schuyler, Catherine (Mrs. Philip), 344
Schuyler, Philip, 142-43; *letter from*, 343-44
Schweizer, Jean Gaspar, 11-13
Schweizer, Jeanneret, and Co.: proposal to purchase U.S. debt to France, 170, 176, 260, 263, 268, 281, 289-90, 324-25, 336, 421-23
Scioto Associates, *see* Scioto Co.
Scioto Co., 227-33; formation of a colony, 228-31; and Ohio Co., 230; second company, 231; survey of, 362; third company, 231
Scioto River, 230
Scotland, 219; and banks, 19; ships for, 435
Scott, Charles (Brig. Gen.), 532, 545-46
Scott, Daniel (Dr.), 27, 62, 148
Scott, Margaret, *see* Page, Margaret Scott
Scott, Thomas, 402-3
"Second Report on the Further Provision Necessary for Establishing Public Credit (Report on a National Bank)" (December 13, 1790), 60, 133, 218
Secretary of State, *see* Jefferson, Thomas
Secretary of Treasury: duties of, 499-500. *See also* Hamilton, Alexander
Secretary of War, *see* Knox, Henry
Sedgwick, Theodore, 402-4
Seely, Charles, 252-53, 295-96
Seizures, 297-98; of distilled spirits, 379-80; and revenue cutter captains, 428. *See also* Collectors of customs
Senate, 124, 344; appointments of, 366, 477; and debt due foreign officers, 561-62; and "Funding Act," 402; message of President to, 41-42; resolution of, 403; rule of, 142-43; and subscribers to the Bank of the U.S., 142-43. *See also* Congress of U.S.
Seneca Indians, 213, 242

Seton, William, 34-35, 146, 206, 277, 357, 397, 541; *letters from,* 4-5, 49-50, 57, 226-27, 241, 276, 345-47, 449, 494-95, 503, 513, 518, 551; *letters to,* 26, 208, 235, 239, 334-35, 485-86, 501, 504, 513, 526; and lighthouse on Cape Henry, Va., 238, 283

Seven Brothers, 543

Seven Years' War, 435

Shelburne, Lord, 17

Shepard, John, 354

Sherburne, Samuel, 201-2

Sherman, Isaac: *letter from,* 9

Sherman, Roger, 9, 111

"Shillelah," 523

Shipbuilding: at Boston, 248-51; at Frenchman's Bay, District of Maine, 521; in New Hampshire, 434-36; at Providence, R.I., 339

Ship registers, 183-84, 208, 224, 272, 553; and frauds, 6; Great Britain, 5-7; Richard Harison's opinion on, 5-7; and surveyors of the ports, 440. *See also* Collectors of customs

Ships: admeasurement of, 441; condemned, 272; entry of, 273-74, 429-30; and forfeitures, 429-30; manifests of, 427, 428-29, 431; nationality of, 5-7; request for information on, 224-25; return of those built, 235; searching of, 427; seizure of, 5-7

Ship timber, 249-51

Short, William, 152-53, 205, 258, 263, 268, 330; on France, 160, 420; Hamilton on, 271; and Holland loans, 288-89, 289-90, of March, 1791, 270-71, 278-79; instructions to, 270-71, 288, 335-36, 356-57, 413, 583, 587-88; *letters from,* 10-13, 51-57, 58-61, 158-61, 170-79, 260-64, 324-25, 412-25, 439, 459-62, 488-93, 534-37, 558-62, 573-76, 577-79, 581-82; *letter from* Antoine Bernard Caillard, 177; *letter from* Thomas Jefferson, 283; *letter from* Ferdinand Le Grand, 178; *letter from* Comte de Montmorin, 176; *letters from* Willink, Van Staphorst, and Hubbard, 425, 461-62, 578-79; *letters to,* 280-83, 335-36, 356-57, 504-5, 519; *letter to* Antoine Bernard Caillard, 177-78; *letters to* Thomas Jefferson, 10-13, 60-61, 160-61, 173-76; *letter to* Ferdinand Le Grand, 179; *letters to* Willink, Van Stap-

horst, and Hubbard, 464, 536-37; and U.S. mint, 285-86

Shrewsbury County, S.C., 190

Silver, 439

Simmons, William: petition of, 141-42

Sinclair, Sir John: *History of the Public Revenue of the British Empire,* 177

Sinking fund: commissioners (trustees) of, 257, 501 (*see also* Adams, John; Hamilton, Alexander; Jay, John; Jefferson, Thomas; Randolph, Edmund); meeting of, 1-2; and purchase of the public debt, 1-2, 257, 501; and western lands, 82

Six Nations, 213, 241, 544-46

Skinner, William, 517; *letters from,* 565-66, 566-69

Smith, ——— (Capt.), 398, 468, 473

Smith, Benjamin, 465-66

Smith, Melancton, 138, 478-79

Smith, Noah, 187, 188, 343-44

Smith, Robert, 354

Smith, Thomas, 15, 32, 305, 452, 453; *letters from,* 32-33, 233-34, 339, 443-46, 456, 467, 507-8; *letters to,* 15, 239, 337, 455-56; Treasury Department circulars to, 394-95, 446-47

Smith, William (Ga.): petition of, 348

Smith, William (Md.), 151, 321-22

Smith, William (Mass.): petition of, 388

Smith, William: vice president of the American Philosophical Society, 29

Smith, William Loughton, 470, 472

Smith, William Stephens, 187, 188, 245-46, 453-54, 475-77, 556-57

Smuggling, 252, 430, 463, 522, 584

Snowden, Isaac: *letter from,* 193-97

Snuff, *see* Duties

Soap, *see* Duties

Society for Establishing Useful Manufactures, 556-57, 591; and Théophile Cazenove, 300-1; foreman for, *see* Parkinson, George; needs of, 571-73; and New Jersey, 300-1; and public debt, 300; subscription to, 300

South: George Washington on, 531

South Carolina, 112, 166, 395; "An Act for loaning to the United States, a Sum of the Indents of this State under certain Limitations therein mentioned" (February 19, 1791), 568; and assumption of state debts,

443; governor of, see Moultrie, William, and Pinckney, Charles; inspector of revenue for, see Cogdell, John; legislature of, 568; lighthouse in, 181, 183; revenue cutter for, 331, 349-50, 531, captain of, see Cochran, Robert; Senate of, 350; state Circuit Court, 152; as subscriber to domestic loan of 1790, 566-68; supervisor of the revenue for, see Stevens, Daniel; surveys of inspection, 190, 368; trade of, 435; U.S. marshal for the District of, see Huger, Isaac; U.S. Representative from, 395 (see also Burke, Ædanus); U.S. Senator from, see Butler, Pierce

Southern states: and Federal District, 255-56

Southwest Territory, 77, 120. See also Territories (U.S.)

Sovereignty, 68; and creation of corporations, 99; and declared powers of Constitution (U.S.), 73-74; and government, 66-67; and legislative power, 72; and state constitutions, 73-74; of states, 73-74, 98; and U.S. Government, 63-134. See also "Opinion on the Constitutionality of an Act to Establish a Bank"

Spain, 69; and England, 42; and meaning of "percent," 391; revolution in colonies of, 246; special U.S. agent to, see Humphreys, David; trade with, 434

Spanish West Indies: trade with, 435

Spartanburg County, S.C., 190

Specie: and banks, 218, 221; and purchases of the public debt, 1-2

Specified powers, see Constitution (U.S.), enumerated powers

Speculation: in the Federal District, 254-56; in Northwest Territory, 360-63; in U.S. debt to France, 283. See also Scioto Co.

Spinola, Christoforo Vincenzo de, 261-62, 324-25, 424, 534-35

Spire, Bishop of, 175

Stadnitski, Pieter, 301

Stanton, Joseph, 158

State Department: appropriation for, 204-5; contingent expenses of, 234-35. See also Jefferson, Thomas

States: accounts of, 201-2, with Army, 3-4, with U.S., 509, 567, 568; and Bank of the U.S., 222, 223; and bankruptcy laws, 79, 109; banks of, 219-20, and Bank of the U.S., 103-4, 110, 590-91; and Constitution (U.S.), 73; constitutions, 68; and Continental treasury, 318-19; creditor states, 567; debtor states, 567, 568; debts, 394-95, certificates of, 144-45, 447, and new emissions, 319-20, purchase of, 301 (see also Assumption of state debts); and Federal District, 255-56; and Federal Government, 22; and foreign loans, 59; and indents, 8; and Indians, 241; Thomas Jefferson on powers of, 77, 108; joint powers with U.S. Government, 73; laws, purchase of, 234-35; and North Carolina, 45-46; paper money of, 93, 387-89; and power of Congress of U.S., 72; and power of incorporation, 77-80, 103, 109; and public debt, 443-46, 474-75, 509-10, 566-69; and public measures, 241-42; ratifying conventions, and power of incorporation, 75, 131; and regulation of foreign coins, 79; reserved powers of, 68, 133; and sovereignty, 73-74, 98; trade among, 126-27

Steel: manufacture of, 166-67. See also Duties

Stein, Philip, 511

Steuben, Frederick William Augustus Henry Ferdinand, baron von, 256

Stevens, Daniel, 151, 188

Stewart, Charles, 138

Stewart, Walter: letter from, 193-97

Stills, 373-74, 378, 380

Stites, Benjamin, 363

Stock (U.S.), 161-62, 169

Stodder, David, 472

Stokes County, N.C., 190

Stratton, Vt., 528

Stuart, David (Dr.), 472

Stull, John (Col.), 321-22

Suffolk, 237, 323

Sugar, see Duties; Tare on goods

Sullivan, John, 514-15

Superintendent of Finance, see Morris, Robert

Supervisors of the revenue, 151, 207, 240, 366-82, 525; appointment of, 186-87; appointment of subordinates, 374-75; and certificates, 375-76; and collectors of customs, 366;

Supervisors of the revenue (*Cont.*)
and collectors of revenue, 376; compensation for, 187; for Connecticut, *see* Chester, John; and counterfeits, 373; for Delaware, *see* Latimer, Henry; and distilleries, 374; duties of, 188-91; for Georgia, *see* Mathews, John; and information on manufactures, 497-98; and inspectors of the ports, 371; and inspectors of the revenue, 382; for Massachusetts, *see* Gorham, Nathaniel; for New Hampshire, *see* Wentworth, Joshua; for New Jersey, *see* Dunham, Aaron; for New York, *see* Smith, William S.; for North Carolina, *see* Polk, William; and oaths, 381-82; for Pennsylvania, *see* Clymer, George; for Rhode Island, 158 (*see also* Dexter, John S.): for South Carolina, *see* Stevens, Daniel; for Vermont, *see* Smith, Noah; for Virginia, *see* Carrington, Edward

"Supplement to the Report on Exports for the Year Ending September 30, 1790" (February 26, 1791), 145-46

Supremacy clause, *see* Constitution (U.S.)

Supreme Court, 135, 141

Surry County, N.C., 190

Surveyors of the port, 370, 430, 529, 542; and admeasurement of ships, 441; of Baltimore, *see* Ballard, Robert; of Barrington, R.I., *see* Phillips, Nathaniel; of Boston, 345 (*see also* Melville, Thomas); and coasting trade, 474; and collectors of customs, 369; compensation of, 440-41, 449, 496-97; of East Greenwich, R.I., *see* Arnold, Thomas; as inspectors of revenue, 191; and manifests of ships, 427; of Middletown, Conn., *see* Sage, Comfort; of Newport, R.I., *see* Lyman, Daniel; of Providence, R.I., *see* Barton, William; of Savannah, Ga., *see* Berrien, John; of Warren, R.I., *see* Phillips, Nathaniel; of Windsor, N.C., *see* Benson, William

Surveys of inspection of revenue, 188-90, 368

Swansea (Swansey), Mass., 163

Swanwick, John, 149-50

Sweden, 58

Swift, 275

Symmes, John Cleves, 405; land spec-

ulation in Northwest Territory, 360-63, 541, 562-63; *letter from* Arthur St. Clair, 363; *letter to* Arthur St. Clair, 363

Tarboro, N.C., 242

Tare on goods, 244-45, 340-41, 350, 355, 483; at Alexandria, Va., 527; calculation of, 442; on cocoa, 147, 341, 390, 468-69, 484-85; on coffee, 147, 244-45, 341, 390, 391, 468-69, 484; on cotton, 469; and duties, 390; on indigo, 390; at Newport, R.I., 468-70; on pepper, 244-45, 341, 390, 391, 468, 484; on pimento, 341, 390, 468, 484; at Portsmouth, N.H., 484-85; regulation of, 399; on rice, 390; on sugar, 147, 244-45, 340-41, 389-90, 391, 468-69, 484; on tea, 391. *See also* Congress of U.S., acts of

Tariffs, 278, 281, 421

Taxes, 89-90; abatement of, in New Hampshire, 435; and banks, 219; in Boston, 549-50; collection of, 245, and banks, 92-96; and common defense, 90; and Constitution (U.S.), 89-90, 115-16, 128-29; direct, 24, 580-81; farming out of, 86, 130; and foreign loans, 324; and general welfare, 90; and incorporation power, 85-87; and Indian wars, 96, 124; indirect, 24; in kind, 93, 121; land, 23, 24; and money, 89-90; poll tax, 23, 24; and public debt, 90, 128, 549-50; and public stock, 591. *See also* Congress of U.S., acts of; Duties; Tonnage duty

Tax power, *see* Congress of U.S.

Tayler, John, 213, 217

Taylor, James: *letters from,* 508-9, 513-14; *letter to,* 520

Taylors Ferry, Va., 243, 471

Tea: Bohea, 20-21; deposit of, 530; importation of, 155-56, 495; and inspector of revenue, 295-96; and officers of inspection, 383-87; and trade with India and China, 20-21. *See also* Congress of U.S., acts of; Duties; Tare on goods

Telfair, Edward, 347-48, 472

Ten Cate and Vollenhoven, 301

Ternant, Jean Baptiste de, 176, 421-23, 439, 448, 535

Territories (U.S.): and powers of Congress, 77, 89, 115-16, 118, 128. *See*

also Northwest Territory; Southwest Territory
Texel Passage, 52, 58
Thatcher, George, 146-47; *letter from*, 234
Thomas, Abishai: *letters from*, 486-87, 508-9, 513-14, 520
Thompson, Ebenezer, 158, 496-97, 585
Thomson, Charles, 139
Tilton, James: Treasury Department circular to, 433-34
Tobacco: French duty on, 11-13, 60-61, 160-61, 174; tax on, for roads and canals, 19. *See also* Duties
Tonnage duty, 155, 204, 259, 273, 474, 479-80, 481; and collectors of customs, 364; and fishing, 479; foreign, 16, 272, 488; and immigration, 18; return of, 479-80
Tracy, Nathaniel, 344-45
Trade and industry: and banks, 218-19, 223. *See also* Commerce
Trading companies: as examples of government corporations, 75, 89, 131, 132
Treasurer of the U.S., 293-94. *See also* Meredith, Samuel
Treasury Department, 306, 447; acting paymaster general of, *see* Howell, Joseph; auditor of, 293-94 (*see also* Wolcott, Oliver, Jr.), clerk of (*see* Freeman, Ezekiel), vacancy of office, 321, 470, 494; books of, 211; certificates, theft of, 273, 284; clerks, compensation of, 141-42; comptroller of, 292-94, 433 (*see also* Eveleigh, Nicholas; Wolcott, Oliver, Jr.), clerk of (*see* Hardy, Joseph), vacancy of office, 334; drafts of, 154, 314, 363-64; and loan office certificates, 329; and new loan certificates, 300; paymaster general of, *see* Pierce, John; and Pennsylvania, 320, 410; register of, 293-94 (*see also* Nourse, Joseph), certificates of, 198; and Scioto Co., 229-30; treasurer of, 293-94 (*see also* Meredith, Samuel)
Treasury Department circular to the governors of the states, June 27, 1791, 509-10
Treasury Department circulars to the captains of the revenue cutters, June 1, 1791, 406-7; June 4, 1791, 426-33
Treasury Department circulars to the collectors of the customs, March 5,

1791, 162-63; March 21, 1791, 209; April 14, 1791, 287-88; May 13, 1791, 340-41; May 25, 1791, 363; May 26, 1791, 365-87; June 1, 1791, 407-9; June 1, 1791, 409-10; July 8, 1791, 538; July 8-12, 1791, 538-39
Treasury Department circulars to the commissioners of loans, February 14, 1791, 34-35; March 9, 1791, 169; March 17, 1791, 198; March 18, 1791, 204; March 25, 1791, 215; April 8, 1791, 257; April 16, 1791, 290; May 2, 1791, 320; May 27, 1791, 394-95; June 4, 1791, 433-34; June 6, 1791, 446-47
Treasury Department circulars to the supervisors of the revenue, June 22, 1791, 497-98; June 25, 1791, 505-6; June 27, 1791, 510-11
Treaties: at Newtown Point, 546; of 1762, 435, 436; of 1783, 477. *See also* France; Great Britain; Morocco
Tromberger, John: *letter from*, 193-97
Troup, Robert, 4-5, 214; on Hamilton, 478-79; *letters from*, 279, 478-79
Troup, —— (Mrs. Robert), 478
Trumbull, Jonathan, 157-58
Turnpikes: and Congress of U.S., 81-82
Tuscany, Duke of, 5
Twine, *see* Duties
Tybee Island, Ga.: lighthouse on, 348-49
Tyrrell County, N.C., 190

Ulster County, N.Y., 528
Union County, S.C., 190
United Netherlands, 69, 87, 117, 177, 288, 412; and John Adams, 307, 308; and assignats, 419; and banks, 221; and information about U.S., 505; loans, *see* Loans, Holland; mint in, 424; tax on foreign loans, 173. *See also* Amsterdam; Public debt; Short, William; Willink, Van Staphorst, and Hubbard
United States, 421; advantages of Bank of the U.S. for, 220-23; Army, appropriation for, 186, clothing for, 334, 354, contracts for supplies of, 164-65, 226-27, 246-48 (*see also* Duer, William; Fowler, Theodosius; Williams, Elie), quartermaster department, 164-65, quartermaster general, *see* Hodgdon, Samuel; attorney for the District of Connecticut, *see* Ed-

United States (*Continued*)

wards, Pierpont, of Massachusetts, *see* Gore, Christopher, of New Hampshire, *see* Sherburne, Samuel, of New York, *see* Harison, Richard, of Pennsylvania, *see* Lewis, William, of Rhode Island, *see* Channing, William; bonds and stocks in Amsterdam, 58, 413, 460-61, 577-79, 581-82; Constitution, *see* Constitution (U.S.); consuls and revenue laws, 304-5; credit, 264, in Europe, 534; customs, *see* Customs officers; debt of, *see* Public credit, Public debt; joint powers with states, 73; judge for the District of Connecticut, *see* Law, Richard, of Georgia, *see* Pendleton, Nathaniel, of Rhode Island, *see* Marchant, Henry, of Virginia, *see* Griffin, Cyrus; judges of, and oaths, 433; laws and British laws, 5-7; loan officers, *see* Commissioners of loans; and loans in Amsterdam, *see* Amsterdam; marshal for the District of New York, *see* Smith, William S., of Pennsylvania, *see* Biddle, Clement, of South Carolina, *see* Huger, Isaac, of Virginia, *see* Carrington, Edward; and "necessary and proper clause," 65-72; North Carolina, account with, 486-87, 508-9; Pennsylvania, account with, 451-53; and people, 22; powers of, 63-134; property of, 127-28; publicity abroad, 260-63, 424-25, 505, 534-35; and sovereignty, 63-134; and states, 22, accounts with, 509, 567, 568, bills of, 387. *See also* Bank of the U.S.

United States bankers in Amsterdam, *see* Willink, Van Staphorst, and Hubbard

United States commissioners at Amsterdam, *see* Willink, Van Staphorst, and Hubbard

United States v *Christopher Backhouse*, 275-76

Updike, Daniel Eldridge, 441

Upper Miami Towns, 544, 546

Usher, George, 30, 37-38, 333

Usher, Hezekiah: petition of, 30, 37-38, 333

Van Eeghen, P. and C., 301

Van Rensselaer, Margaret Schuyler (Mrs. Stephen), 312

Van Rensselaer, Stephen: *letter from,* 346; *letter to,* 312

Van Staphorst, Jacob, 301

Van Staphorst, Nicholaas, 301

Van Staphorst, House of, 414

Venezuela, 246

Vermont, 479; admitted to Union, 166; Assembly of, 344; state attorney, *see* Smith, Noah; supervisor of revenue for, *see* Smith, Noah; Supreme Court of, 344; survey of inspection, 189

Versailles, 308

Vice President of U.S., *see* Adams, John

Vienna: British chargé d'affaires at, *see* Hammond, George

Virginia, 18, 22, 112, 162, 218, 269, 293, 467, 495, 523; and assumption of state debts, 443, 543; commissioner of loans for, *see* Hopkins, John; and foreign loans, 59; governor of, *see* Randolph, Beverley; inspector of revenue for, 280, 405 (*see also* Newton, Thomas, Jr.); and Kentucky, 532; supervisor of revenue for, *see* Carrington, Edward; surveys of inspection of, 189, 207, 368; trade of, 435; U.S. judge for the District of, *see* Griffin, Cyrus; U.S. marshal for the District of, *see* Carrington, Edward; U.S. Representatives from, *see* Brown, John, *and* Parker, Josiah; U.S. Senator from, *see* Monroe, James

Vollenhoven, ——— (Mr.), 301

Von Steuben, *see* Steuben

Wabash Indians, 213, 532; expedition against, 545-46

Wabash River, 546

Wadsworth, Jeremiah, 165-66, 320; *letters to,* 180-81, 279-80

Wake County, N.C., 190

Wales, 7, 136

Walker, Benjamin, 229-33

Walker, Martha (Mrs. Thomas), 589; *letter from,* 337; *letter to,* 526-27

Walker, Thomas, 526

Wall and Tardy, 528

Walley, Thomas: petition of, 388

War: and banks, 220; and public credit, 96, 124

Ward, Joseph: *letter from,* 320; *letter to,* 387-88; petition of, 388

War Department, 248; and contract with William Duer, 247; and invalid pensions, 518. *See also* Knox, Henry

Warren, James, 523, 589

Warren, Mercy (Mrs. James), 589; *letter to,* 522-23

Warren, R.I., 297, 440-41; customs boat for, 297, 333; surveyor of port of, *see* Phillips, Nathaniel

Warren, 310, 398, 473

Warren County, N.C., 190

Washington, George, 97, 99, 124, 130, 146-47, 158, 164, 201, 202-3, 266, 280; and act of Congress, 66; aides-de-camp, *see* Fitzgerald, John, *and* Gibbs, Caleb, *and* Humphreys, David; and American Revolution, 345; appointments by, 179-80, 210, 301-2, 311, 358-59, 366, 398-99, 427, 477; and auditor of Treasury, 322; and Bank of the U.S., 46-49, 50-51, 57-58, 63-134; and British Minister to U.S., 277; and coins, 286; and commercial treaty with Great Britain, 41-45; and contracts, 183, 586-87; and Samuel Dodge, 202-3; and executive departments, 258; and Federal District, 254-56; and foreign loans, 421; and Caleb Gibbs, 345; and Holland loans, 52, 136-38, 335; and Indians, 546; and invalid pensions, 13-14; and laws on emigration of mechanics, 556-57; *letters from,* 50-51, 134-35, 186, 187-91, 205-6, 241-42, 242-43, 330, 331, 349-50, 470-72, 531, 588; *letters to,* 57-58, 62-134, 135, 142-43, 143, 151, 181, 183, 217-23, 269, 270-71, 277-78, 278, 288-89, 290-91, 291-94, 493-94, 540, 540-41, 586-87, 587-88; *letter to* Thomas Jefferson, 242-43; *letter to* Henry Knox, 242-43; and lighthouses, 348-49, 451; messages to Congress, December 8, 1790, 136-38, February 14, 1791, 41-45; and mint, 284, 395; and officers of survey, 374-75; pardoning power of, 312-14, 352-54; and proposal to purchase U.S. debt to France, 11-13, 176, 260; removal power, 72, 106-7; "The Reply of the President of the United States to the speech of the Cornplanter, Half-Town, and Great-Tree, Chiefs and Councillors of the Seneca nation of Indians" (December 29, 1790), 241-42; and revenue cutters, 432, 541, 546; secretaries of, *see* Jackson, William, *and* Lear, Tobias, *and* McHenry, James; and Secretary of Treasury, 499; and William Short's instructions, 356-57, 413, 505, 582-83; southern tour, 201, 203, 207, 242-43, 255, 281, 295, 311, 470-72, 494, 531-32; and veto power, 113; and Oliver Wolcott, Jr., 321

Washington, N.C., 290, 317, 328, 483, 586; collector of customs at, *see* Keais, Nathan; revenue cutter for, 328

Washington County, Md., 322

Washington County, Pa., 189

Washington County, S.C., 190

Watson, James: *letter to,* 265-66

Watt, Alexander, 216

Wayne County, N.C., 190

Weights and measures, 282

Weissenfels, Charles: *letter from,* 337

Weissenfels, Frederick, 337

Weissenfels, George P., Jr.: *letter from,* 337

Wentworth, Joshua, 187, 188; *letter to,* 331; Treasury Department circular to, 498

Wereat, John, 347

Western posts: supply of, 164-65, 438

Western territory, 342-43; and Pennsylvania, 326-27; and post roads, 81-82; and public debt, 82; and sinking fund, 82; speculation in, 213, 228; and U.S. debt to France, 325. *See also* Frontier; Northwest Territory; Southwest Territory

West Indies, 135, 204, 317, 338, 408; and distilled spirits, 591; products of, 483

Westmoreland County, Pa., 189

West Point: supply of, 138-41

Weymouth, Mass., 237, 323

Whipple, Joseph, 317, 521; *letters from,* 10, 16, 40, 243-44, 337-38, 339, 347, 434-36, 457-58, 479-80, 483-85, 514-15, 571, 579; *letters to,* 488, 546-47

Whitaker, John, 190, 358, 393

Widows and orphans: claims of, 513-14, 520

Wilkerson, Abraham: *letter to,* 214

Wilkes County, N.C., 190
Willet, Marinus (Col.), 312, 346
Williamos, Charles, 527-28
Williamos, Louisa Henriette, *see* Rottenbourg, Baroness de
Williams, Elie, 164-65, 438
Williams, John Foster, 530, 569-70; Treasury Department circulars to, 406-7, 426-33
Williams, Jonathan, 29
Williams, Mercy, 322
Williams, Otho H., 15, 28, 301-2, 317, 350-52; *letters from*, 15, 35-37, 338, 389-92, 438, 462-64; *letters to*, 25, 206-7, 235-36, 302-3, 363-64, 400-1, 437-38, 472, 506-7; and office of auditor of Treasury, 321-22; Treasury Department circulars to, 340-41, 409-10, 538-39
Williams, Thomas, 239
Williamsburg, N.C., 243
Williamsburg County, S.C., 190
Williamson, Hugh, 487
Willing, Thomas, 149-50, 210-11, 589-90
Willing, Morris, and Swanwick, 513
Willink, Wilhem and Jan, 59, 414
Willink, Wilhem and Jan, Nicholaas and Jacob Van Staphorst, and Nicholas Hubbard, *see* Willink, Van Staphorst, and Hubbard
Willink, Van Staphorst, and Hubbard, 53, 159-60, 170, 264, 309, 356-57, 413, 415, 459, 489-93, 560; *letter from*, 152-53; *letter from* William Short, 460; *letters to*, 182, 204-5, 521, *letters to* William Short, 425, 461-62, 536-37, 578-79; and loans, 270-71, 424, 425, 519, 561, increase of, 53-55, interest on, 59, 413, 414, 535, 577-79; and U.S. debt to France, 416-17, 534, 558, 559, 575-76

Willkings, M. R.: *letter from*, 295; *letter to*, 464-66
Wilmington, Del.: collector of customs at, *see* Bush, George; deputy collector of customs at, 154-55
Wilmington, N.C., 242, 295, 296, 311, 586; captain of revenue cutter at, *see* Cooke, William; collector of customs at, *see* Read, James
Wilmington County, N.C., 189
Wilson, James, 111-12
Wilson, John, 304, 540
Windsor, N.C., 399
Wines: Madeira, 305. *See also* Duties
Winton County, S.C., 190
Winyaw County, S.C., 190
Withers, Thomas: *letter from*, 295; *letter to*, 464-66
Wolcott, Oliver, Jr.: auditor of the Treasury, 7, 15, 140, 211-12, 224-25, 235, 309, 329, 331-32, 458, chief clerk of, *see* Simmons, William; comptroller of Treasury, 547, 548, appointment as, 470, 493-94; and domestic loan of 1790, 456; Hamilton on, 291-94; and George Washington, 321
Wolf, Charles John Michael de, 573-74, 581
Wolfe, David: *letter from*, 485; *letter to*, 547
Wood, John, 350
Worcester County, Mass., 189
Wray, George, 317
Wylly, Richard: *letters from*, 347-48, 472; *letter to*, 265

Yeaton, Hopley, 514-15
York County, Pa., 189
York County, S.C., 190
Young, William, 149-50

Zacharie, Stephen, 302-3
Zacharie, Coopman, and Co., 303

	DATE DUE		